Lecture Notes in Computer Science 13809

Founding Editors

Gerhard Goos
Juris Hartmanis

Editorial Board Members

The series Lecture Notes in Computer Science (LNCS), including its subseries Lecture Notes in Artificial Intelligence (LNAI) and Lecture Notes in Bioinformatics (LNBI), has established itself as a medium for the publication of new developments in computer science and information technology research, teaching, and education.

LNCS enjoys close cooperation with the computer science R & D community, the series counts many renowned academics among its volume editors and paper authors, and collaborates with prestigious societies. Its mission is to serve this international community by providing an invaluable service, mainly focused on the publication of conference and workshop proceedings and postproceedings. LNCS commenced publication in 1973.

Giampaolo Bella · Mihai Doinea · Helge Janicke
Editors

Innovative Security Solutions for Information Technology and Communications

15th International Conference, SecITC 2022
Virtual Event, December 8–9, 2022
Revised Selected Papers

 Springer

Editors
Giampaolo Bella
University of Catania
Catania, Italy

Mihai Doinea
Bucharest University of Economic Studies
Bucharest, Romania

Helge Janicke
Edith Cowan University
Joondalup, WA, Australia

ISSN 0302-9743   ISSN 1611-3349 (electronic)
Lecture Notes in Computer Science
ISBN 978-3-031-32635-6   ISBN 978-3-031-32636-3 (eBook)
https://doi.org/10.1007/978-3-031-32636-3

This Springer imprint is published by the registered company Springer Nature Switzerland AG
The registered company address is: Gewerbestrasse 11, 6330 Cham, Switzerland

Preface

This volume contains the papers presented at SECITC 2022: The 15th International Conference on Security for Information Technology and Communications held virtually on December 8–9, 2022 and organized by Bucharest University of Economic Studies, Military Technical Academy and the Advanced Technology Institute, Romania.

SECITC brings together computer security researchers, cryptographers, industry representatives and postgraduate students interested in any aspect of information security and privacy. One of SECITC's primary goals is to connect security and privacy researchers from different areas and to provide a forum to enable the knowledge exchange that is necessary for the emergence of new scientific and industrial collaborations.

There were 53 program committee members, widely spread around the world, who contributed with their invaluable knowledge and expertise to the success of this scientific event. Each submission was double-blind reviewed by at least 2, with a median of 3, program committee members. The committee decided to accept 19 of 53 contributions out of which 1 is an invited paper by one of us.

The conference had two guest speakers to whom it wishes to give thanks for their major role of triggering security awareness with their thought-provoking presentations. These are Luca Vigano from King's College London, UK and Erik Poll from Radboud University, The Netherlands.

This volume can be used by researchers, specialists, postgraduate students and security consultants who wish to keep pace with the latest developments in Security for Information Technology and Communication.

December 2022

Giampaolo Bella
Mihai Doinea
Helge Janicke

Organization

Program Committee

Iulian Aciobanitei	Military Technical Academy "Ferdinand I", Romania
Raja Naeem Akram	University of Aberdeen, UK
Elena Andreeva	K U Leuven, Belgium
Ludovic Apvrille	Telecom ParisTech, France
Claudio Ardagna	Universita' degli Studi di Milano, Italy
Josep Balasch	Katholieke Universiteit Leuven, Belgium
Giampaolo Bella	University of Catania, Italy
Lasse Berntzen	University of South-Eastern Norway, Norway
Ion Bica	Military Technical Academy, Romania
Catalin Boja	Bucharest Academy of Economic Studies, Romania
Guillaume Bouffard	National Cybersecurity Agency of France (ANSSI), France
Michele Carminati	Politecnico di Milano, Italy
Christophe Clavier	Université de Limoges, France
Paolo D'Arco	University di Salerno, Italy
Eric Diehl	Sony Pictures, USA
Mihai Doinea	Bucharest University of Economic Studies, Romania
Eric Freyssinet	LORIA, France
Dieter Gollmann	Hamburg University of Technology, Germany
Johann Groszschaedl	University of Luxembourg, Luxembourg
Rémi Géraud	École Normale Supérieure de Paris, France
Helena Handschuh	Rambus, Inc., USA
Shoichi Hirose	University of Fukui, Japan
Xinyi Huang	Fujian Normal University, China
Helge Janicke	Edith Cowan University, Australia
Mehmet Sabir Kiraz	De Montfort University, UK
Diana Maimut	Advanced Technology Institute, Romania
Sjouke Mauw	University of Luxembourg, Luxembourg
Marino Miculan	University of Udine, Italy
Kazuhiko Minematsu	NEC Corporation, Japan
Stig Mjolsnes	Norwegian University of Science and Technology, Norway

Contents

Interactional Freedom and Cybersecurity

Giampaolo Bella[✉][iD]

Dipartimento di Matematica e Informatica, Università degli Studi di Catania,
Catania, Italy
giamp@dmi.unict.it

Abstract. We have become accustomed to the news of more and more
cunning attacks to real-world systems, and equally accustomed to try to
fix them even though further attacks may come. I discuss how to tackle
and ultimately resolve this tedious and infamous attack-fix-loop practice
by distilling out five paradigms to achieve cybersecurity: democratic, dictatorial, beautiful, invisible and explainable security. While each of these
has distinctive features, various combinations, at some rate, of them
may coexist, with the final aim of improving the way security measures
account for the human element. Towards the end of the paper, I conjecture how the paradigms could be used to improve the ultimate security
measure of our times, a Security Operation Centre. May I remark that
many of the observations made below derive from my personal and current understanding and would require a number of experiments to be
fully confirmed.

Keywords: Democratic security · Dictatorial security · Beautiful
security · Invisible Security · Explainable Security

1 Introduction

The Technical System. Engineers build computers, including tiny ones to ani-
mate the smallest IoT device. Computer Scientists build the programs that those
computers execute. History as well as breaking news tell us that each computer
and the suite of programs it runs form, together, a technical system that is
often *vulnerable*. It means that the odds are non-negligible that a criminal finds
a *malicious way* to abuse the resources of that system or to make it work as
the criminal desires, even if it is contrary to the aims of those who built the
system in the first place. Laymen call that malicious way to operate *an attack*.
More precisely, it is a sequence of events to make the targeted system miss some
functional properties and related cybersecurity properties that engineers and

---

My SEICT 2022 co-chairs invited me to deliver a talk, which I entitled *"The Right Level
of Human Interaction to Establish Cybersecurity"*. This is the accompanying paper.

© The Author(s), under exclusive license to Springer Nature Switzerland AG 2023
G. Bella et al. (Eds.): SecITC 2022, LNCS 13809, pp. 1–16, 2023.
https://doi.org/10.1007/978-3-031-32636-3_1

scientists believed would be ensured instead. Cybersecurity properties mean, for example, that anyone who accesses their online bank account is reassured that their login credentials are only going to be shared with the bank, and that police cars on a chase can exchange information that the criminals cannot overhear. They also protect functional properties, such as correctness of satellite trajectory calculations.

With just more examples, this is my gentle introduction to cybersecurity for outsiders, including my primary school son. But the more complicated part is the next one, where I recall that the technical systems demand human interaction, a sort of interplay with their users, itself oriented at pursuing the expected properties mentioned above. An online bank access requires users to follow what is in essence a predefined sequence of steps, also providing relevant information when and where needed. Similarly, policemen must refrain from attempting alternative radio frequencies during the chase or unconventional means of communication in general, and anyone who calculates satellite trajectories ought to remember that the right values must be assigned to the right parameters, with no room for peculiar diversions. All straightforward so far, but there is a clear accent on the humans who interact with the technical systems. Someone or something built humans originally, humans have evolved over the centuries but remain vulnerable, similarly to the technical systems though in different ways. Humans may be biased, may make mistakes and errors, may be deceived and may even be irrational, all at various rates, due to internal forces coming from the self and to external forces coming from society.

The Socio-technical System. It follows that risk sources for cybersecurity are at least two, namely the technical system as well as the humans who interact with it. This is the root of the reason why cybersecurity is an inherently multi-disciplinary problem. Social Scientists and Psychologists, in particular, play a prominent role in understanding people's behaviour in front of technical systems, thereby pursuing the ultimate goal of ensuring cybersecurity over the socio-technical system comprising the technical system and its users. The challenges of reaching that goal begin to come to a focus. Specifically, their human element brings daunting ones, and if I try to summarise them as a research question, the outcome would be along the following lines: *how do we make sure that humans will want to comply with the technical system and will manage to do that?* Compliance here means to interact with the technical system precisely as imagined by those who built it.

It is now time to appeal to some relevant literature, but it is difficult to select the most pertinent publications, so I just mention a few of my own relevant works, chronologically. I included some notion of error by the *oops* rule in my proofs about a version of Kerberos, inspired by Paulson's seminal work [7]. I understood that security properties are not just boolean and, by contrast, are mediated, by those who run them, by means of some level, which can be interpreted as "levels of preference, or of certainty, etc." [3]. It follows that attacks can also be indeliberate, a first hint at a more mentalistic take at the agents who execute the security protocols than the previous interpretation in terms of just computer processes. Also, I explained service security and privacy as a socio-technical problem [5].

We must also consider a few white-paper style articles from highly-reputed sources that virtually every cybersecurity expert will have read. The "IBM Security Services 2014 Cyber Security Intelligence Index" states that *"over 95% of all incidents investigated recognize 'human error' as a contributing factor"*. The "IBM X-Force Threat Intelligence Index 2018" remarks that *"the potentially detrimental impact of an inadvertent insider on IT security cannot be overstated"*, while the 2019 edition of the same report confirms that *"human error continues to facilitate breaches"* and the 2020 publication observes that *"generic botnet malware"* has been *"pushed to users from spam or malvertising"*. A SANS blog page compares humans to machines with their own Operating Systems, the "HumanOS", observing that *"We have to begin investing in securing the HumanOS also, or bad guys will continue to bypass all of our controls and simply target the human end-point"* [17].

Vulnerabilities Due to the Human Element. These observations somehow explain the innumerable vulnerabilities stemming from the human element that take place on a daily basis. Figure 1 depicts two prototypical ones. The left one portrays the deliberate choice of a trivial password to ease the burden of keeping it by heart, a case in which the user's balanced choice is for immediate comfort rather than for a somewhat more far-sighted comfort that a stronger password would have brought in terms of authentication. The right picture has a two-factor, card-and-PIN authentication system for building access whose card-possession factor is baffled by storing the cards next to the PIN pad—clearly anyone could (ab)use any card. The first vulnerability has been addressed by reinforcing the technical system to rule out users' silly choices of extremely obvious passwords, and NIST has published relevant guidelines that are now very widespread [10]. In my experience, however, they are not as pervasively applied as they should be, and perhaps have not yet been fully embraced in the health sector, for example. Of course, I am deliberately leaving aside from this argument the significant issues of human stress and counter-reactions due to the huge number of passwords for each user to remember, as well as those about the security of password managers implemented as computer programs precisely to remove the need for the user to remember all their passwords.

The other vulnerability in Fig. 1 is harder to address because we may follow two approaches that are both demanding and, ultimately, debatable. Fixes at the level of the technical systems are not obvious and, rather, would have to be very creative, hence potentially vulnerable themselves. Enhancements at the human level would, by contrast, have to face and remove pre-established paths of practice of least effort, hence would have to delve deeply into the institutional awareness of the cybersecurity issues and into the overall perception that cybersecurity can no longer be considered a subsidiary feature at the present time. These in Fig. 1 are only meant to serve as extreme examples, of course, but even more realistic ones could be drawn, for example, from the web security domain

Fig. 1. Prototypical vulnerabilities due to the human element (pics from the Internet).

where attacks such as (spear) phishing and cross-site scripting leverage human distraction and general cybersecurity ignorance.

Interactional Freedom. I have already attempted, in the recent years, to increase our understanding of why those that perhaps count as the most challenging vulnerabilities of the socio-technical system are due to its human element. This betrays the fact that the research question stated above has been giving me (and my colleagues!) headaches for years. It is now clearer that a complete answer to the research question would address such vulnerabilities, thereby effectively reducing the security of the socio-technical system to the security of its component technical system, as it was believed a few decades ago.

In this vein, I defined four cybersecurity paradigms, namely the criteria that inspire the security measures for technical systems, how such measures are designed and exposed to the users of the technical systems. These were *democratic security, dictatorial security, beautiful security* and *invisible security* [2]. I am sure that more paradigms exist and just wait to be discovered. For example, another one could come from *explainable security*, due to my colleagues Viganò and Magazzeni. This invited paper will review such paradigms from the standpoint of interaction design and, in particular, of *interactional freedom*. More precisely, *"freedom of interaction is based on the exploitation of a range of perceptual motor skills by offering the user myriad ways to reach the product's functionality"* hence, for example, in an *"alarm clock prototype, freedom of interaction is realized by offering myriad ways to set the wake-up time, instead of a fixed sequential procedure"* [19].

2   Democratic Security

Measures of democratic security strongly suffer the human factor. A somewhat tricky vulnerability was suffered by one of the early functions to share a file saved on a cloud storage system [13]. When a user generated a link that would grant access to the file, that link did not come with a clear policy as it does today, when we can normally decide who the link will work for and for how long. Therefore, when the user shared, in some way, the link with their peer, they were not aware of the full range of consequences. In particular, the file may suffer the following confidentiality vulnerabilities:

– The peer inadvertently put the link in the search bar of their browser rather than in the address bar, causing the connected search engine to index the link, hence enabling various third parties to access the file following some search.
– Moreover, if the file was a text file containing a clickable link to a third party address, humans who clicked on that link caused referral data including the link to be sent to the third party, which was then enabled to access the file.

Technical fixes for this issue were released rather quickly, arguably because addresing the vulnerability purely at the human level would have been much more daunting and time consuming, if at all possible. This is contrary to the unbelievable news that *"Some nuclear facilities do not change the default passwords on their equipment"* [1], which gives us no alternatives to a clear twist in people's mentality on cybersecurity and approach to it.

Looking at democratic security from the standpoint of interactional freedom, it is clear that humans have a lot of that freedom, hence the very name of the paradigm. This observation recalls the example seen above, when a user was allowed to choose a silly password, a likely exaggeration of freedom through their interaction with the technology. As I have pointed out elsewhere, democratic security seems to be the best established paradigm around us, and this perhaps simplifies a conclusion that we ought to move forward, somewhere away from it, by reducing the level of interactional freedom.

This is itself challenging because it is also known that *"For successful human-human communication the expression of emotion is essential"* [19], hence we need to strike a difficult balance to avoid frustration in the users of the security measures, yet ensuring that the freedom that is left does not undermine the measures. Whether that balance can be achieved in general remains an outstanding issue.

3 Dictatorial Security

As it can be gathered by the name, measures of dictatorial security embrace the human element in quite the opposite way as those of the previous type do. It follows that interactional freedom is reduced in this case, ideally zeroed entirely. All of us will have experienced that the mentioned NIST guidelines [10] forcing us to choose passwords that are long enough and contain lowcase, uppercase and special symbols feel rather dictatorial and may be received like a limitation to our creativity. Clearly, those constraints bring the intangible benefit of a robust password, thereby minimising the vulnerability of using weak secrets for authentication measures.

Psychologists tell us that, through our social relations, *"we need interactional freedom to control whether and how we interact with strangers"*, as well as *"we need to be socially included"* [9]. These are rather opposed priorities in general, and there is debate on which one prevails and when. I tend to believe that, most likely, our choices are the outcomes of some combination of both interactional freedom and social inclusion and, further, I hypothesise that this also applies with relatively no jerks to human-to-technology interactions. All the more do I emphasise this hypothesis because technology is becoming more and more an obvious means today, in fact merely a means, and even human-to-technology interactions may be perceived as human-to-human through technology ones eventually. This obviously requires investigation to be confirmed, but is not just looking at whether the user of an online bank account perceives the bank as some technological entity rather than as the human bank manager that used to be the peer in the past. It is also hinting at our century as the definitive milestone where humans and technology cross fade, also thanks to the progress in Artificial Intelligence. As a result, the need for social inclusion may easily stretch over technology in general, as it may already happen for teenagers and their favourite videogames.

Following such arguments, the generality of dictatorial security is even more questionable. Consider a user who connects to a remote host via SSH for the first time. The system will probably display something like this:

```
The authenticity of host www.dmi.unict.it can't
be established.
RSA key fingerprint is
2b:05:ff:64:91:60:24:3a:6e:83:c7:7a:c5:85:0a:41.
Are you sure you want to continue connecting
(yes/no)?
```

For this authentication measure to be made dictatorial, the concluding question would have to be avoided, and the protocol should abort. It would be similar to a browser refusing to render a web site because it could not verify the server's certificate key chain up to a trusted root certificate authority. On one hand, the sense of frustration imposed to users would be out of the question, with their consequent impulse for alternative ideas, including less secure ones, to accomplish the original goal of reaching the server. On the other hand, the challenge would be for us to equip the protocols with secure key certification sub-protocols to deliver the RSA key certificate to the caller before the actual handshake protocol initiates. This is such an extreme problem on the large scale that big-brother like heuristics as Certificate Transparency are getting momentum.

An additional potential limitation of dictatorial security is conceptual and is due to its pervasiveness. In particular, it is not entirely clear how to make all security measures follow this paradigm, if we define a sort of recursive scenario such as the very configuration of the security measures. Then, either we defeat the paradigm and leave the configuration choices to the system administrator's experience and, ultimately freedom, or we must admit the philosophical extreme that the technical systems can self-configure themselves.

4 Beautiful Security

If democratic security feels like a jungle of libertarianism and dictatorial security sounds like an impractical route, we may then recall humans' innate quest for beauty. Due to some inscrutable reasons, humans are attracted to what they find beautiful—or, vice versa, there exists some features that humans are attracted to for inscrutable reasons, and such features are normally addressed as beautiful. This is the fundamental hypothesis of beautiful security.

Beautiful security [2, 8] wants to be the all-encompassing paradigm of a positive user experience, hence something that humans want to comply with by their very nature (indicating both the humans' and the measures' natures in fact!). It may be understood as a more general, in terms of scope, and profound, in terms of human involvement, interpretation of the ploys of incentives, rewards and gamification. While these aim at tangible baits such as remuneration and fun, beauty may seem less tangible but may turn out more decisive in several circumstances, and history is full of countless examples to confirm the claim.

Beautiful security may be understood as more widely-scoped than traditional usable security, whose original aim was to make technical systems and their accompanying measures easy to learn by means of mere use, even without manuals. Although it is noticeable that usable security has gained a wider interpretation, this is certain not to cover the specific element of beauty. It follows that, in general, beautiful security is logically interpreted as a guarantee that humans will want to comply with a security measure that is beautified, while this cannot be concluded in general for a measure that is usable because, for example, users may still want to experience specific choices driven by sheer curiosity (similarly to a kid who drops a glass to experience the consequences).

Another closely related notion is positive security [14], a general one that is not meant to be exclusively applicable to the cyberspace. It aims well beyond *"protecting things we care about from negative consequences"* and *"enables us to engage in activities we value, and have experiences we cherish"* [15]. It is perhaps more abstract than beautiful security, avoiding to pinpoint what the key positive elements could be, which, by contrast, beautiful security identifies to be beauty.

My favourite example of a measure that is beautifully secure is authentication to the web interface of WhatsApp, which requires scanning by the smartphone that hosts the chats the QR code that a browser displays. I always argued that this is extremely more beautiful than, for example, tapping a long alphanumeric string in the smartphone [2]. However, I did not fully understand why until my colleagues and I distilled out what seems to be the four essential dimensions of beautiful security [6]: simplicity, convenience, assurance and modernity. The subjectivity element of beauty becomes more apparent through all four. In short, simplicity refers to easy of use, convenience to minimising time and effort, assurance to getting what is expected, including security, and modernity to adopting something trendy at present. It seems natural to argue that QR-code scanning embodies all dimensions, especially with respect to a long tap-in effort.

The question then arises if we can conceive a sort of beautification procedure, a way to take a security measure and transform it to make it beautiful. A dull way to do this would be to empty the measure altogether, a strategy that would be notably detrimental to security. It follows that any such procedure ought to *combine beauty and security*, and it still remains to be seen how to accomplish this in general. Fassl and Krombhoz focus on the particular measure that enables two people who meet up to authenticate their conversations taking place through their favourite chat system on their smartphones [12]. It is noted that the way this currently works, namely by showing their respective key fingerprint to each other from their phones, may suffer a number of potential barriers. Further to that, I do not believe that this measure is very popular and argue that it could be made more beautiful in many ways, notably by enabling each phone to scan the other one's fingerprint and ultimately confirming success by some audiovisual cues.

There is interactional freedom in beautiful security. In other words, it is as if engineers and scientists did not need to put too much effort in limiting that freedom and, rather, concentrated on how to make the interaction beautiful. In consequence, each user would self-limit their freedom of interaction by being attracted to compliance by the beauty. This is a clear metaphor also for what happens through traditional social relationships. In this light, it seems well worth continuing to deepen our understanding of what constitutes beauty through security measures.

5   Invisible Security

If beautiful security seems to stand at the early kilometres of a long journey, what if we did not need to worry about how security measures are received by their users? This is what invisible security postulates, namely that security measures are invisible and cannot be even perceived by their users although they are in place and perfectly working. The fundamental hypothesis that is leveraged here is that there are no such issues as deliberate or indeliberate human non-compliance with a security measure *if* that measure is invisible for the users.

I observed that invisible security has been known for a while, at least ever since Apple hid a fingerprint reader under the screen activation button of its iPhone 5s. By leveraging the widely established practice that a phone needed to be activated manually prior to being used, Apple found an effective way to make the authentication measure invisible in practice. By contrast, previous routine was to enter a PIN *after* screen activation.

Christianson, Viganò and I took this paradigm and tried to apply it to airport security, specifically to flight boarding [4]. By leveraging biometric authentication through an electronic ID, we conceived boarding-card-less boarding, with the result that, at the gate, a database would inform the airport flight attendant that the current passenger were authenticated and authorised to board the flight that currently stands at the gate. Fewer checks would remain to be performed by the attendant for each passenger, ultimately minimising the attendant's chances of error or of being targeted by malicious activity letting passengers travel to wrong (arbitrary?) destinations [16].

Later, I took invisibility to an extreme and conjectured that simply embedding an authenticated, biometric sample such as a fingerprint in the electronic ID would allow us to entirely dispose with the attendant's role for a human being and to transform it into a mere technical system [2]. Precisely, the passenger would scan their eID and fingerprint, then the technical system would match the live biometric sample to the stored one to authenticate the person and would finally check if that person were correctly registered for the flight at the gate. In principle, no human attendant would be needed anymore, hence zero human risk from that side (but some supervisor would be wise to keep anyway). I was then pleased to find out that Dubai Airport tested an even more developed version, which would make the security measures invisible for passengers too [11]. By storing passengers' IDs in the airport databases (if this is ever conceivable to scale up to all worldwide travellers), passengers would no longer be required to hand out or even carry their IDs. A fish tunnel hiding cameras was built so that passengers who were going through it to reach the gate would be attracted to the fish and stare at them. Here, cameras would recognise individual faces and match them to the database for authentication and authorisation to the flight. The security measures are made invisible for both participants in this prototype.

It is evident that interactional freedom is not an issue with invisible security. Even the potential frustration that dictatorial security may bring is not applicable here, either. We cannot be frustrated by whatever we cannot perceive and, moreover, I think that having to walk in a predetermined airport route for such invisible security measures to work would not be an additional element of frustration because people are already accustomed to that practice while they travel through airports.

There is a notable biometric invasion for invisible security to make sense. Whether this is going to be acceptable in the future on a large scale is hard to tell, but I perceive signs of welcome at present, perhaps due to the current regulations, at least at the European level. This is far from implying that every security measure can be made invisible today! Moreover, invisibility may have negative influences on people's general trust in the very technologies that the measures are meant to secure. For example, it would be very relevant to assess whether the passengers who boarded their flights through the fish tunnel felt that the procedures had been secure enough. Trust tends to reach a plateau and then root after a lapse of time. So, if the fish tunnel ever becomes a standard, then I argue that only after some time would passengers no longer be concerned about it by leveraging the general trustworthiness of the overall boarding experience. This is the same, for example, as with trust on safety—the early patients of X-ray machines as well as the early drivers of cars may have been concerned that they could die, but this is no longer a perceived issue today.

6 Explainable Security

Viganò and Magazzeni warn us that security measures ought to be adequately explained at all levels [18]. Intelligible explanations should be oriented at the expected users in particular, so as to favour acceptance of the measures to the users and, in turn, contribute to user compliance with the measures. Therefore, as seen with the other paradigms, explainability here works as another essential hypothesis—to win the users' compliance by favouring their understanding of what is going on and what is being accomplished. It makes perfect sense to me that, if tools such as written terms of use, privacy policies and more developed ones manage to deliver the relevant explanations to users, then users' attention and, ultimately, willingness to comply will be favoured.

Also in this case, I do not question the essential hypothesis but its precondition, namely the applicability of the paradigm. The real challenge is how to make explanations viable in general, namely whether the paradigm scales up. While this is the same applicability and scalability challenge noted with all other security paradigms, it is clear that explainability may not work well with a large number of users, such as with airport passengers and attendants, unless we find some technical systems to boost it on a large scale. Such tools can be expected to be very dependent on the specific application scenario, for example, we are used to receiving explanations about our trip by audio airport announcements, but these may not be effective in other scenarios.

7 Case Study

Let us consider a Security Operation Centre, normally addressed as a SOC. It is the ultimate line of defence against malicious attacks and typically is a separate institution whose core business is the detection, prevention and response to attacks to the customer institutions. It leverages cutting-edge technologies, including the most modern incarnations of Artificial Intelligence. Here, I see a SOC macroscopically as a socio-technical system whose main functional property is to provide its services and enhance the security measures of the customers.

Of course, a SOC is an obvious target of malicious activity itself. Also for this reason, none of its technical systems is fully independent from human scrutiny and, to confirm this, many job positions as a SOC analyst are available. With this case study, I conjecture various applications of the paradigms discussed above, to some degree. A company called CyberSecurityPlanet installs their new CSP system in the SOC, and the following story summarises the benefits, not only in terms of improved attack detection, prevention and response capabilities but, remarkably, in terms of the overall user experience.

Improved attack detection

Peter was approaching his shift to monitor dozens of monitors in the ExtremeProtection SOC. He frowned: *"And... how many logs will I have to decipher today! And... how many of them are going to be false and such a waste of time!"*. His phone rang, it was Dorothy, his shift supervisor: *"Peter, great news today! These folks from CyberSecurityPlanet finally installed their new CSP system and... you'll be able to interact with it and... guess what, they say you'll be able to get much more accurate outputs with dramatically fewer false alarms, can you believe it?!"*. Peter burst into laughter: *"Hahaha, not a tiny bit, but I'll take a look, goodbye!"*. He then opened the new CSP system and was prompted by a message he had never seen before:

Customer WannaBeSecure.
Event1: 7:58a.m. opening of server cabinet 3
Event2: 8:01a.m. account John runs PowerShell from HR
Event3: 8:02a.m. account Taylor launches GreatDB with user privileges. Please select any risky correlations. Maybe 1 and 2?

Peter froze. Excited at getting such a straight question after years of boring frustration but mostly pensive: *"Well, I remember John doing some admin level stuff before. Even early in the morning. Hey but... last week's headlines had it, yes, bingo!"*. He hurried up to confirm Event1 and Event2 were related, then the tool output:

Customer WannaBeSecure.
Attack detected: physical intrusion in HR, likely to be insider's as cabinet's digital lock is responsive; John's account blasted. Severity: critical

The previous week's news had been that WannaBeSecure was experiencing severe strikes due to new work conditions, and Peter was experienced enough to sense internal threats. Peter clicked to flag the attack to the response team immediately, then sat back and rang Dorothy to tell her the amazing story.

It can be appreciated that the new CSP system is less dictatorial than the previous one, hence more democratic. Still, the level of interactional freedom that it grants Peter, albeit increased, is limited to choosing from (intelligently defined) options. As a result, the attack detection capability of the SOC is more engaging hence perhaps less vulnerable to internal user distraction and is ultimately improved. Elements of beauty that can be identified are simplicity, convenience and assurance, while modernity can be added by elements of augmented reality, as we shall see below. The inherent risk that Peter makes a mistake through his judgment of external conditions to reinforce the learning by the tool is thwarted by the fault-tolerance mechanism that sees the detection team and the response team checking each other's findings.

Improved attack prevention

Peter was amazed on the phone. Five minutes of excitement, laughs and glittering eyes. *"Peter, they even say this damn new thing even anticipates relevant issues and predicts over half the attacks that will happen if you don't react beforehand with something so that they will actually not happen!"*. Peter's laugh was half-mouth this time. And the system prompted:

Customer StrongAsWeAre.
Event: 8:21a.m. account Sally from Cantine runs unprivileged process JohnTheRipper reaching 98
History: Previous similar events never exceeded 2 consecutive minutes.
Attack prediction: Sally is brute-forcing relevant hashes.

Peter was appalled. He killed the process and was going to ring Sally, the customer's contact, for explanations. But the CSP system let him do this with a click through a predefined chat message, and Sally confirmed with a *"not me!"*. So, Peter flagged it as a suspicious intrusion attempt and clicked to involve the response team again. His colleague Donna took it on.

Here, it is clear that CSP embodies the latest Artificial Intelligence techniques. However, beside that, it can be appreciated that Peter's role remains essential, and this makes him feel comfortable with his job. Once more, the system balances the democratic and the dictatorial approaches quite nicely. The system also authenticates Sally using some invisible security measures, which Peter finds convenient while he quickly moves on to the next action. So, elements of beautiful security and of invisible security intertwine.

Improved attack response

Donna had experienced hundreds of such invites, the only difference being that they used to arrive via phone. The new system told her everything she needed to know. Still, she was going to have to connect to StrongAsWeAre via VPN but first brief Sally on the response activities. How boring. Then, she would have had to kill off Sally's main process and reset Sally's account to ask for a new password setup at subsequent login. Donna knew she had to look up the VPN credentials somewhere (but where were they?!) then to enter that weird control panel where it seemed that they had done every effort to hide the password reset button. How annoying. And Sally! One of the most unpleasant ever. She was considering calling her sysadmin friend at StrongAsWeAre to ask the favour of... and the system beeped:

Customer StrongAsWeAre.
Suggested action: full account reset. Click here to inform user and launch reset job.

Donna clicked in amazement — and even got a reply that all processes were smooth, including escalation to Sally's supervisor if her password would not be reset in due time. All super-fast! Following those few clicks and system responses, Donna thought: *"Thank heavens, no phone calls, no Sally so far!"*.

This paragraph shows another instance of the integration of several technologies. First of all, these include all essential ones to let Donna carry out her tasks. Of course, such integration has to be secure so it presupposes a number of measures that are kept invisible. The interaction continues to exhibit a good balance between democratic and dictatorial security, so that some interactional freedom is there, as well as the dimensions of beautiful security, except for modernity. In this particular case, the technology also tries to minimise the possible stress induced by social relations at the professional level by porting these onto the technical system, an outcome that may not be achievable in general.

Improved user experience

The day after, Donna went to work at ExtremeProtection thinking that it was time for her to look for a new job. OK, things had become way smoother and faster, yet she just disliked the workplace and felt oppressed by being surrounded left-to-right by that array of monitors: *"Yes, I'll speak to the line manager. A more managerial position or goodbye!"*. Strangely enough, she was given a pair of smart glasses upon entrance. Some explanations followed and, there she was, wearing a HoloLens pair during her shift. It was like entering a parallel world. She finalised a response activity by staring at a couple of innovative, visual forms and confirming them by a blink and a mouse-click. The HoloLens coloured items according to urgency, and a short beep would come up at different frequencies when she stared at a specific item, depending on its urgency. Perhaps it required a couple of days to fully adjust to but, all in all, it turned out to be much less tiring than the traditional hunt for relevant information through those damn monitors, when she had to prioritise for

> herself what to do first. *"My friends will hear my story tonight!"*, she
> mumbled that afternoon on her way home. What about her new job?

This final part emphasises the improvements to the overall user experience for Donna thanks to the use of a pair of smart glasses. These bring a clear element of modernity, thereby effectively contributing to making the security measure of attack response more beautiful than before. It is also apparent where and how explainable security plays its role—Donna could not have properly interacted with the new, enhanced system without an adequate briefing.

8   Conclusions

This paper summarised my understanding of five modern paradigms to approach cybersecurity problems and, correspondingly, build the measures to face those problems. While democratic and dictatorial security seem the two sides of the same coin, it is clear that they ought to be combined to some extent. It means that we should build security measures that ensure an appropriate level of interactional freedom to the users of the technology that the measures intend to secure, otherwise the human element may source dramatic risks and determine consequent vulnerabilities. Beautiful security and invisible security appear to be more modern. The former is inherently affected by subjectivity, but resolves the issue of making people want to comply with the way security measures are designed and implemented. By contrast, invisible security is less subjective but may hinder people's trust perceptions in the short term.

All these seem reasonable to be intertwined together to some extent, with the ultimate aim of strengthening the socio-technical system that combines a core technical system with its human users. All paradigms may benefit from a conjugation with explainable security, which means that explaining how the security measures work may favour the expected form of user engagement, even by raising awareness through invisible security measures. Interactional freedom was the lens to discuss the paradigms. Some level of freedom was appreciable in all cases, except with invisible security, which, however, makes the measures not apparently there. The arguments developed and the examples provided above form my own way of addressing the research question. It is clear, however, that more technological developments as well as more experiments with human subjects would be needed to fully support such arguments. This is a resource effort that I deem indispensable to resolve the tedious and infamous attack-fix-loop practice that the world is trying to leave behind. Making that effort will turn out less expensive, in the long term, than not making it.

Acknowledgements. I am indebted to all my coauthors for thought-provoking discussions and effective collaborations to develop those thoughts into actual concepts and working prototypes.

References

1. Baylon, C., Brunt, R., Livingstone, D.: Cyber Security at Civil Nuclear Facilities – Chatham House Report (2015). https://www.calameo.com/books/003701328a454e3527bf9
2. Bella, G.: Out to explore the cybersecurity planet. Emerald J. Intellect. Capital **21**(2), 291–307 (2020). https://doi.org/10.1108/JIC-05-2019-0127
3. Bella, G., Bistarelli, S.: Soft constraints for security protocol analysis: confidentiality. In: Ramakrishnan, I.V. (ed.) PADL 2001. LNCS, vol. 1990, pp. 108–122. Springer, Heidelberg (2001). https://doi.org/10.1007/3-540-45241-9_8
4. Bella, G., Christianson, B., Viganò, L.: Invisible security. In: Anderson, J., Matyáš, V., Christianson, B., Stajano, F. (eds.) Security Protocols 2016. LNCS, vol. 10368, pp. 1–9. Springer, Cham (2017). https://doi.org/10.1007/978-3-319-62033-6_1
5. Bella, G., Curzon, P., Lenzini, G.: Service security and privacy as a socio-technical problem. IOS J. Comput. Secur. **23**(5), 563–585 (2015). https://doi.org/10.3233/jcs-150536
6. Bella, G., Ophoff, J., Renaud, K., Sempreboni, D., Viganò, L.: Perceptions of beauty in security ceremonies. Philos. Technol. **35**, 72 (2022). https://doi.org/10.1007/s13347-022-00552-0
7. Bella, G., Paulson, L.C.: Mechanising BAN Kerberos by the inductive method. In: Hu, A.J., Vardi, M.Y. (eds.) CAV 1998. LNCS, vol. 1427, pp. 416–427. Springer, Heidelberg (1998). https://doi.org/10.1007/BFb0028763
8. Bella, G., Viganò, L.: Security is beautiful. In: Christianson, B., Švenda, P., Matyáš, V., Malcolm, J., Stajano, F., Anderson, J. (eds.) Security Protocols 2015. LNCS, vol. 9379, pp. 247–250. Springer, Cham (2015). https://doi.org/10.1007/978-3-319-26096-9_25
9. Brownlee, K.: Being Sure of Each Other: An Essay on Social Rights and Freedoms. Information Security and Cryptography. Oxford University Press (2020)
10. Burr, W.E., Dodson, D.F., Polk, W.T.: NIST special publication 800-63 (2004)
11. Elliott, A.F.: Dubai Airport is replacing security checks with face-scanning fish (2017). https://www.telegraph.co.uk/travel/news/dubai-airport-replaces-security-checks-with-face-scanning-fish/
12. Fassl, M., Krombholz, K.: Why i can't authenticate – understanding the low adoption of authentication ceremonies with autoethnography. In: CHI Conference on Human Factors in Computing Systems (CHI 2023) (2023). https://publications.cispa.saarland/3895/
13. Gilbert, D.: Dropbox and Box Users Accidentally Leaking Private Files Online (2014). https://www.ibtimes.co.uk/dropbox-box-users-accidentally-leaking-private-files-online-1447352
14. Roe, P.: The 'value' of positive security. Rev. Int. Stud. **34**, 777–794 (2008). https://doi.org/10.1017/S0260210508008279
15. Sasse, A., Rashid, A.: Human factors knowledge area issue 1.0. The Cyber Security Body of Knowledge (2019)
16. Ryanair passenger lands in wrong Italian city (2012). http://www.mirror.co.uk/news/uk-news/ryanair-passenger-gets-on-wrong-plane-946207
17. This is Why The Human is the Weakest Link (2021). https://www.sans.org/blog/this-is-why-the-human-is-the-weakest-link/

18. Vigano, L., Magazzeni, D.: Explainable security. In: Proceedings of the 2020 IEEE European Symposium on Security and Privacy Workshops (EuroSPW 2020), pp. 293–300 (2020)
19. Wensveen, S., Overbeeke, K., Djajadiningrat, T., Kyffin, S.: Freedom of fun, freedom of interaction. Interactions **11**, 59–61 (2004). https://doi.org/10.1145/1015530.1015559

Lightweight Permutation-Based Cryptography for the Ultra-Low-Power Internet of Things

Malik Alsahli, Alex Borgognoni, Luan Cardoso dos Santos, Hao Cheng, Christian Franck, and Johann Großschädl[(✉)]

DCS and SnT, University of Luxembourg, 6, Avenue de la Fonte, 4364 Esch-sur-Alzette, Luxembourg
{malik.alsahli.001,alex.borgognoni.001}@student.uni.lu,
{luan.cardoso,hao.cheng,christian.franck,johann.groszschaedl}@uni.lu

Abstract. The U.S. National Institute of Standards and Technology is currently undertaking a process to evaluate and eventually standardize one or more "lightweight" algorithms for authenticated encryption and hashing that are suitable for resource-restricted devices. In addition to security, this process takes into account the efficiency of the candidate algorithms in various hardware environments (e.g. FPGAs, ASICs) and software platforms (e.g. 8, 16, 32-bit microcontrollers). However, while there exist numerous detailed benchmarking results for 8-bit AVR and 32-bit ARM/RISC-V/ESP32 microcontrollers, relatively little is known about the candidates' efficiency on 16-bit platforms. In order to fill this gap, we present a performance evaluation of the final-round candidates ASCON, SCHWAEMM, TINYJAMBU, and XOODYAK on the MSP430 series of ultra-low-power 16-bit microcontrollers from Texas Instruments. All four algorithms were explicitly designed to achieve high performance in software and have further in common that the underlying primitive is a permutation. We discuss how these permutations can be implemented efficiently in Assembly language and analyze how basic design decisions impact their execution time on the MSP430 architecture. Our results show that, overall, SCHWAEMM is the fastest algorithm across various lengths of data and associated data, respectively. XOODYAK has benefits when a large amount of associated data is to be authenticated, whereas TINYJAMBU is very efficient for the authentication of short messages.

1 Introduction

The emergence and rise of *cryptographic permutations* is widely seen one of the most exciting developments in the field of symmetric cryptography during the past 20 years. Formally, a cryptographic permutation is defined as a bijective mapping within $\mathbb{Z}_2^b$ (the bitstrings of length b), designed to behave as a random permutation, i.e. a permutation drawn uniformly at random from the set of all possible permutations that operate on b bits [5]. The width b of a permutation can range from 100 (e.g. PHOTON [17] and other cryptosystems that target the embedded domain) to 1600 (e.g. KECCAK [6]). Permutations are highly flexible and universally-applicable primitives, similar to block ciphers, and can be used to construct e.g. hash functions, message authentication codes, pseudo-random bit-sequence generators, stream ciphers, and even algorithms for authenticated encryption [3,5,7]. However, in contrast to a block cipher, a permutation is an unkeyed primitive, i.e. it does not use any key and, therefore, does not have to perform a key schedule. Another difference is that a cryptographic permutation is usually designed to be efficient only in the forward direction since the inverse permutation is (normally) not needed. In recent years, permutations have also served as building block for the design of "advanced modes" that cover the full functionality of the symmetric portion of modern security protocols. Examples for this relatively new line of research include Blinker [26], the Strobe protocol framework [18], and Stateful Hash Objects (SHO) [23].

Permutations are especially suitable for *lightweight cryptography*, which can be very generally defined as "cryptographic primitives, schemes, and protocols tailored to (extremely) constrained environments" [16]. Examples of such environments include RFID tags, miniature sensors and actuators, and numerous other kinds of devices that form part of the *Internet of Things (IoT)* [32]. The U.S. National Institute of Standards and Technology (NIST) is currently in the process of standardizing lightweight cryptosystems, in particular cryptographic hash functions and algorithms for Authenticated Encryption with Associated Data (AEAD) [20]. Permutation-based designs perform extremely well in this standardization, which is evidenced by the fact that 16 out of 32 s-round candidates, and four out of the ten candidates in the third and final round, use a permutation as low-level primitive [22]. The four permutation-based designs in the (currently still ongoing) final round of NIST's standardization effort are ASCON [15], SPARKLE [2], TINYJAMBU [31], and XOODYAK [12]. However, the finalist TINYJAMBU is a special case since it uses a keyed permutation and can also be classified as a block-cipher-based design (like in [22]). The width of the permutations ranges from 128 bits (TINYJAMBU) over 320 bits (ASCON) up to 384 bits (SPARKLE384, XOODYAK). SPARKLE is a classical Addition-Rotation-XOR (ARX) design, while the other three permutations may be categorized as "AndRX" variants, i.e. they generate non-linearity via logical AND operations instead of modular additions.

The evaluation of candidates for NIST's lightweight cryptography standard takes into account a number of criteria, among which security and performance on software and hardware platforms are particularly important [22]. Regarding software performance, the official NIST document on submission requirements advised the algorithm designers to "consider a wide range of 8-bit, 16-bit, and 32-bit microcontroller architectures" [20, Sect. 3.4]. For most of the final-round candidates, optimized implementations with highly-tuned Assembly segments for the performance-critical parts have been developed for 8-bit and 32-bit platforms, most notably the AVR ATmega [19] and ARM Cortex-M3/M4 [1] series

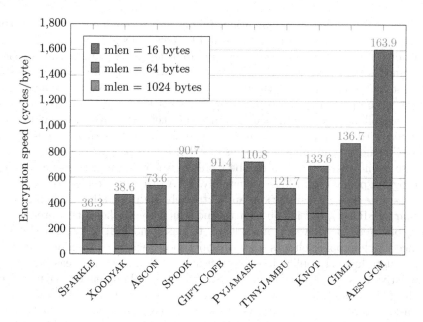

Fig. 1. Comparison of the ten fastest second-round AEAD candidates for encryption of a message with a length of 16, 64, and 1024 bytes (without associated data) on an ARM Cortex-M4F microcontroller. The value above each bar is the encryption speed (in cycles per byte) for a 1024-byte message. For each candidate, the implementation with the best encryption time for 1024 bytes was chosen.

of microcontrollers. These Assembly implementations either come directly from the designers or have been contributed by other developers [30]. Hence, there exist now a large number of implementation results for these two platforms, in particular execution time and binary code size. Detailed benchmarking results have been published by the NIST lightweight cryptography team [21] and some academic research groups, see e.g. [24]. The four permutation-based algorithms are highly efficient in software; for example, SPARKLE, XOODYAK, and ASCON take the top three positions on ARM Cortex-M4F according to NIST's official second-round benchmarking results[1], see Fig. 1. While the efficiency of the ten finalists on 8-bit and 32-bit architectures is well understood, relatively little is known about their performance and binary code size on 16-bit platforms. The only relevant paper we became aware of was published very recently by Blanc et al. [8], who benchmarked reference and optimized C implementations of the final-round candidates on a 16-bit MSP430F1611 microcontroller.

The 16-bit MSP430 platform from Texas Instruments is a particularly interesting target for the benchmarking of lightweight cryptosystems, mainly due to two reasons. First, MSP430 microcontrollers were from the ground up designed

---

[1] At the time of writing this paper, the third (i.e. final) round of evaluation was still going on and NIST had not yet released the round-3 benchmarking results.

with the goal of low power dissipation, taking into account not only the active processing power, but also power in stand-by (resp. sleep) mode, which makes them ideal for many kinds of battery-operated devices, e.g. miniature wireless sensor nodes [14]. Recent members of the MSP430 family support up to seven different *low-power modes* with fine-grain control over active components and instant wake-up thanks to a sophisticated clock system. Furthermore, MSP430 microcontrollers were among the first mass-market IoT platforms that became equipped with *Ferro-electric Random Access Memory (FRAM)*, a non-volatile form of memory combining properties of SRAM with properties of flash within a single memory space, which can be flexibly (re)configured to serve as storage for program or data [25]. More concretely, FRAM features relatively fast write accesses, low power consumption, and extremely high reliability and endurance (similar to SRAM), but is non-volatile and, thus, able to hold its content when being powered off. However, in contrast to flash and EEPROM, FRAM does not need high supply voltages for write operations, which is a major advantage for e.g. data-logging applications. Furthermore, FRAM makes it easy to switch from active to sleep mode and vice versa, thereby enabling energy savings even for short periods of inactivity. Texas Instruments markets the MSP430 line as "ultra-low-power" microcontrollers [29] to emphasize their potency for battery-operated devices. The fact that such devices are widely used in security-critical applications (e.g. sensors for medical monitoring) makes a strong case to assess the performance of the NIST finalists under ultra-low-power regimes.

A second reason as to why MSP430 microcontrollers are an interesting platform for the benchmarking of NIST's candidate algorithms relates to the basic characteristics of the underlying instruction set architecture. The MSP430 is, in essence, a CISC-like memory-to-memory architecture [27], whereas virtually all other benchmarking platforms (especially AVR and ARM) are more RISC-like and based on the load/store paradigm. All data processing instructions of the MSP430 architecture do not necessarily need to have the operands in registers but can also operate directly on data held in memory (without an intermediate register holding) [28]. This contrasts with RISC architectures, where operands have to be first loaded from memory to registers before an instruction can be executed on them. To a certain extent, the ability to directly process data in memory compensates for the (relatively) limited register space of the MSP430 architecture[2]. It is exactly these architectural differences that are interesting in the context of benchmarking. Namely, as argued in [4,9], a lightweight cryptographic algorithm should be fast on a broad range of microcontroller platforms with highly diverse and even divergent characteristics. Collecting benchmarks on a (somewhat) CISC-based architecture like the MSP430 makes sense since the current portfolio of benchmarking platforms is solely RISC-based and does not represent the high diversity of microcontrollers in the IoT.

---

[2] Out of the total of 16 general-purpose registers, only 12 can actually be used by the programmer, which means the usable register space of MSP430 microcontrollers is even smaller than that of the 8-bit AVR architecture (192 vs. 256 bits).

In this paper, we analyze and compare the performance of the permutation-based AEAD algorithms Ascon, Schwaemm, TinyJambu, and Xoodyak on a 16-bit MSP430F1611 microcontroller. However, in contrast to the recent work of Blanc et al. [8], we use carefully-optimized Assembly implementations of the underlying permutations for our evaluation. We developed all implementations from scratch, whereby we aimed for a reasonable trade-off between execution time and code size. Furthermore, we do not only report benchmarking results of the four algorithms for different lengths of associated data and data, but we also aim to analyze and explain *why* the algorithms perform differently on the MSP430 platform. More concretely, we study how basic design decisions of the underlying permutation, such as the *rotation distances* or the *locality* (i.e. the ability to operate on only a part of the state at a time[3]) affect their execution time. To this end, we developed a special tool that is able to simulate MSP430 instructions and gather detailed information about the execution profile of the permutations, e.g. the number of memory accesses. We use this information to compare the (relative) amount of register-to-register operations for each of the permutations, the proportions of clock cycles they spent for rotations and non-linear operations, as well as their throughput in terms of cycles per state-byte and per rate-byte, respectively. We observed significant differences in execution time, not only for the permutations but also for the full AEAD schemes. When taking different lengths of associated data and plaintext (resp. ciphertext) into account, Schwaemm is the best overall performer, mainly because it combines a well-optimizable permutation with an efficient mode of operation.

2 MSP430 Architecture

The MSP430 architecture uses the von-Neumann memory model, which means instructions (i.e. code) and data share a unified address space. There is a single address bus and a single data bus connecting the microcontroller core with the RAM, non-volatile memory (flash or FRAM), and peripheral modules. MSP430 microcontrollers have a total of 16 registers, each 16 bits wide, of which 12 are general working registers, and the remaining four serve a special purpose: r0 is the program counter, r1 is the stack pointer, r2 is a status register, and r3 is used to generate common constants like $-1, 0, 1, 2, 4, 8$. The instruction set is rather minimalist and consists of only 27 core instructions that can be divided into three categories: double-operand instructions (which overwrite one of the operands with the result), single-operand instructions, and jumps. Most of the instructions can not only operate on 16-bit operands, but also on bytes (more concretely, the lower bytes of 16-bit operands) when the instruction is suffixed by .b. The instruction set is orthogonal and supports seven addressing modes

---

[3] As argued in [4], the ability to work locally (i.e. on a part of the state at a time) is an important design criterion to achieve good efficiency on microcontrollers whose register space is too small to store the full state (high locality reduces the need to move state-words between registers and RAM). However, efficiency desiderata like locality have to be carefully balanced with security desiderata like diffusion.

altogether, including modes for direct memory-to-memory transfers without an intermediate register holding [28]. Depending on the addressing mode(s), the latency of double-operand instructions can vary between one clock cycle (when both source and destination operand are held in registers) and six clock cycles (when operands and result are in RAM or non-volatile memory).

As explained in the last section, the MSP430 architecture is more CISC-like than e.g. AVR or ARM since it allows one to execute instructions on operands held in RAM or flash without intermediate register holding. For example, the instruction add.w @r4+, 8(r5) adds two 16-bit words, whereby register r4 and r5 contain the addresses of the operands (resp. result) instead of their actual values. More precisely, the first operand is accessed through the indirect auto-increment addressing mode, which means the value in r4 is a pointer that gets automatically incremented by 2 after the 16-bit word at the target address has been fetched. On the other hand, the effective address of the second operand (and also of the result) is obtained using the indexed addressing mode, i.e. it is the sum of the base address contained in register r5 and the offset of 8 (note that in MSP430 assembly language, the destination of an instruction is always on the right side). Consequently, two loads, an addition, and a store operation are combined into a single memory-to-memory instruction, which (potentially) saves not only code space but also execution time. On a RISC architecture like ARM, such a sequence of operations requires four separate instructions in the best case, and up to twice as much under register pressure. Namely, when all registers are occupied, two registers need to be spilled to free up space for the operands, which costs two push and two pop instructions. To some extent, the ability to execute memory-to-memory instructions compensates for the limited register capacity of the MSP430 architecture. However, since memory accesses generally increase the latency of instructions, finding a good register allocation is still very important to reach high performance.

Shifts or rotations of either 32-bit words or 64-bit words are essential operations of the four permutations we consider in this paper. However, contrary to their ARM counterparts, MSP430 microcontrollers do not feature a fast barrel shifter that would allow them to shift or rotate a 16-bit operand by several bits at a time. Therefore, multi-bit shifts/rotates have to be composed of the single-bit shift and rotate instructions supported by the MSP430 architecture; these are rla.w and rra.w for arithmetic shifts, and rlc.w and rrc.w for rotations via carry [27]. The execution time of shifts/rotations of 32-bit or 64-bit words depends heavily on the shift/rotation distance, whereby the best possible case is a distance of (a multiple of) 16 bits. Rotating a 32-bit or 64-bit word stored in registers by 16 bits is usually free since it only requires adapting the order in which the 16-bit parts are accessed in a subsequent operation. For example, an operation of the form $a = a \oplus (b \ggg 16)$, where a and b are 32-bit words in the register pairs r4,r5 and r6,r7, respectively, takes only two xor.w instructions since the 16-bit rotation of b can be carried out *implicitly*: xor.w r7, r4 and xor.w r6, r5. When a and b are 64-bit words, shifts or rotations by a multiple of 16 bits, i.e. 16, 32, and 48 bits, can be performed implicitly.

Listing 1. Macro for 1-bit left-rotation of a 32-bit word.

```
1:  QROL macro a0, a1
2:      rla.w   a0
3:      rlc.w   a1
4:      adc.w   a0
5:      endm
```

Listing 2. Macro for 1-bit right-rotation of a 32-bit word.

```
1:  QROR macro a0, a1
2:      bit.w   #1, a0
3:      rrc.w   a1
4:      rrc.w   a0
5:      endm
```

Listing 3. Macro for 8-bit left-rotation of a 32-bit word (tr is a scratch register).

```
1:  QROL8 macro a0, a1
2:      swpb    a0
3:      swpb    a1
4:      mov.b   a0, tr
5:      xor.b   a1, tr
6:      xor.w   tr, a0
7:      xor.w   tr, a1
8:      endm
```

Listing 4. Macro for 8-bit right-rotation of a 32-bit word (tr is a scratch register).

```
1:  QROR8 macro a0, a1
2:      mov.b   a0, tr
3:      xor.b   a1, tr
4:      xor.w   tr, a0
5:      xor.w   tr, a1
6:      swpb    a0
7:      swpb    a1
8:      endm
```

The second-fastest shift/rotation distances, after (multiples of) 16 bits, are the ones that are close to multiples of 16 bits, e.g. 1, 15, 17, and 31 bits for 32-bit words. Shifting a 32-bit word held in two registers by one of these distances requires two instructions and takes two cycles, independent of the direction. An additional instruction is necessary for a rotation, whereby again the direction does not matter, i.e. a right-rotation needs the same number of cycles as a left-rotation. Listing 1 and 2 contain Assembly macros (based on directives of the IAR assembler) to rotate a 32-bit word held in registers one bit to the left and to the right, respectively. A rotation by a distance of more than one bit can be composed of these two macros, which confirms the importance of choosing the rotation distances carefully since e.g. a rotation by three bits already costs 12 cycles. However, thanks to the swap-byte instruction swpb, a "shortcut" exists for 8-bit left and right rotation as shown in Listing 3 and 4, respectively. These macros use byte-wise instructions with the .b suffix that only operate on the lower byte of a 16-bit register and set its upper byte to 0. Since the execution time of both macros is only six cycles, they can accelerate rotations by certain distances through a decomposition into 8-bit and 1-bit steps (e.g. a 7-bit right-rotation can be performed by first rotating eight bits right and then one bit to the left). Table 1 summarizes the execution time of optimized implementations of rotations by distances between 1 and 15 bits. As explained earlier, a rotation by a multiple of 16 bits is normally free (up to register-reordering). A rotation by distances of $n > 16$ bits can always be reduced to a $(n \bmod 16)$-bit rotation along with an implicit register-reordering in a subsequent operation.

Table 1. Execution time (in clock cycles) for a rotation of a 32-bit and a 64-bit word over a distance from 1 to 15 bits.

Rotation distance (bits)	1	2	3	4	5	6	7	8	9	10	11	12	13	14	15
Time to rotate a 32-bit word	3	6	9	12	15	12	9	6	9	12	15	12	9	6	3
Time to rotate a 64-bit word	5	10	15	20	25	26	21	16	21	26	25	20	15	10	5

3 Overview of the AEAD Algorithms

In this section, we overview the main properties of the four AEAD algorithms we consider in this paper, namely ASCON, SCHWAEMM, TINYJAMBU V2, and XOODYAK. They all reached the final round of NIST's lightweight cryptography standardization project [22] and are well suited for small microcontrollers.

ASCON. ASCON is not only one of the 10 finalists of NIST's standardization project in lightweight cryptography, but was also selected for the final portfolio of the CAESAR competition. The main AEAD instance of the ASCON suite is ASCON-128 and offers 128-bit security according to [15]. It is based on the so-called Monkey Duplex mode [7] with a stronger keyed initialization and keyed finalization function, respectively, which means the underlying permutation is carried out with an increased number of rounds. Said permutation operates on a 320-bit state (organized in five 64-bit words) by iteratively applying a round function p. The number of rounds is $a = 12$ in the initialization and finalization phase, and $b = 6$ otherwise; the corresponding permutations are referred to as p^a and p^b in the specification. ASCON-128 processes associated data as well as plaintext/ciphertext with a rate of $r = 64$ bits, i.e. the capacity is 256 bits. The hash function of the ASCON suite is a classical sponge construction.

ASCON's round function p is SPN-based and comprises three parts: (i) the addition of an 8-bit round constant c_r to a 64-bit state-word, (ii) a substitution layer that operates across the five words of the state and implements an affine equivalent of the S-box in the χ mapping of KECCAK [6], and (iii) a diffusion layer consisting of linear functions that are similar to the Σ functions in SHA2 and performed on each state-word individually. The S-box maps five input bits to five output bits and is applied to each column of the state, whereby the five state-words are arranged upon each other. It is normally implemented in a bit-sliced fashion using logical ANDs and XORs. The diffusion layer performs an operation of the form $x = x \oplus (x \ggg n_1) \oplus (x \ggg n_2)$ on each word of the state with $n_1 \in \{1, 7, 10, 19, 61\}$ and $n_2 \in \{6, 17, 28, 39, 41\}$ [15].

SPARKLE. The SPARKLE suite submitted to NIST consists of four instances of the AEAD algorithm SCHWAEMM, targeting security levels of 128, 192, and

256 bits, as well as two instances of the hash function ESCH with digest lengths of 256 and 384 bits. All instances are built on top of the SPARKLE permutation family, which consists of three members that differ by the width (i.e. the state size) and the number of steps they execute. SCHWAEMM is based on the highly-efficient BEETLE mode of use [11], whereas ESCH can be classified as a sponge construction. The main instance of SCHWAEMM uses the 384-bit variant of the SPARKLE permutation, i.e. SPARKLE384, with a rate of 256 bits. This variant is also used for ESCH256, the main instance of the hash function ESCH. Besides SPARKLE384, there exists also a smaller and a larger version of the permutation with a width of 256 and 512 bits, respectively (see [2] for details).

SPARKLE384 is a classical ARX design, optimized for high speed on a wide range of 8, 16, and 32-bit microcontrollers. The permutation is performed with a big number of steps, namely 11, for initialization, finalization, and separation between the processing of associated data and the secret message, while a slim (i.e. 7-step) version is used to update the intermediate state. From a high-level point of view, the permutation has an SPN structure and comprises three main parts: (i) a non-linear layer consisting of six parallel ARX-boxes, (ii) a simple linear diffusion layer, (iii) the addition of a step counter and round constant to the 384-bit state. The ARX-box is called ALZETTE and can be seen as a small 64-bit block cipher that operates on two 32-bit words and performs additions modulo 2^{32}, logical XORs, and rotations by 16, 17, 24, and 31 bits [2]. On the other hand, the linear layer is, in essence, a Feistel round with a linear Feistel function, followed by a swap of the left and right half of the state.

TinyJAMBU. TINYJAMBU is, in essence, a permutation-based variant of the AEAD algorithm JAMBU, which was a candidate of the CAESAR competition but did not make it into the final portfolio. A distinguishing feature of TINY-JAMBU is that it uses a keyed permutation and not a public (i.e. unkeyed) one like the other AEAD algorithms. However, according to [22], TINYJAMBU can also be viewed as a block-cipher-based design. In any case, the permutation has a very short width of only 128 bits. There is no key schedule, which means the key-bytes are directly added to the state. The specification [31] describes three variants of TINYJAMBU with key lengths of 128, 192, and 256 bits, whereby the main instance uses a 128-bit key with a 96-bit nonce. Its mode of operation is based on the duplex construction [5], but offers better security in nonce-misuse settings [31, Sect. 6]. Both the associated data and the plaintext/ciphertext are processed at a relatively low rate of 32 bits, i.e. four bytes.

The 128-bit permutation of TINYJAMBU is essentially a Nonlinear Feedback Shift Register (NFSR) whose feedback path consists of four bit-wise XOR and a bit-wise NAND operation. The latter is the only non-linear component of the whole permutation. Several rounds can be computed in parallel (e.g. 32 rounds when the target platform is a 32-bit microcontroller), which benefits software performance. The most costly part of the permutation are special shifts of the form $c = (a \gg n) \vee (b \ll (32 - n))$, where a, b, and c are 32-bit words and the shift distance $n \in \{6, 15, 21, 27\}$. These so-called *funnel shifts* concatenate two

32-bit words into a 64-bit value, shift this 64-bit value n bits left or right, and return the 32 most-significant (left shift) or least-significant (right shift) bits as result. Optimized software implementations combine 128 rounds (i.e. 128 state updates) into a step and execute several steps in a loop. TINYJAMBU processes associated data by iterating the step-loop five times (i.e. 640 rounds), whereas plaintext/ciphertex is processed with eight iterations (i.e. 1024 rounds).

Xoodoo. XOODYAK is a highly versatile cryptographic scheme that is suitable for a wide range of symmetric-key functions including hashing, pseudo-random bit generation, authentication, encryption, and authenticated encryption. At its heart is XOODOO, a lightweight 384-bit permutation [13]. The XOODYAK suite submitted to the NIST lightweight crypto project includes an AEAD algorithm and a hash function; both are built on the Cyclist mode of operation [12]. To perform authenticated encryption, Cyclist has to be initialized in keyed mode with a 128-bit key and nonce, respectively, after which associated data can be absorbed at a rate of 352 bits (i.e. 44 bytes), whereas plaintext/ciphertext gets processed at a rate of 192 bits. On the other hand, when Cyclist is operated in hash mode, the rate is 128 bits (i.e. 256 bits of capacity).

XOODOO was inspired by KECCAK [6] and GIMLI [4] in the sense that the state has the same size and is represented in the same way as in GIMLI, though the round function is similar to KECCAK. Consequently, the state has the form of a 3×4 matrix of 32-bit words, which can be visualized via three horizontal 128-bit planes (one above the other), each consisting of four 32-bit lanes. It is also possible to view the 384-bit state as 128 columns of three bits lying upon another (i.e. each bit belongs to a different plane). The XOODOO permutation executes 12 iterations of a round function of five steps: a column-parity mixing layer θ, a non-linear layer χ, two plane-shifting layers (ρ_{west} and ρ_{east}) between them, and a round-constant addition. Both ρ layers move bits horizontally and perform lane-wise rotations of planes as well as rotations of lanes by 11, 1, and 8 bits to the left. On the other hand, in the parity-computation part of θ and in the χ layer, state-bits interact only vertically, i.e. within 3-bit columns. The θ layer mainly executes XORs and left-rotations by 5 and 14 bits. Finally, the non-linear layer χ applies a 3-bit S-box to each column of the state, which can be computed using logical ANDs, XORs, and bitwise complements.

4 Implementation Details

We developed optimized implementations of the four AEAD algorithms for the purpose of benchmarking and performance analysis using a combination of C and MSP430 Assembly language. More concretely, the underlying permutation is the Assembly component, while the surrounding mode of operation (or mode of use) is written in C. Most of the C source code is based on either reference or optimized implementations provided by the designer teams, but we adapted them to adhere to the low-level benchmarking API introduced in [10] to ensure a consistent evaluation. The MSP430 Assembly code of the four permutations (which we developed from scratch) is based on a common set of special macros for load/store operations (using different addressing modes), arithmetic/logical operations, and shifts/rotations of both 32-bit and 64-bit operands. Our main optimization goal for the permutations was to achieve a good trade-off between execution time and (binary) code size, and therefore we refrained from certain optimization techniques like full loop unrolling, which in the case of MSP430 often only achieve a modest reduction in execution time at the expense of an enormous increase in code size. We devoted a similar amount of optimization time and effort to each of the four permutations to guarantee a fair evaluation and comparison of the performance of the AEAD algorithms.

The rotations performed by the four permutations are composed of macros for 1-bit and 8-bit rotation. As mentioned in Sect. 2, a rotation by a distance of $n > 16$ bits can be split up into a rotation by $k = n \bmod 16$ bits (taking into account that a k-bit rotation in one direction equals a $(16 - k)$-bit rotation in the other direction), followed by a rotation by a multiple of 16 bits, which can usually be performed implicitly (i.e. as part of a subsequent arithmetic/logical or store operation) and is, therefore, free. Since all four permutations use the same set of macros for rotations and other operations on 32/64-bit words, the optimization effort essentially boiled down to finding a good register allocation strategy in order to minimize the number of memory accesses. This includes both explicit accesses in the form of loads and stores, but also implicit accesses that take place when executing instructions where one or both operands reside in memory. A good register allocation is crucial for ASCON, SPARKLE384, and XOODYAK since the size of their state is too big for the register space of the MSP430, which means the state has to be kept in RAM and parts of the state are loaded to registers to reduce the latency of arithmetic/logical instructions executed on them. However, TINYJAMBU's 128-bit state can be entirely kept in the register file throughout the computation of the permutation, in which case still four registers remain available for e.g. storing intermediate results.

As mentioned before, the C implementations of the mode of operation/use of the algorithms are largely based on source codes from the designers, but we modified them to comply with the low-level API given in [10]. The high-level API for authenticated encryption and decryption specified in [20, Sect. 3.5] can be implemented as simple wrappers around the low-level functions. This high-level API represents the plaintext, ciphertext, associated data, key, and nonce as arrays of bytes, i.e. arrays of type **unsigned char**, while the permutations operate on 32-bit or 64-bit words. It is, therefore, tempting to cast a pointer to a byte-array to a pointer to an array of unsigned 32/64-bit integers, e.g. when injecting a block of plaintext (or associated data) into the state. However, the ISO C standard only permits such upcasting of an unsigned-char pointer to an unsigned-integer pointer if the former meets the alignment requirements of the latter (which are more strict), otherwise the result of the cast is undefined. In the case of the MSP430 architecture, a 32-bit or 64-bit integer in memory has to be 2-byte aligned, i.e. its address must be even [27]. As a consequence, the casting of a pointer to a byte-array to a pointer to an unsigned-integer-array is only allowed when the start address of the byte-array is even. If this condition is not satisfied, the plaintext (resp. associated data) blocks have to be copied to an aligned buffer. Alternatively, it is, of course, always possible to process the blocks of plaintext and associated data in a byte-wise way. In the following, we briefly outline how we implemented and optimized the four AEAD algorithms and their permutations for the MSP430 architecture.

ASCON. ASCON is well suited for platforms with small register space because each of the two layers of the permutation needs, at any time, only a part of the state (but never the complete state) in registers. Our MSP430 implementation processes the substitution layer in 16-bit slices, i.e. a 16-bit part of each state-word is loaded, processed, and stored, and these steps are repeated four times in a simple loop. The linear diffusion layer is implemented in a straightforward fashion, i.e. one state-word at a time. In summary, each of the five state-words loaded from (and stored to) RAM twice per round, which means ASCON has relatively high locality. As stated in the last section, the diffusion layer consists of operations of the form $x = x \oplus (x \ggg n_1) \oplus (x \ggg n_2)$; we tried alternative implementation options, e.g. $x = x \oplus ((x \oplus (x \ggg (n_2 - n_1))) \ggg n_1)$, with the goal of minimizing the execution time of the rotations.

ASCON's mode of operation is fairly straightforward to implement on basis of the low-level API from [10]. A peculiarity of ASCON is the byte-order of the five state-words, which is big endian, while MSP430 and most other embedded microcontrollers process and store 32-bit and 64-bit integers using little endian representation. Therefore, the byte-order of 64-bit words that are injected into (or extracted from) the state has to be reversed. Our implementation performs the injection/extraction of words (including endianness conversion) in a byte-by-byte fashion, which has the advantage that we do not need to pay attention to the alignment of the byte-arrays in which the inputs/outputs are stored.

SPARKLE. SPARKLE384, which is the permutation of the primary instance of the SCHWAEMM family, has relatively high locality (though not as high as ASCON) and can, therefore, be well optimized for MSP430. Our implementation of the permutation processes the non-linear layer in a loop and evaluates one ARX-box at a time. An ARX-box computation requires ten registers: four to store two 32-bit state words, two for a 32-bit round constant, further two for an intermediate result, and one each for a pointer to the round-constant and state array, respectively. We integrated the computation of the two temporary values t_x and t_y into the ARX-box layer to reduce the number of memory accesses in the subsequent linear layer. In this way, each 32-bit word of the state is loaded and stored twice per round (similar to ASCON); once in the ARX-box layer and then a second time in the linear layer. However, some further memory accesses are necessary for the round constants and the temporary value t_y, which has to be stored on the stack due to the lack of free registers.

SCHWAEMM's mode of operation uses apart from the permutation also two auxiliary functions: a feedback function ρ and a rate-whitening function $\mathcal{W}$. We merge both functions into a single loop to reduce their execution time. Our C implementation of the mode also optimizes the processing of plaintext, cipher-text, and associated data, which are stored in byte-arrays. We check at runtime whether the pointers to these arrays are sufficiently aligned for an upcasting to uint32_t pointers; when this is the case we directly process the byte-arrays as integer-arrays, otherwise we copy them first to an aligned buffer via memcpy.

TinyJAMBU. TINYJAMBU has the highest locality among all four permuta-tions since the full state can be kept in registers during the computation of the permutation. Nonetheless, some memory accesses are still required to load the key-words in each round. Due to the permutation's high locality, the execution time is dominated by the funnel shifts, which extract a 32-bit word at a certain position within two concatenated 32-bit words (i.e. a 64-bit word). The source code provided by the designers implements these funnel shifts as normal right-shift operations of two concatenated state-words by distances of 6, 15, 21, and 27 bits. However, in MSP430 Assembly language, the four funnel shifts can be performed more efficiently by a 1-bit right-shift-through-carry of a 32-bit word (three instructions), a 1-bit left-shift-through-carry of a 32-bit word (also three instructions), an ordinary 5-bit left-shift of a 48-bit word (15 instructions), and an ordinary 5-bit right-shift of a 64-bit word (20 instructions).

TINYJAMBU processes plaintext/ciphertext and associated data with a rate of four bytes. The low-level encryption/decryption functions check whether the pointers to the byte-arrays containing these inputs are properly aligned for an upcasting to uint32_t pointers; when this is not the case the four bytes to be processed are copied into an aligned buffer, similar to SCHWAEMM. But unlike SCHWAEMM, the input blocks are copied byte by byte using plain C statements since calling memcpy would introduce a significant overhead for four bytes.

Xoodyak. Similar to ASCON and SPARKLE, the state of the XOODOO permu-tation is too big for the register file of a MSP430 microcontroller and, thus, has to be stored in RAM. A straightforward implementation of the five steps of the permutation, one step after another, would require a large number of load and store operations. In order to reduce the number of memory accesses, we tried to integrate (parts of) the plane-shifting layers ρ_{west} and ρ_{east} into the mixing layer θ and non-linear layer χ, respectively. Unfortunately, a full integration is not possible due to the limited register space (at least not when the goal is to achieve a good trade-off between performance and code size), which means the lane-wise rotations within a plane that form part of ρ_{west} and ρ_{east} still have to be implemented as separate steps with their own load and store operations. As a consequence, four state-words are loaded and stored twice per round, and the remaining eight words three times per round. This large number of load/store operations makes XOODOO the permutation with the lowest locality.

Our low-level functions for XOODYAK's Cyclist mode of operation deal with unaligned byte-arrays for associated data and plaintext/ciphertext in the same way as the SCHWAEMM implementation: we first check at runtime whether the pointers to these arrays can be casted to `uint32_t` pointers and use `memcpy` to copy the bytes block-wise into an aligned buffer if this is not the case.

5 Performance Evaluation and Comparison

We compiled and assembled the source code of the four AEAD algorithms with version 7.2 of IAR Embedded Workbench for MSP430[4] and used its integrated cycle-accurate instruction set simulator to determine the execution time of the permutations alone and the high-level encryption functions. Our target device was a MSP430F1611 microcontroller, which comes with 10 kB SRAM and has a flash capacity of 48 kB. In order to be able to examine our implementations of the permutations in more detail, we also developed a tool that emulates the execution of MSP430 instructions step by step and collects information via the execution trace. The tool works with snapshots of registers and memory (since they can be exported from IAR Workbench) and is able to emulate all 27 core instructions of the MSP430 with the supported addressing modes [28]. While the instructions are executed, information about the instruction type, the used addressing mode(s), the number of memory accesses, and so on is recorded.

Table 2. Main characteristics and implementation results of the four permutations.

Characteristic/result	ASCON	SPARKLE	TINYJAMBU	XOODOO
Performance characteristics				
Execution time (cycles)	3510	5946	2454	8985
Number of executed instr.	2369	3811	2134	5191
Average cycles/instruction	1.48	1.56	1.15	1.73
Memory characteristics				
RAM consumption (bytes)	56	76	54	66
– of which is stack (bytes)	16	28	22	18
Code size (bytes)	708	618	652	570
Instruction-type characteristics				
Branching instructions	30	63	8	96
Memory-to-Memory (M2M)	0	21	8	12
Memory-to-Register (M2R)	261	491	146	884
Register-to-Memory (R2M)	254	493	19	789
Register-to-Register (R2R)	1824	2729	1953	3410
Percentage of R2R instr.	77.0%	71.6%	91.5%	65.7%

Table 2 shows various results we obtained for performance, RAM and flash consumption, and the type of instructions executed by each permutation. The

---

[4] http://www.iar.com/products/architectures/iar-embedded-workbench-for-msp430 (accessed on 2022-12-14).

execution time (in cycles) covers all instructions contained in the Assembly file of the permutation, but does not include the generation or passing of function arguments like a pointer to the state or the number of rounds. We can observe that TINYJAMBU has the fastest permutation with just 2454 clock cycles, while XOODOO is by far the worst in terms of execution time. TINYJAMBU's small Cycles-per-Instruction (CPI) ratio of 1.15 means that most of its instructions execute in one cycle, which is only possible when the operands and result are read from and written to registers instead of a location in memory. Indeed, as shown in Table 2, the percentage of Register-to-Register (R2R) instructions in TINYJAMBU's permutation is very high, namely above 91%. Both the CPI and ratio of R2R instructions confirms that TINYJAMBU has high locality. At the opposite end of the spectrum is XOODOO, which has the lowest locality of the four evaluated permutations (evidenced by a CPI of 1.73 and only 65.7% R2R instructions). ASCON has the second-best locality, and SPARKLE is locality-wise approximately in the middle between ASCON and XOODOO.

The RAM footprint (including stack usage) of the four permutations is relatively small and ranges from 54 bytes (TINYJAMBU) to 76 bytes (SPARKLE). In essence, RAM is occupied for the state and, in the case of TINYJAMBU, for the key, while the stack is mainly used for the preservation of callee-saved registers and to store infrequently-used local variables like loop counters. Also the code size of the permutations is relatively similar since the smallest one (XOODOO) and biggest one (ASCON) differ by only 138 bytes, which is roughly 24% of the code size of the former.

Table 3. Detailed execution-time and throughput analysis of the permutations.

Characteristic/result	ASCON	SPARKLE	TINYJAMBU	XOODOO
State size (bytes)	40	48	16	48
Encryption rate (bytes)	8	32	4	24
Authentication rate (bytes)	8	32	4	44
Number of rounds or steps	6	7	8 (5)	12
Execution-time analysis of single round/step				
Cycles per round/step	577 (100%)	844 (100%)	302 (100%)	746 (100%)
– of which are rotations	160 (27.7%)	150 (17.8%)	172 (57.0%)	153 (20.5%)
– of which are non-lin. ops.	20 (3.5%)	48 (5.7%)	8 (2.6%)	24 (3.2%)
Execution-time analysis of full permutation				
Cycles for full permutation	3510 (100%)	5946 (100%)	2454 (100%)	8985 (100%)
– of which are rotations	960 (27.4%)	1050 (17.7%)	1376 (56.1%)	1836 (20.4%)
– of which are non-lin. ops.	120 (3.4%)	336 (5.7%)	64 (2.6%)	288 (3.2%)
Throughput analysis of full permutation				
Cycles per state-byte	87.75	123.88	153.38	187.19
Cycles per rate-byte (enc.)	438.75	185.82	613.50	374.38
Cycles per rate-byte (auth.)	438.75	185.82	387.00	204.20

Table 3 provides more-detailed information about the execution time of the permutations, including an analysis of the cycles spent for shifts/rotations and non-linear operations (i.e. addition in the case of SPARKLE, logical AND for the other three permutations). The table also summarizes the main characteristics of the permutations, e.g. the size of the state, the rate used for authentication and for encryption, and the number of rounds or steps. We analyzed a single round or step of each permutation and determined the overall cycle count, the number of cycles spent for shifts/rotations, and the number of cycles for non-linear operations. The latter was evaluated with help of the specification of the permutation and does not include any add.w or and.w instruction that has no impact on non-linearity, e.g. the adc.w at line 4 of the QROL rotation macro in Listing 1. According to the per-round/step results in Table 3, the rotations are more costly than the non-linear operations, and this holds true for each of the four permutations. However, the relative computational cost of rotations versus non-linear operations is not only determined by the design of the permutation but also by the features of the target architecture. For example, SPARKLE and XOODOO were designed such that, when implemented for a 32-bit ARM micro-controller, each rotation can be "folded" into an arithmetic/logical instruction and both together executed within a single cycle, which makes these rotations basically free. Therefore, when 32-bit ARM is the target architecture, the non-linear operations contribute more cycles to the overall execution time than the rotations, while the opposite is the case for MSP430. To be more concrete, the rotations make up between 17.7% and 56.1% of the overall cycle counts of the permutations on an MSP430F1611 microcontroller. These results underline the importance of choosing the rotation (resp. shift) distances carefully, taking into account both security and efficiency aspects.

As explained in Sect. 2, a shift/rotation of a 32 or 64-bit word by a distance of d bits is fast on MSP430 if either (i) d is a multiple of 16, (ii) d is close to a multiple of 16 (e.g. 1, 2, 14, 15, 17, 18, ...), or (iii) d is a multiple of 8. The SPARKLE permutation performs seven rotations of 32-bit words in each of its ARX-boxes; the distances are 31, 24, 17, 17, 31, 24, and 16 bits. Each distance meets the above requirements, which makes the rotations relatively fast (one is completely free, one takes six cycles, and the other five rotations require three cycles). Overall, the rotations contribute roughly 17.8% to the execution time of SPARKLE. The distances of the rotations carried out by XOODYAK include three that are relatively fast (namely by 1 and 8 bits in ρ_{east} and by 14 bits in θ), but also two slow ones (by 5 bits in θ and 11 bits in ρ_{west}). In summary, the rotations account for 20.4% of the execution time of XOODYAK. The diffusion layer of ASCON includes ten rotations (executed on 64-bit words) by distances of 19, 28, 61, 39, 1, 6, 10, 17, 7, and 41 bits. Only two out of this total of ten distances, namely 1 and 17 bits, can be considered fast according to the above requirements. Though some optimizations are possible (see Sect. 5), our overall verdict is that the rotation distances of ASCON are not particularly "MSP430-friendly," which explains why the rotations consume 27.4% of the permutation cycles. Finally, TINYJAMBU is a special case because it performs funnel shifts instead of actual rotations. As explained in Sect. 5, these funnel shifts can be implemented by two 1-bit shift-through-carry operations on a 32-bit word and two 5-bit shifts (carried out on a 48-bit and a 64-bit word, respectively). The former two are fast but the latter two extremely slow. In summary, the funnel shifts make up 56.1% of TINYJAMBU's overall permutation cycles.

The impact of the rotations (resp. funnel shifts) on the total execution time of the four permutations should not be viewed as completely independent from other efficiency aspects like locality. TINYJAMBU has very high locality and, as a consequence, wastes only few cycles for memory accesses (this is one of the reasons for its relatively fast execution time). Therefore, it is natural that the funnel shifts constitute a large fraction of the execution time, which makes the designers' choice of shift distances appear worse (in relation to the other three permutations) than they are in reality. The opposite is the case for XOODYAK's permutation. Namely, the long execution time of XOODOO (which is partly due to poor locality) makes the rotation distances look less costly than they are.

Since the state size of three of the four permutations differs, it makes sense to analyze the throughput in terms of execution time divided by the state-size in bytes. The results at the bottom of Table 3 show that ASCON wins in this category with a throughput of approximately 87.75 cycles per state-byte. Also contained at the bottom of this table are the throughput figures per rate-byte for encryption and authentication, respectively. The cycles per rate-byte serve as a good benchmark for the efficiency of both the permutation and the mode of operation/use of the corresponding AEAD algorithm. SCHWAEMM employs the BEETLE mode of operation, which allows it to process associated data and plaintext/ciphertext at a rate of 32 bytes. The resulting throughput of 185.82 cycles per rate-byte is the best among the four evaluated AEAD schemes. Also XOODYAK profits from a fairly high rate, namely 24 bytes for encryption, and achieves a throughput of 374.38 cycles per rate-byte. Even though ASCON and TINYJAMBU have fast permutations, their throughput is relatively poor due to a small rate. Note that the throughput of both TINYJAMBU and XOODYAK is much higher for authentication than for encryption; in the former case because of a smaller number of steps and in the latter case due to a higher rate.

Table 4 shows the execution time of the four AEAD algorithms for authentication only (i.e. no plaintext is processed), encryption only (i.e. no associated data is processed) and authenticated encryption (both the associated data and plaintext have the same length). For each scenario, we evaluated the execution time for inputs of three different lengths: short (i.e. 16 bytes), medium (i.e. 128 bytes), and long (i.e. 1024 bytes). The timings in Table 4 are closely correlated with the throughput values at the bottom of Table 3, in particular for medium and long inputs. Therefore, it is not surprising that, overall, SCHWAEMM is the best performer across different lengths of associated data and plaintext. When the inputs are short (i.e. 16 bytes), the execution times of the four algorithms are relatively similar and depend not only on the throughput, but also on the efficiency of operations like initialization, finalization, and computation of the authentication tag. However, for medium-size inputs, SCHWAEMM outperforms XOODYAK, which is (overall) the second-best algorithm, by a factor of 1.89 in the encryption-only case and a factor of approximately 1.45 for authenticated

Table 4. Execution time (in cycles) of the AEAD algorithms for authentication only (dlen = 0), encryption only (adlen = 0), and authenticated encryption (adlen = dlen).

adlen	dlen	Ascon	Schwaemm	TinyJambu	Xoodyak
16	0	25567	20311	18539	28225
128	0	75729	38777	63952	47091
1024	0	477025	214421	427280	243385
0	16	22109	20704	22191	28273
0	128	72957	39618	93168	74865
0	1024	479707	221080	661008	420299
16	16	32834	30748	28680	28377
128	128	133842	68126	145073	93838
1024	1024	941924	425268	1076241	635566

encryption. Finally, in the authentication-only scenario, the speed-up factor is smaller, namely about 1.21 for associated data of medium length and a bit less for longer lengths. Ascon and TinyJambu are around two times slower than Schwaemm for both medium and long inputs.

6   Conclusions

In this paper, presented a performance analysis of the four AEAD algorithms Ascon, TinyJambu, Schwaemm, and Xoodyak on a 16-bit MSP430 microcontroller. We developed carefully-optimized Assembler implementations of the underlying permutations, whereby we aimed for a reasonable trade-off between execution time and (binary) code size. Our results show that the shift/rotation distances and the locality have a significant impact on the performance of the permutations. TinyJambu's permutation has very high locality since its entire state can be kept in registers. The permutation of Ascon and Sparkle have the second and third-bast locality; each word of their state needs to be loaded from RAM and written back to RAM twice per round or step. Xoodoo shows the worst locality of the four permutations. On the other hand, when it comes to rotation distances, Sparkle is the winner since the majority of its rotations can be executed in only three clock cycles. Xoodoo and TinyJambu perform a mix of fast and slow rotations (resp. shifts), while almost all of the rotation distances of Ascon's permutation are not well-suited for MSP430. The actual performance of each of the four AEAD algorithms does not only depend on the permutation, but also the rate for encryption and authentication. Our results show that Schwaemm is clearly the best overall performer across different use cases (authentication only, encryption only, and authenticated encryption) and input lengths. When encrypting a 128-byte plaintext, Schwaemm is 1.89 times faster than Xoodyak and outperforms Ascon by a factor of 1.84. Xoodyak is more competitive when a large amount of associated data is processed, whereas

TinyJambu is particularly efficient for the authentication of very short blocks of associated data (up to approximately 16 bytes).

Acknowledgements. The last author was supported by the Fonds National de la Recherche (FNR) Luxembourg under CORE grant C19/IS/13641232. The source code is available online at http://github.com/johgrolux/aead430.

References

1. Arm Limited. ARM Cortex-M3 Processor Technical Reference Manual, Revision r2p1 (2016). http://developer.arm.com/documentation/100165/latest
2. Beierle, C., et al.: Lightweight AEAD and hashing using the Sparkle permutation family. IACR Trans. Symmetric Cryptol. **2020**(S1), 208–261 (2020)
3. Bernstein, D.J.: The Salsa20 family of stream ciphers. In: Robshaw, M., Billet, O. (eds.) New Stream Cipher Designs. LNCS, vol. 4986, pp. 84–97. Springer, Heidelberg (2008). https://doi.org/10.1007/978-3-540-68351-3_8
4. Bernstein, D.J., et al.: GIMLI: a cross-platform permutation. In: Fischer, W., Homma, N. (eds.) CHES 2017. LNCS, vol. 10529, pp. 299–320. Springer, Cham (2017). https://doi.org/10.1007/978-3-319-66787-4_15
5. Bertoni, G., Daemen, J., Peeters, M., Van Assche, G.: Cryptographic sponge functions (2011). http://keccak.team/files/CSF-0.1.pdf
6. Bertoni, G., Daemen, J., Peeters, M., Van Assche, G.: The Keccak reference, version 3.0 (2011). http://keccak.team/files/Keccak-reference-3.0.pdf
7. Bertoni, G., Daemen, J., Peeters, M., Van Assche, G.: Permutation-based encryption, authentication and authenticated encryption. In: Record of the 1st ECRYPT II Workshop on New Directions in Authenticated Encryption (DIAC 2012), pp. 159–170 (2012)
8. Blanc, S., Lahmadi, A., Le Gouguec, K., Minier, M., Sleem, L.: Benchmarking of lightweight cryptographic algorithms for wireless IoT networks. Wireless Netw. **28**(8), 3453–3476 (2022)
9. Cardoso dos Santos, L., Großschädl, J.: An evaluation of the multi-platform efficiency of lightweight cryptographic permutations. In: Ryan, P.Y.A., Toma, C. (eds.) SecITC 2021. LNCS, vol. 13195, pp. 75–90. Springer, Cham (2022). https://doi.org/10.1007/978-3-031-17510-7_6
10. Cardoso dos Santos, L., Großschädl, J., Biryukov, A.: FELICS-AEAD: benchmarking of lightweight authenticated encryption algorithms. In: Belaïd, S., Güneysu, T. (eds.) CARDIS 2019. LNCS, vol. 11833, pp. 216–233. Springer, Cham (2020). https://doi.org/10.1007/978-3-030-42068-0_13
11. Chakraborti, A., Datta, N., Nandi, M., Yasuda, K.: Beetle family of lightweight and secure authenticated encryption ciphers. IACR Trans. Cryptogr. Hardw. Embed. Syst. **2018**(2), 218–241 (2018)
12. Daemen, J., Hoffert, S., Peeters, M., Van Assche, G., Van Keer, R.: Xoodyak, a lightweight cryptographic scheme. IACR Trans. Symmetric Cryptol. **2020**(S1), 60–87 (2020)
13. Daemen, J., Hoffert, S., Van Assche, G., Van Keer, R.: The design of Xoodoo and Xoofff. IACR Trans. Symmetric Cryptol. **2018**(4), 1–38 (2018)
14. Dang, D., Plant, M., Poole, M.: Wireless connectivity for the Internet of Things (IoT) with MSP430 microcontrollers (MCUs) (2014). Texas Instruments white paper. http://www.ti.com/lit/wp/slay028/slay028.pdf

15. Dobraunig, C., Eichlseder, M., Mendel, F., Schläffer, M.: Ascon v1.2: lightweight authenticated encryption and hashing. J. Cryptol. **34**(3), 33 (2021)
16. Gligor, V.D.: Light-weight cryptography - how light is light? Keynote presentation at the Information Security Summer School, Florida State University (2005). Slide deck. http://www.sait.fsu.edu/conferences/2005/is3/resources/slides/gligorv-cryptolite.ppt
17. Guo, J., Peyrin, T., Poschmann, A.: The PHOTON family of lightweight hash functions. In: Rogaway, P. (ed.) CRYPTO 2011. LNCS, vol. 6841, pp. 222–239. Springer, Heidelberg (2011). https://doi.org/10.1007/978-3-642-22792-9_13
18. Hamburg, M.: The STROBE protocol framework. Cryptology ePrint Archive, Report 2017/003 (2017). http://eprint.iacr.org/2017/003
19. Microchip Technology Inc. 8-bit Atmel Microcontroller with 128KBytes In-System Programmable Flash: ATmega128, ATmega128L (2011). http://ww1.microchip.com/downloads/en/DeviceDoc/doc2467.pdf
20. National Institute of Standards and Technology (NIST). Submission Requirements and Evaluation Criteria for the Lightweight Cryptography Standardization Process (2018). http://csrc.nist.gov/CSRC/media/Projects/Lightweight-Cryptography/documents/final-lwc-submission-requirements-august2018.pdf
21. National Institute of Standards and Technology (NIST). Benchmarking of lightweight cryptographic algorithms on microcontrollers (2020). http://github.com/usnistgov/Lightweight-Cryptography-Benchmarking
22. National Institute of Standards and Technology (NIST). Status Report on the Second Round of the NIST Lightweight Cryptography Standardization Process. Internal Report 8369 (2021). http://nvlpubs.nist.gov/nistpubs/ir/2021/NIST.IR.8369.pdf
23. Perrin, T.: Stateful hash objects: API and constructions (2018). Specification. http://github.com/noiseprotocol/sho_spec
24. Renner, S., Pozzobon, E., Mottok, J.: NIST LWC software performance benchmarks on microcontrollers (2020). http://lwc.las3.de
25. Rzehak, V.: Low-power FRAM microcontrollers and their applications (2019). Texas Instruments white paper. http://www.ti.com/lit/wp/slaa502/slaa502.pdf
26. Saarinen, M.-J.O.: Beyond modes: building a secure record protocol from a cryptographic sponge permutation. In: Benaloh, J. (ed.) CT-RSA 2014. LNCS, vol. 8366, pp. 270–285. Springer, Cham (2014). https://doi.org/10.1007/978-3-319-04852-9_14
27. Texas Instruments Inc. MSP430 Family Architecture Guide and Module Library. TI literature number SLAUE10B (1996). http://www.ti.com/sc/docs/products/micro/msp430/userguid/ag_01.pdf
28. Texas Instruments, Inc. MSP430x1xx Family User's Guide (Rev. F) (2006). Manual. http://www.ti.com/lit/ug/slau049f/slau049f.pdf
29. Texas Instruments Inc. MSP430 Ultra-Low-Power Microcontrollers (2013). Product bulletin. http://www.ti.com/lit/sg/slab034w/slab034w.pdf
30. Weatherley, R.: Lightweight cryptography primitives documentation (2021). http://rweather.github.io/lwc-finalists/index.html
31. Wu, H., Huang, T.: TinyJAMBU: a family of lightweight authenticated encryption algorithms (Version 2) (2021). Specification. http://csrc.nist.gov/CSRC/media/Projects/lightweight-cryptography/documents/finalist-round/updated-spec-doc/tinyjambu-spec-final.pdf
32. Yan, L., Zhang, Y., Yang, L.T., Ning, H.: The Internet of Things: From RFID to the Next-Generation Pervasive Networked Systems. Auerbach Publications (2008)

Bridges Connecting Encryption Schemes

Mugurel Barcau[1,2], Cristian Lupaşcu[1,3], Vicenţiu Paşol[1,2],
and George C. Ţurcaş[1,4(✉)]

[1] certSIGN – Research and Innovation, Bucharest, Romania
{alexandru.barcau,cristian.lupascu,vicentiu.pasol,
george.turcas}@certsign.ro
[2] Institute of Mathematics "Simion Stoilow" of the Romanian Academy,
Bucharest, Romania
[3] Ferdinand I Military Technical Academy, Bucharest, Romania
[4] Babeş-Bolyai University, Cluj-Napoca, Romania

Abstract. The present work investigates a type of morphisms between
encryption schemes, called bridges. By associating an encryption scheme
to every such bridge, we define and examine their security. Inspired by the
bootstrapping procedure used by Gentry to produce fully homomorphic
encryption schemes, we exhibit a general recipe for the construction of
bridges. Our main theorem asserts that the security of a bridge reduces
to the security of the first encryption scheme together with a technical
additional assumption.

Keywords: Encryption scheme · Homomorphic encryption ·
IND-CPA security

1 Introduction

The idea of switching ciphertexts encrypted using the same scheme from one
secret key to another appears in the literature under the name of Proxy Re-
Encryption (see [14] and the references within). More recently, a general method
of converting ciphertexts from one encryption scheme to another was introduced
in [15] under the name of Universal Proxy Re-Encryption. In practice, Proxy Re-
Encryption between two distinct (arbitrary) schemes is very difficult to realize,
as the general methods proposed in [15] make use of hard to achieve protocols
such as indistinguishability obfuscation. In this work, we focus on unidirectional
such protocols between two distinct encryption schemes and call them *bridges*
(see Definition 3).

Bridges are important tools in the context of Hybrid Homomorphic Encryption (see for example [12] and [13]), where the owner encrypts its data using a
symmetric cipher and sends the encryption to a server together with his symmetric key encrypted under a homomorphic encryption scheme. The server first
homomorphically performs the decryption circuit of the symmetric cipher to
transform the initial ciphertext into one that allows homomorphic computation
and then proceeds with the desired computations. The result of this computation

G. Bella et al. (Eds.): SecITC 2022, LNCS 13809, pp. 37–64, 2023.
https://doi.org/10.1007/978-3-031-32636-3_3

can only be decrypted by the data owner. Apart from other possible applications, there is another motivation for studying these primitives which comes from the perspective of viewing encryption schemes in a categorical context, where bridges play the role of morphisms in an appropriate category.

In his remarkable work on fully homomorphic encryption, C. Gentry [17] used a *Recrypt* procedure in order to transform a somewhat homomorphic encryption scheme into a fully homomorphic encryption scheme. To be precise, Gentry's *Recrypt* algorithm takes as input a ciphertext together with certain encryptions of the secret key under a different key and evaluates homomorphically the decryption algorithm in order to produce an encryption of the same plaintext under the new key. Under the definition we propose, the *Recrypt* algorithm is a bridge from a somewhat homomorphic encryption scheme to itself. The recipe can be extended to produce a bridge from any encryption scheme to any somewhat homomorphic encryption scheme that can correctly evaluate the decryption circuit of the former.

Perhaps connected to the same idea is the work in [11], where maps between two encryption schemes are used to construct a 2-party computation protocol, called an Encryption Switching Protocol (ESP). The examples proposed in [11] and [7] consist of two encryptions schemes over the same plaintext, which has a structure of a ring, and switching protocols between them. One of the schemes is homomorphic with respect to addition and the other is homomorphic for the multiplication. An ESP of this form can be used to construct a secure general 2-party computational protocol.

Switching between one encryption scheme to another, in order to securely perform a sequence of homomorphic operations, is a recurrent theme in the literature. In this respect, it is important to formally define and analyze the security implications of such protocols, which represents the main goal of the present work. We shall call a map (or a morphism) between encryption schemes satisfying certain properties a *bridge*. The terminology is borrowed from [4], where the expression "bridge between encryption schemes" is briefly used in reference to a hybrid solution for switching between FHE schemes in order to optimize performance of certain homomorphic computations on encrypted data.

Our Contribution. In this paper, we first propose a general definition for a bridge, formalizing the conditions under which an algorithm that publicly transforms encrypted data from one scheme to another should perform. We provide a general recipe, inspired by Gentry's idea, for the construction of bridges and then apply it to give various examples. This general recipe can be modified in various ways and we demonstrate this by presenting a variant of it. We also present an additional example of a bridge that does not fall in the category of Gentry type bridges. We canonically associate to any bridge an encryption scheme and then define the security of a bridge as being the security of its associated encryption scheme. This association is widely used in mathematics when someone needs to replace a morphism between two objects by an object. More precisely, it consists in substituting a map by its graph, whenever this is possible. We prove a general theorem (Theorem 2) asserting that the security of a bridge reduces to the security of the first encryption scheme together with a technical additional assumption. We show that the latter technicality is in fact a natural condition by proving that bridges obtained using Gentry's *Recrypt* idea satisfy this assumption (Proposition 2). The security analysis provided here is finer than the corresponding security analysis made on Proxy Re-Encryption schemes. Our definition of IND-CPA security of the bridge and Cohen's HRA security definition (see [10]) are equivalent (all players are honest) and thus Cohen's simulatability theorem (see Theorem 5 of [10]) is vacuous in the case discussed in this paper. Our work is accompanied by three appendices. In the first two, we present examples of bridges (of different types). Comments on the performance of the implementations of these examples are to be found in the last appendix.

Organization. The article is organized as follows. Section 2 consists of some mathematical background and preliminaries about encryption schemes used in the rest of the article. It starts by recalling some terminology and theoretical facts about finite distributions. In the same section, we also give the definition of a bridge. The contributions in Sect. 3 regard the security of a bridge between two encryption schemes. The main result of our paper (Theorem 2) is proved in this section. In Sect. 4, we show that Gentry's *Recrypt* algorithm gives a general recipe for the construction of bridges. Using the main result from the previous section, we prove that bridges generated using this recipe are secure. The appendices are organised as follows. By representing the decryption circuit of a specific encryption scheme in four different ways, we give in appendix A, four different examples of bridges from the same encryption scheme to various FHE schemes. A bridge with empty bridge key, not following the recipe presented in Sect. 4, connecting the GM and SYY encryption schemes is exhibited in appendix B. Its security follows from results in Sect. 3. The homomorphic evaluation of a comparison circuit is presented as an application to the latter bridge. In the last appendix of this article, we report on the results of several experiments involving the implementation of the bridges introduced in the first two appendices.

2 Preliminaries

In all our definitions, we denote the security parameter by λ. We say that a function $\mu : \mathbb{N} \to [0, +\infty)$ is a negligible function if for any positive integer c there exists a positive integer N_c, such that $\mu(n) < \dfrac{1}{n^c}$ for all $n \geq N_c$.

2.1 Finite Distributions

A finite probability distribution is a probability distribution with finite support. If X is a finite distribution, we denote by $|X|$ its support. If X and Y are finite distributions, then a morphism $\varphi : Y \to X$ is a map of sets (still denoted by) $\varphi : |Y| \to |X|$ such that

$$\Pr\{X = x\} = \sum_{y \in \varphi^{-1}(x)} \Pr\{Y = y\}.$$

for all $x \in |X|$. Notice that if $\varphi^{-1}(x)$ is empty then $\Pr\{X = x\} = 0$, which means that φ is surjective onto $\{x \in |X| \mid \Pr\{X = x\} \neq 0\}$. The composition of two morphisms is a morphism and the identity map $1_{|X|} : |X| \to |X|$ gives rise to a morphism of distributions $1_X : X \to X$ so that the class of finite distributions together with all morphisms between them forms a category denoted $\mathscr{F}in\mathscr{D}ist$. As usual, two finite distributions are isomorphic if there exist a morphism between them that has an inverse. If X is a finite distribution, then the slice category (cf. [2]) $\mathscr{F}in\mathscr{D}ist_X$ of X-distributions consists of pairs (Y, φ) where Y is a finite distribution and $\varphi : Y \to X$ is a morphism of finite distributions. A morphism of X-distributions $f : (Y_1, \varphi_1) \to (Y_2, \varphi_2)$, consists of a morphism of finite distributions $f : Y_1 \to Y_2$ such that the following diagram

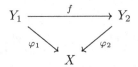

is commutative.

If $x \in |X|$ with $\Pr\{X = x\} \neq 0$ and (Y, φ) is an X-distribution then the *fiber of Y over x* is the finite distribution $Y|_{X=x}$ with support $\varphi^{-1}(x)$ and

$$\Pr\{Y|_{X=x} = y\} = \frac{\Pr\{Y = y\}}{\Pr\{X = x\}}, \text{ for all } y \in \varphi^{-1}(x).$$

If (Y_1, φ_1) and (Y_2, φ_2) are two X-distributions we construct the following product $Y_1 \times_X Y_2$. The support of this distribution is

$$|Y_1 \times_X Y_2| := \{(y_1, y_2) \mid y_1 \in |Y_1|, y_2 \in |Y_2| \text{ such that } \varphi_1(y_1) = \varphi_2(y_2)\}.$$

If $x = \varphi_1(y_1) = \varphi_2(y_2)$ and $\Pr\{X = x\} \neq 0$, then

$$\Pr\{Y_1 \times_X Y_2 = (y_1, y_2)\} := \frac{\Pr\{Y_1 = y_1\} \cdot \Pr\{Y_2 = y_2\}}{\Pr\{X = x\}}.$$

Moreover, when $\Pr\{X = x\} = 0$, then

$$\Pr\{Y_1 \times_X Y_2 = (y_1, y_2)\} := 0.$$

Finally, the structural morphism of $\psi : |Y_1 \times_X Y_2| \to X$ is $\psi := \varphi_1 \circ \mathrm{pr}_1 = \varphi_2 \circ \mathrm{pr}_2$, where $\mathrm{pr}_i : |Y_1 \times_X Y_2| \to |Y_i|, i \in \{1, 2\}$ are the usual projections.

We remark that $|Y_1 \times_X Y_2|$ is the usual fiber product in the category of sets, but $Y_1 \times_X Y_2$ is not a fiber product in the category $\mathscr{F}in\mathscr{D}ist$. However, the distribution $Y_1 \times_X Y_2$ is a product in the following sense. If one constructs the distribution of triples (x, y_1, y_2): x is chosen from $|X|$ according to X, y_1 and y_2 are chosen independently from $\varphi_1^{-1}(x)$ and $\varphi_2^{-1}(x)$ according to Y_1 and Y_2 respectively, then one obtains a distribution isomorphic to $Y_1 \times_X Y_2$.

Any finite distribution whose support is a one-point set is a final object in $\mathscr{F}in\mathscr{D}ist$. We shall denote by $Y_1 \times Y_2$ the product $Y_1 \times_X Y_2$, where X is any of the final objects of $\mathscr{F}in\mathscr{D}ist$.

Notice that if Y is an X-distribution, then the distribution $X \times_X Y$ is isomorphic to Y as X-distributions (here we view X as an X-distribution via the identity map). We will sometimes identify the distribution $X \times_X Y$ with Y without mentioning it, if this is clear from the context. Morally, $X \times_X Y$ is the distribution Y whose associated map φ is known.

If $\{X_\lambda\}_{\lambda \in \mathbb{N}}$, $\{Y_\lambda\}_{\lambda \in \mathbb{N}}$ are ensembles of finite distributions then we define a morphism from the latter to the former as being a set of morphisms of finite distributions $\varphi_\lambda : Y_\lambda \to X_\lambda$ for all λ. One can verify immediately that ensembles of finite distributions together with morphisms form a category. If we fix an ensemble $\{X_\lambda\}_\lambda$, then we obtain the slice category of $\{X_\lambda\}_\lambda$-ensembles of finite distributions. In this category we define, as before, the product of the two ensembles $\{Y_\lambda\}_\lambda$, $\{Z_\lambda\}_\lambda$ as $\{Y_\lambda \times_{X_\lambda} Z_\lambda\}_\lambda$.

The first part of the following statement is Definition 2 from [20].

Definition 1. *An ensemble $\{X_\lambda\}_\lambda$ of finite distributions is polynomial-time constructible if there exists a PPT algorithm A such that $A(1^\lambda) = X_\lambda$, for every λ. An $\{X_\lambda\}_\lambda$-ensemble of finite distributions $\{(Y_\lambda, \varphi_\lambda)\}_\lambda$ is polynomial-time constructible on fibers if there exist a PPT algorithm A, such that for any $x_\lambda \in |X_\lambda|$ we have $A(1^\lambda, x_\lambda) = Y_\lambda|_{X_\lambda = x_\lambda}$.*

We will also use the following notion of computational (or polynomial) indistinguishability from [21] and [20].

Definition 2. *Two ensembles of finite distributions $\{X_\lambda\}_\lambda$ and $\{Y_\lambda\}_\lambda$ are called computationally indistinguishable if for any PPT distinguisher D, the quantity*

$$|\Pr\{D(X_\lambda) = 1\} - \Pr\{D(Y_\lambda) = 1\}|$$

is negligible as a function of λ.

When referring to ensembles of finite distributions, we will leave out the subscript λ if this is clear from the context.

2.2 Encryption Schemes and Bridges

A public key (or asymmetric) encryption scheme

$$\mathscr{S} = (\text{KeyGen}_{\mathscr{S}}, \text{Enc}_{\mathscr{S}}, \text{Dec}_{\mathscr{S}})$$

is a triple of PPT algorithms as follows:

- **Key Generation.** The algorithm $(sk, pk) \leftarrow \text{KeyGen}_{\mathscr{S}}(1^\lambda)$ takes a unary representation of the security parameter λ and outputs a secret decryption key sk and a public encryption key pk;
- **Encryption.** The algorithm $c \leftarrow \text{Enc}_{\mathscr{S}}(pk, m)$ takes the public key pk and a message $m \in \mathscr{P}$ and outputs a ciphertext $c \in \mathscr{C}$;
- **Decryption.** The algorithm $m^\star \leftarrow \text{Dec}_{\mathscr{S}}(sk, c)$ takes the secret key sk and a ciphertext $c \in \mathscr{C}$ and outputs a message $m^\star \in \mathscr{P}$;

where the finite sets $\mathscr{P}$ and $\mathscr{C}$ represent the plaintext space, respectively the ciphertext space. The algorithms above must satisfy the correctness property

$$\Pr\left\{\operatorname{Dec}_{\mathscr{S}}(sk, \operatorname{Enc}_{\mathscr{S}}(pk, m)) = m\right\} = 1 - \operatorname{negl}(\lambda),$$

where the probability is taken over the experiment of running the key generation and encryption algorithms and choosing uniformly $m \leftarrow \mathscr{P}$.

A private key (or symmetric) encryption scheme is a public key encryption scheme for which the public and secret keys are equal.

We say that an instance pk of the public key, or an instance sk of the secret key, is of *level* λ_0 if it is outputted by the key generation algorithm whose input is the unary representation of λ_0.

Remark 1. In the language of ensembles of finite distributions, the public keys of an encryption scheme form an SK-ensemble of finite distributions, where SK is the ensemble of secret keys. Moreover, an encryption scheme is just a collection of PK-ensembles of finite distributions indexed by the plaintext space that are polynomial-time constructible on fibers (here PK is the ensemble of public keys).

A homomorphic (public-key) encryption scheme

$$\mathscr{H} = (\operatorname{KeyGen}_{\mathscr{H}}, \operatorname{Enc}_{\mathscr{H}}, \operatorname{Dec}_{\mathscr{H}}, \operatorname{Eval}_{\mathscr{H}})$$

is a quadruple of PPT algorithms such that $(\operatorname{KeyGen}_{\mathscr{H}}, \operatorname{Enc}_{\mathscr{H}}, \operatorname{Dec}_{\mathscr{H}})$ is a public-key encryption scheme and the $\operatorname{KeyGen}_{\mathscr{H}}$ algorithm also outputs an additional evaluation key evk besides sk and pk, where the **Homomorphic Evaluation** algorithm $\operatorname{Eval}_{\mathscr{H}}$ takes the evaluation key evk, a circuit $f : \mathscr{P}^{\ell} \to \mathscr{P}$ and a set of ℓ ciphertexts $c_1, ..., c_{\ell} \in \mathscr{C}$, and outputs a ciphertext c_f.

We say that a homomorphic encryption scheme $\mathscr{H}$ is $\mathcal{C}$-*homomorphic* for a class of functions $\mathcal{C} = \{\mathcal{C}_{\lambda}\}_{\lambda \in \mathbb{N}}$, if for any sequence of functions $f_{\lambda} \in \mathcal{C}_{\lambda}$ and respective inputs $\mu_1, ..., \mu_{\ell} \in \mathscr{P}$ (where $\ell = \ell(\lambda)$), it holds that

$$\Pr[\operatorname{Dec}_{\mathscr{H}}(sk, \operatorname{Eval}_{\mathscr{H}}(evk, f_{\lambda}, c_1, ..., c_{\ell})) \neq f_{\lambda}(\mu_1, ..., \mu_{\ell})] = \operatorname{negl}(\lambda),$$

where $(pk, sk, evk) \leftarrow \operatorname{KeyGen}_{\mathscr{H}}(1^{\lambda})$ and $c_i \leftarrow \operatorname{Enc}_{\mathscr{H}}(pk, \mu_i)$ for all i.

In addition, a homomorphic encryption scheme $\mathscr{H}$ is *compact* if there exist a polynomial $s = s(\lambda)$ such that the output length of $\operatorname{Eval}_{\mathscr{H}}$ is at most s bits long, regardless of f or the number of inputs.

An encryption scheme is called *fully homomorphic (FHE)* if it is homomorphic for the class of all boolean functions and it satisfies the compactness condition.

We now give the definition of a bridge:

Definition 3. *Let $\mathscr{S}_j = (\mathscr{P}_j, \mathscr{C}_j, \operatorname{KeyGen}_j, \operatorname{Enc}_j, \operatorname{Dec}_j)$, $j \in \{1, 2\}$ be two encryption schemes. A bridge $\mathbf{B}_{\iota, f}$ from $\mathscr{S}_1$ to $\mathscr{S}_2$ consists of:*

1. *An injective function $\iota : \mathscr{P}_1 \to \mathscr{P}_2$ such that:*
   (a) ι is computable by a deterministic polynomial time algorithm;

(b) there exists a deterministic polynomial time algorithm which computes $\iota^{-1} : \mathscr{P}_2 \to \mathscr{P}_1$, i.e. outputs the symbol $\perp$ if the input is not in the image of ι and the preimage of the input otherwise,

2. *A PPT bridge key generation algorithm, which has the following three stages. First, the algorithm gets the security parameter λ and uses it to run the key generation algorithm of $\mathscr{S}_1$ in order to obtain a pair of keys sk_1, pk_1. In the second stage the algorithm uses sk_1 to find a secret key sk_2 of level λ for $\mathscr{S}_2$, and then calls the key generation algorithm of $\mathscr{S}_2$ to produce pk_2. In the final stage, the algorithm takes as input the quadruple (sk_1, pk_1, sk_2, pk_2) and outputs a bridge key bk.*

3. *A PPT algorithm f which takes as input the bridge key bk and a ciphertext $c_1 \in \mathscr{C}_1$ and outputs a ciphertext $c_2 \in \mathscr{C}_2$,*

such that

$$Pr\{\mathrm{Dec}_2(sk_2, f(bk, \mathrm{Enc}_1(pk_1, m))) = \iota(m)\} = 1 - \mathrm{negl}(\lambda),$$

where the probability is taken over the experiment of running the key generation and encryption algorithms and choosing uniformly $m \leftarrow \mathscr{P}_1$.

Notice that the definition above includes the case in which any of the two schemes is symmetric. Also, the plaintext spaces are fixed, i.e. they do not depend on the security parameter λ. One can define a bridge between encryption schemes for which the plaintext spaces do depend on λ, as in the case of RSA or Paillier cryptosystems. However, in this article we are considering only the former situation.

Remark 2. The bridge key generation algorithm does not necessarily output all possible pairs (sk_1, sk_2). Even though any secret key sk_1 of the scheme $\mathscr{S}_1$ may be outputted by the key generation algorithm of the bridge, only few sk_2's may occur. The bridge key generation algorithm produces the following $\{SK_{1,\lambda}\}_\lambda$-ensembles of finite distributions $\{SK_{2,\lambda}\}_\lambda$, $\{PK_{i,\lambda}\}_\lambda, i \in \{1,2\}$, and $\{BK_\lambda\}_\lambda$. The morphisms between these ensembles of finite distributions are illustrated in Fig. 1.

We mentioned earlier the idea of thinking of a bridge as a (category theoretical) morphism between encryption schemes. Although we do not claim to have defined a category, from this point of view, it is natural to address the existence of identity morphisms. We briefly explain below that the identity map between one encryption scheme to itself is a bridge.

Example 1. If $\mathscr{S}$ is an encryption scheme, then the identity map $\mathscr{C} \to \mathscr{C}$ gives rise to a bridge. The bridge key generation algorithm generates a unique secret key sk and two (independently generated) public keys pk_1, pk_2 corresponding to this secret key. The algorithm outputs $(sk, pk_1, sk, pk_2, \mathrm{NIL})$. We emphasize that the bridge key and the choices of pk_1 and pk_2 do not play any role in the evaluation of the bridge map.

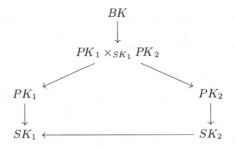

Fig. 1. Probability distributions for bridges.

3   The Security of a Bridge

The aim of this section is to define and investigate the IND-CPA security of a bridge. We start by defining and extending the notion of IND-CPA security of a scheme and then we move to the discussion concerning the security of a bridge.

Definition 4. (IND-CPA Security). *Let $\mathscr{S} = (\mathrm{KeyGen}_{\mathscr{S}}, \mathrm{Enc}_{\mathscr{S}}, \mathrm{Dec}_{\mathscr{S}})$ be a public key encryption scheme. We define an experiment $\mathrm{Exp}_b[\mathcal{A}]$ parameterized by a bit $b \in \{0,1\}$ and an efficient (PPT) adversary $\mathcal{A}$:*

$$\mathrm{Exp}_b[\mathcal{A}](1^\lambda) : 1.\ (pk, sk) \longleftarrow \mathrm{KeyGen}_{\mathscr{S}}(1^\lambda)$$
$$2.\ (m_0, m_1) \longleftarrow \mathcal{A}(1^\lambda, pk)$$
$$3.\ \mathrm{ct} \longleftarrow \mathrm{Enc}_{\mathscr{S}}(pk, x_b)$$
$$4.\ b' \longleftarrow \mathcal{A}(\mathrm{ct})$$
$$5.\ \mathrm{return}(b')$$

The advantage of adversary $\mathcal{A}$ against the IND-CPA security of the scheme is

$$\mathrm{Adv}^{IND\text{-}CPA}[\mathcal{A}](\lambda) := |\Pr\{\mathrm{Exp}_0[\mathcal{A}](1^\lambda) = 1\} - \Pr\{\mathrm{Exp}_1[\mathcal{A}](1^\lambda) = 1\}|,$$

where the probability is over the randomness of $\mathcal{A}$ and of the experiment. We say that the scheme is IND-CPA secure if for any efficient adversary $\mathcal{A}$, the advantage $\mathrm{Adv}^{IND\text{-}CPA}[\mathcal{A}]$ is negligible as a function of λ. In the case of a symmetric encryption scheme, the adversary $\mathcal{A}$ is given access to an encryption oracle.

Remark 3. As in the previous definition, when considering the security of a private encryption scheme, it is standard to replace the public key by an encryption oracle. From this point of view, a symmetric encryption scheme is a public encryption scheme whose public key consists of the access to an encryption oracle. Although we will give security definitions and proofs for public key encryption schemes, unless otherwise specified, these can be extended to the symmetric key setting using the above paradigm.

Let $\mathscr{S}$ be an encryption scheme and let K be some data outputted by an oracle whose input is the triple $(1^\lambda, sk_{\mathscr{S}}, pk_{\mathscr{S}})$. We shall denote by $\mathscr{S}[K]$ the encryption scheme whose public key is the pair $(pk_{\mathscr{S}}, K)$, and the encryption and decryption algorithms are exactly as in $\mathscr{S}$. The only difference between the schemes $\mathscr{S}$ and $\mathscr{S}[K]$ is related to their security. More precisely, an adversary attacking the scheme $\mathscr{S}[K]$ has more information than an adversary attacking $\mathscr{S}$. We say that an adversary $\mathcal{A}$ attacking $\mathscr{S}[K]$ is an adversary attacking $\mathscr{S}$ *with knowledge* K. For example, K can be a set consisting of $\mathscr{S}$-encryptions of the bit representation of the secret key, as used in [18] for the bootstrapping procedure. It is commonly assumed that such K's do not affect the security of the encryption scheme, assumption called *circular security*. The following definition aims to generalize the *circular security* assumption for some general data K.

Definition 5. *We say that some knowledge K is negligible for an encryption scheme $\mathscr{S}$ if for any adversary $\mathcal{A}$ attacking $\mathscr{S}[K]$ there exists an adversary $\mathcal{A}'$ attacking $\mathscr{S}$ such that*

$$|\mathrm{Adv}^{IND\text{-}CPA}[\mathcal{A}](\lambda) - \mathrm{Adv}^{IND\text{-}CPA}[\mathcal{A}'](\lambda)|$$

is negligible as a function of λ.

Notice that any adversary attacking $\mathscr{S}$ gives rise, in the obvious way, to an adversary attacking $\mathscr{S}[K]$, so that if K is negligible for $\mathscr{S}$ then the IND-CPA security of $\mathscr{S}$ is equivalent to the IND-CPA security of $\mathscr{S}[K]$.

In order to define the IND-CPA security of a bridge, we shall associate to it, in a canonical way, an encryption scheme; the security of the bridge will be, by definition, the security of the associated encryption scheme. Let $\mathbf{B}_{\iota,f}$ be a bridge, then the associated encryption scheme

$$\mathscr{G}_f = (\mathscr{P}_{\mathscr{G}_f}, \mathscr{C}_{\mathscr{G}_f}, \mathrm{KeyGen}_{\mathscr{G}_f}, \mathrm{Enc}_{\mathscr{G}_f}, \mathrm{Dec}_{\mathscr{G}_f})$$

is defined as follows. The plaintext space is $\mathscr{P}_{\mathscr{G}_f} = \mathscr{P}_1$, and the ciphertext space is $\mathscr{C}_{\mathscr{G}_f} = \mathscr{C}_1 \times \mathscr{C}_2$. The algorithm $\mathrm{KeyGen}_{\mathscr{G}_f}$ uses the key generation algorithm of the bridge to get $sk_1, pk_1, sk_2, pk_2, bk$. The secret key $sk_{\mathscr{G}_f}$ is the pair (sk_1, sk_2), and the public key $pk_{\mathscr{G}_f}$ is (pk_1, pk_2, bk).

For any $m \in \mathscr{P}_{\mathscr{G}_f}$, its encryption is defined by:

$$\mathrm{Enc}_{\mathscr{G}_f}(pk_{\mathscr{G}_f}, m) := (a, f(bk, b)),$$

where $a, b \leftarrow \mathrm{Enc}_1(pk_1, m)$. Finally, the decryption of a ciphertext $c_{\mathscr{G}_f} = (c_1, c_2) \in \mathscr{C}_1 \times \mathscr{C}_2$ is obtained using the formula:

$$\mathrm{Dec}_{\mathscr{G}_f}(sk_{\mathscr{G}_f}, c_{\mathscr{G}_f}) := \mathrm{Dec}_1(sk_1, c_1).$$

We notice that the decryption of $\mathscr{G}_f$ satisfies

$$\mathrm{Dec}_{\mathscr{G}_f}\left(sk_{\mathscr{G}_f}, (a, f(bk, b))\right) = \iota^{-1}\left(\mathrm{Dec}_2(sk_2, f(bk, b))\right),$$

for any $(a, f(bk, b)) \leftarrow \mathrm{Enc}_{\mathscr{G}_f}(pk_{\mathscr{G}_f}, m)$ with overwhelming probability, due to the third condition in the definition of a bridge. One can immediately verify that the correctness of the encryption scheme $\mathscr{G}_f$ follows from the correctness of $\mathscr{S}_1$.

Remark 4. The notation and construction are inspired by the construction of the graph of a function.

Now we define the IND-CPA security of a bridge.

Definition 6. *The IND-CPA security of the bridge* $\mathbf{B}_{\iota,f}$ *is the IND-CPA security of its associated encryption scheme* $\mathscr{G}_f$.

We have the following immediate result.

Proposition 1. *If a bridge* $\mathbf{B}_{\iota,f}$ *is IND-CPA secure, then the encryption scheme* $\mathscr{S}_1$ *is also IND-CPA secure.*

Proof. Indeed, we can associate to any adversary $\mathcal{A}_1$ which is trying to break the IND-CPA security of $\mathscr{S}_1$, an adversary $\mathcal{A}_f$ for the encryption scheme $\mathscr{G}_f$, as follows. For any pair $(a, f(bk, b))$ proposed by the challenger to $\mathcal{A}_f$, where $a, b \leftarrow \mathrm{Enc}_1(m)$, the attacker $\mathcal{A}_f$ sends the triple (λ, pk_1, a) to $\mathcal{A}_1$ and returns the output of $\mathcal{A}_1(\lambda, pk_1, a)$.

It is clear that

$$\mathrm{Adv}^{\mathrm{IND\text{-}CPA}}[\mathcal{A}_f](\lambda) = \mathrm{Adv}^{\mathrm{IND\text{-}CPA}}[\mathcal{A}_1](\lambda),$$

and the result follows. □

In the next theorem, the encryption scheme $\mathscr{S}_1[PK_{\mathscr{G}_f}]$ is the scheme $\mathscr{S}_1$ with knowledge $PK_{\mathscr{G}_f}$. Namely, after running the key generation algorithm of $\mathscr{S}_1$ and receiving the pair (sk_1, pk_1), the challenger has access to an oracle that runs the second part of the key generation algorithm of the bridge to get sk_2, pk_2, bk. Thus, an IND-CPA attacker on this scheme will receive pk_1, pk_2, bk.

Theorem 1. *The encryption scheme* $\mathscr{S}_1[PK_{\mathscr{G}_f}]$ *is IND-CPA secure if and only if* $\mathscr{G}_f$ *is IND-CPA secure.*

Proof. We first show that if $\mathscr{G}_f$ is IND-CPA secure, then $\mathscr{S}_1[PK_{\mathscr{G}_f}]$ is IND-CPA secure. Suppose $\mathcal{A}$ is an IND-CPA attacker on $\mathscr{S}_1[PK_{\mathscr{G}_f}]$ scheme. We construct the following adversary $\mathcal{B}$ attacking the IND-CPA security of $\mathscr{G}_f$ as follows. At start, $\mathcal{B}$ takes as input $(1^\lambda, pk_{\mathscr{G}_f})$ and executes the program $\mathcal{A}(1^\lambda, pk_{\mathscr{G}_f})$. The attacker $\mathcal{B}$ receives $(m_0, m_1) \leftarrow \mathcal{A}(1^\lambda, pk_{\mathscr{G}_f})$ and sends this pair to its challenger. The latter samples $b \leftarrow \{0, 1\}$ and returns to $\mathcal{B}$ the challenge $c = (c_1, f(bk, c_1'))$, where $c_1, c_1' \leftarrow \mathrm{Enc}_1(pk_1, m_b)$. Finally, $\mathcal{B}$ terminates by outputting the bit $b' \leftarrow \mathcal{A}(c_1)$. One obtains that

$$\mathrm{Adv}_{\mathscr{G}_f}^{\mathrm{IND\text{-}CPA}}[\mathcal{B}](\lambda) = \mathrm{Adv}_{\mathscr{S}_1[PK_{\mathscr{G}_f}]}^{\mathrm{IND\text{-}CPA}}[\mathcal{A}](\lambda),$$

which proves this implication.

To prove the other implication, we first point out that using a standard hybrid argument one can show that the IND-CPA security of an encryption scheme is equivalent to its 2-IND-CPA security (see [26] for a detailed discussion). As opposed to the IND-CPA game, in the 2-IND-CPA game the attacker receives from the challenger two encryptions of m_b, instead of one.

Suppose that $\mathcal{B}$ is an IND-CPA attacker on $\mathcal{G}_f$. We construct a 2-IND-CPA attacker $\mathcal{A}$ for the scheme $\mathcal{S}_1[PK_{\mathcal{G}_f}]$ as follows. The attacker $\mathcal{A}$ receives as input $(1^\lambda, pk_{\mathcal{G}_f})$ and sends this to $\mathcal{B}$. On this input, the attacker $\mathcal{B}$ produces two messages $m_0, m_1 \in \mathcal{P}_1$ which are sent to $\mathcal{A}$ and the latter passes them to its challenger. After receiving m_0, m_1, the challenger of $\mathcal{A}$ chooses $b \leftarrow \{0,1\}$ and returns $c_1, c_1' \leftarrow \mathrm{Enc}_1(m_b)$ to the attacker $\mathcal{A}$. The attacker $\mathcal{A}$, knowing bk, is able to compute $f(bk, c_1') \in \mathcal{C}_2$ and finishes by outputting $b' \leftarrow \mathcal{B}(c_1, f(bk, c_1'))$. Now, one can verify that

$$\mathrm{Adv}_{\mathcal{S}_1[PK_{\mathcal{G}_f}]}^{2-\mathrm{IND-CPA}}[\mathcal{A}](\lambda) = \mathrm{Adv}_{\mathcal{G}_f}^{\mathrm{IND-CPA}}[\mathcal{B}](\lambda).$$

By the discussion in the previous paragraph, the scheme $\mathcal{S}_1[PK_{\mathcal{G}_f}]$ is 2-IND-CPA secure, so that $\mathcal{A}$ has negligible advantage. The last equality shows that $\mathcal{B}$ has also negligible advantage, which ends the argument. □

Recall that the *bridge key generation algorithm* produces the following ensembles of $\{SK_{1,\lambda}\}_\lambda$ distributions: $\{PK_{1,\lambda}\}_\lambda$, $\{PK_{2,\lambda}\}_\lambda$ and $\{BK_\lambda\}_\lambda$. Let $\mathcal{F}$ be the ensemble of finite distributions of triples (pk_1, pk_2, bk). Note that $\pi_1 : \mathcal{F} \to PK_1$ is a morphism of finite distributions, so $\mathcal{F}$ is a PK_1-distribution as discussed in Sect. 2.1.

Theorem 2. *Assume that $\mathcal{S}_1$ is IND-CPA secure and there exists a polynomial time constructible on fibers ensemble of PK_1-distributions $\widetilde{\mathcal{F}}$ which is computational indistinguishable from $\mathcal{F}$. Then the bridge $\mathbf{B}_{i,f}$ is IND-CPA secure.*

Proof. Without losing generality we assume that $\mathcal{P}_1 = \{0,1\}$. By the above theorem, it is enough to prove that $\mathcal{S}_1[PK_{\mathcal{G}_f}]$ is IND-CPA secure. We do the proof by contradiction, so we suppose that $\mathcal{A}$ is an adversary attacking the scheme $\mathcal{S}_1[PK_{\mathcal{G}_f}]$ with non-negligible advantage. We think of $\mathcal{A}$ as being a distinguisher between the ensembles of distributions $\mathcal{F} \times_{PK_1} \mathrm{Enc}_1(PK_1, 0)$ and $\mathcal{F} \times_{PK_1} \mathrm{Enc}_1(PK_1, 1)$. The first claim is that, if $\mathcal{A}$ can distinguish with non-negligible advantage between these two distributions then $\mathcal{A}$ distinguishes with non-negligible advantage between $\widetilde{\mathcal{F}} \times_{PK_1} \mathrm{Enc}_1(PK_1, 0)$ and $\widetilde{\mathcal{F}} \times_{PK_1} \mathrm{Enc}_1(PK_1, 1)$. To prove the claim we suppose that this is not the case and we construct a distinguisher $\mathcal{D}$ for the distributions $\mathcal{F}$ and $\widetilde{\mathcal{F}}$. As the ensemble of distributions $\widetilde{\mathcal{F}}$ is computationally indistinguishable from $\mathcal{F}$, for every λ, the distribution $\widetilde{\mathcal{F}}_\lambda$ consists of triples of the form (pk_1, α, β).

The distinguisher $\mathcal{D}$ runs as follows. It first receives a triple (pk_1, x, y) from the challenger, chooses at random a bit $b \leftarrow \{0,1\}$ and encrypts b using pk_1 to obtain a ciphertext c. The distinguisher $\mathcal{D}$ sends the quadruple (pk_1, x, y, c) to $\mathcal{A}$ and outputs

$$\mathcal{D}(pk_1, x, y) := \begin{cases} 1 & \text{if } \mathcal{A}(pk_1, x, y, c) = b \\ 0 & \text{otherwise} \end{cases}.$$

We note that the labels $b = 1$ and $b = 0$, as outputted by $\mathcal{A}$, correspond to the ensembles $\mathscr{F}$ and $\widetilde{\mathscr{F}}$, respectively. Notice that

$$\Pr\left\{\mathrm{Exp}_1[\mathcal{D}] = 1\right\} = \frac{1}{2}\Pr\left\{\mathrm{Exp}_0[\mathcal{A}|_{\mathscr{F}}] = 0\right\} + \frac{1}{2}\Pr\left\{\mathrm{Exp}_1[\mathcal{A}|_{\mathscr{F}}] = 1\right\},$$

where $\mathrm{Exp}_b[\mathcal{A}|_{\mathscr{F}}]$ means that in the experiment Exp_b the challenger chooses the triple $(pk_1, x, y) = (pk_1, pk_2, bk)$ according to $\mathscr{F}$. Using analogous notation for $\widetilde{\mathscr{F}}$, we have:

$$\Pr\left\{\mathrm{Exp}_0[\mathcal{D}] = 1\right\} = \frac{1}{2}\Pr\left\{\mathrm{Exp}_0[\mathcal{A}|_{\widetilde{\mathscr{F}}}] = 1\right\} + \frac{1}{2}\Pr\left\{\mathrm{Exp}_1[\mathcal{A}|_{\widetilde{\mathscr{F}}}] = 0\right\}.$$

Since the advantage of $\mathcal{A}|_{\mathscr{F}}$ is non-negligible, there exists a positive integer k such that

$$\left|\Pr\left\{\mathrm{Exp}_1[\mathcal{D}] = 1\right\} - \frac{1}{2}\right| > \frac{1}{\lambda^k} \tag{1}$$

for infinitely many λ's. Also, since $\mathrm{Adv}[\mathcal{A}|_{\widetilde{\mathscr{F}}}](\lambda) = \mathrm{negl}(\lambda)$, we have

$$\left|\Pr\left\{\mathrm{Exp}_0[\mathcal{D}] = 1\right\} - \frac{1}{2}\right| = \mathrm{negl}(\lambda). \tag{2}$$

From (1) and (2) we infer that

$$\mathrm{Adv}[\mathcal{D}](\lambda) = \left|\Pr\left\{\mathrm{Exp}_1[\mathcal{D}] = 1\right\} - \Pr\left\{\mathrm{Exp}_0[\mathcal{D}] = 1\right\}\right|$$

is non-negligible, which contradicts the assumption about the computational indistinguishability of the two distributions $\mathscr{F}$ and $\widetilde{\mathscr{F}}$.

Now we use $\mathcal{A}|_{\widetilde{\mathscr{F}}}$ to construct an adversary $\mathcal{B}$ on $\mathscr{S}_1$. After receiving the pair (pk_1, c) (as before $c \leftarrow \mathrm{Enc}_1(pk_1, b)$) from the challenger, $\mathcal{B}$ is using the sampling algorithm of $\widetilde{\mathscr{F}}$ to get a triple (pk_1, α, β). The adversary $\mathcal{B}$ sends (pk_1, α, β, c) to $\mathcal{A}|_{\widetilde{\mathscr{F}}}$ and outputs the bit received from it. It is clear that

$$\mathrm{Adv}[\mathcal{B}](\lambda) = \mathrm{Adv}[\mathcal{A}|_{\widetilde{\mathscr{F}}}](\lambda)$$

so that $\mathcal{B}$ breaks the IND-CPA security of $\mathscr{S}_1$ with non-negligible advantage, and this contradicts our assumption.   □

4   A General Recipe for Constructing Bridges

As we shall explain in what follows, the *Recrypt* algorithm, used in the bootsrapping procedure that transforms a somewhat homomorphic encryption scheme into a fully homomorphic encryption scheme (see [18]), can be adapted to our situation in order to give a general recipe for the construction of a bridge. We will call this method *Gentry's recipe* and say that the bridges obtained using it are of *Gentry type*.

Let us consider an encryption scheme

$$\mathscr{S} = (\mathscr{P}_{\mathscr{S}}, \mathscr{C}_{\mathscr{S}}, \text{KeyGen}_{\mathscr{S}}, \text{Enc}_{\mathscr{S}}, \text{Dec}_{\mathscr{S}})$$

and a homomorphic encryption scheme

$$\mathscr{H} = (\mathscr{P}_{\mathscr{H}}, \mathscr{C}_{\mathscr{H}}, \text{KeyGen}_{\mathscr{H}}, \text{Enc}_{\mathscr{H}}, \text{Dec}_{\mathscr{H}}, \text{Eval}_{\mathscr{H}}),$$

such that $\mathscr{P}_{\mathscr{H}}$ has a ring structure and there exists an injective map $\iota : \mathscr{P}_{\mathscr{S}} \hookrightarrow \mathscr{P}_{\mathscr{H}}$ satisfying the properties 1.(a)-(b) in Definition 3.

In this construction, the key generation algorithm is as follows. First, it runs $\text{KeyGen}_{\mathscr{S}}(1^\lambda)$ to sample from the distribution $SK_{\mathscr{S}}$ and then, independently, it runs $\text{KeyGen}_{\mathscr{H}}(1^\lambda)$ to sample from $SK_{\mathscr{H}}$. We point out that the distribution SK_2 in the definition of the bridge is in fact the product $SK_{\mathscr{S}} \times SK_{\mathscr{H}}$ and the map $SK_2 \to SK_1$ (see Fig. 1) is the projection on the first component $SK_{\mathscr{S}} \times SK_{\mathscr{H}} \to SK_{\mathscr{S}}$. Samples for the public keys $pk_{\mathscr{S}}$ and $pk_{\mathscr{H}}$ are generated, independently, using the key generation algorithms of the two schemes. Given a quadruple $(sk_{\mathscr{S}}, pk_{\mathscr{S}}, sk_{\mathscr{H}}, pk_{\mathscr{H}})$ constructed as above, the algorithm creates bk as the vector of encryptions of all the bits of $sk_{\mathscr{S}}$ under $pk_{\mathscr{H}}$ (see below). This is how the distribution of bridge keys BK is obtained.

The PPT algorithm f mentioned in the third part of Definition 3 is in this case the homomorphic evaluation (in $\mathscr{H}$) of the algorithm $\text{Dec}_{\mathscr{S}}$. We need to realise $\text{Dec}_{\mathscr{S}}$ as a map $\mathscr{P}_{\mathscr{H}}^\ell \to \mathscr{P}_{\mathscr{H}}$, and for this we use the ring structure on $\mathscr{P}_{\mathscr{H}}$. Suppose that the ciphertext space $\mathscr{C}_{\mathscr{S}}$ is a subset of $\{0,1\}^n$ and that the set of secret keys is a subset of $\{0,1\}^e$, so that $\text{Dec}_{\mathscr{S}} : \{0,1\}^e \times \{0,1\}^n \to \mathscr{P}_{\mathscr{S}}$. We construct the map $\widetilde{\text{Dec}}_{\mathscr{S}} : \mathscr{P}_{\mathscr{H}}^e \times \mathscr{P}_{\mathscr{H}}^n \to \mathscr{P}_{\mathscr{H}}$ as follows. Letting $\mathscr{P}_{\mathscr{H}}$ be a subset of $\{0,1\}^m$, we have that $\iota \circ \text{Dec}_{\mathscr{S}} : \{0,1\}^e \times \{0,1\}^n \to \mathscr{P}_{\mathscr{H}}$ is a vector $(g_1, ..., g_m)$ of boolean circuits expressed using XOR and AND gates. Let $\tilde{g}_i : \mathscr{P}_{\mathscr{H}}^e \times \mathscr{P}_{\mathscr{H}}^n \to \mathscr{P}_{\mathscr{H}}$ be the circuit obtained by replacing each XOR(x,y)- gate by $x \oplus y := 2(x+y) - (x+y)^2$ and each AND(x,y) gate by $x \otimes y := x \cdot y$, where $+$ and $\cdot$ are the addition and multiplication in $\mathscr{P}_{\mathscr{H}}$. Notice that the subset of $\mathscr{P}_{\mathscr{H}}$ consisting of its zero element $0_{\mathscr{H}}$ and its unit $1_{\mathscr{H}}$ together with $\oplus$ and $\otimes$ is a realisation of the field with two elements inside $\mathscr{P}_{\mathscr{H}}$. In other words, if $c = (c[1], ..., c[n]) \in \mathscr{C}_{\mathscr{S}}$ and $sk_{\mathscr{S}} = (sk[1], ..., sk[e])$ is the secret key, then $\tilde{g}_i(sk[1]_{\mathscr{H}}, ..., sk[e]_{\mathscr{H}}, c[1]_{\mathscr{H}}, ..., c[n]_{\mathscr{H}}) = m_{\mathscr{H}}$ if $g_i(sk[1], ..., sk[e], c[1], ..., c[n]) = m$ for all i, where $m \in \{0,1\}$. For an element $x \in \mathscr{P}_{\mathscr{H}}$, we let $[x = 1_{\mathscr{H}}]$ be the equality test, which returns 1 if $x = 1_{\mathscr{H}}$ and 0 otherwise. Finally, $\widetilde{\text{Dec}}_{\mathscr{S}} : \mathscr{P}_{\mathscr{H}}^e \times \mathscr{P}_{\mathscr{H}}^n \to \{0,1\}^m$ is defined by:

$$([\tilde{g}_i(y_1, ..., y_e, x_1, ..., x_n) = 1_{\mathscr{H}}])_{i=\overline{1,m}}.$$

One can verify that

$$\widetilde{\text{Dec}}_{\mathscr{S}}(sk[1]_{\mathscr{H}}, ..., sk[e]_{\mathscr{H}}, c[1]_{\mathscr{H}}, ..., c[n]_{\mathscr{H}}) = \iota \circ \text{Dec}_{\mathscr{S}}(sk, c).$$

Now we are ready to define the bridge map. Given a ciphertext $c \in \mathscr{C}_{\mathscr{S}}$, the algorithm f first encrypts the n bits of c (viewed as elements of $\mathscr{P}_{\mathscr{H}}$) under

$pk_{\mathscr{H}}$ and retains these encryptions in a vector $\tilde{c}$. The bridge key bk is obtained by encrypting the bits of $sk_{\mathscr{S}}$ under $pk_{\mathscr{H}}$. Then, the algorithm outputs:

$$f(bk, c) = \mathrm{Eval}_{\mathscr{H}}\left(evk_{\mathscr{H}}, \widetilde{\mathrm{Dec}}_{\mathscr{S}}, bk, \tilde{c}\right)$$

Assuming that $\mathscr{H}$ can evaluate $\widetilde{\mathrm{Dec}}_{\mathscr{S}}$ we have:

$$\begin{aligned}
\mathrm{Dec}_{\mathscr{H}}\left(f(bk, c)\right) &= \mathrm{Dec}_{\mathscr{H}}\left(\mathrm{Eval}_{\mathscr{H}}\left(evk_{\mathscr{H}}, \widetilde{\mathrm{Dec}}_{\mathscr{S}}, bk, \tilde{c}\right)\right) \\
&= \iota\left(\mathrm{Dec}_{\mathscr{S}}\left(\mathrm{Dec}_{\mathscr{H}}(bk), \mathrm{Dec}_{\mathscr{H}}(\tilde{c})\right)\right) \\
&= \iota\left(\mathrm{Dec}_{\mathscr{S}}(sk_{\mathscr{S}}, c)\right)
\end{aligned}$$

which shows that third condition in the definition of a bridge is satisfied.

Remark 5. The above construction relies on the fact that the plaintext space of $\mathscr{H}$, being a ring, can be used to simulate an $\mathbb{F}_2$-structure inside it.

An example of the above construction can be found in [19], where the authors managed to homomorphically evaluate the AES-128 circuit (encryption and decryption) using an optimized implementation of the BGV scheme [5]. Once the plaintext spaces and the embedding ι are fixed, the evaluation of this decryption circuit can be seen as a Gentry type bridge. The bridge key consists of the BGV encryptions of the eleven AES round keys (see Sect. 4 of [19]). We note that here the round keys are embedded in the plaintext, so it was not necessary to encrypt the bits of the round keys, as discussed at the beginning of the section. This results in a simpler homomorphic evaluation of AES decryption. Nonetheless, this bridge is essentially obtained using Gentry's recipe.

4.1   On the Security of Gentry Type Bridges

The aim of this subsection is to show that if $\mathscr{S}$ and $\mathscr{H}$ are IND-CPA secure, then any Gentry type bridge $B_{\iota, f}$ from $\mathscr{S}$ to $\mathscr{H}$ is IND-CPA secure. The plan is to apply Theorem 2 to the above construction.

Recall that $\mathscr{F}$ is the ensemble of finite distributions of triples $(pk_{\mathscr{S}}, pk_{\mathscr{H}}, bk)$, where bk is a vector of encryptions of the form $(bk[1], ..., bk[e])$ with $bk[i] \leftarrow \mathrm{Enc}_{\mathscr{H}}(pk_{\mathscr{H}}, sk[i]_{\mathscr{S}})$ for all i. Next, let $\widetilde{\mathscr{F}}$ be the ensemble of finite distributions of triples $(pk_{\mathscr{S}}, pk_{\mathscr{H}}, \widetilde{bk})$, where $pk_{\mathscr{S}}$, $pk_{\mathscr{H}}$ are independently outputted by $\mathrm{KeyGen}_{\mathscr{S}}$ and $\mathrm{KeyGen}_{\mathscr{H}}$, respectively and $\widetilde{bk} := (\widetilde{bk}[1], ..., \widetilde{bk}[e])$ with $\widetilde{bk}[i] \leftarrow \mathrm{Enc}(pk_{\mathscr{H}}, 0_{\mathscr{H}})$ for all $i \in \overline{1, e}$. Notice that $\widetilde{\mathscr{F}}$ is polynomial-time constructible on fibers as a $PK_{\mathscr{S}}$-ensemble of finite distributions (see Definition 1). Let us remark that one can choose $\widetilde{\mathscr{F}}$ in a different way, setting $\widetilde{bk}$ to be a vector of encryptions of any fixed e-long bit vector. If the scheme $\mathscr{H}$ is IND-CPA secure, then one can prove by a standard hybrid argument (see the next proposition) that the two versions are in fact computational indistinguishable. Therefore, the choice of the particular fixed bit vector that is encrypted to get $\widetilde{bk}$ does not matter.

Proposition 2. *If $\mathscr{H}$ is IND-CPA secure, then the ensembles $\mathscr{F}$ and $\widetilde{\mathscr{F}}$ are computationally indistinguishable.*

Proof. Let $\mathcal{D}$ be a distinguisher between the two ensembles $\mathscr{F}$ and $\widetilde{\mathscr{F}}$. We denote by $\mathscr{G}_i$ the distribution of triples $(pk_{\mathscr{S}}, pk_{\mathscr{H}}, x)$ where the pair $(pk_{\mathscr{S}}, pk_{\mathscr{H}})$ is chosen exactly as in the case of $\mathscr{F}$, or $\widetilde{\mathscr{F}}$, and $x := (x[1], ..., x[e])$ where $x[j] \leftarrow$ $\text{Enc}(pk_{\mathscr{H}}, sk_{\mathscr{S}}[j])$ for all $j \in \overline{1, i}$ and $x[j] \leftarrow \text{Enc}(pk_{\mathscr{H}}, 0)$ for all $j \in \overline{i+1, e}$. Notice that $\{\mathscr{G}_{e(\lambda)}\}_\lambda$ is the same as $\mathscr{F}$, and $\{\mathscr{G}_0\}_\lambda$ is $\widetilde{\mathscr{F}}$. For each $i \in \overline{1, e}$ we construct an attacker $\mathcal{B}_i$ on the scheme $\mathscr{H}$ as follows. The attacker receives from the challenger the triple $(1^\lambda, pk_{\mathscr{H}}, c)$, where c is either an encryption of 0 or an encryption of 1. The attacker uses $\text{KeyGen}_{\mathscr{S}}$ to generate a pair $(sk_{\mathscr{S}}, pk_{\mathscr{S}})$ and then constructs an e-long vector y as follows: $y[j] \leftarrow \text{Enc}(pk_{\mathscr{H}}, sk_{\mathscr{S}}[j])$ for $j < i$, $y[i] = c$, and $y[j] \leftarrow \text{Enc}(pk_{\mathscr{H}}, 0)$ for $j > i$. Then the attacker $\mathcal{B}_i$ runs $\mathcal{D}(1^\lambda, pk_{\mathscr{S}}, pk_{\mathscr{H}}, y)$ and outputs $sk[i]$ if the answer received from $\mathcal{D}$ is $\mathscr{F}$ and 0 otherwise. Basically, $\mathcal{D}$ can be used as a distinguisher between the ensembles $\{\mathscr{G}_{i-1}\}_\lambda$ and $\{\mathscr{G}_i\}_\lambda$, which gives rise to $\mathcal{B}_i$. Notice that

$$\text{Adv}^{\text{IND-CPA}}[\mathcal{D}](\lambda) \leq \sum_{i=1}^{e(\lambda)} \text{Adv}^{\text{IND-CPA}}[\mathcal{B}_i](\lambda),$$

where we used the fact that the advantage of $\mathcal{B}_i$ is equal to the advantage of $\mathcal{D}$ as a distinguisher between $\mathscr{G}_i$ and $\mathscr{G}_{i-1}$. Since $\mathscr{H}$ is IND-CPA secure and $e(\lambda)$ is polynomial in λ, we get that $\mathcal{D}$ has negligible advantage.

The result of Proposition 2 combined with Theorem 2 yields the following result:

Theorem 3. *Assume that $\mathscr{S}$ and $\mathscr{H}$ are both IND-CPA secure, then any Gentry type bridge $\mathbf{B}_{\iota, f}$ from $\mathscr{S}$ to $\mathscr{H}$ is IND-CPA secure.*

4.2   A Variant of Gentry's Recipe

The aim of this subsection is to give a new variant of Gentry's recipe for the construction of bridges. For this, we need first to introduce the product of two encryption schemes. Suppose that $\mathscr{S}_i = (\mathscr{P}_i, \mathscr{C}_i, \text{KeyGen}_i, \text{Enc}_i, \text{Dec}_i)$, $i \in \{1, 2\}$ are two encryption schemes, then the product $\mathscr{S}_1 \times \mathscr{S}_2$ is defined as follows. The plaintext space is defined as $\mathscr{P}_1 \times \mathscr{P}_2$ and the ciphertext space as $\mathscr{C}_1 \times \mathscr{C}_2$. The Key Generation algorithm of the product scheme uses independently the key generation algorithms of the two schemes to produce two pairs (sk_1, pk_1) and (sk_2, pk_2) of keys and sets the secret key as (sk_1, sk_2), and sets the public key as (pk_1, pk_2). An encryption of a message $(m_1, m_2) \in \mathscr{P}_1 \times \mathscr{P}_2$ is just a pair (c_1, c_2), where $c_1 \leftarrow \text{Enc}_1(pk_1, m_1)$ and $c_2 \leftarrow \text{Enc}_2(pk_2, m_2)$. Finally, the decryption of (c_1, c_2) is $(\text{Dec}_1(sk_1, c_1), \text{Dec}_2(sk_2, c_2))$. In the same way, one can define the product of $p \geq 2$ encryption schemes. If $\mathscr{H}$ is an encryption scheme, we shall denote by $\mathscr{H}^p$ the product of p copies of $\mathscr{H}$.

Now, we describe this new construction. We use the same notations as in the beginning of this section, and we assume that $\mathscr{P}_{\mathscr{H}} = \{0, 1\}$. Let

$\iota : \mathscr{P}_{\mathscr{S}} \hookrightarrow \{0,1\}^p$ be a representation of the plaintext space of $\mathscr{S}$, which can be viewed as the map $\iota : \mathscr{P}_{\mathscr{S}} \hookrightarrow \mathscr{P}_{\mathscr{H}}^p$, by identifying $\{0,1\}^p$ with the plaintext space of $\mathscr{H}^p$. We construct a bridge from $\mathscr{S}$ to $\mathscr{H}^p$ as follows. Notice that the decryption algorithm of $\mathscr{S}$ is in fact a p-long vector of boolean algorithms $g_i :$ $\{0,1\}^e \times \{0,1\}^n \to \{0,1\}$, that is $\mathrm{Dec}_{\mathscr{S}}(sk_{\mathscr{S}},c) = (g_1(sk_{\mathscr{S}},c), ..., g_p(sk_{\mathscr{S}},c))$, where $\{0,1\}^n$ and $\{0,1\}^e$ correspond to $\mathscr{C}_{\mathscr{S}}$ and the support of secret keys of $\mathscr{S}$, respectively. The bridge key bk is obtained by encrypting the bits of $sk_{\mathscr{S}}$ under each component of the public key of $\mathscr{H}^p$.

The bridge map f is the vector obtained by homomorphically evaluating the circuits g_i in $\mathscr{H}$. More precisely

$$f(bk,c) = (\mathrm{Eval}_{\mathscr{H}}(evk_{\mathscr{H}}, g_i, bk, \tilde{c}))_{i=\overline{1,p}},$$

where $\tilde{c}$ is defined as above. Notice that, if $c \leftarrow \mathrm{Enc}(pk_{\mathscr{S}}, m)$ then

$$\mathrm{Dec}_{\mathscr{H}^p}(f(bk,c)) = \iota(m).$$

Security. As in the previous subsection, it can be shown that if $\mathscr{S}$ and $\mathscr{H}$ are IND-CPA secure, then the bridge is also IND-CPA secure. The proof is very similar to that of Proposition 2, hence omitted here.

5   Conclusions

Access to secure and efficient bridges between homomorphic encryption schemes would be helpful for applications of cloud computing on sensitive data. Investigating theoretical results for proving the security of such protocols is therefore an important topic. Our main theorem is such a tool, and a particular case of it recovers the already known security of Gentry-type bridges.

Acknowledgements. The authors are indebted to George Gugulea and Mihai Togan for helpful discussions and comments during the preparation of this work. We are also grateful to the anonymous reviewers for useful suggestions.

A   Examples of Gentry Bridges

The aim of this appendix is to emphasize the fact that, for an encryption scheme $\mathscr{S}$, different representations for the decryption algorithm $\mathrm{Dec}_{\mathscr{S}}$ give rise to different bridges from $\mathscr{S}$ to a FHE scheme $\mathscr{H}$. For practical applications, one can select the appropriate representation that best suits the implementation of the desired application. Having this in mind, we chose to exhibit the encryption scheme CSGN introduced in [3] and implemented in [8], whose decryption algorithm admits at least four fundamentally different representations. We shall restrict ourselves in discussing the security of these bridges, because the security of the CSGN scheme is not entirely understood.

A.1 Description of the CSGN Scheme

We give a brief description of the CSGN scheme. For more details regarding the parameter selection, we refer to [3]. The plaintext space is the field $\mathbb{F}_2$ and the ciphertext space of this scheme is $\mathbb{F}_2^n$ with the monoid structure defined by component-wise multiplication. A simplified version of the scheme is defined as follows.

- KeyGen$_{\text{CSGN}}(1^\lambda)$: Choose dimension parameters n, d and s of size poly(λ), a uniformly random subset S of $\{1, 2, \ldots, n\}$ of size s, and a finite distribution X on $\{1, 2, \ldots, d\}$ according to [3]. Set the secret key sk to be the characteristic function of S, viewed as a bit vector.
- Enc$_{\text{CSGN}}$: To encrypt 0, choose first $k \in \{1, 2, \ldots, d\}$ according to X and then choose uniformly at random d numbers $i_1, \ldots, i_d$ from the set $\{1, 2, \ldots, n\}$, such that exactly k of them are in S. Finally, output the vector in $\mathbb{F}_2^n$ whose components corresponding to the indices $i_1, \ldots, i_d$ are equal to 0 and the others are equal to 1. To encrypt 1, choose uniformly at random d numbers $i_1, \ldots, i_d$ from the set $\{1, 2, \ldots, n\}$, such that none of them is in S, and output the resulting vector in $\mathbb{F}_2^n$ as before.
- Dec$_{\text{CSGN}}$: To decrypt a ciphertext c using the secret key sk, output 0 if c has at least one component equal to 0 corresponding to an index from S and 1, otherwise.

The output of the decryption algorithm can be written as

$$\text{Dec}_{\text{CSGN}}(sk, c) = \prod_{i \in S} c_i.$$

Notice that, the decryption map is a homomorphism of monoids from $(\mathbb{F}_2^n, \cdot)$ to the monoid $(\mathbb{F}_2, \cdot)$ with the usual multiplication.

   In what follows, we present four variants of bridges from the CSGN scheme, denoted by $\mathscr{S}$, to various FHE schemes. The latter are going to be denoted by $\mathscr{H}$. Also, the pairing $\langle \cdot, \cdot \rangle : R^n \times R^n \to R$ will always be the standard inner product over the ring R.

A.2 1st Bridge

Let $\mathscr{H}$ be any FHE scheme with plaintext space the field with two elements; hence, the map ι is the identity map. The secret key $sk_{\mathscr{S}}$ can be represented by the n-dimensional standard vectors e_i, where $i \in S$. The bridge key generation algorithm encrypts each entry of the vectors e_i, $i \in S$ using $pk_{\mathscr{H}}$ to obtain the bridge key $bk = \{\widetilde{e}_1, \ldots, \widetilde{e}_s\}$, a set of vectors consisting of the aforementioned encryptions.

   We remark that the decryption algorithm of $\mathscr{S}$ may be written as

$$\text{Dec}_{\mathscr{S}}(sk_{\mathscr{S}}, c) = \prod_{i \in S} \langle c, e_i \rangle,$$

so that the bridge algorithm f is as follows:

$$f(bk, c) = \prod_{i=1}^{s} \langle c, \tilde{e}_i \rangle = \prod_{i=1}^{s} \left(\sum_{c[j]=1} \tilde{e}_i[j] \right).$$

For simplicity, we chose the trivial encryptions as the encryptions of the bits of c with $\mathscr{H}$.

A.3   2nd Bridge

We are in the same setting as before, where both plaintext spaces are $\mathbb{F}_2$. Recall that the secret key $sk_{\mathscr{S}}$ is the characteristic function of the set S, represented as an n-dimensional bit vector. Then, the decryption of $\mathscr{S}$ can be alternatively written as

$$\text{Dec}_{\mathscr{S}}(sk_{\mathscr{S}}, c) = \prod_{i=1}^{n} \left(1 - (1 - c[i]) sk_{\mathscr{S}}[i] \right) = \prod_{c[i]=0} (1 - sk_{\mathscr{S}}[i]).$$

The bridge key bk is constructed as $bk := \{ \widetilde{sk_{\mathscr{S}}}[1], ..., \widetilde{sk_{\mathscr{S}}}[n] \}$, where for every i, $\widetilde{sk_{\mathscr{S}}}[i]$ is an encryption of $1 - sk_{\mathscr{S}}[i]$ under $pk_{\mathscr{H}}$. Finally, the bridge is given by

$$f(bk, c) = \prod_{c[i]=0} \widetilde{sk_{\mathscr{S}}}[i].$$

Remark 6. The last formula shows that this bridge can be constructed even if the scheme $\mathscr{H}$ is homomorphic only with respect to multiplication. For example, it can be used when $\mathscr{H} = \mathscr{S}$ obtaining something that resembles the key-switching technique in some FHE schemes.

A.4   3rd Bridge

Here, the scheme $\mathscr{H}$ can be any FHE scheme with plaintext space the finite field $\mathbb{F}_p$, where p is a prime (for example the BGV and B/FV schemes, see [5,6] and [16]).

The bridge key generation algorithm instantiates $\text{KeyGen}_{\mathscr{S}}(1^{\lambda})$ and then $\text{KeyGen}_{\mathscr{H}}(1^{\lambda})$, assuring that the characteristic of $\mathscr{P}_{\mathscr{H}}$ is larger than the Hamming weight of $sk_{\mathscr{S}}$, that is $p > s$. It then chooses positive integers $x_1, ..., x_s$ such that $p = 1 + x_1 + \cdots + x_s$, and fixes a bijection $\varphi : S \to \{1, ..., s\}$. Consider the vector $sk \in \mathbb{F}_p^n$, where $sk[i] = 0$ if $sk_{\mathscr{S}}[i] = 0$ and $sk[i] = x_{\varphi(i)}$, otherwise. For every $i \in \{1, ..., n\}$, write $\widetilde{sk}[i]$ for an encryption of $sk[i]$ under $pk_{\mathscr{H}}$. In this case, the bridge key bk is the set of $\mathscr{H}$ encryptions $bk = \{ \widetilde{sk}[1], ..., \widetilde{sk}[n] \}$.

We remark that if $\iota : \mathbb{F}_2 \hookrightarrow \mathbb{F}_p$ denotes the usual embedding, then the decryption of $\mathscr{S}$ satisfies

$$\text{Dec}_{\mathscr{S}}(sk_{\mathscr{S}}, c) = \iota^{-1} \left(1 - \left(1 + \langle c, sk \rangle_{\mathbb{F}_p} \right)^{p-1} \right).$$

The bridge map is defined as

$$f(bk, c) = \text{Enc}_{\mathscr{H}}(pk_{\mathscr{H}}, 1) - \left(\text{Enc}_{\mathscr{H}}(pk_{\mathscr{H}}, 1) + \sum_{c[i]=1} \widetilde{sk}[i] \right)^{p-1},$$

where the additions, subtractions and exponentiation on the right hand side are homomorphic operations on the ciphertexts of $\mathscr{H}$.

Remark 7. As mentioned in the discussion following Definition 3, one can develop a theory of bridges for which the plaintext spaces of the two encryption schemes vary with λ along the same lines. The bridge constructed here falls in this category because the plaintext space of $\mathscr{H}$ is chosen after the size of the secret key is selected, as part of the Setup/KeyGen algorithm.

A.5 4th Bridge

This bridge is based on an idea used in [1] for the bootstrapping procedure of the GSW scheme. Notice that if c is a ciphertext in $\mathscr{S}$, encrypted using $pk_{\mathscr{S}}$, then c decrypts to 1 if and only if the inner product $\langle c, sk_{\mathscr{S}} \rangle_{\mathbb{Z}} = s$, namely

$$\text{Dec}_{\mathscr{S}}(sk_{\mathscr{S}}, c) = [\langle c, sk_{\mathscr{S}} \rangle_{\mathbb{Z}} = s],$$

where $[x = y]$ is, as before, the equality test.

We observe that in the computation of the inner product $\langle c, sk_{\mathscr{S}} \rangle_{\mathbb{Z}}$ one uses only the additive structure of $\mathbb{Z}$ (also $\mathbb{Z}_m$ with $m > s$ would be sufficient for our purposes). To find a representation of the cyclic group $(\mathbb{Z}_m, +)$, one needs first to embed it into the symmetric group $\mathfrak{S}_m$. The generator $1 \in \mathbb{Z}_m$ is sent by this injective homomorphism to the cyclic permutation $\pi_1 \in \mathfrak{S}_m$, defined as $\pi_1(i) = i + 1$ for $1 \leq i < m$ and $\pi_1(m) = 1$. On the other hand, the group $\mathfrak{S}_m$ is isomorphic to the multiplicative group of m-by-m permutation matrices, that is matrices with 0 or 1 entries, having exactly one nonzero element in each row and each column. The isomorphism maps the permutation $\pi \in \mathfrak{S}_m$ to the matrix $M_\pi = [e_{\pi(1)}, ..., e_{\pi(m)}]$, where $e_i \in \{0, 1\}^m$ is the ith standard basis vector. The composition of these two homomorphisms gives us an embedding for the cyclic group $(\mathbb{Z}_m, +)$. For implementation purposes, it is good to notice that the permutation matrices in the image of this embedding can be represented more compactly by just their first column, because the remaining columns are just the successive cyclic shifts of this column.

Let us explain how the bridge is constructed. Let $m = s + 1$ and take $sk = (sk[1], ..., sk[n])$ to be the aforementioned representation of the secret key $sk_{\mathscr{S}}$, that is $sk[i] = M_{\pi_1}$ if $sk_{\mathscr{S}} = 1$ and $sk[i]$ is the identity matrix otherwise. Set $\widetilde{sk}[i]$ to be an encryption of $sk[i]$ under $pk_{\mathscr{H}}$ for all $i \in \overline{1, n}$, meaning that we encrypt with $\mathscr{H}$ each entry of the matrix $sk[i]$. The bridge key bk consists of $\{\widetilde{sk}[1], \ldots, \widetilde{sk}[n]\}$.

The algorithm f takes as input bk and c and computes the matrix

$$P^c := \prod_{c[i]=1} \widetilde{sk}[i],$$

where the right hand side is a product of encrypted matrices, performed homomorphically in $\mathscr{C}_{\mathscr{H}}$. We remark that the last entry of the first row of P^c is an encryption of the value returned by the equality test $[\langle c, sk_{\mathscr{S}}\rangle_{\mathbb{Z}} = s]$. Consequently, we let the output of the bridge map be

$$f(bk, c) := P^c_{1,s+1}.$$

B   Entangled Encryption Schemes

Informally, we say that two encryption schemes $\mathscr{S}$ and $\mathscr{H}$ are *entangled* if there is a bridge with empty bridge key from one to another.

In this appendix we give an example of such a bridge. In this example, the secret key of $\mathscr{S}$ and $\mathscr{H}$ are identical.

We believe that whenever two encryption schemes $\mathscr{S}$ and $\mathscr{H}$ are entangled, there is a relation between the ensembles of distributions of their secret keys. We regard this as an interesting question for future research.

The presented bridge does not follow Gentry's recipe. We start by recalling the Goldwasser-Micali and Sander-Young-Yung encryption schemes. A bridge from the former to the latter is then presented. The presentation is followed by an interesting application of this bridge.

B.1   Goldwasser-Micali Cryptosystem

The Goldwasser-Micali encryption scheme is an asymmetric key encryption algorithm developed by Shafi Goldwasser and Silvio Micali in [22]. If p, q are two primes and $N = p \cdot q$, then let $J_1(N) := \{x \in (\mathbb{Z}/N\mathbb{Z})^\times | \left(\frac{x}{N}\right) = 1\}$ be the multiplicative group of invertible integers modulo N with Jacobi symbol equal to 1. The GM-encryption scheme $(\mathbb{Z}/2\mathbb{Z}, J_1(N), \text{KeyGen}_{GM}, \text{Enc}_{GM}, \text{Dec}_{GM})$ is given as follows:

- **KeyGen**(1^λ): Choose two primes $p = p(\lambda), q = q(\lambda)$ of size λ and let $N = pq$. Choose $\eta \in (\mathbb{Z}/N\mathbb{Z})^\times$ such that $\left(\frac{\eta}{p}\right) = \left(\frac{\eta}{q}\right) = -1$, which yields that $\eta \in J_1(N)$. The public key is the pair $(N, \gamma := \eta \cdot u^2)$, where u is a random element of $(\mathbb{Z}/N\mathbb{Z})^\times$. The secret key is the pair (p, q).
- **Enc**: To encrypt $m \in \mathbb{Z}/2\mathbb{Z}$, choose a random $\xi \in \mathbb{Z}/N\mathbb{Z}$ and let $\text{Enc}_{GM}(m) = \gamma^m \xi^2$.
- **Dec**: To decrypt $c \in J_1(N)$, compute the Jacobi symbol $\left(\frac{c}{p}\right)$. Set $\text{Dec}_{GM}(c) = 0$ if the answer is 1 and $\text{Dec}_{GM}(c) = 1$ if the answer is -1.

The GM-encryption scheme is homomorphic with respect to addition in $\mathbb{Z}/2\mathbb{Z}$ and multiplication in $J_1(N)$, i.e.

$$\text{Dec}_{GM}(c_1 \cdot c_2) = \text{Dec}_{GM}(c_1) + \text{Dec}_{GM}(c_2)$$

for all $c_1, c_2 \in J_1(N)$.

B.2   The Sander-Young-Yung Cryptosystem

In this part of the appendix we present a homomorphic encryption scheme over the multiplicative monoid $(\mathbb{Z}/2\mathbb{Z}, \cdot)$ introduced in [25]. To describe the scheme we shall use the encryption scheme of Goldwasser-Micali, which was recalled above.

- **Keygen(1^λ):** Choose two primes $p = p(\lambda)$, $q = q(\lambda)$ as in the Goldwasser-Micali scheme. Choose $\ell = \ell(\lambda)$ of size $\Theta(\lambda)$. Compute $N = pq$. The public key and secret keys are the same as in the Goldwasser-Micali scheme.
- **Enc:** If $m = 1$ set $v = (0, ..., 0) \in \{0, 1\}^\ell$. If $m = 0$ set $v = (v_1, ..., v_n) \in \{0, 1\}^\ell$, where the components v_i are randomly chosen in $\{0, 1\}$, not all equal to 0. Encrypt each component of v with the Goldwasser-Micali scheme to get a vector in $\mathscr{C}_{SYY} := J_1(N)^\ell$.
- **Dec:** To recover the plaintext from the ciphertext $c \in \mathscr{C}$, first decrypt each component of c using the decryption algorithm of the Goldwasser-Micali scheme, and then if the obtained vector is the 0-vector the message decrypts to 1, else to 0.

Let us describe an operation $\odot$ on the ciphertext space $\mathscr{C}_{SYY}$. If x and y are two ciphertexts then $z := x \odot y$ is defined as follows:

1. Choose uniformly at random two $\ell \times \ell$ matrices over $\mathbb{Z}/2\mathbb{Z}$ until two nonsingular matrices $A = (a_{ij})$ and $B = (b_{ij})$ are found.
2. If $x = (x_1, ..., x_\ell)$, $y = (y_1, ..., y_\ell)$, then compute

$$z_i = \prod_{j, a_{ij}=1} x_j \cdot \prod_{j, b_{ij}=1} y_j$$

for all i.

3. Pick uniformly at random $r_1, ..., r_\ell \in (\mathbb{Z}/N\mathbb{Z})^\times$ and set $z = (z_1 r_1^2, ..., z_\ell r_\ell^2)$.

Let us denote by v_c the bit vector obtained by applying the decryption algorithm of the Goldwasser-Micali scheme componentwise to the ciphertext $c \in \mathscr{C}$. If $z := x \odot y$ then Step 2 above is equivalent to:

$$v_z = Av_x + Bv_y,$$

where the operations are the usual addition and multiplication in $\mathbb{Z}/2\mathbb{Z}$. Notice that $\mathrm{Dec}_{SYY}(z) \neq \mathrm{Dec}_{SYY}(x) \cdot \mathrm{Dec}_{SYY}(y)$ if and only if $Av_x + Bv_y = \mathbf{0}$ (here $\mathbf{0}$ is the zero vector in $(\mathbb{Z}/2\mathbb{Z})^\ell$), and $v_x \neq \mathbf{0}$, $v_y \neq \mathbf{0}$. Since $v_x \neq \mathbf{0}$ and A is nonsingular, the product Av_x can be any nonzero vector in $(\mathbb{Z}/2\mathbb{Z})^\ell$, and in fact any such vector occurs with the same probability. Of course, the same is true for Bv_y such that the situation described above occurs with probability $\leq \dfrac{1}{2^\ell}$. In other words, except with exponentially small probability, we have that

$$\mathrm{Dec}_{SYY}(x \odot y) = \mathrm{Dec}_{SYY}(x) \cdot \mathrm{Dec}_{SYY}(y).$$

B.3   A Bridge from GM to SYY

Here, we construct a bridge from the Goldwasser-Micali encryption scheme to the Sander-Young-Yung encryption scheme. After generating a secret key (p, q) of GM, the key generation algorithm of the bridge sets the same pair (p, q) as the secret key for the SYY encryption scheme. Then, the public keys for the two encryption schemes are generated independently using their respective key generation algorithms. After that, the bridge key generation algorithm does not output anything, i.e. the support of the distribution BK is the empty set.

Now, for $c \in J_1(N)$, choose uniformly at random a non-singular matrix $A \in \mathrm{GL}_\ell(\mathbb{Z}/2\mathbb{Z})$ and compute

$$t_i = \prod_{j, a_{ij}=1} c\gamma' = (c\gamma')^{|\{j\,|\,a_{ij}=1\}|}$$

for all $i \in \overline{1, \ell}$, where γ' is the second component of the public key of the SYY scheme. Pick uniformly at random $r_1, \dots, r_\ell \in (\mathbb{Z}/N\mathbb{Z})^\times$ and set

$$f(c) = (t_1 r_1^2, \dots, t_\ell r_\ell^2).$$

If $\mathrm{Dec}_{GM}(c) = 1$, then $\mathrm{Dec}_{GM}(c\gamma') = 0$ so that $\mathrm{Dec}_{GM}(t_i) = 0$, $\forall i$. Therefore, $v_{f(c)} = \mathbf{0}$ and hence $\mathrm{Dec}_{SYY}(f(c)) = 1$. On the other hand, if $\mathrm{Dec}_{GM}(c) = 0$, then $\mathrm{Dec}_{GM}(c\gamma') = 1$, and since A is nonsingular there exist $i \in \overline{1, \ell}$ such that $\mathrm{Dec}_{GM}(t_i) = 1$. We get that $v_{f(c)} \neq \mathbf{0}$, equivalently $\mathrm{Dec}_{SYY}(f(c)) = 0$.

Remark 8. The security of this bridge reduces to the security of the GM scheme (see [22]) using Theorem 2. Indeed, the bridge key distribution is empty, thus trivially polynomial-time constructible on fibers. On the other hand, the security of SYY encryption scheme can be easily reduced to the security of GM (see [25]). Alternatively, one can use Theorem 1 instead of 2. To see this, note that in the notation of Sect. 3, the public key of the scheme attached to this bridge $PK_{\mathscr{G}_f}$ consists of just GM's public key and the security of $GM[PK_{\mathscr{G}_f}]$ is equivalent to the security of GM.

B.4   An Application

As an application of the above bridge we show that the comparison circuit can be evaluated homomorphically. For this, let $\boldsymbol{x} = (x_1, x_2, \dots, x_n)$ and $\boldsymbol{y} = (y_1, y_2, \dots, y_n)$ be two bit vectors. The two vectors coincide if and only if

$$(x_1 + y_1 + 1) \cdot \dots \cdot (x_n + y_n + 1) = 1,$$

so that the comparison circuit $[\boldsymbol{x} = \boldsymbol{y}]$ is defined by

$$[\boldsymbol{x} = \boldsymbol{y}] := (x_1 + y_1 + 1) \cdot \dots \cdot (x_n + y_n + 1).$$

Suppose now that $c = (c_1, ..., c_n)$ and $d = (d_1, ..., d_n)$ are encryptions of the vectors x, y with the Goldwasser-Micali cryptosystem. To homomorphically evaluate the comparison circuit, we compute:

$$\text{Eval}([x = y], c, d) := \left(\left(\left((f(c_1 \cdot d_1 \cdot \gamma) \odot f(c_2 \cdot d_2 \cdot \gamma)) \odot ... \right) \odot f(c_n \cdot d_n \cdot \gamma) \right) \right).$$

Notice that $\text{Dec}_{SYY} (\text{Eval}([x = y], c, d)) = [x = y]$, except with negligible probability in the security parameter.

We end this appendix with the following reflection. When two encryption schemes admit the construction of a bridge which has an empty bridge key, this may be interpreted as some sort of entanglement between the schemes. Along the same line of thought, if one can prove that such a bridge cannot be constructed, the encryption schemes may be regarded as being independent.

C   Experiments

We conducted experiments for the bridges described in Appendices A and B. For each of the four different bridges in Appendix A, we compare the results of the homomorphic evaluation of a circuit consisting of only one monomial in the following two ways. First, we encrypt each factor of the monomial and perform the homomorphic multiplications of these factors using the CSGN scheme. Then, bridges described in Appendix A are applied, in turn, to obtain a ciphertext in a fully (leveled) homomorphic encryption scheme based on (R)LWE. We compare this to the alternative option of evaluating the monomial directly on encryptions in the FHE scheme. If the degree of the monomial is larger than a certain threshold, the first procedure outperforms the second in terms of speed. We identified this threshold for each of the FHE schemes in which we performed experiments.

These computations were carried on a virtual machine having an Intel CPU (I7-4770, 4 cores, 3.4 GHz, 12 GB RAM), using a single threaded implementation. Table 1 consists of an overview of the processing times for each bridge using the implementations of BGV, BFV and TFHE schemes, namely the HElib [23], SEAL [24] and TFHE [9] software libraries. In the first two columns of the table, one can find the version of the bridge that was implemented, the FHE target scheme and the security parameters for the two schemes. The timings are measured such that all encryptions maintain approximately the same security level λ and listed in the last two columns. The small variation in λ is due to parameter tuning in the different software libraries.

The reason we are missing an implementation for our third bridge using the TFHE library comes from the lack of flexibility in choosing as plaintext space a ring of characteristic $p > 2$ in this library. Additionally, we felt that adapting the TFHE library was beyond the scope of our work. Also, the timing for running the fourth bridge in BGV and BFV could not be measured because of large memory usage, which exceeded the virtual machine RAM. Moreover, regarding the fourth bridge, the implementation is optimized to store only the first column

Table 1. Bridge evaluation.

Bridge (CSGN-λ)	$LWE(\lambda)$	$ENC(Bridgekey)$	$Bridgetime$
$1^{st}(125)$	BGV(121)	69 s	2.6 s
$1^{st}(125)$	TFHE(128)	186 ms	38.33 s
$1^{st}(125)$	BFV(128)	38.97 s	209.95 ms
$2^{nd}(125)$	BGV(114)	14.6 s	68.28 s
$2^{nd}(125)$	TFHE(128)	2.94 ms	1049 ms
$2^{nd}(125)$	BFV(128)	698 ms	2.24 s
$3^{rd}(120)$	BGV(145)	7.65 s	248 ms
$3^{rd}(120)$	BFV(128)	8.2 s	156.46 ms
$4^{th}(115)$	TFHE(128)	162.6 ms	989.4 s

of each associated bit in the secret key, while the matrix multiplications involve only homomorphic algebraic operations on encryptions from the first column of the matrices.

There is no doubt that homomorphically evaluating a circuit whose polynomial representation has a large number of monomials of low degree using the bridge is inefficient and there is little hope for optimizations in terms of speed. However, if some monomials have large degree, one might choose to do so, because first performing multiplications in the CSGN scheme, followed by additions in the (R)LWE setting might result in lower noise growth. Moreover, by increasing the multiplicative depth of the circuit, we observe that its evaluation is faster using the bridge than evaluating the circuit entirely in the (R)LWE schemes. This can be observed in the figures below.

Since the multiplication in the CSGN scheme is inexpensive, the evaluation time in the bridge using BGV, BFV and TFHE is almost constant as it essentially consists only of the evaluation time of the bridge algorithm for one CSGN ciphertext. Small variations in execution time for the bridge are due to the CPU scheduling process. The drops in evaluation times occur when the instruction-specific and data-specific cache at different levels in the CPU is filled with numerous repetitive instructions. The timings for evaluating the circuit entirely in the BGV or BFV scheme grow linearly with the degree of the monomial. We notice that in the TFHE case, the running time of the evaluation starts growing expo-

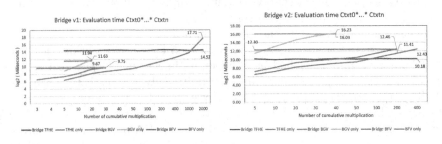

Fig. 2. The first and second bridges.

nentially in the number of multiplications, at some point. This is explained by the fact that the TFHE software library goes automatically into bootstrapping, whereas in the HElib and SEAL software libraries we can choose parameters in which one can evaluate the circuit without the costly bootstrapping procedure (Figs. 2 and 3).

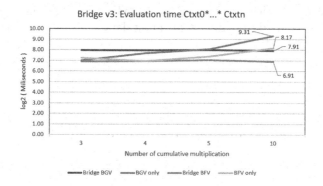

Fig. 3. The third bridge - BGV & BFV.

We now report on the implementation of the bridge from the Goldwasser-Micali encryption scheme to the Sander-Young-Yung encryption scheme constructed in the Appendix B. In the table below, one can find the timings required for running the bridge, as well as the ones needed for the homomorphic evaluation of the comparison circuit. The measurements were performed on an Intel I7-1068NG7 CPU laptop with 32 GB of RAM. Since the parameter ℓ of the SYY

Table 2. Homomorphic evaluation of comparison circuit using GM-SYY bridge.

n	$\log_2(N)$	GM·	SYY⊙	GM $\to$ SYY	$[x = y]$
4	1024	0.002 ms	10.02 ms	4.54 ms	58.35 ms
4	2048	0.003 ms	29.96 ms	11.64 ms	164.44 ms
4	4096	0.008 ms	84.01 ms	32.82 ms	467.43 ms
8	1024	0.003 ms	10.70 ms	4.77 ms	123.98 ms
8	2048	0.004 ms	30.12 ms	11.89 ms	336.27 ms
8	4096	0.008 ms	84.65 ms	33.46 ms	945.26 ms
16	1024	0.002 ms	10.8 ms	4.87 ms	251.44 ms
16	2048	0.004 ms	29.69 ms	11.55 ms	660.17 ms
16	4096	0.008 ms	85.49 ms	33.71 ms	1907.78 ms
32	1024	0.003 ms	10.4 ms	4.69 ms	484.10 ms
32	2048	0.004 ms	30.29 ms	11.82 ms	1348.44 ms
32	4096	0.009 ms	82.51 ms	32.34 ms	3576.41 ms

scheme does not have an impact on the security, but rather on the probability to correctly decrypt the ciphertext $\left(\geq 1 - \dfrac{1}{2^{\ell}} \right)$, we fix ℓ to be 50.

The parameters n and N in Table 2 stand for the bit-lengths of $\boldsymbol{x}, \boldsymbol{y}$ and, respectively, the Goldwaser-Micalli modulus. The timings required for the one homomorphic operation in each scheme can be found in the third and the fourth columns. We notice that the timings presented above grow linearly with the number of bits required to represent the input data. This can be observed in the following figure (Fig. 4).

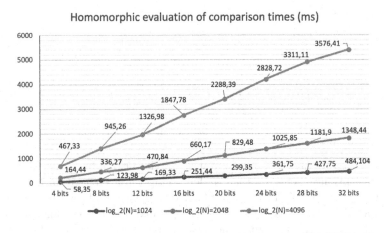

Fig. 4. Evaluation times for the comparison circuit using GM-SYY bridge.

References

1. Alperin-Sheriff, J., Peikert, C.: Faster bootstrapping with polynomial error. In: Garay, J.A., Gennaro, R. (eds.) CRYPTO 2014. LNCS, vol. 8616, pp. 297–314. Springer, Heidelberg (2014). https://doi.org/10.1007/978-3-662-44371-2_17
2. Awodey, S.: Category Theory, 2nd edn. Oxford University Press, Oxford (2010)
3. Barcau, M., Paşol, V., Pleşca, C.: Monoidal encryption over $(\mathbb{F}_2, \cdot)$. In: Lanet, J.-L., Toma, C. (eds.) SECITC 2018. LNCS, vol. 11359, pp. 504–517. Springer, Cham (2019). https://doi.org/10.1007/978-3-030-12942-2_37
4. Boura, C., Gama, N., Georgieva, M., Jetchev, D.: CHIMERA: combining ring-LWE-based fully homomorphic encryption schemes. J. Math. Cryptol. **14**(1), 316–338 (2020)
5. Brakerski, Z., Gentry, C., Vaikuntanathan, V.: (Leveled) fully homomorphic encryption without bootstrapping. ACM Trans. Comput. Theory **6**(13(3)), 1–36 (2014)

6. Brakerski, Z.: Fully homomorphic encryption without modulus switching from classical GapSVP. In: Safavi-Naini, R., Canetti, R. (eds.) CRYPTO 2012. LNCS, vol. 7417, pp. 868–886. Springer, Heidelberg (2012). https://doi.org/10.1007/978-3-642-32009-5_50

7. Castagnos, G., Imbert, L., Laguillaumie, F.: Encryption switching protocols revisited: switching modulo p. In: Katz, J., Shacham, H. (eds.) CRYPTO 2017. LNCS, vol. 10401, pp. 255–287. Springer, Cham (2017). https://doi.org/10.1007/978-3-319-63688-7_9

8. certSIGN RD: CSGN GitHub repository. https://github.com/certFHE/CSGN. Accessed 20 May 2021

9. Chillotti, I., Gama, N., Georgieva, M., Izabachène, M.: TFHE: fast fully homomorphic encryptionover the torus. J. Cryptol. **33**, 34–91 (2020)

10. Cohen, A.: What about bob? The inadequacy of CPA security for proxy reencryption. PKC (2), 287–316 (2019)

11. Couteau, G., Peters, T., Pointcheval, D.: Encryption switching protocols. In: Robshaw, M., Katz, J. (eds.) CRYPTO 2016. LNCS, vol. 9814, pp. 308–338. Springer, Heidelberg (2016). https://doi.org/10.1007/978-3-662-53018-4_12

12. Dobraunig, C., et al.: Rasta: a cipher with low ANDdepth and few ANDs per bit. In: Shacham, H., Boldyreva, A. (eds.) CRYPTO 2018. LNCS, vol. 10991, pp. 662–692. Springer, Cham (2018). https://doi.org/10.1007/978-3-319-96884-1_22

13. Dobraunig, C., Grassi, L., Helminger, L., Rechberger, C., Schofnegger, M., Walch, R.: Pasta: a case for hybrid homomorphic encryption. In: Cryptology ePrint Archive (2021)

14. Dodis, Y., Ivan, A.: Proxy cryptography revisited. In: Proceedings of the Tenth Network and Distributed System Security Symposium, February 2003

15. Dottling, N., Nishimaki, R.: Universal Proxy Re-Encryption, Cryptology ePrint Archive, Report 2018/840, to appear in PKC '21

16. Fan, J., Vercauteren, F.: Somewhat Practical Fully Homomorphic Encryption, IACR Cryptol. ePrint Arch., vol. 2012, p. 144 (2012)

17. Gentry, C: A fully homomorphic encryption scheme. PhD thesis, Stanford University (2009)

18. Gentry, C.: Computing arbitrary functions of encrypted data. Commun. ACM **53**(3), 97–105 (2010)

19. Gentry, C., Halevi, S., Smart, N.P.: Homomorphic evaluation of the AES circuit. In: Safavi-Naini, R., Canetti, R. (eds.) CRYPTO 2012. LNCS, vol. 7417, pp. 850–867. Springer, Heidelberg (2012). https://doi.org/10.1007/978-3-642-32009-5_49

20. Goldreich, O.: A note on computational indistinguishability. Inf. Process. Lett. **34**(6), 277–281 (1990)

21. Goldwasser, S., Micali, S.: Probabilistic encryption and how to play mental poker keeping secret all partial information, In: STOC 1982: Proceedings of the fourteenth annual ACM symposium on Theory of computing, pp. 365–377. Association for Computing Machinery, New York, NY (1982)

22. Goldwasser, S., Micali, S.: Probabilistic encryption. J. Comput. Syst. Sci. **28**(2), 270–299 (1984)

23. HElib library homepage: An Implementation of homomorphic encryption by Halevi and Shoup. https://github.com/shaih/HElib/

24. Redmond, W.A.: Microsoft Research, Microsoft SEAL (release 3.6), November 2020. https://github.com/Microsoft/SEAL

25. Sander, T., Young, A., Yung, M.: non-interactive crypto computing for NC^1. In: FOCS 1999: Proceedings of the 40th Annual Symposium on Foundations of Com-

puter Science, pp. 554–566. IEEE Computer Society, NW Washington, DC, United States (1999)
26. Smart, N.: Cryptography Made Simple. Springer, Cham (2016). https://doi.org/10.1007/978-3-319-21936-3

Superpoly Recovery of Grain-128AEAD Using Division Property

Debasmita Chakraborty$^{(\boxtimes)}$ and Santu Pal

Indian Statistical Institute, Kolkata, Kolkata, India
debasmitachakraborty1@gmail.com, santu.pal@niser.ac.in

Abstract. The cube attack is a powerful cryptanalytic technique against stream ciphers. Cube attacks exploit the algebraic properties of symmetric ciphers by recovering a particular polynomial, the superpoly, and subsequently, the secret key. Nowadays, the division property-based approach has become very popular, allowing us to recover the exact superpoly cleverly. However, the computational cost to recover the superpoly becomes prohibitive as the number of rounds of the cipher increases. In this paper, we study NIST lightweight 3rd round candidate Grain-128AEAD in the light of division property-based cube attacks. We first introduce some good cubes of dimensions 91, 92, 93, 94, and then we construct an algorithm to find conditional key bits for the cubes of Grain-128AEAD mentioned above. Next, we apply three-subset division property without unknown subset-based cube attacks to recover exact superpolies for 192, 193, 194, 195-round Grain-128AEAD in the weak-key setting, which are the longest till now. Moreover, we are able to find good cubes that are used to build distinguishers of Grain-128AEAD in the weak-key setting. In particular, we show that Grain-128AEAD can be distinguished from a random source up to 193-rounds in the weak-key setting, which is the best zero-sum distinguisher of Grain-128AEAD till now using division property-based cube attacks.

Keywords: Cube attack · Division property · Three-subset division property · MILP · Grain-128AEAD

1 Introduction

Cube attack, proposed by Dinur and Shamir [6] at EUROCRYPT 2009, is one of the most powerful cryptanalytic techniques against symmetric cryptosystems. The target of cube attack is to recover secret variables from the simplified polynomial called superpoly. To mount a cube attack, one first recovers the superpoly in an offline phase. Then, the value of the superpoly is obtained by querying the encryption oracle and computing the summation. From the equation between the superpoly and its value, information about the secret key can be revealed. Therefore, the superpoly recovery is a central step in the cube attack.

G. Bella et al. (Eds.): SecITC 2022, LNCS 13809, pp. 65–80, 2023.
https://doi.org/10.1007/978-3-031-32636-3_4

Traditional cube attacks [6,8,25,31] regard ciphers as black boxes so the superpolies are recovered experimentally. Only linear or quadratic superpolies are applicable. At CRYPTO 2017, [27] Todo *et al* treated the polynomial as non-blackbox and applied Conventional Bit-based Division Property (CBDP) to cube attacks on stream ciphers for the first time. Then, at CRYPTO 2018, Wang *et al* [29] improved it by introducing flag and term enumeration techniques. For CBDP based cube attacks, the superpolies of large cubes can be recovered by the theoretical method. But the theory of CBDP cannot ensure that the superpoly of a cube is non-constant. Hence the key recovery attack may be just a distinguishing attack. To solve this problem, at ASIACRYPT 2019, Wang *et al* [30] proposed the cube attack based on Bit-based Division Property using Three Subsets (BDPT) and proved that BDPT without an unknown subset can recover the accurate superpoly of cube attack. Then, at EUROCRYPT 2020, Hao *et al* [11] proposed a new modeling method for the BDPT without an unknown subset. Their algorithm is more efficient, and it can improve existing key-recovery attacks on many ciphers. Moreover, in [13,15] the authors embedded the monomial prediction technique into a nested framework, which allows them to recover superpolies and in [31], the authors also developed a pure algebraic method to recover the exact superpoly. However, as the number of rounds of the cipher increases, such useful cubes are hard to find.

One of the most significant security criteria for a keyed cryptographic primitive is its unpredictable behaviour concerning any randomly chosen key from the whole key space. When a key is used with a given cipher, it is considered to be *weak* if it causes the cipher to behave in an undesirable way (like it reduces the algebraic degree significantly). Many attacks in the weak-key setting for block cipher [12,16], as well as stream ciphers [23,26] have been presented. However, finding a weak-key set is a computationally hard problem. For example, the invariant subspace attack [18,19], is a general weak-key attack, that is known in the literature. Recently, cube attacks that investigate key conditions which may lead to weak-key attacks, have been proposed in [21,22].

Table 1. Previous Works of Superpoly Recovery for Grain-128AEAD using Division Property

Round	Number of Cubes	Cube Size	Time	References
190	–	95	–	[11]
191	2	95–96	–	[15]
192	1	94	45 days	[13]

Related Works. NIST has launched a process for soliciting, evaluating, and standardising lightweight cryptographic algorithms suited for use in limited contexts. In August 2018, NIST issued a call for algorithms to be considered for lightweight cryptography standards. There were initially 57 submissions and

NIST released ten candidates following the third round of pruning. Grain-128AEAD is one of these candidates. Grain-128AEAD is designed by modifying the authentication module of Grain-128a. Grain-128a has been adopted as an ISO standard for radio frequency identification (RFID) devices. Further, the encryption module of Grain-128AEAD and Grain-128a are the same. The cryptanalysis of the encryption module of Grain-128a can be applied to the cryptanalysis of the encryption module of Grain-128AEAD.

As Grain-128AEAD is one of the candidates in the competition by NIST, the cryptanalysis of Grain-128AEAD is an important research area. In 2012, Lehmann et al [20] proposed an attack using the conditional cube tester on Grain-128a of 177 KSA (Key Scheduling Algorithm) round in the single key setup and 189 KSA round in the weak-key setup. Recently, Ma et al [24] and Karlsson et al [17] proposed a differential attack and nonrandomness detectors on Grain-128a up to 195 and 203 KSA rounds, respectively in the weak-key setup. Readers may refer to [2–5,7,28] for detailed cryptanalytic results on the Grain family. Moreover, using the concept of division property-based cube attacks, exact superpolies for 190, 191, 192-round Grain-128AEAD have been recovered efficiently using which key-recovery attacks are also mounted [11,13,15] (The results we have listed in Table 1). But, for these cube attacks, the cube dimensions are on the higher side. Now, the following question arises in our mind:

Can we reduce the cube dimension and recover exact superpoly of the cube for higher round Grain-128AEAD?

1.1 Our Contributions

To address this question, we begin by studying the most popular cipher Grain-128AEAD in the light of division property-based cube attacks. Our primary focus is to reduce the cube dimension of Grain-128AEAD and recover exact superpoly using those cubes for higher round Grain-128AEAD. The details of our technical contributions are listed as follows:

Finding Cubes and Searching Conditional Key Bits. First, we search for good cubes with less dimensions than the previous division property-based cube attacks for which we can recover superpoly efficiently (which is illustrated in Sect. 3.1). Here, we use the cube dimensions of Grain-128AEAD as 91, 92, 93, and 94. Therefore, our other important contribution is to search for conditional key bits for which we can efficiently recover superpolies of above-mentioned cubes of Grain-128AEAD (which is described in Sect. 3.2). To do this, we provide an algorithm (Algorithm 1) using which we can set conditions on key bits which depend on cube variables.

Application on Grain-128AEAD. As for the application of our concept, we apply three-subset division property without unknown subset in order to recover exact superpoly of Grain-128AEAD of our cubes in the weak-key setting. As a result of this, we find exact superpolies of 192-195 round Grain-128AEAD in the weak-key setting which are the best results on Grain-128AEAD till now. Moreover, we also present a zero-sum distinguisher of 193-round Grain-128AEAD which is the longest distinguisher of Grain-128AEAD using division property-based cube attacks. The detailed results are shown in Table 2.

Table 2. Summarization of our Superpoly Recovery Results for Grain-128AEAD in the Weak-Key Setup using Division Property

Round	Number of Cubes	Cube Size	Time	References
192	2	91, 92	2 min	Sect. 4
193	2	92, 94	7 min	Sect. 4
194	1	93	1 h	Sect. 4
195	1	94	7 days	Sect. 4

1.2   Organization of the Paper

This paper is organized as follows: In Sect. 2, we briefly recall some background knowledge and the relationship between the division property and cube attack. In Sect. 3, we construct good cubes and propose an algorithm to construct appropriate weak-key conditions to perform cube attack on Grain-128AEAD. Therefore, we show some results (superpoly recovery, zero-sum distinguisher) on Grain-128AEAD in Sect. 4. At last we conclude the paper in Sect. 5.

2   Preliminaries

2.1   Notations

Let $\mathbb{F}_2$ denote the finite field $\{0,1\}$ and $\boldsymbol{a} = (a_0, a_1, \ldots, a_{n-1}) \in \mathbb{F}_2^n$ be an n-bit vector, where a_i denotes the i-th bit of a. For n-bit vectors $\boldsymbol{x}$ and $\boldsymbol{u}$, define $\boldsymbol{x}^{\boldsymbol{u}} = \prod_{i=0}^{n-1} x_i^{u_i}$. Then, for any $\boldsymbol{k} \in \mathbb{F}_2^n$ and $\boldsymbol{k}' \in \mathbb{F}_2^n$, define $\boldsymbol{k} \succeq \boldsymbol{k}'$ if $k_i \geq k_i'$ holds for all $i = 0, 1, \ldots, n-1$, and define $\boldsymbol{k} \succ \boldsymbol{k}'$ if $k_i > k_i'$ holds for all $i = 0, 1, \ldots, n-1$. For a subset $\mathcal{I} \subseteq \{0, 1, ..., n-1\}$, $\boldsymbol{u}_{\mathcal{I}}$ denotes an n-dimensional bit vector $(u_0, u_1, \ldots, u_{n-1})$ satisfying $u_i = 1$ if $i \in \mathcal{I}$ and $u_i = 0$ otherwise. We simply write $\mathbb{K} \leftarrow \boldsymbol{k}$ when $\mathbb{K} = \mathbb{K} \cup \{\boldsymbol{k}\}$ and $\mathbb{K} \rightarrow \boldsymbol{k}$ when $\mathbb{K} = \mathbb{K} \setminus \{\boldsymbol{k}\}$. And $|\mathbb{K}|$ denotes the number of elements in the set $\mathbb{K}$. We denote $[n] = \{1, 2, \ldots, n\}$, $\boldsymbol{1} = 1^n$, and $\boldsymbol{0} = 0^n$.

2.2   Specification of Grain128AEAD

Grain-128AEAD [14] is a member of the Grain family and also one of the winner of the NIST LWC standardization process. Grain-128AEAD inherits many specifications from Grain-128a, which was proposed in 2011 [1]. There are four differences between Grain-128AEAD and Grain-128a: (i) larger Macs, (ii) no encryption-only mode, (iii) initialization hardening, and (iv) keystream limitation. These differences do not come only from the requirement for the NIST LWC standardization process but also from recent cryptanalysis results against Grain-128a [10].

The internal state is represented by two 128-bit states, $(b_0, b_1, \ldots, b_{127})$ and $(s_0, s_1, \ldots, s_{127})$. The 128-bit key K is loaded to the first register b, and the 96-bit initialization vector is loaded to the second register s. The other state bits are set to 1 except for the last one bit in the second register. Namely, the initial states are represented as

$$\begin{cases} (b_0, b_1, \ldots, b_{127}) = (K_1, K_2, \ldots, K_{128}) \\ (s_0, s_1, \ldots, s_{127}) = (IV_1, IV_2, \ldots, IV_{96}, 1, 1, \ldots, 1, 0) \end{cases}$$

We denote IV is a set consisting of $IV_1, IV_2, \ldots, IV_{96}$. The pseudo-code of the update function in the initialization is given as follows.

$$\begin{cases} g \leftarrow b_0 + b_{26} + b_{56} + b_{91} + b_{96} + b_3 b_{67} + b_{11} b_{13} + b_{17} b_{18} + b_{27} b_{59} \\ \quad + b_{40} b_{48} + b_{61} b_{65} + b_{68} b_{84} + b_{88} b_{92} b_{93} b_{95} + b_{22} b_{24} b_{25} + b_{70} b_{78} b_{82}, \\ f \leftarrow s_0 + s_7 + s_{38} + s_{70} + s_{81} + s_{96}, \\ h \leftarrow b_{12} s_8 + s_{13} s_{20} + b_{95} s_{42} + s_{60} s_{79} + b_{12} b_{95} s_{94}, \\ z \leftarrow h + s_{93} + b_2 + b_{15} + b_{36} + b_{45} + b_{64} + b_{73} + b_{89}, \\ (b_0, b_1, \ldots, b_{127}) \leftarrow (b_1, \ldots, b_{127}, g + s_0 + z), \\ (s_0, s_1, \ldots, s_{127}) \leftarrow (s_1, \ldots, s_{127}, f + z). \end{cases}$$

In the initialization, the state is updated 256 times without producing an output. After the initialization, the update function is tweaked such that z is not fed to the state, and z is used as a pre-output key stream. Hereinafter, we assume that the first bit of the pre-output key stream can be observed. Note that there is no difference between Grain128a and Grain-128AEAD under this assumption.

2.3   Cube Attack and Division Property

Cube Attack. The cube attack was proposed by Dinur and Shamir in [6]. A cipher is regarded as a public Boolean function whose input is divided into two parts: secret variables x and public ones v. Then, the ANF of the Boolean function is represented as

$$f(x, v) = \bigoplus_{u \in \mathbb{F}_2^{n+m}} a_u^f (x \,\|\, v)^u.$$

For a set of indices $\mathcal{I} = \{i_1, i_2, \ldots, i_{|\mathcal{I}|}\} \subset \{1, 2, \ldots, m\}$, which is referred as cube indices, $t_{\mathcal{I}}$ denotes a monomial as $t_{\mathcal{I}} = v_{i_1} \cdot v_{i_2} \cdots v_{i_{|\mathcal{I}|}}$. The Boolean function $f(x, v)$ can also be decomposed as

$$f(x, v) = t_{\mathcal{I}} \cdot p(x, v) + q(x, v).$$

Let $C_\mathcal{I}$, which is referred as a cube (defined by $\mathcal{I}$), be a set of $2^{|\mathcal{I}|}$ values where variables in $\{v_{i_1}, v_{i_2}, \ldots, v_{i_\mathcal{I}}\}$ are taking all possible combinations of values, and all remaining variables are fixed to any value. The sum of f over all values of the cube $C_\mathcal{I}$ is

$$\bigoplus_{C_\mathcal{I}} f(\boldsymbol{x}, \boldsymbol{v}) = \bigoplus_{C_\mathcal{I}} t_\mathcal{I} \cdot p(\boldsymbol{x}, \boldsymbol{v}) + \bigoplus_{C_\mathcal{I}} q(\boldsymbol{x}, \boldsymbol{v}) = p(\boldsymbol{x}, \boldsymbol{v})$$

because $t_\mathcal{I} = 1$ for only one case in $C_\mathcal{I}$ and each term in $q(\boldsymbol{x}, \boldsymbol{v})$ misses at least one variable from $\{v_{i_1}, v_{i_2}, \ldots, v_{i_\mathcal{I}}\}$. Then, $p(\boldsymbol{x}, \boldsymbol{v})$ is called the superpoly of the cube $C_\mathcal{I}$, and the goal of the cube attack is to recover the superpoly.

Division Property. The division property is formally developed as the generalization of the integral property, and it has been initially used to evaluate the integral distinguisher. Now, the relationship between the division property and the ANF of public functions is discussed below:

Definition 1. (Three-Subset Division Property without Unknown Subset [11]). $\mathbb{X}$ be a multi set whose elements take a value of $\mathbb{F}_2^n$. Let $\tilde{\mathbb{L}}$ be also a multi set whose elements also take a value of $\mathbb{F}_2^n$. When the multi-set $\mathbb{X}$ has three-subset division property without unknown subset $(\mathcal{T}_{\tilde{\mathbb{L}}}^{1^n})$, it fulfills the following conditions:

$$\bigoplus_{x \in \mathbb{X}} x^u = \begin{cases} 1, & \text{if there are odd number of } \boldsymbol{u}\text{'s in } \tilde{\mathbb{L}} \\ 0, & \text{otherwise} \end{cases}$$

Using this definition, the authors also defined three-subset division trail and explained the propagation rules of COPY, XOR and AND in [11].

Mixed Integer Linear Programming (MILP). MILP is a kind of optimization or feasibility program whose objective function and constraints are linear, and the variables can be continuous or integers. Generally, an MILP model M consists of variables $M.var$, constraints $M.con$, and the objective function $M.obj$. MILP models can be solved by solver like Gurobi [9]. If there is no feasible solution, the solver will returns infeasible. And if there are feasible solutions, the solver will returns the optimal value of the objective function. When there is no objective function in M, the MILP solver will only return whether M is feasible or not.

Algorithm to Recover ANF Coefficients of Public Function [11]. Let f be a Boolean function whose input denotes an n-bit string $\boldsymbol{x} = (x_1, x_2, \ldots, x_n)$, and let it consist of the iteration of simple public functions. Then, the algebraic normal form of f is represented as

$$f(\boldsymbol{x}) = \bigoplus_{u \in \mathbb{F}_2^n} a_{\boldsymbol{u}}^f x^u$$

Our goal is to recover the value of a_u^f for some u. To do this, we have to first construct MILP model that represents the three-subset division property without unknown subset of the function f. The authors in [11] proposed an algorithm (Algorithm 1 in [11]) which recovers an ANF coefficient a_u^f. The initial three-subset division property without unknown subset is defined by u, and the number of feasible solutions is enumerated by using the MILP solver. Note that the efficiency of Algorithm 1 in [11] depends on the number of feasible solutions.

3 Superpoly Recovery for Grain-128AEAD Using Weak Keys

The most important and challenging part of the cube attack is to recover the ANF of the superpoly of the cube. As Grain-128AEAD is a finalist in a recent NIST competition, it will be challenging to recover the superpoly of such cipher. Before recovering the superpoly, one needs to search for a good cube of the cipher. If one works on a weak-key setting, another important task is finding conditional key variables, which leads to the recovery of the superpoly of the cube.

3.1 Cube Searching Algorithm for Grain-128AEAD

Constructing a cube-searching algorithm nowadays is a crucial task for a cube attack. Many such algorithms exist for such purposes as maximum last zero, and maximum last α $(0 \leq \alpha \leq 1)$. The last method gives a better cube searching for Grain-128a. So we have used this algorithm to find a better result. In the paper [4], the authors have found a cube of $\{63, 64, 66, 68, 69\}$ of size five to mount a distinguishing attack for 191 round in a single key scenario. They construct the cube of size five from a cube of size one.

Following a similar method, we also start to find the cube of size one. The best cube of size one is $\{s_{69}\}$ because it attains the maximum last alpha round at 123. By similar process, we get the cube variables s_{68}, s_{67}, s_{66}, s_{65}, s_{64} simultaneously. As those cube variables expose some weakness of the Boolean functions at particular rounds, so we again work with those cube variables. The variables mentioned above are crucial in getting a distinguisher for Grain-128a. But our challenge is tougher and more exciting. We want to recover the superpoly of the Boolean function at some particular round using the division property. As we know, a small dimensional cube will not be useful for superpoly recovery in the division property-based cube attacks. Due to the success of our cube variables in the previous attack on Grain-128a, we decide to work with the complement of the set of cube variables. As superpoly searching is lengthy and time-consuming process, so we start to find the superpoly using the cube of size $96 - 2 = 94$. As previously cube of sizes $96, 95$ was used, so we used a cube of less size to reduce the complexity of superpoly recovery. Then we decrease the cube size one by one, following less complexity for superpoly recovery. Also, we vary the initialization round to reduce the complexity. Finally, we find the best trade off between the initialization round and cube size to get better complexity.

Algorithm 1: Searching for Conditional Bits Corresponding to Chosen Cubes

---

Input: Set of strong variables[a] $\mathcal{S}$
Output: Set of Conditional key variables $\mathcal{W}$
begin
    Start with a single element from $\mathcal{S}$ and store it in $\mathcal{C}$
    while $|\mathcal{C}| \leq |\mathcal{S}|$ **do**
        Choose the cube variables as $IV \setminus \mathcal{C}$
        Store the conditional key variables from SAGE corresponding to variables in $IV \setminus \mathcal{C}$ in $\mathcal{W}$.
        Also, store conditional key variables from structure observation of the cipher in $\mathcal{W}$
        Run division property-based cube attacks using the cube $IV \setminus \mathcal{C}$
        if *Superpoly corresponding to $IV \setminus \mathcal{C}$ is recovered* **then**
          | Take $\mathcal{W}$ as a set of conditional key bits
        end
        else
          Add some additional conditional key variables in $\mathcal{W}$
          Run division property-based cube attacks
          Repeat Else part until superpoly is recovered
        end
        Take another subset $\mathcal{C}$ of $\mathcal{S}$ and repeat the while part.
    end
    return $\mathcal{W}$
end

---

[a] The set of those variables in IV using which we can construct good cubes for Grain-128AEAD.

3.2 Searching Weak-Key Domain for Grain-128AEAD

Putting conditions on key and IV variables plays an important role in upgrading the attacks on any cipher. Conditions on the variables help us to find weaknesses in the corresponding Boolean function at a particular round. In the previous paper [4], the authors found the conditions on key bits corresponding to cube variables using SAGE software. Also, some conditions are found using the structure observation with theoretical analysis. We have also followed their approaches. But the conditions retrieved for corresponding cubes do not help us to recover superpoly using division property-based approaches. So again, we try to find the additional conditions to recover the superpoly. We try to find the subset of key bits which contributes to superpoly recovery. As the division property-based attack takes all IV bits as zero, we do not worry about the conditions on IV bits. The selection of key bits is made in the following way:

In our case, we have implemented the algorithm on the different rounds of Grain-128AEAD in the following way.

- We collect the strong variables of Grain-128AEAD as $\mathcal{S} = \{s_{42}, \cdots, s_{69}\}$.
- The conditions on key variables for each strong variable are given in Table 3.
- Select an element say r from $\mathcal{S}$ and take $IV \setminus \{r\}$ as cube. Therefore, collect all corresponding conditional key bits from Table 3 in the set $\mathcal{W}$ corresponding to the chosen cube.
- Also, we collect the conditional key variables getting through the structure observation of Grain-128AEAD in the set $\mathcal{W}$ (Given in the last of this section).
- For example, we take $IV \setminus \{s_{69}, s_{68}\}$ as a cube for 195-round Grain-128AEAD and run the division property-based cube attacks to recover the superpoly.
- As we can not recover the superpoly, we add some additional conditional key variables $b_{42}, b_{43}, b_{44}, b_{45}, b_{72}, b_{73}, b_{76}, b_{77}, b_{121}, b_{122}, b_{123}, b_{124}, b_{126}, b_{127}$ in the set $\mathcal{W}$.
- Again, we run the program. This time, we recover the superpoly for 195-round Grain-128AEAD. Similar way, we find $\mathcal{W}$ for different cubes and recover superpolies.

Note 1. As the running of division property-based cube attack is a time-consuming process, we optimize the $\mathcal{W}$ set as much as possible.

Table 3. Conditions on key variables for 1-dimensional cubes

Cube	Conditions on key variables	Cube	Conditions on key variables
$\{s_{42}\}$	$b_{46} = b_{50} = b_{95} = 0$	$\{s_{56}\}$	$b_{60} = b_{64} = b_{109} = 0$
$\{s_{43}\}$	$b_{47} = b_{51} = b_{96} = 0$	$\{s_{57}\}$	$b_{61} = b_{65} = b_{110} = 0$
$\{s_{44}\}$	$b_{48} = b_{52} = b_{97} = 0$	$\{s_{58}\}$	$b_{62} = b_{66} = b_{111} = 0$
$\{s_{45}\}$	$b_{49} = b_{53} = b_{98} = 0$	$\{s_{59}\}$	$b_{63} = b_{67} = b_{112} = 0$
$\{s_{46}\}$	$b_{50} = b_{54} = b_{99} = 0$	$\{s_{60}\}$	$b_{64} = b_{68} = b_{113} = 0$
$\{s_{47}\}$	$b_{51} = b_{55} = b_{100} = 0$	$\{s_{61}\}$	$b_{65} = b_{69} = b_{114} = 0$
$\{s_{48}\}$	$b_{52} = b_{56} = b_{101} = 0$	$\{s_{62}\}$	$b_{66} = b_{70} = b_{115} = 0$
$\{s_{49}\}$	$b_{53} = b_{57} = b_{102} = 0$	$\{s_{63}\}$	$b_{67} = b_{71} = b_{80} = b_{116} = 0$
$\{s_{50}\}$	$b_{54} = b_{58} = b_{103} = 0$	$\{s_{64}\}$	$b_{68} = b_{72} = b_{117} = 0$
$\{s_{51}\}$	$b_{55} = b_{59} = b_{104} = 0$	$\{s_{65}\}$	$b_{69} = b_{73} = b_{118} = 0$
$\{s_{52}\}$	$b_{56} = b_{60} = b_{105} = 0$	$\{s_{66}\}$	$b_{70} = b_{74} = b_{119} = 0$
$\{s_{53}\}$	$b_{57} = b_{61} = b_{106} = 0$	$\{s_{67}\}$	$b_{71} = b_{75} = b_{120} = 0$
$\{s_{54}\}$	$b_{58} = b_{62} = b_{107} = 0$	$\{s_{68}\}$	$b_{72} = b_{76} = b_{121} = 0$
$\{s_{55}\}$	$b_{59} = b_{63} = b_{108} = 0$	$\{s_{69}\}$	$b_{73} = b_{77} = b_{122} = 0$

From the structure observation, the additional conditional key bits for the above
cubes are $b_{64}, b_{67}, b_{70} - b_{74}, b_{76} - b_{87}, b_{91}, b_{94}, b_{95}, b_{102}, b_{104}, b_{105}, b_{108}, b_{110}, b_{112} - b_{114}, b_{116}, b_{118}, b_{119}, b_{121}, b_{122}, b_{125}$.

3.3 Division Property-Based Cube Attack for Grain-128AEAD

The most important part of a cube attack is to recover the superpoly, and we simply call it the *superpoly recovery* in this paper. In [11], the authors explained how three-subset division property without unknown subset can be used as a tool to analyze ANF coefficients of the superpoly for a public Boolean function.

Superpoly Recovery. The encryption module of Grain-128AEAD is regarded as a public boolean function $f(x, v)$ whose input is divided into two parts: secret variable x and public variable v. Now, we construct MILP model $\mathcal{M}$ where the encryption module of Grain-128AEAD is represented by the context of division property as described in Algorithm 5 in [11]. Here, we denote x and v as the MILP variables corresponding to secret and public variables and in our case, $x = (b_0^0, \ldots, b_{127}^0)$, and $v = (s_0^0, \ldots, s_{127}^0)$. Therefore, to represent the initial division property, elements of v indexed by $\mathcal{I}$ (cube indices) are constrained by 1 and the elements of v indexed by the other IV indices are constrained by 0. Moreover, we add the constraints corresponding to weak-key conditions in MILP model $\mathcal{M}$.

After constructing MILP model $\mathcal{M}$ with initial division property corresponding to cube and non-cube indices and weak-key conditions, we solve MILP model $\mathcal{M}$ as all monomials that could be involved in the superpoly can be found as feasible solutions (Algorithm 2 in [11]). Finally, we enumerate feasible solutions and finally get the superpoly of Grain-128AEAD corresponding to the cube $C_{\mathcal{I}}$ where $\mathcal{I}$ be the cube indices. Although using this method, we can accurately find superpoly of the cube $C_{\mathcal{I}}$, it is practically impossible to enumerate all feasible solutions when there are too many solutions.

After recovering the superpoly, an attacker can retrieve the information regarding the Boolean function of the cipher. Also, the attacker can use the drawbacks in the superpoly to find loopholes in the output function of the cipher, which leads to a distinguishing attack. Further, one can extend it to a key recovery attack using a sufficient number of superpolies.

4   Experimental Results

We apply the three-subset division property without unknown subset based cube attacks on the encryption module of Grain-128AEAD in the weak-key setting. First, we search appropriate cubes and weak-key using Algorithm 1, and therefore using division property-based cube attack technique we accurately recover the superpolies for 192-195 rounds using cube sizes 91, 92, 93, 94 respectively in the weak-key setting where the size of the corresponding weak-key class is 2^{43}. The details of our results are given in Table 4. These are the best-known attacks on Grain-128AEAD in the weak-key setting till now. Moreover, we construct zero-sum distinguishers on 192-193 round Grain-128AEAD in the weak-key setting which are the longest distinguisher in this direction. The detailed parameters of *superpoly recovery* of 192-round and 193-round Grain-128AEAD and zero-sum distinguishers are in the following subsections. The recovered superpoly for 194-round Grain-128AEAD is in the Appendix A.

Superpoly Recovery for 192-Round Grain-128AEAD. The cube indices of size 91 to recover superpoly of 192-Round Grain-128AEAD are

$$\mathcal{I} = \{1, 2, \ldots, 65, 71, \ldots, 96\}$$

and $IV_{66} = IV_{67} = IV_{68} = IV_{69} = IV_{70} = 0$. Therefore, we get the superpoly corresponding to $C_\mathcal{I}$ which is represented as the sum of 2 monomials, and the following

$$p(\boldsymbol{x}) = x_{40}x_{42} + x_{29}$$

is the recovered superpoly, where $\boldsymbol{x} = (x_1, x_2, \ldots, x_{128})$ denotes the secret key, i.e., $x_i = K_i$. This superpoly is a balanced Boolean function because there is a monomial x_{29} that is independent of other monomials.

Superpoly Recovery for 193-Round Grain-128AEAD. The cube indices of size 92 to recover superpoly of 193-Round Grain-128AEAD are

$$\mathcal{I} = \{1, 2, \ldots, 66, 71, \ldots, 96\}$$

and $IV_{67} = IV_{68} = IV_{69} = IV_{70} = 0$. Therefore, we get the superpoly corresponding to $C_\mathcal{I}$ which is represented as the sum of 38 monomials, and the following

$$
\begin{aligned}
p(\boldsymbol{x}) &= 1 + x_{43} + x_{42}x_{43} + x_{41} + x_{40}x_{42}x_{43} + x_{39}x_{41} + x_{39}x_{40} \\
&\quad + x_{38} + x_{36}x_{38} + x_{35}x_{36} + x_{33} + x_{33}x_{35} + x_{32} + x_{32}x_{36} \\
&\quad + x_{31}x_{41}x_{42} + x_{31}x_{40}x_{41} + x_{31}x_{35}x_{37} + x_{30} + x_{29}x_{38} \\
&\quad + x_{29}x_{36}x_{37} + x_{29}x_{34}x_{37} + x_{29}x_{31} + x_{28} + x_{28}x_{42}x_{43} \\
&\quad + x_{28}x_{36}x_{38} + x_{28}x_{29} + x_{28}x_{29}x_{37} + x_{26} + x_{26}x_{29} + x_{25} \\
&\quad + x_{25}x_{28} + x_{24} + x_{24}x_{43} + x_{24}x_{32} + x_{24}x_{31} + x_{22} + x_{21} + x_{18}
\end{aligned}
$$

is the recovered superpoly, where $\boldsymbol{x} = (x_1, x_2, \ldots, x_{128})$ denotes the secret key, i.e., $x_i = K_i$. This superpoly is a balanced Boolean function because there are monomials x_{22}, x_{21}, and x_{18} that are independent of other monomials.

Zero-Sum Distinguishers for 192-193 Round Grain-128AEAD. To construct the cube attack against 192-round Grain-128AEAD, we choose the cube indices of size 92 as follows:

$$\mathcal{I} = \{1, 2, \ldots, 66, 71, \ldots, 96\}$$

where $IV_{67} = IV_{68} = IV_{69} = IV_{70} = 0$. Therefore, in the weak-key setting, we find that the superpoly does not involve secret key (where $\boldsymbol{x} = (x_1, x_2, \ldots, x_{128})$

denotes the secret key). Hence, the cube attack against 192-round Grain-128AEAD is a zero-sum distinguisher.

Moreover, the cube attack against 193-round Grain-128AEAD is also a zero-sum distinguisher where we choose the cube indices of size 94 as follows:

$$\mathcal{I} = \{1, 2, \ldots, 68, 71, \ldots, 96\}$$

where $IV_{69} = IV_{70} = 0$. This is the longest zero-sum distinguisher on Grain-128AEAD using division property-based cube attack best known to us.

Table 4. Results of Superpoly Recovery for Different Cubes on Grain-128AEAD

Cube size	Cube variables	Round	Additional Conditional Key Variables
91	$IV \setminus \{s_{65}, s_{66}, s_{67}, s_{68}, s_{69}\}$	192	$b_{42}, b_{43}, b_{44}, b_{45}, b_{69}, b_{70}, b_{71}, b_{72}, b_{73}$ $b_{74}, b_{75}, b_{76}, b_{77}, b_{118}, b_{119}, b_{120}$ $b_{121}, b_{122}, b_{123}, b_{124}, b_{126}, b_{127}$
92	$IV \setminus \{s_{66}, s_{67}, s_{68}, s_{69}\}$	193	$b_{42}, b_{43}, b_{44}, b_{45}, b_{70}, b_{71}, b_{72}, b_{73}$ $b_{74}, b_{75}, b_{76}, b_{77}, b_{119}, b_{120}$ $b_{121}, b_{122}, b_{123}, b_{124}, b_{126}, b_{127}$
93	$IV \setminus \{s_{67}, s_{68}, s_{69}\}$	194	$b_{42}, b_{43}, b_{44}, b_{45}, b_{71}, b_{72}, b_{73}, b_{75}, b_{76}, b_{77}$ $b_{120}, b_{121}, b_{122}, b_{123}, b_{124}, b_{126}, b_{127}$
94	$IV \setminus \{s_{68}, s_{69}\}$	195	$b_{42}, b_{43}, b_{44}, b_{45}, b_{72}, b_{73}, b_{76}, b_{77}$ $b_{121}, b_{122}, b_{123}, b_{124}, b_{126}, b_{127}$

5   Conclusion and Future Work

In this paper, we revisit division property-based cube attacks and study NIST lightweight 3rd round candidate Grain-128AEAD in the light of cube attacks based on division property. First, we find some good cubes and propose an algorithm to find conditional key bits for our cubes of Grain-128AEAD. Therefore, we efficiently apply three-subset division property without unknown subset based cube attacks on Grain-128AEAD and recover superpolies up to 195 rounds in the weak-key setting which are best-known results on Grain-128AEAD till now. Moreover, we find zero-sum distinguishers on 193-round Grain-128AEAD which is the longest distinguisher in this direction.

As, it is hard to find good cubes with less dimension in order to construct division property-based cube attacks, how to construct an efficient cube searching algorithm so that we can recover exact superpolies of higher rounds Grain-128AEAD is an open problem. Moreover, in the single-key setup, how to mount distinguishing as well as key recovery attacks on stream ciphers efficiently using division property will be nice future work.

Acknowledgement. The authors would like to thank the anonymous reviewers for their valuable comments and suggestions.

A   Detailed Result for Cube Attacks Against Grain-128AEAD

The cube indices of size 93 to recover superpoly of 194-Round Grain-128AEAD are

$$\mathcal{I} = \{1, 2, \ldots, 67, 71, \ldots, 96\}$$

and $IV_{68} = IV_{69} = IV_{70} = 0$. Therefore, we get the superpoly corresponding to $C_{\mathcal{I}}$ which is represented as the sum of 38 monomials, and the following

$$
\begin{aligned}
p(\boldsymbol{x}) &= 1 + x_{43} + x_{42}x_{43} + x_{41} + x_{41}x_{42} + x_{40}x_{43} + x_{40}x_{42} + x_{40}x_{41} \\
&+ x_{40}x_{41}x_{43} + x_{40}x_{41}x_{42} + x_{39} + x_{39}x_{41} + x_{39}x_{40} + x_{39}x_{40}x_{41}x_{42} \\
&+ x_{38}x_{43} + x_{38}x_{41}x_{43} + x_{38}x_{41}x_{42} + x_{38}x_{40} + x_{38}x_{39} + x_{38}x_{39}x_{41}x_{42} \\
&+ x_{37}x_{39}x_{40} + x_{37}x_{38} + x_{36}x_{40} + x_{35} + x_{35}x_{37}x_{41} + x_{35}x_{37}x_{40} \\
&+ x_{34}x_{36} + x_{34}x_{35}x_{40} + x_{34}x_{35}x_{38} + x_{33} + x_{33}x_{42} + x_{33}x_{41}x_{43} \\
&+ x_{32}x_{33} + x_{31} + x_{31}x_{42} + x_{31}x_{40} + x_{31}x_{39}x_{40} + x_{31}x_{36} \\
&+ x_{31}x_{33} + x_{30}x_{43} + x_{30}x_{41}x_{42} + x_{30}x_{40}x_{42} + x_{30}x_{40}x_{41} \\
&+ x_{30}x_{38} + x_{30}x_{37} + x_{30}x_{35}x_{37} + x_{30}x_{33} + x_{30}x_{33}x_{37} + x_{30}x_{32} \\
&+ x_{30}x_{32}x_{41} + x_{30}x_{32}x_{40} + x_{30}x_{31} + x_{30}x_{31}x_{41} + x_{29} + x_{29}x_{41}x_{42} \\
&+ x_{29}x_{40} + x_{29}x_{38} + x_{29}x_{35}x_{37}x_{41} + x_{29}x_{33} + x_{29}x_{32}x_{41} + x_{29}x_{30}x_{39} \\
&+ x_{29}x_{30}x_{33} + x_{28} + x_{28}x_{41} + x_{28}x_{41}x_{43} + x_{28}x_{40} + x_{28}x_{35}x_{40} \\
&+ x_{28}x_{35}x_{40}x_{41} + x_{28}x_{33} + x_{28}x_{31} + x_{28}x_{31}x_{40} + x_{28}x_{30} \\
&+ x_{28}x_{30}x_{40} + x_{28}x_{30}x_{40} + x_{28}x_{30}x_{38} + x_{28}x_{30}x_{35}x_{40} + x_{28}x_{30}x_{31} \\
&+ x_{28}x_{29}x_{39} + x_{27} + x_{27}x_{40} + x_{26}x_{40} + x_{26}x_{38} + x_{25}x_{40} + x_{25}x_{30}x_{40} \\
&+ x_{24}x_{41}x_{43} + x_{24}x_{40} + x_{24}x_{40}x_{41} + x_{24}x_{38} + x_{24}x_{30}x_{41} + x_{24}x_{30}x_{40} \\
&+ x_{24}x_{30}x_{39} + x_{24}x_{29}x_{41} + x_{24}x_{26} + x_{23} + x_{23}x_{40} + x_{23}x_{30} \\
&+ x_{23}x_{29} + x_{22} + x_{22}x_{40} + x_{21} + x_{21}x_{38}x_{40} + x_{21}x_{33} \\
&+ x_{21}x_{31}x_{40}x_{41} + x_{21}x_{31}x_{34}x_{36} + x_{21}x_{27} + x_{21}x_{26}x_{31}x_{40}x_{42} + x_{21}x_{26}x_{30} \\
&+ x_{21}x_{26}x_{29}x_{31} + x_{21}x_{26}x_{28}x_{31} + x_{21}x_{23}x_{31} + x_{20}x_{42}x_{43} + x_{20}x_{40} \\
&+ x_{20}x_{40}x_{42}x_{43} + x_{20}x_{38} + x_{20}x_{38}x_{40} + x_{20}x_{37}x_{39} + x_{20}x_{36} + x_{20}x_{36}x_{38} \\
&+ x_{20}x_{35} + x_{20}x_{35}x_{36} + x_{20}x_{33} + x_{20}x_{33}x_{35}x_{36} + x_{20}x_{32} + x_{20}x_{32}x_{41}x_{42} \\
&+ x_{20}x_{32} + x_{20}x_{32}x_{41}x_{42} + x_{20}x_{32}x_{35}x_{36} + x_{20}x_{29}x_{37}x_{41}x_{42} \\
&+ x_{20}x_{29}x_{36}x_{38} + x_{20}x_{29}x_{36}x_{37} + x_{20}x_{29}x_{35}x_{37} + x_{20}x_{29}x_{31} \\
&+ x_{20}x_{29}x_{30}x_{37} + x_{20}x_{29}x_{30}x_{32} + x_{20}x_{28} + x_{20}x_{28}x_{39}x_{40} + x_{20}x_{28}x_{37} \\
&+ x_{20}x_{28}x_{33}x_{35} + x_{20}x_{28}x_{32} + x_{20}x_{28}x_{32}x_{35} + x_{20}x_{28}x_{29} + x_{20}x_{27} \\
&+ x_{20}x_{26} + x_{20}x_{25} + x_{20}x_{25}x_{29} + x_{20}x_{24}x_{32} + x_{20}x_{24}x_{29}x_{37} \\
&+ x_{20}x_{24}x_{28} + x_{20}x_{23} + x_{20}x_{23}x_{29}x_{32} + x_{20}x_{22}x_{28} + x_{20}x_{22}x_{28} \\
&+ x_{20}x_{22}x_{24} + x_{20}x_{21} + x_{20}x_{21}x_{40}x_{42} + x_{20}x_{21}x_{23}x_{29} + x_{20}x_{21}x_{22} \\
&+ x_{19}x_{20}x_{29} + x_{18}x_{20} + x_{17}x_{40} + x_{17}x_{38} + x_{13} + x_{11}x_{20}
\end{aligned}
$$

is the recovered superpoly, where $x = (x_1, x_2, \ldots, x_{128})$ denotes the secret key, i.e., $x_i = K_i$.

As the superpoly for 195-round Grain-128AEAD contains a huge number of terms, therefore we can not present it here.

References

1. Ågren, M., Hell, M., Johansson, T., Meier, W.: Grain-128a: a new version of grain-128 with optional authentication. Int. J. Wirel. Mob. Comput. **5**(1), 48–59 (2011)
2. Aumasson, J.P., Dinur, I., Henzen, L., Meier, W., Shamir, A.: Efficient FPGA implementations of high-dimensional cube testers on the stream cipher grain-128. IACR Cryptol. ePrint Arch., p. 218 (2009)
3. Banik, S., Maitra, S., Sarkar, S., Meltem Sönmez, T.: A chosen IV related key attack on grain-128a. In: Boyd, C., Simpson, L. (eds.) ACISP 2013. LNCS, vol. 7959, pp. 13–26. Springer, Heidelberg (2013). https://doi.org/10.1007/978-3-642-39059-3_2
4. Dalai, D.K., Pal, S., Sarkar, S.: Some conditional cube testers for grain-128a of reduced rounds. IEEE Trans. Comput. **71**(6), 1374–1385 (2022)
5. Dinur, I., Güneysu, T., Paar, C., Shamir, A., Zimmermann, R.: An experimentally verified attack on full grain-128 using dedicated reconfigurable hardware. In: Lee, D.H., Wang, X. (eds.) ASIACRYPT 2011. LNCS, vol. 7073, pp. 327–343. Springer, Heidelberg (2011). https://doi.org/10.1007/978-3-642-25385-0_18
6. Dinur, I., Shamir, A.: Cube attacks on tweakable black box polynomials. In: Joux, A. (ed.) EUROCRYPT 2009. LNCS, vol. 5479, pp. 278–299. Springer, Heidelberg (2009). https://doi.org/10.1007/978-3-642-01001-9_16
7. Dinur, I., Shamir, A.: Breaking grain-128 with dynamic cube attacks. In: Joux, A. (ed.) FSE 2011. LNCS, vol. 6733, pp. 167–187. Springer, Heidelberg (2011). https://doi.org/10.1007/978-3-642-21702-9_10
8. Fouque, P.-A., Vannet, T.: Improving key recovery to 784 and 799 rounds of trivium using optimized cube attacks. In: Moriai, S. (ed.) FSE 2013. LNCS, vol. 8424, pp. 502–517. Springer, Heidelberg (2014). https://doi.org/10.1007/978-3-662-43933-3_26
9. Gurobi Optimization, LLC. Gurobi Optimizer Reference Manual (2021)
10. Hamann, M., Krause, M.: On stream ciphers with provable beyond-the-birthday-bound security against time-memory-data tradeoff attacks. Cryptogr. Commun. **10**(5), 959–1012 (2018)
11. Hao, Y., Leander, G., Meier, W., Todo, Y., Wang, Q.: Modeling for three-subset division property without unknown subset. In: Canteaut, A., Ishai, Y. (eds.) EUROCRYPT 2020. LNCS, vol. 12105, pp. 466–495. Springer, Cham (2020). https://doi.org/10.1007/978-3-030-45721-1_17
12. Hawkes, P.: Differential-linear weak key classes of IDEA. In: Nyberg, K. (ed.) EUROCRYPT 1998. LNCS, vol. 1403, pp. 112–126. Springer, Heidelberg (1998). https://doi.org/10.1007/BFb0054121
13. He, J., Hu, K., Preneel, B., Wang, M.: Stretching cube attacks: improved methods to recover massive superpolies. IACR Cryptol. ePrint Arch., p. 1218 (2022)
14. Hell, M., Johansson, T., Meier, W., Sönnerup, J., Yoshida, H.: An AEAD variant of the grain stream cipher. In: Carlet, C., Guilley, S., Nitaj, A., Souidi, E.M. (eds.) C2SI 2019. LNCS, vol. 11445, pp. 55–71. Springer, Cham (2019). https://doi.org/10.1007/978-3-030-16458-4_5

15. Hu, K., Sun, S., Todo, Y., Wang, M., Wang, Q.: Massive superpoly recovery with nested monomial predictions. In: Tibouchi, M., Wang, H. (eds.) ASIACRYPT 2021. LNCS, vol. 13090, pp. 392–421. Springer, Cham (2021). https://doi.org/10.1007/978-3-030-92062-3_14

16. Kara, O., Manap, C.: A new class of weak keys for blowfish. In: Biryukov, A. (ed.) FSE 2007. LNCS, vol. 4593, pp. 167–180. Springer, Heidelberg (2007). https://doi.org/10.1007/978-3-540-74619-5_11

17. Karlsson, L., Hell, M., Stankovski, P.: Not so greedy: enhanced subset exploration for nonrandomness detectors. In: Mori, P., Furnell, S., Camp, O. (eds.) ICISSP 2017. CCIS, vol. 867, pp. 273–294. Springer, Cham (2018). https://doi.org/10.1007/978-3-319-93354-2_13

18. Leander, G., Abdelraheem, M.A., AlKhzaimi, H., Zenner, E.: A cryptanalysis of PRINTCIPHER: the invariant subspace attack. In: Rogaway, P. (ed.) CRYPTO 2011. LNCS, vol. 6841, pp. 206–221. Springer, Heidelberg (2011). https://doi.org/10.1007/978-3-642-22792-9_12

19. Leander, G., Minaud, B., Rønjom, S.: A generic approach to invariant subspace attacks: cryptanalysis of robin, iSCREAM and zorro. In: Oswald, E., Fischlin, M. (eds.) EUROCRYPT 2015. LNCS, vol. 9056, pp. 254–283. Springer, Heidelberg (2015). https://doi.org/10.1007/978-3-662-46800-5_11

20. Lehmann, M., Meier, W.: Conditional differential cryptanalysis of grain-128a. In: Pieprzyk, J., Sadeghi, A.-R., Manulis, M. (eds.) CANS 2012. LNCS, vol. 7712, pp. 1–11. Springer, Heidelberg (2012). https://doi.org/10.1007/978-3-642-35404-5_1

21. Li, Z., Bi, W., Dong, X., Wang, X.: Improved conditional cube attacks on keccak keyed modes with MILP method. In: Takagi, T., Peyrin, T. (eds.) ASIACRYPT 2017. LNCS, vol. 10624, pp. 99–127. Springer, Cham (2017). https://doi.org/10.1007/978-3-319-70694-8_4

22. Li, Z., Dong, X., Wang, X.: Conditional cube attack on round-reduced ASCON. IACR Trans. Symm. Cryptol. **2017**(1), 175–202 (2017)

23. Liu, F., Isobe, T., Meier, W., Sakamoto, K.: Weak keys in reduced AEGIS and tiaoxin. IACR Trans. Symm. Cryptol. **2021**(2), 104–139 (2021)

24. Ma, Z., Tian, T., Qi, W.-F.: Improved conditional differential attacks on grain v1. IET Inf. Secur. **11**(1), 46–53 (2017)

25. Mroczkowski, P., Szmidt, J.: The cube attack on stream cipher trivium and quadraticity tests. Fundam. Informaticae **114**(3–4), 309–318 (2012)

26. Rohit, R., Sarkar, S.: Diving deep into the weak keys of round reduced ascon. IACR Trans. Symm. Cryptol. **2021**(4), 74–99 (2021)

27. Todo, Y., Isobe, T., Hao, Y., Meier, W.: Cube attacks on non-blackbox polynomials based on division property. In: Katz, J., Shacham, H. (eds.) CRYPTO 2017. LNCS, vol. 10403, pp. 250–279. Springer, Cham (2017). https://doi.org/10.1007/978-3-319-63697-9_9

28. Todo, Y., Isobe, T., Meier, W., Aoki, K., Zhang, B.: Fast correlation attack revisited. In: Shacham, H., Boldyreva, A. (eds.) CRYPTO 2018. LNCS, vol. 10992, pp. 129–159. Springer, Cham (2018). https://doi.org/10.1007/978-3-319-96881-0_5

29. Wang, Q., Hao, Y., Todo, Y., Li, C., Isobe, T., Meier, W.: Improved division property based cube attacks exploiting algebraic properties of superpoly. In: Shacham, H., Boldyreva, A. (eds.) CRYPTO 2018. LNCS, vol. 10991, pp. 275–305. Springer, Cham (2018). https://doi.org/10.1007/978-3-319-96884-1_10

30. Wang, S., Hu, B., Guan, J., Zhang, K., Shi, T.: MILP-aided method of searching division property using three subsets and applications. In: Galbraith, S.D., Moriai, S. (eds.) ASIACRYPT 2019. LNCS, vol. 11923, pp. 398–427. Springer, Cham (2019). https://doi.org/10.1007/978-3-030-34618-8_14

31. Ye, C., Tian, T.: A new framework for finding nonlinear superpolies in cube attacks against trivium-like ciphers. In: Susilo, W., Yang, G. (eds.) ACISP 2018. LNCS, vol. 10946, pp. 172–187. Springer, Cham (2018). https://doi.org/10.1007/978-3-319-93638-3_11

On Single-Server Delegation of RSA

Giovanni Di Crescenzo[1], Matluba Khodjaeva[2]([✉]), Ta Chen[1],
Rajesh Krishnan[1], David Shur[1], Delaram Kahrobaei[3], and Vladimir Shpilrain[4]

[1] Peraton Labs, Basking Ridge, NJ, USA
{gdicrescenzo,tchen,rkrishnan,dshur}@peratonlabs.com
[2] CUNY John Jay College of Criminal Justice, New York, NY, USA
mkhodjaeva@jjay.cuny.edu
[3] CUNY Graduate Center, New York, NY, USA
dkahrobaei@gc.cuny.edu
[4] City University of New York, New York, NY, USA
vshpilrain@ccny.cuny.edu

Abstract. In delegated computation research, the main problem asks how a computationally weaker client device can obtain help from one or more computationally stronger servers to perform some computation. Desirable solution requirements include correctness of the computation, privacy of the inputs, high probability detection of any malicious behavior of a server, low client online runtime, low communication complexity, low client storage complexity, and minimal server trust.

In this paper we investigate the problem of single-server delegated computation of the encryption and decryption algorithms in the ubiquitously applied RSA public-key cryptosystem. Our contribution includes state-of-the-art summaries, the first delegated computation protocol for small-exponent RSA encryption, a delegated computation protocol for RSA decryption with improved server runtime and client storage, and an upper bound on the impact of communication on client device energy, which may be of independent interest.

1 Introduction and Model

The area of server-aided cryptography, or delegation/outsourcing of cryptographic primitives, is mainly concerned with the following problem: "how can a computationally weaker client delegate cryptographic computations to computationally superior servers?"

This problem has been first discussed in [1,18,28] and a first formal model has been produced in [23]. In the past few years, this problem is seeing an increased interest because of the shift of modern computation paradigms towards cloud/fog/edge computing, large-scale computations over big data, Internet of Things, etc. A solution to this problem is an interactive protocol between a client and one or more servers (Fig. 1), where the client holding an input x wants to

© The Author(s), under exclusive license to Springer Nature Switzerland AG 2023
G. Bella et al. (Eds.): SecITC 2022, LNCS 13809, pp. 81–101, 2023.
https://doi.org/10.1007/978-3-031-32636-3_5

get help from the server(s) in computing $F(x)$, where F is a publicly known function, and the main desired properties of this delegated computation of $F(x)$ are:

1. *result correctness*: if client and server(s) honestly follow their instructions, at the end of the protocol the client obtains $F(x)$;
2. *input/output ϵ_p-privacy*: only minimal or no information about x and/or $F(x)$ is revealed to the server(s); here, [23] formally defines privacy in the sense of simulatability of the client's messages (as in the area of secure multiparty computation), and [4,22] considers input privacy in the sense of input indistinguishability; that is, even malicious servers cannot distinguish which out of two different inputs was used in a protocol's execution, except possibly with very small probability ϵ_p;
3. *result ϵ_s-security*: even malicious server(s) should not be able, except possibly with very small probability (i.e., $\epsilon_s = 2^{-\lambda}$, for some statistical parameter λ) to convince the client to accept a result different than $F(x)$.

Following, for instance, [35], protocols can be partitioned into (a) an offline phase, where input x is not yet known, but somewhat expensive computation can be performed by the client deployer or even the temporarily unconstrained client's device, and stored on the client's device, and (b) an online phase, where we assume the client's resources are limited, and thus the client needs the server's help to compute $F(x)$. Accordingly, the desired efficiency properties are:

4. *resource efficiency*: client's runtime t_C in the online phase should be significantly smaller than the runtime t_F for computing $F(x)$ without delegation; use of other resources like communication complexity cc, client's storage complexity sc and offline phase runtime t_P, should also be minimized.

To capture distinct input scenarios, we say that an input x to F is

- *public-online* if x is unknown in the offline phase but known to both parties in the online phase;
- *private-online* if x is unknown in the offline phase but known to C in the online phase;
- *private-offline* if x is known to C starting from the offline phase but unknown to S.

The RSA Functions. Let p, q be primes of the same length, let $n = p \cdot q$, $\phi(n) = (p-1) \cdot (q-1)$, and let $\mathbb{Z}_n^*$ denote the set of integers coprime with n. We consider the group $(\mathbb{Z}_n^*, \cdot)$, where $\cdot$ denotes multiplication modulo n. Let e, d denote integers such that $\gcd(e, \phi(n)) = 1$ and $e \cdot d = 1 \mod \phi(n)$. In this group, with parameter values n, e, d, we define the following functions:

1. *Multiplication with RSA moduli*, defined as $\mathsf{Mult}_n : (a, b) \in \mathbb{Z}_n^* \times \mathbb{Z}_n^* \to c \in \mathbb{Z}_n^*$, such that $c = a \cdot b \mod n$.
2. *Large-exponent RSA encryption exponentiation*, defined, for $e \in \mathbb{Z}_{\phi(n)}$, as $\mathsf{leExp}_{n,e} : m \in \mathbb{Z}_n^* \to c \in \mathbb{Z}_n^*$, such that $c = m^e \mod n$.

3. *Small-exponent RSA encryption exponentiation*, defined, for $e \in \{0,1\}^a$, as
   $\mathsf{seExp}_{n,e,a} : m \in \mathbb{Z}_n^* \to c \in \mathbb{Z}_n^*$, such that $c = m^e \bmod n$.
4. *RSA decryption exponentiation* as $\mathsf{dExp}_{n,e,d} : c \in \mathbb{Z}_n^* \to y \in \mathbb{Z}_n^*$, such that $y = c^d \bmod n$.

We consider Mult_n as a modular multiplication function with 2 public online inputs, $\mathsf{seExp}_{n,e}$ and $\mathsf{leExp}_{n,e,a}$ as base-private-online exponent-public-offline exponentiation functions, and $\mathsf{dExp}_{n,e,d}$ as a base-public-online exponent-private-offline exponentiation function. The textbook algorithm for a non-delegated computation of functions $\mathsf{leExp}_{n,e}$, $\mathsf{seExp}_{n,e,a}$ and $\mathsf{dExp}_{n,e,d}$ is the *square-and-multiply* algorithm, which requires up to $2|e|$ multiplications modulo n, but see, e.g. [21], for algorithms with a slightly improved constant.

This Paper. Single-server delegation protocols provably satisfying the defined properties of result correctness, input/output-privacy, result-security and resource efficiency, have been proposed for some operations often found in cryptographic protocols (see, e.g., [14]), including: large/small-exponent exponentiation in discrete logarithm groups (see, e.g., [8,15]), large-exponent RSA encryption exponentiation (see, e.g., [10]), pairings (see, e.g., [3,11,12]), multiplication modulo large primes (see, e.g., [13]). Earlier work [4–7,16,23,27] showed solutions provably satisfying a subset of these properties. There are also results for sufficiently large arbitrary circuits (starting with [22]). In this paper, we consider the problem of delegating computations in the widely used RSA public-key cryptosystem.

We show the *first* single-server protocol for efficient delegated computation of *small-exponent* RSA encryption (i.e., the RSA variant which is implemented in many popular cryptography software libraries). Single-server delegation of small-exponent exponentiation in the RSA group is not adequately solved by a direct use of single-server delegation of large-exponent exponentiation in the same group (as from, e.g., [4,9,10]). This is because delegated computation would be less expensive for the client than non-delegated computation only for a small range of ϵ_s values, not ruling out a constant probability that a malicious server convinces the client of an incorrect result.

We also show a solution for single-server delegation of RSA decryption, improving server runtime and client storage over the best known protocol [26]. Both our protocol and the protocol from [26] have potentially large communication complexity. A review of past work, including several failed attempts to reduce communication complexity, can be found in Appendix A.

Analyzing the impact of both computation and communication to the energy consumption of resource-constrained devices is an important problem (see, e.g., [30]), and is especially of interest in the protocols presented in this paper since their communication is somewhat larger (for the protocol on RSA encryption) or can be significantly larger (for the protocol on RSA decryption) than the computation result. Accordingly, we show an upper bound, of independent interest, to estimate the energy consumption on a resource-constrained device of both communication and computation in a delegated computation protocol. In our example evaluation of this upper bound, we show that relatively to a specific device (Giant Gecko) and a specific choice of network technology (TCP over Ethernet communication), our delegation protocol for small-exponent RSA encryption does reduce device energy. This derivation may or may not generalize to other devices and/or communication technologies, but our upper bound can be evaluated for those.

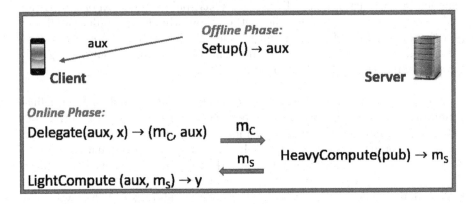

Fig. 1. Delegated computation of $y = F(x)$: system architecture.

2   Delegation of Small-Exponent RSA Encryption

In this section we investigate the delegation of function $\mathsf{seExp}_{n,e,a}$ where the input base is private online and the short, a-bit, exponent e is public offline, with special focus on the case $e = 65537$ since this is the most used exponent for RSA encryption in applied cryptography software libraries. Using past solutions [4, 9,10], at best we can achieve client-efficient single-server delegation of large-exponent RSA encryption where result ϵ_s-security only holds up to a constant ϵ_s value. In the rest of this section, we focus on solving the same problem, while achieving *arbitrarily small* values of ϵ_s.

Our solution consists of combining the following 3 ingredients: (1) a sub-protocol that performs the delegation of function Mult_n computing modular multiplication of two public online inputs in the RSA group; (2) a subprotocol that performs the delegation of function $\mathsf{seExp}_{n,e,a}$ computing modular exponentiation of a public online base to a public online exponent in the RSA group, using ingredient (1) as a subprotocol for delegating multiplication; (3) a base randomization technique to efficiently reduce the problem of delegating private-base exponentiation to delegating public-base exponentiation, where the latter is performed using ingredient (2).

About ingredient (1), we achieve this protocol as an extension of our previous protocol in [13] for delegating multiplication of two public online inputs modulo *a prime*. The extension requires only minor description changes and no technical difficulty, but for completeness we include this protocol in Appendix B. In this protocol, the client only performs reductions modulo n, multiplications modulo much smaller primes, and other lower-order operations.

About ingredient (2), we note that our previous protocol in [15] solves the same problem in a ring modulo *a prime*. Thus, we combine this latter protocol with ingredient (1) to obtain a solution in the RSA group. The resulting protocol, included in Appendix C for completeness, can be seen as an optimized simulation of the (iterative) square and multiply algorithm for modular exponentiation, while using ingredient (1) to delegate the computation of squares and multiplications modulo n in this algorithm.

In ingredient (3), the client precomputes $v = u^{-e} \mod n$ in the offline phase, for some random value $u \in \mathbb{Z}_n^*$, and then does the following in the online phase: it randomizes the input base x by multiplying it by u, and uses ingredient (2) to delegate the exponentiation of the value $m \cdot u \mod n$ (which is uniformly distributed in $\mathbb{Z}_n^*$ and does not need to be kept private) to the exponent e, and then multiplies the result of this latter delegation by v to obtain the desired output of function $\mathsf{seExp}_{n,e,a}$ on input x.

The resulting protocol achieves the following theorem.

Theorem 1. Let σ be a computational security parameter, let λ be a statistical security parameter, and let $\mathcal{P}_{e,pub}$ be the single-server protocol for delegating computation of small-exponent RSA encryption exponentiation in the input case where the base is public online and the a-bit exponent is public offline, satisfying 1-correctness, unbounded $2^{-\lambda}$-security and $(t_F', t_S', t_P', t_C', cc', sc', mc')$-efficiency, such as the one described in Appendix C. There exist (constructively) a single-server protocols $\mathcal{P}_{e,priv}$ for delegating computation of small-exponent exponentiation in the input case where the base is private online and the a-bit exponent is public offline, satisfying 1-decryption-correctness, 1-bounded privacy, $2^{-\lambda}$-security and $(t_F, t_S, t_P, t_C, cc, sc, mc)$-efficiency, where

- $t_F = t_F'$, $t_S \le t_S' + O(\sigma)$,
- $t_P = t_P' + 1$ group exponentiation with random base + 1 inverse,
- $t_C \le t_C' + 2$ multiplications $\mod n$,
- $cc \le cc' + O(\sigma)$, $sc = sc' + 1$, and $mc = 2$.

Description of $\mathcal{P}_{e,priv}$. By $\mathcal{P}_{e,pub} = (\mathsf{Offline}_{e,pub}, S_{e,pub}, C_{e,pub})$ we denote a protocol for the delegation of small-exponent exponentiation with public online base and public offline exponent, such as the protocol in Appendix C. We now formally describe protocol $\mathcal{P}_{e,priv}$ for the delegation of small-exponent exponentiation $\mathsf{seExp}_{n,e,a}(x) = x^e \mod n$ in a group $\mathbb{Z}_n^*$, where x is private online and e is public offline.

Offline Input: $1^\sigma, 1^\lambda, 1^a$, $n \in \{0,1\}^\sigma$, $e \in \{0,1\}^a$
Offline phase of $\mathcal{P}_{e,priv}$:

1. Run the offline-phase algorithm $\mathsf{Offline}_{e,pub}$ from protocol $\mathcal{P}_{e,pub}$
2. Store the resulting output *out* on C's device

3. Randomly choose $u \in \mathbb{Z}_n^*$ and set $v := u^{-e} \bmod n$
4. Store v on C's device

Online Input to C: $1^\sigma, 1^\lambda, 1^a, n \in \{0,1\}^\sigma, x \in \mathbb{Z}_n^*, e \in \{0,1\}^a$
Online Input to S: $1^\sigma, 1^\lambda, 1^a, n \in \{0,1\}^\sigma, e \in \{0,1\}^a$
Online phase of $\mathcal{P}_{e,priv}$:

1. C sets $z = x \cdot u \bmod n$ and sends z to S
2. C delegates the computation $z^e \bmod n$ to S, as follows:
   C runs $C_{e,pub}$ and sends the resulting message to S
   S receives C's message, runs $S_{e,pub}$ and sends the resulting message to C
   C receives S's message, and runs $C_{e,pub}$ to compute protocol's output y_z
3. C computes $y = y_z \cdot v \bmod n$ and **returns**: y

Properties of $\mathcal{P}_{e,priv}$. The efficiency properties of $\mathcal{P}_{e,priv}$ follow by protocol inspection, and by observing that in $\mathcal{P}_{e,priv}$ there is only one call to subprotocol $\mathcal{P}_{e,pub}$. In particular, we note that: (1) in the online phase of $\mathcal{P}_{e,priv}$, the client C only performs 2 multiplications modulo n and any operations required to run the client algorithm of $\mathcal{P}_{e,pub}$; (2) the offline phase runtime includes one exponentiation and one inverse mod n, in addition to the runtime of the offline phase of $\mathcal{P}_{e,pub}$.

The 1-*correctness* property of $\mathcal{P}_{e,priv}$ follows by observing that at the end of the protocol C can compute $y = x^e \bmod n$ with probability 1. First, we observe that at the end of the execution of subprotocol $\mathcal{P}_{e,pub}$ on input z, C can compute $y_z = z^e \bmod n$, thanks to the 1-correctness of subprotocol $\mathcal{P}_{e,pub}$. Then, we can see that the value y computed by C at the end of the protocol satisfies $y = y_z \cdot v = z^e \cdot u^e = x^e \cdot u^e \cdot u^{-e} \bmod n = x^e \bmod n$, as desired.

The α-*bounded input privacy* property, for $\alpha = 1$, is easily seen to be satisfied since message z sent by C is uniformly distributed in $\mathbb{Z}_n^*$ as so is u.

The α-*bounded* $2^{-\lambda}$-*security* property, where $\alpha = 1$, of $\mathcal{P}_{e,priv}$ directly follows by combining its α-bounded input privacy property with the α-bounded $2^{-\lambda}$-security property of protocol $\mathcal{P}_{e,pub}$. First, we observe that if S returns a correct value at the end of subprotocol $\mathcal{P}_{e,pub}$, then the 1-correctness property implies that C returns a correct output $y = x^e \bmod n$ with probability 1. Then we observe that the value z sent by C to S is uniformly distributed in $\mathbb{Z}_n^*$ and does not leak any information helping S in violating the security of property of protocol $\mathcal{P}_{e,pub}$. Thus, the probability that C accepts a value $y \neq x^e \bmod n$ is exactly the probability that C accepts an incorrect result in the execution of protocol $\mathcal{P}_{e,pub}$.

Performance. We carried out a software implementation on a macOS Big Sur Version 11.4 laptop with a 3.2 GHz Apple M1 processor with 8 cores (4 performance cores and 4 efficiency cores at 1/10th of the power) and 16 GB RAM. We implemented protocol $\mathcal{P}_{e,priv}$ and, for comparison purposes, the restriction to small exponents of the protocol from [10]. The two protocols were coded in Python 3.8 using the gmpy2 package.

In our implementation runtime analysis, as a small exponent, we used $e = 65537$, for which $a = 17$, and used specific and practical parameter ranges for the security parameter λ and the computational parameter σ. Specifically, we have considered $\sigma \in \{2048, 3072\}$, which correspond to security levels 112 and 128, respectively. Moreover, we have considered $\lambda \in \{10, 20, 30, 40\}$, as an event happening with probability between 2^{-10} and 2^{-40} has occurrence expectancy between 1 in about one thousand and less than 1 in about 1 trillion protocol executions, respectively.

Table 1 reports performance results relative to $\mathcal{P}_{e,priv}$ as well as the protocol from [10] for the delegation of $\mathsf{seExp}_{\mathsf{n,e,a}}(x) = x^e \bmod n$, where $|n| = \sigma$.

Average runtime values for non-delegated computation of $\mathsf{seExp}_{\mathsf{n,e,a}}(x)$, denoted as t_F, as well as for the client's program in the online phase, denoted as t_C, are showed for the mentioned varying values of statistical parameter λ, security parameter σ and length a of exponent e. All values were computed by averaging across 100 random and independent offline and online phases of the protocol for a fixed size, randomly and independently chosen σ-bit number n, $x \in \mathbb{Z}_n^*$ and $e = 65537$. Most of our analysis focused on client's online runtime t_C and its improvements over non-delegated computation runtime t_F.

Main takeaways are that, depending on values of λ, the ratio t_F/t_C, capturing the runtime improvement due to delegated computation, is in $[1.194, 1.251]$ when $\sigma = 2048$, or in $[1.777, 1.800]$ when $\sigma = 3072$.

Another important takeaway is that the previous work protocol from [10], originally designed for arbitrary $e \in \mathbb{Z}_{\phi(n)}$, and providing significant efficient client runtime gains for large values of e, did not do so for small values of e. In particular, when run for the small value $e = 65537$, it was never competitive, in that for all considered values of λ and σ, the client's online runtime t_C was significantly higher than the non-delegated computation t_F.

Table 1. Performance of Protocol $\mathcal{P}_{e,priv}$ to delegate $y = x^e \bmod n$ where $e = 65537$, $a = 17$, $\sigma = 2048, 3072$. Quantities t_F, t_P, t_C, t_S are measured in seconds.

Our protocol $\mathcal{P}_{e,priv}$								
λ	10		20		30		40	
σ	2048	3072	2048	3072	2048	3072	2048	3072
$t_F =$	3.73E-05	7.24E-05	3.41E-05	7.17E-05	3.38E-05	7.19E-05	3.37E-05	7.20E-05
$t_P =$	9.16E-05	1.32E-04	8.45E-05	1.40E-04	9.44E-05	1.45E-04	1.01E-04	1.49E-04
$t_C =$	2.98E-05	4.08E-05	2.86E-05	4.01E-05	2.82E-05	4.00E-05	2.82E-05	4.03E-05
$t_S =$	6.38E-05	1.18E-04	6.12E-05	1.15E-04	6.06E-05	1.15E-04	6.07E-05	1.15E-04
$t_F/t_C =$	1.251	1.777	1.194	1.789	1.200	1.800	1.195	1.787
Protocol in [10]								
$t_F =$	3.44E-05	7.05E-05	3.45E-05	7.08E-05	3.52E-05	7.17E-05	3.42E-05	7.07E-05
$t_P =$	1.25E-04	2.29E-04	1.25E-04	2.29E-04	1.26E-04	2.35E-04	1.25E-04	2.30E-04
$t_C =$	6.60E-05	1.36E-04	1.13E-04	2.27E-04	1.56E-04	3.16E-04	1.97E-04	4.00E-04
$t_S =$	6.82E-05	1.41E-04	6.83E-05	1.41E-04	6.93E-05	1.44E-04	6.83E-05	1.41E-04
$t_F/t_C =$	0.521	0.519	0.306	0.312	0.226	0.227	0.174	0.177

We also estimated the minimum exponent size a (rounded to the nearest multiple of 10) for the protocol in [10] to be more client-efficient than ours. Results, obtained with 10 independent runs, are included in Table 2.

Table 2. Exponent size a values for which, as λ, σ vary, $R \leq 1$, where R = ratio of C's online runtime in the protocol from [10] to C's online runtime in protocol $\mathcal{P}_{e,priv}$.

λ	10	20	30	40
$\sigma = 2048$	$a = 30; R = 0.83$	$a = 50; R = 0.85$	$a = 60; R = 0.95$	$a = 90; R = 0.97$
$\sigma = 3072$	$a = 60; R = 0.89$	$a = 90; R = 0.98$	$a = 140; R = 0.98$	$a = 180; R = 1.00$

3   Single-Server Delegation of RSA Decryption

In this section we investigate the delegation of RSA decryption. Past work is reviewed in Appendix A. Here, we show a new protocol with improved server runtime and client storage with respect to the best known single-server protocol (i.e.,, [26]). Formally, we achieve the following theorem.

Theorem 2. Let σ be a computational security parameter, let λ be a statistical security parameter, let b, k be parameters such that $b^k \geq 2^\sigma$, and let $\mathcal{P}_{e,pub}$ be the single-server protocol for delegating computation of RSA encryption exponentiation in the input case where the base is public online and the exponent is public offline, satisfying 1-correctness, unbounded $2^{-\lambda}$-security and $(t'_F, t'_S, t'_P, t'_C, cc', sc', mc')$-efficiency, such as the protocol in Sect. 2 for the small exponent case, or the protocol in [10] for the large exponent case. There exist (constructively) a single-server protocol $\mathcal{P}_d$ for delegating computation of RSA decryption exponentiation in the input case where the base is public online and the exponent is private offline, satisfying 1-decryption-correctness; 1-bounded ϵ_p privacy for some ϵ_p negligible in σ; $2^{-\lambda}$-security; and efficiency with parameters $(t_F, t_S, t_P, t_C, cc, sc, mc)$, where

- $t_F = 1$ exponentiation in $\mathbb{Z}_n^*$; $t_S \leq t'_S + k$ exponentiations,
- $t_P = t'_P + 2k$ exponentiations + 1 inverse, $t_C \leq t'_C + k + 1$ multiplications,
- $cc \leq cc' + b + k - 2$, $sc = sc' + 3$, and $mc = 3$.

We split the proof of the theorem into 2 parts. First, in Sect. 3.1, we show a technique that transforms a single-server RSA decryption delegation protocol $\mathcal{P}_{d,1}$ that satisfies result correctness and input privacy (and no result security) into a protocol $\mathcal{P}'_{d,1}$ that satisfies all 3 properties, using our protocols for delegation of RSA encryption. Next, in Sect. 3.2, we show a single-server RSA decryption delegation protocol $\mathcal{P}_{d,2}$ that only satisfies result correctness and input privacy and slightly improves on the best known solution, although still requiring significant communication complexity. The protocol $\mathcal{P}_d$ claimed by the theorem is then obtained as the protocol $\mathcal{P}'_{d,1}$ obtained after first setting $\mathcal{P}_{d,1} = \mathcal{P}_{d,2}$, and then applying the transformation in Sect. 3.1 to $\mathcal{P}_{d,1}$. We note that protocol $\mathcal{P}_d$ improves the server runtime and storage complexity of the best known result (i.e., applying the transformation in Sect. 3.1 to the result in [26]). On the other hand, it still requires somewhat high communication complexity for typical parameter values of b, k. The approach of reducing communication with shorter vector-type representations of d has appeared in many past efforts, starting with [28], and none of them has been proved secure, as also discussed in Appendix A.

3.1 A Transformation to Achieve the Result's Security Property

We observe that if there exists a delegation protocol $\mathcal{P}_{d,1}$ for the RSA decryption exponentiation function $\mathsf{dExp}_{n,e,c} : c \to c^d \bmod n$ satisfying result correctness and input privacy, then we can construct a delegation protocol $\mathcal{P}'_{d,1}$ for the same function, satisfying result correctness, input privacy, and result ϵ-security.

Let $\mathsf{eExp}_{n,e} : x \to x^e \bmod n$ denote an RSA encryption exponentiation function. Note that when $e \in \mathbb{Z}_{\phi(n)}$, we have that $\mathsf{eExp}_{n,e} = \mathsf{leExp}_{n,e}$, and when $e \in \{0,1\}^a$, for some small value a, we have that $\mathsf{eExp}_{n,e} = \mathsf{seExp}_{n,e,a}$.

Let $\mathcal{P}_e$ denote a delegation protocol for $\mathsf{eExp}_{n,e}$, satisfying correctness, input privacy, and ϵ-security. $\mathcal{P}_e$ can be instantiated using the protocol from [10] when $\mathsf{eExp}_{n,e} = \mathsf{leExp}_{n,e}$, or the protocol in Sect. 2, when $\mathsf{eExp}_{n,e} = \mathsf{seExp}_{n,e}$. Given protocols and $\mathcal{P}_{d,1}$ and $\mathcal{P}_e$, we construct protocol $\mathcal{P}'_{d,1}$ as follows:

1. The offline phase of $\mathcal{P}'_{d,1}$ runs the offline phase of $\mathcal{P}_{d,1}$ and $\mathcal{P}_e$
2. In the online phase, C has input c, e, d, n and S has input c, e, n
3. Given these inputs, C and S run the online phase of protocol $\mathcal{P}_{d,1}$, thus returning m to C
4. C and S run the online phase of protocol $\mathcal{P}_e$ on input m, e, n, thus returning $c' = m^e \bmod n$ to C
5. C checks that $c = c'$; if yes, C **returns:** m

We note that $\mathcal{P}'_{d,1}$ preserves the efficiency of $\mathcal{P}_{d,1}$ in all metrics; in particular, if C is efficient in $\mathcal{P}_{d,1}$, then C is also efficient in $\mathcal{P}'_{d,1}$, where it only performs 2 additional exponentiations to a λ-bit exponent in the online phase, to achieve the result ϵ_s-security property, for $\epsilon_s = 2^{-\lambda}$. In practice λ can be set much smaller than $|n|$; e.g., $\lambda = 50$. Finally, note that with respect to $\mathcal{P}_{d,1}$, protocol $\mathcal{P}'_{d,1}$ requires two additional messages, the computation of two exponentiations in the offline phase, and C's computation of two λ-bit-exponent exponentiations in the online phase, when requiring result ϵ_s-security.

3.2 A Protocol with Improved Server Runtime and Client Storage

We show a 1-server protocol $\mathcal{P}_{d,2} = (C, S)$ for the delegated computation of $\mathsf{dExp}_{n,e,d} : c \to c^d \bmod n$.

Informally, protocol $\mathcal{P}_{d,2}$ goes as follows. The secret exponent d is considered in its b-ary representation $d = \sum_{i=0}^{k-1} d_i \cdot b^i$, for some tunable parameter $b \geq 2$. Note that $c^d \bmod n$ can thus be seen as a product of exponentiations with bases

c^{d_i} and powers of b as exponent. In this protocol C sends random masks of these bases and asks S to compute the product of exponentiation to the known power-of-b exponents. Upon receiving values from S, C removes the masks by using a product of exponentiations computed offline, and thus recovers $c^d \mod n$.

A formal description of protocol $\mathcal{P}_{d,2}$ follows. (Its properties are discussed in Table 3 and Appendix A). Let G be a pseudo-random generator.

Input to C and S: n, e, c and parameter base b; also, let k be the minimum value such that $b^k > n$.

Private input to C: $d \in \mathbb{Z}_{\phi(n)}$

Offline phase instructions:

1. Write private exponent d in base b; i.e., $d = (d_{k-1}, \ldots, d_1, d_0)_b = \sum_{i=0}^{k-1} d_i \cdot b^i$, where $d_i \in [0, b-1]$ for $i \in \{0, \ldots, k-1\}$
2. Pseudo-randomly choose $u_0, \ldots, u_{k-1} \in \mathbb{Z}_n^*$ using G on input a random seed s, and set $v_0 := (\prod_{i=0}^{k-1} u_i^{b^i})^{-1} \mod n$
3. Store $((d_{k-1}, \ldots, d_1, d_0)_b, s, v_0)$ on C's device.

Online phase instructions:

1. S sets $B_1 := c$ and computes $B_j := B_{j-1} \cdot c \mod n$, for $j = 2, \ldots, b-1$
   S sends $B_2, \ldots, B_{b-1}$ to C
2. C sets $B_0 := 1$, $B_1 := c$, and computes $z_i := B_{d_i} \cdot u_i \mod n$ for $i = 0, \ldots k-1$
   C sends $z_0, \ldots, z_{k-1}$ to S
3. S computes $w_0 := \prod_{i=0}^{k-1} z_i^{b^i} \mod n$ and
   S sends w_0 to C
4. C **returns:** $m := w_0 \cdot v_0 \mod n$,

Table 3. Comparing our RSA Decryption delegation protocol $\mathcal{P}_{d,2}$ with [26], which also provably satisfies correctness, input privacy and client efficiency, but no result security. We are not aware of other previous work provably satisfying this set of properties, but see Appendix A for a discussion of previous work.

Protocol	t_C # of mult	t_S # of exp	cc	sc	mc	ϵ_p	# Servers
[26] [§2C]	$k+1$	$2b-2$	$b+k+1$	b	3	0	1
$\mathcal{P}_{d,2}$	$k+1$	k	$b+k-2$	3	3	negligible	1

4   On the Impact of Communication on Client Energy

In this section we show our upper bounds on the estimated energy due to a resource-constrained device's computation and communication during an execution of a delegated computation protocol, from which we derive that for a particular device and network environment, delegation of RSA encryption does reduce device energy consumption.

Let $\mathcal{P}$ denote a delegation protocol for function F, let dn denote a device name, and de denote the network environment. By $E_{dn}(F)$ we denote the energy consumed by device dn when running a (non-delegated) computation of function F. By $E_{dn,de}^{cc}(F,\mathcal{P},m)$ we denote the energy consumed during the device dn's communication (i.e., data sending and receiving) in an execution of delegation protocol $\mathcal{P}$ for function F in network environment ne, where this communication totals to m data bytes. Our goal is to estimate (an upper bound of) the ratio $\rho_{dn,de}^{cc}(m) = E_{dn,de}^{cc}(F,\mathcal{P},m)/E_{dn}(F)$ as a function of the number m of data bytes communicated in $\mathcal{P}$. Towards this goal, we use the following definitions:

- icd_F: average current draw during a non-delegated computation of F
- $icd_{\mathcal{P},F}$: average current draw during a client's program in an execution of delegation protocol $\mathcal{P}$ for F
- icd_{aes}: average current draw during both computation and communication of AES-encrypted data
- t_F: runtime of a computation of F
- $t_{aes}(m)$: runtime for computation and communication of m AES-encrypted data blocks, of 256 bits each
- $\rho_{aes,F}$: ratio between runtime of a computation of F and runtime of 1 AES-encrypted data block (i.e., 256 bits).

We also make the following, arguably reasonable, assumptions:

1. Device energy consumption during a given operation is well approximated by the product of (instantaneous) average current draw and the time of the device operation, whether the latter is runtime or communication or both.
2. Device energy consumption due to communication of m data bytes in $\mathcal{P}$ is smaller than or equal to the device energy consumption during both computation and communication of m AES-encrypted bytes.

For functions F such that $icd_F \geq icd_{aes}$, we then derive that $\rho_{dn,de}^{cc}(m)$ is

$$\sim \frac{E_{dn,de}^{cc}(F,\mathcal{P},m)}{icd_F \cdot t_F} \leq \frac{icd_{aes} \cdot t_{aes}(m)}{icd_F \cdot t_F} \leq \frac{icd_{aes} \cdot t_{aes}(m)}{icd_{aes} \cdot t_F} = \frac{t_{aes}(m)}{\rho_{aes,F} \cdot t_{aes}(1)}, \tag{1}$$

where the approximation follows from Assumption 1, the first inequality follows from Assumption 2, the second inequality follows since we consider functions F such that $icd_F \geq icd_{aes}$, and the equality follows from the definition of $\rho_{aes,F}$.

We used Giant Gecko [38] as a resource-constrained IoT client device, since it has a popular low-power consuming processor (i.e., EFM32). On this device, using TCP communication over Ethernet as network environment, and considering F = short-exponent exponentiation in RSA encryption, we measured $\rho_{aes,F} = 1434$, $t_{aes}(1) = 2.71$ ms, and $t_{aes}(m)$, as depicted in Fig. 2 (left). (Here, runtimes are measured on a single execution as Giant Gecko shows no significant runtime changes across multiple executions of the same program.)

We now use the above bound to derive considerations on the client energy on our RSA encryption delegation protocol from Sect. 2. In both cases, above

Assumptions 1 and 2 seem reasonable, and so seems also the condition $icd_F \geq icd_{aes}$, where F is RSA-encryption exponentiation with exponent $e = 65537$.

In the case of protocol $\mathcal{P}_{e,priv}$, we have that $cc = 34$ group elements, and thus 8704B, and we derive, using Fig. 2 (left), that $t_{aes}(m) = 43.5149$ ms, and

$$\rho_{dn,de}(m) \leq \frac{t_{aes}(m)}{\rho_{aes,F} \cdot t_{aes}(1)} \leq \frac{43.5149}{1434 \cdot 2.7565} \leq 0.01101 = 1.101\%.$$

Thus, the communication in $\mathcal{P}_{e,priv}$ increases client energy by $\leq 1.11\%$ of the energy taken by non-delegated computation.

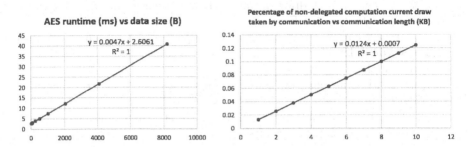

Fig. 2. (Left): Runtime of AES encryption in CBC mode on Giant Gecko vs data size. (Right): Percentage non-delegated computation current draw taken by (AES-encrypted) communication on a Giant Gecko vs communication length (in KB).

To evaluate the impact on energy consumption due to computation, we can similarly define $E_{dn}^{rt}(F, \mathcal{P})$ as the energy consumed during the device dn's computation in an execution of delegation protocol $\mathcal{P}$ for function F, and ratio $\rho_{dn}^{rt} = E_{dn}^{rt}(F, \mathcal{P})/E_{dn}(F)$. Similarly as before, we make Assumption 1 and for all functions F such that $icd_F \geq icd_{\mathcal{P},F}$, we derive that

$$\rho_{dn}^{rt} \leq t_C/t_F. \tag{2}$$

The energy consumption ratio due to both computation and communication can then be expressed as $\rho_{dn}^{rt} + \rho_{dn,de}^{cc}(m)$ which are bounded using the just discussed upper bounds (1) and (2). In particular, for RSA encryption with exponent $e = 65537$, upper bound (1) can be set as the inverse of the t_F/t_C values in Table 1, which are all ≤ 0.8375, and upper bound (2) can be set as the above computed value 0.0111. This totals to ≤ 0.8486, which confirms energy reduction through delegation.

We caution the reader that these energy derivations may or may not generalize to other devices and/or other network technologies. However, our assumptions and upper bounds can be evaluated for such different computation and communication environments.

5   Conclusions and Directions for Future Research

Encouraged by recent research that successfully delegates exponentiation, multiplication and pairing operations in algebraic structures of cryptographic interest, we revisited the problem of delegating the computation of RSA encryption and decryption, which have attracted a large amount of solution proposals and attacks for 30+ years. We produced the first single-server protocol for efficient delegated computation of small-exponent RSA encryption (i.e., the RSA variant which is implemented in many popular cryptography software libraries). We also produced a solution for efficient delegated computation of RSA decryption which slightly improves the previously best protocol from [26]. We showed an upper bound to estimate the energy consumption on a resource-constrained device of both communication and computation in a delegated computation protocol, which can be of independent interest, and we gave example evaluation of this upper bound for a specific device and network technology and derived conclusions on when delegated computation reduces (or does not reduce) device energy.

Acknowledgements. Many thanks to the SEC-ITC 2022 reviewers for very useful comments. Work by Matluba Khodjaeva was supported by the NSF CNS - CISE MSI Research Expansion grant N2131182 and PSC CUNY Cycle 53. Work by Giovanni Di Crescenzo, Ta Chen, Rajesh Krishnan and David Shur was supported by the Defense Advanced Research Projects Agency (DARPA), contract n. HR001120C0156. Approved for Public Release, Distribution Unlimited. The U.S. Government is authorized to reproduce and distribute reprints for Governmental purposes notwithstanding any copyright annotation hereon. Disclaimer: The views and conclusions contained herein are those of the authors and should not be interpreted as necessarily representing the official policies or endorsements, either expressed or implied, of DARPA, or the U.S. Government.

A   On Delegation of RSA Decryption

Previous Work. In [28], the first paper proposing delegation of cryptographic algorithms, the authors presented two protocols for the delegation of RSA decryption. The basic idea of such a protocols was as follows: the client sends some randomized masking of exponent d to the server; the server computes exponentiations to exponents related to the masking, and sends the results to the client; finally, the client uses the mask computation to turn the received exponentiation results into the desired $x^d \mod n$ exponentiation. The specific masking used in the first of their protocols was

$$d = f_1 d_1 + \cdots + f_M d_M \mod \phi(n),$$

for some random integers $d_1, \ldots, d_M$ send by the client to the server, some random bits $f_1, \ldots, f_M$ kept secret by the client, and some small value M. While this might seem an interesting approach, in that recovering d might seem to require exhaustive search of all possible vectors $(f_1, \ldots, f_M)$, about 20 papers were published containing faster attacks to their protocols and/or proposing protocol variants and improvements, as well as faster attacks to these variants. The reader is referred to Sect. 2 of [24] and Sect. 1.2 of [29] for a detailed discussion of these papers. All of these results were published before the introduction of a formal delegation model [23], and therefore protocols were described without proofs for their properties, other than sometimes claiming security against all previous attacks. For some of these papers, it might be interesting to study if their techniques suffice to provably achieve some of the properties formally defined in the more recent delegation models. In particular, some of these attacks were based on an attacker's knowledge of signatures, which would not necessarily be part of the adversary model when considering decryption delegation.

More recently, protocols were proposed [17,19,20,32,34,36] where the RSA exponent was hidden in one or more linear equations depending on a random value t in the exponent group. According to our analysys of these protocols: (a) a full-domain value t would perfectly hide the RSA secret key from the server, but require client work comparable to non-delegated computation of RSA decryption; (b) a smaller-size value t would reduce the client's work but also proportionally reduce the work needed to derive the RSA secret key. Properties (a) and (b) imply that these protocols do not simultaneously satisfy input privacy and client resource efficiency. Indeed, the variant of this approach used in [34] was broken by [7] using lattice-based cryptanalysis techniques.

Other exponent masking attempts were proposed in [31,33], where the exponent was masked by a multiple of the group order. This would seem a potentially interesting and valid idea, since, on one hand the random value would mask d, and on the other hand the server's exponentiation to a multiple of the group order would cancel out and allow C to recover an exponentiation to the original exponent. However, these protocols were broken in [2] using lattice-based cryptanalysis techniques.

Finally, [7] proves, in the generic group model, lower bounds on the efficiency of delegation protocols for a class of functions, including one that has some similarity to RSA decryption: public-online-base private-offline-exponent exponentiation in prime-order groups. These results are summarized in Table 4. We note that it is yet unknown if these results can be extended to RSA groups. Even if they were, it would still be possible to design RSA decryption delegation protocols with non-trivial improvements over non-delegated computation.

Properties of Our Protocol. $\mathcal{P}_{2,d}$. The *efficiency* properties are verified by protocol inspection; in particular,

- C's *online runtime complexity* consists of $k+1$ multiplications, which improves over non-delegated multiplication by a multiplicative factor of $\geq \log b$;
- S's *runtime complexity* consists of only k exponentiations, and $b + k - 2$ multiplications in $\mathbb{Z}_n^*$;
- the *offline runtime complexity* consists of 1 product of k exponentiations with k random bases, 1 inversion in $\mathbb{Z}_n^*$, and time linear in $|d|$;
- with respect to *round complexity*, $\mathcal{P}_{d,2}$ requires 3 messages between C and S;

Table 4. Summary of lower bound results from Theorems in [7] for protocols for the delegation of public-online-base private-offline-exponent exponentiation in prime order groups, in the generic group model, where s is an arbitrary integer. Each row represents a barrier in the sense that a protocol with a better improvement factor than what written in the 2nd column, in a scenario with protocol parameters as described in columns 3–5, would imply an efficient attack that successfully violates input privacy.

Lower Bound	Improvement Factor (over non-deleg sq and mult alg)	Offline Client Exponentiations	Online Server Exponentiations	# of rounds
Thm. 2	4	$O(1)$	1	1
Thm. 3	$(s+1)/2$	$O(1)$	s	1
Thm. 4	$\ell + 2$	$\ell = O(1)$	1	1
Thm. 5	8	$O(1)$	2	2
Thm. 6	$(4 + (s+1)^2)/2$	$O(1)$	s	2
Thm. 7	2^{s+1}	$O(1)$	s	s

– with respect to *communication complexity*, the online phase of $\mathcal{P}_{d,2}$ requires the transfer of $b + k - 1$ values in $\mathbb{Z}_n^*$.

To show the *correctness* property, we note that if C and S follow the protocol, C outputs $m = c^d \bmod n$ since $d = (d_{k-1}, \ldots, d_1, d_0)_b = \sum_{i=0}^{k-1} d_i \cdot b^i$ and

$$
m = w_0 \cdot v_0 = \prod_{i=0}^{k} z_i^{b^i} \cdot (\prod_{i=0}^{k} u_i^{b^i})^{-1}
$$

$$
= \prod_{i=0}^{k} (B_{d_i} \cdot u_i)^{b^i} \cdot \prod_{i=0}^{k} u_i^{-b^i} = \prod_{i=0}^{k} (B_{d_i})^{b^i} = \prod_{i=0}^{k} (c^{d_i})^{b^i} = c^{\sum_{i=0}^{k} d_i \cdot b^i} = c^d
$$

The *privacy* property of the protocol against a malicious S follows by observing that C's message to S is a sequence of pseudo-random values in $\mathbb{Z}_n^*$ and is thus pseudo-independent from d. Specifically, the values sent by C to S are $z_0, \ldots, z_k$ where $z_i = B_{d_i} \cdot u_i \bmod n$ for all $i = 0, \ldots, k-1$ and $z_k = m \cdot u_k \bmod n$. Note that as $u_0 \ldots, u_k$ are chosen as pseudo-random values in $\mathbb{Z}_n^*$ using G's output on input a random seed s, even $z_0, \ldots, z_k$ are pseudo-random values in $\mathbb{Z}_n^*$. Thus, under the assumption that G is pseudo-random, the probability that any efficient malicious S learns some additional information about private exponent d, is negligible.

B Delegation of Multiplication in $\mathbb{Z}_n^*$

We show how a quasilinear-time client can delegate modular multiplication in the group $\mathbb{Z}_n^*$, where n is an RSA group, in the input case where both factors are public online. (Here, by quasilinear-time client we mean a client that only performs modular additions/subtractions, reductions modulo small primes, and/or multiplications of small integers modulo small primes). The delegation protocol is obtained as a direct generalization of the analogue protocol in [13] for modular multiplication in the group $\mathbb{Z}_p^*$, where p is a prime. It turns out that after replacing a prime modulus with a non-prime modulus in the protocol from [13], all protocol's poperties still hold, with only syntactic changes to their proofs.

Informal Description of $\mathcal{P}_m$. The protocol in [13] improves Yao's generalization [37] of Pippenger's idea (see, e.g., example 2 in [25]) to efficiently verify integer equations modulo small primes, and adapts it from $\mathbb{Z}$ to $\mathbb{Z}_p^*$. In that protocol, a server would send the product w of the two input integers a and b, and the integer equation $w = a \cdot b$ is verified modulo a small random prime chosen by the client. Directly extending the protocol from [13], a server sends quotient w_0 and reminder w_1 of the division of w by n, and the integer equation $w_0 \cdot n + w_1 = a \cdot b$ is verified modulo a small random prime by the client, which can then obtain w_1 as the desired $a \cdot b \mod n$ value.

Formal Description of $\mathcal{P}_m$. Consider algebraic group $\mathbb{Z}_n^*$. We now formally describe a 1-server protocol $\mathcal{P}_m = (C, S)$ for the delegation of multiplication of public online group values a and b in $\mathbb{Z}_n^*$, where $|a| = |b| = \sigma$, and with statistical parameter λ. By $\pi(x)$ we denote the number of prime integers $\leq x$.
Offline Input: $1^\sigma, 1^\lambda, n \in \{0,1\}^\sigma$
Offline phase instructions:

1. Randomly chooses a prime $t < 2^\eta$, where $\eta = \lceil \lambda + \log_2 \lambda + \log_2(\pi(2\sigma)) \rceil$
2. Compute $n' = n \mod t$
3. **Return:** (t, n') and store this pair on C's device

Online Input to C and S: $1^\sigma, 1^\lambda, n \in \{0,1\}^\sigma, a, b \in \mathbb{Z}_n^*$
Online Input to C: t, n'
Online phase instructions:

1. S computes $w := a \cdot b$ (i.e., the product, over $\mathbb{Z}$, of a, b, considered as integers)
   S computes w_0, w_1 such that $w = w_0 \cdot n + w_1$ (over $\mathbb{Z}$), where $0 \leq w_1 < n$
   S sends w_0, w_1 to C
2. C computes $w'_0 := w_0 \mod t$ and $w'_1 := w_1 \mod t$
   C computes $a' := a \mod t$ and $b' := b \mod t$
   If $a' \cdot b' \neq w'_0 \cdot n' + w'_1 \mod t$ then
        C **returns:** $\perp$ and the protocol halts
   C **returns:** $y := w_1$

In [13], protocol $\mathcal{P}_m$ is proved to satisfy 1-correctness, unbounded $2^{-\lambda}$-security and $(t_F, t_S, t_P, t_C, cc, sc, mc)$-efficiency, where $cc = 2$, $sc = 2$, $mc = 2$, $t_F = 1$ multiplication mod p, $t_C = 4$ η-bit-modulus reductions + 2 η-bit-values multiplications + 1 η-bit-value addition, $t_S = 1$ multiplication + 1 division mod n, and $t_P = 1$ η-bit random prime generation + 1 η-bit-modulus reduction. In particular, C's online computations only consist of 4 reductions modulo q and 2 multiplications modulo q, where q is a small, η-bit, modulus.

C   Public-Base Small-Exponent Exponentiation in $\mathbb{Z}_n^*$

We show how to delegate small-exponent exponentiation in the RSA group $\mathbb{Z}_n^*$, in the input case where the base is public online and the exponent is public offline. This is obtained as a direct extension of the analogue result from [15] in the algebraic group $\mathbb{Z}_p^*$, where p is a prime. The extension consists of replacing the subprotocol for delegating multiplication mod p with the subprotocol for delegating multiplication mod n from Appendix B. We obtain the following

Theorem 3. Let σ be computational security parameter, let λ be a statistical security parameter, and let $\mathcal{P}_m$ be the single-server protocol for delegating computation of the multiplication operation in group $\mathbb{Z}_n^*$, satisfying 1-correctness, unbounded $2^{-\lambda}$-security and $(t'_F, t'_S, t'_P, t'_C, cc', sc', mc')$-efficiency, as described in Appendix B. There exist (constructively) a single-server protocols $\mathcal{P}_{e,pub}$ for delegating computation of small-exponent exponentiation in the same group for the input case where base $x \in \mathbb{Z}_n^*$ is public online and exponent $e \in \{0,1\}^a$ is public offline, satisfying unbounded 1-decryption-correctness, unbounded $2^{-\lambda}$-security, and $(t_F, t_S, t_P, t_C, cc, sc, mc)$-efficiency, where

- $t_F \leq 2a \cdot t'_F,\ t_S \leq 2a \cdot t'_S,\ t_P = t'_P,\ t_C \leq 2a \cdot t'_C,$
- $cc \leq 2a \cdot cc' + 2,\ sc = sc',$ and $mc = 2.$

Informal Description of $\mathcal{P}_{e,pub}$. Analogously as in [15], our protocol $\mathcal{P}_{e,pub}$ can be seen as an optimized simulation of the (iterative) square and multiply algorithm for modular exponentiation, while using a multiplication delegation subprotocol, such as the scheme $\mathcal{P}_m$ in Appendix B, to compute squares and multiplications modulo n in this algorithm. A first optimization consists of running all executions of protocol $\mathcal{P}_m$ in parallel instead of sequentially. Specifically, sequential black-box runs of protocol $\mathcal{P}_m$ at each squaring or multiplication step would result in up to $2a$ messages, where $a = \lceil \log(x+1) \rceil$. Instead, since the online phase of $\mathcal{P}_m$ only consists of a single message from S to C, and at the end of the protocol, both S and C can compute the computation result, all executions of $\mathcal{P}_m$ can be run in parallel, and so $\mathcal{P}_e$ consists of a single message from S to C. As a second optimization, we observe that the offline phase of $\mathcal{P}_m$ can be only run once, even if we run the online phase of the same protocol up to $2a$ times. This follows from the unbounded security property of $\mathcal{P}_m$, which we use to keep C's storage complexity independent on a. Finally, we note that in the executions of protocol $\mathcal{P}_m$, we set statistical parameter $\lambda_m = \lambda + \lceil \log(2a) \rceil$, where λ is the statistical parameter desired for protocol $\mathcal{P}_e$, to guarantee enough verification confidence for all (up to) $2a$ squares or multiplications.

Formal Description of $\mathcal{P}_{e,pub}$. By $\mathcal{P}_m = (\text{Offline}_m, S_m, C_m)$ we denote a protocol for the delegation of $a \cdot b \bmod n$ with statistical parameter λ_m, where a and b are public online, such as the protocol in Appendix B. In particular, the notation $(q, r) \leftarrow S_m(out, a, b)$ refers to an execution of the $\mathcal{P}_m$ server's algorithm with offline-phase input out and online-phase inputs a, b, returning message (q, r) for C, such that $a \cdot b = q \cdot n + r$, where $0 \le r < n$. Similarly, the notation $d \leftarrow C_m(out, q, r)$ refers to an execution of the $\mathcal{P}_m$ client's algorithm with offline-phase input out, online-phase inputs a, b, and server's message (q, r), and returning decision bit d where $d = 1/0$ depending on whether C_m accepts/does not accept the statement $r = a \cdot b \mod n$. We now formally describe protocol $\mathcal{P}_{e,pub}$ to delegate small-exponent exponentiation $\mathsf{seExp}_{n,e,a}(x) = x^e \mod n$ in a group $\mathbb{Z}_n^*$, where x is public online and e is public offline.

Offline Input: $1^\sigma, 1^\lambda, 1^a, \ n \in \{0, 1\}^\sigma$, public exponent $e \in \{0, 1\}^a$
Offline phase of $\mathcal{P}_e$:

1. Run the offline-phase algorithm $\mathsf{Offline}_m$ from protocol $\mathcal{P}_m$
2. Store the resulting output out on C's device

Online Input to C and S: $1^\sigma, 1^\lambda, 1^a, \ n \in \{0, 1\}^\sigma$, $x \in \mathbb{Z}_n^*$, $e \in \{0, 1\}^a$
Online phase of $\mathcal{P}_e$:

1. S sets $z = x$, $y = 1$ and $i = 1$
2. While $e > 1$ do
    if e is even then
        S computes $(q_{1i}, r_{1i}) = S_m(z, z)$
        S sets $z = r_{i1}$, $q_{2i} = r_{2i} = 0$, $i = i + 1$ and $e = e/2$
    if e is odd then
        S computes $(q_{1i}, r_{1i}) = S_m(z, y)$ and $(q_{2i}, r_{2i}) = S_m(z, z)$
        S sets $y = r_{i1}$, $z = r_{i2}$, $i = i + 1$ and $e = (e - 1)/2$
3. S computes $(q, r) = S_m(z, y)$
4. S sends $((q_{11}, r_{11}, q_{21}, r_{21}), \ldots, (q_{1a}, r_{1a}, q_{2a}, r_{2a}), (q, r))$ to C
5. C sets $y = 1$ and $i = 1$
6. While $e > 1$ do
    if e is even then
        C computes $d_{1i} = C_m(out, q_{1i}, r_{1i})$
        if $d_{1i} = 0$ then C halts
        else C sets $z = r_{i1}$, $i = i + 1$ and $e = e/2$
    if e is odd then
        C computes $d_{1i} = C_m(out, q_{1i}, r_{1i})$ and $d_{2i} = C_m(out, q_{2i}, r_{2i})$
        if $d_{1i} = 0$ or $d_{2i} = 0$ then C halts
        else C sets $y = r_{i1}$, $z = r_{i2}$, $i = i + 1$ and $e = (e - 1)/2$
7. C computes $l = C_m(out, q, r)$
8. If $l = 0$ then C halts else C **returns:** $y = r$

Properties of $\mathcal{P}_{e,pub}$. The efficiency properties of $\mathcal{P}_{e,pub}$ follow by protocol inspection, and by observing that $\mathcal{P}_{e,pub}$ runs $\mathcal{P}_m$ up to $2a$ times, with statistical parameter $\lambda_m = \lambda + \lceil \log(2a) \rceil$. In particular, we note that: (1) the online phase of $\mathcal{P}_{e,pub}$ consists of a single round message complexity from C to S and then followed by S to C since it parallelizes the $\le 2a$ executions of protocol $\mathcal{P}_m$; (2) the offline phase runtime includes the runtime of one execution of the offline phase of $\mathcal{P}_m$; only one thanks to the unbounded security of $\mathcal{P}_m$.

The 1-*correctness* property of $\mathcal{P}_{e,pub}$ follows by observing that at the end of the protocol C can compute $y = x^e \mod n$ with probability 1. This follows by combining these 2 facts: (1) At the end of each execution of subprotocol $\mathcal{P}_m$ on input (a, b), C can compute $a \cdot b \mod n$; (2) If subprotocol $\mathcal{P}_m$ allows C to obtain a (delegated) computation of multiplication $\mod n$, then protocol $\mathcal{P}_{e,pub}$ allows C to obtain a (delegated) computation of the output of the iterative version of the square-and-multiply algorithm for exponentiation $\mod n$ and obtain $r = z^e \mod n = x^e \mod n$. Fact (1) follows from the 1-correctness of subprotocol $\mathcal{P}_m$. Fact (2) follows by induction on variable i in the while loops in protocol $\mathcal{P}_e$, after observing that protocol $\mathcal{P}_{e,pub}$ realizes the square-and-multiply algorithm, where computation of multiplications is delegated via $\mathcal{P}_m$.

The *unbounded* $2^{-\lambda}$-*security* property of $\mathcal{P}_{e,pub}$ follows from the 1-correctness property of $\mathcal{P}_{e,pub}$, the unbounded $2^{-\lambda}$-security property of protocol $\mathcal{P}_m$ and the setting $\lambda_m = \lambda + \lceil \log(2a) \rceil$. First, we observe that if S returns correct values when running protocol $\mathcal{P}_m$, then the 1-correctness property implies that C returns a correct output $y = x^e \mod n$ with probability 1. Thus, the probability ϵ_s that C accepts a value $y \neq x^e \mod n$ is upper bounded by the probability that C accepts an incorrect result in any one of the $\leq 2a$ executions of protocol $\mathcal{P}_m$. By a union bound, we have that

$$\epsilon_s \leq \sum_{i=1}^{2a} \frac{1}{2^{\lambda_m}} \leq \sum_{i=1}^{2a} \frac{1}{2^{\lambda + \lceil \log(2a) \rceil}} \leq \frac{1}{2^\lambda} \sum_{i=1}^{2a} \frac{1}{2a} = 2^{-\lambda}.$$

References

1. Abadi, M., Feigenbaum, J., Kilian, J.: On hiding information from an oracle. In J. Comput. Syst. Sci. **39**(1), 21–50 (1989)
2. Bouillaguet, C., Martinez, F., Vergnaud, D.: Cryptanalysis of modular exponentiation outsourcing protocols. Comput. J. **65**(9), 2299–2314 (2022)
3. Canard, S., Devigne, J., Sanders, O.: Delegating a pairing can be both secure and efficient. In: Boureanu, I., Owesarski, P., Vaudenay, S. (eds.) ACNS 2014. LNCS, vol. 8479, pp. 549–565. Springer, Cham (2014). https://doi.org/10.1007/978-3-319-07536-5_32
4. Cavallo, B., Di Crescenzo, G., Kahrobaei, D., Shpilrain, V.: Efficient and secure delegation of group exponentiation to a single server. In: Mangard, S., Schaumont, P. (eds.) RFIDSec 2015. LNCS, vol. 9440, pp. 156–173. Springer, Cham (2015). https://doi.org/10.1007/978-3-319-24837-0_10
5. Chen, X., Li, J., Ma, J., Tang, Q., Lou, W.: New algorithms for secure outsourcing of modular exponentiations. Comput. Secur.-ESORICS **2012**, 541–556 (2012)
6. Chevallier-Mames, B., Coron, J.-S., McCullagh, N., Naccache, D., Scott, M.: Secure delegation of elliptic-curve pairing. In: Gollmann, D., Lanet, J.-L., Iguchi-Cartigny, J. (eds.) CARDIS 2010. LNCS, vol. 6035, pp. 24–35. Springer, Heidelberg (2010). https://doi.org/10.1007/978-3-642-12510-2_3. eprint.iacr.org/2005/150
7. Chevalier, C., Laguillaumie, F., Vergnaud, D.: Privately outsourcing exponentiation to a single server: cryptanalysis and optimal constructions. Algorithmica **83**, 72–115 (2021). also, Proc. ESORICS '16: 261–278, Springer
8. Di Crescenzo, G., Khodjaeva, M., Kahrobaei, D., Shpilrain, V.: Practical and secure outsourcing of discrete log group exponentiation to a single malicious server. In: Proceedings of 9th ACM CCSW, pp. 17–28 (2017)

9. Di Crescenzo, G., Khodjaeva, M., Kahrobaei, D., Shpilrain, V.: Efficient and secure delegation of exponentiation in general groups to a single malicious server. Math. Comput. Sci. **14**(3), 641–656 (2020). Also in IMCS 2018
10. Di Crescenzo, G., Khodjaeva, M., Kahrobaei, D., Shpilrain, V.: Secure delegation to a single malicious server: exponentiation in RSA-type Groups. In: Proceedings of 7th IEEE Conference on Communications and Network Security, CNS 2019, pp. 1–9 (2019)
11. Di Crescenzo, G., Khodjaeva, M., Kahrobaei, D., Shpilrain, V.: Secure and efficient delegation of elliptic-curve pairing. In: Conti, M., Zhou, J., Casalicchio, E., Spognardi, A. (eds.) ACNS 2020. LNCS, vol. 12146, pp. 45–66. Springer, Cham (2020). https://doi.org/10.1007/978-3-030-57808-4_3
12. Di Crescenzo, G., Khodjaeva, M., Kahrobaei, D., Shpilrain, V.: Secure and efficient delegation of pairings with online inputs. In: Liardet, P.-Y., Mentens, N. (eds.) CARDIS 2020. LNCS, vol. 12609, pp. 84–99. Springer, Cham (2021). https://doi.org/10.1007/978-3-030-68487-7_6
13. Di Crescenzo, G., Khodjaeva, M., Shpilrain, V., Kahrobaei, D., Krishnan, R.: Single-server delegation of ring multiplications from quasilinear-time clients. In: Proceedings of 14th International Conference on Security of Information and Networks (SIN), pp. 1–8 (2021)
14. Di Crescenzo, G., Khodjaeva, M., Kahrobaei, D., Shpilrain, V.: A survey on delegated computation. In: Proceedings of DLT 2022. LNCS, vol. 13257, pp. 33–53. Springer, Heidelberg (2022). https://doi.org/10.1007/978-3-031-05578-2_3
15. Di Crescenzo, G., Khodjaeva, M., Krishnan, R., Shur, D.: Single-server delegation of small-exponent exponentiation from quasi-linear clients and applications. In: Proceedings of the ACM CCS 4th Workshop on CPS & IoT Security (CPSIoTSec 2022) (2022)
16. Dijk, M., Clarke, D., Gassend, B., Suh, G., Devadas, S.: Speeding up exponentiation using an untrusted computational resource. Des. Codes Cryptogr. **39**(2), 253–273 (2006)
17. Ding, Y., Xu, Z., Ye, J., Choo, K.-K.R.: Secure outsourcing of modular exponentiations under single untrusted program model. Int. J. Comput. Syst. Sci. **90**, 1–13 (2017)
18. Feigenbaum, J.: Encrypting problem instances: or ..., can you take advantage of someone without having to trust him? In: Williams, H.C. (ed.) CRYPTO 1985. LNCS, vol. 218, pp. 477–488. Springer, Heidelberg (1986). https://doi.org/10.1007/3-540-39799-X_38
19. Fu, A., Li, S., Yu, S., Zhang, Y., Sun, Y.: Privacy-preserving composite modular exponentiation outsourcing with optimal checkability in single untrusted cloud server. J. Netw. Comp. App. **118**, 102–112 (2018)
20. Fu, A., Zhu, Y., Yang, G., Yu, S., Yu, Y.: Secure outsourcing algorithms of modular exponentiations with optimal checkability based on a single untrusted cloud server. Cluster Comput. **21**, 1933–1947 (2018)
21. Galbraith, S.: Mathematics of Public-Key Cryptography. Cambridge Press, Cambridge (2018). version 2.0
22. Gennaro, R., Gentry, C., Parno, B.: Non-interactive verifiable computing: outsourcing computation to untrusted workers. In: Rabin, T. (ed.) CRYPTO 2010. LNCS, vol. 6223, pp. 465–482. Springer, Heidelberg (2010). https://doi.org/10.1007/978-3-642-14623-7_25
23. Hohenberger, S., Lysyanskaya, A.: How to securely outsource cryptographic computations. In: Kilian, J. (ed.) TCC 2005. LNCS, vol. 3378, pp. 264–282. Springer, Heidelberg (2005). https://doi.org/10.1007/978-3-540-30576-7_15

24. Horng, G.: A secure server-aided RSA signature computation protocol for smart cards. J. Inf. Sci. Eng. **16**, 847–855 (2000)
25. Kaminski, M.: A note on probabilistically verifying integer and polynomial products. J. ACM **36**(1), 142–149 (1989)
26. Kawamura, S., Shimbo, A.: Fast server-aided secret computation protocols for modular exponentiation. IEEE J. Sel. Areas Commun. **11**(5), 778–784 (1993)
27. Ma, X., Li, J., Zhang, F.: Outsourcing computation of modular exponentiations in cloud computing. Cluster Comput. **16**(4), 787–796 (2013)
28. Matsumoto, T., Kato, K., Imai, H.: Speeding up secret computations with insecure auxiliary devices. In: Goldwasser, S. (ed.) CRYPTO 1988. LNCS, vol. 403, pp. 497–506. Springer, New York (1990). https://doi.org/10.1007/0-387-34799-2_35
29. Mefenza, T., Vergnaud, D.: Cryptanalysis of server-aided RSA protocols with private-key splitting. Comput. J. **62**(8), 1194–1213 (2019)
30. Meulenaer, G., Gosset, F., Standaert, F.-X., Pereira, O.: On the energy cost of communication and cryptography in wireless sensor networks. In: IEEE International Conference on Wireless & Mobile Computing, Networking & Communication (2008)
31. Rangasamy, J., Kuppusamy, L.: Revisiting single-server algorithms for outsourcing modular exponentiation. In: Chakraborty, D., Iwata, T. (eds.) INDOCRYPT 2018. LNCS, vol. 11356, pp. 3–20. Springer, Cham (2018). https://doi.org/10.1007/978-3-030-05378-9_1
32. Ren, Y., Dong, M., Qian, Z., Zhang, X., Feng, G.: Efficient algorithm for secure outsourcing of modular exponentiation with single server. IEEE Trans. Cloud Comput. **9**, 145–154 (2021)
33. Su, Q., Zhang, R., Xue, R.: Secure outsourcing algorithms for composite modular exponentiation based on single untrusted cloud. Comput. J. **63**, 1271 (2020)
34. Wang, Y., et al.: Securely outsourcing exponentiations with single untrusted program for cloud storage. In: Kutyłowski, M., Vaidya, J. (eds.) ESORICS 2014. LNCS, vol. 8712, pp. 326–343. Springer, Cham (2014). https://doi.org/10.1007/978-3-319-11203-9_19
35. Wasserman, H., Blum, M.: Software reliability via run-time result-checking. J. ACM **44**(6), 826–849 (2019). Proceedings of IEEE FOCS 94, 2019
36. Ye, J., Wang, J.: Secure outsourcing of modular exponentiation with single untrusted server. In: 18th International Conference on Network-Based Information Systems (2015)
37. Yao, A.: A lower bound to palindrome recognition by probabilistic Turing Machines. Technical Report STAN-CS-77-647 (1977)
38. https://www.silabs.com/mcu/32-bit-microcontrollers/efm32-giant-gecko

Constructing Pairing Free Unbounded Inner Product Functional Encryption Schemes with Unbounded Inner Product Policy

Subhranil Dutta$^{(\boxtimes)}$, Ratna Dutta, and Sourav Mukhopadhyay

Department of Mathematics, Indian Institute of Technology Kharagpur, Kharagpur, India
subhranildutta@iitkgp.ac.in, {ratna,sourav}@maths.iitkgp.ac.in

Abstract. *Inner product functional encryption* (IPFE) is a promising advanced cryptographic primitive for the inner product function class that facilitates fine-grained access control of sensitive data in an untrusted cloud environment and has an expanding range of applications in the context of cloud security, health-record access control, network privacy, data security on mobile devices, Internet of Things (IoT) and many more. We address the open problem of constructing public key unbounded IPFE (UIPFE) schemes that do not use bilinear pairings. Our main results are as follows:

- We design the *first* post-quantum secure public key UIPFE scheme in the random oracle model with adaptive security based on the Learning With Errors (LWE) assumption with leads to low computation cost.
- Furthermore, we develop a public key *unbounded zero inner product predicate* **IPFE** (UZP-IPFE) scheme that allows a successful decryption if an inner product policy is satisfied. We support the conjectured security of our candidate by analysis and prove that the scheme achieves security in the *selective weak attribute-hiding* model under the LWE assumption. The scheme offers linear-size ciphertext and constant-size secret keys. We emphasize that our construction presents the *first* post-quantum secure UZP-IPFE scheme in an unbounded scenario preserving attribute-hiding property.

More interestingly, when contrasted with the existing similar schemes, all our schemes exhibit favourable results in terms of communication overhead and secret key size.

Keywords: Inner product functional encryption · unbounded · attribute-hiding

1 Introduction

Inner product functional encryption (IPFE) refers to a specific class of functional encryption (FE) [8] initiated by Abdalla et al. [1] where a sophisticated secret

© The Author(s), under exclusive license to Springer Nature Switzerland AG 2023
G. Bella et al. (Eds.): SecITC 2022, LNCS 13809, pp. 102–116, 2023.
https://doi.org/10.1007/978-3-031-32636-3_6

key sk_y corresponding to the vector $y \in \mathbb{Z}^\ell$ reveals the inner product $\langle x, y \rangle$ by decrypting the ciphertext ct_x associated with the message vector $x \in \mathbb{Z}^\ell$. Significant research efforts have been put into these constructs in various ways during the last few years, like [2,3,6,7,9,10,16]. Due to linear functionality, IPFE bears an inherent security loss. More explicitly, an adversary can learn the entire message vector x from ct_x using any set $\mathcal{S}$ of ℓ-secret keys queries. Abdalla et al. [2] mitigated the leakage by introducing fine-grained access control in IPFE or *attribute-based IPFE* (AB-IPFE) where the decryptor learns the inner product depending on an access policy. In such a scheme, a secret key $\mathsf{sk}_{y,v}$ and the ciphertext $\mathsf{ct}_{x,w}$ are generated corresponding to the key vector y, predicate v and the message vector x, attribute w, respectively. The decryption successfully recovers $\langle x, y \rangle$ if a relation $R(w, v)$ holds. Consequently, the adversary can not extract unwanted information about x from $\mathsf{ct}_{x,w}$ with the help of $\mathcal{S}$ if some of the associated secret keys correspond to a policy v such that $R(w, v)$ does not hold. Here, we focus on a specific subclass of AB-IPFE called *inner product predicate IPFE* (IP-IPFE), where a successful decryption happens only when the relation R (defined as the inner product between the predicate vector v and the attribute vector w) satisfies. It can be viewed as the composition between *predicate encryption* (PE) and IPFE. From the security perspective of IP-IPFE, *payload-hiding* is a primary requirement where the ciphertext hides only the message x. *Attribute-hiding* (AH) is a more robust security notion that guarantees the ciphertext $\mathsf{ct}_{w,x}$ hides both message x and attribute w vectors. One version of IP-IPFE is *zero IP-IPFE* (ZP-IPFE) where the decryptor can recover $\langle x, y \rangle$ by decrypting $\mathsf{ct}_{w,x}$ using a secret key $\mathsf{sk}_{v,y}$ if the policy $\langle w, v \rangle = 0$ holds.

Most of the IPFEs are 'bounded' as they can only compute the inner product between bounded length vectors, which are fixed while generating public parameters. *Unbounded IPFE* (UIPFE) is gaining interest as it enables public parameter generation without any prior information about the length of any vector. The first UIPFE schemes were concurrently and independently proposed by Dufour-Sans et al. [10] and Tomida et al. [16]. Dufour-Sans et al. [10] designed public key UIPFE constructions with the succinct public key, master secret key and the functional secret keys in the random oracle model, whereas Tomida et al. [16] presented *private and public* UIPFE schemes in the standard model. One observation is that all the constructions of UIPFE require the computation on a bilinear map. This motivates us to ask the following questions:

1. *Can we construct a public key **UIPFE** scheme without using a bilinear map?*
2. *Is it possible to construct a public unbounded **IPFE** scheme with an inner product policy whereby decryption outputs the inner product between the unbounded length of the key and message vectors only when the inner product between unbounded size attribute and predicate vectors vanishes?*

Our Contribution and Techniques. We affirmatively answer the above questions. To be more specific, using the underlying standard assumption, we build the concrete UIPFE schemes that follow.

1. Firstly, we present a public key UIPFE scheme based on LWE in the random oracle model with *adaptive indistinguishability* (Adp-IND) security. Adaptive

Table 1. Comparison among existing UFE schemes for linear policy/functions.

	$|ct|$	$|sk|$	#P	Pol. Func.	unbounded (att, msg)	Assum	Security	ROM /Std. Model
[13]	$(15|\mathcal{D}|+5)\cdot|\mathbb{G}_1|+|\mathbb{G}_T|$	$15|\mathcal{D}||\mathbb{G}_1|+5|\mathbb{G}_1|$	$|\mathcal{D}'|+1$	IP,×	√,×	DLIN	Adp-FAH	Std. Model
[10]	$(|\mathcal{D}|+1)|\mathbb{G}_1|$	$|\mathbb{G}_2|$	$|\mathcal{D}'|+1$	×,IP	×,√	DBDH	Sel-IND	ROM
[16]	$4|\mathcal{D}||\mathbb{G}_1|$	$4|\mathcal{D}'||\mathbb{G}_2|$	$|\mathcal{D}'|$	×,IP	×,√	SXDH	Fully-FH	Std. Model
	$7|\mathcal{D}||\mathbb{G}_1|$	$7|\mathcal{D}'||\mathbb{G}_2|$	$|\mathcal{D}'|$	×,IP	×,√	SXDH	Adp-IND	Std. Model
Our work	$\mathcal{O}(|\mathcal{D}|)\,|\mathbb{Z}_q|$	$\mathcal{O}(1)|\mathbb{Z}_q|$	–	×,IP	×,√	LWE	Adp-IND	ROM
	$\mathcal{O}(|\mathcal{D}|)|\mathbb{Z}_q|$	$\mathcal{O}(1)|\mathbb{Z}_q|$	–	IP,IP	√,√	LWE	Sel-WAH	ROM

Adp-FAH, Sel-IND, Fully-FH: adaptive full attribute-hiding, selective indistinguishability, fully functional-hiding; DLIN, DBDH, SXDH: decisional linear, decisional bilinear Diffie Hellman, symmetric external Diffie-Hellman; $|ct|$, $|sk|$: size of ciphertext, secret key; $|\mathcal{D}|$, $|\mathcal{D}'|$: size of message vector and key vector; $|\mathbb{G}_1|$, $|\mathbb{G}_2|$, $|\mathbb{G}_T|$: size of the an element of the group $\mathbb{G}_1$ and $\mathbb{G}_2$ respectively; ROM, Std. Model: random oracle model, standard model; Pol., Func., att, msg, IP: policy, functionality, attribute, message and inner product; q: large prime integer; #P: number of pairing computation

in the sense that the adversary can query for secret keys to the key generation oracle at any instant of security experiment. This scheme bears a constant size secret key and linear size ciphertext. For more details, we refer to the full version for the scheme and security analysis.

2. Next, we propose an unbounded ZP-IPFE (UZP-IPFE) which is a composition of UIPFE with an unbounded zero inner product policy. In other words, the decryption recovers $\langle x, y \rangle$ if the inner product between two unbounded predicate vector v and attribute vector w is zero. Our scheme achieves *selective weak attribute-hiding indistinguishability* (Sel-WAH-IND) security under the LWE assumption in the random oracle model. Note that, in selective security model, the adversary submits the challenge attribute pair before asking the secret keys, and weak-attribute hiding refers that the adversary is restricted to secret key query $\mathsf{sk}_{v,y}$ for the vector pair (v, y) such that $\langle w, v \rangle \neq 0$. For the details, we refer to Sect. 4 for the scheme and security analysis.

In Table 1, we depict the efficiency, functionality and hardness assumptions of our UIPFEs and compare the matrices with that of existing UFEs. In this study, the decryptor computes $\langle x, y \rangle$ between the message $x = (x_i)_{i \in \mathcal{D}}$ and key vector $y = (y_i)_{i \in \mathcal{D}'}$ whenever $\mathcal{D} = \mathcal{D}'$.

2   Unbounded Zero Predicate **IPFE**

Unbounded zero predicate inner product functional encryption UZP-IPFE = (Setup, KeyGen, Enc, Dec) scheme consists following PPT algorithms:

- Setup$(1^\lambda) \rightarrow$ (mpk, msk): On input a security parameter λ, this algorithm outputs a master public key mpk and a master secret key msk.
- KeyGen(mpk, msk, v, y) $\rightarrow \mathsf{sk}_{v,y}$: Takes mpk, msk, a key vector $y = (y_i)_{i \in \mathcal{D}_y} \in \mathcal{Y}_\lambda$ and a predicate vector $v = (v_i)_{i \in \mathcal{D}_v} \in \mathcal{V}_\lambda$ as input, this algorithm outputs secret key $\mathsf{sk}_{v,y}$ where $\mathcal{D}_y, \mathcal{D}_v \subseteq \mathbb{N}$ are the finite index sets of y and v respectively.

- $\mathsf{Enc}(\mathsf{mpk}, \boldsymbol{w}, \boldsymbol{x}) \to \mathsf{ct}_{w,x}$: On input mpk, a message vector $\boldsymbol{x} = (x_i)_{i \in \mathcal{D}_x} \in \mathcal{X}_\lambda$ with an attribute vector $\boldsymbol{w} = (w_i)_{i \in \mathcal{D}_w} \in \mathcal{W}_\lambda$, this algorithm outputs a ciphertext $\mathsf{ct}_{w,x}$ where $\mathcal{D}_x, \mathcal{D}_w \subseteq \mathbb{N}$ are the finite index sets of $\boldsymbol{x}$ and $\boldsymbol{w}$ respectively.
- $\mathsf{Dec}(\mathsf{mpk}, \mathsf{sk}_{v,y}, \mathsf{ct}_{w,x}) \to d$ or $\bot$: Using $\mathsf{sk}_{v,y}$ the algorithm decrypts $\mathsf{ct}_{w,x}$ and outputs a decrypted value $d \in \mathbb{Z}$ or a special symbol $\bot$ indicating failure.

Correctness: UZP-IPFE scheme is said to be *correct* if for all $\lambda \in \mathbb{N}$, $\boldsymbol{x} \in \mathcal{X}_\lambda$, $\boldsymbol{w} \in \mathcal{W}_\lambda$, $\boldsymbol{y} \in \mathcal{Y}_\lambda$, $\boldsymbol{v} \in \mathcal{V}_\lambda$ s.t $\mathcal{D}_x = \mathcal{D}_y$, $\mathcal{D}_w = \mathcal{D}_v$ and $\langle \boldsymbol{w}, \boldsymbol{v} \rangle = 0$ we have

$$\Pr\left[d = \sum_{i \in \mathcal{D}_x \cap \mathcal{D}_y} x_i y_i \left| \begin{array}{l} (\mathsf{mpk}, \mathsf{msk}) \leftarrow \mathsf{UZP\text{-}IPFE.Setup}(1^\lambda) \\ \mathsf{sk}_{v,y} \leftarrow \mathsf{UZP\text{-}IPFE.KeyGen}(\mathsf{mpk}, \mathsf{msk}, v, y) \\ \mathsf{ct}_{w,x} \leftarrow \mathsf{UZP\text{-}IPFE.Enc}(\mathsf{mpk}, w, x) \\ d \leftarrow \mathsf{UZP\text{-}IPFEDec}(\mathsf{mpk}, \mathsf{sk}_{v,y}, \mathsf{ct}_{w,x}) \end{array} \right. \right] \geq 1 - \mathsf{negl}(\lambda)$$

Note that the notion of public UIPFE (pubUIPFE) is a particular case of UZP-IPFE if we simply ignore predicate $\boldsymbol{v}$, attribute vector $\boldsymbol{w}$ used in above syntax.

Definitiom 1 (*Sel-WAH-IND* security). *The selective weak attribute-hiding indistinguishability-based* (Sel-WAH-IND) *security for an* UZP-IPFE = (UZP-IPFE. *Setup,* UZP-IPFE.KeyGen, UZP-IPFE.Enc, UZP-IPFE.Dec) *is formalized by the following experiment* $\mathsf{Expt}^{\mathsf{Sel\text{-}WAH\text{-}IND}}_{\mathcal{A}, \mathsf{UZP\text{-}IPFE}}(\lambda)$ *between the adversary* $\mathcal{A}$ *and challenger* $\mathcal{B}$.

Setup: *A first submits two distinct challenge attribute vectors* $\boldsymbol{w}^{(0)}, \boldsymbol{w}^{(1)}$ *with the same index set* $\mathcal{D}_{w^{(0)}} = \mathcal{D}_{w^{(1)}} = \mathcal{D}_w$ *(say) to* $\mathcal{B}$ *who in turn generates* $(\mathsf{mpk}, \mathsf{msk}) \leftarrow \mathsf{UZP\text{-}IPFE.Setup}(1^\lambda)$ *and sends* mpk *to* $\mathcal{A}$.

Key query phase: *The adversary* $\mathcal{A}$ *is allowed to make adaptively the following queries polynomially many times.*

– Key queries: *The adversary* $\mathcal{A}$ *sends* $\boldsymbol{y} = (y_i)_{i \in \mathcal{D}_y} \in \mathcal{Y}_\lambda$, $\boldsymbol{v} = (v_i)_{i \in \mathcal{D}_v} \in \mathcal{V}_\lambda$ *to* $\mathcal{B}$ *for the secret key such that* $\langle \boldsymbol{v}, \boldsymbol{w}^{(0)} \rangle \neq 0, \langle \boldsymbol{v}, \boldsymbol{w}^{(1)} \rangle \neq 0$. *In response,* $\mathcal{B}$ *forms* $\mathsf{sk}_{v,y} \leftarrow \mathsf{UZP\text{-}IPFE.KeyGen}(\mathsf{mpk}, \mathsf{msk}, v, y)$ *and hands it to* $\mathcal{A}$.

Challenge phase: *The adversary* $\mathcal{A}$ *submits two distinct message vectors* $\boldsymbol{x}^{(0)} = (x_i^{(0)})_{i \in \mathcal{D}_{x^{(0)}}} \in \mathcal{X}_\lambda$ *and* $\boldsymbol{x}^{(1)} = (x_i^{(1)})_{i \in \mathcal{D}_{x^{(1)}}} \in \mathcal{X}_\lambda$ *with same index set* $\mathcal{D}_{x^{(0)}} = \mathcal{D}_{x^{(1)}} = \mathcal{D}_x$. *If* $\langle \boldsymbol{v}, \boldsymbol{w}^{(0)} \rangle = \langle \boldsymbol{v}, \boldsymbol{w}^{(1)} \rangle = 0$ *for any key queried vector* $\boldsymbol{y} \in \mathcal{Y}_\lambda, \boldsymbol{v} \in \mathcal{V}_\lambda$, *then it is required that* $\langle \boldsymbol{x}^{(0)}, \boldsymbol{y} \rangle = \langle \boldsymbol{x}^{(1)}, \boldsymbol{y} \rangle$. *The challenger* $\mathcal{B}$ *randomly selects a bit* β *from* $\{0,1\}$, *notationally,* $\beta \xleftarrow{\$} \{0,1\}$ *and computes the challenge ciphertext* $\mathsf{ct}_{w^{(\beta)}, x^{(\beta)}} \leftarrow \mathsf{UZP\text{-}IPFE.Enc}(\mathsf{mpk}, \boldsymbol{w}^{(\beta)}, \boldsymbol{x}^{(\beta)})$ *and gives it to* $\mathcal{A}$.

$\mathcal{A}$ *can again make secret key queries corresponding to the vectors* $\boldsymbol{y}$ *and* $\boldsymbol{v}$ *with the same restrictions as mentioned in the key query phase.*

Guess: $\mathcal{A}$ *guesses a bit* β' *and the experiment outputs 1 if* $\beta = \beta'$.

An UZP-IPFE *scheme is said to be Sel-WAH-IND secure if for all* PPT *adversary* $\mathcal{A}$, *there exists a negligible function* negl *such that for all* $\lambda \in \mathbb{N}$,

$$\mathsf{Adv}^{\mathsf{Sel\text{-}WAH\text{-}IND}}_{\mathcal{A}}(\lambda) = |\Pr[\mathsf{Expt}^{\mathsf{Sel\text{-}WAH\text{-}IND}}_{\mathcal{A}, \mathsf{UZP\text{-}IPFE}}(\lambda) = 1]| \leq \frac{1}{2} + \mathsf{negl}(\lambda)$$

2.1   Lattices Preliminaries [2,5]

We recall here some important Theorems, Lemmas, and due to space constraints, other preliminaries will be included in the full version.

Lemma 1 *[15]. Let $q = q(n)$ be a prime and $\alpha = \alpha(n) \in (0, 1)$ satisfies $\alpha \cdot q > 2\sqrt{n}$. If there exists an efficient algorithm that can solve $\mathsf{LWE}_{q,\alpha,n}$, then there exists an efficient quantum algorithm for approximating the shortest independent vectors problem (SIVP) and decisional version of the shortest vector problem (GapSVP) in the ℓ_2 norm, in the worst case, to within $\mathcal{O}(n/\alpha)$ factors.*

Learning with errors (LWE) [15]: Let q be a prime, α be a real number and $s \xleftarrow{\$} \mathbb{Z}_q^n$. The oracles $\mathcal{O}_s$ or $\mathcal{O}_\$$ is defined as:

- $\mathcal{O}_s$ outputs $(a, a^\top s + x)$ where $a \xleftarrow{\$} \mathbb{Z}_q^n$, $x \xleftarrow{\$} \mathfrak{D}_{\mathbb{Z}_q,\alpha q}$[1] are fresh and independently sampled. The oracle $\mathcal{O}_\$$ outputs uniform elements from $\mathbb{Z}_q^n \times \mathbb{Z}_q$.

Define a oracle $\mathcal{O}$ which is either $\mathcal{O}_s$ or $\mathcal{O}_\$$ across all calls. The $\mathsf{LWE}_{q,\alpha,n}$ problem is to distinguish between the oracles $\mathcal{O}_s$ or $\mathcal{O}_\$$ given access to oracle $\mathcal{O}$.

Lemma 2 *[5]. Let q, n, m be positive integers with $q \geq 2$ and $m \geq 6n \log q$. Then there is a PPT algorithm $\mathsf{TrapGen}(1^n, 1^m, q)$ that outputs a pair $(\mathbf{A} \in \mathbb{Z}_q^{n \times m}, \mathbf{T_A} \in \mathbb{Z}_q^{m \times m})$ such that $\mathbf{A}$ is statistically close to uniform in $\mathbb{Z}_q^{n \times m}$ and $\mathbf{T_A}$ is a basis for $\Lambda_q^\perp(\mathbf{A})$ satisfying $\|\widetilde{\mathbf{T}}_\mathbf{A}\| \leq \mathcal{O}(\sqrt{n \log q})$ and $\|\mathbf{T_A}\| \leq \mathcal{O}(n \log q)$ with overwhelming probability in n.*

Lemma 3   (Sampling algorithm *[2,4]). We now discuss two sampling algorithms to sample a short vector from a specified lattices.*

- $\mathsf{SamplePre}(\mathbf{A}, \mathbf{T_A}, \sigma, \mathbf{U}) \to \mathbf{Z}$: *On input a matrix $\mathbf{A} \in \mathbb{Z}_q^{n \times m}$, trapdoor $\mathbf{T_A} \in \mathbb{Z}_q^{m \times m}$, any $\sigma \geq L \cdot \omega(\sqrt{\log n})$ and randomly chosen $\mathbf{U} \in \mathbb{Z}_q^{n \times \ell}$, this algorithm outputs a matrix $\mathbf{Z} \in \mathbb{Z}^{m \times \ell}$ such that $\mathbf{U} = \mathbf{A} \cdot \mathbf{Z}$. Additionally, the following two distributions are statistically close.[2]*

$$\left\{ (\mathbf{A}, \mathbf{Z}, \mathbf{U}) \,\middle|\, \begin{array}{l} (\mathbf{A}, \mathbf{T_A}) \leftarrow \mathsf{TrapGen}(1^n, 1^m, q), \\ \mathbf{Z} \leftarrow \mathsf{SamplePre}(\mathbf{A}, \mathbf{T_A}, \sigma, \mathbf{U}) \\ where\ \mathbf{U} \xleftarrow{\$} \mathbb{Z}^{n \times \ell} \end{array} \right\} \approx_s \left\{ (\mathbf{A}, \mathbf{Z}, \mathbf{A} \cdot \mathbf{Z}) \,\middle|\, \begin{array}{l} \mathbf{A} \xleftarrow{\$} \mathbb{Z}_q^{n \times m}, \mathbf{Z} \xleftarrow{\$} \mathfrak{D}_{\mathbb{Z}^{m \times \ell}, \sigma} \\ \|z_i\| \leq \sigma\sqrt{m}\ \forall i \in [\ell]\ where\ z_i \\ denotes\ the\ i\text{-}th\ column\ of\ \mathbf{Z}. \end{array} \right\}$$

- $\mathsf{Sampleleft}(\mathbf{A}, \mathbf{B}, \mathbf{T_A}, u, \sigma)$: *On input the matrix $\mathbf{A} \in \mathbb{Z}_q^{n \times m}$, a 'good basis' $\mathbf{T_A} \in \Lambda_q^\perp(\mathbf{A})$, a matrix $\mathbf{B} \in \mathbb{Z}_q^{n \times m_1}$, $u \in \mathbb{Z}_q^n$ and a Gaussian parameter σ, the algorithm outputs a vector $\mathbf{e} \in \mathbb{Z}^{(m + m_1)}$ distributed statistically close to $\Lambda_q^u(\mathbf{F})$ satisfying $\mathbf{F} \cdot \mathbf{e} = u$ where $\mathbf{F} = (\mathbf{A} \| \mathbf{B})$.*

---

[1] Here $\mathfrak{D}_{\mathbb{Z}_q,\alpha q}$ is the discrete Gaussian distribution [5] over $\mathbb{Z}_q$ with center 0 with standard deviation αq and $\widetilde{\mathbf{R}}$ stands the Gram-Schmidt orthogonalization.

[2] For a vector u and matrix $\mathbf{W}$, $\|u\|$ represents the ℓ_2 norm and $\|\mathbf{W}\|$ represents ℓ_2 norm of the longest column of $\mathbf{W}$.

- Sampleright($\mathbf{A}, \mathbf{B}, \mathbf{R}, \mathbf{T_B}, \boldsymbol{u}, \sigma$): *On input the matrices* $\mathbf{A} \in \mathbb{Z}_q^{n \times k}$, $\mathbf{R} \in \{-1, 1\}^{k \times m}$, *a full rank matrix* $\mathbf{B} \in \mathbb{Z}_q^{n \times m}$ *with its 'good basis'* $\mathbf{T_B} \in \Lambda_q^\perp(\mathbf{B})$, *a vector* $\boldsymbol{u} \in \mathbb{Z}_q^n$ *and a Gaussian parameter* σ, *the algorithm outputs a vector* $\mathfrak{e} \in \mathbb{Z}^{(m+k)}$ *distributed statistically close to* $\Lambda_q^{\boldsymbol{u}}(\mathbf{F})$ *satisfying* $\mathbf{F} \cdot \mathfrak{e} = \boldsymbol{u}$ *where* $\mathbf{F} = (\mathbf{A} || \mathbf{AR} + \mathbf{B})$.

Theorem 1. *Let* $q > 2, n < m, \sigma > ||\widetilde{\mathbf{T}}_\mathbf{A}|| \cdot \omega(\sqrt{\log(m + m_1)})$. *Then the algorithm* Sampleleft *outputs a vector* $\mathfrak{e} \in \mathbb{Z}^{(m+m_1)}$ *distributed statistically close to* $\mathfrak{D}_{\Lambda_q^{\boldsymbol{u}}(\mathbf{F}),\sigma}$ *where* $\mathbf{F} = (\mathbf{A} || \mathbf{B})$.

Theorem 2. *Let* $q > 2, n < m, \sigma > ||\widetilde{\mathbf{T}}_\mathbf{A}|| \cdot s_\mathbf{R} \cdot \omega(\sqrt{\log m})$. *Then the algorithm* Sampleright *outputs a vector* $\mathfrak{e} \in \mathbb{Z}^{(m+k)}$ *distributed statistically close to* $\mathfrak{D}_{\Lambda_q^{\boldsymbol{u}}(\mathbf{F}),\sigma}$ *where* $\mathbf{F} = (\mathbf{A} || \mathbf{AR} + \mathbf{B})$. *Note that,* $s_\mathbf{R}$ *is defined as* $s_\mathbf{R} = \sup_{||\boldsymbol{x}|| \in S^{m-1}} ||\mathbf{R}\boldsymbol{x}||$ *where* S^m *is the m-sphere defined as* $\{||\boldsymbol{x}|| \in \mathbb{R}^{m+1} : ||\boldsymbol{x}|| = 1\}$.

Lemma 4. *[11] If* $\mathbf{S} \xleftarrow{\$} \{-1, 1\}^{r \times k}$, *then* $\Pr[||\mathbf{S}|| > 12\sqrt{r + k}] \leq e^{-(k+r)}$.

Lemma 5. *Consider a matrix* $\mathbf{R}$ *be chosen uniformly in* $\mathbb{Z}_q^{m \times k}$ mod q *where* $k = k(n)$ *and satisfies* $m > (n + 1) \log q + \omega(\log n)$ *with* $q > 2$ *is square free. Let* $\mathbf{A} \in \mathbb{Z}_q^{n \times m}$, $\mathbf{B} \in \mathbb{Z}_q^{n \times k}$ *be matrices chosen uniformly random. Then for all vectors* $\boldsymbol{v} \in \mathbb{Z}_q^m$, *then* $(\mathbf{A}, \mathbf{AR}, \mathbf{R}^\top \boldsymbol{v}) \approx_s (\mathbf{A}, \mathbf{B}, \mathbf{R}^\top \boldsymbol{v})$.

Lemma 6 (Bounding Gaussian Noise). *[12] Let* Λ *be an n-dimensional lattice with center* $\boldsymbol{c} \in \text{span}(\Lambda)$ *(where* $\text{span}(\Lambda) = \{\mathbf{B}\boldsymbol{y} : \boldsymbol{y} \in \mathbb{R}^n\}$, $\mathbf{B}$ *being the basis of* Λ), $\epsilon \in (0, 1) \cap \mathbb{R}$ *and* $\sigma \geq \eta_\epsilon(\Lambda)$ *where* $\eta_\epsilon(\Lambda)$ *be smoothing parameter[3] of n-dimensional lattice* Λ. *Then* $\Pr[||\boldsymbol{x} - \boldsymbol{c}|| > \sigma \cdot \sqrt{n}] \leq \frac{1+\epsilon}{1-\epsilon} \cdot \frac{1}{2^n}$ *for all* $\boldsymbol{x} \xleftarrow{\$} \mathfrak{D}_{\Lambda,\sigma,\boldsymbol{c}}$.

3 Our LWE Based pubUIPFE

In this section, we present our pubUIPFE scheme integrating the technique of ALS-IPFE scheme [6]. Our UIPFE scheme has the message space $\mathcal{X}_\lambda$ over the set $\{0, 1, \ldots, P(\lambda) - 1\}$ and the secret keys space $\mathcal{Y}_\lambda$ over the set $\{0, 1, \ldots, V(\lambda) - 1\}$. The length of message and the secret key vectors are $< \ell_{\max}$ for some integer $\ell_{\max}$. Consider a hash function $\mathcal{H} : \mathbb{N} \rightarrow \mathbb{Z}_q^n$ and $\langle \boldsymbol{x}, \boldsymbol{y} \rangle < K$ where $K = \text{poly}(\lambda)$.

- Setup(1^λ) → (mpk, msk): The algorithm works as follows:

  - Defines the parameters $n = n(\lambda), m = m(\lambda)$ and $q = q(\lambda)$.
  - Runs TrapGen($1^n, 1^m, q$) → $(\mathbf{A}, \mathbf{T_A})$ such that $\mathbf{A} \in \mathbb{Z}_q^{n \times m}$ and outputs mpk $= (n, m, \mathbf{A}, P, V, K, q, \sigma, \alpha, \rho, \mathcal{H})$, and msk $= \mathbf{T_A} \in \mathbb{Z}_q^{m \times m}$.

- KeyGen(mpk, msk, $\boldsymbol{y} \in \mathcal{Y}_\lambda$) → sk$_{\boldsymbol{y}}$: This algorithm works as follows:

---

[3] The smoothing parameter $\eta_\epsilon(\Lambda)$ to be the smallest s such that $\rho_{1/\sigma}(\Lambda^* - \{0\}) \leq \epsilon$ for n-dimensional lattice Λ and positive real ϵ.

- Computes the matrix $\mathbf{U}' = (\boldsymbol{u}_{i'_1} || \boldsymbol{u}_{i'_2} || \cdots || \boldsymbol{u}_{i'_{\ell'}}) \in \mathbb{Z}_q^{n \times \ell'}$ where $\boldsymbol{u}_{i'_j} = \mathcal{H}(i'_j) \in \mathbb{Z}_q^n$ for each $i'_j \in \mathcal{D}'$.
- Runs SamplePre $(\mathbf{A}, \mathbf{T_A}, \rho, \mathbf{U}') \to \mathbf{Z} \in \mathbb{Z}^{m \times \ell'}$ satisfying $\mathbf{U}' = \mathbf{A} \cdot \mathbf{Z} \in \mathbb{Z}^{n \times \ell'}$.
- Sets the secret key $\mathsf{sk}_{\boldsymbol{y}} = (\boldsymbol{y}, \boldsymbol{y}^\top \mathbf{Z}^\top)$.

• Enc(mpk, $\boldsymbol{x} \in \mathcal{X}_\lambda) \to \mathsf{ct}_{\boldsymbol{x}}$: This algorithm executes the following steps:

- Samples a column vector $\boldsymbol{s} \xleftarrow{\$} \mathbb{Z}_q^n$, $\boldsymbol{e}_1 \xleftarrow{\$} \mathfrak{D}_{\mathbb{Z}^m, \sigma}$ and $\boldsymbol{e}_2 \xleftarrow{\$} \mathfrak{D}_{\mathbb{Z}^\ell, \sigma}$.
- Computes $\mathbf{U} = (\boldsymbol{u}_{i_1} || \boldsymbol{u}_{i_2} || \cdots || \boldsymbol{u}_{i_\ell}) \in \mathbb{Z}_q^{n \times \ell}$ where $\boldsymbol{u}_{i_j} = \mathcal{H}(i_j) \in \mathbb{Z}_q^n \ \forall i_j \in \mathcal{D}$.
- Outputs the ciphertext $\mathsf{ct}_{\boldsymbol{x}} = (\boldsymbol{c}_1, \boldsymbol{c}_2)$ associated with the vector $\boldsymbol{x}$ as

$$\boldsymbol{c}_1 = \mathbf{A}^\top \boldsymbol{s} + \boldsymbol{e}_1 \in \mathbb{Z}_q^m, \quad \boldsymbol{c}_2 = \mathbf{U}^\top \boldsymbol{s} + \boldsymbol{e}_2 + \left\lfloor \frac{q}{K} \right\rfloor \boldsymbol{x} \in \mathbb{Z}_q^\ell$$

• Dec(mpk, $\mathsf{sk}_{\boldsymbol{y}}, \mathsf{ct}_{\boldsymbol{x}}) \to \mu / \perp$: Decryption proceeds as follows:

- Computes $\mu' = \boldsymbol{y}^\top \boldsymbol{c}_2 - (\boldsymbol{y}^\top \mathbf{Z}^\top) \boldsymbol{c}_1$ if $\mathcal{D} = \mathcal{D}'$ otherwise outputs $\perp$.
- Outputs $\mu \in \{0, 1, \ldots, K-1\}$ which minimizes $\left| \lfloor \frac{q}{K} \rfloor \cdot \mu - \mu' \right|$.

Correctness: If $\mathcal{D} = \mathcal{D}'$, then we have

$$\mu' = \boldsymbol{y}^\top \boldsymbol{c}_2 - (\boldsymbol{y}^\top \mathbf{Z}^\top) \boldsymbol{c}_1 = \left\lfloor \frac{q}{K} \right\rfloor \langle \boldsymbol{x}, \boldsymbol{y} \rangle + \boldsymbol{y}^\top \boldsymbol{e}_2 - (\boldsymbol{y}^\top \mathbf{Z}^\top) \boldsymbol{e}_1 = \left\lfloor \frac{q}{K} \right\rfloor \langle \boldsymbol{x}, \boldsymbol{y} \rangle + noise$$

By the SamplePre algorithm of Lemma 3, every column of $\mathbf{Z} \in \mathbb{Z}^{m \times \ell}$ is bounded above by $\rho \sqrt{m}$, i.e., $\|\mathbf{Z}\| \leq \rho \sqrt{m\ell}$ and $\|\boldsymbol{y}\| \leq V \sqrt{\ell}$ as $\boldsymbol{y} \in \mathcal{Y}_\lambda$. Since $\boldsymbol{e}_2 \xleftarrow{\$} \mathfrak{D}_{\mathbb{Z}^\ell, \sigma}$, we have $\|\boldsymbol{e}_2\| \leq \sqrt{\ell} \sigma$ as long as $\sigma \geq \omega(\sqrt{\log n})$. Therefore, $\|\boldsymbol{y}^\top \cdot \boldsymbol{e}_2\| \leq V \ell \sigma$. By the choice of parameter, $\sigma \geq 2C' \alpha q (\sqrt{m} + \sqrt{n} + \sqrt{\ell})$ and C' is a constant, and $\|(\boldsymbol{y}^\top \cdot \mathbf{Z}^\top) \cdot \boldsymbol{e}_1\| \leq \rho \sigma m \ell V$. Therefore, $|noise| \leq \rho \sigma m \ell V + V \ell \sigma$ with high probability. To ensure the correct decryption, we set $|noise| \leq \frac{q}{2K}$ which can be achieved by setting $q \geq 2K(\rho \sigma m \ell_{\max} V + V \ell_{\max} \sigma)$.

Parameter Setting. We first set the parameters n, m, q, ρ, σ as in ALS-IPFE of [2,14]. To fulfil the correctness of our pubUIPFE scheme, we modify our parameters accordingly to satisfy the ALS-IPFE parameters.

- For generating a short basis $\mathbf{T_A} \subset \Lambda_q^\perp(\mathbf{A})$ for a random matrix $\mathbf{A} \in \mathbb{Z}_q^{n \times m}$, run TrapGen$(1^n, 1^m, q)$ algorithm by setting $m \geq 6n \log q$ (see Lemma 2).
- For the algorithm SamplePre$(\mathbf{A}, \mathbf{T_A}, \rho, \mathbf{U})$, we set $\rho \geq L \cdot \omega(\sqrt{\log n})$ where $L = m^{2.5}$ (see Lemma 3).
- From the correctness of ALS-IPFE (as in [2,6,14]), we have $\sigma \geq \omega(\sqrt{\log n})$.
- For the hardness of LWE$_{q,\alpha,n}$ with $\alpha q > 2\sqrt{n}$, $\alpha \in (0,1) \cap \mathbb{R}$ (Lemma 1).
- The number α must satisfy $\alpha \leq \frac{\sigma}{2C'q(\sqrt{m}+\sqrt{n}+\sqrt{\ell_{\max}})}$ where C' is a constant.
- Prime $q > 2$ must satisfy $q \geq 2K(\rho \sigma m \ell_{\max} V + V \ell_{\max} \sigma)$ where $K = \ell_{\max} PV$. This does not mean that such upper bounds are required while generating system parameters. We sufficiently can chose a large prime q to make sure the above inequality holds and hence the correctness, security also follow[4].

Note that with this parameter setting of [2,6,14], ALS-IPFE is correct and secure..
Due the space constraints, we discuss the security proof in full version.

---

[4] Observe that, the bit-lengths of system parameters such as master keys and ciphertexts scale with $\log q$, but not q or the upper bounds $\ell_{\max}$.

4 Our LWE Based UZP-IPFE

We construct a UZP-IPFE scheme using the framework of predicate encryption of Agrawal et el. [5]. We consider the following hash functions $\mathcal{H}_1 : \mathbb{Z} \times ([k] \cup \{0\}) \to \mathbb{Z}_q^{n \times m}$, $\mathcal{H}_2 : \mathbb{Z} \to \mathbb{Z}_q^n$ which are modelled as random oracles in the security analysis. In addition, we consider $\langle x, y \rangle < K$ where $K = \text{poly}(\lambda)$.

- Setup$(1^\lambda) \to (\text{mpk}, \text{msk})$: The algorithm works as follows:

  - Defines the parameters $n = n(\lambda), m = m(\lambda), r = r(\lambda)$ and $q = q(\lambda)$.
  - Runs TrapGen$(1^n, 1^m, q) \to (\mathbf{A}, \mathbf{T_A})$ such that $\mathbf{A} \in \mathbb{Z}_q^{n \times m}$ and $\mathbf{T_A} \in \mathbb{Z}_q^{m \times m}$.
  - Outputs $\text{mpk} = (n, m, k = \lceil \log_r q \rceil, \mathbf{A}, q, \alpha, \sigma, P, V, r, K, \mathcal{H}_1, \mathcal{H}_2)$, $\text{msk} = \mathbf{T_A}$.

- KeyGen$(\text{mpk}, \text{msk}, \boldsymbol{v} \in \mathbb{Z}_q^{|\mathcal{D}_v|}, \boldsymbol{y} \in \mathcal{Y}_\lambda) \to \text{sk}_{\boldsymbol{v}, \boldsymbol{y}}$: The algorithm works as follows:

  - Sets $v_i \equiv \widehat{v}_i \mod q$ and expresses $\widehat{v}_i = \sum_{\gamma=0}^k v_{i,\gamma} r^\gamma$ where $v_{i,\gamma} \in [0, r-1] \cap \mathbb{Z}$ and computes $\mathcal{H}_1(i, \gamma) = \mathbf{A}_{i,\gamma} \in \mathbb{Z}_q^{n \times m} \; \forall \; i \in \mathcal{D}_v, \gamma \in \{0, 1, \ldots, k\} = [k] \cup \{0\}$.
  - Sets $\mathbf{C_v} = \sum_{i \in \mathcal{D}_v} \sum_{\gamma=0}^k v_{i,\gamma} \mathbf{A}_{i,\gamma} \in \mathbb{Z}_q^{n \times m}$ with $\mathbf{A_v} = (\mathbf{A} \parallel \mathbf{C_v}) \in \mathbb{Z}_q^{n \times 2m}$.
  - Runs Sampleleft$(\mathbf{A}, \mathbf{C_v}, \mathbf{T_A}, \boldsymbol{u}_j, \sigma) \to \mathbf{e}_j \in \mathbb{Z}^{2m}$ so that $(\mathbf{A} \parallel \mathbf{C_v}) \cdot \mathbf{e}_j = \boldsymbol{u}_j$ $\mod q$ for all $j \in \mathcal{D}_y$ where $\mathcal{H}_2(j) = \boldsymbol{u}_j \in \mathbb{Z}_q^n$ and generates $\mathbf{E} = (\mathbf{e}_{j_1} \parallel \mathbf{e}_{j_2} \parallel \cdots \parallel \mathbf{e}_{j_{|\mathcal{D}_y|}}) \in \mathbb{Z}^{2m \times |\mathcal{D}_y|}$ if $\mathcal{D}_y = \{j_1, j_2, \ldots, j_{|\mathcal{D}_y|}\}$.
  - Outputs the secret key $\text{sk}_{\boldsymbol{v}, \boldsymbol{y}} = (\boldsymbol{y}, \mathbf{E}\boldsymbol{y})$.

- Enc$(\text{mpk}, \boldsymbol{w} \in \mathbb{Z}_q^{|\mathcal{D}_w|}, \boldsymbol{x} \in \mathcal{X}_\lambda) \to \text{ct}_{\boldsymbol{w}, \boldsymbol{x}}$: The algorithm works as follows:

  - Chooses $\mathbf{B} \xleftarrow{\$} \mathbb{Z}_q^{n \times m}$ and $\boldsymbol{s} \xleftarrow{\$} \mathbb{Z}_q^n, \boldsymbol{e} \xleftarrow{\$} \mathfrak{D}_{\mathbb{Z}^m, \alpha}$.
  - Sets $\mathcal{H}_1(i, \gamma) = \mathbf{A}_{i,\gamma} \in \mathbb{Z}_q^{n \times m}$ and $\mathbf{R}_{i,\gamma} \xleftarrow{\$} \{-1, 1\}^{m \times m} \forall i \in \mathcal{D}_w, \gamma \in \{0, 1, \ldots, k\}$,
  - Computes $\boldsymbol{c}_0 = \mathbf{A}^\top \boldsymbol{s} + \boldsymbol{e} \in \mathbb{Z}_q^m; \boldsymbol{c}_{i,\gamma} = (\mathbf{A}_{i,\gamma} + r^\gamma w_i \mathbf{B})^\top \boldsymbol{s} + \mathbf{R}_{i,\gamma}^\top \boldsymbol{e} \in \mathbb{Z}_q^m$.
  - Generates $\mathbf{U} = (\boldsymbol{u}_{j_1} \parallel \boldsymbol{u}_{j_2} \parallel \cdots \parallel \boldsymbol{u}_{j_{|\mathcal{D}_x|}}) \in \mathbb{Z}_q^{n \times |\mathcal{D}_x|}$ where $\mathcal{H}_2(j_\iota) = \boldsymbol{u}_{j_\iota} \in \mathbb{Z}_q^n$ for all $j_\iota \in \mathcal{D}_x = \{j_1, j_2, \ldots, j_{|\mathcal{D}_x|}\}$.
  - Sets $\boldsymbol{c}' = \mathbf{U}^\top \boldsymbol{s} + \boldsymbol{x} \lfloor \frac{q}{K} \rfloor + \boldsymbol{f} \in \mathbb{Z}_q^{|\mathcal{D}_x|}$ where $\boldsymbol{f} \xleftarrow{\$} \mathfrak{D}_{\mathbb{Z}^{|\mathcal{D}_x|}, \alpha}$.
  - Outputs the ciphertext $\text{ct}_{\boldsymbol{w}, \boldsymbol{x}} = (\boldsymbol{c}_0, \{\boldsymbol{c}_{i,\gamma}\}_{i \in \mathcal{D}_w, \gamma \in ([k] \cup \{0\})}, \boldsymbol{c}')$.

- Dec$(\text{mpk}, \text{sk}_{\boldsymbol{v}, \boldsymbol{y}}, \text{ct}_{\boldsymbol{w}, \boldsymbol{x}}) \to d$ or $\perp$: It decrypts $\text{ct}_{\boldsymbol{w}, \boldsymbol{x}}$ using $\text{sk}_{\boldsymbol{v}, \boldsymbol{y}}$ as follows:

  - If $\mathcal{D}_v = \mathcal{D}_w, \mathcal{D}_y = \mathcal{D}_x$, then decryption proceeds, otherwise outputs $\perp$.
  - Computes $\boldsymbol{c}_v = \sum_{i \in \mathcal{D}_v} \sum_{\gamma=0}^k v_{i,\gamma} \boldsymbol{c}_{i,\gamma} \in \mathbb{Z}_q^m$.
  - Sets $\boldsymbol{c} = \begin{bmatrix} \boldsymbol{c}_0 \\ \boldsymbol{c}_v \end{bmatrix} \in \mathbb{Z}_q^{2m}$ and computes $z = \boldsymbol{y}^\top \boldsymbol{c}' - (\mathbf{E}\boldsymbol{y})^\top \boldsymbol{c}$.
  - Outputs $d \in \{0, 1, \ldots, K-1\}$ which minimizes $|\lfloor \frac{q}{K} \rfloor d - z|$.

Correctness: If $\mathcal{D}_v = \mathcal{D}_w, \mathcal{D}_y = \mathcal{D}_x$ with $\langle \boldsymbol{w}, \boldsymbol{v} \rangle = 0 \mod q$. We have

$$\boldsymbol{c}_v = \sum_{i \in \mathcal{D}_v} \sum_{\gamma=0}^k v_{i,\gamma} \boldsymbol{c}_{i,\gamma} = \mathbf{C}_v^\top \boldsymbol{s} + \langle \boldsymbol{w}, \boldsymbol{v} \rangle \mathbf{B}^\top \boldsymbol{s} + \sum_{i \in \mathcal{D}_v} \sum_{\gamma=0}^k v_{i,\gamma} \mathbf{R}_{i,\gamma}^\top \boldsymbol{e} \mod q$$

$$= \mathbf{C}_v^\top \boldsymbol{s} + \mathbf{R}_v \boldsymbol{e} \mod q \; [\text{Sets, } \mathbf{R}_v = \sum_{i \in \mathcal{D}_v} \sum_{\gamma=0}^k v_{i,\gamma} \mathbf{R}_{i,\gamma}^\top \text{ with } \langle \boldsymbol{w}, \boldsymbol{v} \rangle = 0]$$

Hence, $c = \begin{bmatrix} c_0 \\ c_v \end{bmatrix} = \begin{pmatrix} \mathbf{A}^\top s + e \\ \mathbf{C}_v^\top s + \mathbf{R}_v e \end{pmatrix} = \mathbf{A}_v^\top s + \begin{pmatrix} e \\ \mathbf{R}_v e \end{pmatrix} \mod q$. Therefore, $(\mathbf{E} \cdot y)^\top c = y^\top \mathbf{E}^\top \left[\mathbf{A}_v^\top s + \begin{pmatrix} e \\ \mathbf{R}_v e \end{pmatrix} \mod q \right] = y^\top \mathbf{U}^\top s + (\mathbf{E} \cdot y)^\top \begin{pmatrix} e \\ \mathbf{R}_v e \end{pmatrix} \mod q$. Also we have, $\mathbf{A}_v \mathbf{E} = \mathbf{U}$ since $\mathbf{A}_v \mathfrak{e}_{j_\iota} = u_{j_\iota}$ for all $j_\iota \in \mathcal{D}_y = \{j_1, j_2, \ldots, j_{|\mathcal{D}_y|}\} = \mathcal{D}_x$ where $\mathbf{E} = (\mathfrak{e}_{j_1} \| \mathfrak{e}_{j_2} \| \cdots \| \mathfrak{e}_{j_{|\mathcal{D}_y|}})$ and $\mathbf{U} = (u_{j_1} \| u_{j_2} \| \cdots \| u_{j_{|\mathcal{D}_x|}})$. So in the decryption phase, the decryptor computes

$$z = y^\top c' - (\mathbf{E} \cdot y)^\top c = \langle x, y \rangle \left\lfloor \frac{q}{K} \right\rfloor + y^\top f - (\mathbf{E}y)^\top \begin{pmatrix} e \\ \mathbf{R}_v e \end{pmatrix} \mod q = \langle x, y \rangle \left\lfloor \frac{q}{K} \right\rfloor + noise$$

To obtain as the inner product $\langle x, y \rangle$ as output, it suffices to set the parameters so that with overwhelming probability, we have

$$|noise| = |y^\top f - (\mathbf{E}y)^\top (e \| \sum_{i \in \mathcal{D}_v} \sum_{\gamma=0}^{k} v_{i,\gamma} \mathbf{R}_{i,\gamma}^\top e)| < \frac{q}{2K}$$

We express $\mathbf{E} = \begin{bmatrix} \mathbf{E}_1 \\ \mathbf{E}_2 \end{bmatrix}$ where $\mathbf{E}_i \in \mathbb{Z}_q^{m \times |\mathcal{D}_y|}$ for $i = 1, 2$. Then

$$y^\top \left[f - \mathbf{E}_1^\top e - \mathbf{E}_2^\top \mathbf{R}_v e \right] = y^\top f - \left(\mathbf{E}_1 \cdot y + \left(\sum_{i \in \mathcal{D}_v} \sum_{\gamma=0}^{k} v_{i,\gamma} \mathbf{R}_{i,\gamma} \right) \mathbf{E}_2 \cdot y \right)^\top e$$

From Theorem 1 and Lemma 6, we have, $\|\mathbf{E} \cdot y\| \leq \sigma V \sqrt{2m|\mathcal{D}_y|}$ with overwhelming probability. Again by Lemma 4, we have $\|\mathbf{R}_{i,\gamma} \cdot (\mathbf{E}_2 \cdot y)\| \leq 12\sqrt{2m} \cdot \|\mathbf{E}_2 \cdot y\|$ with high probability. As $v_{i,\gamma} \in [0, r-1]$, it can be written as follows:

$$\left\| \mathbf{E}_1 \cdot y + \left(\sum_{i \in \mathcal{D}_v} \sum_{\gamma=0}^{k} v_{i,\gamma} \mathbf{R}_{i,\gamma} \right) \mathbf{E}_2 \cdot y \right\| < \left(1 + 12\sqrt{2m} \cdot |\mathcal{D}_v| \cdot (1+k) \cdot r \right) \cdot \sigma V \sqrt{2m|\mathcal{D}_y|} = a(\text{say})$$

Therefore, the noise is bounded by $|noise| < a\alpha\sqrt{m} + V\alpha|\mathcal{D}_x|$. For the correct decryption, the absolute value of the noise must be less than $\frac{q}{2K}$. It is suffices to choose q and α satisfying $q > 2K[a\alpha\sqrt{m} + V\alpha\ell_{max}]$ where ℓ_{max} is the upper bound of the length of message-attribute vectors and the key-predicate vectors corresponding to which the secret keys are issued.

4.1   Security

Theorem 3. *Assuming the decisional* $\mathsf{LWE}_{q,\alpha,n}$ *assumption holds, then* UZP-IPFE *scheme as described above achieves* Sel-WAH-IND *in the random oracle model security as per Definition 1.*

Proof. Let us consider a PPT adversary $\mathcal{A}$ against Sel-WAH-IND security of our UZP-IPFE scheme. We can construct an algorithm $\mathcal{B}$ that breaks the $\mathsf{LWE}_{q,\alpha,n}$ assumption using $\mathcal{A}$ as a subroutine. We prove the security via a series of Games. The security games between adversary $\mathcal{A}$ and challenger $\mathcal{B}$ as describe below.

Game 0: Similar experiment $\mathsf{Expt}_{\mathcal{A},\mathsf{UZP\text{-}IPFE}}^{\mathsf{Sel\text{-}WAH\text{-}IND}}(\lambda)$ for $\beta = 0$ as described Definition 1.

$(\mathsf{mpk}, \mathsf{msk}) \leftarrow \mathsf{sim.Setup}(1^\lambda, \boldsymbol{w}^*)$: On input the security parameter λ, selectively chosen attribute vector $\boldsymbol{w}^* = (w_i^*)_{i \in \mathcal{D}_{\boldsymbol{w}^*}}$, the algorithm proceeds as follows:

- Chooses the parameters $n = n(\lambda), m = m(\lambda), q = q(\lambda), r = r(\lambda)$ which is an integers and the Gaussian parameter $\sigma = \sigma(\lambda)$ which are the real numbers.
- Selects a matrix $\mathbf{A} \xleftarrow{\$} \mathbb{Z}_q^{n \times m}$.
- Generates $(\mathbf{B}^*, \mathbf{T}_{\mathbf{B}^*}) \leftarrow \mathsf{TrapGen}(1^n, 1^m, q)$.
- Picks two hash functions $\mathcal{H}_1 : \mathbb{Z} \times ([k] \cup \{0\}) \to \mathbb{Z}_q^{n \times m}, \mathcal{H}_2 : \mathbb{Z} \to \mathbb{Z}_q^n$.
- Chooses $\mathbf{R}_{i,\gamma}^* \xleftarrow{\$} \{-1, 1\}^{m \times m}$, sets $\mathbf{A}_{i,\gamma} = \mathbf{A}\mathbf{R}_{i,\gamma}^* - r^\gamma \cdot w_i^* \cdot \mathbf{B}^*$ for all $(i, \gamma) \in (\mathcal{D}_{\boldsymbol{w}^*} \times [k] \cup \{0\})$.
- Outputs mpk $=$ $(n, m, k, \mathbf{A}, q, \alpha, \sigma, P, V, r, K, \mathcal{H}_1, \mathcal{H}_2)$ and msk $=$ $(\mathbf{T}_{\mathbf{B}^*}, \mathbf{B}^*, \boldsymbol{w}^*, \{\mathbf{A}_{i,\gamma}, \mathbf{R}_{i,\gamma}^*\}_{i \in \mathcal{D}_{\boldsymbol{w}^*}, \gamma \in ([k] \cup \{0\})})$.

Fig. 1. The algorithm sim.Setup run by the challenger $\mathcal{B}$.

$\mathsf{sk}_{v,y} \leftarrow \mathsf{sim.KeyGen}(\mathsf{mpk}, \mathsf{msk}, \boldsymbol{v}, \boldsymbol{y})$: This algorithm takes input the master public key mpk, the master secret key msk and key-predicate vector pair $\boldsymbol{v} = (v_i)_{i \in \mathcal{D}_{\boldsymbol{v}}}, \boldsymbol{y} = (y_i)_{i \in \mathcal{D}_{\boldsymbol{y}}}$ do as follows:

- If $\langle \boldsymbol{v}, \boldsymbol{w}^* \rangle = 0$ then returns $\perp$.
- Computes $v_i \equiv \widehat{v}_i \pmod{q}$ and expresses $\widehat{v}_i = \sum_{\gamma=0}^{k} v_{i,\gamma} r^\gamma$ where $v_{i,\gamma} \in [0, r-1]$ for all $i \in \mathcal{D}_{\boldsymbol{v}}, \gamma \in ([k] \cup \{0\})$.
- Sets $\mathbf{C}_{\boldsymbol{v}} = \sum_{i \in \mathcal{D}_{\boldsymbol{v}}} \sum_{\gamma=0}^{k} v_{i,\gamma} \mathbf{A}_{i,\gamma} \in \mathbb{Z}_q^{n \times m}$ and computes $\mathbf{A}_{\boldsymbol{v}} = (\mathbf{A} \parallel \mathbf{C}_{\boldsymbol{v}}) \in \mathbb{Z}_q^{n \times 2m}$.
- Computes $\mathcal{H}_2(i) = \boldsymbol{u}_i$ for all $i \in \mathcal{D}_{\boldsymbol{y}}$.
- Generates $\boldsymbol{e}_i \leftarrow \mathsf{Sampleright}(\mathbf{A}, -\langle \boldsymbol{w}^*, \boldsymbol{v} \rangle \mathbf{B}^*, \sum_{i \in \mathcal{D}_{\boldsymbol{v}}} \sum_{\gamma=0}^{k} v_{i,\gamma} \mathbf{R}_{i,\gamma}^*, \mathbf{T}_{\mathbf{B}^*}, \boldsymbol{u}_i, \sigma)$ such that $\left[\mathbf{A} \parallel \mathbf{A} \left(\sum_{i \in \mathcal{D}_{\boldsymbol{v}}} \sum_{\gamma=0}^{k} v_{i,\gamma} \mathbf{R}_{i,\gamma}^* \right) - \sum_{i \in \mathcal{D}_{\boldsymbol{v}}} \sum_{\gamma=0}^{k} v_{i,\gamma} r^\gamma w_i^* \mathbf{B}^* \right] \boldsymbol{e}_i = \boldsymbol{u}_i$ for all $i \in \mathcal{D}_{\boldsymbol{y}}$
- Forms the matrix $\mathbf{E} \in \mathbb{Z}^{2m \times |\mathcal{D}_{\boldsymbol{y}}|}$ by concatenating all the pre-generated $\boldsymbol{e}_i$ vectors, i.e., $\mathbf{E} = (\boldsymbol{e}_{i_1} \parallel \boldsymbol{e}_{i_2} \parallel \cdots \parallel \boldsymbol{e}_{i_{|\mathcal{D}_{\boldsymbol{y}}|}})$ where $\mathcal{D}_{\boldsymbol{y}} = \{i_1, i_2, \ldots, i_{|\mathcal{D}_{\boldsymbol{y}}|}\}$.
- Outputs $\mathsf{sk}_{v,y} = (\boldsymbol{y}, \mathbf{E} \cdot \boldsymbol{y})$.

Fig. 2. The algorithm sim.KeyGen run by the challenger $\mathcal{B}$.

$\mathsf{ct}_{\boldsymbol{w}^*, \boldsymbol{x}^*} \leftarrow \mathsf{sim.Enc}(\mathsf{mpk}, \mathsf{msk}, \boldsymbol{w}^*, \boldsymbol{x}^*)$: This algorithm works in the same way as UZP-IPFE.Enc algorithm except the following:

- Uses the pre-defined matrix $\mathbf{B}^* \in \mathbb{Z}_q^{n \times m}$ generated by sim.Setup instead of the matrix $\mathbf{B} \in \mathbb{Z}_q^{n \times m}$ during UZP-IPFE algorithm.
- Here $\mathbf{R}_{i,\gamma}^* \in \{-1, 1\}^{m \times m}$ is generated by sim.Setup to compute the challenge ciphertext components $c_{i,\gamma}$ for all $i \in \mathcal{D}_{\boldsymbol{w}^*}, \gamma \in \{0, 1, \ldots, k\}$ instead of using $\mathbf{R}_{i,\gamma}$ selected during UZP-IPFE.Enc algorithm.

Fig. 3. The algorithm sim.Enc run by the challenger $\mathcal{B}$.

Game 1: This game is identical to the Game 0 except that the challenger $\mathcal{B}$ uniformly chooses $\mathbf{A}_{i,\gamma} \xleftarrow{\$} \mathbb{Z}_q^{n \times m}$ in both challenge ciphertext $\mathsf{ct}_{\boldsymbol{w}^{(0)}, \boldsymbol{x}^{(0)}} = (c_0, \{c_{i,\gamma}\}_{i,\gamma}, \boldsymbol{c}')$ and the secret keys $\mathsf{sk}_{\boldsymbol{v}^{(j)}, \boldsymbol{y}^{(j)}} = (\boldsymbol{y}^{(j)}, \mathbf{E}\boldsymbol{y}^{(j)})$.

Game 2: $\mathcal{B}$ runs the sim.Setup algorithm, as described in Fig. 1, on input the selectively chosen attribute vector $\boldsymbol{w}^* = \boldsymbol{w}^{(0)}$ and $\mathcal{B}$ responds the secret key queries $\mathsf{sk}_{\boldsymbol{v}^{(j)}, \boldsymbol{y}^{(j)}}$ and the challenger ciphertext $\mathsf{ct}_{\boldsymbol{w}^{(0)}, \boldsymbol{x}^{(0)}}$ by using the sim.KeyGen and sim.Enc algorithms as presented in Fig. 2 and 3, respectively.

Game 3: Game 3 is similar to Game 2 except that in sim.Enc phase, $\mathcal{B}$ uniformly chooses $\boldsymbol{u}_i \xleftarrow{\$} \mathbb{Z}_q^n$ for all $i \in \mathcal{D}_{\boldsymbol{x}}$ instead of generating it using hash function $\mathcal{H}_2$.

Game 4: The challenger $\mathcal{B}$ chooses uniformly random components from the ciphertext space and returns it as the challenge ciphertext.

Game 5: The challenger $\mathcal{B}$ runs the algorithm sim.Setup with the challenge attribute $\boldsymbol{w}^* = \boldsymbol{w}^{(1)}$ and responds to the adversary's secret key queries by running sim.KeyGen algorithm. The challenger $\mathcal{B}$ returns the challenge ciphertext by picking uniformly random elements from the ciphertext space.

Game 6: Game 6 is the same as Game 5 except that the challenge ciphertext is generated by executing the algorithm sim.Enc where the matrix $\mathbf{U} \in \mathbb{Z}_q^{n \times |\mathcal{D}_x|}$ is constructed from the hash function $\mathcal{H}_2$ instead of choosing uniformly, i.e., the challenge ciphertext is generated using the algorithm sim.Enc over the challenge vector pair $(\boldsymbol{w}^{(1)}, \boldsymbol{x}^{(1)})$.

Game 7: Same as experiment $\mathsf{Expt}_{\mathcal{A},\mathsf{UZP\text{-}IPFE}}^{\mathsf{Sel\text{-}WAH\text{-}IND}}(\lambda)$ for $\beta = 1$ as described Definition 1. □

Using the simulated algorithms of Fig. 1 to 3, we show that the successive games are indistinguishable under the decisional LWE assumption.

Lemma 7. *The adversarial view of Game 0 and Game 1 are computationally indistinguishable.*

Proof. All hash queries corresponding to the indices of $\mathcal{D}_v$ produce random matrices assuming that the hash functions $\mathcal{H}_1$ is modelled as a random oracle. Thus, Game 0 and Game 1 are computationally indistinguishable. □

Lemma 8. *The adversarial view of Game 1 and Game 2 are statistically close.*

Proof. We have to show that the distribution of the challenge ciphertext and the master public keys in both the games are indistinguishable, i.e., the honestly generated public parameters and ciphertext are statistically close to the public parameters and the ciphertext generated by sim.Setup and sim.Enc algorithms. In Game 1, matrix $\mathbf{A}$ is generated by using Trap.Gen algorithm where in Game 2, it is chosen uniformly random over $\mathbb{Z}_q^{n \times m}$. By Lemma 2, it can be concluded that matrix $\mathbf{A}$ is statistically close to a uniform matrix over $\mathbb{Z}_q^{n \times m}$ for $m \geq 6n \log q$. To show that ciphertext components $\{c_{i,\gamma}\}_{i,\gamma}$ are statistically close in Game 1 and Game 2, we first argue that $\{\mathbf{A}_{i,\gamma}\}_{i,\gamma}$ are indistinguishable in both games.

$\underline{\{\mathbf{A}_{i,\gamma}\}\ indistinguishability.}$ We observe that $\mathbf{A}_{i,\gamma} \in \mathbb{Z}_q^{n \times m}$ is uniformly random in Game 1, and in Game 2, $\mathbf{A}_{i,\gamma} = \mathbf{A}\mathbf{R}_{i,\gamma}^* - r^\gamma w_i^{(0)}\mathbf{B}^*$, which are statistically close as the matrices $\mathbf{R}_{i,\gamma}^* \xleftarrow{\$} \{-1,1\}^{m \times m}$, $\mathbf{B}^* \xleftarrow{\$} \mathbb{Z}_q^{n \times m}$ for all $i \in \mathcal{D}_{w^{(0)}}, \gamma \in ([k] \cup \{0\})$.

$\underline{\{c_{i,\gamma}\}\ indistinguishability.}$ In Game 1, the challenge ciphertext are computed as $c_{i,\gamma} = (\mathbf{A}_{i,\gamma} + r^\gamma w_i^{(0)}\mathbf{B}^*)^\top s + \mathbf{R}_{i,\gamma}^{*\top} e$ for all $i \in \mathcal{D}_{w^{(0)}}, \gamma \in ([k] \cup \{0\})$ with $\mathbf{R}_{i,\gamma}^* \xleftarrow{\$} \{-1,1\}^{m \times m}$, $\mathbf{B}^* \xleftarrow{\$} \mathbb{Z}_q^{n \times m}$. In contrast, the corresponding challenge ciphertext in Game 2 is set as

$$c_{i,\gamma} = (\mathbf{A}\mathbf{R}_{i,\gamma}^* - r^\gamma w_i^{(0)}\mathbf{B}^* + r^\gamma w_i^{(0)}\mathbf{B}^*)^\top s + \mathbf{R}_{i,\gamma}^{*\top} e = \mathbf{R}_{i,\gamma}^{*\top} c_0 \text{ as } c_0 = \mathbf{A}^\top s + e$$

where $\mathbf{R}_{i,\gamma}^* \in \{-1,1\}^{m \times m}$ is the same matrix as used to compute $\mathbf{A}_{i,\gamma} = \mathbf{A}\mathbf{R}_{i,\gamma}^* - r^\gamma w_i^{(0)}\mathbf{B}^*$. The main difference between the Game 1 and Game 2 is that the matrix $\mathbf{R}^*_{i,\gamma}$ is used in Game 2 in both sim.Setup and sim.Enc algorithms to generate the public parameters and the challenge ciphertext but in Game 1, $\mathbf{R}^*_{i,\gamma}$ and $\mathbf{B}^*$ are picked randomly during UZP-IPFE.Enc phase. We show below that the joint distribution of $(\mathbf{A}, \{\mathbf{A}_{i,\gamma}, \mathbf{c}_{i,\gamma}\}_{i,\gamma})$ are statistically close in both the Game 1 and Game 2. Then for all fixed $\mathbf{B}^*, \boldsymbol{w}^{(0)}$ and $\boldsymbol{e} \in \mathbb{Z}_q^m$, we have

$$\left(\mathbf{A}, \mathbf{A}\mathbf{R}^*_{i,\gamma} - r^\gamma w_i^{(0)} \mathbf{B}^*, \mathbf{R}^{*\top}_{i,\gamma} e\right) \approx_s \left(\mathbf{A}, \mathbf{A}_{i,\gamma}, \mathbf{R}^{*\top}_{i,\gamma} e\right)$$

as $\mathbf{A}_{i,\gamma}, \mathbf{R}^*_{i,\gamma}$ are uniformly chosen from $\mathbb{Z}_q^{n \times m}$ and $\{-1,1\}^{m \times m}$ respectively. Therefore, if we extend this over all the $i \in \mathcal{D}_{\boldsymbol{w}^{(0)}}, \gamma \in [k] \cup \{0\}$, we get

$$\left(\mathbf{A}, \{\mathbf{A}\mathbf{R}^*_{i,\gamma} - r^\gamma w_i^{(0)} \mathbf{B}^*, \mathbf{R}^{*\top}_{i,\gamma} e\}_{i,\gamma}\right) \approx_s \left(\mathbf{A}, \{\mathbf{A}_{i,\gamma}, \mathbf{R}^{*\top}_{i,\gamma} e\}_{i,\gamma}\right)$$

From the indistinguishability of $\mathbf{A}_{i,\gamma}$ for all i, γ, we conclude that

$$\left(\mathbf{A}, \{\mathbf{A}\mathbf{R}^*_{i,\gamma} - r^\gamma w_i^{(0)} \mathbf{B}^*, (\mathbf{A}\mathbf{R}^*_{i,\gamma} - r^\gamma w_i^{(0)} \mathbf{B}^* + r^\gamma w_i^{(0)} \mathbf{B}^*)^\top \boldsymbol{s} + \mathbf{R}^{*\top}_{i,\gamma} e\}_{i,\gamma}\right)$$
$$\approx_s \left(\mathbf{A}, \{\mathbf{A}_{i,\gamma}, (\mathbf{A}_{i,\gamma} + r^\gamma w_i^{(0)} \mathbf{B}^*)^\top \boldsymbol{s} + \mathbf{R}^{*\top}_{i,\gamma} e\}_{i,\gamma}\right)$$

Note that the left-hand side of the above inclusion is the joint distribution of $\mathbf{A}_{i,\gamma}, \mathbf{c}_{i,\gamma}$ in Game 2, whereas the right-hand side is the distribution in Game 1.

Therefore, the output distribution of UZP-IPFE.KeyGen algorithm in Game 1 is statistically close to sim.KeyGen algorithm in Game 2 using the Theorem 1, 2 since the secret keys are generated in Game 1 using Sampleleft algorithm and in Game 2, we use Sampleright algorithm. Assuming σ is sufficiently large, this follows from the properties of the algorithms Sampleleft and Sampleright. To fulfil both the requirements, we explicitly discuss in the parameter setting using Theorem 1 and 2. This completes the proof of the lemma.

Lemma 9. *In adversarial view of $\mathcal{A}$, the Game 2 and Game 3 are computationally indistinguishable.*

Proof. Since $\mathcal{H}_2$ is modelled as a random oracle, all hash queries of $\mathcal{H}_2$ corresponding to the index sets $\mathcal{D}_{\boldsymbol{x}^{(0)}}, \mathcal{D}_{\boldsymbol{y}^{(j)}}$ will generate random vectors. Therefore, Game 2 and Game 3 are indistinguishable to each other.

Lemma 10. *The adversarial view of $\mathcal{A}$ in Game 3 and Game 4 are computationally indistinguishable if the decisional-LWE assumption holds.*

Proof. Suppose we are given $(m + |\mathcal{D}_{\boldsymbol{x}^{(0)}}|)$ many LWE instances $(\boldsymbol{a}_i, \widehat{z}_i) \in \mathbb{Z}_q^n \times \mathbb{Z}_q$, $(\boldsymbol{u}_j, z_j) \in \mathbb{Z}_q^n \times \mathbb{Z}_q$ for all $i \in \{1, 2, \ldots, m\}, j \in \mathcal{D}_{\boldsymbol{x}^{(0)}}$ where either $\widehat{z}_i = \langle \boldsymbol{a}_i, \boldsymbol{s} \rangle + e_i$ and $z_j = \langle \boldsymbol{u}_j, \boldsymbol{s} \rangle + f_j$ for some fixed secret vector $\boldsymbol{s} \xleftarrow{\$} \mathbb{Z}_q^n$ and the discrete Gaussian error quantity $e_i \xleftarrow{\$} \mathfrak{D}_{\mathbb{Z},\alpha}, f_j \xleftarrow{\$} \mathfrak{D}_{\mathbb{Z},\alpha}$ or $\widehat{z}_i, z_j$ are uniform in $\mathbb{Z}_q$. Let

$$\mathbf{A} = (\boldsymbol{a}_1, \boldsymbol{a}_2, \ldots, \boldsymbol{a}_m) \in \mathbb{Z}_q^{n \times m}, \mathbf{U} = (\boldsymbol{u}_j)_{j \in \mathcal{D}_{\boldsymbol{x}^{(0)}}} \in \mathbb{Z}_q^{|\mathcal{D}_{\boldsymbol{x}^{(0)}}| \times n}$$
$$\boldsymbol{c}_0 = (\langle \boldsymbol{a}_1, \boldsymbol{s} \rangle + e_1, \langle \boldsymbol{a}_2, \boldsymbol{s} \rangle + e_2, \ldots, \langle \boldsymbol{a}_m, \boldsymbol{s} \rangle + e_m) = (\widehat{z}_1, \widehat{z}_2, \ldots, \widehat{z}_m) \in \mathbb{Z}_q^m$$
$$\boldsymbol{c}' = (\langle \boldsymbol{u}_j, \boldsymbol{s} \rangle + f_j + x_j \lfloor \frac{q}{K} \rfloor)_{j \in \mathcal{D}_{\boldsymbol{x}^{(0)}}} = (z_j + x_j \lfloor \frac{q}{K} \rfloor)_{j \in \mathcal{D}_{\boldsymbol{x}^{(0)}}}$$

Given the LWE instances as above, the challenger $\mathcal{B}$ simulates the public parameters, challenge ciphertext and the secret keys as follows:

Public Parameter. $\mathcal{B}$ runs sim.Setup algorithm and sets the matrix $\mathbf{A}$ from the given LWE instances.

Secret Key. $\mathcal{B}$ executes sim.KeyGen algorithm and uses the matrix $\mathbf{U}$ from LWE instances to generate j-th secret key corresponding to the vector pair $(\boldsymbol{y}^{(j)}, \boldsymbol{v}^{(j)})$.

Challenge Ciphertext. The challenger $\mathcal{B}$ outputs $(\boldsymbol{c}_0, \{\boldsymbol{c}_{i,\gamma}\}_{i,\gamma}, \boldsymbol{c}')$ where $\boldsymbol{c}_{i,\gamma} = \mathbf{R}_{i,\gamma}^{*\top} \boldsymbol{c}_0 \ \forall i \in \mathcal{D}_{\boldsymbol{w}^{(0)}}, \ \gamma \in [k] \cup \{0\}$ and $\boldsymbol{c}_0, \boldsymbol{c}'$ are set from the given LWE instances.

In sim.Enc algorithm, the challenge ciphertext components $\boldsymbol{c}_{i,\gamma}, \boldsymbol{c}'$ are set as $\boldsymbol{c}_{i,\gamma} = \mathbf{R}_{i,\gamma}^{*\top}(\mathbf{A}^\top \boldsymbol{s} + \boldsymbol{e})$ and $\boldsymbol{c}' = \mathbf{U}^\top \boldsymbol{s} + \boldsymbol{x} \cdot \lfloor \frac{q}{K} \rfloor + \boldsymbol{f}$. It follows that if $\hat{z}_i = \langle \boldsymbol{a}_i, \boldsymbol{s} \rangle + e_i$ and $z_j = \langle \boldsymbol{u}_j, \boldsymbol{s} \rangle + f_j$ then the simulated $\boldsymbol{c}_{i,\gamma}$ and $\boldsymbol{c}'$ the simulator described above have identical distribution as in Game 3. Otherwise, if $\hat{z}_i, z_j$ are randomly chosen from $\mathbb{Z}_q$, the simulated challenge ciphertext is $(\boldsymbol{c}_0, \{\widetilde{\mathbf{R}}^{*\top} \boldsymbol{c}_0\}_{i,\gamma}, \widetilde{\boldsymbol{c}})$ where $\widetilde{\mathbf{R}}^*$ is concatenation of matrices $\mathbf{R}_{i,\gamma}$ for all i, γ. Therefore, by the Leftover hash Lemma 5, the quantities $\mathbf{A}\widetilde{\mathbf{R}}^*$ and $\widetilde{\mathbf{R}}^{*\top} \boldsymbol{c}_0$ are independently and uniformly sampled. Thus, the ciphertext components are uniformly random and the simulation described above is identical to Game 4 challenger. Thus any adversary that can distinguish between Game 3 and 4 can solve the decisional LWE problem.

Lemma 11. *In adversarial view in Game 4 and Game 5 are identically close.*

Proof. Since the challenge attribute vector $\boldsymbol{w}^{(1)}$ does not appear in the public parameters of sim.Setup algorithm in Game 4 and Game 5. So we can conclude that Game 4 and Game 5 are identically close.

Lemma 12. *The adversarial view of $\mathcal{A}$ in Game 5 and Game 6 are computationally indistinguishable if decisional-LWE holds.*

Lemma 13. *In adversarial view in Game 6 and Game 7 are indistinguishable.*

– Proof of Lemma 12 and 13 follows from Lemma 9, 10 and 8 respectively.

Let $\mathsf{E}^{(i)}$ be the output of the experiment between $\mathcal{A}$ interacting with the challenger in Game i. From the hybrid argument we have $|\Pr[\mathsf{E}^{(i)} = 1] - \Pr[\mathsf{E}^{(i+1)} = 1]| \leq \frac{1}{\mathsf{poly}(\lambda)} \ \forall i \in \{0, 1, \ldots, 6\}$. Therefore, $|\Pr[\mathsf{E}^{(0)} = 1] - \Pr[\mathsf{E}^{(7)} = 1]| \leq \frac{1}{\mathsf{poly}(\lambda)}$.

Parameter Settings. We explicitly discuss the settings of parameters n, m, k, r, σ, K required for the correctness and the security of the scheme.

- From the correctness of the scheme, we have $q > 2K[a\alpha\sqrt{m} + V\alpha\ell_{\max}]$ where $a = (1 + 12\sqrt{2m} \cdot \ell_{\max} \cdot (1 + k) \cdot r) \cdot \sigma V\sqrt{2m\ell_{\max}}$ and $\ell_{\max}$ is the upper bound of message-attribute vectors corresponding to which ciphertext are generated and key-predicate vectors corresponding to which the secret keys are issued.
- For TrapGen algorithm of Lemma 2, we get $m \geq 6n \log q$.
- For the setup algorithm of our UZP-IPFE, by the Lemma 2, we set $\|\widetilde{\mathbf{T}}_\mathbf{A}\| = \mathcal{O}(\sqrt{n \log q})$ and Sampleleft algorithm of UZP-IPFE.KeyGen algorithm as per Theorem 1 and Lemma 2, we set $\sigma > \|\widetilde{\mathbf{T}}_\mathbf{A}\| \cdot \omega(\sqrt{\log m}) = \mathcal{O}(\sqrt{n \log q}) \cdot \omega(\sqrt{\log m})$.

- For the description of sim.KeyGen and sim.Setup algorithm, we have $||\widetilde{\mathbf{T}}_{\mathbf{B}^*}|| = \mathcal{O}(\sqrt{n \log q})$ and the algorithm Sampleright (as the Theorem 2) in sim.KeyGen phase, we get $\sigma \geq ||\widetilde{\mathbf{T}}_{\mathbf{A}}|| \cdot s_{\mathbf{R}} \cdot \omega(\sqrt{\log m})$. Note that, $s_{\mathbf{R}} = \sup_{\{x: ||x||=1\}} ||\mathbf{R}x||$, therefore, $s_{\mathbf{R}} = \mathcal{O}(|\mathcal{D}_v|(\log_r q + 1)\sqrt{m})$ with a high probability. Plugging this value into above inequality of σ, we see that it suffices to choose $\sigma \geq ||\widetilde{\mathbf{T}}_{\mathbf{A}}|| \cdot \mathcal{O}(|\mathcal{D}_v|(\log_r q + 1)\sqrt{m}) \cdot \omega(\sqrt{\log m})$. So combining the above two bound over σ, we get $\sigma \geq \omega(m\ell_{\max} \log q \sqrt{\log m})$ using the relation $m \geq 6n \log q$.

- Form the hardness of $\mathsf{LWE}_{q,\alpha,n}$ assumption of Lemma 1, we have $\alpha q > 2\sqrt{n}$.

Acknowledgments. This work was supported by the Council of Scientific & Industrial Research (CSIR) (Grant No. 09/081(1336)/2019-EMR-I) and Indian Space Research Organization (ISRO) (Grant No. STC0322).

References

1. Abdalla, M., Bourse, F., De Caro, A., Pointcheval, D.: Simple functional encryption schemes for inner products. In: Katz, J. (ed.) PKC 2015. LNCS, vol. 9020, pp. 733–751. Springer, Heidelberg (2015). https://doi.org/10.1007/978-3-662-46447-2_33
2. Abdalla, M., Catalano, D., Gay, R., Ursu, B.: Inner-product functional encryption with fine-grained access control. In: Moriai, S., Wang, H. (eds.) ASIACRYPT 2020. LNCS, vol. 12493, pp. 467–497. Springer, Cham (2020). https://doi.org/10.1007/978-3-030-64840-4_16
3. Abdalla, M., Gay, R., Raykova, M., Wee, H.: Multi-input inner-product functional encryption from pairings. In: Coron, J.-S., Nielsen, J.B. (eds.) EUROCRYPT 2017. LNCS, vol. 10210, pp. 601–626. Springer, Cham (2017). https://doi.org/10.1007/978-3-319-56620-7_21
4. Agrawal, S., Boneh, D., Boyen, X.: Efficient lattice (H)IBE in the standard model. In: Gilbert, H. (ed.) EUROCRYPT 2010. LNCS, vol. 6110, pp. 553–572. Springer, Heidelberg (2010). https://doi.org/10.1007/978-3-642-13190-5_28
5. Agrawal, S., Freeman, D.M., Vaikuntanathan, V.: Functional encryption for inner product predicates from learning with errors. In: Lee, D.H., Wang, X. (eds.) ASIACRYPT 2011. LNCS, vol. 7073, pp. 21–40. Springer, Heidelberg (2011). https://doi.org/10.1007/978-3-642-25385-0_2
6. Agrawal, S., Libert, B., Stehlé, D.: Fully secure functional encryption for inner products, from standard assumptions. In: Robshaw, M., Katz, J. (eds.) CRYPTO 2016. LNCS, vol. 9816, pp. 333–362. Springer, Heidelberg (2016). https://doi.org/10.1007/978-3-662-53015-3_12
7. Benhamouda, F., Bourse, F., Lipmaa, H.: CCA-secure inner-product functional encryption from projective hash functions. In: Fehr, S. (ed.) PKC 2017. LNCS, vol. 10175, pp. 36–66. Springer, Heidelberg (2017). https://doi.org/10.1007/978-3-662-54388-7_2
8. Boneh, D., Sahai, A., Waters, B.: Functional encryption: definitions and challenges. In: Ishai, Y. (ed.) TCC 2011. LNCS, vol. 6597, pp. 253–273. Springer, Heidelberg (2011). https://doi.org/10.1007/978-3-642-19571-6_16
9. Datta, P., Okamoto, T., Tomida, J.: Full-hiding (unbounded) multi-input inner product functional encryption from the k-linear assumption. In: Abdalla, M., Dahab, R. (eds.) PKC 2018. LNCS, vol. 10770, pp. 245–277. Springer, Cham (2018). https://doi.org/10.1007/978-3-319-76581-5_9

10. Dufour-Sans, E., Pointcheval, D.: Unbounded inner-product functional encryption with succinct keys. In: Deng, R.H., Gauthier-Umaña, V., Ochoa, M., Yung, M. (eds.) ACNS 2019. LNCS, vol. 11464, pp. 426–441. Springer, Cham (2019). https://doi.org/10.1007/978-3-030-21568-2_21
11. Litvak, A.E., Pajor, A., Rudelson, M., Tomczak-Jaegermann, N.: Smallest singular value of random matrices and geometry of random polytopes. Adv. Math. **195**(2), 491–523 (2005)
12. Micciancio, D., Regev, O.: Worst-case to average-case reductions based on Gaussian measures. SIAM J. Comput. **37**(1), 267–302 (2007)
13. Okamoto, T., Takashima, K.: Fully secure unbounded inner-product and attribute-based encryption. In: Wang, X., Sako, K. (eds.) ASIACRYPT 2012. LNCS, vol. 7658, pp. 349–366. Springer, Heidelberg (2012). https://doi.org/10.1007/978-3-642-34961-4_22
14. Pal, T., Dutta, R.: Attribute-based access control for inner product functional encryption from LWE. In: Longa, P., Ràfols, C. (eds.) LATINCRYPT 2021. LNCS, vol. 12912, pp. 127–148. Springer, Cham (2021). https://doi.org/10.1007/978-3-030-88238-9_7
15. Regev, O.: On lattices, learning with errors, random linear codes, and cryptography. In: STOC, pp. 84–93. ACM (2005)
16. Tomida, J., Takashima, K.: Unbounded inner product functional encryption from bilinear maps. In: Peyrin, T., Galbraith, S. (eds.) ASIACRYPT 2018. LNCS, vol. 11273, pp. 609–639. Springer, Cham (2018). https://doi.org/10.1007/978-3-030-03329-3_21

Efficient Distributed Keys Generation of Threshold Paillier Cryptosystem

Amirreza Hamidi$^{(\boxtimes)}$ and Hossein Ghodosi

James Cook University, Townsville, QLD, Australia
amirreza.hamidi@my.jcu.edu.au, hossein.ghodosi@jcu.edu.au

Abstract. Paillier cryptosystem is the building block of many cryptographic protocols. The secure keys generation without a trusted dealer
is an essential scheme in a distributed system since the dealer may be
under the threat of a single point of attack.

We present a distributed keys generation scheme of the threshold
Paillier's encryption system using efficient multiparty computation. Our
scheme consists of two offline and online phases where the offline phase
can be implemented at any time well in advance of the computation
phase. Both the public and the private keys are computed and verified
in the presence of at least $n \geq t + 1$ participants in the actual online
phase. This gives an improvement on the previous studies where at least
a number of $2t + 1$ parties are required for the keys generation. Furthermore, the private communication complexity of our scheme is $O(n^2)$ field
elements with no broadcast communication overhead which improves on
the total communication complexity of [21]. Our protocol maintains the
security against a static active adversary corrupting up to t participants
with the small probability of error using message authentication codes.
Also, the computed keys are t-private, i.e., any subset of equal or less
than t parties cannot gain any information about the factorization of N.

Keywords: Distributed Keys Generation · Threshold Paillier
Cryptosystem · Multiparty Computation · Statistical Security · Secure
Distributed Cryptography

1 Introduction

In threshold cryptography, all the parties are required to participate and cooper-
ate in the system to perform a secure cryptographic computation. One may think
of using a trusted dealer to generate public and private keys of the encryption
system. It is a trivial task as the dealer publishes the public key and distributes
the private key among the participants such that all the qualified parties collaboratively can decrypt the ciphertext. However, this system cannot be reliable
and secure in practice, since all the secret information can be leaked, changed
or even deleted by an adversary carrying out a single point of attack on the
dealer. Thus, the important notion of distributed key generation is the solution

© The Author(s), under exclusive license to Springer Nature Switzerland AG 2023
G. Bella et al. (Eds.): SecITC 2022, LNCS 13809, pp. 117–132, 2023.
https://doi.org/10.1007/978-3-031-32636-3_7

to generate the keys in a form of the secret shared among the participants such that it would not be available in a single location.

Generating an RSA modulus N (which is the product of two prime numbers) in a distributed fashion has been an important research topic in threshold cryptography. It is the core of many cryptographic protocols in which the computations are executed without giving any information about the factorization of N to equal or less than a number of threshold participants in the system. Numerous number of studies have been undertaken in the field of distributed RSA key generation, see e.g. [6,10,11,15–18,23]. Boneh and Franklin (1997) [6] proposed the first RSA key generation for a two-party setting. Their protocol was secure against a passive adversary and they used a trusted third party for the security purpose. [23] employed pro-active secret sharing and a computationally bounded verifiable secret sharing in their RSA key generation protocol. A robust protocol with honest majority was suggested by [16] using the technique of secret sharing over the integers. [10] proposed a threshold RSA scheme with an efficient security method of zero-knowledge proofs, based on the hardness of discrete logarithm, where the modulus N is a product of two safe primes. Nevertheless, their protocol requires an honest third party to generate and distribute the signature keys. [11] presented an efficient and robust protocol with honest majority that the cost of going from passive security to active security is a constant factor and any fault or malicious behaviour can be detected. However, the cost of this efficiency is a simplification assumption in which their protocol is just limited to the number of three parties.

Paillier cryptosystem [22], due to its additive homomorphic feature, is an important building block of many cryptographic frameworks, see e.g. [1,5,7,12]. It has the same public key and the ciphertexts' algebraic structure as the RSA encryption scheme, however, the private key and the decryption procedure of the Pillier encryption do not follow from the RSA system. Therefore, a different type of distributed keys generation technique is required for the threshold Paillier cryptosystem. Nishide and Sakurai (2010) [21] conducted the first study of the Paillier's distributed keys generation and proposed a protocol with the honest majority. They employed the multiparty computation method of [4] and the Pedersen's verifiable secret sharing, which is based on the hardness of discrete logarithm, such that the protocol holds the security against an active adversary corrupting the minority of the parties. Their protocol has the private point-to-point communication complexity $O(n^2)$ field elements, determined by the factor $6n^2$, and broadcasts $O(tn)$ field elements for the process of the shares verification where t is the threshold number of the parties, and at least $n \geq 2t + 1$ participants are required to generate the keys. An important question remaining here is that whether can the keys generation of the Paillier's system be improved? Recently, [18] presented a system for threshold keys generation of the RSA and Paillier's cryptosystems in the two-party setting. Their protocol maintains the security against an active adversary using the commitment scheme (zero-knowledge proof) of ElGamal encryption.

1.1   Our Contribution

In this study, we present a scheme for distributed keys generation of the threshold Paillier encryption system without a trusted dealer. Our protocol maintains the security against a static active adversary corrupting at most t participants where only one honest party is required to detect any malicious behaviour using message authentication codes. Furthermore, the keys are t-private, i.e. any set of equal or less than t parties cannot obtain any information about the factorization of N. Our protocol has two phases, a preprocessing offline phase and an online computation phase, where the offline phase can be implemented at any time before running the actual online phase. The offline phase is executed just for one time in the whole protocol and random shares of a triple, computed in this phase, can be used for the generation process of both the public and private keys. This idea allows us to give a faster computation phase than the protocol of [21] as the computation of the random preprocessed information can be carried out without needing the inputs required for the keys generation. The communication complexity of our protocol is bounded to $O(n^2)$ field elements without any broadcast communication, and the required number of participants in the online phase is just $n \geq t + 1$ giving the improvements on the scheme of [21].

To achieve these goals, we employ the technique of hyper-invertible matrices, presented in [3], to generate the sharings of a random triple in the offline phase. One may think of using the Beaver's multiparty computation scheme [2] to generate the threshold sharings of the keys, however, we propose another multiparty computation approach with the same communication overhead/rounds as the Beaver's scheme meaning that our method can be considered as an alternative approach to it. Moreover, we use the distributed biprimarily test for an RSA modulus, presented in [6], and we give a non-interactive zero-knowledge proof technique to make the players commit to their shares in this test.

The remaining structure of this paper is designed as follows: Sect. 2 describes the required materials for our protocol. Section 3 presents the actual scheme with the security proofs. Finally, Sect. 4 gives the conclusion.

2   Preliminaries

2.1   Secret Sharing

In Shamir's secret sharing [24], a dealer distributes a secret value s among n participants using a random polynomial $f(x) = \sum_{i=0}^{t} a_i x^i \mod q$ where $a_0 = s$ and q is a prime number. We also use the Shamir's secret sharing over the integers, as a variant of [24], which was first introduced by [15] and modified by [16]. In this scheme, the secret s must be $s \in [0, I]$ where I is the interval for s. The free constant term $a_0 = \Delta \cdot s$ and the integer coefficients a_i, $1 \leq i \leq t$ are randomly chosen from the interval $a_i \in [0, K\Delta^2 I]$ where $\Delta = n!$ and $K = 2^\sigma$. Note that σ is the statistical security parameter and K is chosen such that $1/K$ is negligible. Each party P_i (for $i = 1, 2, \ldots, n$) is given the share $f_i \leftarrow f(i)$, and to reconstruct the secret a set of at least $t + 1$ participants pools their shares and compute the constant term as:

$$\Delta \cdot f(0) = \Delta \cdot \sum_{i=1}^{t+1} f_i \cdot l_{0,i}$$

where $l_{0,i}$ is the Lagrange coefficient of P_i. Finally, since $\Delta \cdot f(0) = \Delta^2 s$, the parties calculate $s = \frac{\Delta \cdot f(0)}{\Delta^2}$.

Clearly, the secret s cannot be leaked to any subset of less than $t + 1$ parties with information-theoretic security for the normal Shamir's secret sharing and σ bits statistical security for the Shamir's secret sharing over the integers. Furthermore, this method is linear meaning that a player can compute a share of any linear function with no interaction.

We denote the normal t-sharings $[s]_t$ as a set of the shares generated by the normal secret sharing from a random polynomial with the degree t and the secret s, and also $[s]_t^Z$ is denoted as the same t-sharings setting except that the secret sharing scheme is over the integers. Without loss of generality, the secret addition of two values s and r distributed by the normal secret sharing $[s]_t$ and the secret sharing over the integers $[r]_t^Z$ can be reconstructed by having the parties pool their shares and compute it over the field as:

$$s + r = \frac{1}{\Delta^2} \sum_{i=1}^{n} ([\Delta^2 \cdot s]_t + [\Delta \cdot r]_t^Z) \times l_{0,i}$$

2.2 Threshold Paillier Cryptosystem with a Trusted Dealer

The Paillier cryptosystem [22] is a public key encryption system which holds semantic security according to the decisional composite residuosity (DCR) assumption. This assumption implies that given a ciphertext encrypted under the problem of DCR, a probabilistic polynomial time adversary has a negligible advantage to guess the corresponding plaintext [8]. More formally:

Definition 1. *Let x_0 and x_1 be encrypted under a k-bits public key encryption system based on the problem of DCR assumption. Suppose a probabilistic polynomial time adversary $\mathcal{A}$ obtains an encryption of x_β for a random $\beta \in \{0, 1\}$. Let $\mathcal{A}$ can guess the values x_0 and x_1 with the probabilities $p_0(\mathcal{A}, k)$ and $p_1(\mathcal{A}, k)$, respectively. The encryption system is semantically secure, if $|p_0(\mathcal{A}, k) - p_1(\mathcal{A}, k)| \leq \varepsilon$ where ε is negligible in k.*

We now describe the algorithm of threshold Pailler encryption system where a trusted party generates and distributes the keys.

Keys Generation: A trusted dealer invokes a probabilistic algorithm $\mathsf{Gen}(1^k)$ to generate a pair of the keys $(pk, sk) \leftarrow \mathsf{Gen}(1^k)$. The public key is an RSA modulus $pk \leftarrow N$ where $N = pq$ and $\gcd(N, \phi(N)) = 1$ such that p and q are two safe primes, i.e., $p = 2p' + 1$ and $q = 2q' + 1$ where p' and q' are prime numbers as well. That is because to make sure that there is a sufficiently large number of generators in the cyclic group of N^2 [21].

The private key sk is the Euler's totient $sk = p'q' = \phi(N)/4$ where $\phi(N) = (p-1)(q-1)$. The dealer chooses a random $\beta \in Z_N^*$, and he masks the private key as $\theta = \beta \cdot \phi(N)/4 \bmod N$ and distributes the t-sharings over the integers $[\theta]_t^Z$. Also, θ is added to the public key, i.e. $pk = (N, \theta)$.

Encryption: A probabilistic algorithm $\mathsf{Enc}_{\mathsf{pk}}(m, r)$ is invoked to encrypt a plaintext $m \in Z_N$ and compute the ciphertext $c \leftarrow \mathsf{Enc}_{\mathsf{pk}}(m, r)$ as follows:

$$\mathsf{Enc}_{\mathsf{pk}}(m, r) = g^m \cdot r^N \bmod N^2$$

where the simplest value for g is $g = N + 1$ an element in $Z_{N^2}^*$ and r is a random number in Z_N^*.

Decryption: The parties execute the deterministic algorithm $\mathsf{Dec}_{\mathsf{sk}}(c)$ to decrypt and obtain the plaintext $m \leftarrow \mathsf{Dec}_{\mathsf{sk}}(c)$. To achieve the threshold decryption, each party P_i computes the decryption share $c_i = c^{2\Delta \cdot [\theta]_t^Z} \bmod N^2$ and publishes it. He also makes a proof of correct commitment to his share using the zero-knowledge proof technique described in [14]. The parties compute the plaintext as follows:

$$m = L(\prod_{i=1}^{t+1} c_i^{2l_{0,i}} \bmod N^2) \cdot (4\Delta^2 \cdot \theta)^{-1} \bmod N$$

where the function $L(x)$ is defined as $L(x) = \frac{x-1}{N}$.

2.3   Generating Random Triples Based on Hyper-Invertible Matrices

We employ the technique of hyper-invertible matrices, described in [3], which can be used to generate random t-sharings of a triple in the offline pre-processing phase. We recommend to refer to [3] for more detail. In a hyper-invertible matrix, every square sub-matrix is invertible. Namely:

Definition 2. *A $m \times n$ matrix is hyper-invertible, if for any sets of rows $R \subseteq \{1, \ldots, m\}$ and columns $C \subseteq \{1, \ldots, n\}$ with $|R| = |C| > 0$, the matrix M_C^R is invertible such that it consists of the intersections between the rows in R and the columns in C.*

This matrix has a symmetry feature where a linear mapping of n points, for instance $(x_1, \ldots, x_n)$ to $(y_1, \ldots, y_n)$, can be computed using two sets of fixed elements. More specifically, each party P_i generates a random value s_i and distributes it with two degrees t and t' denoted by the double sharings $[s_i]_{t,t'}$ (note that it denotes two separate vectors of sharings with the thresholds t and t')

among the participants. Each party can now compute two new sets of sharings of a new random value r_i with the same degrees t and t' using the hyper-invertible matrix M as follows:

$$([r_1]_{t,t'}, \ldots, [r_n]_{t,t'}) = M([s_1]_{t,t'}, \ldots, [s_n]_{t,t'})$$

Note that each vector of sharings $[r_i]_t$ lies on a random polynomial $g(.)$ of degree t. Now a number of at least $2t + 1$ participants are required to generate the sharings of a random triple $(ab = c)$ where each player calculates a share of degree $2t$ as:

$$[d_i]_{2t} = [a_i]_t [b_i]_t - [r_i]_{2t}$$

A set of $2t+1$ participants reconstruct the value d_i. Finally, each party calculates a share of c_i with the degree t as follows:

$$[c_i]_t = a_i \cdot b_i - r_i + [r_i]_t$$

Each party now holds the t-sharings $[a_i]_t$, $[b_i]_t$ and $[c_i]_t$ of the triple $a_i b_i = c_i$.

2.4   Message Authentication Code

The message authentication code (MAC) is an information-theoretic method to authenticate an output in a multiparty computation system. The output can be manipulated by an active adversary in the form of a shared secret in the system. Since this method offers a more efficient computationally unbounded security compared to other verifiable secret sharing schemes, it has been used in multiparty computation systems to detect any inconsistency or malicious behaviour, see e.g. [1,9,13,19].

A prover party sending a message m calculates the MAC value, denoted by $\gamma_\alpha(m)$, as $\gamma_\alpha(m) = \alpha \cdot m$ in the field of the computation where α is the MAC key generated by the verifier. The verifier party accepts m if the equation of the MAC value is correct, otherwise outputs *fail* representing the detection of dishonest behaviour and the protocol is aborted. Clearly, this method is linear and parties can use a global MAC key α, as an additive secret of the each player's random key α_i, to verify the computation output. In this case, the probability of cheating ε without being detected is equivalent to guessing the global MAC key α over the field, i.e., $\varepsilon = 1/\mathbb{F}$.

Definition 3. *A MAC scheme with the key space $\mathcal{K}$ is ε-secure to validate an output m in the field $\mathbb{F}$, where there is a computationally unbounded adversary $\mathcal{A}$ deviating from the system to compute an output m' such that:*

$$\{\forall \alpha \in \mathcal{K}, m \in \mathbb{F}, \exists\, m', m' \leftarrow \mathcal{A} |\ Pr[\gamma_\alpha(m) = \alpha \cdot m' \wedge m \neq m'] < \varepsilon\}$$

2.5   Security

We present the security of our scheme based on the ideal/real models. The ideal model achieves the highest level of security as there exists no type of adversary in this model. It is assumed a simulator $\mathcal{S}$ takes inputs from the participants and executes the functionality $\mathcal{F}$ such that the players do not interact directly with each other. The model is denoted by $IDEAL_{\mathcal{F},\mathcal{S}}$. On the other hand, the participants with the presence of a computationally bounded adversary $\mathcal{A}$ implement the protocol Π in the real model denoted by $REAL_{\Pi,\mathcal{A}}$. The protocol Π is said to be secure, if the ideal model $IDEAL_{\mathcal{F},\mathcal{S}}$ and the real model $REAL_{\Pi,\mathcal{A}}$ are computationally indistinguishable [20]. This implies that $\mathcal{S}$ simulates the adversary in the ideal model by trying to change the actual output without being detected.

We assume there exists a static active adversary in our scheme which intends to deviate from the protocol and change the outcome in the fashion of malicious behaviour. A static (non-adaptive) adversary corrupts the players before running the scheme. The correctness and the privacy of our scheme is maintained against at most t corrupted parties in the presence of at least $n \geq t + 1$ participants.

3   Our Distributed Keys Generation Scheme

In this section, we present our scheme to generate the public and private keys of the threshold Paillier cryptosystem in the distributed form. Our method includes two offline and online phases, where the public key and the shares of the private key are computed and verified in the actual online computation phase in the presence of only $n \geq t + 1$ participants.

3.1   Pre-processing Phase

This phase can be executed at any time before running the actual online phase and it is needed only once for the generation process of the both keys. We use the technique of hyper-invertible matrices, described in the Sect. 2.3, to generate the shares of a random triple in the presence of at least $2t + 1$ parties where the majority is honest. Any inconsistency of the computation can be detected by the MAC scheme. The participants do not reveal the global MAC key as they locally calculate the checking shares to authenticate the output.

Note that the computations of this phase and the public key generation must be in the order of a field greater than the public key N. Hence, according to [21], the participants pick a large prime number P such that at least $P > [n(3 \times 2^{k-1})]^2 > 2N$ where n is the number of participants and k is the security parameter which is also used to determine the range of two primes p and q for the generation of the public key. It is recommended to choose a large value for k such that the bit length of P is at least greater than 1024 bits [25]. Figure 1 shows the protocol Π_{Triple} to generate and verify t-sharings of a random triple.

Theorem 1. *The protocol Π_{Triple} is unconditionally secure against a static active adversary $\mathcal{A}$ corrupting up to t parties with small probability of error.*

Proof. Let H and C represent the honest and corrupted parties in the ideal model, respectively. Suppose $\{P_1, \ldots, P_t\} \in C$ and $\{P_{t+1}, \ldots, P_n\} \in H$. The simulator $\mathcal{S}$ sends the list of the corrupted parties to the functionality. Also, $\mathcal{S}$

Output: Each Party P_i obtains t-sharings $[a]_t$, $[b]_t$ and $[c]_t$ of the triple $ab = c$.

- Each player P_i (for $i = 1, \ldots, 2t + 1$) generates a random MAC key α_i in $\mathbb{F}_P$ and sends it to the other participants P_j ($j \neq i$).

- Given the sharings $[a']_t$, $[b']_t$ and $[s]_{t,2t}$ of three random values a', b' and s in the order of $\mathbb{F}_P$, each P_i locally computes the sets of the t-sharings $[a]_t$, $[b]_t$ and the double-sharings $[r]_{t,2t}$ using the hyper-invertible matrix M as:

$$([a]_t, [b]_t, [r]_{t,2t}) = M([a']_t, [b']_t, [s]_{t,2t})$$

- P_i computes a random $2t$-sharing as follows:

$$[a]_t[b]_t - [r]_{2t} = [c - r]_{2t}$$

and a set of at least $2t + 1$ participants opens the value $c - r$.

- Each P_i computes the new t-sharing of c as:

$$[c]_t = c - r + [r]_t$$

Verification

- The participants repeat the steps above with another round of hyper-invertible matrix technique to compute new random double sharings $[r']_{t,2t}$ from random given sharings $[s']_{t,2t}$. Also, each party calculates the global MAC key α as the additive secret of the random MAC keys $\alpha = \sum_{i=1}^{n} \alpha_i$ and computes the random $2t$-sharing:

$$\alpha[a]_t[b]_t - \alpha[r']_{2t} = \alpha[c - r']_{2t}$$

and they obtain the value $\alpha(c - r')$. Each P_i computes a MAC value share of c as follows:

$$[\gamma(c)]_t = \alpha(c - r') + \alpha[r']_t$$

- Finally, to validate the shares of the triple, P_i locally calculates:

$$[\sigma(c)]_t = [\gamma(c)]_t - \alpha \cdot [c]_t$$

and a set of at least $t + 1$ parties pools their shares $[\sigma(c)]_t$ and reconstructs $\sigma(c)$. The shares of the triple are consistent iff $\sigma(c) = 0$, otherwise the protocol *fails* and outputs $\perp$.

Fig. 1. The protocol Π_{Triple} for generating t-sharings of a random triple.

picks random values $[c']_t$, α' and $[\gamma'(c)]_t$ for the inputs of the corrupted parties. This is analogous to the condition where $\mathcal{A}$ introduces the errors δ_c, δ_α and $\delta_{\gamma(c)}$ to the real model which can be denoted as $[c']_t = [c]_t + \delta_c$, $\alpha' = \alpha + \delta_\alpha$ and $[\gamma'(c)]_t = [\gamma(c)]_t + \delta_{\gamma(c)}$, respectively. $\mathcal{S}$ executes the functionality and the honest parties detect any inconsistency in the system with the probability $1 - 1/\mathbb{F}_P$ because $\sigma'(c) \neq 0$. Therefore, the ideal and the real models are computationally indistinguishable.

The communication complexity of the protocol Π_{Triple} is linear $O(n)$. Now, the participants need to check the multiplication correctness of the triple generated in this protocol. This can be achieved by sacrificing another random triple [9]. Figure 2 illustrates the protocol $\Pi_{\text{CheckTriple}}$ to check the multiplication correctness of the triple. If the check is passed successfully, each party holds the t-sharings $[a]_t$, $[b]_t$ and $[c]_t$ as the outputs of the offline phase.

- Another set of triple t-sharings $[f]_t$, $[g]_t$ and $[h]_t$ (where $f \cdot g = h$) are generated by having the participants implement the protocol Π_{Triple} once again. Also the players pick a random value t_r in the field.

- Each party computes the new t-sharings $[\rho]_t = t_r \cdot [a]_t - [f]_t$ and $[\tau]_t = [b]_t - [g]_t$. At least $t + 1$ participants obtain the random values ρ and τ.

- P_i locally calculates a checking share as follows:

$$[\sigma_{Check}]_t = t_r \cdot [c]_t - [h]_t - \tau \cdot [f]_t - \rho \cdot [g]_t - \tau.\rho$$

and the players open σ_{Check}. The check is OK iff $\sigma_{Check} = 0$, otherwise the protocol *fails* and outputs $\bot$.

Fig. 2. The protocol $\Pi_{\text{CheckTriple}}$ for checking the multiplication correctness of the triple.

3.2 Online Phase

The public and private keys of the threshold Paillier cryptosystem are computed and verified in this phase. A number of $n \geq t+1$ participants are able to perform this phase which is an improvement on the scheme of [21] where at least $2t + 1$ parties are required to generate the keys. Moreover, we use the MAC scheme to authenticate the keys output which is less expensive than the protocol of [21] using the Pedersen's VSS based on the hardness of discrete logarithm.

Note that one can employ the Beaver's scheme [2] to compute the shares of the keys, however, we present our multiparty computation approach which has the same efficient communication overhead and reconstruction rounds as the Beaver's scheme.

Distributed Public Key Generation

Inspired by the study of [6], the participants collaboratively generate two primes p and q using the notion of Blum integers, since about $1/4$ of all RSA modulus are Blum integers. The proactive secret sharing method allows the parties to redistribute the shares of the two primes such that no less than t players can gain their actual values, i.e., the factorization of N remains t-private. Figure 3 shows the protocol Π_{pk} to generate the public key of the Paillier's encryption system. The computations are performed in the order of P as it described in the pre-processing phase.

Theorem 2. *The protocol* Π_{pk} *maintains statistical security against a static active adversary* $\mathcal{A}$ *which corrupts at most* t *participants with low probability of error.*

Proof. Without loss of generality, suppose $\{P_1, \ldots, P_t\} \in C$ and $P_{t+1} \in H$ where C and H represent the sets of corrupted and honest parties in the ideal model, respectively. The simulator $\mathcal{S}$ sends a list of corrupted parties to the functionality. Also, $\mathcal{S}$ sends the random values $[p_i']_t$, $[q_i']_t$ and α_{t+1}' to the functionality which simulate the errors $[p_i']_t = [p_i]_t + \delta_p$, $[q_i']_t = [q_i]_t + \delta_q$ and $\alpha_{t+1}' = \alpha_{t+1} + \delta_{\alpha_{t+1}}$ by $\mathcal{A}$ in the real model. Any inconsistency in the initial shares can be detected with small probability of error. $\mathcal{S}$ chooses random sharings $[y']_t$, $[z']_t$ and the random MAC key α' and sends them to the functionality. This is analogous to the condition where $\mathcal{A}$ introduces the errors $[y']_t = [y]_t + \delta_y$, $[z']_t = [z]_t + \delta_z$ and $\alpha' = \alpha + \delta_\alpha$ to the real model. The functionality is implemented and P_{t+1} can detect any malicious behaviour for obtaining y and z with the probability $1 - 1/\mathbb{F}_P$. Finally, $\mathcal{S}$ picks random $[N']_t$ and $\gamma'([N]_t)$ which can be considered as simulating the errors $[N']_t = [N]_t + \delta_N$ and $\gamma'([N]_t) = \gamma([N]_t) + \delta_{\gamma_N}$ in the real model. $\mathcal{S}$ executes the functionality and P_{t+1} detects any malicious behaviour in the computation with the error probability $1/\mathbb{F}_P$. Hence, the ideal and the real models are statistically indistinguishable with the security parameter k.

If $\{P_1, \ldots, P_{t+1}\} \in H$, the participants open the random values $y = p + a$ and $z = q - b$. Each party computes a share of the public key $[N]_t$ and the parties pool their shares and obtain the public key which can be written as:

$$N = \frac{(p + a) \cdot (q + b) + (q - b) \cdot (p - a)}{2} - c$$
$$= \frac{2(N + c)}{2} - c$$

$\square$

The total communication complexity for generating the Paillier's public key in the protocol Π_{pk} is $O(n^2)$ field elements with no broadcast communication which improves on the total communication overhead of [21] which is bounded to the private communication complexity $O(n^2)$ plus the broadcast coomunication overhead $O(tn)$. The public key N needs to be checked for small prime divisors up to some upper bound B. According to [25], it is more efficient in practice to check for the small prime divisors after computing N instead of checking the individual primes p and q for it. This implies that N must be checked for dividing to any prime divisor smaller than B.

Distributed Biprimarily Test

The participants need to check the multiplication correctness of N that whether it is a product of two primes p and q without revealing the primes. [6] gave a scheme for this test using the Euler's theorem. We propose a technique of non-interactive zero-knowledge proof to make the participants commit to the

---

Output: A set S of $n \geq t+1$ participants obtains a public key N modulo P.

- The participants choose random values p_i, $q_i \in [2^{k-1}, 2^k - 1]$ where k, as described in the section 3.1, is the security parameter such that the party P_1 calculates $p_1 = q_1 = 3 \mod 4$ and the every other party, except P_1, picks $p_i = q_i = 0 \mod 4$. Each party P_i distributes the t-sharings $[p_i]_t$ and $[q_i]_t$ in the order of P.

- Player P_j $(j \neq i)$ generates a random MAC key $\alpha_j \in Z_P$, and sends it to the party P_i . P_i replies with the MAC values $\gamma_{\alpha_j}([p_i]_t) = \alpha_j \cdot [p_i]_t$ and $\gamma_{\alpha_j}([q_i]_t) = \alpha_j \cdot [q_i]_t$.

- P_j accepts the shares $[p_i]_t$ and $[q_i]_t$ iff $\gamma_{\alpha_j}([p_i]_t) = \alpha_j \cdot [p_i]_t$ and $\gamma_{\alpha_j}([q_i]_t) = \alpha_j \cdot [q_i]_t$, otherwise he broadcasts *fail* and the protocol is aborted.

- After verifying the initial shares, each party $P_i \in S$ computes the new t-sharings of the primes using one round of pro-activization as $[p]_t = \sum_{i=1}^n [p_i]_t$ and $[q]_t = \sum_{i=1}^n [q_i]_t$.

- P_i calculates the random sharings $[y]_t = [p]_t + [a]_t$ and $[z]_t = [q]_t - [b]_t$. The parties obtain the values y and z.

- Each party calculates the global MAC key α as the additive secret of the random MAC keys $\alpha = \sum_{i=1}^n \alpha_i$. Then, each party $P_i \in S$ computes the MAC value shares of y and z as:

$$\gamma([y]_t) = \alpha([p]_t + [a]_t)$$

$$\gamma([z]_t) = \alpha([q]_t - [b]_t)$$

- P_i locally calculates the t-sharings $[\sigma(y)]_t = \gamma([y]_t) - \alpha[y]_t$ and $[\sigma(z)]_t = \gamma([z]_t) - \alpha[z]_t$. The parties open the checking values $\sigma(y)$ and $\sigma(z)$. The protocol *continues* iff $\sigma(y) = 0$ and $\sigma(z) = 0$, otherwise it *fails* and is aborted.

- P_i computes a share of the public key N as follows:

$$[N]_t = \frac{y \cdot ([q]_t + [b]_t) + z \cdot ([p]_t - [a]_t)}{2} - [c]_t$$

and a set of at least $t+1$ participants obtains the public key N. Each $P_i \in S$ computes a MAC value share of the public key as follows:

$$\gamma([N]_t) = \frac{\alpha \cdot y \cdot ([q]_t + [b]_t) + \alpha \cdot z \cdot ([p]_t - [a]_t)}{2} - \alpha \cdot [c]_t$$

- P_i locally computes:

$$[\sigma(N)]_t = \gamma([N]_t) - \alpha[N]_t$$

and the parties open $\sigma(N)$. The public key output N is *OK* iff $\sigma(N) = 0$, otherwise the protocol *fails* and outputs $\perp$.

Fig. 3. The protocol Π_{pk} for distributed public key generation of the Paillier cryptosystem.

values they reveal for this test. Figure 4 presents the protocol $\Pi_{\text{Biprimarily}}$ for distributed biprimarily test of N. Note that each participant already holds the random values p_i and q_i and their shares from the protocol Π_{pk}.

- The participants pick a random generator $g \in Z_N^*$ such that Jacobi $\left(\frac{g}{N}\right) = 1$.

- Party P_1 computes $\phi_1(N) = N + 1 - p_1 - q_1$ and every other participant, except P_1, calculates $\phi_i(N) = -(p_i + q_i)$. Each party P_i computes $\nu_i = g^{\phi_i(N)/4} \bmod N$ and reveals it.

- Each $P_i \in S$ proves that he has committed to a correct value of ν_i. Namely, all parties conduct a non-interactive zero-knowledge proof to verify ν_i as follows:

  - Every P_j $(j = 1, \ldots, n)$ computes $d_j = g^{1/4([p_i]_t \cdot l_{0,j} + [q_i]_t \cdot l_{0,j})} \bmod N$, where $l_{0,j}$ is the Lagrange coefficient of the party P_j and $[p_i]_t$ and $[p_i]_t$ are the shares he received from P_i in the protocol Π_{pk}. He publishes d_j.

  - The parties compute:

  $$e_i = \nu_i \cdot \prod_{j=1}^{n} d_j \bmod N$$

  - For the inputs commitment of P_1, all the participants examine that whether $\log_g(e_1)$ is equal to $1/4(N + 1)$. If Ok the commitment is successful, otherwise the protocol *fails*.

  - For the inputs commitment of other parties except P_1, the participants check that whether $e_i = 1$, i.e., g^0. The commitment is successful if it is Ok, otherwise the protocol *fails*.

- The participants check that whether $\prod_{i=1}^{n} \nu_i = \pm 1 \bmod N$. If it *fails*, N is not biprime and is discarded.

Fig. 4. The protocol $\Pi_{\text{Biprimarily}}$ for the distributed biprimarily test of N.

The correctness proof of the zero-knowledge technique and the test can be found in the appendix. In the case that N is not biprime, the test may fail with the probability $\frac{1}{2}$. Therefore, the test must be repeated for few m iterations to reduce the error probability which gives the probability 2^{-m} for accepting N, if N is not biprime. However, in practice the probability that a non-biprime N passes even one iteration of this test is actually much less than $\frac{1}{2}$ [6].

Output: Each party of a set S of $n \geq t+1$ participants computes the t-sharing of the masked private key $[\theta]_t^Z$ over the integers.

- Each party $P_i \in S$ generates a random number $\beta_i \in Z_N^*$. He distributes the t-sharings over the integers $[\phi_i(N)]_t^Z$ and $[\beta_i]_t^Z$ among the participants.

- Every other player P_j $(j \neq i)$ picks a random MAC key $\alpha_j \in Z_N^*$ and sends it to P_i who replies with the corresponding MAC values of the shares as $\gamma_{\alpha_j}([\phi_i(N)]_t^Z) = \alpha_j \cdot [\phi_i(N)]_t^Z$ and $\gamma_{\alpha_j}([\beta_i]_t^Z) = \alpha_j \cdot [\beta_i]_t^Z$.

- P_j accepts the shares $[\phi_i(N)]_t^Z$ and $[\beta_i]_t^Z$ iff $\gamma_{\alpha_j}([\phi_i(N)]_t^Z) = \alpha_j \cdot [\phi_i(N)]_t^Z$ and $\gamma_{\alpha_j}([\beta_i]_t^Z) = \alpha_j \cdot [\beta_i]_t^Z$, otherwise the protocol *fails*.

- Each P_i calculates the new t-sharings of the secrets by pro-activization as $[\phi(N)]_t^Z = \sum_{i=1}^n [\phi_i(N)]_t^Z$ and $[\beta]_t^Z = \sum_{i=1}^n [\beta_i]_t^Z$.

- P_i calculates the random t-sharings $[y']_t = [\phi(N)]_t^Z + [a]_t$ and $[z']_t = [\beta]_t^Z - [b]_t$, and the parties open the random values y' and z' (see section 2.1).

- Every party calculates the global MAC key $\alpha = \sum_{i=1}^n \alpha_i$. Each $P_i \in S$ computes the MAC value shares of y' and z' as:

$$\gamma([y']_t) = \alpha([\phi(N)]_t^Z + [a]_t)$$

$$\gamma([z']_t) = \alpha([\beta]_t^Z - [b]_t)$$

- Every party locally calculates the t-sharings $[\sigma(y')]_t = \gamma([y']_t) - \alpha[y']_t$ and $[\sigma(z')]_t = \gamma([z']_t) - \alpha[z']_t$, and the participants obtain the checking values $\sigma(y')$ and $\sigma(z')$. The protocol *fails* iff $\sigma(y) \neq 0$ or $\sigma(z) \neq 0$, otherwise it *continues*.

- P_i computes a share of θ over the integers as follows:

$$[\theta]_t^Z = \frac{y' \cdot ([\beta]_t^Z + [b]_t) + z' \cdot ([\phi(N)]_t^Z - [a]_t)}{2} - [c]_t$$

- Also, P_i computes a MAC value share of θ over the integers as:

$$\gamma([\theta]_t^Z) = \frac{\alpha \cdot y' \cdot ([\beta]_t^Z + [b]_t) + \alpha \cdot z' \cdot ([\phi(N)]_t^Z - [a]_t)}{2} - \alpha \cdot [c]_t$$

- P_i locally computes:

$$[\sigma(\theta)]_t^Z = \gamma([\theta]_t^Z) - \alpha[\theta]_t^Z$$

and a set of at least $t+1$ participants reconstructs $\sigma(\theta)$. The generation of the private key shares is *OK* iff $\sigma(\theta) = 0$, otherwise the protocol is aborted and outputs $\perp$.

Fig. 5. The protocol Π_{sk} for the private key generation of the threshold Paillier system.

Distributed Private Key Generation

The participants start this stage while they are holding the public key N and the additive shares of the private key $\phi(N)$ from the protocol Π_{pk}. Recall that the idea is to mask the private key by a random number $\beta \in Z_N^*$ i.e., $\theta = \beta \cdot \phi(N)/4$ (see Sect. 2.2). Note that the private key can be written as $\phi(N) = N - p - q + 1$. We use the similar multiparty computation approach to the protocol Π_{pk} to compute the t-sharings of θ. Figure 5 shows the protocol Π_{sk} for the distributed generation of the threshold Paillier's private key.

Theorem 3. *The protocol Π_{sk} is statistically secure against a static active adversary $\mathcal{A}$ corrupting up to t parties with the negligible probability of error.*

Proof. The security proof follows the proof of the protocol Π_{pk}.

Note that the final step of the threshold decryption is to reveal the public key $\theta = \beta \cdot \phi(N) \bmod N$ (see Sect. 2.2), however, the participants hold the t-sharings $[\theta]_t^Z$ over the integers. Thus, in order to deal with this issue, the parties transform the t-sharings $[\theta]_t^Z$ to the normal t-sharings $[\Delta^2 \cdot \theta]_t$ in the order of Z_N^*, by locally reducing the shares modulo N, and then they pool their new t-sharings to reconstruct θ in Z_N^* [25].

4   Conclusion

Distributed keys generation of encryption systems without a trusted dealer has been an important topic in the field of threshold cryptography. In this paper, we give an efficient scheme for distributed keys generation of the threshold Paillier cryptosystem using multiparty computation. Our protocol has two offline and online phases. We employ the technique of hyper-invertible matrices to generate random t-sharings of a triple in the offline phase which can happen at any time before the actual online computation. Also, these shares are authenticated and the multiplication correctness of the triple is checked. The public and the private keys are computed and verified in the presence of at least $n \geq t + 1$ participants which gives an improvement on the scheme of [21] where at least $2t + 1$ parties are required for that purpose. Moreover, a distributed biprimarily test with a technique of non-interactive zero-knowledge proof, to check the commitment of the players' inputs, is implemented to examine the correctness of the public key factorization.

Our scheme preserves the statistical security against a non-adaptive active adversary corrupting at most t participants with the low probability of error using message authentication codes. Furthermore, the computed keys are t-private. The private communication complexity to generate the keys is $O(n^2)$ field elements with no broadcast communication overhead which also improves on the protocol of [21] where the private communication complexity is the same as our scheme but the broadcast overhead is (nt).

Acknowledgement. The authors would like to acknowledge the anonymous reviewers for their comments.

A   Correctness of the Protocol $\Pi_{\text{Biprimarily}}$

For the zero-knowledge proof of each party P_i, the term $\prod_{j=1}^{n} d_j \bmod N = g^{1/4(p_i+q_i)} \bmod N$ due to the homomorphism of discrete logarithm in the base g. Since $\phi_1(N) = N+1-p_1-q_1$, the party P_1 proves that he has committed to the correct value of ν_1 by having all the parties compute $e_1 = g^{1/4(N+1)} \bmod N$. For every other party except P_1, the commitment value is $e_i = g^0 \bmod N$ because $\phi_i(N) = -(p_i + q_i)$.

For the biprimarily test, note that $\phi(N) = N+1-p-q$ and $\prod_{i=1}^{n} \nu_i = g^{\phi(N)/4}$. Since the Jacobi $(\frac{g}{N}) = 1$ and due to the Euler's theorem, the parties check that $g^{\phi(N)/4} = \pm 1 \bmod N$.

References

1. Baum, C., Damgård, I., Toft, T., Zakarias, R.: Better preprocessing for secure multiparty computation. In: Manulis, M., Sadeghi, A.-R., Schneider, S. (eds.) ACNS 2016. LNCS, vol. 9696, pp. 327–345. Springer, Cham (2016). https://doi.org/10.1007/978-3-319-39555-5_18

2. Beaver, D.: Efficient multiparty protocols using circuit randomization. In: Feigenbaum, J. (ed.) CRYPTO 1991. LNCS, vol. 576, pp. 420–432. Springer, Heidelberg (1992). https://doi.org/10.1007/3-540-46766-1_34

3. Beerliová-Trubíniová, Z., Hirt, M.: Perfectly-secure MPC with linear communication complexity. In: Canetti, R. (ed.) TCC 2008. LNCS, vol. 4948, pp. 213–230. Springer, Heidelberg (2008). https://doi.org/10.1007/978-3-540-78524-8_13

4. Ben-Or, M., Goldwasser, S., Wigderson, A.: Completeness theorems for non-cryptographic fault-tolerant distributed computation. In: Proceedings of the Twentieth Annual ACM Symposium on Theory of Computing, pp. 1–10 (1988)

5. Bendlin, R., Damgård, I., Orlandi, C., Zakarias, S.: Semi-homomorphic encryption and multiparty computation. In: Paterson, K.G. (ed.) EUROCRYPT 2011. LNCS, vol. 6632, pp. 169–188. Springer, Heidelberg (2011). https://doi.org/10.1007/978-3-642-20465-4_11

6. Boneh, D., Franklin, M.: Efficient generation of shared RSA keys. In: Kaliski, B.S. (ed.) CRYPTO 1997. LNCS, vol. 1294, pp. 425–439. Springer, Heidelberg (1997). https://doi.org/10.1007/BFb0052253

7. Cramer, R., Damgård, I., Nielsen, J.B.: Multiparty computation from threshold homomorphic encryption. In: Pfitzmann, B. (ed.) EUROCRYPT 2001. LNCS, vol. 2045, pp. 280–300. Springer, Heidelberg (2001). https://doi.org/10.1007/3-540-44987-6_18

8. Damgård, I., Jurik, M.: A generalisation, a simplification and some applications of Paillier's probabilistic public-key system. In: Kim, K. (ed.) PKC 2001. LNCS, vol. 1992, pp. 119–136. Springer, Heidelberg (2001). https://doi.org/10.1007/3-540-44586-2_9

9. Damgård, I., Keller, M., Larraia, E., Pastro, V., Scholl, P., Smart, N.P.: Practical covertly secure MPC for dishonest majority – or: breaking the SPDZ limits. In: Crampton, J., Jajodia, S., Mayes, K. (eds.) ESORICS 2013. LNCS, vol. 8134, pp. 1–18. Springer, Heidelberg (2013). https://doi.org/10.1007/978-3-642-40203-6_1

10. Damgård, I., Koprowski, M.: Practical threshold RSA signatures without a trusted dealer. In: Pfitzmann, B. (ed.) EUROCRYPT 2001. LNCS, vol. 2045, pp. 152–165. Springer, Heidelberg (2001). https://doi.org/10.1007/3-540-44987-6_10

11. Damgård, I., Mikkelsen, G.L.: Efficient, robust and constant-round distributed RSA key generation. In: Micciancio, D. (ed.) TCC 2010. LNCS, vol. 5978, pp. 183–200. Springer, Heidelberg (2010). https://doi.org/10.1007/978-3-642-11799-2_12

12. Damgård, I., Orlandi, C.: Multiparty computation for dishonest majority: from passive to active security at low cost. In: Rabin, T. (ed.) CRYPTO 2010. LNCS, vol. 6223, pp. 558–576. Springer, Heidelberg (2010). https://doi.org/10.1007/978-3-642-14623-7_30

13. Damgård, I., Pastro, V., Smart, N., Zakarias, S.: Multiparty computation from somewhat homomorphic encryption. In: Safavi-Naini, R., Canetti, R. (eds.) CRYPTO 2012. LNCS, vol. 7417, pp. 643–662. Springer, Heidelberg (2012). https://doi.org/10.1007/978-3-642-32009-5_38

14. Fouque, P.-A., Poupard, G., Stern, J.: Sharing decryption in the context of voting or lotteries. In: Frankel, Y. (ed.) FC 2000. LNCS, vol. 1962, pp. 90–104. Springer, Heidelberg (2001). https://doi.org/10.1007/3-540-45472-1_7

15. Frankel, Y., Gemmell, P., MacKenzie, P.D., Yung, M.: Optimal-resilience proactive public-key cryptosystems. In: Proceedings 38th Annual Symposium on Foundations of Computer Science, pp. 384–393. IEEE (1997)

16. Frankel, Y., MacKenzie, P.D., Yung, M.: Robust efficient distributed RSA-key generation. In: Proceedings of the Thirtieth Annual ACM Symposium on Theory of Computing, pp. 663–672 (1998)

17. Gennaro, R., Jarecki, S., Krawczyk, H., Rabin, T.: Robust and efficient sharing of RSA functions. In: Koblitz, N. (ed.) CRYPTO 1996. LNCS, vol. 1109, pp. 157–172. Springer, Heidelberg (1996). https://doi.org/10.1007/3-540-68697-5_13

18. Hazay, C., Mikkelsen, G.L., Rabin, T., Toft, T., Nicolosi, A.A.: Efficient RSA key generation and threshold Paillier in the two-party setting. J. Cryptol. **32**(2), 265–323 (2019)

19. Ishai, Y., Kushilevitz, E., Meldgaard, S., Orlandi, C., Paskin-Cherniavsky, A.: On the power of correlated randomness in secure computation. In: Sahai, A. (ed.) TCC 2013. LNCS, vol. 7785, pp. 600–620. Springer, Heidelberg (2013). https://doi.org/10.1007/978-3-642-36594-2_34

20. Lindell, Y.: How to simulate it-a tutorial on the simulation proof technique. In: Tutorials on the Foundations of Cryptography, pp. 277–346 (2017)

21. Nishide, T., Sakurai, K.: Distributed Paillier cryptosystem without trusted dealer. In: Chung, Y., Yung, M. (eds.) WISA 2010. LNCS, vol. 6513, pp. 44–60. Springer, Heidelberg (2011). https://doi.org/10.1007/978-3-642-17955-6_4

22. Paillier, P.: Public-key cryptosystems based on composite degree residuosity classes. In: Stern, J. (ed.) EUROCRYPT 1999. LNCS, vol. 1592, pp. 223–238. Springer, Heidelberg (1999). https://doi.org/10.1007/3-540-48910-X_16

23. Rabin, T.: A simplified approach to threshold and proactive RSA. In: Krawczyk, H. (ed.) CRYPTO 1998. LNCS, vol. 1462, pp. 89–104. Springer, Heidelberg (1998). https://doi.org/10.1007/BFb0055722

24. Shamir, A.: How to share a secret. Commun. ACM **22**(11), 612–613 (1979)

25. Veugen, T., Attema, T., Spini, G.: An implementation of the Paillier crypto system with threshold decryption without a trusted dealer. Cryptology ePrint Archive (2019)

Statistical Tests for Symmetric Primitives
An Application to NIST Lightweight Finalists

Emanuele Bellini(ID), Yun Ju Huang[✉](ID), and Mohamed Rachidi

Technology Innovation Institute, Cryptography Research Center, Abu Dhabi, UAE
{emanuele.bellini,yunju.huang,mohamed.rachidi}@tii.ae
https://www.tii.ae/cryptography

Abstract. In this work, we show the results of the NIST statistical tests performed on different datasets generated from the output of all possible reduced-round versions of the finalists of the NIST Lightweight standardization process and some of the most popular symmetric ciphers. The objective of the experiment is to provide a metric that compares how conservative or aggressive the choice of the number of rounds is for each candidate. This comparison can add up to the other comparison studies being carried out before the closing of the last round of the NIST Lightweight standardization process, which is supposed to end in late 2022. Note that a similar analysis was also performed during the Advanced Encryption Standard selection in 1999 and 2000 and later in 2011 for the SHA-3 candidates.

Keywords: Statistical tests · Lightweight cipher · NIST standardization process · block cipher · permutation

1 Introduction

In August 2018, NIST initiated a process to solicit, evaluate, and standardize lightweight cryptographic algorithms suitable for use in constrained environments where the performance of current NIST cryptographic standards is not acceptable. The cryptographic algorithms were requested to provide authenticated encryption with associated data (AEAD) functionality, and optionally, the hashing function.

Since then, the cryptographic community has contributed to the cryptanalysis and benchmarks on different software and hardware platforms of the initial 57 submissions. The ten finalists were selected on March 29, 2021: ASCON, Elephant, GIFT-COFB, Grain128-AEAD, ISAP, Photon-Beetle, Romulus, Sparkle, TinyJambu, and Xoodyak. Besides performance benchmarks, there are not many works comparing the security choices of each cipher. Mostly, this is due to the difficulty of defining an objective and fair metric. In this work, we try to address this problem, following the well-known approach of using (reduced-round versions of) cryptographic primitives as random number generators and measuring the quality of their output through statistical tests.

© The Author(s), under exclusive license to Springer Nature Switzerland AG 2023
G. Bella et al. (Eds.): SecITC 2022, LNCS 13809, pp. 133–152, 2023.
https://doi.org/10.1007/978-3-031-32636-3_8

1.1   Our Contribution

In what follows, we re-propose a similar analysis as the one performed by NIST for the AES standardization process [2,11], and by Sulak, in 2011, during the SHA-3 selection [12]. In particular, we show the results of the NIST statistical tests performed on different datasets generated from the output of all possible reduced-round versions of the finalists of the NIST Lightweight standardization process. In the analysis, we also include some of the most popular ciphers, such as AES, PRESENT, DES and ChaCha.

Even if the primitives of the NIST Lightweight standardization process are not meant to be used as random number generators, we still believe this analysis to be of interest, especially as our results can be considered as a metric to compare how conservative the choice of the number of rounds in each candidate.

1.2   Organization

The remainder of this paper is structured as follows. In Sect. 2, we overview relevant related works. In Sect. 3, we describe the statistical tests methodology. In Sect. 4, we describe our results. In Sect. 5, we draw our conclusions.

2   Related Works

The concept of *confusion* and *diffusion* have been introduced by Shannon in his seminal work on the theory of secrecy systems [10]. Shannon defined confusion as the capacity of an algorithm to create a very complex and involved relationship between the key and the ciphertext and diffusion as the property that the redundancy in the statistics of the plaintext is "dissipated" into the statistics of the ciphertext. One way to incorporate this concept in the analysis of a symmetric cipher is using statistical tests to measure the bias of certain bits of the cipher with respect to other bits.

While Knuth's empirical statistical tests [6] were already defined in the late sixties, it was only in the late nineties that statistical test suites started to become more and more popular to systematically test the cryptographic properties of random number generators and stream ciphers. As an example, see Marsaglia's DIEHARD tests [7], Brown's DIEHARDER tests [4], or NIST Statistical Test Suite [1]. In this work, rather than testing random number generators, we consider a different number of tests to identify statistical biases in the output bits of a full or reduced round block cipher or cryptographic permutation, without any knowledge of the internal structure of the cipher (*black box scenario*).

One of the first works we are aware of tackling this problem is by Gustafson et al., in 1997 [5]. In this work, the authors essentially define three ways of generating a dataset related to the block cipher input and output of every round. Each dataset measures the deviation from an expected distribution using different metrics. The first type of datasets is intended to capture possible relations between ciphertext and plaintext. The second type of datasets is intended to capture possible relations between differences of 1-bit differences on plaintext and corresponding ciphertext, called *avalanche vectors*. This second type of datasets seems to detect non-randomness for a higher number of rounds (5 vs. 3) in the case study (DES) presented by the authors. It is worth mentioning that this kind of test is somehow the black box analog of differential cryptanalysis. A black box test analog to linear cryptanalysis is presented as well. However, no practical results are reported in the paper for this test. The idea of the avalanche vector test is derived from the so-called *strict avalanche criterion*, a property defined for SBoxes by Webster and Tavares in 1986 [15]. This criterion, applied to a block cipher, says that each output bit should change with a probability of one-half whenever either a single plaintext bit is flipped (*strict plaintext avalanche criterion*, SPAC) or a single key bit is flipped (*strict key avalanche criterion*, SKAC). The third type of datasets defined in [5] is intended to capture possible relations between subsets of ciphertext bits and plaintext bits. Due to the large number of these subsets, this test does not seem very practical unless only a few subsets are selected. In their use case, this test did not perform better than the analysis of the avalanche vectors.

Between 1999 and 2000, NIST released the analysis of the Advanced Encryption Standard candidate algorithms concerning some statistical properties (including the ones in [5]) that could be measured from different types of output generated by each candidate [2,11]. The statistical properties were defined in the so-called NIST Statistical Test Suite. At the time, this test suite was in preparation. The test suite was finalized in 2001 [9] and then finally superseded by [1] in 2010. In the context of AES standardization, the purpose of these tests was to demonstrate the suitability of candidate algorithms as random number generators. The 1999 analysis included 15 encryption algorithms, and required to generate more than 135 data sets (9 data sets for each algorithm), for a total of almost 29 billion bits (about 3.6 Gigabytes), only for testing the 128-bit key version of each encryption algorithm. In the 2000 analysis, only the 192 and 256-bit key versions of the 5 finalists (Mars, RC6, Rijndael, Serpent and Twofish) were analyzed, with respect to basically the same set of tests[1]. Note that all statistical tests were performed both for full and partial rounds (the test required several months on several SUN Ultra workstations), but, due to resource constraints, partial round testing was limited to only one of the datasets (the low-density plaintext dataset).

A similar analysis considering different datasets was performed in [14] (2005) and extended in [12] (2011), where the tests were applied to both the AES and SHA-3 candidates. Additionally, in [12], a set of additional tests was performed, namely: the Strict Avalanche Criterion Test ("Whenever one input bit is changed, every output bit should change with probability a half to achieve ideal diffusion"), the Linear Span Test ("The distance of a boolean function to the set of all affine functions should be large. This property is measured in terms

---

[1] The data sets were reduced from 9 to 8 (removing the Random Plaintext/Random 128-Bit Keys dataset). The statistical tests contained one extra test, the Serial Test, with respect to 1999. Precisely, 16 core statistical tests that, under different parameter inputs, could be viewed as 189 statistical tests.

of nonlinearity, and it is a concept related to confusion. Evaluates an algorithm by examining the linear dependence of the outputs formed from a highly linearly dependent set of inputs), the Collision Test (counts the number of collisions in a portion of the output corresponding to a random subset of the input set), and the Coverage Test (takes a subset of the input set and examines the size of the corresponding output set).

In 2019, Perov [8] exploited neural networks to study statistical properties of reduced round SIMON block cipher [3]. He converted a list of ciphertexts into an image format, to be fed to a convolutional neural network consisting of 17 layers called Inception v3 [13]. He showed consistent results with the ones found by applying the NIST Statistical Test Suite, with the advantage that his dataset only needs 2^{12} samples, rather than the 2^{27} samples required by the NIST suite. For a smaller number of samples, the NIST suite reports anomalies for some of the tests, such as approximate entropy test, non-overlapping patterns test, and a test for arbitrary deviations. In this case, deviations in all rounds, including the full rounds of the number of AES algorithm, were detected.

3 Statistical Tests

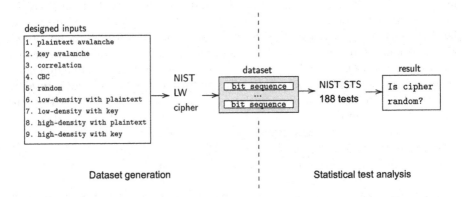

Fig. 1. The two phase of the statistical test: dataset generation and NIST statistical test analysis.

The statistical test activity can be divided into two phases: the *dataset generation* and the *statistical tests* as shown in Fig. 1. For both phases, we followed the approach taken by NIST during the analysis of the AES candidates [2, 11]. The target of the analysis is the underlying primitives of the candidates, not the authenticated encryption nor the hash constructions as a whole. This means we considered the underlying permutations or block ciphers.

In what follows, we briefly review the methodology used to perform the statistical test analysis during the AES and SHA-3 selection, describe the experimental parameters, and present the experimental results in the next session.

3.1   Dataset

As shown in Fig. 1, we first need to generate the dataset to run a statistical test. In this paper, we call the bitstrings generated by the cipher *bit sequences*, or just *sequences*, and define a *dataset* as a set of sequences generated for the different purposes shown in Table 1:

Table 1. The categories of dataset [2, 11].

dataset type	input variant	purpose
avalanche	plaintext or key	testing the diffusion of 1-bit difference in plaintext or key
plaintext-ciphertext correlation	plaintext	testing the correlation between plaintext and ciphertext
cipher block chaining mode	plaintext	testing the encryption with CBC mode
random	plaintext	testing the correlation between each block
low density	plaintext or key	testing the randomness of the ciphertext with inputs being mostly 0 s
high density	plaintext or key	testing the randomness of the ciphertext with inputs being mostly 1 s

We generated each of the above datasets for every round of the primitive used in NIST LW cipher candidates. However, the datasets containing the keyword "key" could only be generated for the block ciphers.

3.2   Statistical Test

A statistical test suite contains several tests for different randomness properties. An example of the statistical tests is the frequency monobit test, which accumulates the weights of 0s and 1s in one sequence and checks if there is any bias. Another example of the statistical tests is the frequency test within a block, which checks the proportion of 1s within arbitrary length blocks.

In [1], the randomness distinguisher problem is formulated as a statistical test to test a specific *null hypothesis* $\mathcal{H}_0$, which asserts that the sequence being tested is *random*. The alternative hypothesis is $\mathcal{H}_a$, which states that the tested sequence is *not random*. When applying a sequence for a specific test, a conclusion is made that either accepts or rejects the null hypothesis. If the $\mathcal{H}_0$ is accepted, we say the tested sequence is random. If the $\mathcal{H}_a$ is accepted, the $\mathcal{H}_0$ is rejected, and the tested sequence is not random. These two hypotheses can be concluded in Table 2.

Table 2. Null ($\mathcal{H}_0$) and alternative ($\mathcal{H}_a$) hypothesis [1].

True Situation	Conclusion	
	Accept $\mathcal{H}_0$	Accept $\mathcal{H}_a$ (reject $\mathcal{H}_0$)
Data is random ($\mathcal{H}_0$ is true)	No error	Type I error
Data is not random ($\mathcal{H}_a$ is true)	Type II error	No error

The probability of a Type I error shown in Table 2 is often called the *level of significance* of the test, denoted as α. The value α is commonly set to 0.01 in cryptographic testing. A *P-value*, also called the tail probability, is the probability that the tested sequence is more random than a sequence generated by a perfect random number generator. If a *P-value* $= 1$, then the tested sequence is perfectly random. On the other hand, if a *P-value* $= 0$, the tested sequence is absolutely non-random. In the statistical tests, if a *P-value* $\geq \alpha$, the tested sequence appears to be random.

In this paper, we choose the significance level α to be 0.01, which indicates that among 100 sequences tested, we expect, on average, one truly random sequence to be rejected. If a *P-value* ≥ 0.01, the corresponding sequence would be considered random with a confidence of 99.9%.

3.3 NIST Statistical Test Suits

The NIST Statistical Test Suite (NIST STS) [1] was used to perform the statistical tests. This suite consists of 15 core statistical tests that, under different parameter inputs, can be viewed as 188 statistical tests as shown in Table 3. Lempel-Ziv Compression test, stated in [1], is not implemented here.

Table 3. The 188 statistical tests in the NIST STS

statistical test	test ID	statistical test	test ID	statistical test	test ID
Monobit	1	Rank	7	Approximate Entropy	159
Block Frequency	2	Spectral DFT	8	Random Excursions	160–167
Cusum	3–4	Aperiodic Templates	9–156	Random Excursions Variant	168–185
Runs	5	Periodic Template	157	Serial	186–187
Long Runs of Ones	6	Universal Statistical	158	Linear Complexity	188

4 Experimental Results

The total data generated for the plaintext/key avalanche dataset is 190,964,711,424 bits (i.e., 191 Giga Bytes). The approximate time to generate this dataset is 4 h. The total data generated for the plaintext/ciphertext correlation dataset is 62,326,878,208 bits (i.e., 62 Giga Bytes). The approximate time to generate all this dataset is 2 h. The total data generated for the CBC mode dataset is 96,945,713,280 bits (i.e., 97 Giga Bytes). The approximate time to generate all this dataset is 45 days. The random dataset has the same size as the plaintext/ciphertext correlation one, and it takes 1.5 h to finish the task. The total data generated for the plaintext/key low-density dataset is 50,866,290,688 bits (i.e., 51 Giga Bytes). The approximate time to generate all this dataset is 5 min. The plaintext/key high-density dataset has the same size and similar time spent. We generated a total of around 514 Giga Bytes datasets for the test. All the parameters follow the parameters used in [11], and the adapted change will be stated in the following sub-sections. The dataset generation has been performed using the NumPy library and an independent non-optimized python implementation of each cipher.

The NIST STS [1] was used for the statistical test, and the significance level α was 0.01. The total time to execute all statistical tests was approximately 40 days.

All experiments were executed in one of the following machines:

- Server 1 and 2: 16 Intel(R) Xeon(R) Gold 5222 CPUs, each with 4-cores, 3.80 GHz, 252G RAM
- Server 3: 112 Intel(R) Xeon(R) Platinum 8280 CPUs, each with 28-cores, 2.70 GHz, 1152G RAM

We report a summary of the results of the tests in Table 4. In the table, when we say that an underlying primitive is random at round r, we mean it passed 186 tests (of 188 tests) at round r and kept stable for further rounds. The datasets of Grain-128, which is a stream cipher, are not applying the NIST STS here.

4.1 Plaintext and Key Avalanche

Unlike the AES candidates, the underlying primitives differ in their block size. To make the test results comparable, we fixed the bit length of the sequences

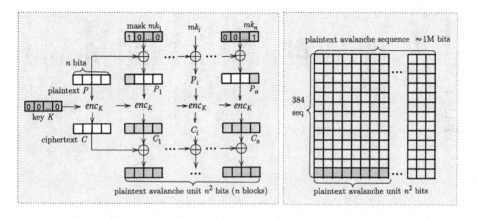

Fig. 2. Illustration of the plaintext avalanche dataset generation.

Table 4. Comparison of Randomness of NIST LW cipher candidates and other classical ciphers.

Nist Cipher	LW Underlying Primitives	Block Size	Key Size	Passed NIST Statistical Tests (Randomness) at Round−[Min, Max Round used in scheme]								
				Avalanche		Plaintext/Ciphertext Correlation	CBC	Random	Low Density		High Density	
				Plaintext	Key				Plaintext	Key	Plaintext	Key
SPN-based Permutation												
Ascon	Ascon's Permutation	320	-	4|[6, 12]	-	1|[6, 12]	1|[6, 12]	1|[6, 12]	-	-	-	-
Elephant	Dumbo: Elephant-Spongent-π[160]	160		8|80	-	1|80	1|80	1|80	-	-	-	-
	Jumbo: Elephant-Spongent-π[176]	176		8|90	-	1|90	1|90	1|90	-	-	-	-
	Delirium: Elephant-Keccak-f[200]	200		3|18	-	1|18	1|18	1|18	-	-	-	-
ISAP	Ascon's Permutation	320		4|[1, 12]	-	1|[1, 12]	1|[1, 12]	1|[1, 12]	-	-	-	-
PHOTON-Beetle	Keccak-p[400]	400		3|[1, 20]	-	1|[1, 20]	1|[1, 20]	1|[1, 20]	-	-	-	-
	PHOTON256	256		3|12	-	1|12	1|12	1|12	-	-	-	-
Xoodyak	Xoodoo	384		4|12	-	1|12	1|12	1|12	-	-	-	-
SPARKLE (SCHWAEMM and ESCH)	Sparkle256ns	256		3|[7, 10]	-	1|[7, 10]	1|[7, 10]	1|[7, 10]	-	-	-	-
	Sparkle384ns	384		3|[7, 11]	-	1|[7, 11]	1|[7, 11]	1|[7, 11]	-	-	-	-
	Sparkle512ns	512		3|[8, 12]	-	1|[8, 12]	1|[8, 12]	1|[8, 12]	-	-	-	-
Keyed Permutation												
TinyJambu	TinyJambu-128 P1024	128	128	17|[20, 32]	19|[20, 32]	4|[20, 32]	4|[20, 32]	1|[20, 32]	14|[20, 32]	17|[20, 32]	14|[20, 32]	17|[20, 32]
	TinyJambu-192 P1152	128	192	17|[20, 36]	21|[20, 36]	4|[20, 36]	4|[20, 36]	1|[20, 36]	14|[20, 36]	17|[20, 36]	14|[20, 36]	17|[20, 36]
	TinyJambu-256 P1280	128	256	17|[20, 40]	23|[20, 40]	4|[20, 40]	4|[20, 40]	1|[20, 40]	15|[20, 40]	19|[20, 40]	14|[20, 40]	20|[20, 40]
SPN-based Block Cipher												
GIFT-COFB	GIFT-128	128	128	8|40	10|40	2|40	2|40	1|40	7|40	9|40	7|40	8|40
Tweakable Block Cipher												
Romulus	SKINNY-128-384+	128	384	7|40	8|40	1|40	1|40	1|40	6|40	8|40	6|40	8|40
Non NIST LW cipher underlying Primitives												
-	AES	128	128	3|10	3|10	1|10	1|10	1|10	2|10	3|10	2|10	3|10
-	SPECK	128	128	9|32	9|32	2|32	1|32	1|32	8|32	9|32	8|32	8|32
-	DES	64	56	6|16	6|16	2|16	2|16	1|16	5|16	5|16	5|16	5|16
ChaCha20	ChaCha Permutation	512	-	4|20	-	1|20	-	1|20	-	-	-	-
-	Present	64	80	8|31	8|31	4|31	2|31	1|31	7|31	7|31	9|31	10|31
-	Present	64	128	8|31	9|31	4|31	2|31	1|31	8|31	8|31	7|31	8|31

Table 5. Parameters for Plaintext/Key Avalanche Dataset.

Nist LW cipher	Underlying Primitives	Block Size	Key Size	Sequences	Plaintext			Key		
					Sample Size	Samples per Seq	Bits per Seq	Sample Size	Samples per Seq	Bits per Seq
SPN-based Permutation										
Ascon	Ascon's Permutation	320	–	384	102400	11	1126400	–	–	–
Elephant	Dumbo: Elephant-Spongent-π[160]	160	–	384	25600	41	1049600	–	–	–
	Jumbo: Elephant-Spongent-π[176]	176	–	384	30976	34	1053184	–	–	–
	Delirium: Elephant-Keccak-f[200]	200	–	384	40000	27	1080000	–	–	–
ISAP	Ascon's Permutation	320	–	384	102400	11	1126400	–	–	–
	Keccak-p[400, 16], Keccak-p[400, 20]	400	–	384	160000	7	1120000	–	–	–
PHOTON-Beetle	PHOTON$_{256}$	256	–	384	65536	16	1048576	–	–	–
Xoodyak	Xoodoo	384	–	384	147456	8	1179648	–	–	–
Keyed Permutation										
TinyJambu	TinyJambu-128 P_{640}, P_{1024}	128	128	384	16384	64	1048576	16384	64	1048576
	TinyJambu-192 P_{640}, P_{1152}	128	192	384	16384	64	1048576	24576	43	1056768
	TinyJambu-256 P_{640}, P_{1280}	128	256	384	16384	64	1048576	32768	32	1048576
SPN-based Block Cipher										
GIFT-COFB	GIFT-128	128	128	384	16384	64	1048576	16384	64	1048576
Tweakable Block Cipher										
Romulus	SKINNY-128-384+	128	384	384	16384	64	1048576	49152	22	1081344
Non NIST LW cipher underlying Primitives										
–	AES	128	128	384	16384	64	1048576	16384	64	1048576
–	SPECK	128	128	384	16384	64	1048576	16384	64	1048576
–	DES	64	56	384	4096	256	1048576	3584	293	1050112
ChaCha20	ChaCha Permutation	512	–	384	262144	4	1048576	–	–	–
–	Present	64	80	384	4096	256	1048576	5120	205	1049600
–	Present	64	128	384	4096	256	1048576	8192	128	1048576

that are input the NIST STS at 10^6 bits. For the generation of plaintext/key avalanche datasets with a block bit size equal to 128 bits, we followed the settings in [11]. For primitives with larger output block sizes, we use a fair number of avalanche samples in one sequence, which makes the input sequence length of each of the underlying primitives about the same size. Here, one avalanche sample means the total derived blocks with one fixed input. For example, one avalanche sample of ASCON contains 320 blocks, and the sample size is $320 \cdot 320$ bits, that is 102,400 bits. The Table 5 shows the parameters of each cipher for the plaintext/key avalanche datasets generation. A total of 384 sequences per primitive have been generated for both plaintext and key avalanche datasets. An illustration of the plaintext avalanche dataset is shown in Fig. 2. For SPN-based primitives, the encryption is done without a key. To get a key avalanche dataset, switch the setting of plaintext and key in Fig. 2.

As shown in Table 4, most schemes produce a dataset that looks indistinguishable from random after a few rounds compared to the total round suggested. With abuse of notation, we say that the cipher *reaches randomness* at a certain round. In Spongent-π, it reaches randomness at 1/10 of the recommended rounds. On the other hand, TinyJambu P reaches randomness at 1/2 of the suggested rounds.

Table 6. Parameters for Correlation and Random Dataset.

NIST LW cipher	Underlying Primitives	Block Size	Key Size	Sequence	Blocks per Seq	Bits per Seq
SPN-based Permutation						
Ascon	Ascon's Permutation	320	–	128	3252	1040640
Elephant	Dumbo: Elephant-Spongent-π[160]	160	–	128	6503	1040480
	Jumbo: Elephant-Spongent-π[176]	176	–	128	5912	1040512
	Delirium: Elephant-Keccak-f[200]	200	–	128	5202	1040400
ISAP	Ascon's Permutation	320	–	128	3252	1040640
	Keccak-p[400, 16], Keccak-p[400, 20]	400	–	128	2601	1040400
PHOTON-Beetle	PHOTON$_{256}$	256	–	128	4064	1040384
Xoodyak	Xoodoo	384	–	128	2710	1040640
Keyed Permutation						
TinyJambu	TinyJambu-128 P_{640}, P_{1024}	128	128	128	8128	1040384
	TinyJambu-192 P_{640}, P_{1152}	128	192	128	8128	1040384
	TinyJambu-256 P_{640}, P_{1280}	128	256	128	8128	1040384
SPN-based Block Cipher						
GIFT-COFB	GIFT-128	128	128	128	8128	1040384
Tweakable Block Cipher						
Romulus	SKINNY-128-384+	128	384	128	8128	1040384
Non NIST LW cipher underlying Primitives						
–	AES	128	128	128	8128	1040384
–	SPECK	128	128	128	8128	1040384
–	DES	64	56	128	16256	1040384
ChaCha20	ChaCha Permutation	512	–	128	2032	1040384
–	Present	64	80, 128	128	16256	1040384

In Sect. A, we report the detailed progression of the NIST tests passing as the round increases for each cipher. We report only the avalanche dataset progression due to space constraints.

4.2 Plaintext/Ciphertext Correlation

Here as well, for the primitives with 128 block bit size, we have used the parameters shown in [11], and reported in Table 6, for the generation of the dataset for this type of statistical tests. For larger block sizes, we have used fewer blocks in a sequence. Please refer to Table 6 for detailed parameters. A total of 128 sequences per primitive have been generated for this type of test. The illustration is shown in Fig. 3.

As shown in Table 4, most of the underlying primitives with SPN-based structure show good randomness in this test, reaching randomness already at round 2. However, for other types, especially TinyJambu P and PRESENT, the inputs and outputs are highly correlated in the first 3 rounds.

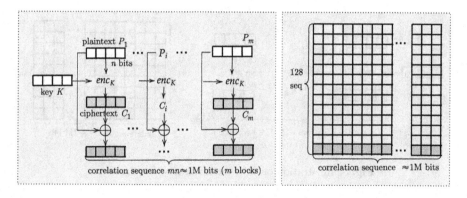

Fig. 3. Illustration of the correlation dataset generation.

4.3   CBC Mode

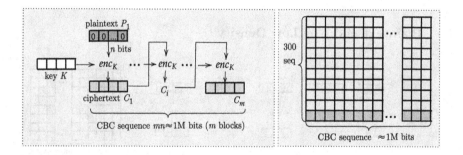

Fig. 4. Illustration of the CBC dataset generation.

The CBC results, as shown in Table 4, are quite similar to the plaintext/ciphertext correlation dataset. They reach randomness for these 2 types of tests in the same round. The dataset parameters are also similar to the parameters of the plaintext/ciphertext correlation dataset, except that a total of 300 sequences are tested. The illustration is shown in Fig. 4. Similar to the plaintext/ciphertext correlation dataset, the primitives with SPN-based structure are random after the first round. Therefore, we will not show the detail of the behavior of randomness here either.

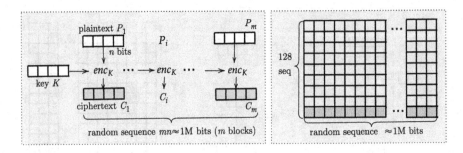

Fig. 5. Illustration of the random dataset generation.

4.4 Random

The random dataset setup shares the same parameters with the plaintext/ciphertext correlation dataset, described in Table 6. As shown in Table 4, all the underlying primitives reach randomness after the first round. The illustration of the dataset is shown in Fig. 5

4.5 Plaintext and Key Low Density

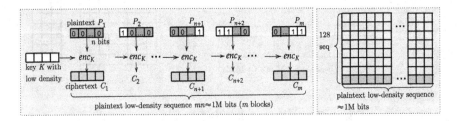

Fig. 6. Illustration of the plaintext low-density dataset generation.

The low-density dataset generation requires a key. Hence, for the underlying primitives belonging to the SPN-based permutation class, the low/high-density test is not applicable. For other types of underlying primitives, with 128 bits as block bit size for the plaintext and the key, we use the parameters given in [11], which are 8257 blocks with all possible low-density inputs. For larger key sizes, we discard some weight-2 low-density sequences (two 1 s in the sequence) and still make 8257 blocks in one sequence to fit the proper sequence size. A total of 128 sequences are generated for the test. The illustration of the plaintext low-density dataset generation is shown in Fig. 6. To get the key low-density dataset, switch the setting of plaintext and key.

As shown in Table 4, the SKINNY-128-384+ cipher reaches randomness faster than other primitives in proportion to the total number of rounds. Moreover, Table 4 tells us that randomness is reached faster when the key is fixed and the plaintexts vary, rather than a fixed plaintext with keys that vary.

4.6   Plaintext and Key High Density

The high-density datasets share the same parameters as the low-density datasets, which are 8257 blocks in each sequence, for a total of 128 sequences. We also discard some weight-2 high-density sequences for the larger key size (two 0s in the sequence). For each primitive, the high and low-density tests present almost the same results. The high-density dataset generation is the same as shown in Fig. 6, but switch the '0's and '1's to make the data high-density (Fig. 7).

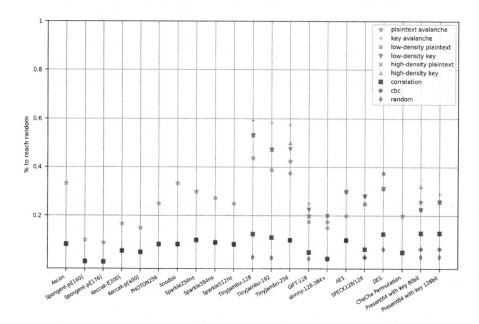

Fig. 7. The randomness rounds comparison between each ciphers with different dataset.

5   Conclusions

According to Table 4, we can see that most of the underlying primitives reach randomness after the first three rounds out of the total number of rounds. For Spongent-π, this proportion is much higher, which seems to indicate a very conservative choice in the number of rounds of this cipher.

In some schemes, the underlying primitives have a different number of rounds. Ascon and the Sparkle family choose these parameters more conservatively. On the other hand, we can see that some cipher like ISAP and TinyJambu seems more aggressive in having some none random choice when doing a small task such as initialization or associated data encryption.

A   NIST Statistical Test Results of Underlying Primitives for the Avalanche Dataset

Due to the page limit, we only report the avalanche dataset results for all the ciphers that we analyzed (Figs. 8, 9, 10, 11, 12, 13, 14, 15, 16, 17, 18 and 19).

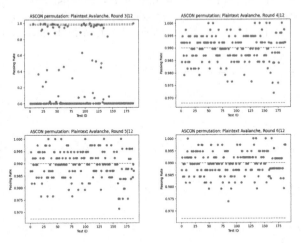

Fig. 8. Test for ASCON permutation with avalanche datasets from round 3 to 6.

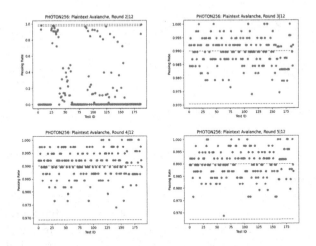

Fig. 9. Test for PHOTON$_{256}$ with avalanche datasets from round 2 to 5.

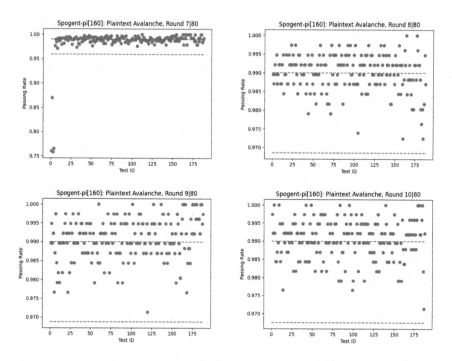

Fig. 10. Test for Spongent-π[160] with avalanche datasets from round 7 to 10.

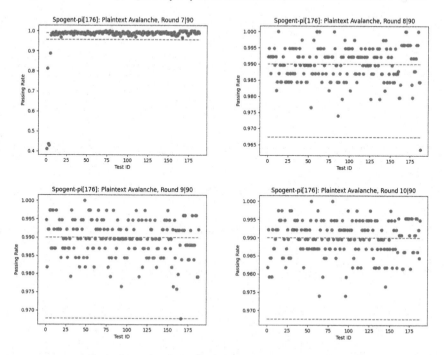

Fig. 11. Test for Spongent-π[176] with avalanche datasets from round 7 to 10.

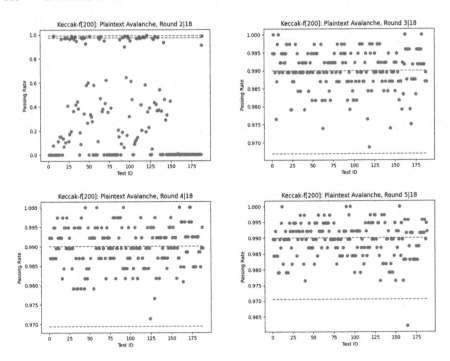

Fig. 12. Test for Keccak-$f[200]$ with avalanche datasets from round 2 to 5.

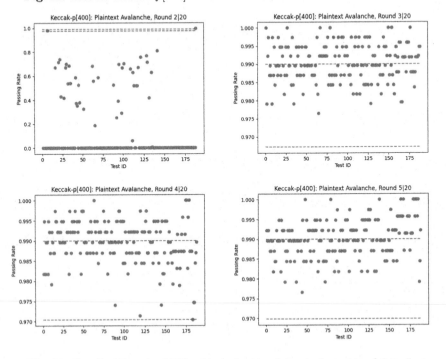

Fig. 13. Test for Keccak-$p[400]$ with avalanche datasets from round 2 to 5.

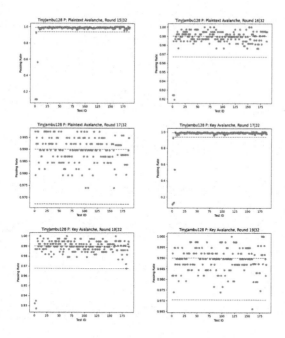

Fig. 14. Test for TinyJambu-128 P with plaintext/key avalanche datasets from round 15 to 17 and 17 to 19.

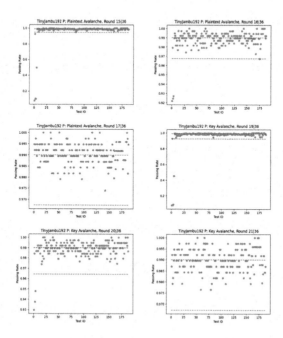

Fig. 15. Test for TinyJambu-192 P with plaintext/key avalanche datasets from round 15 to 17 and 19 to 21.

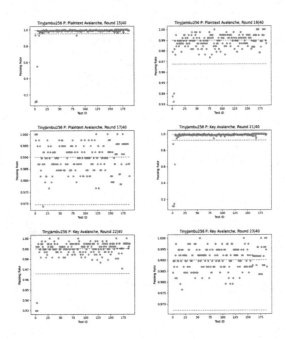

Fig. 16. Test for TinyJambu-256 P with plaintext/key avalanche datasets from round 15 to 17 and 21 to 23.

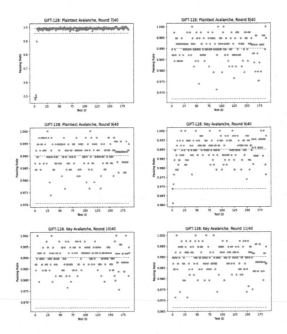

Fig. 17. Test for GIFT-128 with plaintext/key avalanche datasets from round 7 to 9 and 9 to 11.

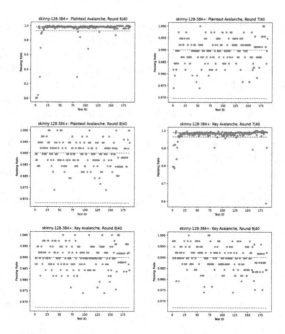

Fig. 18. Test for skinny-128-384+ with plaintext/key avalanche datasets from round 6 to 8 and 7 to 9.

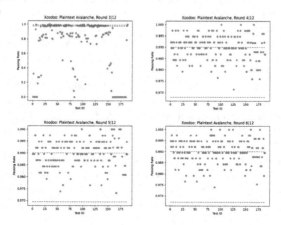

Fig. 19. Test for Xoodoo with avalanche datasets from round 3 to 6.

References

1. Bassham, L., et al.: Special Publication (NIST SP) - 800-22 Rev 1a: A Statistical Test Suite for Random and Pseudorandom Number Generators for Cryptographic Applications, September 2010. https://tsapps.nist.gov/publication/get_pdf.cfm?pub_id=906762

2. Bassham, L., Soto, J.: NISTIR 6483: randomness testing of the advanced encryption standard finalist candidates. NIST Internal or Interagency Reports (2000)
3. Beaulieu, R., Shors, D., Smith, J., Treatman-Clark, S., Weeks, B., Wingers, L.: The SIMON and SPECK families of lightweight block ciphers. IACR Cryptology ePrint Archive 2013/404 (2013). http://eprint.iacr.org/2013/404
4. Brown, R.G.: Dieharder: A Random Number Test Suite Version 3.31.1 (2021). https://webhome.phy.duke.edu/rgb/General/dieharder.php
5. Gustafson, H., Dawson, E., Golić, J.D.: Automated statistical methods for measuring the strength of block ciphers. Stat. Comput. **7**(2), 125–135 (1997). https://doi.org/10.1023/A:1018521732085
6. Knuth, D.: The Art of Computer Programming, Volume 2: Seminumerical Algorithms (1969)
7. Marsaglia, G., Tsang, W.W., et al.: Some difficult-to-pass tests of randomness. J. Stat. Softw. **7**(3), 1–9 (2002)
8. Perov, A.: Using machine learning technologies for carrying out statistical analysis of block ciphers. In: 2019 International Multi-Conference on Engineering, Computer and Information Sciences (SIBIRCON), pp. 0853–0856 (2019). https://doi.org/10.1109/SIBIRCON48586.2019.8958281
9. Rukhin, A., et al.: Special Publication (NIST SP) - 800-22: A Statistical Test Suite for Random and Pseudorandom Number Generators for Cryptographic Applications, May 2001
10. Shannon, C.E.: Communication theory of secrecy systems. Bell Syst. Tech. J. **28**(4), 656–715 (1949). https://doi.org/10.1002/j.1538-7305.1949.tb00928.x
11. Soto, J.: NISTIR 6390: randomness testing of the advanced encryption standard candidate algorithms. NIST Internal or Interagency Reports (1999)
12. Sulak, F.: Statistical analysis of block ciphers and hash functions. Ph.D. thesis, Graduate School of Applied Mathematics of Middle East Technical University, February 2011. https://open.metu.edu.tr/bitstream/handle/11511/20626/index.pdf?sequence=1
13. Szegedy, C., Vanhoucke, V., Ioffe, S., Shlens, J., Wojna, Z.: Rethinking the inception architecture for computer vision. In: 2016 IEEE Conference on Computer Vision and Pattern Recognition, CVPR 2016, Las Vegas, NV, USA, 27–30 June 2016, pp. 2818–2826. IEEE Computer Society (2016). https://doi.org/10.1109/CVPR.2016.308
14. Toz, D., Doğanaksoy, A., Turun, M.S.: Statistical analysis of block ciphers. In: Ulusal Kriptologi Sempozyumu, Ankara, Turkey, pp. 56–66 (2005)
15. Webster, A.F., Tavares, S.E.: On the design of S-boxes. In: Williams, H.C. (ed.) CRYPTO 1985. LNCS, vol. 218, pp. 523–534. Springer, Heidelberg (1986). https://doi.org/10.1007/3-540-39799-X_41

MILP-Aided Cryptanalysis
of the FUTURE Block Cipher

Murat Burhan İlter[1,2(✉)] and Ali Aydın Selçuk[3]

[1] Institute of Applied Mathematics, Middle East Technical University,
Ankara, Turkey
ilter.muratb@gmail.com
[2] Aselsan Inc., Ankara, Turkey
[3] Department of Computer Engineering, TOBB University of Economics
and Technology, Ankara, Turkey
aselcuk@etu.edu.tr

Abstract. FUTURE is a recently proposed, lightweight block cipher. It
has an AES-like, SP-based, 10-round encryption function, where, unlike
most other lightweight constructions, the diffusion layer is based on an
MDS matrix. Despite its relative complexity, it has a remarkable hardware performance due to careful design decisions.

In this paper, we conducted a MILP-based analysis of the cipher, where
we incorporated exact probabilities rather than just the number of active
S-boxes into the model. Through the MILP analysis, we were able to
find differential and linear distinguishers for up to 5 rounds of FUTURE,
extending the known distinguishers of the cipher by one round.

Keywords: FUTURE · MILP · differential cryptanalysis · linear
cryptanalysis

1 Introduction

FUTURE is a new 64-bit lightweight block cipher, recently proposed by Gupta
et al. [5]. It is a 10-round, AES-like cipher that operates on 4-bit nibbles rather
than bytes. FUTURE is interesting as being one of the few lightweight cipher
designs where the diffusion layer is based on an MDS matrix. It is also remarkable
for the lightweight construction of its MDS matrix and the S-box: Designers of
FUTURE obtained the MDS matrix to have a minimal cost by multiplying
four sparse matrices, and obtained the S-box by the composition of four low-
hardware-cost S-boxes. The authors benchmarked hardware implementations on
FPGA and ASIC and compared FUTURE to several well-known lightweight
ciphers in the literature with respect to size, critical path, and throughput.
FUTURE ended up giving the best results among the compared algorithms in
many respects [5].

Mixed integer linear programming (MILP) is a well-known optimization
method to find the optimal solution of a linear objective function, subject to

G. Bella et al. (Eds.): SecITC 2022, LNCS 13809, pp. 153–167, 2023.
https://doi.org/10.1007/978-3-031-32636-3_9

a given set of linear constraints. It has found widespread application in security analysis of ciphers and hash functions over the past decade [8,12,14]. By encoding the internal structure of a cipher as a set of linear constraints, and the characteristic to be found as the objective function, a search for optimal characteristics can be carried out using general tools, such as the Gurobi optimizer [6]. MILP analyses have been particularly effective for lightweight ciphers where the models are more tractable, and the exact optimal characteristics can be found [8–10,12–14]. For general, non-lightweight ciphers such as AES, MILP has been used to prove differential and linear lower bounds [8,12].

A preliminary MILP analysis of FUTURE was given in the design paper [5]. The authors solved MILP models to find the minimum number of active S-boxes in a characteristic. They concluded that 4-round differential and linear distinguishers were possible, but five or more rounds of FUTURE should be safe from such distinguishers.

In this paper, we conduct a more detailed MILP analysis of FUTURE, where we incorporate the exact differential and linear probabilities of the cipher into the MILP model. We work with exact probabilities rather than the number of active S-boxes, with an increased complexity of the model. After applying several techniques to increase the effectiveness of the MILP search, our analysis obtains 5-round differential and linear distinguishers for the cipher.

The organization of the rest of this paper is as follows: Application of MILP techniques in cryptography is surveyed in Sect. 2. FUTURE is described in Sect. 3. The construction details of our MILP models are described in Sect. 4. The MILP models for differential and linear cryptanalysis are given in Sect. 5 and Sect. 6, respectively. The paper is concluded in Sect. 7.

2   Related Work

Mouha et al. [8] proposed using MILP techniques to find lower bounds on the number of active S-boxes in cryptanalysis of word-oriented ciphers. They investigated linear and differential cryptanalysis of the AES and Enocoro ciphers by this technique and obtained the desired lower bounds.

Sun et al. [12] improved Mouha et al.'s technique to find the exact minimum number of active S-boxes for bit-oriented block ciphers. They modeled PRESENT-80 by MILP for single-key and related-key differential analysis.

Sun et al. [14] gave the first MILP-based analysis that used H-representation and logical condition modeling to obtain an exact representation of an S-box. They analyzed the ciphers SIMON, Serpent, LBlock, and DESL, and obtained some significant results of differential cryptanalysis and related key attacks on these ciphers.

Sun et al. [13] improved this technique further to incorporate the probability (or, bias) information into the MILP model and to find the optimal characteristic with the highest probability (or, bias). In this work, the probability information of possible linear and differential patterns was encoded within an S-box representation. They studied SIMON48, LBlock, DESL, and PRESENT-128 ciphers and improved results for linear, differential, and related-key cryptanalysis.

Sasaki and Todo [9] further improved the technique of [13] by adding a MILP-based optimization phase to the algorithm to obtain a minimized representation of S-boxes with smallest number of constraints.

MILP modeling has more recently been applied to different cryptanalysis methods, such as the cube attack [4], and impossible differential cryptanalysis [9].

Different types of ciphers, besides bit-oriented, lightweight ciphers, have also been analyzed by MILP: Sun et al. [10] applied the technique to analyze ARX-based ciphers. Sun et al. [11] showed how to model differential propagation over an MDS matrix multiplication by MILP. Abdelkhalek et al. [1] and Boura and Coggia [2] modeled ciphers with 8 × 8 S-boxes by MILP.

Efficiency improvements on various components of MILP models have also been studied in the literature. Fu et al. [3] provided a way to reduce the number of constraints needed to model an XOR operation. Yin et al. [16] and Ilter and Selcuk [7] proposed more efficient ways to model multiple combined XOR operations.

3   FUTURE

FUTURE is an AES-like block cipher, where the operations are carried out on nibbles rather than bytes. It has a 10-round lightweight structure, designed for low latency and low hardware cost. The S-box and the MDS matrix are designed especially to be efficient in hardware. The FUTURE block size is 64 bits, and the key length is 128 bits.

The Round Function. The basic round operations of FUTURE are SubCell, MixColumn, ShiftRow, and AddRoundKey. The MixColumn operation is omitted in the final round. The state of the cipher is denoted by a 4 × 4 matrix X where each entry is a nibble; i.e., $s_i \in \{0,1\}^4$ for $0 \le i \le 15$:

$$X = \begin{pmatrix} s_0 & s_4 & s_8 & s_{12} \\ s_1 & s_5 & s_9 & s_{13} \\ s_2 & s_6 & s_{10} & s_{14} \\ s_3 & s_7 & s_{11} & s_{15} \end{pmatrix}$$

The round function is presented in Fig. 1.

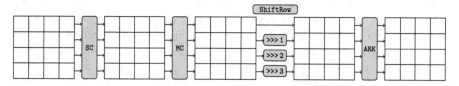

Fig. 1. Round function of FUTURE

SubCell. The 4 × 4 S-box of FUTURE which is a composition of 4 different lightweight S-boxes is given in Table 1.

Table 1. S-box of FUTURE

Input	0	1	2	3	4	5	6	7	8	9	A	B	C	D	E	F
Output	1	3	0	2	7	E	4	D	9	A	C	6	F	5	8	B

MixColumn. The finite field multiplication of FUTURE is done over $GF(2^4) = GF(2)/\langle x^4 + x + 1\rangle$. The state matrix entries are considered elements in $GF(2^4)$ and multiplied with the MDS matrix M, as $X \leftarrow MX$:

$$M = \begin{pmatrix} 8 & 9 & 1 & 8 \\ 3 & 2 & 9 & 9 \\ 2 & 3 & 8 & 9 \\ 9 & 9 & 8 & 1 \end{pmatrix}$$

ShiftRow. The ith row of the state matrix ($0 \leq i \leq 3$) is shifted to the right, depending on the value of i:

$$\begin{pmatrix} s_0 & s_4 & s_8 & s_{12} \\ s_1 & s_5 & s_9 & s_{13} \\ s_2 & s_6 & s_{10} & s_{14} \\ s_3 & s_7 & s_{11} & s_{15} \end{pmatrix} \leftarrow \begin{pmatrix} s_0 & s_4 & s_8 & s_{12} \\ s_{13} & s_1 & s_5 & s_9 \\ s_{10} & s_{14} & s_2 & s_6 \\ s_7 & s_{11} & s_{15} & s_3 \end{pmatrix}$$

AddRoundKey. The 64-bit round key is XORed to the state of the cipher.

4   Construction of MILP Models

The MILP approach has been widely used in cryptanalysis since Mouha et al. [8] introduced the technique. The main idea is to find the optimal solution of an objective function (e.g., the minimum number of active S-boxes or the maximum differential probability) with respect to certain constraints, according to the MILP model of a given cipher. The technique was first used to find the minimum number of active S-boxes in a characteristic [8,12]. It was later refined by Sun et al. [14] to find the optimal characteristic with the maximum differential probability or the maximum linear bias. In this paper, our objective function will be to maximize the differential probability (or linear bias) of a characteristic.

We need to model cipher components as constraints to construct a MILP model to analyze differential and linear characteristics. Therefore, the S-box, permutation, and matrix multiplication over a finite field are represented by linear inequalities with binary variables. This section provides an overview of the MILP modeling of block cipher components, such as the nibble-oriented S-box, MDS matrix multiplication, and permutation.

The number of variables and constraints in a MILP model affects its solution time dramatically. Hence, efficient cipher component modeling is essential to obtain a shorter solution time. With this aim in mind, we modeled the XOR operations by generalizing the idea of Fu et al. [3].

Gurobi optimizer [6] v.9.5.2 is used to solve the MILP models, and Sage-Math [15] is used to calculate the H-representations. The experiments are carried out on a 2.3 GHz Quad-Core Intel Core i5 processor with 8 GB RAM.

4.1   S-Box

Lower bounds for the minimum number of active S-boxes can be obtained via using the branch number of S-boxes, as Mouha et al. [8] showed. Sun et al. [14] provided a method in which S-box is modeled to find exact solutions.

Let a 4×4 bijective S-box have the input (x_0, x_1, x_2, x_3) and the output (y_0, y_1, y_2, y_3). The following inequalities of binary variables can be used to represent the activity of this S-box and $A = 1$ means that the S-box is active.

$$x_0 - A \leq 0$$
$$x_1 - A \leq 0$$
$$x_2 - A \leq 0$$
$$x_3 - A \leq 0$$
$$x_0 + x_1 + x_2 + x_3 - A \geq 0$$
$$4(x_0 + x_1 + x_2 + x_3) - (y_0 + y_1 + y_2 + y_3) \geq 0$$
$$4(y_0 + y_1 + y_2 + y_3) - (x_0 + x_1 + x_2 + x_3) \geq 0$$

Furthermore, if exact probability bounds are sought, the Difference Distribution Table (DDT) or the Linear Approximation Table (LAT) should be included in the model. Sun et al. [14] proposed a greedy approach to model the DDT (LAT), which was later improved by Sasaki and Todo [9]. Our model is based on Sasaki and Todo's approach:

Suppose we want to model a 4×4 S-box with the probability of a difference,

$$p = Pr[(x_0, x_1, x_2, x_3) \rightarrow (y_0, y_1, y_2, y_3)],$$

and there are three distinct probabilities in its DDT such as $2^{-3}, 2^{-2}$, and 1. The probability information is encoded in two bits as (π_0, π_1), denoting the binary encoding of $- \log_2 p$ as:

$$(\pi_0, \pi_1) = (0, 0) \implies p = 1$$
$$(\pi_0, \pi_1) = (0, 1) \implies p = 2^{-2}$$
$$(\pi_0, \pi_1) = (1, 1) \implies p = 2^{-3}$$

Then, we encode input, output, and probability information in a binary vector, defined as:

$$\mathcal{E} := (x_0, x_1, x_2, x_3, y_0, y_1, y_2, y_3, \pi_0, \pi_1).$$

H-representation is a method for representing input vectors as a set of linear inequalities, which is an intersection of halfspaces. We calculate the H-representation of $\mathcal{E}$, denoted by $\mathcal{H}(\mathcal{E})$, and obtain a set of linear inequalities.

Via the H-representation, we obtain a list of inequalities such as:

$$(\gamma_{0,0}, \gamma_{0,1}, \cdots, \gamma_{0,9}) \cdot \mathcal{E} + \gamma_{0,10} \le 0$$

$$\vdots$$

$$(\gamma_{t-1,0}, \gamma_{t-1,1}, \cdots, \gamma_{t-1,9}) \cdot \mathcal{E} + \gamma_{t-1,10} \le 0$$

where $\gamma_{i,j}$ are integer coefficients, $0 \le j \le 10$ and $0 \le i < t$, where t denotes the total number of inequalities computed in H-representation.

Some of the inequalities calculated in H-representation may possibly be redundant. In order to eliminate the redundant inequalities, a MILP instance is built and solved. The solution provides a minimized set of constraints that represents the S-box with its DDT (or, LAT). Further details of the H-representation construction can be found in [14] and [9].

4.2   Permutation

Let the input of the permutation Π be a_i and the output of the permutation be b_i for $0 \le i < n$, where n is the block size of the permutation. In order to model this operation, binary variables b_i are defined to represent the output. Then, equations representing the permutation operation, $b_i = \Pi(a_i)$ for $0 \le i < n$, are added to the MILP model as constraints.

4.3   MDS Matrix Multiplication

Mouha et al. [8] modeled matrix multiplication with the branch number of the linear transformation. The solution obtained by this method yields lower bounds on the number of active S-boxes.

MDS matrix multiplication can be carried out by shift and XOR operations over the base field. Sun et al. [11] provided a method to model matrix multiplication with binary XOR operation. This representation can be used to model differential propagation. In order to model linear propagation, we need a different representation which is discussed in Sect. 6.1.

4.4   XOR Operation

There are several different ways to model a binary XOR operation by MILP in the literature. Mouha et al. [8] provided a method that requires 4 constraints and 3 variables to model a 1-XOR operation, i.e., $c = a \oplus b$, where $a, b, c, d_1 \in \{0, 1\}$, as follows:

$$a + b + c \ge 2d_1$$
$$d_1 \ge a$$
$$d_1 \ge b$$
$$d_1 \ge c$$

The operation $d = a \oplus b \oplus c$, where $a, b, c, d \in \{0, 1\}$, is called a 2-XOR operation. It can be modeled via Mouha's approach with 8 constraints and 5 variables. Alternatively, Yin et al. [16] provided a method to model 2-XOR operation, which requires the following 8 constraints and 4 variables:

$$a + b - c + d \geq 0$$
$$a + b + c - d \geq 0$$
$$-a + b + c + d \geq 0$$
$$a - b + c + d \geq 0$$
$$-a - b + c - d \geq -2$$
$$a - b - c - d \geq -2$$
$$-a + b - c - d \geq -2$$
$$-a - b - c + d \geq -2$$

Dummy variables are not used in this approach.

Fu et al. [3] implemented a method to model a 1-XOR operation with a single constraint as follows:

$$a + b + c = 2d_1$$

where $a, b, c, d_1 \in \{0, 1\}$. In this work, we extend this approach to the n-XOR case. The timing comparison of the proposed n-XOR method and the method provided in [7] are given in Appendix.

In Table 2, constraints are given to model XOR operations up to 5-XOR.

Table 2. Constraints of n-XOR

n-XOR	XOR	Constraint
1	$a \oplus b = c$	$a + b + c = 2d_1$
2	$a \oplus b \oplus c = d$	$a + b + c + d = 4d_1 - 2d_2$
3	$a \oplus b \oplus c \oplus d = e$	$a + b + c + d + e = 4d_1 - 2d_2$
4	$a \oplus b \oplus c \oplus d \oplus e = f$	$a + b + c + d + e + f = 6d_1 - 4d_2 - 2d_3$
5	$a \oplus b \oplus c \oplus d \oplus e \oplus f = g$	$a + b + c + d + e + f + g = 6d_1 - 4d_2 - 2d_3$

6-XOR ($a \oplus b \oplus c \oplus d \oplus e \oplus f \oplus g = h$) can be modeled via the following equality:

$$a + b + c + d + e + f + g + h = 8d_1 - 6d_2 - 4d_3 - 2d_4.$$

Also, 7-XOR ($a \oplus b \oplus c \oplus d \oplus e \oplus f \oplus g \oplus h = i$) can be modeled as:

$$a + b + c + d + e + f + g + h + i = 8d_1 - 6d_2 - 4d_3 - 2d_4.$$

In general, for an even value of n, the n-XOR operation $a_0 \oplus a_1 \oplus \cdots \oplus a_n = b$ is modeled as,

$$a_0 + a_1 + \cdots + a_n + b = (n+2)d_1 - \left(nd_2 + (n-2)d_3 \cdots + 2d_{(n/2)+1}\right),$$

and for an odd value of n:

$$a_0 + a_1 + \cdots + a_n + b = (n+1)d_1 - \left((n-1)d_2 + (n-3)d_3 + \cdots + 2d_{(n-1/2)+1}\right).$$

4.5   Construction of the Objective Function

The objective function of a MILP model can be constructed either to minimize the number of active S-boxes or to maximize the probability of a characteristic. Models that involve probabilities are preferred whenever possible because they yield the exact best characteristic; but they also tend to be larger and much harder to solve. The MILP analysis in the original FUTURE paper [5] focused on the number of active S-boxes. We chose to work with the exact probabilities instead.

The objective function in differential cryptanalysis is to maximize the characteristic's overall probability $\prod_i p_i$, where p_i denotes the individual round probability. Therefore, the objective function for the differential MILP model becomes to minimize $\sum_i(\pi_{i,0} + 2\pi_{i,1})$, for $(\pi_{i,0}, \pi_{i,1})$ denoting $-\log_2 p_i$ in binary.

The objective function in linear cryptanalysis is to maximize the approximation's overall bias $\prod_i b_i$, where b_i denotes the individual round biases (in absolute value). For $(\pi_{i,0}, \pi_{i,1})$ denoting $-\log_2 b_i$ in binary, the objective function for the linear MILP model is to minimize $\sum_i(\pi_{i,0} + 2\pi_{i,1})$.

5   Differential Cryptanalysis of FUTURE

In this section, we describe the details of the MILP model constructed for differential cryptanalysis of FUTURE and how it is implemented in practice.[1]

5.1   Differential MILP Model Construction

The round function elements of FUTURE, namely the SubCell, MixColumn, and ShiftRow operations, are modeled for differential cryptanalysis using the techniques described below:

SubCell. The DDT is calculated for the S-box of FUTURE, which contains three non-zero values; 2, 4, and 16. As described in Sect. 4.1, we encoded each input, output, and probability information as a vector, and computed the H-representation using SAGE. The solution returned 333 inequalities including redundant ones. We utilized Sasaki and Todo's approach and obtained 18 inequalities to represent the S-box's differential behavior.

---

[1] https://github.com/murat-ilter/future-bc.

MixColumn. In order to represent the MDS matrix, the primitive matrix representation provided by [10] is utilized for differential propagation. FUTURE's MDS matrix M contains the field elements **1**, **2**, **3**, **8**, **9** from $GF(2^4)$. Field multiplication by these scalars in $GF(2^4)$ is a linear transformation over $GF(2)$, represented via the following matrices:

$$1 = \begin{pmatrix} 1\,0\,0\,0 \\ 0\,1\,0\,0 \\ 0\,0\,1\,0 \\ 0\,0\,0\,1 \end{pmatrix} \quad 2 = \begin{pmatrix} 0\,1\,0\,0 \\ 0\,0\,1\,0 \\ 1\,0\,0\,1 \\ 1\,0\,0\,0 \end{pmatrix} \quad 3 = \begin{pmatrix} 1\,1\,0\,0 \\ 0\,1\,1\,0 \\ 1\,0\,1\,1 \\ 1\,0\,0\,1 \end{pmatrix} \quad 8 = \begin{pmatrix} 1\,0\,0\,1 \\ 1\,1\,0\,0 \\ 0\,1\,1\,0 \\ 0\,0\,1\,0 \end{pmatrix} \quad 9 = \begin{pmatrix} 0\,0\,0\,1 \\ 1\,0\,0\,0 \\ 0\,1\,0\,0 \\ 0\,0\,1\,1 \end{pmatrix}$$

Let $M_{\mathcal{PR}}$ denote the 16×16 binary matrix which is the primitive representation of M over $GF(2)$, obtained by replacing the field elements in M by the 4×4 binary matrices given above. For the state matrices Y and Z where $Z = MY$, let $Y_{\mathcal{B}}$ and $Z_{\mathcal{B}}$ denote the 16×4 binary matrices, where each column vector is obtained from the corresponding column vector of Y and Z by replacing each field element from $GF(2^4)$ by its binary representation over $GF(2)$. Hence, the MDS matrix multiplication over these binary vectors becomes,

$$Z_{\mathcal{B}} = M_{\mathcal{PR}} Y_{\mathcal{B}}.$$

The 1's in each row of $M_{\mathcal{PR}}$ indicate the elements to be XORed when a column vector is multiplied by $M_{\mathcal{PR}}$.

To model the differential propagation over each MDS matrix multiplication, we need 64 new constraints and 204 new binary d_i dummy variables.

ShiftRow. The binary variables resulting from the MixColumn operation are permuted through the ShiftRow operation. Then, 64 new binary variables are introduced and assigned to these results.

AddRoundKey. Since we model a single-key differential cryptanalysis, there is no need to model the XOR operation with the round key.

5.2   Search Strategy

The number of variables and constraints used in the MILP model increases as more rounds are added to the model, and the solution time increases exponentially as a result. Zhou et al. [17], in their MILP analysis of the GIFT cipher, added extra constraints to the model, to limit the number of active S-boxes in each round and hence to restrict the solution space. We adopted a similar approach to obtain differential characteristics of FUTURE. For instance, the 4-round differential characteristic is obtained by adding the following four constraints:

$$A_0^0 + A_1^0 + \cdots A_{15}^0 = 4$$
$$A_0^1 + A_1^1 + \cdots A_{15}^1 = 1$$
$$A_0^2 + A_1^2 + \cdots A_{15}^2 = 4$$
$$A_0^3 + A_1^3 + \cdots A_{15}^3 = 16$$

where A_j^i stands for the jth S-box in the ith round. These extra constraints are used to determine the number of active S-boxes in each round, such as 4-1-4-16 in this example search strategy.

In Table 3, the best differential probabilities are given with respect to the search strategies we tried.

5.3 Results

The differential characteristic probabilities up to five rounds are given in Table 3.

Table 3. The search strategies tried and the maximum differential probabilities obtained for FUTURE up to 5 rounds

# of rounds	Extra Constraint	Max. Diff. Prob.	# of Var.	# of Cons.
2	1-4	2^{-10}	620	930
3	4-1-4	2^{-18}	1064	1458
4	4-1-4-16	2^{-51}	1508	1986
	1-4-16-4	2^{-55}		
	16-4-1-4	2^{-50}		
	4-16-4-1	2^{-53}		
5	4-1-4-16-4	2^{-63}	1952	2518
	1-4-16-4-1	2^{-58}		
	2-16-4-1-2	2^{-61}		
	2-4-16-4-1	2^{-58}		
	1-4-16-4-2	2^{-61}		

A 5-round characteristic with 2^{-58} probability has been found through our searches. Remarkably, one of these characteristics involves 27 active S-boxes, which is not the minimum number of active S-boxes for 5 rounds.

Designers of FUTURE provided a 4-round differential characteristic with a probability of 2^{-62}. We were able to obtain the probability 2^{-58} for a 5-round characteristic. The details of the 5-round characteristic is given in Table 4.

6 Linear Cryptanalysis of FUTURE

In this section, we describe the details of the MILP model constructed for linear cryptanalysis of FUTURE and how it is implemented in practice. We focus on how a linear approximation of the S-box can be transformed into a linear approximation of the round function, propagating through the MDS matrix multiplication.

Table 4. Differential characteristic of FUTURE for 5 round

Round	Difference	Diff. Prob.
Input	0704 0000 0000 0000	1
1	4000 0700 0050 0007	2^{-4}
2	6161 1C16 4482 3262	2^{-13}
3	0000 0000 0000 6122	2^{-48}
4	0000 0000 0002 0000	2^{-56}
5	0090 0001 8000 0900	2^{-58}

6.1 Linear MILP Model Construction

SubCell. We calculated the LAT for FUTURE's S-box, and, as described in Sect. 4.1, we encoded each input, output, and bias (in absolute value) information as a vector. Then we computed the H-representation. The solution returned 505 inequalities including redundant ones. We utilized Sasaki and Todo's approach and obtained 18 inequalities to represent the S-box's linear behavior.

MixColumn. Let $M_{\mathcal{PR}}$ be the 16×16 binary matrix which is the primitive representation of M over $GF(2)$, as explained in Sect. 5.1, and let $Y_{\mathcal{B}}$ and $Z_{\mathcal{B}}$ be the 16×4 binary matrices, where each column vector is obtained from the corresponding column vector of Y and Z by replacing each field element from $GF(2^4)$ by its binary representation over $GF(2)$. Hence, $Z_{\mathcal{B}} = M_{\mathcal{PR}} Y_{\mathcal{B}}$. We can transform a linear mask on each column of $Y_{\mathcal{B}}$ into a linear mask of the corresponding column of $Z_{\mathcal{B}}$ along the following lines:

Let y and z be column vectors such that $z = M_{\mathcal{PR}} y$, and β^T be the 16-bit row vector (linear mask) indicating the active bits of y in a linear approximation. Then, the corresponding linear mask γ^T on z can be calculated as follows:

$$z = M_{\mathcal{PR}} y$$
$$M_{\mathcal{PR}}^{-1} z = y$$
$$\beta^T M_{\mathcal{PR}}^{-1} z = \beta^T y$$

Hence, $\gamma^T z = \beta^T y$ for,

$$\gamma^T = \beta^T M_{\mathcal{PR}}^{-1}.$$

We need 64 new constraints and 200 new binary d_i dummy variables are needed to model linear propagation over each MDS matrix multiplication,

ShiftRow. The binary variables resulting from the MixColumn operation are permuted through the ShiftRow operation. 64 new binary variables are defined and assigned to these results as introduced in Sect. 4.2.

AddRoundKey. There is no need to model the XOR operation with the round key since linear cryptanalysis is conducted.

6.2   Search Strategy

As explained in Sect. 5.2, the number of variables and constraints used in the MILP model increases as more rounds are added to the model, and the solution time increases exponentially as a result. To tackle this problem and to keep the MILP search within practical limits, we add extra constraints that indicate the number of active S-boxes in each round. The search strategies we used in our search of linear approximations of FUTURE are listed in Table 5.

6.3   Results

The linear approximation biases (in absolute values) up to five rounds are given in Table 5. A 5-round approximation with a bias of 2^{-31} has been found through our searches. The details of the 5-round characteristic is given in Table 6.

Table 5. The search strategies tried and the maximum linear biases obtained for FUTURE up to 5 rounds

# of rounds	Extra Constraint	Max. Linear Bias	# of Var.	# of Cons.
2	1-4	2^{-6}	616	930
3	4-1-4	2^{-10}	1056	1458
4	16-4-1-4	2^{-26}	1496	1986
5	1-4-16-4-1	2^{-32}	1936	2518
	1-4-16-4-2	2^{-31}		
	2-4-16-4-1	2^{-32}		

Table 6. Linear characteristic of FUTURE for 5-round

Round	Input Mask	Linear Bias
Input	0000 0000 0090 0000	1
1	0080 0001 1000 0900	2^{-2}
2	1EF4 79B4 338A FF41	2^{-6}
3	0000 0000 8D73 0000	2^{-25}
4	0000 0000 D000 0F00	2^{-29}
5	0150 00E7 D007 8500	2^{-31}

7 Conclusion

FUTURE is a new, promising lightweight cipher designed for low latency and low hardware cost, based on an AES-like structure. In this paper, we conducted a MILP-based analysis of the cipher to find single-key differential and linear distinguishers. We incorporated the DDT and LAT probabilities into the model and obtained some previously unknown characteristics up to five rounds.

As an additional contribution, we showed an efficient way to model an n-XOR operation with one constraint. The proposed method can be used to improve the MILP models of various cryptanalysis methods in the literature.

The 5-round distinguishers we discovered improve the known distinguishers of FUTURE by one round. Nevertheless, they cannot be extended to the full version of the cipher, and hence do not pose an immediate threat to its security. FUTURE still enjoys a reasonable security margin.

Appendix

We compare the solution times of differential and linear characteristic of FUTURE modeled with the n-XOR method and the method proposed by Ilter and Selcuk [7] in Table 7 and Table 8.

Table 7. Timing comparison of XOR methods for differential characteristics of FUTURE

Round	Ext. Cons.	[7]			This paper		
		# of Var.	# of Cons.	Time (s.)	# of Var.	# of Cons.	Time (s.)
2	–	416	4961	4	620	929	2
3	4-1-4	656	10545	30	1064	1457	2
4	16-4-1-4	896	15621	445	1508	1986	193
4	4-1-4-16	896	15621	478	1508	1986	54

Table 8. Timing comparison of XOR methods for linear characteristics of FUTURE

Round	Ext. Cons.	[7]			This paper		
		# of Var.	# of Cons.	Time (s.)	# of Var.	# of Cons.	Time (s.)
2	–	416	5217	61	616	929	11
3	4-1-4	656	10036	10	1056	1460	1
4	16-4-1-4	896	14853	579	1496	1989	13
4	4-1-4-16	896	14853	260	1496	1989	27

As shown in Table 7 and in Table 8, the proposed n-XOR method uses fewer constraints to model xor operation, leading to shortening solution time.

References

1. Abdelkhalek, A., Sasaki, Y., Todo, Y., Tolba, M., Youssef, A.M.: MILP modeling for (large) S-boxes to optimize probability of differential characteristics. IACR Trans. Symmetric Cryptol. **2017**(4), 99–129 (2017)
2. Boura, C., Coggia, D.: Efficient MILP modelings for Sboxes and linear layers of SPN ciphers. IACR Trans. Symmetric Cryptol. **2020**(3), 327–361 (2020)
3. Fu, K., Wang, M., Guo, Y., Sun, S., Hu, L.: MILP-based automatic search algorithms for differential and linear trails for speck. In: Peyrin, T. (ed.) FSE 2016. LNCS, vol. 9783, pp. 268–288. Springer, Heidelberg (2016). https://doi.org/10.1007/978-3-662-52993-5_14
4. Funabiki, Y., Todo, Y., Isobe, T., Morii, M.: Several MILP-aided attacks against SNOW 2.0. In: Camenisch, J., Papadimitratos, P. (eds.) CANS 2018. LNCS, vol. 11124, pp. 394–413. Springer, Cham (2018). https://doi.org/10.1007/978-3-030-00434-7_20
5. Gupta, K.C., Pandey, S.K., Samanta, S.: FUTURE: a lightweight block cipher using an optimal diffusion matrix. In: Batina, L., Daemen, J. (eds.) AFRICACRYPT 2022. LNCS, vol. 13503, pp. 28–52. Springer, Cham (2022). https://doi.org/10.1007/978-3-031-17433-9_2
6. Gurobi Optimization Inc.: Gurobi optimizer reference manual (2018). http://www.gurobi.com
7. Ilter, M.B., Selçuk, A.A.: A new MILP model for matrix multiplications with applications to KLEIN and PRINCE. In: SECRYPT, pp. 420–427 (2021)
8. Mouha, N., Wang, Q., Gu, D., Preneel, B.: Differential and linear cryptanalysis using mixed-integer linear programming. In: Wu, C.-K., Yung, M., Lin, D. (eds.) Inscrypt 2011. LNCS, vol. 7537, pp. 57–76. Springer, Heidelberg (2012). https://doi.org/10.1007/978-3-642-34704-7_5
9. Sasaki, Yu., Todo, Y.: New algorithm for modeling S-box in MILP based differential and division trail search. In: Farshim, P., Simion, E. (eds.) SecITC 2017. LNCS, vol. 10543, pp. 150–165. Springer, Cham (2017). https://doi.org/10.1007/978-3-319-69284-5_11
10. Sun, L., Wang, W., Liu, R., Wang, M.: MILP-aided bit-based division property for ARX-based block cipher. Cryptology ePrint Archive (2016)
11. Sun, L., Wang, W., Wang, M.Q.: MILP-aided bit-based division property for primitives with non-bit-permutation linear layers. IET Inf. Secur. **14**(1), 12–20 (2020)
12. Sun, S., Hu, L., Song, L., Xie, Y., Wang, P.: Automatic security evaluation of block ciphers with S-bP structures against related-key differential attacks. In: Lin, D., Xu, S., Yung, M. (eds.) Inscrypt 2013. LNCS, vol. 8567, pp. 39–51. Springer, Cham (2014). https://doi.org/10.1007/978-3-319-12087-4_3
13. Sun, S., et al.: Towards finding the best characteristics of some bit-oriented block ciphers and automatic enumeration of (related-key) differential and linear characteristics with predefined properties. IACR Cryptology ePrint Archive 2014/747 (2014)
14. Sun, S., Hu, L., Wang, P., Qiao, K., Ma, X., Song, L.: Automatic security evaluation and (related-key) differential characteristic search: application to SIMON, PRESENT, LBlock, DES(L) and other bit-oriented block ciphers. In: Sarkar, P., Iwata, T. (eds.) ASIACRYPT 2014. LNCS, vol. 8873, pp. 158–178. Springer, Heidelberg (2014). https://doi.org/10.1007/978-3-662-45611-8_9
15. The Sage Developers: SageMath, the Sage Mathematics Software System (Version 9.2) (2020). https://www.sagemath.org

16. Yin, J., et al.: Improved cryptanalysis of an ISO standard lightweight block cipher with refined MILP modelling. In: Chen, X., Lin, D., Yung, M. (eds.) Inscrypt 2017. LNCS, vol. 10726, pp. 404–426. Springer, Cham (2018). https://doi.org/10.1007/978-3-319-75160-3_24
17. Zhu, B., Dong, X., Yu, H.: MILP-based differential attack on round-reduced GIFT. In: Matsui, M. (ed.) CT-RSA 2019. LNCS, vol. 11405, pp. 372–390. Springer, Cham (2019). https://doi.org/10.1007/978-3-030-12612-4_19

Easy-ABE: An Easy Ciphertext-Policy Attribute-Based Encryption

Ahmad Khoureich Ka[(✉)] 📵

Université Alioune Diop de Bambey, Bambey, Senegal
ahmadkhoureich.ka@uadb.edu.sn

Abstract. Attribute-Based Encryption is widely recognized as a leap forward in the field of public key encryption. It allows to enforce an access control on encrypted data. Decryption time in ABE schemes can be long depending on the number of attributes and pairing operations. This drawback hinders their adoption on a broader scale.

In this paper, we propose a non-monotone CP-ABE scheme that has no restrictions on the size of attribute sets and policies, allows fast decryption and is adaptively secure under the CBDH-3 assumption. To achieve this, we approached the problem from a new angle, namely using a set membership relation for access structure. We have implemented our scheme using the Java Pairing-Based Cryptography Library (JPBC) and the source code is available on GitHub.

Keywords: attribute-based encryption · CBDH-3 assumption · non-monotone · random oracle model

1 Introduction

Traditionally, access control was applied to protect unencrypted data stored on servers. But the problem with this system is that if a server is compromised, the attacker gains direct access to unencrypted data. A solution to this problem appeared in 2005 on the proposal of Amit Sahai and Brent Waters [33] called attribute-based encryption. It allows to enforce fine-grained and flexible access controls over encrypted data.

Attribute-Based Encryption (ABE) is widely recognized as a leap forward in the field of public key encryption. It has numerous applications, ranging from cloud services [25], internet of things [3], video streaming [30], to healthcare systems [15].

ABE offers the possibility to encrypt for multiple recipients at once. Those who wanted to access the plaintext from the ciphertext simply had to have the necessary attributes to satisfy the ciphertext's built-in access control. ABE comes in two flavors: Key-Policy Attribute-Based Encryption (KP-ABE) in which the access policy is embedded in the recipients' secret keys and Ciphertext-Policy Attribute-Based Encryption (CP-ABE) in which the access policy is embedded in the ciphertext. However, the design of such schemes faces many practical

G. Bella et al. (Eds.): SecITC 2022, LNCS 13809, pp. 168–183, 2023.
https://doi.org/10.1007/978-3-031-32636-3_10

difficulties that hinder their wide adoption. A practical ABE scheme must have the following essential properties: [2, 34]:

1. no restriction on the size of policies and attribute sets (unboundedness)
2. arbitrary string as an attribute (large universe);
3. based on the fast Type-3 pairings;
4. small number of pairings for decryption;
5. adaptive security under standard assumptions.

Many proposals have been made but few [2, 34] satisfy the properties mentioned above. We believe that a practical ABE scheme of simple structure and more efficient can be constructed.

In this paper, we propose a non-monotonic ciphertext-policy attribute-based encryption denoted Easy-ABE. Our scheme not only offers constant-size secret keys, but also adds the above five properties. Compared to FAME [2], the most efficient scheme in the literature (to our knowledge), our scheme performs much better. We have also implemented our scheme using the Java Pairing-Based Cryptography Library (JPBC) [13] and the source code is available on GitHub [22].

1.1 Related Work

Attribute-Based Encryption is a natural extension of Identity Based Encryption [7,8]. It comes in two flavors: Key-Policy ABE and Ciphertext-Policy ABE. The first KP-ABE scheme was presented by Goyal et al. [19]. Ciphertext-Policy ABE was first proposed by Bethencourt et al. [6] who prove its security under the Decisional Bilinear Diffie-Hellman (DBDH) assumption. It is followed by the work of Cheung et al. [12] in which access structures are AND gates on positive and negative attributes. They improve the security of their scheme by applying the Canetti-Halevi-Katz technique to obtain a chosen ciphertext attack (CCA) security.

Other ABE schemes have emerged focusing on constant-size ciphertexts [4,11,14,16,21,35–37]. In [4], the private key size is linear in the number of attributes of the user. To address the efficiency problem that plagues many schemes due to high computational cost [35] also provides constant computational cost useful when computational and bandwidth issues are major concerns. [20,23,27] have designed constant-size secret key schemes. Besides the constant-size secret key, [27] provides low computational and storage overhead with an expressive AND-gate access structure.

Some schemes take scalability into account. They are called unbounded schemes. Unboundedness is an essential property for an ABE scheme because it allows adding new attributes without having to redeploy the scheme. Lewko and Waters [26] were the first to present such a scheme followed by [2,10,15,28,32,34]. In [15] unboundedness is obtained by limiting the attribute elements in the ciphertexts to only those associated with the attribute group keys of the ciphertext attributes.

Most of the schemes in the literature are monotonous since it is natural to admit that a user having more attributes than required to access an information must have access to that information. But this could give rise to conflict of interest. Non-monotonic ABE schemes have also been proposed [15,28,29,34]. But some of these proposals [28,29] are inefficient when it comes to decryption and storage.

Many ABE schemes [12,15,16,19,20,27,29,32,35,37] offering various attractive properties (such as constant-size ciphertexts, constant-size secret key, scalability, unboundedness) have been shown to be secure only in the selective security model which is weaker than the adaptive security enjoyed by our scheme. The problem with selective security is that for the deployment of the scheme one adversary have to declare the access structure he wants to attack. Which is very unlikely to happen in reality.

Building efficient schemes has been the goal of [2,34]. Their schemes are based on the fast Type-3 pairings, have simultaneously unboundedness, large universe, fast decryption and are adaptively secure under standard assumptions. However, [2] is more efficient than [34] but is less expressive since it does not support negation and multi-use of attributes like [34].

1.2   Organization

This paper is structured as follows: after the introduction, Sect. 2 presents the notations, terminologies and tools necessary for the formal description of our proposal in Sect. 3. The proof of security of our scheme is done in Sect. 4. In Sect. 5, we compare the performance of Easy-ABE to other schemes available in the literature. Section 6 concludes this work.

2   Preliminaries

In this section, we present the notations, terminologies and tools necessary for the presentation of Easy-ABE.

2.1   Access Structures

We denote by $\mathcal{U} = \{A_1, A_2, \cdots, A_l\}$ the universe of attributes where $A_{i,i=1,...,l}$ are attributes. In our scheme, a set of user attributes $\mathcal{S} \subseteq \mathcal{U}$ is mapped to an $|\mathcal{U}|$-bit string $\omega = b_l \cdots b_1$ where $l = |\mathcal{U}|$ and

$$b_i = \begin{cases} 0 & \text{if } A_i \notin \mathcal{S} \\ 1 & \text{otherwise} \end{cases}$$

In the rest of the paper, we call ω a user attribute string. For example, if $\mathcal{S} = \{A_2, A_4, A_5\}$, the user attribute string ω will be $0 \cdots 011010 \in \{0, 1\}^l$.

To generate the user's secret key, ω will be taken as a binary number in $\mathbb{Z}_p^*$ and then mapped to a group element. Representing ω in reverse order (of the indexes) makes our schema scalable since by expanding the universe of attributes (addition of new attributes) the keys generated before the expansion remain valid and no re-encryption of data is needed. For example, if $\mathcal{U}$ expands to $\{A_1, A_2, \cdots, A_l, \cdots, A_n\}$, the user attribute set $\mathcal{S} = \{A_2, A_4, A_5\}$ will be represented by $0\cdots011010 \in \{0,1\}^n$ and will remain unchanged when considered as a binary number. This representation of the set of user attributes guarantees unboundedness and large universe (since any arbitrary string can be used as an attribute) to our scheme.

Definition 1. (Access Structure). *We say that an access structure $\mathbb{A} \subseteq \{0,1\}^n$ is the set of authorized user attribute strings. That is a user attribute string ω is authorized if and only if $\omega \in \mathbb{A}$.*

From our definition of the access structure, it is clear that our scheme is non-monotonic since a monotonic access structure is defined as follows:

Definition 2. (Monotonic Access Structure [2]). *If $\mathcal{U}$ denotes the universe of attributes, then an access structure $\mathbb{A}$ is a collection of non-empty subsets of $\mathcal{U}$, i.e., $\mathbb{A} \in 2^{\mathcal{U}}\backslash\emptyset$. It is called monotone if for every $B, C \subseteq \mathcal{U}$ such that $B \subseteq C, B \in \mathbb{A} \Rightarrow C \in \mathbb{A}$.*

Although it is non-monotonic, Easy-ABE becomes monotonic if it is accepted for a user to query for a secret key associated to a subset of her/his set of attributes.

The access structure can also be defined without the use of a universe of attributes by considering directly the set of binary strings representing authorized users identities. For example, informations on citizen id card can be hashed to serve as user attribute string.

2.2   Ciphertext-Policy ABE

A Ciphertext-Policy Attribute-Based Encryption consists of four algorithms (adapted from [6]):

- **Setup**(λ): The algorithm takes a security parameter λ and outputs the system parameters params, a master public key mpk and a master secret key msk.
- **Encrypt**(mpk, $\mathbb{A}$, m): The algorithm takes the master public key mpk, a set of authorized user attribute strings $\mathbb{A}$ and a message m then outputs a ciphertext ct.
- **KeyGen**(mpk, msk, ω): The algorithm takes the master public key mpk, the master secret key msk and a user attribute string ω then outputs a secret key sk.
- **Decrypt**(ct, sk): The algorithm takes a ciphertext ct and a secret key sk then outputs the plaintext m or $\perp$.

2.3   Security Model

In this paper, we are interested in indistinguishability under chosen plaintext attack (IND-CPA) modelled by the following IND-CPA game between a challenger $\mathcal{C}$ and an adversary $\mathcal{A}$:

- **Setup.** $\mathcal{C}$ runs the Setup algorithm of a CP-ABE scheme denoted Π with the security parameter λ as input and gives params and mpk to $\mathcal{A}$.
- **Phase 1.** $\mathcal{A}$ can make repeated (at will) secret key queries for user attribute strings ω and receives from $\mathcal{C}$ their corresponding secret keys.
- **Challenge.** $\mathcal{A}$ submits a set of user attribute strings $\mathbb{A}$ and two messages m_0, m_1 of the same length. One restriction should be noted: the intersection of $\mathbb{A}$ and the set of user attribute strings used for secret key queries must be empty. $\mathcal{C}$ randomly selects $b \in \{0,1\}$, encrypts the message m_b and sends the result to the $\mathcal{A}$.
- **Phase 2.** Similar to phase 1 with the restriction that the intersection of $\mathbb{A}$ and the set of user attribute strings used for secret key queries must be empty.
- **Guess.** The adversary outputs a guess b' of b. We say that $\mathcal{A}$ succeeded if $b' = b$.

The advantage of an adversary $\mathcal{A}$ in the IND-CPA game is defined as

$$\mathsf{Adv}_{\Pi}^{\mathcal{A}}(\lambda) = \Pr[b' = b] - \frac{1}{2}$$

Definition 3. *A CP-ABE scheme Π is fully or adaptively IND-CPA secure if for any polynomial time adversary $\mathcal{A}$, $\mathsf{Adv}_{\Pi}^{\mathcal{A}}$ is negligible, that is to say $\mathsf{Adv}_{\Pi}^{\mathcal{A}}$ is smaller than the inverse of any polynomial, for all large enough values of λ.*

2.4   Bilinear Maps and Diffie-Hellman Assumption

Let $\mathbb{G}_1$, $\mathbb{G}_2$ and $\mathbb{G}_T$ be three cyclic groups of prime order p. A bilinear pairing is a map $e : \mathbb{G}_1 \times \mathbb{G}_2 \to \mathbb{G}_T$ with the following properties [9,17]:

1. Bilinearity: $e(g_1 g_1', g_2 g_2') = e(g_1, g_2)e(g_1, g_2')e(g_1', g_2)e(g_1', g_2')$ for all $g_1, g_1' \in \mathbb{G}_1, g_2, g_2' \in \mathbb{G}_2$.
2. Non-degeneracy: for any $g_1 \in \mathbb{G}_1$, if $e(g_1, g_2) = 1$ for all $g_2 \in \mathbb{G}_2$, then $g_1 = 1$ (and similarly with $\mathbb{G}_1$, $\mathbb{G}_2$ reversed).
3. Computability: The map e is efficiently computable. ·

The pairing is asymmetric when $\mathbb{G}_1 \neq \mathbb{G}_2$ and of Type-3 when no efficiently-computable isomorphism is known from $\mathbb{G}_2$ to $\mathbb{G}_1$ (or from $\mathbb{G}_1$ to $\mathbb{G}_2$).

Definition 4. *(Bilinear group generator [17]). For the purpose of simplicity we say that an asymmetric bilinear group generator is an algorithm $\mathcal{G}$ that takes as input a security parameter λ and outputs a description of three groups $\mathbb{G}_1$, $\mathbb{G}_2$ and $\mathbb{G}_T$ of prime order p. We assume that this description permits efficient (polynomial-time in λ) group operations and random sampling in each group. The algorithm also outputs an efficiently computable map $e : \mathbb{G}_1 \times \mathbb{G}_2 \to \mathbb{G}_T$ and generators g_1 and g_2 for $\mathbb{G}_1$ and $\mathbb{G}_2$, respectively.*

Definition 5. (Computational Bilinear Diffie-Hellman Problem in Type-3 (CBDH-3) [9]). *Given $g_1^\alpha, g_1^\beta, g_1^\gamma \in \mathbb{G}_1$ and $g_2^\beta, g_2^\gamma \in \mathbb{G}_2$ for $\alpha, \beta, \gamma \in_R \mathbb{Z}_p^*$, the CBDH-3 problem is to compute the Type-3 pairing value $e(g_1, g_2)^{\alpha\beta\gamma}$. The CBDH-3 assumption asserts that CBDH-3 problem is hard. That is to say for all PPT adversaries $\mathcal{A}$ the advantage:*

$$\mathsf{Adv}_{\mathsf{CBDH\text{-}3}}^{\mathcal{A}}(\lambda) = \Pr\left[\mathcal{A}\left(\begin{array}{c} pair\text{-}grp, \\ g_1^\alpha, g_1^\beta, g_1^\gamma \in \mathbb{G}_1, \\ g_2^\beta, g_2^\gamma \in \mathbb{G}_2 \end{array}\right) = e(g_1, g_2)^{\alpha\beta\gamma} \left|\begin{array}{c} pair\text{-}grp \leftarrow \mathcal{G}(\lambda), \\ \alpha, \beta, \gamma \in_R \mathbb{Z}_p^* \end{array}\right.\right]$$

is negligible in λ, where $pair\text{-}grp = (p, \mathbb{G}_1, \mathbb{G}_2, \mathbb{G}_T, g_1, g_2, e)$.

2.5   Some Cryptographic Primitives

In this section, we briefly present some cryptographic primitives used in our scheme.

Symmetric Encryption Scheme. A symmetric encryption scheme (SYM) is a pair of probabilistic polynomial-time algorithms (Enc, Dec) such that:

1. The encryption algorithm Enc takes as input a key $k \in \{0,1\}^n$ (n is related to a security parameter) and a plaintext message $m \in \{0,1\}^*$, and returns a ciphertext $c \in \{0,1\}^*$.
2. The decryption algorithm Dec takes as input a key k and a ciphertext c, and returns a message m.

It is required that for all k and m, $\mathsf{Dec}_k(\mathsf{Enc}_k(m)) = m$.

The symmetric encryption scheme is said to be secure in the sense of INDistinguishability under Chosen-Plaintext Attacks (IND-CPA) if from the encryption of one of its two messages, the adversary cannot tell which one has been encrypted even if it has knowledge of encryptions of many other messages of its choice.

Message Authentication Codes. A message authentication code (MAC) is a pair of probabilistic polynomial-time algorithms (Mac, Vrfy) such that:

1. The tag-generation algorithm Mac takes as input a key $k \in \{0,1\}^n$ (n is related to a security parameter) and a message $m \in \{0,1\}^*$, and returns a tag t.
2. The verification algorithm Vrfy takes as input a key k, a message m and a tag t. It returns 1 indicating that t is valid, thus m is authentic and 0 indicating that t is invalid, thus m is unauthentic.

It is required that for all k and m, $\mathsf{Vrfy}_k(m, \mathsf{Mac}_k(m)) = 1$.

The message authentication code is said to satisfy Strong Unforgeability under Chosen-Message Attacks (SUF-CMA) it is computationally infeasible for the adversary to provide a new tag t for a message m even if it has knowledge of many other tags for messages of its choice [5].

Key Derivation Function. Formally, a key derivation function (KDF) is define in [24] as an algorithm that takes as input four arguments: a value σ sampled from a source of keying material, a value l indicating the length of the secret key to return, and two additional arguments, a salt value r defined over a set of possible salt values and a context variable c, both of which are optional, i.e., can be set to the null string or to a constant.

Informally, the key derivation function is said to be secure if its output distribution is computationally indistinguishable from the uniform distribution over $\{0,1\}^l$.

In our scheme, the source of keying material is an algebraic group.

2.6 Diffie-Hellman Integrated Encryption Scheme

Abdalla et al. [1] suggested a method for encrypting strings using the Diffie-Hellman assumption. The method is called Diffie-Hellman Integrated Encryption Scheme (DHIES) and is secure against chosen-ciphertext attack. The version [18] we describe here uses a symmetric encryption scheme $\mathsf{SYM} = (\mathsf{Enc}, \mathsf{Dec})$ a message authentication code $\mathsf{MAC} = (\mathsf{Mac}, \mathsf{Vrfy})$ and a key derivation function KDF.

Let $\mathbb{G}$ be a finite cyclic group of order p generated by g. Let $a \in_R \mathbb{Z}_p^*$ and $h = g^a$. The public key is $(\mathbb{G}, g, h)$ and the private key is a.

Encrypt(m, h): To encrypt $\mathsf{m} \in \{0,1\}^*$, do the following:

1. Choose a random $k \in \mathbb{Z}_p^*$ and set $c_1 = g^k$
2. Set $\kappa = \mathsf{KDF}(h^k, l_1 + l_2)$ and parse κ as $\kappa_1 \| \kappa_2$ where κ_1 and κ_2 are l_1 and l_2 bit binary strings respectively.
3. Set $c_2 = \mathsf{Enc}_{\kappa_1}(\mathsf{m})$ and $c_3 = \mathsf{Mac}_{\kappa_2}(c_2)$.
4. Transmit the ciphertext (c_1, c_2, c_3).

Decrypt(c_1, c_2, c_3, a):

1. Compute $\kappa = \mathsf{KDF}(c_1^a, l_1 + l_2)$ and parse it as $\kappa_1 \| \kappa_2$ where κ_1 and κ_2 are l_1 and l_2 bit binary strings respectively.
2. Check whether $\mathsf{Vrfy}_{\kappa_2}(c_3, \mathsf{Mac}_{\kappa_2}(c_2)) = 1$ (if not then return $\perp$ and halt).
3. Return $\mathsf{m} = \mathsf{Dec}_{\kappa_1}(c_2)$.

3 Easy-ABE: Our CP-ABE Scheme

In this section, we give a formal description of the four algorithms (Setup, Encrypt, KeyGen and Decrypt) that characterise Easy-ABE:

Setup(λ): To produce the system parameters params, the master public key mpk and the master secret key msk, the algorithm performs the following steps:

(1) Run $\mathcal{G}(\lambda)$ to obtain $(p, \mathbb{G}_1, \mathbb{G}_2, \mathbb{G}_T, g_1, g_2, e)$.

(2) Choose two cryptographic hash functions:

$$H_1 : \{0,1\}^n \to \mathbb{G}_1 \quad \text{and} \quad H_2 : \mathbb{G}_T \to \mathbb{Z}_p^*$$

(3) Choose two random exponents α and $\beta \in \mathbb{Z}_p^*$.
(4) Since our scheme uses a Diffie-Hellman Integrated Encryption Scheme (DHIES) [1], choose an IND-CPA secure symmetric encryption scheme SYM = (Enc, Dec) a SUF-CMA secure message authentication code MAC = (Mac, Vrfy) and a secure key derivation function KDF.
(5) Return the system parameters, the master public key and the master secret key:

$$\text{params} = (H_1, H_2, \text{SYM}, \text{MAC}, \text{KDF})$$

$$\text{mpk} = (g_1, g_1^\alpha, g_1^\beta, g_2, g_2^\beta)$$

$$\text{msk} = (\alpha, \beta)$$

KeyGen(mpk, msk, ω): To produce the user secret key for the user attribute string ω, the algorithm performs the following steps:

(1) Compute $h_\omega = H_1(\omega) \in \mathbb{G}_1$.
(2) Pick a random $r \in \mathbb{Z}_p^*$ and return the secret key

$$\text{sk} = (g_1^{\alpha\beta} h_\omega^r, g_2^r)$$

Encrypt(mpk, $\mathbb{A}$, m): To encrypt a message m $\in \{0,1\}^*$ under the set of authorized user attribute strings $\mathbb{A}$, the algorithm performs the following steps:

(1) Pick a random exponent $s \in \mathbb{Z}_p^*$.
(2) Compute $h_\omega = H_1(\omega) \in \mathbb{G}_1$, $\quad \forall \omega \in \mathbb{A}$.
(3) Compute $\sigma = H_2(e(g_1^\alpha, g_2^\beta)^s)$
(4) Perform a DHIES [1].
  (a) Pick a random $k \in \mathbb{Z}_p^*$, set $c_1 = g_1^\beta g_1^k$.
  (b) Compute $\kappa = \text{KDF}(c_1^\sigma, l_1 + l_2)$ and split the binary string κ in two substrings κ_1 and κ_2 of length l_1 and l_2 respectively ($\kappa = \kappa_1 || \kappa_2$). l_1 and l_2 must match the key lengths of the underlying SYM and MAC schemes respectively.
  (c) Compute $c_2 = \text{Enc}_{\kappa_1}(m)$ and $c_3 = \text{Mac}_{\kappa_2}(c_2)$.
(5) Return the ciphertext:

$$\text{ct} = (c_1, c_2, c_3, g_2^s, \{h_\omega^s\}_{\omega \in \mathbb{A}})$$

Decrypt(ct, sk): To decrypt the ciphertext ct with the user secret key sk, the algorithm performs the following steps:

(1) Find h_ω^s in ct with the same index ω as in $g_1^{\alpha\beta} h_\omega^r$ in sk. If the search fails then return $\perp$ and halt.

(2) Otherwise, let h_ω^s be the returned value from the search then compute:

$$\rho = e(g_1^{\alpha\beta} h_\omega^r, g_2^s)/e(h_\omega^s, g_2^r)$$
$$= e(g_1, g_2)^{\alpha\beta s} e(h_\omega, g_2)^{rs}/e(h_\omega, g_2)^{sr}$$
$$= e(g_1, g_2)^{\alpha\beta s} \tag{1}$$

(3) Compute $\sigma = H_2(\rho)$.
(4) Recover m with DHIES [1].
  (a) Compute $\kappa = \mathsf{KDF}(c_1^\sigma, l_1 + l_2)$ and split the binary string κ in two substrings κ_1 and κ_2 of length l_1 and l_2 respectively ($\kappa = \kappa_1 || \kappa_2$). l_1 and l_2 must match the key lengths of the underlying SYM and MAC schemes respectively.
  (b) Compute $b = \mathsf{Vrfy}_{\kappa_2}(c_3, \mathsf{Mac}_{\kappa_2}(c_2))$, if $b = 0$ then return $\perp$ and halt.
  (c) Otherwise, compute $\mathsf{m} = \mathsf{Dec}_{\kappa_1}(c_2)$.
(5) Return the plaintext m.

4   Security Analysis

The security of Easy-ABE is based on the hardness of the Computational Bilinear Diffie-Hellman Problem in Type-3 (CBDH-3). Assuming that the underlying primitives (SYM, MAC and KDF) are secure, we show that the proposed scheme has ciphertext indistinguishability against chosen plaintext attack (IND-CPA) in the random oracle model.

Theorem 1. *Let H_1 and H_2 be two random oracles. Let SYM be a symmetric encryption scheme, let MAC be a message authentication code and let KDF be a key derivation function. If there exists an IND-CPA adversary $\mathcal{A}$ that has advantage $\epsilon(\lambda)$ against Easy-ABE by making q secret key queries and a challenge set of size m of user attribute strings, then there exists a simulator that solves the CBDH-3 problem with advantage at least $m\epsilon(\lambda)/q$ and a running time $\mathcal{O}(time(\mathcal{A}))$.*

Proof. The simulator is given a random instance of the CBDH-3 problem: g_1, g_1^a, g_1^b, $g_1^c \in \mathbb{G}_1$ and g_2, g_2^b, $g_2^c \in \mathbb{G}_2$ for a, b and c randomly choosen from $\mathbb{Z}_p^*$. The simulator must output the solution of the CBDH-3 problem that is $e(g_1, g_2)^{abc} \in \mathbb{G}_T$. The groups $\mathbb{G}_1$, $\mathbb{G}_2$ and $\mathbb{G}_T$ are of prime order p, g_1 and g_2 are generators of $\mathbb{G}_1$ and $\mathbb{G}_2$ respectively.

Now we describe how the simulator uses adversary $\mathcal{A}$ to solve the CBDH-3 problem in the following IND-CPA security game:

Setup: The simulator runs the Setup algorithm of Easy-ABE and sends to $\mathcal{A}$ the system parameters and the master public key:

$$\mathsf{params} = (H_1, H_2, \mathsf{SYM}, \mathsf{MAC}, \mathsf{KDF})$$

$$\mathsf{mpk} = (g_1, g_1^a, g_1^b, g_2, g_2^b)$$

Note that the two hash functions H_1 and H_2 are random oracles controlled by the simulator as described below.

H_1-**queries:** The adversary $\mathcal{A}$ can send an H_1 query at any time. Therefore the simulator maintains a list initially empty of the form $(\omega, t, h_\omega) \in \{0,1\}^n \times \mathbb{Z}_p^* \times \mathbb{G}_1$. This list is denoted H_1-list. When a query $H_1(\omega)$ is received, the simulator checks if the tuple (ω, t, h_ω) is in the list. If yes responds with $H_1(\omega) = h_\omega$. Otherwise it picks a random $t \in \mathbb{Z}_p^*$, computes $h_\omega = g_1^a g_1^t \in \mathbb{G}_1$, adds the tuple (ω, t, h_ω) to the list and responds with $H_1(\omega) = h_\omega$.

H_2-**queries:** The adversary $\mathcal{A}$ can send an H_2 query at any time. Therefore the simulator maintains a list initially empty of the form $(x, y) \in \mathbb{G}_T \times \mathbb{Z}_p^*$. This list is denoted H_2-list. When a query $H_2(x)$ is received, the simulator checks if the tuple (x, y) is in the list. If yes responds with $H_2(x) = y$. Otherwise, it picks a random $y \in \mathbb{Z}_p^*$, adds the tuple (x, y) to the list and responds with $H_2(x) = y$.

Phase 1: The adversary $\mathcal{A}$ can send secret key queries for user attribute strings $\{\omega_i\}_{i=1 \,..\, l}$ of its choice. Therefore, the simulator maintains a list initially empty of the form $(\omega_i, \mathsf{sk}_i = (\mu_i, \nu_i))$. This list is denoted sk-list. When a secret key query for $\omega_i \in \{0,1\}^n$ is received, the simulator runs the H_1-**queries** algorithm to obtain the tuple $(\omega_i, t_i, h_{\omega_i})$ corresponding to ω_i from the H_1-list, picks a random $r \in \mathbb{Z}_p^*$ and responds to $\mathcal{A}$ with

$$\mathsf{sk}_i = \left((g_1^b)^{-t_i} h_{\omega_i}^r, g_2^r / g_2^b\right) \tag{2}$$

The simulator adds the tuple $(\omega_i, \mathsf{sk}_i)$ to the sk-list. One can see that sk_i is a valid secret key because

$$(g_1^b)^{-t_i} h_{\omega_i}^r = g_1^{ab} g_1^{-ab} g_1^{-bt_i} (g_1^a g_1^{t_i})^r = g_1^{ab} (g_1^a g_1^{t_i})^{(r-b)} = g_1^{ab} h_{\omega_i}^{(r-b)} = g_1^{ab} h_{\omega_i}^{\tilde{r}}$$

which shows that (2) satisfies $(g_1^{ab} h_{\omega_i}^{\tilde{r}}, g_2^{\tilde{r}})$ matching the definition of a secret key in the **KeyGen** algorithm of Easy-ABE.

Challenge: When the adversary feels ready for the challenge, it submits a set of user attribute strings $\mathbb{A}$ and two messages $m_0, m_1 \in \{0,1\}^*$ of the same length. If there is an ω present at the same time in both $\mathbb{A}$ and sk-list then the simulator terminates its interactions with $\mathcal{A}$ and outputs abort. Otherwise the simulator selects $m_{b,b \in \{0,1\}}$, picks two random $c_2, c_3 \in \{0,1\}^*$ (with the appropriate lengths related to the output-length of Enc and Mac), m random $s_i \in \mathbb{Z}_p^*$ where $m = |\mathbb{A}|$ the number of elements in $\mathbb{A}$. The simulator responds to $\mathcal{A}$ with the ciphertext

$$\mathsf{ct} = (g_1^c, c_2, c_3, g_2^c, \{(g_1^c)^{s_i}\}_{i=1 \,..\, m}) = (g_1^c, c_2, c_3, g_2^c, \{(g_1^{s_i})^c\}_{i=1 \,..\, m})$$

Note that the tuple (g_1^c, c_2, c_3) is indistinguishable from the encryption of a random message m as in the real ciphertext since the underlying primitives (SYM, MAC and KDF) are secure [31]. Also, note that from the H_1-**queries** algorithm each $\omega \in \mathbb{A}$ is mapped to a random element $h_\omega \in \mathbb{G}_1$ as the $g_1^{s_i}$ for $i = 1 \,..\, m$ are random in $\mathbb{G}_1$. Therefore, ct is a valid ciphertext.

One can see that with a secret key of the form $\mathsf{sk}_i = (g_1^{ab} g_1^{s_i r}, g_2^r)$ for $i \in [1 .. m]$ the solution $e(g_1, g_2)^{abc}$ of the instance of the CBDH-3 problem given to the simulator appears in the **Challenge** phase.

Phase 2: $\mathcal{A}$ sends more secret key queries for user attribute strings $\{\omega_i\}_{i=l+1 .. q}$ of its choice as in **Phase 1** with the restriction that none of the ω_i is in the set of user attribute strings $\mathbb{A}$ used in the **Challenge** phase.

Guess: Adversary $\mathcal{A}$ outputs its guess $b' \in \{0, 1\}$. The simulator selects a random tuple $(\omega_j, \mathsf{sk}_j = (\mu_j, \nu_j))$ from the sk-list, computes $\rho = e(\mu_j, g_2^c)/e(g_1^{s_i c}, \nu_j)$ for an $i \in [1 .. m]$ and outputs ρ as the solution to the given instance of CBDH-3 problem.

The fact that the secret keys and the ciphertext sent to $\mathcal{A}$ from queries are valid justifies that the view of $\mathcal{A}$ when used by the simulator is distributed identically to $\mathcal{A}$'s view in a real attack against Easy-ABE.

The simulator outputs the correct solution when $b' = b$ and there is a tuple in the H_1-list of the form $(*, *, g^{s_i})_{i \in [1 .. m]}$ produced when the **Phase 1** algorithm is run. Let H_1-sublist be the subset of H_1-list containing tuples produced by executions of the **Phase 1** algorithm and let $\mathcal{E}$ be the event that the simulator's output is correct. Let $\mathcal{B}$ be the event that there exist an $i \in [1 .. m]$ such that the tuple $(*, *, g^{s_i})$ appears in H_1-sublist. We have:

$$\Pr[b' = b] = \Pr[b' = b \mid \mathcal{B}] \cdot \Pr[\mathcal{B}] + \Pr[b' = b \mid \overline{\mathcal{B}}] \cdot \Pr[\overline{\mathcal{B}}]$$
$$\leq \Pr[b' = b \mid \mathcal{B}] + \Pr[b' = b \mid \overline{\mathcal{B}}] \cdot \Pr[\overline{\mathcal{B}}] \tag{3}$$

If event $\mathcal{B}$ does not occur, then the view of $\mathcal{A}$ in its interactions with the simulator is independent of $e(g_1, g_2)^{abc}$. Therefore $\Pr[b' = b \mid \overline{\mathcal{B}}] = 1/2$ and (3) becomes:

$$\Pr[b' = b] \leq \Pr[b' = b \mid \mathcal{B}] + \frac{1}{2}\Pr[\overline{\mathcal{B}}] \leq \Pr[b' = b \mid \mathcal{B}] + \frac{1}{2} \tag{4}$$

which leads to

$$\Pr[b' = b \mid \mathcal{B}] \geq \Pr[b' = b] - \frac{1}{2} = \mathsf{Adv}_{\Pi}^{\mathcal{A}}(\lambda) = \epsilon \tag{5}$$

To complete the proof of the theorem, we have:

$$\Pr[\mathcal{E}] = \Pr[b' = b \wedge \mathcal{B}]$$
$$= \Pr[b' = b \mid \mathcal{B}] \cdot \Pr[\mathcal{B}]$$
$$= \Pr[b' = b \mid \mathcal{B}] \cdot \Pr[\exists i \text{ s.t. } (*, *, g^{s_i}) \in H_1\text{-sublist}]$$
$$\geq \epsilon \cdot \sum_{i=1}^{m} \Pr[(*, *, g^{s_i}) \in H_1\text{-sublist}] = m\epsilon/q$$

$\square$

5   Theoretical Comparison

We compare Easy-ABE with FAME by Agrawal and Chase [2]. FAME satisfies the five essential properties: based on the fast Type-3 pairings, adaptive security, unboundedness, large universe, fast decryption.

In this comparison, we are interested in two metrics that are the computational cost and storage cost. For the computational cost, we compare the number of multiplications, exponentiations, hash function calls and pairings in key-generation, encryption and decryption algorithms, see Tables 1, 2 and 3. For the storage cost we compare the number of group elements in secret keys and ciphertexts, see Table 4.

Table 1. Comparison of the number of operations for Key generation. T denotes the number of attributes.

Scheme	Key generation					
	$\mathbb{G}_1$			$\mathbb{G}_2$		
	Mul	Exp	Hash	Mul	Exp	Hash
Our	1	2	1	–	1	–
FAME [2]	$8T + 9$	$9T + 9$	$6(T + 1)$	–	3	–

Table 2. Comparison of the number of operations for encryption. m is the size of access structure $\mathbb{A}$ and n_1, n_2 are the dimensions of the monotone span programs (MSP).

Scheme	Encryption					
	$\mathbb{G}_1$			$\mathbb{G}_2$		
	Mul	Exp	Hash	Mul	Exp	Hash
Our	1	$m + 2$	m	–	1	–
FAME [2]	$12n_1n_2 + 6n_1$	$6n_1$	$6(n_1 + n_2)$	–	3	–

From these tables, it is clear that our scheme is more efficient than FAME [2] in terms of computational cost and storage cost. FAME in turn works slightly better than [34]. However, the latter is more expressive since it can deal with natural negation and multi-use of attributes. It should be noted that in the comparison we did not take into account the running time of the symmetric encryption scheme, the running time of the message authentication code and the complexity of the search algorithm used in the first step of our decryption algorithm.

Table 3. Comparison of the number of operations for decryption. I is the number of attributes used in decryption.

Scheme	Decryption			
	Multiplication			Pairing
	$\mathbb{G}_1$	$\mathbb{G}_2$	$\mathbb{G}_T$	
Our	–	–	1	2
FAME [2]	$6I + 3$	–	6	6

Table 4. Comparison of the storage cost of secret key and ciphertext. m is the size of access structure $\mathbb{A}$, T denotes the number of attributes; and n_1, n_2 are the dimensions of the monotone span programs (MSP).

Scheme	Storage cost			
	Key size		Ciphertext size	
	$\mathbb{G}_1$	$\mathbb{G}_2$	$\mathbb{G}_1$	$\mathbb{G}_2$
Our	1	1	$m + 1$	1
FAME [2]	$3(T + 1)$	3	$3n_1$	3

6   Conclusion

In this paper, we have proposed a ciphertext-policy attribute-based encryption scheme denoted Easy-ABE that is efficient in terms of computationnal and storage cost. Our scheme is non-monotonic but can be monotonic when it is accepted for a user to query for a secret key associated to a subset of her/his set of attributes. Easy-ABE has the five essential properties required for a practical ABE scheme: it is based on the fast Type-3 pairings, is adaptively secure under CBDH-3 assumption, has unboundedness, large universe and fast decryption.

With the use of DHIES, we believe that our scheme has indistinguishable encryptions under a chosen-ciphertext attack, but this remains to be proven. It would be interesting to prove it without resorting to the random oracle heuristic.

Acknowledgements. We would like to thank the anonymous reviewers for their detailed and insightful comments on an early draft of this paper.

References

1. Abdalla, M., Bellare, M., Rogaway, P.: The oracle Diffie-Hellman assumptions and an analysis of DHIES. In: Naccache, D. (ed.) CT-RSA 2001. LNCS, vol. 2020, pp. 143–158. Springer, Heidelberg (2001). https://doi.org/10.1007/3-540-45353-9_12
2. Agrawal, S., Chase, M.: Fame: fast attribute-based message encryption. In: CCS 2017. Association for Computing Machinery, New York (2017). https://doi.org/10.1145/3133956.3134014

3. Ambrosin, M., et al.: On the feasibility of attribute-based encryption on internet of things devices. IEEE Micro **36**(6), 25–35 (2016). https://doi.org/10.1109/MM. 2016.101

4. Attrapadung, N., Herranz, J., Laguillaumie, F., Libert, B., de Panafieu, E., Ràfols, C.: Attribute-based encryption schemes with constant-size ciphertexts. Theoret. Comput. Sci. **422**, 15–38 (2012). https://doi.org/10.1016/j.tcs.2011.12.004

5. Bellare, M., Namprempre, C.: Authenticated encryption: relations among notions and analysis of the generic composition paradigm. J. Cryptol. **21**(4), 469–491 (2008). https://doi.org/10.1007/s00145-008-9026-x

6. Bethencourt, J., Sahai, A., Waters, B.: Ciphertext-policy attribute-based encryption. In: 2007 IEEE Symposium on Security and Privacy (SP 2007), pp. 321–334 (2007). https://doi.org/10.1109/SP.2007.11

7. Boneh, D., Boyen, X.: Secure identity based encryption without random oracles. In: Franklin, M. (ed.) CRYPTO 2004. LNCS, vol. 3152, pp. 443–459. Springer, Heidelberg (2004). https://doi.org/10.1007/978-3-540-28628-8_27

8. Boneh, D., Franklin, M.: Identity-based encryption from the weil pairing. In: Kilian, J. (ed.) CRYPTO 2001. LNCS, vol. 2139, pp. 213–229. Springer, Heidelberg (2001). https://doi.org/10.1007/3-540-44647-8_13

9. Chatterjee, S., Menezes, A.: On cryptographic protocols employing asymmetric pairings - the role of ψ revisited. Discret. Appl. Math. **159**(13), 1311–1322 (2011). https://doi.org/10.1016/j.dam.2011.04.021

10. Chen, J., Gong, J., Kowalczyk, L., Wee, H.: Unbounded ABE via bilinear entropy expansion, revisited. In: Nielsen, J.B., Rijmen, V. (eds.) EUROCRYPT 2018. LNCS, vol. 10820, pp. 503–534. Springer, Cham (2018). https://doi.org/10.1007/ 978-3-319-78381-9_19

11. Chen, J., Wee, H.: Semi-adaptive attribute-based encryption and improved delegation for boolean formula. In: Abdalla, M., De Prisco, R. (eds.) SCN 2014. LNCS, vol. 8642, pp. 277–297. Springer, Cham (2014). https://doi.org/10.1007/978-3-319-10879-7_16

12. Cheung, L., Newport, C.: Provably secure ciphertext policy ABE. In: CCS 2007, pp. 456–465. Association for Computing Machinery, New York (2007). https://doi. org/10.1145/1315245.1315302

13. De Caro, A., Iovino, V.: jPBC: Java pairing based cryptography. In: Proceedings of the 16th IEEE Symposium on Computers and Communications, ISCC 2011, Kerkyra, Corfu, Greece, 28 June–1 July 2011, pp. 850–855. IEEE (2011). http:// gas.dia.unisa.it/projects/jpbc/

14. Doshi, N., Jinwala, D.C.: Fully secure ciphertext policy attribute-based encryption with constant length ciphertext and faster decryption. Secur. Commun. Netw. **7**(11), 1988–2002 (2014). https://doi.org/10.1002/sec.913

15. Edemacu, K., Jang, B., Kim, J.: CESCR: CP-ABE for efficient and secure sharing of data in collaborative ehealth with revocation and no dummy attribute. PLoS ONE **16**(5), e0250992 (2021). https://doi.org/10.1371/journal.pone.0250992

16. Emura, K., Miyaji, A., Nomura, A., Omote, K., Soshi, M.: A ciphertext-policy attribute-based encryption scheme with constant ciphertext length. In: Bao, F., Li, H., Wang, G. (eds.) ISPEC 2009. LNCS, vol. 5451, pp. 13–23. Springer, Heidelberg (2009). https://doi.org/10.1007/978-3-642-00843-6_2

17. Freeman, D.M.: Converting pairing-based cryptosystems from composite-order groups to prime-order groups. In: Gilbert, H. (ed.) EUROCRYPT 2010. LNCS, vol. 6110, pp. 44–61. Springer, Heidelberg (2010). https://doi.org/10.1007/978-3-642-13190-5_3

18. Galbraith, S.D.: Mathematics of Public Key Cryptography. Cambridge University Press (2012). https://doi.org/10.1017/CBO9781139012843

19. Goyal, V., Pandey, O., Sahai, A., Waters, B.: Attribute-based encryption for fine-grained access control of encrypted data. In: Proceedings of the 13th ACM Conference on Computer and Communications Security, CCS 2006, pp. 89–98. Association for Computing Machinery, New York (2006). https://doi.org/10.1145/1180405.1180418

20. Guo, F., Mu, Y., Susilo, W., Wong, D.S., Varadharajan, V.: CP-ABE with constant-size keys for lightweight devices. IEEE Trans. Inf. Forensics Secur. 9(5), 763–771 (2014). https://doi.org/10.1109/TIFS.2014.2309858

21. Herranz, J., Laguillaumie, F., Ràfols, C.: Constant size ciphertexts in threshold attribute-based encryption. In: Nguyen, P.Q., Pointcheval, D. (eds.) PKC 2010. LNCS, vol. 6056, pp. 19–34. Springer, Heidelberg (2010). https://doi.org/10.1007/978-3-642-13013-7_2

22. Ka, A.K.: Easyabe (2022). https://github.com/khoureich/EasyABE.git

23. Kothari, R., Choudhary, N., Jain, K.: CP-ABE scheme with decryption keys of constant size using ECC with expressive threshold access structure. In: Mathur, R., Gupta, C.P., Katewa, V., Jat, D.S., Yadav, N. (eds.) Emerging Trends in Data Driven Computing and Communications. SADIC, pp. 15–36. Springer, Singapore (2021). https://doi.org/10.1007/978-981-16-3915-9_2

24. Krawczyk, H.: Cryptographic extraction and key derivation: the HKDF scheme. In: Rabin, T. (ed.) CRYPTO 2010. LNCS, vol. 6223, pp. 631–648. Springer, Heidelberg (2010). https://doi.org/10.1007/978-3-642-14623-7_34

25. Kumar, N.S., Lakshmi, G.R., Balamurugan, B.: Enhanced attribute based encryption for cloud computing. Procedia Comput. Sci. 46, 689–696 (2015). https://doi.org/10.1016/j.procs.2015.02.127. Proceedings of the International Conference on Information and Communication Technologies, ICICT 2014, 3–5 December 2014 at Bolgatty Palace & Island Resort, Kochi, India

26. Lewko, A., Waters, B.: Unbounded HIBE and attribute-based encryption. In: Paterson, K.G. (ed.) EUROCRYPT 2011. LNCS, vol. 6632, pp. 547–567. Springer, Heidelberg (2011). https://doi.org/10.1007/978-3-642-20465-4_30

27. Odelu, V., Das, A.K.: Design of a new CP-ABE with constant-size secret keys for lightweight devices using elliptic curve cryptography. Secur. Commun. Netw. 9(17), 4048–4059 (2016). https://doi.org/10.1002/sec.1587

28. Okamoto, T., Takashima, K.: Fully secure unbounded inner-product and attribute-based encryption. In: Wang, X., Sako, K. (eds.) ASIACRYPT 2012. LNCS, vol. 7658, pp. 349–366. Springer, Heidelberg (2012). https://doi.org/10.1007/978-3-642-34961-4_22

29. Ostrovsky, R., Sahai, A., Waters, B.: Attribute-based encryption with non-monotonic access structures. In: CCS 2007, pp. 195–203. Association for Computing Machinery, New York (2007). https://doi.org/10.1145/1315245.1315270

30. Papanis, J.P., Papapanagiotou, S.I., Mousas, A.S., Lioudakis, G.V., Kaklamani, D.I., Venieris, I.S.: On the use of attribute-based encryption for multimedia content protection over information-centric networks. Trans. Emerg. Telecommun. Technol. 25(4), 422–435 (2014). https://onlinelibrary.wiley.com/doi/abs/10.1002/ett.2722

31. Rogaway, P.: Evaluation of some blockcipher modes of operation. Cryptography Research and Evaluation Committees (CRYPTREC) for the Government of Japan (2011)

32. Rouselakis, Y., Waters, B.: Practical constructions and new proof methods for large universe attribute-based encryption. In: Proceedings of the 2013 ACM SIGSAC

Conference on Computer & Communications Security, CCS 2013, pp. 463–474. Association for Computing Machinery, New York (2013). https://doi.org/10.1145/2508859.2516672

33. Sahai, A., Waters, B.: Fuzzy identity-based encryption. In: Cramer, R. (ed.) EURO-CRYPT 2005. LNCS, vol. 3494, pp. 457–473. Springer, Heidelberg (2005). https://doi.org/10.1007/11426639_27

34. Tomida, J., Kawahara, Y., Nishimaki, R.: Fast, compact, and expressive attribute-based encryption. In: Kiayias, A., Kohlweiss, M., Wallden, P., Zikas, V. (eds.) PKC 2020. LNCS, vol. 12110, pp. 3–33. Springer, Cham (2020). https://doi.org/10.1007/978-3-030-45374-9_1

35. Zhang, Y., Zheng, D., Chen, X., Li, J., Li, H.: Computationally efficient ciphertext-policy attribute-based encryption with constant-size ciphertexts. In: Chow, S.S.M., Liu, J.K., Hui, L.C.K., Yiu, S.M. (eds.) ProvSec 2014. LNCS, vol. 8782, pp. 259–273. Springer, Cham (2014). https://doi.org/10.1007/978-3-319-12475-9_18

36. Zhao, Y., Xie, X., Zhang, X., Ding, Y.: A revocable storage CP-ABE scheme with constant ciphertext length in cloud storage. Math. Biosci. Eng. **16**(5), 4229–4249 (2019). https://www.aimspress.com/article/doi/10.3934/mbe.2019211

37. Zhou, Z., Huang, D.: On efficient ciphertext-policy attribute based encryption and broadcast encryption: extended abstract. In: Proceedings of the 17th ACM Conference on Computer and Communications Security, CCS 2010, pp. 753–755. Association for Computing Machinery, New York (2010). https://doi.org/10.1145/1866307.1866420

MOTUS: How Quantized Parameters Improve Protection of Model and Its Inference Input

Hiromasa Kitai, Naoto Yanai[(⊠)] [ID], Kazuki Iwahana [ID], Masataka Tatsumi, and Jason Paucl Cruz [ID]

Osaka University, 1-5 Yamadaoka, Suita, Osaka, Japan
yanai@ist.osaka-u.ac.jp

Abstract. Protecting a machine learning model and its inference inputs with secure computation is important for providing services with a valuable model. In this paper, we discuss how a model's parameter quantization works to protect the model and its inference inputs. To this end, we present an investigational protocol, *MOTUS*, based on ternary neural networks whose parameters are ternarized. Through extensive experiments with MOTUS, we found three key insights. First, ternary neural networks can avoid accuracy deterioration due to modulo operations of secure computation. Second, the increment of model parameter candidates significantly improves accuracy more than an existing technique for accuracy improvement, i.e., batch normalization. Third, protecting both a model and inference inputs reduces inference throughput four to seven times to provide the same level of accuracy compared with existing protocols protecting only inference inputs. Our source code is publicly available via GitHub.

1 Introduction

A machine learning process needs a large number of computational resources. Consequently, many Machine-Learning-as-a-Service (MLaaS) hosts the computation process of a machine learning model instead of a model owner, e.g., Microsoft Azure or Google Cloud. When a MLaaS hosts a machine learning model, there are two standpoints of privacy protection, i.e., parameters of the trained model itself [8,10,12,17,21,29,30,34,35,43,51] and inference inputs from clients [5,6,13,15,18,27,28,33,37–39,41,52]. (Hereafter, we refer parameters of the trained model to a model for the sake of convenience.) There are several important reasons for protection of a model according to Sun et al [47]. A model is an enormously important asset for the model owner because it often includes human, data, and computing costs. A leaked model also facilitates malicious actors to find adversarial inputs to bypass or confuse existing machine learning services. On the other hand, inference inputs may be privately sensitive for clients in many services [27], e.g., facial recognition, cancer testing, and genomic test. Therefore, both model and inference inputs should be protected even on

G. Bella et al. (Eds.): SecITC 2022, LNCS 13809, pp. 184–202, 2023.
https://doi.org/10.1007/978-3-031-32636-3_11

MLaaS and then secure computation techniques are used for instantiating these protections.

To this end, neural networks with quantized parameters, i.e., binarized neural networks [11] with $(+1, -1)$ or ternary neural networks [26] with $(+1, 0, -1)$, have attracted attention [1,2,7,8,12,21,37,41,53]. Roughly speaking, these neural networks can reduce computational complexity by quantizing model parameters. Nevertheless, to the best of the author's knowledge, it has remained unclear how neural networks with quantized parameters benefit the protection of a model and inference inputs.

In this paper, we answer the following questions: (1) How do quantized parameters benefit inference throughput and accuracy for the protection of a model and inference inputs? (2) What is essential for quantized parameters to improve the accuracy?

The above questions are non-trivial. Existing works [23,24,36] have often focused on improving inference throughput and accuracy by designing machine-learning-friendly secure computation. However, these works did not discuss quantized parameters. We investigate how inference throughput and accuracy are affected by quantized parameters when using typical secure computation. It is not implied from the existing works from the viewpoints of quantized parameters. Furthermore, the accuracy given by quantized parameters deteriorates compared to general neural networks because a model with quantized parameters often suffers from poor convergence due to the low expressiveness [41]. While there are existing techniques [8,21,37] for improving the accuracy by introducing batch normalization [16] into quantized neural networks, such an extension of neural networks may be somewhat complicated. In contrast, we investigate whether adding parameter candidates improves the accuracy compared to the existing techniques. It is quite a different question from the existing techniques.

In this paper, we present a novel investigational protocol based on ternary neural networks [26], named *Model-Oblivious Ternary neUral networkS (MOTUS)*, for the protection of a model and inference inputs based on secret sharing. Through extensive experiments with MOTUS compared to existing protocols [1,8,10,21,29,30,37], we demonstrate the following three key insight as our contributions:

(1) The first insight is that *neural networks with quantized parameters can ideally avoid the accuracy deterioration by modulo operations of secure computation.* In particular, for binarized neural networks and ternary neural networks, we show that the accuracies of neural networks with the protection of a model and inference inputs are identical to their original neural networks. Consequently, they can also provide higher accuracies for small-size neural networks than several existing protocols [8,10,29,30] with floating-point operations by virtue of avoiding accuracy deterioration.

(2) The second key insight is that *the accuracy is improved significantly by increasing parameter candidates for neural networks with quantized parameters.* Notably, increasing parameter candidates works better than introducing a typical technique for improving accuracy, i.e., batch normalization [16]. We

demonstrate the above insight by comparing MOTUS with XONN [37] based on binarized neural networks and SOTERIA [1] based on ternary neural networks.

(3) The third key insight is that *protection of a model will reduce the inference throughput four to seven times than protection of only inference inputs* to provide the same level of accuracies according to comparison with existing works [9,27] based on the same secure computation library [14]. Our source code is released on GitHub for subsequent work and reproducibility.

Related Work. This section describes related works regarding the protection of a model and inference inputs.

Protection of Model: To the best of our knowledge, the protection of a model was first discussed in E2DM [17]. The protection of a model can also be achieved by protecting the training phase with secure computation [30] (also known as private training). Specifically, it can be realized by keeping the model secret with secure computation during the training phase and not recovering the original model. Experiments of SecureML [30] were conducted in the above manner. Hence, existing protocols [4,10,29,32,34,35,40,43,49,51] for protecting the training phase. The works described above concentrated on improving secure computation but did not discuss neural networks with quantized parameters. Several works [12,20] have designed protocols for the protection of a model by converting model parameters to fixed-point operations. These works can mitigate the accuracy deterioration. However, the ReLU, sigmoid, and softmax activation functions, which are potentially unsuitable for secure computation, are utilized.

Closest works to our work are QUOTIENT [2] and SOTERIA [1], which are based on ternary neural networks. QUOTIENT contains the ReLU function, which is unsuitable for quantized parameters, as activation function. In contrast, SOTERIA contains ternary weight parameters and a binary activation function. SOTERIA is the closest to MOTUS except for the use of batch normalization [16]. Therefore, we compare MOTUS with SOTERIA. Although a ternary activation function [3] has been proposed, a construction based on it is an open problem, to the best of our knowledge.

The next important works are MOBIUS [21] and FLASH [8]. These works have discussed the protection of a model and inference inputs on binarized neural networks. The motivation of MOBIUS is to extend binarized neural networks for secure computation, and FLASH further introduces novel secure computation techniques. We also compare MOTUS with MOBIUS since the same library is used for implementation.

Protection of Inference Inputs: There are many works for the protection of inference inputs on neural networks with quantized parameters [1,2,7,37, 41,42,46]. Among them, XONN [37] extended architectures of binarized neural networks [11] for secure computation. Specifically, it combines batch normalization [16] with an activation function, and all the computations are defined as bit operations to improve the inference throughput. We hence compare MOTUS with XONN to show the overhead of the protection of a model. Recently, some optimization technique [41] of XONN was shown. The performance of MOTUS can be improved by the same technique in [41].

2 Preliminaries

This section provides background on secure computation. We first describe secret sharing as a building block and then show secure computation based on the secret sharing.

A t-out-of-n secret sharing scheme over a finite domain D consists of the following two algorithms: $([\![x]\!]_1, \ldots, [\![x]\!]_n) \leftarrow$ Share(x): Share takes $x \in D$ as input, and outputs $[\![x]\!]_1, \ldots, [\![x]\!]_n \in D$; $x \leftarrow$ Reconst$([\![x]\!]_1, \ldots, [\![x]\!]_t)$: Reconst takes $[\![x]\!]_1, \ldots, [\![x]\!]_t \in D$ as input, and outputs $x \in D$.

In the above algorithms, for $i \in \{1, \ldots, n\}$, $[\![x]\!]_i$ is called the i-th share of x. We denote $[\![x]\!] = ([\![x]\!]_1, \ldots, [\![x]\!]_n)$ as their shorthand. Any less than t shares of x over the t-out-of-n secret sharing scheme jointly give no information on x, whereas any $\geq t$ shares jointly determine x by using Reconst. Secret sharing schemes are proposed typically on finite domains, e.g., the ring of integers $\mathbb{Z}_M$ modulo M, where M is a positive integer greater than 1, and an ℓ-length binary string [45]. An i-th share of an ℓ-dimensional vector $\boldsymbol{v} = (x_1, \ldots, x_\ell)$ over a domain D consists of i-th shares of its components and is denoted by $[\![\boldsymbol{v}]\!]_i := ([\![x_1]\!]_i, \ldots, [\![x_\ell]\!]_i)$. Analogously, an i-th share of a matrix is defined in the same way. Therefore, a secret sharing scheme over vectors, matrices, and tensors, among others, can be defined.

We define secure computation protocols utilized in this work. The following computations are defined over the ring of integers $\mathbb{Z}_M = \{0, \ldots, M-1\}$ modulo M.

$[\![c]\!] \leftarrow$ ADD$([\![a]\!], [\![b]\!])$: ADD takes shares $[\![a]\!]$ and $[\![b]\!]$ of $a \in \mathbb{Z}_M$ and $b \in \mathbb{Z}_M$, respectively, as inputs, then outputs a share $[\![c]\!]$ of $a + b = c \in \mathbb{Z}_M$.

$[\![c]\!] \leftarrow$ ADDConst$([\![a]\!], b)$: ADDConst takes share $[\![a]\!]$ of $a \in \mathbb{Z}_M$ and $b \in \mathbb{Z}_M$ as inputs, then outputs a share $[\![c]\!]$ of $a + b = c \in \mathbb{Z}_M$.

$[\![c]\!] \leftarrow$ MUL$([\![a]\!], [\![b]\!])$: MUL takes shares $[\![a]\!]$ and $[\![b]\!]$ of $a \in \mathbb{Z}_M$ and $b \in \mathbb{Z}_M$, respectively, as inputs, then outputs a share $[\![c]\!]$ of $a \times b = c \in \mathbb{Z}_M$.

$[\![c]\!] \leftarrow$ MULConst$([\![a]\!], b)$: MULConst takes share $[\![a]\!]$ of $a \in \mathbb{Z}_M$ and $b \in \mathbb{Z}_M$ as inputs, then outputs a share $[\![c]\!]$ of $a \times b = c \in \mathbb{Z}_M$.

$[\![c]\!] \leftarrow$ Half$([\![a]\!])$: Half takes a share $[\![a]\!]$ of $a \in \mathbb{Z}_M$ as input, then outputs a share $[\![1]\!]$ if $a \leq \lfloor M/2 \rfloor$ over the integers, $[\![0]\!]$ otherwise.

In this paper, we utilize the ABY library [14], two-party secure computation over the ring of integers modulo $M = 2^m$ ($m = 8, 16, 32,$ or 64). We note that any secure computation library [19, 23, 24, 29, 34, 36, 49] based on secret sharing can be used.

3 Problem Description

This section recalls system and threat models for the protection of a model and inference inputs. Hereafter, we assume image classification as a task of a machine learning model. Let C denote the number of channels in an input, H the height, W the width, $\mathcal{C}$ a finite set of labels. A machine learning model is defined as a function $M : \mathbb{Z}^{C \times H \times W} \to \mathcal{C}$.

System Model. We define three kinds of entities, i.e., a client, a model owner, and two computational resource providers who delegate computations on the model. First, the model owner trains a model with plaintexts, i.e., without secure computation, and then generates shares of the trained model for $(2, 2)$-secret sharing. Next, the model owner sends the shares of the model to the resource providers. The resource providers then interact with each other to compute an inference result of the model when a client requests to execute an inference. Here, the inference result for each resource provider remains in the form of shares, and it is recovered only in the client's local environment.

Threat Model. We focus on the semi-honest adversary, i.e., an adversary follows a protocol but tries to learn the client's or model owner's data. The client generates shares for the $(2, 2)$-secret sharing as an input to the inference on the model and then sends the shares to the resource providers who host the model. We then assume the use of a secure channel, and the transport layer security can instantiate it (TLS) in a similar manner as in prior works [27,30]. Then, the following security notions are discussed:

Protection of Inference Inputs: An adversary cannot learn clients' input unless the adversary corrupts the two resource providers.

Protection of a Model: An adversary cannot learn the model unless the adversary corrupts the two resource providers.

We do not aim to hide the size of the clients' input, the network architecture provided by the model owner, and which secure computation protocols are used. Such information can be protected by adding dummy layers [27]. Besides, model extraction attacks [50] to obtain a substitute model in local via inference results are out of the scope of this work. We also note that the model extraction attacks can be prevented by watermarking [48] to check the model ownership.

4 Methodology

This section presents MOTUS, an investigational protocol for the protection of a model and inference inputs, as our research methodology. We evaluate the impact of neural networks with quantized parameters for the questions in Sect. 1 through MOTUS. To this end, ternary neural networks [26] are introduced in MOTUS. Although the original ternary neural networks contain $-1, 0, +1$ in only weight matrices and convolutional filters as quantized parameters, we first extend ternary neural networks by several techniques [21,37]. We then describe algorithms of MOTUS with the extended ternary neural networks.

4.1   Extension of Ternary Neural Networks

We extend ternary neural networks. In particular, while an activation function of the original ternary neural networks [26] is the ReLU function based on floating-point operations, we introduce the sign function [11] based on fixed-point operations through the two techniques described below instead of the ReLU function. We describe intuition due to the page limitation. (See Appendix A for detail.)

The first technique is the MOBIUS transformation [21], where batch normalization layers are converted to fixed-point operations from shift-based operations [11]. The batch normalization can improve accuracy in general [16] while that in the original binarized neural networks [11] needed the shift-based operations approximating inputs. The MOBIUS transformation scales up inputs of batch normalization layers with the trained parameters to provide fixed-point operations instead of shift-based operations. It can then provide higher accuracy than the original binarized neural networks.

The second technique is the BN+BA technique [37] that combines batch normalization and activation layers. The sign function [11] that approximates inputs with either $+1$ for a positive value or -1 for a negative value is utilized in activation layers of the original binarized neural networks instead of the ReLU function. When an activation layer with the sign function follows a batch normalization layer, the BN+BA technique combines them into a single layer. Outputs of the layer are then closed to $+1$ or -1, keeping the accuracy improvement by batch normalization.

Furthermore, inspired by XONN [37], we also present *ActMaxPooling*, which combines activation and max-pooling layers. Inputs of a max-pooling layer following an activation layer are binarized to $+1$ or -1 because of the sign function. An operation to choose a maximum value in the max-pooling layer is then identical to the OR operation for any element with the window size by converting -1 to 0 [37]. Consequently, ActMaxPooling is compatible with the BN+BA technique, and we introduce ActMaxPooling by combining it with the BN+BA technique.

Algorithm 1. SecureActMaxPooling

Input: $[\![b]\!] \in \mathbb{Z}_M^{FN \times OH \times OW}$: Shares of input vectors
Output: $[\![output]\!] \in \mathbb{Z}_M^{FN \times OH/2 \times OW/2}$
1: **for** $i = 0$ to $OH/2 - 1$ **do**
2:    **for** $j = 0$ to $OW/2 - 1$ **do**
3:       **for** $k = 0$ to $FN - 1$ **do**
4:          $[\![X_k]\!] \leftarrow \mathsf{OR}(\mathsf{Half}([\![b_{2i,2j,k}]\!]), \mathsf{Half}([\![b_{2i,2j+1,k}]\!]))$
5:          $[\![Y_k]\!] \leftarrow \mathsf{OR}(\mathsf{Half}([\![b_{2i+1,2j,k}]\!]), \mathsf{Half}([\![X_k]\!]))$
6:          $[\![Z_k]\!] \leftarrow \mathsf{OR}(\mathsf{Half}([\![b_{2i+1,2j+1,k}]\!]), \mathsf{Half}([\![Y_k]\!]))$
7:          $[\![S_k]\!] \leftarrow \mathsf{MULConst}([\![Z_k]\!], 2)$
8:          $[\![output_{i,j,k}]\!] \leftarrow \mathsf{ADDConst}([\![S_k]\!], -1)$
9:       **end for**
10:    **end for**
11: **end for**

Hereafter, we refer the above combination, including the BN+BA technique, to ActMaxPooling.

It is expected that inference throughput and accuracy of any neural network with quantized parameters are improved for the protection of a model compared to the original ternary neural networks, although we only discuss ternary neural networks (and binarized neural networks) in this paper.

4.2   Algorithms of MOTUS

We describe the algorithms of MOTUS below. In particular, secure computation of ActMaxPooling and convolution layers are described below. Although secure computation protocols for full connection, batch normalization, and activation layers are utilized in experiments described later, we follow MOBIUS [21] for these protocols. We omit the details of them due to the page limitation.

Secure ActMaxPooling Layer: A secure computation protocol of ActMax-Pooling is constructed by comparing whether each shared value is greater than or equal to 0.5, i.e., Half because the max-pooling layer returns a value from 0 to +1 as described in the previous section. More specifically, the secure computation protocol of ActMaxPooling, named SecureActMaxPooling Protocol, is shown in Algorithm 1.

Here, a modulus M is chosen similarly with MOBIUS [21].

Secure Convolution Layer: We describe how to convert the process of convolution layers to matrix operations for the use of secure computation. For any matrix W, X, the following relation is defined for matrix W', X':

$$W = \begin{pmatrix} w_{11} & w_{12} \\ w_{21} & w_{22} \end{pmatrix}, X = \begin{pmatrix} x_{11} & x_{12} & x_{13} \\ x_{21} & x_{22} & x_{23} \\ x_{31} & x_{32} & x_{33} \end{pmatrix} \Rightarrow \begin{pmatrix} w_{11} & w_{12} & w_{21} & w_{22} \end{pmatrix} \times \begin{pmatrix} x_{11} & x_{12} & x_{21} & x_{22} \\ x_{12} & x_{13} & x_{22} & x_{23} \\ x_{21} & x_{22} & x_{31} & x_{32} \\ x_{22} & x_{23} & x_{32} & x_{33} \end{pmatrix}.$$

That is, a 2-dimensional convolution operation between a (2×2)-filter W and a (3×3)-input X are represented by a dot product between a (1×4)-matrix W' and a (4×4)-matrix X'. Hereafter, let FH be the height of the filter, FW the width, FN the number, OH the height of the output, OW the width. A 2-dimensional convolution operation between a $(FH \times FW)$-filter W and a $(H \times W)$-input X is represented by a dot product between a $(1 \times FH \cdot FW)$-matrix W' and a $(FH \cdot FW \times OH \cdot OW)$-matrix X'. Similarly, a 3-dimensional convolution operation between a $(FN \times C \times FH \times FW)$-filter W and a $(C \times H \times W)$-input is represented by a dot product between a $(FN \times C \cdot FH \cdot FW)$-matrix W' and a $(C \cdot FH \cdot FW \times OH \cdot OW)$-matrix X'.

The secure computation protocol of convolution layers, i.e., SecureConvolution, is constructed with a dot product between shares as shown in Algorithm 2.

Here, an output of a convolution layer is a 3-dimension matrix, and thereby the batch normalization is executed on a 3-dimension input. For the batch normalization with a 3-dimension input, each mini-batch is utilized as the entire training data. In doing so, for a set of output data on a convolution layer, a

Algorithm 2. SecureConvolution

Input: $[\![input]\!] \in \mathbb{Z}_M^{C \times H \times W}$:
  $[\![W]\!] \in \mathbb{Z}_M^{FN \times C \times FH \times FW}$:
Output: $[\![output]\!] \in \mathbb{Z}_M^{FN \times OH \times OW}$
Procedure:
  1: $[\![input]\!] \in \mathbb{Z}_M^{C \cdot FH \cdot FW \times OH \cdot OW} \leftarrow$ Reshape $([\![input]\!])$
  2: $[\![W]\!] \in \mathbb{Z}_M^{FN \times C \cdot FH \cdot FW} \leftarrow$ Reshape $([\![W]\!])$
  3: **for** $i = 0$ to FN **do**
  4:   **for** $j = 0$ to OH $\cdot$ OW **do**
  5:     **for** $k = 0$ to C $\cdot$ FH $\cdot$ FW **do**
  6:       $[\![X_i]\!] \leftarrow$ MUL$([\![W_{i,k}]\!], [\![input_{k,j}]\!])$
  7:       $[\![output_{i,j}]\!] \leftarrow$ ADD$([\![output_{i,j}]\!], [\![X_i]\!])$
  8:     **end for**
  9:   **end for**
 10: **end for**
 11: $[\![output]\!] \in \mathbb{Z}_M^{FN \times OH \times OW} \leftarrow$ Reshape $([\![output]\!])$

---

batch normalization parameter u is computed by executing the normalization for each channel of the 3-dimensions. For the protection of inference inputs, additions between shares are executed for each channel. We also show the security analysis of MOTUS in Appendix B.

We also consider a further extension of MOTUS to improve the inference throughput. In particular, by *partially* leaking a model as a moderate setting of the protection of a model, the number of secure computations can be reduced by sharing the location of 0's for quantized parameters because entries of 0's in a matrix can avoid multiplications [44]. such an extension is insufficient for existing protocols [8,21,37] based on binarized neural networks because they contain only +1 and −1. We omit the detail of the above technique due to the page limitation. (See the full version of this paper [22] for detail.)

5   Experiments

This section describes experimental evaluations of MOTUS on the MNIST and CIFAR10 datasets. The primary purpose of the experiments is to confirm advantages of quantized parameters for inference throughput and accuracy. To this end, we first identify that quantized parameters can avoid the accuracy deterioration caused by modulo operations of secure computation by comparing the original neural networks [11,26]. We then evaluate MOTUS compared with existing protocols [1,9,21,27,29,30,37].

5.1   Implementation

MOTUS was implemented in C++ with the ABY library [14]. The ABY library is a secure computation library in the two-party setting and contains three types of shares, i.e., *Arithmetic*, *Boolean*, and *Yao*. These shares have different operations, and the ABY library provides efficient conversions between the shares. The arithmetic shares are used in arithmetic operations, such as additions and multiplications. Algorithm 2 was implemented with the arithmetic shares. On the other hand, Algorithm 1 requires Half and OR operations on secure computation, which are provided by the boolean or Yao shares. Since the arithmetic shares cannot be directly converted into boolean shares, we utilized the Yao shares in Algorithm 1. The Half and OR operations based on the Yao shares are computed faster than the boolean shares according to the benchmark [14].

In terms of the share size, the ABY library includes four parameters as a modulus M, i.e., $8, 16, 32$, and 64 bits. The MNIST and CIFAR10 datasets can be evaluated with the 32-bit parameter [21], and hence we adopted the 32-bit parameters. Our implementation was not optimized yet unlike SecureML [30], and we did not implement the padding process. Implementations of the remaining algorithms follow MOBIUS [21] as described in Sect. 4.2.

We conduct experiments on two AmazonEC2 c4.8xlarge machines running Linux with 60 GB of RAM. A model is trained with plaintexts in advance with the Chainer framework. The two machines are hosted in the same region as a LAN setting with four gigabytes per second as bandwidth. We then compare MOTUS with protocols for the protection of a model [21,29,30] and those for the protection of inference inputs [1,9,27,37] as baselines. We note that MOBIUS, EzPC [9], SecureML [30] and MiniONN [27] were implemented with the ABY library on almost the same-sized architectures. Architectures are shown in Table 3 in Appendix.

5.2   Results

Comparison with the Original Networks. Figure 1 shows an accuracy comparison of MOTUS and the original ternary neural networks [26] for the number of neurons on the MNIST dataset. Likewise, Fig. 2 shows a comparison of

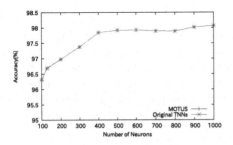

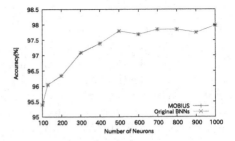

Fig. 1. Accuracy comparison between MOTUS and the original ternary neural networks (Original TNNs): Although a single line appears in this figure, two lines with different colors are identical.

Fig. 2. Accuracy comparison between MOBIUS and the original binarized neural networks (Original BNNs): The same result as Fig. 1 was obtained.

MOBIUS [21] with the original binarized neural networks [11] to identify the effect in parameter candidates.

As shown in Fig. 1, the accuracy of MOTUS is rigorously identical to the original ternary neural networks. The same result is obtained between MOBIUS and binarized neural networks as shown in Fig. 2. These results are strong evidence that neural networks with quantized parameters can avoid accuracy deterioration by secure computation, even for the protection of a model and inference inputs. Besides, comparing Fig. 1 with Fig. 2, the accuracy in Fig. 1 is higher than that in Fig. 2. It indicates that the increase of parameter candidates will improve accuracy.

Comparison of MOTUS with the Existing Protocols. The results are shown in Table 1 and Table 2.

Table 1. Performance of MOTUS on MNIST dataset in comparison with existing works. In the first column, MOTUS (partial) means the extension of MOTUS with the partial protection of a model described in the full version [22]. In the second column, the check-mark means the achievement of the protection of a model and "partial" means the partial protection of a model. In the third column, "NA" means that convolution neural networks cannot specify the number of neurons. The fifth column refers to the time dependent of input for secure computation, whereas the seventh column refers to the time independent of the input. We refer to the values in each paper except for MOBIUS, and the parenthesized values in the XONN columns are the reproduced results in [1]. The symbol "-" means that the value has not been described in the corresponding work.

		Protection of Model	Neurons	Accuracy [%]	On-line Time [sec]	Off-line Time [sec]	Total Time [sec]	Networks
Arc1	SecureML [30]	✓	128	93.1	0.18	4.7	4.88	Fixed-point
	ABY3 [29]	✓	128	94.0	0.003	0.005	0.008	Fixed-point
	MiniONN [27]		128	97.6	0.14	0.9	1.04	Fixed-point
	EzPC [9]		128	97.6	-	-	0.70	Floating-point
	MOBIUS [21]	✓	128	96.1	0.06	0.67	0.73	Binaraized
	XONN [37]		128	97.6 (95.9)	-	-	0.13	Binaraized
	SOTERIA [1]		128	96.4	0.04	0.03	0.07	Ternary
	MOTUS	✓	128	96.7	0.06	0.69	0.75	
			500	97.8	0.31	3.52	3.83	Ternary
			1000	98.0	0.83	10.09	10.9	
	MOTUS (partial)	✓	128	96.7	0.03	0.37	0.40	
			500	98.0	0.13	2.02	2.15	Ternary
			1000	98.1	0.37	5.59	5.96	
Arc2	ABY3 [29]	✓	NA	98.3	0.003	0.005	0.008	Fixed-point
	MiniONN [27]		NA	99.0	0.4	99.0	1.28	Fixed-point
	EzPC [9]		NA	99.0	-	-	0.600	Floating-point
	MOBIUS [21]	✓	NA	97.4	0.20	2.14	2.34	Binaraized
	XONN [37]		NA	98.6 (97.2)	-	-	0.16	Binarized
	SOTERIA [1]		NA	97.3	0.06	0.08	0.15	Ternary
	MOTUS	✓	NA	97.6	0.20	2.08	2.28	Ternary
	MOTUS (partial)	Partial	NA	97.6	0.11	1.21	1.32	Ternary
Arc3	MiniONN [27]		NA	99.0	5.74	3.58	9.32	Fixed-point
	EzPC [9]		NA	99.2	-	-	5.10	Floating-point
	MOBIUS [21]	✓	NA	97.3	0.39	4.00	4.39	BNN
	XONN [37]		NA	99.0 (96.7)	-	-	0.15	Binaraized
	SOTERIA [1]		NA	97.4	0.08	0.07	0.15	Ternary
	MOTUS	✓	NA	97.8	0.39	4.00	4.39	Ternary
	MOTUS (partial)	Partial	NA	97.8	0.29	2.12	2.41	Ternary
	MOBIUS [21]	✓	NA	98.8	1.76	24.16	25.9	Binaraized
Arc4	MOTUS	✓	NA	98.9	1.76	24.15	25.9	Ternary
	MOTUS (partial)	Partial	NA	98.9	1.36	13.51	14.9	

Table 2. Performance of MOTUS on CIFAR-10 dataset in comparison with existing works. The setting is common with Table 1 except for the architectures. We note that the architectures on the columns from MiniONN to SOTERIA slightly differ from Arc6 for kernels. Meanwhile, we implemented an evaluation of MOBIUS in full scratch.

		Protection of Model	Accuracy [%]	On-line Time [sec]	Off-line Time [sec]	Total Time [sec]	Networks
Arc5	MOBIUS [21]	✓	62.84	14.89	223.88	238.8	Binarized
	XONN [37]		80.0 (71.97)	-	-	15.1	Binarized
	SOTERIA [1]		73.14	8.56	6.14	14.7	Ternary
	MOTUS	✓	66.75	14.57	219.56	234.1	Ternary
	MOTUS (partial)	Partial	66.75	11.93	121.8	133.7	Ternary
Arc6	MiniONN [27]		81.61	72	472	544	Fixed-point
	EzPC [9]		81.61	-	-	265.6	Floating-point
	MOBIUS [21]	✓	76.98	116.95	1809.24	1926.2	Binarized
	XONN [37]		81.8 (72.66)	-	-	5.8	Binarized
	SOTERIA [1]		72.52	3.48	2.95	6.4	Ternary
	MOTUS	✓	78.96	117.89	1806.24	1924.1	Ternary
	MOTUS (partial)	Partial	78.96	91.45	1022.17	1113.6	Ternary

MNIST: As shown in Table 1, MOTUS achieves a higher accuracy on Arc1 than the existing protocols for the protection of a model, i.e., SecureML, ABY3 and MOBIUS. Notably, the accuracy of MOTUS is more than two points higher compared to these works. It is considered that such a high accuracy could be obtained by avoiding accuracy deterioration. In contrast, the accuracy of MOTUS is proportionally lower than ABY3 on Arc2. It is considered that ABY3 is based on fixed-point operations, which can provide more suitable expressiveness for convolution layers than quantized parameters. Since accuracies of Trident [10] and FLASH [8] for the protection of a model are the same as ABY3, similar observations will be obtained between MOTUS and them. Meanwhile, MOTUS always outperforms MOBIUS because MOTUS contains more parameter candidates by virtue of ternary neural networks.

Interestingly, MOTUS achieves higher accuracies for all the architectures than XONN and SOTERIA, despite providing the protection of a model. For instance, MOTUS achieves 96.7% accuracy on Arc1, which is higher than 95.9% of XONN[1] and 96.4% of SOTERIA, respectively. Likewise, the accuracy of MOTUS is 1.1 points higher than XONN and 0.4 points higher than SOTERIA on Arc3, respectively. We believe that these higher accuracies can be obtained by the techniques described in Sect. 4.1. More precisely, compared to XONN, the accuracy was improved by the increase of parameter candidates for ternary neural networks. Furthermore, compared to SOTERIA, MOTUS contains batch normalization, which is not used in SOTERIA.

---

[1] The accuracy follows the value presented in the SOTERIA paper [1].

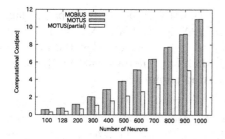
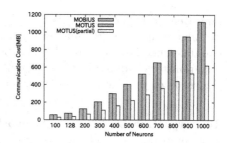

Fig. 3. Computational cost: We measured the computational cost on MOBIUS, MOTUS and its partial setting MOTUS for neurons.

Fig. 4. Communication cost: The setting is common with Fig. 3.

CIFAR-10: As shown in Table 2, the accuracy of MOTUS achieves 3.91 points higher on Arc5 and 6.3 points higher on Arc6 than MOBIUS. Similar to the results on MNIST, these accuracies could be obtained by ternary neural networks.

However, the accuracy of MOTUS is lower than XONN and SOTERIA. The reason is that we did not implement the padding process. MOTUS would achieve higher accuracy than XONN and SOTERIA if the convolution layers were fully implemented. Meanwhile, MOTUS outperforms these works on Arc6. Although the architectures of XONN and SOTERIA are slightly different from Arc6 for the number of kernels, Arc6 in [31] would provide high accuracies even on the existing works.

6 Discussion

This section discusses considerations about the experimental results. In particular, accuracy improvement, comparison between ternary/binarized neural networks, and the trade-off between accuracy and computational cost are discussed below.

Accuracy Improvement. According to Sect. 5.2, neural networks with quantized parameters can provide higher accuracies for the protection of a model in simple architectures such that convolution layers are not utilized in comparison with ABY3 [29] based on secret sharing. We believe that quantized parameters can ideally avoid the accuracy deterioration even for the protection of a model as shown in Fig. 1 and Fig. 2. In contrast, ABY3 would provide higher accuracy than quantized parameters in proportion to the complexity of network architectures because they use floating-point operations, whose expressiveness is higher than quantized parameters.

Next, from the comparison with XONN [37] and SOTERIA [1] in Table 1, the increase of parameter candidates has a significant effect on the accuracy improvement rather than introducing the batch normalization [16]. In particular, in Table 1, an accuracy difference between MOTUS and XONN is larger than one difference between MOTUS and SOTERIA. It is evident that the increase of parameter candidates is more significant than batch normalization to improve the accuracy in neural networks with quantized parameters.

Ternary/Binarized Neural Networks. We measured the computational and communication costs of MOTUS and MOBIUS [21] for the number of neurons on Arc1. The results are shown in Fig. 3 and Fig. 4. According to the figures, the computational and communication costs are identical between MOTUS and MOBIUS. It indicates that the number of the dot product between matrices for secure computation is independent of the setting of quantized parameters. Besides, the accuracy for MOTUS could be improved by increasing parameter candidates, as shown in Sect. 5.2. We thus believe that a higher accuracy for the protection of a model will be achieved without increasing the computational cost by providing more parameter candidates. Although we leave as an open question to find such parameters, we believe that truly quantized parameters from $-N$ to $+N$ for any integer N [7,12] will realize the same-level accuracy for the protection of a model with fixed-point operations.

Finally, as shown in Fig. 3 and Fig. 4, the computational cost and the communication cost for MOTUS are almost linear for the number of neurons. The performance for any number of neurons can thus be measured approximately.

Trade-Off Between Accuracy and Computational Cost. We compare MOTUS with EzPC [9] based on the ABY library [14] to discuss the trade-off between accuracy and computational cost for inference. MOTUS requires four to seven times the computational cost compared to EzPC to achieve the same-level accuracy. For instance, the total time for EzPC was 0.70 s with 97.6% accuracy on Arc1, while MOTUS was 3.83 s with 97.8% accuracy for 500 neurons. Even for CIFAR-10, EzPC was 265.6 s with 81.61% accuracy on Arc6 while MOTUS was 1924 s with 78.96% accuracy. The above differences indicate that the protection of a model with quantized parameters needs four to seven times the computational cost compared to only the protection of inference inputs with floating-point operations because more complicated architectures are necessary than floating-point operations.

7   Conclusion

In this paper, we presented MOTUS, an investigational protocol based on ternary neural networks [26] for the protection of a model. The key insight was that neural networks with quantized parameters could ideally avoid accuracy deterioration by secure computation. Remarkably, the increase of parameter candidates for quantized parameters significantly affects the accuracy improvement rather than batch normalization [16]. As might have been unexpected, achieving the protection of a model needs four to seven times longer computational cost compared to a protocol for the protection of inference inputs. We are confident that our results improve knowledge about achieving the protection of a model. In the future, we plan to design a protocol based on an architecture whose parameter is more generalized to $-N$ and $-+N$ for any integer N, i.e., quantized neural networks [7,12]. The accuracy can be improved strikingly by utilizing such an architecture. We are also in the process of evaluating neural networks with quantized parameters in the case of malicious security.

Acknowledgments. This research was supported in part by JST, CREST Grant Number JPMJCR21M5, Japan.

Code Availability. Our implementation is available from https://github.com/schrms/MOTUS.

A   Transformation of Batch Normalization into Integers

We recall the transformation technique [21] of batch normalization parameters into fixed-point operations. The transformation technique was initially introduced for binarized neural networks, while we utilize it for ternary neural networks.

On the conventional batch normalization [16], Eq. (1) is computed to output $\hat{x}_i$ for an output vector x_i on full connection layers and convolution layers, where let γ_i and β_i be training parameters, μ_i and σ_i^2 be the means and the variance of training data, and ϵ be a positive constant.

$$\hat{x}_i = \gamma_i \frac{x_i - \mu_i}{\sqrt{\sigma_i^2 + \epsilon}} + \beta_i. \tag{1}$$

Then, computation on the equation is transformed into integers. To do this, the equation is converted to the form of $\hat{x}_i = s_i x_i + t_i$, where s_i and t_i are defined as Eq. (2):

$$s_i = \frac{\gamma_i}{\sqrt{\sigma_i^2 + \epsilon}}, \quad t_i = \beta_i - \frac{\gamma_i \mu_i}{\sqrt{\sigma_i^2 + \epsilon}}. \tag{2}$$

Next, we describe the BN+BA technique [37]. To introduce technique, the sign function as an activation layer is placed after a batch normalization layer. In particular, since γ_i is experimentally positive, the following equation holds because s_i is positive:

$$Sign\left(\hat{x}_i\right) = \begin{cases} +1 \ (s_i x_i + t_i \geq 0) \\ -1 \ (s_i x_i + t_i < 0) \end{cases} \Leftrightarrow \begin{cases} +1 \left(x_i + \lfloor \frac{t_i}{s_i} \rfloor \geq 0\right) \\ -1 \left(x_i + \lfloor \frac{t_i}{s_i} \rfloor < 0\right) \end{cases} \tag{3}$$

That is, operations of batch normalization layers except for the output layer are identical to $x_i + \lfloor \frac{t_i}{s_i} \rfloor$ and therefore can be replaced with fixed-point operations.

Hereafter, for the sake of convenience, let u_i be $\lfloor \frac{t_i}{s_i} \rfloor$ where u_i is a batch normalization parameter. We also denote by IntegerBatchNorm the batch normalization with the MOBIUS technique described in Sect. 4.1.

On the other hand, for output of batch normalization layers on the output layer, a scale parameter q is experimentally found, and then s_i and t_i are transformed into integers by multyplying q and rounding off digits after the decimal point. Next, for an output vector x_i of full connection layers and convolution layers, Eq. (4) is computed for the batch normalization.

$$\hat{x}'_i = s'_i x_i + t'_i \ (s'_i = \lfloor qs_i \rfloor, t'_i = \lfloor qt_i \rfloor). \tag{4}$$

Because the batch normalization is based on integer operations, the magnitude relationship between output values for our transformation is identical to that of output values without the transformation as long as a modulus M is large enough. That is, an inference result is unaffected by our transformation. Hereafter, we denote by s'_i, t'_i the batch normalization parameters via the above transformation and by BatchNorm a batch normalization in the output layer.

B   Security Analysis

We discuss the security of MOTUS against a semi-honest adversary in a similarly argument with existing works [18,27,37]. In MOTUS, a model owner generates shares of a trained model with $(2, 2)$-secret sharing and then sends the shares to two resource providers. Under this situation, the model by the model owner is utilized as shares under the resource provider and a client. The client then generates shares of inputs for inference with the $(2, 2)$-secret sharing and then sends one of the shares to one of the resource providers. The resource providers then execute secure computation with the shares of the inputs and those of the model, and return shares of an inference result to the client. In doing so, the resource providers can compute an inference result without recovering the original data from shares, i.e., without knowing the inputs from the client and the trained model itself. Consequently, if a secure computation protocol against a semi-honest adversary is utilized as a building block of MOTUS, the protection of a model and inference inputs are achieved against the semi-honest adversary under the composition theorem [25].

C   Architectures

We describe the datasets and their architectures below. The MNIST dataset contains 70,000 images of handwritten digits from 0 to 9, i.e., 60,000 training and 10,000 test samples. Each sample has 784 features based on 28 × 28 pixels image with a grayscale value between 0–255. Four network architectures were utilized as shown in Table 3 in Appendix, i.e., Arc1–Arc4. Arc1–Arc3 are identical to XONN [37] and MOBIUS [21] and also similar to SOTERIA [1] except for the batch normalization.

Table 3. Architectures for experimental evaluations. In this table, "FC" means a full connection layer, "CONV" means a convolution layer, and "BN" means a batch normalization layer. Likewise, "IBN2D" means an integer batch normalization layer on 2-dimension, "IBN3D" means an integer batch normalization layer on 3-dimension, "Act" means an activation layer, and "MAXPOOL" means a max-pooling layer. Finally, we also denote by "d" the number of neurons.

Type	Kernels/Nodes	Type	Kernels/Nodes
MNIST (Arc1)		CIFAR-10 (Arc5)	
1 FC + IBN2D + Act	d	1 CONV 3 × 3 + IBN3D + Act	64
2 FC + IBN2D + Act	d	2 CONV 3 × 3 + IBN3D + Act	64
3 FC + BN	10	3 MAXPOOL 2 × 2	-
		4 CONV 3 × 3 + IBN3D + Act	64
MNIST (Arc2)		5 CONV 3 × 3 + IBN3D + Act	64
1 CONV 5 × 5 + IBN3D + Act	5	6 MAXPOOL 2 × 2	-
2 FC + IBN2D	100	7 CONV 3 × 3 + IBN3D + Act	64
3 FC + BN	10	8 CONV 1 × 1 + IBN3D + Act	64
MNIST (Arc3)		9 CONV 1 × 1 + IBN3D + Act	64
1 CONV 5 × 5 + IBN3D + Act	16	10 FC + BN	10
2 MAXPOOL 2 × 2	-	CIFAR-10 (Arc6)	
3 CONV 5 × 5 + IBN3D + Act	16	1 CONV 3 × 3 + IBN3D + Act	128
4 MAXPOOL 2 × 2	-	2 CONV 3 × 3 + IBN3D + Act	128
5 FC + IBN2D + Act	100	3 CONV 3 × 3 + IBN3D + Act	128
6 FC + BN	10	4 MAXPOOL 2 × 2	-
MNIST (Arc4)		5 CONV 3 × 3 + IBN3D + Act	256
1 CONV 5 × 5 + IBN3D + Act	16	6 CONV 3 × 3 + IBN3D + Act	256
2 MAXPOOL 2 × 2	-	7 CONV 3 × 3 + IBN3D + Act	256
3 CONV 5 × 5 + IBN3D + Act	16	8 MAXPOOL 2 × 2	-
4 MAXPOOL 2 × 2	-	9 CONV 2 × 2 + IBN3D + Act	512
5 FC + IBN2D + Act	512	10 CONV 1 × 1 + IBN3D + Act	512
6 FC + BN	10	11 CONV 1 × 1 + IBN3D + Act	512
		12 FC + BN	10

References

1. Aggarwal, A., Carlson, T.E., Shokri, R., Tople, S.: Soteria: in search of efficient neural networks for private inference (2020). arXiv preprint arXiv:2007.12934
2. Agrawal, N., Shahin Shamsabadi, A., Kusner, M.J., Gascón, A.: QUOTIENT: two-party secure neural network training and prediction. In: Proceedings of CCS, pp. 1231–1247. ACM (2019)
3. Alemdar, H., Leroy, V., Prost-Boucle, A., Pétrot, F.: Ternary neural networks for resource-efficient AI applications. In: Proceedings of IJCNN 2017, pp. 2547–2554. IEEE (2017)
4. Attrapadung, N., et al.: Adam in private: secure and fast training of deep neural networks with adaptive moment estimation. Proc. Privacy Enhancing Technol. **2022**(4), 746–767 (2022)

5. Barni, M., Orlandi, C., Piva, A.: A privacy-preserving protocol for neural-network-based computation. In: Proceedings of Multimedia and Security 2006, pp. 146–151. ACM (2006)
6. Bost, R., Popa, R.A., Tu, S., Goldwasser, S.: Machine learning classification over encrypted data. In: Proceedings of NDSS 2015. Internet Society (2015)
7. Bourse, F., Minelli, M., Minihold, M., Paillier, P.: Fast homomorphic evaluation of deep discretized neural networks. In: Shacham, H., Boldyreva, A. (eds.) CRYPTO 2018. LNCS, vol. 10993, pp. 483–512. Springer, Cham (2018). https://doi.org/10.1007/978-3-319-96878-0_17
8. Byali, M., Chaudhari, H., Patra, A., Suresh, A.: Flash: fast and robust framework for privacy-preserving machine learning. Proc. Privacy Enhancing Technol. **2020**(2), 459–480 (2020)
9. Chandran, N., Gupta, D., Rastogi, A., Sharma, R., Tripathi, S.: Ezpc: programmable and efficient secure two-party computation for machine learning. In: Proceedings of IEEE EuroS&P 2019, pp. 496–511. IEEE (2019)
10. Chaudhari, H., Rachuri, R., Suresh, A.: Trident: efficient 4PC framework for privacy preserving machine learning. In: Proceedings of NDSS 2020. The Internet Society (2020)
11. Courbariaux, M., Hubara, I., Soudry, D., El-Yaniv, R., Bengio, Y.: Binarized neural networks: training deep neural networks with weights and activations constrained to +1 or -1. arXiv preprint, arXiv:1602.02830 (2016)
12. Dalskov, A.P.K., Escudero, D., Keller, M.: Secure evaluation of quantized neural networks. Proc. Privacy Enhancing Technol. **2020**(4), 355–375 (2020)
13. Dathathri, R., et al.: Chet: an optimizing compiler for fully-homomorphic neural-network inferencing. In: Proceedings of PLDI 2019, pp. 142–156. ACM (2019)
14. Demmler, D., Schneider, T., Zohner, M.: Aby - a framework for efficient mixed-protocol secure two-party computation. In: Proceedings of NDSS 2015. Internet Society (2015)
15. Dowlin, N., et al.: Cryptonets: applying neural networks to encrypted data with high throughput and accuracy. In: Proceedings of ICML 2016, pp. 201–210 (2016)
16. Ioffe, S., Szegedy, C.: Batch normalization: accelerating deep network training by reducing internal covariate shift. In: Proceedings of ICML 2015, pp. 448–456 (2015)
17. Jiang, X., Kim, M., Lauter, K., Song, Y.: Secure outsourced matrix computation and application to neural networks. In: Proceedings of CCS 2018, pp. 1209–1222. ACM (2018)
18. Juvekar, C., Vaikuntanathan, V., Chandrakasan, A.: Gazelle: a low latency framework for secure neural network inference. In: Proceedings of USENIX Security 2018, pp. 1651–1668. USENIX Association (2018)
19. Keller, M.: MP-SPDZ: a versatile framework for multi-party computation. In: Proceedings of CCS 2020, pp. 1575–1590. ACM (2020)
20. Keller, M., Sun, K.: Secure quantized training for deep learning. In: Proceedings of ICML 2022. PMLR, vol. 162, pp. 10912–10938. PMLR (2022)
21. Kitai, H., et al.: Mobius: model-oblivious binarized neural networks. IEEE Access **7**, 139021–139034 (2019)
22. Kitai, H., Yanai, N., Iwahana, K., Masataka, T., Cruz, J.P.: Motus: how quantized parameters improve protection of models and their inference inputs (2022)
23. Knott, B., Venkataraman, S., Hannun, A.Y., Sengupta, S., Ibrahim, M., van der Maaten, L.: Crypten: secure multi-party computation meets machine learning. In: Proceedings of NeurIPS 2021, vol. 34 (2021)

24. Kumar, N., Rathee, M., Chandran, N., Gupta, D., Rastogi, A., Sharma, R.: Cryptflow: secure tensorflow inference. In: Proceedings of IEEE S&P, pp. 1646–1663. IEEE (2020)
25. Kushilevitz, E., Lindell, Y., Rabin, T.: Information-theoretically secure protocols and security under composition. SIAM J. Comput. **39**, 2090–2112 (2010)
26. Li, F., Liu, B.: Ternary weight networks (2016). arXiv preprint, arXiv:1605.04711
27. Liu, J., Juuti, M., Lu, Y., Asokan, N.: Oblivious neural network predictions via minionn transformations. In: Proceedings of CCS 2017, pp. 619–631. ACM (2017)
28. Lou, Q., Bian, S., Jiang, L.: Autoprivacy: automated layer-wise parameter selection for secure neural network inference. In: Proceedings of NeurIPS 2020, vol. 33, pp. 8638–8647. Curran Associates Inc. (2020)
29. Mohassel, P., Rindal, P.: Aby3: a mixed protocol framework for machine learning. In: Proceedings of CCS 2018, pp. 35–52. ACM (2018)
30. Mohassel, P., Zhang, Y.: Secureml: a system for scalable privacy-preserving machine learning. In: Proceedings of IEEE S&P 2017, pp. 19–38. IEEE (2017)
31. Nishida, N., et al.: Efficient secure neural network prediction protocol reducing accuracy degradation. IEICE Trans. Fundam. Electron. Commun. Comput. Sci. **103-A**(12), 1367–1380 (2020)
32. Niu, Y., Ali, R.E., Avestimehr, S.: 3LegRace: privacy-preserving DNN training over tees and GPUs. Proc. Privacy Enhancing Technol. **2022**(4), 183–203 (2022)
33. Orlandi, C., Piva, A., Barni, M.: Oblivious neural network computing via homomorphic encryption. EURASIP J. Inf. Secur. **1**, 2007 (2007)
34. Patra, A., Schneider, T., Suresh, A., Yalame, H.: ABY2.0: improved mixed-protocol secure two-party computation. In: Proceedings of USENIX Security 2021, pp. 2165–2182. USENIX Association (2021)
35. Patra, A., Suresh, A.: Blaze: blazing fast privacy-preserving machine learning. In: Proceedings of NDSS 2020. The Internet Society (2020)
36. Rathee, D., et al.: CrypTFlow2: practical 2-party secure inference. In: Proceedings of CCS 2020, pp. 325–342. ACM (2020)
37. Riazi, M.S., Samragh, M., Chen, H., Laine, K., Lauter, K.E., Koushanfar, F.: XONN: XNOR-based oblivious deep neural network inference. In: Proceedings of USENIX Security 2019, pp. 1501–1518. USENIX Association (2019)
38. Riazi, M.S., Weinert, C., Tkachenko, O., Songhori, E.M., Schneider, T., Koushanfar, F.: Chameleon: a hybrid secure computation framework for machine learning applications. In: Proceedings of ASIACCS 2018, pp. 707–721. ACM (2018)
39. Rouhani, B.D., Riazi, M.S., Koushanfar, F.: Deepsecure: scalable provably-secure deep learning. In: Proceedings of DAC 2018, pp. 2:1–2:6. ACM (2018)
40. Ryffel, T., Tholoniat, P., Pointcheval, D., Bach, F.R.: AriaNN: low-interaction privacy-preserving deep learning via function secret sharing. Proc. Privacy Enhancing Technol. **2022**(1), 291–316 (2022)
41. Samragh, M., Hussain, S., Zhang, X., Huang, K., Koushanfar, F.: On the application of binary neural networks in oblivious inference. In: Proceedings of CVPR 2021, pp. 4630–4639 (2021)
42. Sanyal, A., Kusner, M., Gascon, A., Kanade, V.: TAPAS: tricks to accelerate (encrypted) prediction as a service. In: Proceedings of ICML 2018, vol. 80, pp. 4497–4506. PMLR (2018)
43. Sav, S., et al.: POSEIDON: privacy-preserving federated neural network learning. In: Proceedings of NDSS 2021. Internet Society (2021)
44. Schoppmann, P., Gascón, A., Raykova, M., Pinkas, B.: Make some ROOM for the zeros: data sparsity in secure distributed machine learning. In: Proceedings of CCS 2019, pp. 1335–1350. ACM (2019)

45. Shamir, A.: How to share a secret. Commun. ACM **22**(11), 612–613 (1979)
46. Shen, L., et al.: Abnn2: secure two-party arbitrary-bitwidth quantized neural network predictions. In: Proceedings of DAC 2022, pp. 361–366. ACM (2022)
47. Sun, Z., Sun, R., Lu, L., Mislove, A.: Mind your weight(s): a large-scale study on insufficient machine learning model protection in mobile apps. In: Proceedings of USENIX Security 2021, pp. 1955–1972. USENIX Association (2021)
48. Szyller, S., Atli, B.G., Marchal, S., Asokan, N.: Dawn: dynamic adversarial watermarking of neural networks, pp. 4417–4425. ACM (2021)
49. Tan, S., Knott, B., Tian, Y., Wu, D.J.: CryptGPU: fast privacy-preserving machine learning on the GPU. In: Proceedings of IEEE S&P 2021, pp. 1021–1038 (2021)
50. Tramèr, F., Zhang, F., Juels, A., Reiter, M.K., Ristenpart, T.: Stealing machine learning models via prediction APIs. In: Proceedings of USENIX Security 2016, pp. 601–618. USENIX Association (2016)
51. Wagh, S., Gupta, D., Chandran, N.: SecureNN: 3-party secure computation for neural network training. Proc. Privacy Enhancing Technol. **2019**(3), 26–49 (2019)
52. Zhang, Q., Xin, C., Wu, H.: GALA: greedy computation for linear algebra in privacy-preserved neural networks. In: Proceedings of NDSS 2021. Internet Society (2021)
53. Zhu, W., Wei, M., Li, X., Li, Q.: Securebinn: 3-party secure computation for binarized neural network inference. In: Atluri, V., Di Pietro, R., Jensen, C.D., Meng, W. (eds.) ESORICS 2022, vol. 13556, pp. 275–294. Springer, Cham (2022). https://doi.org/10.1007/978-3-031-17143-7_14

Lightweight Authentication Using Noisy Key Derived from Physically Unclonable Function

Yuichi Komano[1]($\boxtimes$) ⓘ, Mitsugu Iwamoto[2] ⓘ, Kazuo Ohta[2,3] ⓘ,
and Kazuo Sakiyama[2] ⓘ

[1] Toshiba Corporation, 1 Komukai-Toshiba-Cho, Saiwai-ku, Kawasaki, Japan
komano@net.it-chiba.ac.jp
[2] The University of Electro-Communications, 1-5-1 Chofugaoka, Chofu, Tokyo, Japan
{mitsugu,kazuo.ohta,sakiyama}@uec.ac.jp
[3] National Institute of Advanced Industrial Science and Technology, 2-3-26, Aomi,
Koto-ku, Tokyo, Japan

Abstract. Internet of things (IoT) systems consist of many devices that send their sensor data to cloud servers. Cryptographic authentication is essential for maintaining the consistency of these systems, and lightweight authentication in particular is required because most IoT devices are resource-constrained. Physically unclonable functions (PUF) are promising tools for protecting such devices from cyber-attacks. It can *naturally* generate a unique but noisy (*i.e.*, erroneous) key for a device without implementing costly secure key storage in the device. However, a costly error correction technique is required to remove the noise. In this paper, we propose a lightweight authentication scheme with a noisy key (i.e., an uncorrected key) *naturally* derived from a PUF. The security of our scheme is based on a combinatorial problem with small noise. We also discuss its security and feasibility.

Keywords: physically unclonable function · authentication · Internet of Things

1 Introduction

Internet of things (IoT) is widely expected to make our lives more intelligent, efficient, and comfortable. In IoT systems, devices are located everywhere and exchange data such as sensing data and control information. Because most of these devices are resource-constrained, they can act as weak points in the system. Securing such devices is an emerging challenge.

Physically unclonable functions (PUFs) are promising primitives for improving the security of resource-constrained devices. It *naturally* generates unique but noisy data for each device from the detailed characteristics of the device, similar

---

Y. Komano—Presently, the author is with Chiba Institute of Technology, Japan.

G. Bella et al. (Eds.): SecITC 2022, LNCS 13809, pp. 203–221, 2023.
https://doi.org/10.1007/978-3-031-32636-3_12

to biometric objects (such as the iris and fingerprints) for a human. Examples include SRAM-PUF [7,8] which is based on the initial states of SRAM cells, and arbiter-PUF [6,12] which is based on logic delays in a dual-rail circuit. Like biometric objects, cloning of a PUF is expected to be difficult. Therefore, PUFs are regarded as *a secure key storage* for replacing costly secure non-volatile memory[1] (NVM).

From the number of challenge-response pairs (CRPs) which PUF can produce, PUFs are classified into *weak* PUF and *strong* PUF. The CRP space of weak PUF grows in a polynomial order for the security parameter such as length of challenge, whereas that of strong PUF grows in an exponential order for the security parameter. Hence, in general, the weak PUF is suitable for key generation, whereas the strong PUF is suitable for challenge-response-based device authentication.

Among the security requirements for IoT systems, authenticity is the most important because unauthorized devices or incorrect data break the consistency and reliability of the system. Although there are several cryptographic techniques for authenticating devices and data, it is difficult for resource-constrained devices to execute such cryptographic techniques including lots of computation.

1.1 Lightweight Authentication Protocols

Several researchers have reported lightweight authentication protocols. There are *two classes* of protocols: protocols that use *a pre-stored secret key* and those that use *a noisy key* dynamically derived from a PUF.

For *the former class*, *a non-PUF-based authentication protocol* has been proposed by Kiltz et al. [10] (see Appendix A.2 for detail). This protocol assumes a device is authenticated by a server with an authentication data which is computed by the device using two steps: multiplying a matrix by the pre-stored secret key and adding logical noise to the multiplied data. The secret key is shared between the device and the server in advance and is stored in the device's NVM. During verification, the server reproduces the multiplied data using the shared secret key and accepts the authenticated data if the distance between the reproduced data and the authentication data is small. The scheme can be *proven to be secure* if a learning parity with noise (LPN) problem [2] is hard.

The *latter class*, *PUF-based authentication protocols*, is further divided into *two sub-classes*: protocols *retrieving a stable key using helper data*, and those *without retrieving a stable key*. The helper data is an error correction code for retrieving a stable key from noisy PUF output. Because the helper data include no sensitive data regarding the output of PUF or key, they can be stored in non-secure NVM.

In *the first sub-class*, the device retrieves a stable key and then computes cryptographic authentication data using the retrieved key. Examples of key retrieval instantiations include *the fuzzy extractor* [4] and *the pattern matching key generation* [3,11,20]. In this approach, the material cost of the NVM and the computation cost of the key retrieval are problematic.

---

[1] Storing a key in NVM increases both the material cost and the manufacturing cost of storing the key using secure equipment.

An example of *the second sub-class* is called a *helper-data-free PUF-based authentication protocol*. The seminal works on this type of protocol are [5,21]. Later, protocols that were more secure against active attacks were proposed in [16,23,30]. However, since these protocols use raw PUF outputs as authentication data and attacks by reusing PUF outputs that have already been used for authentication have become possible. To prevent these kinds of attack, these protocols use a (strong) PUF that can generate a large enough number of fresh bits for all of the authentications executed throughout the life-cycle of the device. See Appendix A.1 for the protocol of [16] as an example.

1.2   Our Contribution

In this paper, we propose a lightweight authentication protocol using a noisy key. Our work is inspired by the non-PUF-based authentication protocol of Kiltz et al. [10].

Unlike previous helper-data-free PUF-based authentication protocols [16,23, 30], our protocol does not use, as authentication data, the raw noisy PUF output as it is. More precisely, an exclusive-OR (XOR) of l bits randomly selected from the noisy key is used as the authentication data. If the bits in the noisy key are uniformly random and mutually independent, the authentication data are indeterminable if at least one of the l bits is undetermined, and conversely, each XORed bit from the authentication data is indeterminable unless the other $l - 1$ bits are determined.

To our knowledge, this is the first proposal of a helper-data-free PUF-based authentication protocol that allows *reuse of the PUF output* with *provable security*. To discuss the security, we formally give a security model of the protocol.

The security of our protocol relies on the difficulty of *a combinatorial problem*. Let us consider information leakage of the noisy key bits from the authentication data. When a device generates an authentication data, the authentication data are generated by one equation for the l XORed bits. Another equation is generated each time the device performs authentications, until eventually we have a linear system of equations made up of these equations. If the equation system is unsolvable, our protocol is secure even if the bits in the noisy key are reused for multiple authentications.

We also test the feasibility of the protocol by simulation and experiments with some parameters. This test shows the applicability of our protocol to IoT systems consisting of resource-constrained devices.

1.3   Organization

The remainder of this paper is organized as follows. Section 2 gives definitions of the PUF and the authentication protocol. Section 3 proposes a concrete protocol and discusses its security. We then discuss the feasibility of our protocol by simulations and experiments, in Sect. 4. In Sect. 5, we discuss applications and security of our protocol. Finally, Sect. 6 concludes this paper.

2   Definition

Throughout this paper, we use the following notations:

- $\{0,1\}^k$: a set of k-bit strings for some integer k
- $[a,b]$: a set of integers from a to b for integers $a < b$
- hw: the Hamming weight function $\{0,1\}^* \to \mathbb{Z}$, which, for an input with arbitrary length, returns the number of 1's in the input
- $\sharp\mathcal{L}$: the cardinal number of a set $\mathcal{L}$
- $\mathbf{s}_{\downarrow\mathbf{v}}$: a bit string which is a concatenation of (i-th) bits extracted from $\mathbf{s}$, where the corresponding (i-th) bit of $\mathbf{v}$ is 1, for bit strings $\mathbf{s}, \mathbf{v}$ with same length

Let us first review the definition of PUFs [24].

Definition 1 (PUF). *A family of functions is called a family of* PUF *if it satisfies the following conditions.*

1. *The output of each function can be obtained in polynomial steps.*
2. *It is* physically and mathematically *difficult to clone a function even if the input-output pairs of the function are observed, except all input-output pairs are observed.*
3. *It is difficult to predict the output of each function.*
4. *Although the output may include a small amount of noise, the signal-to-noise ratio is high enough that the noise can be removed by using an error correcting technique.*

We then formalize the definitions of the authentication protocol using a noisy key and its security.

Definition 2 (Authentication protocol using a noisy key). *Assume that the device being authenticated by a server includes a mechanism for generating a noisy key. Also assume that the server authenticating the device securely stores the initial key generated during enrollment of the device. The authentication protocol between the device and the server is executed as follows:*

1. *The server sends a challenge to the device.*
2. *The device generates a noisy key and computes a response from both the challenge and the noisy key. The device then sends the response to the server.*
3. *The server checks the validity of the response based on both the challenge and the stored key. If it is valid, then the server accepts the device, otherwise it rejects the device.*

We say that an authentication protocol using a noisy key is correct *if the server accepts legitimate devices.*

Definition 3 (Secure authentication protocol using a noisy key). *Let us consider an adversary $\mathcal{A}$ who is not able to access the noisy key directly. We say that $\mathcal{A}$ breaks the authentication protocol using a noisy key in $(\epsilon, q_h, q_a, \tau)$ if $\mathcal{A}$, within time bound τ, succeeds in forging a response with probability more than ϵ in the following game:*

1. If $\mathcal{A}$ is in the random oracle model (see below), it outputs queries to the oracle O_H and receives the corresponding outputs.
2. $\mathcal{A}$ outputs challenges to the authentication oracle O_A, and receives the corresponding responses.
3. $\mathcal{A}$ requests a challenge and receives it.
4. $\mathcal{A}$ makes queries to O_H as in Step 1. The number of queries made in Steps 1 and 4 is at most q_h in total.
5. $\mathcal{A}$ makes queries to O_A as in Step 2. The number of queries made in Steps 2 and 5 is at most q_a in total.
6. $\mathcal{A}$ outputs a forged response corresponding to the challenge received in Step 3.

If such an adversary does not exist, we say that the authentication protocol with a noisy key is secure in $(\epsilon, q_h, q_a, \tau)$.

We review the definition of the random oracle [1].

Definition 4 (Random Oracle). *We say that a map H from $\{0,1\}^*$ to $\mathcal{L}$ is a random oracle if it satisfies:*

1. *for an input x, it uniquely outputs $y = H(x)$, and*
2. *for a new input x, the probability where $H(x)$ equals $y \in \mathcal{L}$ is $1/\sharp\mathcal{L}$.*

3   Proposed Protocol

We first explain our idea, then give its construction and discuss its security.

3.1   Idea

Our protocol is inspired by the non-PUF-based authentication protocol proposed by Kiltz et al. [10]. That protocol (see Appendix A.2 and Fig. 3) sums up the partial bits of the digital secret key and then adds logical noise to the sum to generate a response (authentication data).

Unfortunately, if we simply replace the digital secret key $\mathbf{s}$ in the protocol with a noisy key $\widetilde{\mathbf{s}}$, the resulting protocol does not work correctly. This is because the matrix multiplication, $\mathbf{R}^T \cdot \widetilde{\mathbf{s}}_{\downarrow \mathbf{v}}$ in Fig. 3, diffuses the noise of the noisy key into many bits in the response. *Our idea* is to construct an authentication protocol using a noisy key as follows:

1. The device computes n single-bit responses where each response is an XOR of l bits selected from the noisy key. Let us assume that the noise is small enough, e.g., less than 15% as discussed in [15,26] for the PUF. By setting l appropriately, we can expect that some of the responses are noise-free and useful for authentication.
2. The device sends n single-bit responses to the server as authenticated data. We choose the parameter n appropriately to make attacks using random responses infeasible.

3. The server accepts the device if more than $k-1$ responses pass the verification. Even with a small amount of noise, some of the single-bit responses flip. Therefore, we choose appropriate k so that the authentication is tolerable against noise.

In the protocol of [10], the device adds logical noise to the response in order to make it difficult to learn (attack) the secret key bits from responses. Although our protocol does not use logical noise, the physical noise of the PUF output prevents the attack.

Note that in the protocol of [10], the secret key is digital data that are reused for multiple authentications. Similarly, our protocol allows us to reuse the noisy key (raw output of PUF) for multiple authentications which may enable us to use a weak PUF for device authentication without reproducing a stable key.

As in the previous protocols, the device uses its own randomness aside from the secret key and challenge received from the server to compute the response in order to prevent active attacks from a malicious server. This randomness makes the bit positions used for computing the response unpredictable by the server, which it makes the analysis difficult even if the server maliciously sends a challenge for analyzing the noisy key.

3.2   Construction

Let us assume that the device generates an L-bit noisy key $\widetilde{\mathbf{y}}$ from the PUF and that the server securely stores the L-bit key $\mathbf{y}$ initially loaded during enrollment.

Each time an authentication is executed, the device generates $\widetilde{\mathbf{y}}$. It then computes a response $(\mathbf{b}, \mathbf{z})$ (authentication data) using $\widetilde{\mathbf{y}}$. The server uses the stored secret key $\mathbf{y}$ to check the validity of $(\mathbf{b}, \mathbf{z})$. Figure 1 shows the procedure.

Let $\mathcal{L}$ be a set of L-bit strings with a Hamming weight of l, and let $H : \{0,1\}^* \rightarrow \mathcal{L}$ be a function that outputs, for each input, an element from $\mathcal{L}$ uniformly at random[2]. Let $\mathbf{y}_{\downarrow \mathbf{v}} \in \{0,1\}^l$ be an l-bit substring consisting of j-th bit of $\mathbf{y}$, where j-th bit of $\mathbf{v}$ is 1. For example, assuming that $l = 4$, $\mathbf{y} = 1101$, and $\mathbf{v} = 1010$, $\mathbf{y}_{\downarrow \mathbf{v}}$ is a two-bit string 10 extracted from the underlined parts of $\mathbf{y} = \underline{1}1\underline{0}1$. Note that, in Fig. 1, $z_i = \mathsf{hw}(\mathbf{x}) \bmod 2$ means exclusive-or of bits in bit string $\mathbf{x}$.

3.3   Security Considerations

To discuss the security, we first introduce an assumption for the PUF. We call this assumption *linearly unpredictable*.

---

[2] H (random oracle) is instantiated by a hash function. Because a hash function can be used for checking message integrity and so on, it is implemented in lots of security devices to which our protocol can be applied. Hence, we believe that implementing the hash function is not an additional cost, rather than implementing an error correction designed with PUF characteristics to remove output noises.

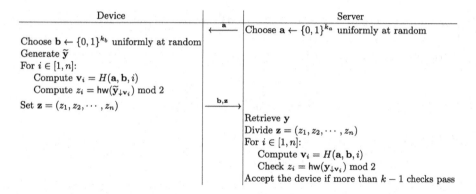

Fig. 1. Our protocol.

Definition 5 (linearly unpredictable PUF). *Let* PUF *be a function that, given an input of arbitrary length if necessary, outputs an L-bit string[3]. Let $l < L$ and $p_{i,j} \in [1, L]$ be integers. We call this* PUF *linearly unpredictable in $(\epsilon, L, l, m_1, m_2, \tau)$ if it satisfies the following properties:*

1. *Its output bits are mutually independent.*
2. *Each output bit flips with probability α independently.*
3. *Any adversary $\mathcal{A}$, who interacts with a challenger $\mathcal{C}$ within the time bound τ, cannot achieve an advantage $\mathsf{Adv} = |\Pr[C' = 1|C = 1] - \Pr[C' = 1|C = 0]|$ of more than ϵ, where C and C' are random variables for c and c' in the following game, respectively.*
   (a) *From a PUF oracle O_P, $\mathcal{A}$ receives $(l + 1)$-tuples $\{(p_{i,1}, \cdots, p_{i,l}, z_i)\}_{i \in [1, m_1]}$ for random $p_{i,j}$, where z_i equals $y_{i,1} \oplus \cdots \oplus y_{i,l}$ and $y_{i,j}$ is a $p_{i,j}$-th bit of the L-bit PUF output.*
   (b) *From a challenger $\mathcal{C}$, $\mathcal{A}$ receives $(l + 1)$-tuples $\{(\widetilde{p}_{i,1}, \cdots, \widetilde{p}_{i,l}, \widetilde{z}_i)\}_{i \in [1, m_2]}$ for random $\widetilde{p}_{i,j}$, where $\mathcal{C}$ sets $\widetilde{z}_i$ as follows: $\mathcal{C}$ first chooses $c \in \{0, 1\}$ at random. If $c = 0$, $\mathcal{C}$ sets $\widetilde{z}_i$ with a random bit in $\{0, 1\}$. If $c = 1$, $\mathcal{C}$ sets $\widetilde{z}_i$ with $\widetilde{y}_{i,1} \oplus \cdots \oplus \widetilde{y}_{i,l}$ where $\widetilde{y}_{i,j}$ is a $\widetilde{p}_{i,j}$-th bit of the output.*
   (c) *$\mathcal{A}$ guesses c as $c' \in \{0, 1\}$ and outputs it.*

We expect that the noise in the PUF output makes it difficult to learn (or maliciously analyze) the characteristics of the output. The above definition can be regarded as a variant of the well-known cryptographic assumptions of learning with errors (LWE, [22]) and learning parity with noise (LPN, [2]).

Our protocol is proven to be secure if the underlying PUF is linearly unpredictable (Definition 5) in the random oracle model (Definition 4). For the security, the following theorem holds.

---

[3] For example, if SRAM-PUF is used, the string is the initial states of L SRAM cells from the top (with no input) or from the address indicated by the input. Or, if an $(n$-XOR) arbiter-PUF is used, the string is a concatenation of L outputs for L inputs.

Theorem 1. *Let* $k = \delta n$ *for* $\delta \in (0.5, 1)$*, where* $\sum_{i=k}^{n} \frac{\binom{n}{i}}{2^i}$ *is negligible. If a PUF is linearly unpredictable in* $(\epsilon', L, l, nq_a, n, \tau')$*, our authentication protocol is secure in* $(\epsilon, q_h, q_a, \tau)$ *in the random oracle model, where* $\tau' \approx \tau$ *and*

$$\epsilon' \geq \frac{1}{q_h + nq_a}\epsilon - \frac{1}{2^{k_b}} - \sum_{i=k}^{n} \frac{\binom{n}{i}}{2^i}$$

hold.

The proof is given in Appendix B.

3.4   Notes

In Fig. 1, the device generates a whole $\widetilde{\mathbf{y}} \in \{0, 1\}^L$ and then extracts an l-bit substring $\widetilde{\mathbf{y}}_{\downarrow \mathbf{v}_i}$. Instead of generating the entire substring, the device can generate the necessary bits of $\widetilde{\mathbf{y}}$ for which the corresponding bits of $\mathbf{v}$ are 1. Furthermore, instead of extraction of $\widetilde{\mathbf{y}}_{\downarrow \mathbf{v}}$, the device may compute the inner product of $\widetilde{\mathbf{y}}$ and $\mathbf{v}$ in modulo 2 and set the result to z_i.

As explained in Sect. 3.1, we remove the addition of the logical noise. From a security perspective, if the PUF output is noise-less, the PUF characteristics can be easily analyzed from the responses of our authentication protocol. Therefore, if the noise is too small (before aging, for example), adding a small amount of logical noise may be a solution for enhancing security.

Our device authentication protocol can be extended to a message authentication code (MAC, [19]) scheme. Assume that the device wants to authenticate a message $\mathbf{m}$ to the server. To do so, the device replaces $\mathbf{a}$ with $\mathbf{m}$ and computes a response by itself, and then sends the $\mathbf{m}$ and the response to the server as the message and the corresponding MAC, respectively.

4   Feasibility

In this section, we discuss the feasibility of our protocol. We first check the validity of the assumption in Definition 5, and then discuss the parameters of our protocol by simulation and experiments to show that our protocol works correctly.

4.1   Validity of Our Assumption

We first discuss the validity of the assumption of Definition 5. We estimate the hardness of the assumption using a Python library (scikit-learn library for Python 3.6) for the support vector machine (SVM). The machine learning trains the model with $m_1 = 1,000,000$ instances, and then tries to distinguish the games $m_2 = 100,000$ times. The simulations are performed as follows, with parameters $L \in \{128, 256, \cdots, 8192\}$ and $\alpha \in \{0.15, 0.035\}$, respectively:

Table 1. Validity of our assumption.

α	l	L	P_{Succ}	P_{Fail}	Diff
0.15	2	512	0.6319	0.5753	5.66×10^{-2}
		1024	0.5865	0.5897	3.25×10^{-3}
		2048	0.5416	0.5257	1.59×10^{-2}
		4096	0.5446	0.5327	1.20×10^{-2}
		8192	0.5311	0.5359	4.40×10^{-3}
0.035	2	512	0.6541	0.4822	0.172
		1024	0.5909	0.4966	9.44×10^{-2}
		2048	0.5676	0.5472	2.04×10^{-2}
		4096	0.5348	0.5347	1.21×10^{-4}
		8192	0.5379	0.5323	4.85×10^{-3}
0.035	8	512	0.6442	0.6401	4.09×10^{-3}
		1024	0.5603	0.5562	4.18×10^{-3}
		2048	0.5345	0.5335	1.98×10^{-3}
		4096	0.5339	0.5350	1.03×10^{-3}
		8192	0.5237	0.5226	1.15×10^{-3}

1. Generate an L-bit random string **y** as the PUF output
2. Repeat the following steps 1,000,000 times:
   (a) Randomly choose $p_1, \cdots, p_l \in [1, L]$ as the indices (that is, the bit position to be extracted)
   (b) Extract bits $y_1, \cdots, y_l$ from **y** with the indices $p_1, \cdots, p_l$
   (c) Flip each bit y_i to y_i' with probability α, independently
   (d) Compute $z = y_1' \oplus \cdots \oplus y_l'$
   (e) Add $(p_1, \cdots, p_l, z)$ into the dataset for the machine leaning
3. Train the model with SVM library, with the default parameter ($C = 1.0$)
4. Repeat the following steps 100,000 times:
   (a) Randomly choose $\widetilde{p}_1, \cdots, \widetilde{p}_l \in [1, L]$ as the indices
   (b) Extract bits $\widetilde{y}_1, \cdots, \widetilde{y}_l$ from **y** with the indices $\widetilde{p}_1, \cdots, \widetilde{p}_l$
   (c) Flip each bit $\widetilde{y}_i$ to $\widetilde{y}_i'$ with probability α independently
   (d) Compute $\widetilde{z} = \widetilde{y}_1' \oplus \cdots \oplus \widetilde{y}_l'$
   (e) Predict $\widetilde{z}'$
5. Estimate the probabilities $P_{Succ} = \Pr[\widetilde{Z}' = 1 | \widetilde{Z} = 1]$ and $P_{Fail} = \Pr[\widetilde{Z}' = 1 | \widetilde{Z} = 0]$ where $\widetilde{Z}$ and $\widetilde{Z}'$ are the random variables for $\widetilde{z}$ and $\widetilde{z}'$, respectively

We show the results in Table 1. In this table, Diff. is the difference in probabilities $|P_{Succ} - P_{Fail}|$. From the table, we can conclude that for each (α, l), prediction of $\widetilde{z}$ becomes more difficult with larger L. More specifically, we have two facts. First, for each (α, l), both P_{Succ} and P_{Fail} fall to 0.5 if L is enlarged from 512-bit (64-byte) to 8192-bit (1 KiB). These probabilities are expected to further decrease if a PUF with larger L, more than 1 KiB for example, is used.

Table 2. Relationship between α and β.

$\alpha = 0.15$		$\alpha = 0.035$	
l	β	l	β
2	0.2550	2	0.0676
4	0.3800	4	0.1260
8	0.4712	8	0.2202
16	0.4983	16	0.3434

Second, in comparing the cases for $(\alpha, l) = (0.15, 2)$ and $(\alpha, l) = (0.035, 2)$, the difficulty of the learning increases with the amount of noise. As discussed in Sect. 3.4, if α is too small, adding logical noise may be a solution for enhancing the security.

Although the above simulations estimate the hardness of a problem that is slightly different from Definition 5, we expect that the problem in Definition 5 is also hard with appropriate parameters from this result.

4.2   Feasibility Test with Simulation

Assume that each bit of the noisy key (for simplicity, PUF output hereinafter) is random in $\{0, 1\}$ and mutually independent, and that it flips with probability α independently. The correctness and security of our protocol relates to the parameters L, l, α, n, k, q_a, and q_h.

Let us first discuss the relationship between the correctness and the parameters α, l, n, and k. Note that if the odd bit(s) in the l-bit substring flip(s), the response z_i also flips. By letting β denote the probability of this, we have

$$\beta = \sum_{k=1}^{l/2} \binom{l}{2k-1} \alpha^{2k-1} (1-\alpha)^{l-(2k-1)}.$$

Table 2 shows the relationship between l and β for $\alpha \in \{0.15, 0.035\}$. In the case for $\alpha = 0.15$ and $l = 16$, β is almost 0.5. That is, the response z_i is random and independent from the secret $\widetilde{\mathbf{y}}_{\downarrow \mathbf{v}_i}$. In this case, the correctness cannot be satisfied. If we use PUF with $\alpha = 0.15$, the authentication may correctly work if $l = 2$ ($\beta = 0.2550$) or at most $l = 4$ ($\beta = 0.3800$). Alternately, if we can use an error-less PUF with $\alpha = 0.035$, β is about 0.1 or less than 0.25 for $l = 2$ or $l = 8$, respectively, and the authentication may correctly work with these parameters.

We next discuss the relationship between the correctness and (n, k) for these (α, l). Table 3 shows the results, where P_{Succ} means the success probability with which the server accepts the legitimate device for parameter (α, l, n, k) and P_{Bad} means the probability with which the server accepts a malicious device that sends the server n single-bit randomnesses. From the table, for $\alpha = 0.15$, the server accepts legitimate and illegitimate devices with probabilities of almost 1 and less than 4×10^{-5}, respectively, with parameters $(l, n, k) = (2, 256, 160)$. P_{Bad} can

Table 3. Relationship between the correctness and (α, l, n, k).

$\alpha = 0.15, \ell = 2$				$\alpha = 0.035, \ell = 2$				$\alpha = 0.035, \ell = 8$			
n	k	P_{Succ}	P_{Bad}	n	k	P_{Succ}	P_{Bad}	n	k	P_{Succ}	P_{Bad}
64	40	0.9882	0.0300	64	40	1	0.0300	64	40	0.9985	0.0300
128	80	0.9990	0.0030	128	80	1	0.0030	128	80	1	0.0030
256	160	1	3.8×10^{-5}	256	160	1	3.8×10^{-5}	256	160	1	3.8×10^{-5}
512	320	1	8.4×10^{-9}	512	320	1	8.4×10^{-9}	512	320	1	8.4×10^{-9}

be decreased if large parameters are used. Similarly, in the case of $\alpha = 0.035$, the server accepts legitimate and illegitimate devices with probabilities of almost 1 and less than 4×10^{-5}, respectively, with parameters $(l, n, k) = (2, 256, 160)$.

In both cases, for each (α, l), if we enlarge (n, k), we can increase P_{Succ} (and decrease P_{Bad}). Hence, there is a trade-off between such probabilities and computation and communication costs.

4.3 Feasibility Test with Experiments

We finally check the feasibility of the protocol by toy experiments. In these experiments, we prepare two Nucleo-F401RE boards[4] by STMicroelectronics. We load 4096-bit initial SRAM states on each board and regard them as the output of 4096-bit SRAM-PUF. These experiments are performed at room temperature with the power supplied by the USB interface. The average bit error rates for 4096-bit SRAM cells for two boards were 3.30% and 3.57%, respectively.

We set $k_a = k_b = 128$. That is, we assume that $\mathbf{a}$ and $\mathbf{b}$ are 128-bit randomnesses. We implement H as the composition of the enumerative encoding [25,29] and SHA-256 [18]. That is, for an input $(\mathbf{a}, \mathbf{b}, i)$, we first compute $h = \text{SHA-256}(\mathbf{a}, \mathbf{b}, i) \mod \binom{L}{l}$, and then encode h with the enumerative encoding to derive $\mathbf{v}_i \in \mathcal{L}$.

Table 4 shows the experimental results, which are similar to the simulations for $\alpha = 0.035$ in Table 3. For each parameter, we execute 1,000 authentications with each of legitimate and illegitimate devices, Our experiments show that, as in the simulation, we can increase P_{Succ} (and decrease P_{Bad}) by increasing (n, k).

If we use the SRAM-PUF in other conditions (high/low power supply and/or temperature) or if we use other PUF devices, the bit error rate may change as summarized in Chap. 4 of [14]. The correctness of our protocol depends on the bit rate. If a PUF with a bit error rate of less than 15% (as discussed in [15,26]) is used, our simulation for $\alpha = 0.15$ ensures that our protocol works correctly by selecting adequate (n, k).

5   Discussion

Let us discuss the applicability of our protocol to IoT devices in terms of security and efficiency.

---

[4] http://www.st.com/en/evaluation-tools/nucleo-f401re.html (accessible on October 18, 2022).

Table 4. Experimental Results.

l	n	k	P_{Succ}	P_{Bad}	l	n	k	P_{Succ}	P_{Bad}
2	64	40	1	0.028	8	64	40	0.968	0.029
2	128	80	1	0.003	8	128	80	0.996	0.004
2	256	160	1	0	8	256	160	1	0

5.1 Application to IoT Devices

IoT systems require secure and low-cost authentication protocols. There are three possible solutions: (i) lightweight authentication protocols based on a digital secret key such as [10,13], (ii) PUF-based authentication protocols with an error correction such as the fuzzy extractor, and (iii) helper data free PUF-based authentication protocols such as [16,30] and ours. As discussed in the introduction, the third one is suitable for tiny devices.

Whereas the raw bits of the PUF output are transmitted by previous protocols [16,30], our protocol does not transmit the unaltered raw bits. Therefore, unlike previous protocols, the PUF output can be reused. That is, our protocol can be securely realized with a weak PUF.

Our experiments in Sect. 4.3 show that our protocol is executable by resource-constrained and mass-produced, in other words, tiny and cheap devices. The protocol consists of lightweight computations such as a hash function and some bit operations suitable for such devices. The communication cost is also adequate; receiving a 128-bit challenge and transmitting a 128-bit randomness for avoiding active attacks and a 128-bit response, for example.

5.2 Security and Efficiency

Although the appropriate parameters need to be investigated by further research according to the security requirements of individual applications, let us discuss the security and efficiency of our protocol with the parameters already discussed. Assume a weak PUF with 4 KiB input space, such as 4 KiB SRAM, where the noise is at most 15%. With the PUF, let us consider our protocol with $(l, n, k) = (2, 128, 80)$. More than 536 million ($\approx \binom{32768}{2}$) responses can then be used, which allows us to use our protocol up to more than 4 million ($536/n = 536/128 > 4$ million) times. In this case, the transmitted data for each authentication are 128-bit **a**, 128-bit **b**, and 128-bit **z**, as discussed in the previous subsection.

Our protocol is proven to be secure if the underlying PUF is linearly unpredictable. Although an ideal PUF in which the output bits are uniformly random and mutually independent creates a linearly unpredictable PUF, the reverse does not hold in general. This means that constructing a linearly independent PUF is easier than constructing an ideal PUF. Our protocol and security proof might give a new direction for PUF design and development suitable for authentication in IoT systems.

Finally, let us discuss the (in)security against side channel attacks. Some references [9,17,28] have reported the (in)security of the PUF and the error correction, namely, the fuzzy extractor. In this paper, we regard the PUF as a black box for generating random but unique data and assume a PUF with less side channel leakage. Let us consider the leakage from other parts than the PUF. In general, the side channel information tends to be leaked when complex non-linear operations are performed. Our protocol does not use the complex fuzzy extractor but instead uses lightweight linear XOR operations that are thought to leak less information. Moreover, XOR allows us to easily use masking, which is one of the basic countermeasures against side channel attacks. Therefore, our protocol is potentially robust against these attacks.

6 Conclusions

We proposed a helper-data-free PUF-based authentication protocol that allows devices to reuse the PUF output. Because it does not require helper data stored in NVM nor a costly strong PUF with a large number of fresh output bits, our protocol is suitable for low-cost devices. Although the authentication might not be rigorous for some of the parameters discussed in Sect. 4, it is suitable for IoT systems, which work correctly if most of the data are correct and reliable. The estimation of adequate parameters for a specific application, including the selection of PUF type, is the target of future work.

Moreover, we gave a security proof for our protocol if the underlying PUF is linearly unpredictable. Although constructing a linearly unpredictable PUF is an open problem, it is easier than constructing an ideal PUF. Hence, our result is not only of theoretical interest but bridges the gap between research on PUF device development and application of PUF to authentication protocols.

Acknowledgements. We thank the anonymous referees, whose comments have helped us improve the presentation of the paper. This work was supported by Grant-in-Aid for Scientific Research (JP18H05289, JP18K11293, JP21H03395, JP22H03590).

A Related Works

We give a review of the helper-data-free PUF-based authentication protocol *Slender PUF* as a previous work on an authentication protocol using a noisy key. We then review a non-PUF-based authentication that relates to our protocol.

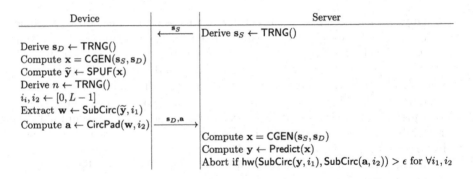

Fig. 2. Improved Slender PUF [23].

A.1   Helper-Data-Free PUF-Based Authentication: Slender PUF

We first review Slender PUF, which was proposed by Majzoobi et al. [16]. Rostami et al. [23] then improved it to enhance the security against learning attacks[5], by adding circularity operations such as SubCirc and CircPad. In Slender PUF and its improvement, the device is assumed to include a PUF. The server is also assumed to learn the model of the PUF and securely store the model during enrollment of the device. Yu et al. [30] also proposed a variant of Slender PUF, which treated selected bits from the PUF output, instead of the circulative data, as the response.

Figure 2 shows the protocol of Rostami et al. [23]. In this figure, TRNG, CGEN, and SPUF are a true number generator, a challenge generator, and a strong PUF with an L-bit output, respectively. $\mathsf{SubCirc}(\mathbf{y}, i_1)$ is a function that extracts an m-bit substring $\mathbf{w}$ from the i_1-th bit of the L-bit PUF output $\mathbf{y}$, for an integer $i_1 < L$ and the predetermined m. In SubCirc, the L-bit PUF output is used in a circular manner. That is, if $i_1 + m > L$, the remainder of the substring is taken from the beginning of $\mathbf{y}$. $\mathsf{CircPad}(\mathbf{w}, i_2)$ is a function that pads the m-bit substring $\mathbf{w}$ with random bits to create an L'-bit string where $L' > m$. Specifically, CircPad generates an L'-bit string $\mathbf{a}'$ at random, replaces a substring of $\mathbf{a}'$ from its i_2-th bit with $\mathbf{w}$, and returns the resulting substring as $\mathbf{a}$. In this process, the L'-bit string $\mathbf{a}'$ is used in a circular manner. That is, if $i_2 + m > L'$, the remainder of the substring is taken from the beginning of $\mathbf{a}'$. $\mathsf{Predict}(\mathbf{x})$ is a function that, for an input $\mathbf{x}$, returns $\mathsf{SPUF}(\mathbf{x})$ from the trained PUF model. ϵ is a prefixed threshold.

Because this protocol transmits the circulative raw bits of the PUF output, the PUF output cannot be reused in order to prevent forgery attacks using previous responses. Hence, it requires a strong PUF as a building block. Although we omit the details, the original Slender PUF [16] and another variant [30] also require a strong PUF for similar reasons.

---

[5] Against some PUF instantiations, attacks that learn the model of the PUF from the known input–output pairs have been reported.

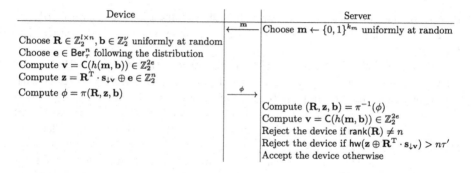

Device	Server
	Choose $\mathbf{m} \leftarrow \{0,1\}^{km}$ uniformly at random
Choose $\mathbf{R} \in \mathbb{Z}_2^{l \times n}, \mathbf{b} \in \mathbb{Z}_2^{\nu}$ uniformly at random	
Choose $\mathbf{e} \in \mathsf{Ber}_{\tau}^n$ following the distribution	
Compute $\mathbf{v} = \mathsf{C}(h(\mathbf{m}, \mathbf{b})) \in \mathbb{Z}_2^{2e}$	
Compute $\mathbf{z} = \mathbf{R}^{\mathrm{T}} \cdot \mathbf{s}_{\downarrow \mathbf{v}} \oplus \mathbf{e} \in \mathbb{Z}_2^n$	
Compute $\phi = \pi(\mathbf{R}, \mathbf{z}, \mathbf{b})$	
	Compute $(\mathbf{R}, \mathbf{z}, \mathbf{b}) = \pi^{-1}(\phi)$
	Compute $\mathbf{v} = \mathsf{C}(h(\mathbf{m}, \mathbf{b})) \in \mathbb{Z}_2^{2e}$
	Reject the device if $\mathsf{rank}(\mathbf{R}) \neq n$
	Reject the device if $\mathsf{hw}(\mathbf{z} \oplus \mathbf{R}^{\mathrm{T}} \cdot \mathbf{s}_{\downarrow \mathbf{v}}) > n\tau'$
	Accept the device otherwise

Fig. 3. 2-round lightweight device authentication based on MAC_1 [10].

A.2 Non-PUF-Based Authentication

Kiltz et al. [10] proposed a lightweight authentication protocol with man-in-the-middle security implied by their secure MAC. Figure 3 shows the protocol that we refer to while constructing our protocol later. In this figure, $\mathbf{s}_{\downarrow \mathbf{v}} \in \{0,1\}^l$ denotes, for $\mathbf{s}, \mathbf{v} \in \{0,1\}^{2l}$ such that $\mathsf{hw}(\mathbf{v}) = l$, an l-bit string, which is a concatenation of (i-th) bits extracted from $\mathbf{s}$, where the corresponding (i-th) bit of $\mathbf{v}$ is 1. Ber_{τ} denotes the Bernoulli distribution parameterized by $\tau \in (0, 1/2)$. $\mathbf{R}^{\mathrm{T}}$ and $\mathsf{rank}(\mathbf{R})$ denote a transpose and a rank of matrix $\mathbf{R}$, respectively.

In this protocol, the device and the server digitally share secret keys: a $2l$-bit secret key $\mathbf{s}$ and a pair of secret functions (C, h, π), where C is a public function from $\mathbb{Z}_2^{\nu}$ to $\mathbb{Z}_2^{2l}$ whose output satisfies both $\mathsf{hw}(\mathsf{C}(\mathbf{x})) = l$ and $\mathsf{hw}(\mathsf{C}(\mathbf{x}) \oplus \mathsf{C}(\mathbf{x}')) \geq 0.9l$, for arbitrary inputs $\mathbf{x} \neq \mathbf{x}'$, h is a pairwise independent permutation, and π is a permutation.

As in the figure, the device computes a response by adding a small amount of logical noise $\mathbf{e}$, chosen from the Bernoulli distribution, to the product of the matrix and secret vector. The server reproduces the response in a similar manner to the device, and accepts the device if the distance of these responses is small enough. Note that the noise makes it difficult for an adversary to recover the secret vector from the response. The scheme can be proven to be secure if the learning parity with noise (LPN, [2]) problem is hard.

B   Proof Sketch of Theorem 1

In this subsection, we give a sketch of security proof for our protocol.

Sketch of Proof: We give a proof by contradiction. Namely, we show that if an adversary $\mathcal{A}$ against our protocol exists, then we can construct a reduction $\mathcal{B}$ that, by using $\mathcal{A}$ as a subroutine, breaks the linear unpredictability of the underlying PUF.

$\mathcal{A}$ is an adversary who forges a response of the authentication protocol. $\mathcal{A}$ makes queries to a random oracle O_H and an authentication oracle O_A, and then, $\mathcal{A}$ asks $\mathcal{B}$ to send a challenge $\mathbf{a}^*$ to $\mathcal{A}$. After that, $\mathcal{A}$ continues to make queries to the above two oracles, and then $\mathcal{A}$ outputs a forged response $(\mathbf{b}^*, \mathbf{z}^*)$ for $\mathbf{a}^*$. Note that $\mathcal{A}$ is disallowed to output $(\mathbf{b}^*, \mathbf{z}*)$ where O_A returns $(\mathbf{b}^*, \mathbf{z}^*)$ for query $\mathbf{a}^*$.

$\mathcal{B}$ interacts with $\mathcal{A}$ to break the linear unpredictability of the PUF. $\mathcal{B}$ is allowed to access the PUF oracle O_P to obtain the XOR of PUF outputs with positions indicating the output bits to be XORed. With the replies of O_P, $\mathcal{B}$ simulates O_H and O_A in order for $\mathcal{A}$ to work correctly. If $\mathcal{B}$ succeeds, $\mathcal{B}$ can obtain a forgery from $\mathcal{A}$, and, with this forgery, $\mathcal{B}$ tries to break the underlying assumption of the PUF.

The proof uses the game hopping technique [27] with four steps from Game_0 (original game for $\mathcal{A}$ to break the authentication protocol) to Game_4 (where $\mathcal{B}$ breaks the assumption) below. In each game, $\mathcal{B}$ interacts with $\mathcal{A}$ to receive a forged response. Here, S_i denotes an event where $\mathcal{B}$ receives a forgery that passes the verification from $\mathcal{A}$ in Game_i $(i \in [0, 4])$.

Overview of Games:

In the proof, we consider five games.

Game_0 is an original/real game where $\mathcal{A}$ tries to break the security of our authentication protocol. Note that in the random oracle model, we assume that H is a random oracle. That is, $\mathcal{A}$ obtains the output of H not from a computation, but from a query to oracle O_H outside of $\mathcal{A}$.

In Game_1, we modify the entity who invokes the PUF. In Game_0, $\mathcal{B}$ (which interacts with $\mathcal{A}$) invokes PUF by itself. However, because our proof goal is to construct $\mathcal{B}$, which breaks the security assumption of the PUF that is located outside of $\mathcal{B}$, we let $\mathcal{B}$ ask the PUF output to O_P, not to invoke PUF by itself.

In Game_2, we modify $\mathcal{A}$ to ask O_H about $H(\mathbf{a}^*, \mathbf{b}^*, i)$ as for the forgery $(\mathbf{a}^*, \mathbf{b}^*, \mathbf{z}^*)$, in advance.

Game_3 and Game_4 are the main parts of this proof. In this proof, $\mathcal{B}$ tries to distinguish the real world from the random one, by using $\mathcal{A}$ as a subroutine.

The basic strategy for constructing $\mathcal{B}$ is as follows. From the challenger $\mathcal{C}$, $\mathcal{B}$ receives $\{(\widetilde{p}_{i,1}, \cdots, \widetilde{p}_{i,l}, \widetilde{z}_i)\}$ as an instance. Let us consider the case where $\mathcal{B}$ receives a forged response $(\mathbf{b}^*, \mathbf{z}^*)$ corresponding to $\{(\widetilde{p}_{i,1}, \cdots, \widetilde{p}_{i,l})\}$ from $\mathcal{A}$. If $c = 1$, then, for more than or equal to k i's, z_i^* is expected to be equal to $\widetilde{z}_i$. However, if $c = 0$, because $\widetilde{z}_i$'s are random and independent from PUF outputs, z_i^* can be equal to $\widetilde{z}_i$ for about $n/2$ i's. Hence, $\mathcal{B}$ can distinguish between whether the number of equations $\{z_i^* = \widetilde{z}_i\}$ exceeds the threshold k or not.

To make $\mathcal{A}$ output forged response corresponding to $\{(\widetilde{p}_{i,1}, \cdots, \widetilde{p}_{i,l})\}_i$, $\mathcal{B}$ needs to embed it in the simulation of the answer of O_H. In Game_3, $\mathcal{B}$ decides when $\mathcal{B}$ embed them on queries to O_H. To do so, $\mathcal{B}$ looks for the query from $\mathcal{A}$ to O_H on $(\mathbf{a}^*, \mathbf{b}^*, *)$. Note that $\mathcal{A}$ is a black-box adversary and $\mathcal{A}$ may not query $(\mathbf{a}^*, \mathbf{b}^*, 1), (\mathbf{a}^*, \mathbf{b}^*, 2), \cdots$ in sequential, but in random order. Therefore, at step 10(b) in Game_3, $\mathcal{B}$ also checks whether it is the first query on $(\mathbf{a}^*, \mathbf{b}^*)$.

Finally, in Game_4, we let $\mathcal{B}$ distinguish the worlds by a threshold k.

<u>Probability Estimation:</u> From above discussions,

$$\begin{aligned}
\epsilon' &= |\Pr[c' = 1 | c = 1] - \Pr[c' = 1 | c = 0]| \\
&\geq \Pr[S_4 | c = 1] - \Pr[\mathsf{Bad}_2] \\
&= \Pr[S_3] - \Pr[\mathsf{Bad}_2] \\
&\geq \frac{1}{q_h + nq_a} \Pr[S_2] - \Pr[\mathsf{Bad}_2] \\
&\geq \frac{1}{q_h + nq_a} (\Pr[S_0] - \Pr[\mathsf{Bad}_1]) - \Pr[\mathsf{Bad}_2] \\
&= \frac{1}{q_h + nq_a} (\epsilon - \Pr[\mathsf{Bad}_1]) - \Pr[\mathsf{Bad}_2] \\
&\geq \frac{1}{q_h + nq_a} \epsilon - \frac{1}{2^{k_b}} - \sum_{i=k}^{n} \frac{\binom{n}{i}}{2^i}
\end{aligned}$$

holds, where Bad_i denotes an event where $\mathcal{A}$'s views are different between Game_{i-1} and Game_i. □

References

1. Bellare, M., Rogaway, P.: Random oracles are practical: a paradigm for designing efficient protocols. In: Denning, D.E., Pyle, R., Ganesan, R., Sandhu, R.S., Ashby, V. (eds.) CCS 1993, Proceedings of the 1st ACM Conference on Computer and Communications Security, pp. 62–73. ACM (1993)

2. Blum, A., Furst, M., Kearns, M., Lipton, R.J.: Cryptographic primitives based on hard learning problems. In: Stinson, D.R. (ed.) CRYPTO 1993. LNCS, vol. 773, pp. 278–291. Springer, Heidelberg (1994). https://doi.org/10.1007/3-540-48329-2_24

3. Delvaux, J., Verbauwhede, I.: Attacking PUF-based pattern matching key generators via helper data manipulation. In: Benaloh, J. (ed.) CT-RSA 2014. LNCS, vol. 8366, pp. 106–131. Springer, Cham (2014). https://doi.org/10.1007/978-3-319-04852-9_6

4. Dodis, Y., Ostrovsky, R., Reyzin, L., Smith, A.: Fuzzy extractors: how to generate strong keys from biometrics and other noisy data. SIAM J. Comput. **38**, 97–139 (2008)

5. Gassend, B., Clarke, D., Van Dijk, M., Devadas, S.: Silicon physical random functions. In: Proceedings of the 9th ACM Conference on Computer and Communications Security, CCS 2002, pp. 148–160. ACM (2002)

6. Gassend, B., Lim, D., Clarke, D.E., van Dijk, M., Devadas, S.: Identification and authentication of integrated circuits. Concurr. Practi. Exp. **16**(11), 1077–1098 (2004)

7. Guajardo, J., Kumar, S.S., Schrijen, G.-J., Tuyls, P.: FPGA intrinsic PUFs and their use for IP protection. In: Paillier, P., Verbauwhede, I. (eds.) CHES 2007. LNCS, vol. 4727, pp. 63–80. Springer, Heidelberg (2007). https://doi.org/10.1007/978-3-540-74735-2_5

8. Holcomb, D.E., Burleson, W.P., Fu, K.: Initial SRAM state as a fingerprint and source of true random numbers for RFID tags. In: Conference on RFID Security 2007. IEEE (2007)

9. Karakoyunlu, D., Sunar, B.: Differential template attacks on PUF enabled crypto-graphic devices. In: 2010 IEEE International Workshop on Information Forensics and Security, WIFS 2010, pp. 1–6. IEEE (2010)

10. Kiltz, E., Pietrzak, K., Cash, D., Jain, A., Venturi, D.: Efficient authentication from hard learning problems. In: Paterson, K.G. (ed.) EUROCRYPT 2011. LNCS, vol. 6632, pp. 7–26. Springer, Heidelberg (2011). https://doi.org/10.1007/978-3-642-20465-4_3

11. Komano, Y., Ohta, K., Sakiyama, K., Iwamoto, M., Verbauwhede, I.: Single-round pattern matching key generation using physically unclonable function. Secur. Commun. Netw. **2019**, 1719585:1–1719585:13 (2019)

12. Lim, D.: Extracting secret keys from integrated circuits. Master's thesis, Massachusetts Institute of Technology (MIT) (2004)

13. Lyubashevsky, V., Masny, D.: Man-in-the-middle secure authentication schemes from LPN and weak PRFs. In: Canetti, R., Garay, J.A. (eds.) CRYPTO 2013. LNCS, vol. 8043, pp. 308–325. Springer, Heidelberg (2013). https://doi.org/10.1007/978-3-642-40084-1_18

14. Maes, R.: Physically Unclonable Functions: Constructions. Properties and Applications. Springer, Heidelberg (2014). https://doi.org/10.1007/978-3-642-41395-7

15. Maes, R., Tuyls, P., Verbauwhede, I.: Low-overhead implementation of a soft decision helper data algorithm for SRAM PUFs. In: Clavier, C., Gaj, K. (eds.) CHES 2009. LNCS, vol. 5747, pp. 332–347. Springer, Heidelberg (2009). https://doi.org/10.1007/978-3-642-04138-9_24

16. Majzoobi, M., Rostami, M., Koushanfar, F., Wallach, D.S., Devadas, S.: Slender PUF protocol: a lightweight, robust, and secure authentication by substring matching. In: 2012 IEEE Symposium on Security and Privacy Workshops, pp. 33–44. IEEE Computer Society (2012)

17. Merli, D., Schuster, D., Stumpf, F., Sigl, G.: Side-channel analysis of pufs and fuzzy extractors. In: McCune, J.M., Balacheff, B., Perrig, A., Sadeghi, A.-R., Sasse, A., Beres, Y. (eds.) Trust 2011. LNCS, vol. 6740, pp. 33–47. Springer, Heidelberg (2011). https://doi.org/10.1007/978-3-642-21599-5_3

18. National Institute of Standards and Technology (NIST). Federal information processing standards publication (FIPS) 180-4, secure hash standard (SHS) (2015)

19. National Institute of Standards and Technology (NIST). Recommendation for block cipher modes of operation: the CMAC mode for authentication (2016)

20. Paral, Z.S., Devadas, S.: Reliable and efficient PUF-based key generation using pattern matching. In: 2011 IEEE International Symposium on Hardware-Oriented Security and Trust (HOST2011), pp. 128–133. IEEE (2011)

21. Ranasinghe, D.C., Engels, D.W., Cole, P.H.: Security and privacy: modest proposals for low- cost RFID systems. In: Auto-ID Labs Research Workshop, pp. 58–64. IEEE (2004)

22. Regev, O.: On lattices, learning with errors, random linear codes, and cryptography. J. ACM **56**(6), 34:1–34:40 (2009)

23. Rostami, M., Majzoobi, M., Koushanfar, F., Wallach, D.S., Devadas, S.: Robust and reverse-engineering resilient PUF authentication and key-exchange by substring matching. IEEE Trans. Emerging Topics Comput. **2**(1), 37–49 (2014)

24. Sadeghi, A.-R., Naccache, D. (eds.): Towards Hardware-Intrinsic Security. Springer, Heidelberg (2010). https://doi.org/10.1007/978-3-642-14452-3

25. Pieter, J., Schalkwijk, M.: An algorithm for source coding. IEEE Trans. Inf. Theory **18**(3), 395–399 (1972)

26. Schaller, A., Arul, T., van der Leest, V., Katzenbeisser, S.: Lightweight anti-counterfeiting solution for low-end commodity hardware using inherent PUFs. In: Holz, T., Ioannidis, S. (eds.) Trust 2014. LNCS, vol. 8564, pp. 83–100. Springer, Cham (2014). https://doi.org/10.1007/978-3-319-08593-7_6

27. Shoup, V.: Sequences of games: a tool for taming complexity in security proofs. IACR Cryptology ePrint Archive **2004**, 332 (2004)

28. Tebelmann, L., Pehl, M., Sigl, G.: EM side-channel analysis of BCH-based error correction for PUF-based key generation. In: Chang, C.-H., Rührmair, U., Zhang, W. (eds.) Proceedings of the 2017 Workshop on Attacks and Solutions in Hardware Security, ASHES@CCS 2017, Dallas, TX, USA, 3 November 2017, pp. 43–52. ACM (2017)

29. Uyematsu, T., Iwata, K., Okamoto, E.: An efficient algorithm for enumerative coding. IEICE Trans. **J80-A**(3), 573–575 (1997)

30. (Mandel) Yu, M.-D., M'Raïhi, D.., Verbauwhede, I., Devadas, S.: A noise bifurcation architecture for linear additive physical functions. In: 2014 IEEE International Symposium on Hardware-Oriented Security and Trust, HOST 2014, pp. 124–129. IEEE Computer Society (2014)

Card-Based Zero-Knowledge Proof Protocol for Pancake Sorting

Yuichi Komano[1]([⊠])🆔 and Takaaki Mizuki[2]🆔

[1] Toshiba Corporation, 1 Komukai-Toshiba-Cho, Saiwai-ku, Kawasaki, Japan
komano@net.it-chiba.ac.jp
[2] Tohoku University, 6–3 Aramaki-Aza-Aoba, Aoba-ku, Sendai, Japan
mizuki+lncs@tohoku.ac.jp

Abstract. Assume that, given a sequence of n integers from 1 to n arranged in random order, we want to sort them, provided that the only acceptable operation is a prefix reversal, which means to take any number of integers (sub-sequence) from the left of the sequence, reverse the order of the sub-sequence, and return them to the original sequence. This problem is called "pancake sorting," and sorting an arbitrary sequence with the minimum number of operations restricted in this way is known to be NP-hard. In this paper, we consider applying the concept of zero-knowledge proofs to the pancake sorting problem. That is, we design a physical zero-knowledge proof protocol in which a user (the prover) who knows how to sort a given sequence with ℓ operations can convince another user (the verifier) that the prover knows this information without divulging it.

Keywords: Zero-knowledge proof · Card-based cryptography · Pancake sorting

1 Introduction

"Pancake sorting" [27] is a problem of sorting a given sequence of n integers from 1 to n by using only "prefix reversals," which rearrange a sub-sequence of any length taken from the left in the reverse order. In this paper, we apply the concept of zero-knowledge proofs to the pancake sorting problem and propose a physical zero-knowledge proof protocol for the pancake sorting problem. This paper begins by explaining the pancake sorting problem in detail.

1.1 Pancake Sorting Problem

We take a sequence of five integers $(3, 5, 2, 1, 4)$ as an example. For this sequence, let us reverse its prefixes of lengths 2, 5, 4, and 3 in this order one by one, so that the sequence is rearranged as

$$(\underline{3, 5}, 2, 1, 4) \rightarrow (\underline{5, 3, 2, 1, 4}) \rightarrow (\underline{4, 1, 2, 3}, 5) \rightarrow (\underline{3, 2, 1}, 4, 5) \rightarrow (1, 2, 3, 4, 5).$$

Y. Komano—Presently, the author is with Chiba Institute of Technology, Japan.

G. Bella et al. (Eds.): SecITC 2022, LNCS 13809, pp. 222–239, 2023.
https://doi.org/10.1007/978-3-031-32636-3_13

Thus, the sorting (in ascending order) is completed in four *prefix reversals*. The four prefix reversals above can be represented as a sequence $(2, 5, 4, 3)$ that consists of the lengths in the prefix reversals; such a sequence of prefix reversal lengths completing the sorting is called a *solution* to a given sequence (to be sorted).

This kind of sorting problem is called *pancake sorting* [27]; the name comes from the problem of sorting a stack of pancakes of distinct diameters in order of diameter size by repeatedly flipping over a number of pancakes at the top with a spatula.

Let us formalize this problem. Let $n \geq 1$, and let $(x_1, x_2, \ldots, x_n)$ be an input sequence that consists of n integers randomly arranged from 1 to n. Such a sequence of n integers can be regarded as a permutation on $\{1, 2, \ldots, n\}$. That is, when S_n denotes the symmetric group of degree n, the sequence $(x_1, x_2, \ldots, x_n)$ can be represented by the following permutation $x \in S_n$:

$$x = \begin{pmatrix} 1 & 2 & 3 & \cdots & n \\ x_1 & x_2 & x_3 & \cdots & x_n \end{pmatrix}.$$

Next, let us also express the prefix reversal operations in terms of permutation as follows. For each i such that $1 \leq i \leq n$, the operation of a prefix reversal of length i is represented by the following permutation $\mathsf{sw}_i \in S_n$:

$$\mathsf{sw}_i = \begin{pmatrix} 1 & 2 & 3 & \cdots & i-2 & i-1 & i \\ i & i-1 & i-2 & \cdots & 3 & 2 & 1 \end{pmatrix}.$$

Thus, $(y_1, y_2, \ldots, y_\ell) \in \{1, 2, \ldots, n\}^\ell$ is a solution to a sequence $x \in S_n$ if and only if

$$\mathsf{sw}_{y_\ell} \circ \mathsf{sw}_{y_{\ell-1}} \circ \cdots \circ \mathsf{sw}_{y_1} \circ x = \mathsf{id}$$

holds, where $\mathsf{id} \in S_n$ denotes the identity. Note that the above permutation sw_i is equal to its inverse sw_i^{-1}. That is, $\mathsf{sw}_i = \mathsf{sw}_i^{-1}$ holds for every i, $1 \leq i \leq n$. Note furthermore that $\mathsf{sw}_1 = \mathsf{id}$.

Following this formulation, we can check, for example, that the above sequence $(3, 5, 2, 1, 4)$ and its solution $(2, 5, 4, 3)$ satisfy

$$\mathsf{sw}_3 \circ \mathsf{sw}_4 \circ \mathsf{sw}_5 \circ \mathsf{sw}_2 \circ \begin{pmatrix} 1\,2\,3\,4\,5 \\ 3\,5\,2\,1\,4 \end{pmatrix} = \mathsf{id}.$$

1.2 Computational Complexity of Pancake Sorting

Since the pancake sorting problem was introduced in the 1970s, many researchers have reported algorithms for minimizing the number of prefix reversals and their lower bounds.

Among all the solutions to a sequence $x \in S_n$, any solution with the minimum number of prefix reversals is said to be *optimal*; we denote the minimum number of prefix reversals as $\alpha(x)$, that is, the length of any optimal solution to x. For example, because the length of the solution $(2, 5, 4, 3)$ to the sequence $(3, 5, 2, 1, 4)$

is four and there is no solution whose length is smaller than four, it is an optimal solution and we have $\alpha((3,5,2,1,4)) = 4$[1]. We also write $h(n)$ as the longest length of optimal solutions to sequences of n integers. That is, we define

$$h(n) := \max\{\alpha(x) \mid x \in S_n\}$$

for every $n \geq 1$.

Table 1. Values of $h(n)$.

n	1	2	3	4	5	6	7	8	9	10	11	12	13	14	15	16	17	18	19
$h(n)$ (OEIS A058986)	0	1	3	4	5	7	8	9	10	11	13	14	15	16	17	18	19	20	22

As shown in Table 1, the values of $h(n)$ have been obtained up to $n = 19$ by numerical calculations or observations (e.g., [2,9,10,19,30]), and they are registered in the On-Line Encyclopedia of Integer Sequences (OEIS) as OEIS A058986[2]. Finding the values of $h(n)$ for $n \geq 20$ is an open problem.

As general upper and lower bounds on $h(n)$, Gates and Papadimitriou [12] showed that $\frac{17}{16}n \leq h(n) \leq \frac{5n+5}{3}$ in 1979. Since then, the bounds on $h(n)$ have been analyzed, and the best lower and upper bounds currently known are $\frac{15}{14}n \leq h(n)$ [19] and $h(n) \leq \frac{18}{11}n$ [8], respectively.

In contrast, the complexity of finding its optimal solution given an arbitrary sequence $x \in S_n$ (sorting by prefix reversals, or MIN-SBPR) had been unsolved for many years, until in 2012 Bulteau, Fertin, and Rusu [3,4] proved that this problem, MIN-SBPR, is NP-hard.

1.3   Contribution

As explained in Sect. 1.2, MIN-SBPR is an NP-hard problem, and hence, there are possible situations where it is valuable to be the only one who knows a solution to a particular sequence of a pancake sorting problem. Therefore, we will attempt to apply the concept of the *zero-knowledge proof* [13] to the pancake sorting problem.

Suppose that there are two users, a prover P and a verifier V, and only the prover P knows a solution $(y_1, y_2, \ldots, y_\ell)$ of length ℓ to a sequence $x \in S_n$. Assume furthermore that P wants to convince V that P knows the solution without leaking any information about the solution. Our contribution is to propose a zero-knowledge proof protocol for the pancake sorting problem that achieves this goal. The proposed protocol is a so-called *physical* zero-knowledge proof protocol that can be executed using a physical deck of cards.

---

[1] In this way, we sometimes use the terms "sequence" and "permutation" interchangeably.

[2] https://oeis.org/A058986.

The following is an example of a game where the proposed protocol will be useful. When a sequence $(12, 19, 20, 4, 13, 17, 5, 10, 16, 15, 11, 1, 7, 14, 3, 6, 18, 8, 2, 9)$ of size $n = 20$ of the pancake sorting problem is given, multiple players try to find a solution to it, and a player wins the game if he/she finds the solution with the shortest length. In this case, if a player discloses the solution to other players, another player who sees the solution may take it as his/her own achievement or may use it as a hint for finding a solution to the next game, which makes the game less fun. Therefore, a player who has found a solution of certain length first convinces other players that he/she knows the solution without leaking any information using our zero-knowledge proof protocol, and then the player discloses the solution after gaining sufficient recognition so that he/she can correctly claim the achievements or be judged as a winner of the game.

In addition, we expect that our proposed protocol can be used as a good educational tool for teaching lay-people the concept of zero-knowledge proof as well as the sorting problem. Furthermore, as will be explained in Sect. 6, our proposed technique can be applied to more general problems (beyond the pancake sorting problem).

1.4 Related Work

One problem similar to the pancake sorting problem is *Topswops* [25,26,45]. In Topswops, for a sequence of integers, a prefix reversal of the first k integers, where k is the leading integer of the sequence, is repeated until the leading integer becomes 1. Recently, the authors constructed a physical zero-knowledge proof protocol that can verify that a Topswops game terminates with a predefined number of prefix reversals while the input sequence of integers is kept confidential [29]. Although pancake sorting is similar to Topswops, what is being kept secret in the zero-knowledge proofs is different. In the former, the solution should be kept secret, whereas in the latter, the input sequence of integers should be kept secret.

In addition, numerous physical zero-knowledge proof protocols for pencil puzzles have been constructed to date using a physical deck of cards. Examples are Akari [5], Cryptarithmetic [22], Hashiwokakero (Bridges) [63], Heyawake [53], Hitori [50,53], Juosan [39], Kakuro [5,40], KenKen [5], Makaro [6,66], Masyu [32], Nonogram [7,54], Norinori [11], Numberlink [58,60], Nurikabe [50,53], Nurimisaki [48], Ripple Effect [61,62], Shikaku [65], Slitherlink [32,33], Sudoku [14,55, 57,67,68], Suguru [49,52], Takuzu [5,39], and Usowan [51].

Card-based cryptography that performs cryptographic tasks using a deck of physical cards has been growing rapidly in recent years [42,43]. Hot topics include secure and efficient protocols in the private model [1,35,46], multi-valued-output symmetric function evaluation [64,71], information leakage due to operative errors [44], graph automorphism shuffles [41], secure sorting [16], multi-valued protocols with a direction encoding [76], the half-open action [38], card-minimal protocols [15,28], and single-shuffle protocols [31,73]. Furthermore, very recently, Shinagawa and Nuida [74] showed that a certain single-shuffle protocol implies the existence of a private simultaneous messages protocol; this is the first successful and amazing result that directly connects 'physical' protocols with 'digital' protocols. It should be noted that several studies [34,56,75] on card-based cryptography were reported in the previous SecITC conferences.

2   Preliminaries

In this section, we first explain the physical properties of cards used in this paper, then describe how to encode permutations and integers using cards, and finally introduce the "pile-scramble shuffle" [21], which will be used in our protocol. Hereinafter, n denotes the size of a pancake sorting problem (i.e., the length of an input sequence of integers).

2.1   Physical Cards

In this paper, two types of physical cards are used:

> **Integer cards** Each card has an integer from 1 to n written on its face, such as $\boxed{1}\boxed{2}\boxed{3}\cdots\boxed{n}$, and the reverse side of every card has the same pattern $\boxed{?}$.
> **Black and red cards** Each card has a ♣ or ♡ symbol on its face, and the back of every card has the same pattern $\boxed{?}$.

We use the notation

$$\boxed{?}_{i}$$

to denote a face-down integer card whose face is $\boxed{i}$ for an integer $1 \leq i \leq n$.

2.2   Permutation Commitment

As explained in Sect. 1.1, a sequence of integers and an operation of prefix reversal in the pancake sorting problem are represented by permutations. Therefore, we introduce a method to represent permutations with integer cards, as often used in card-based cryptography [20,67].

To represent a permutation $\pi \in S_n$, we simply use n integer cards $\boxed{1}\boxed{2}\boxed{3}\cdots\boxed{n}$ and arrange them according to the values of $\pi(1), \pi(2), \ldots, \pi(n)$:

$$\boxed{\pi(1)}\boxed{\pi(2)}\boxed{\pi(3)} \ldots \boxed{\pi(n)}.$$

Consider turning over these n cards: we call n face-down cards

$$\boxed{?}_{\pi(1)} \boxed{?}_{\pi(2)} \boxed{?}_{\pi(3)} \cdots \boxed{?}_{\pi(n)}$$

a *permutation commitment* to $\pi \in S_n$. For example, a permutation commitment to $\mathsf{sw}_3 \in S_n$ (corresponding to a prefix reversal of length 3) is

$$\boxed{?}\boxed{?}\boxed{?}\boxed{?}\boxed{?} \cdots \boxed{?}\boxed{?}_{3\ 2\ 1\ 4\ 5 \quad n-1\ n}.$$

In the following, we write a permutation commitment to $\pi \in S_n$ as

$$\pi : \boxed{?}\boxed{?} \cdots \boxed{?} \quad \text{or} \quad \underset{\pi}{\underbrace{\boxed{?}}} .$$

2.3   Integer Commitment

As explained in Sect. 2.2, a sequence $x \in S_n$ and a prefix reversal sw_i are represented with permutation commitments. Another important element of the pancake problem is a 'solution,' and hence, we introduce "integer commitments" here to express the solution with cards.

With $n - 1$ black cards and one red card, let us encode integers from 1 to n as

$$\boxed{\heartsuit}\boxed{\clubsuit}\boxed{\clubsuit} \cdots \boxed{\clubsuit}\boxed{\clubsuit} = 1$$
$$\boxed{\clubsuit}\boxed{\heartsuit}\boxed{\clubsuit} \cdots \boxed{\clubsuit}\boxed{\clubsuit} = 2$$
$$\boxed{\clubsuit}\boxed{\clubsuit}\boxed{\heartsuit} \cdots \boxed{\clubsuit}\boxed{\clubsuit} = 3$$
$$\vdots$$
$$\boxed{\clubsuit}\boxed{\clubsuit}\boxed{\clubsuit}\boxed{\clubsuit} \cdots \boxed{\clubsuit}\boxed{\heartsuit} = n.$$

That is, the position of the red card $\boxed{\heartsuit}$ determines the integer. Following this encoding rule, we will call a sequence of face-down cards an *integer commitment*. Such an encoding rule is often used in card-based cryptography [37,59,77].

According to convention, we write an integer commitment to i, $1 \le i \le n$, as the symbol $E_n(i)$:

$$E_n(i) : \boxed{?}\boxed{?}\boxed{?} \cdots \boxed{?},$$

where only the i-th card is $\boxed{\heartsuit}$ and the remaining $n - 1$ cards are $\boxed{\clubsuit}$ as mentioned above.

2.4   Pile-Scramble Shuffle and Composition of Permutations

A *pile-scramble shuffle* [21] is a shuffling operation by which several piles of cards of the same size are shuffled.

As an example, suppose that we have three permutation commitments to a sequence $x \in S_n$, the identity $\mathsf{id} \in S_n$, and a prefix reversal $\mathsf{sw}_i \in S_n$:

$$x : \boxed{?}\boxed{?}\boxed{?} \cdots \boxed{?}$$
$$\mathsf{id} : \boxed{?}\boxed{?}\boxed{?} \cdots \boxed{?}$$
$$\mathsf{sw}_i : \boxed{?}\boxed{?}\boxed{?} \cdots \boxed{?}.$$

Considering each (vertical) column consisting of three cards as a single pile, we apply a pile-scramble shuffle to the n piles; then, the transition is as follows:

$$
\begin{bmatrix} \boxed{?}\,\boxed{?}\,\boxed{?} \cdots \boxed{?} \\ \boxed{?}\,\boxed{?}\,\boxed{?} \cdots \boxed{?} \\ \boxed{?}\,\boxed{?}\,\boxed{?} \cdots \boxed{?} \end{bmatrix}
\quad \rightarrow \quad
\begin{array}{l}
r \circ x : \boxed{?}\,\boxed{?}\,\boxed{?} \cdots \boxed{?} \\
r \circ \text{id} : \boxed{?}\,\boxed{?}\,\boxed{?} \cdots \boxed{?} \\
r \circ \text{sw}_i : \boxed{?}\,\boxed{?}\,\boxed{?} \cdots \boxed{?},
\end{array}
$$

where $r \in S_n$ is a uniformly distributed random permutation generated by the pile-scramble shuffle.

We then turn over the bottom row, namely the permutation commitment to $r \circ \text{sw}_i$, and sort the vertical columns without collapsing them based on the n integers appearing in the bottom row. With this sort, $(r \circ \text{sw}_i)^{-1}$ acts upon the top two rows, and the cards are rearranged as follows (note that $\text{sw}_i = \text{sw}_i^{-1}$ holds):

$$
\begin{array}{l}
\text{sw}_i \circ x : \boxed{?}\,\boxed{?}\,\boxed{?} \cdots \boxed{?} \\
\text{sw}_i : \boxed{?}\,\boxed{?}\,\boxed{?} \cdots \boxed{?} \\
\phantom{\text{sw}_i :} \boxed{1}\,\boxed{2}\,\boxed{3} \cdots \boxed{n}.
\end{array}
$$

Thus, the above series of operations allows us to compose permutations of the prefix reversal sw_i and of the sequence x, while the permutation commitment to sw_i remains intact. The proposed protocol in this paper uses this technique, which originally comes from the "permutation division protocol" developed by Hashimoto et al. [17,18].

3 Proposed Protocol

In this section, we propose a physical zero-knowledge proof protocol for the pancake sorting problem using permutation and integer commitments.

Let $x \in S_n$ be an input sequence and let $y = (y_1, y_2, \ldots, y_\ell)$ be a solution to x with length ℓ. That is, $\text{sw}_{y_\ell} \circ \text{sw}_{y_{\ell-1}} \circ \cdots \circ \text{sw}_{y_1} \circ x = \text{id}$ holds. Assume that the sequence x and the length of the solution ℓ are public information and that only the prover P knows the solution y (i.e., the verifier V does not know y).

3.1 Concept

As seen in Sect. 2.4, from permutation commitments to x and sw_i, it is easy to construct a composition of permutations $\text{sw}_i \circ x$. A permutation commitment to the input sequence x can be created publicly. Thus, if the prover P prepares permutation commitments to $\text{sw}_{y_1}, \text{sw}_{y_2}, \ldots, \text{sw}_{y_\ell}$ corresponding to the solution $y = (y_1, y_2, \ldots, y_\ell)$, then by composing them, we have

$$
\text{sw}_{y_\ell} \circ \text{sw}_{y_{\ell-1}} \circ \cdots \circ \text{sw}_{y_1} \circ x : \boxed{?}\,\boxed{?}\,\boxed{?} \cdots \boxed{?}.
$$

By turning over this permutation commitment and checking that it is the identity id, we can guarantee that the prover P knows y. Based on these ideas, we propose our protocol as described below.

Note that if the prover P directly creates and places permutation commitments to $\mathsf{sw}_{y_1}, \ldots, \mathsf{sw}_{y_\ell}$ by himself/herself, then we cannot guarantee that they surely correspond to some prefix reversals; therefore, we need a more elaborate way to arrange permutation commitments to $\mathsf{sw}_{y_1}, \ldots, \mathsf{sw}_{y_\ell}$.

3.2 Protocol Description

First of all, as an input to our protocol, a prover P, who knows a solution $y = (y_1, y_2, \ldots, y_\ell)$, creates integer commitments $E_n(y_1), E_n(y_2), \ldots, E_n(y_\ell)$ corresponding to $(y_1, y_2, \ldots, y_\ell)$ in secret and places them on the table as follows:

$$
\begin{aligned}
E_n(y_1) &: \boxed{?}\boxed{?} \cdots \boxed{?} \\
E_n(y_2) &: \boxed{?}\boxed{?} \cdots \boxed{?} \\
&\quad\vdots \\
E_n(y_\ell) &: \boxed{?}\boxed{?} \cdots \boxed{?}.
\end{aligned}
\tag{1}
$$

In addition, $n + 2$ sets of integer cards $\boxed{1}\boxed{2}\boxed{3} \cdots \boxed{n}$ as additional cards are prepared.

Our protocol is executed with the above cards as input. Because our protocol is non-interactive (cf. [36]), it may be executed individually by either the prover P or by the verifier V (or even by any third party).

Protocol 1 (Proposed protocol).

1. Using additional $n + 2$ sets of integer cards, arrange $n + 2$ permutation commitments to $\mathsf{sw}_1, \mathsf{sw}_2, \ldots, \mathsf{sw}_n$, x, and id, as follows:

$$
\underbrace{\boxed{?}}_{\mathsf{sw}_1}\ \underbrace{\boxed{?}}_{\mathsf{sw}_2} \cdots \underbrace{\boxed{?}}_{\mathsf{sw}_n}
$$

$$
\begin{aligned}
x &: \boxed{?}\boxed{?}\boxed{?} \cdots \boxed{?} \\
\mathsf{id} &: \boxed{?}\boxed{?}\boxed{?} \cdots \boxed{?}.
\end{aligned}
$$

2. Take the permutation commitments to $\mathsf{sw}_1, \mathsf{sw}_2, \ldots, \mathsf{sw}_n$, and place them along with the integer commitments $E_n(y_1), E_n(y_2), \cdots, E_n(y_\ell)$ of Eq. (1) as follows:

$$
\underbrace{\boxed{?}}_{\mathsf{sw}_1}\ \underbrace{\boxed{?}}_{\mathsf{sw}_2} \cdots \underbrace{\boxed{?}}_{\mathsf{sw}_n}
$$

$$
\begin{aligned}
E_n(y_1) &: \boxed{?} \quad \boxed{?} \quad \cdots \quad \boxed{?} \\
E_n(y_2) &: \boxed{?} \quad \boxed{?} \quad \cdots \quad \boxed{?} \\
&\qquad\quad\vdots \\
E_n(y_\ell) &: \boxed{?} \quad \boxed{?} \quad \cdots \quad \boxed{?}.
\end{aligned}
$$

Note that in the first row, the permutation commitment to sw_{y_i} for each i, $1 \leq i \leq \ell$, appears in the column where the card ♡ appears in the $(i+1)$-th row[3].

3. Apply a pile-scramble shuffle[4]:

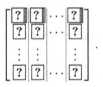

Because the pile-scramble shuffle does not change within each vertical column, the above statement "in the first row, the permutation commitment to sw_{y_i} appears in the column where the card ♡ appears in the $(i+1)$-th row" remains valid. Therefore, we turn over the integer commitment in the second row, and identify the permutation commitment $\underbrace{\boxed{?}}_{\mathsf{sw}_{y_1}}$ above ♡:

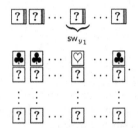

4. Use the permutation commitment to sw_{y_1} just identified and the permutation commitments to x and id to construct a composition of permutations $\mathsf{sw}_{y_1} \circ x$ (still holding a permutation commitment to sw_{y_1}), as described in Sect. 2.4:

$$x : \boxed{?}\,\boxed{?}\,\cdots\,\boxed{?} \quad\quad \begin{bmatrix} \boxed{?}\,\boxed{?}\,\cdots\,\boxed{?} \\ \boxed{?}\,\boxed{?}\,\cdots\,\boxed{?} \\ \boxed{?}\,\boxed{?}\,\cdots\,\boxed{?} \end{bmatrix} \quad\quad \mathsf{sw}_{y_1} \circ x : \boxed{?}\,\boxed{?}\,\cdots\,\boxed{?}$$

$$\mathsf{id} : \boxed{?}\,\boxed{?}\,\cdots\,\boxed{?} \quad \rightarrow \quad\quad\quad \rightarrow \quad \mathsf{sw}_{y_1} : \boxed{?}\,\boxed{?}\,\cdots\,\boxed{?}$$

$$\mathsf{sw}_{y_1} : \boxed{?}\,\boxed{?}\,\cdots\,\boxed{?} \quad\quad\quad\quad\quad\quad\quad\quad\quad \boxed{1}\,\boxed{2}\,\cdots\,\boxed{n}.$$

5. Return $\underbrace{\boxed{?}}_{\mathsf{sw}_{y_1}}$ obtained in the previous step to its original position in Step (3) and remove the second row:

$$\underbrace{\boxed{?}\,\boxed{?}\,\cdots\,\boxed{?}\,\cdots\,\boxed{?}}_{\mathsf{sw}_{y_1}}$$

$$\boxed{?}\,\boxed{?}\,\cdots\,\boxed{?}\,\cdots\,\boxed{?}.$$

$$\vdots\quad\vdots\quad\quad\vdots\quad\quad\vdots$$

$$\boxed{?}\,\boxed{?}\,\cdots\,\boxed{?}\,\cdots\,\boxed{?}$$

---

[3] Here, $E_n(y_1)$ is the second row, $E_n(y_2)$ is the third row, and so on.

[4] Instead of a pile-scramble shuffle, one may use a "pile-shifting shuffle" [47,72].

6. Repeat Steps (3) through (5) $\ell - 1$ times, but do not execute the process corresponding to Step (5) in the last iteration. That is, we identify the permutation commitments from sw_{y_2} to sw_{y_ℓ} and compose them sequentially to the composition of permutations $\mathsf{sw}_{y_1} \circ x$. Finally, we obtain the composition of permutations as follows:

$$\mathsf{sw}_{y_\ell} \circ \mathsf{sw}_{y_{\ell-1}} \circ \cdots \circ \mathsf{sw}_{y_1} \circ x : \boxed{?}\boxed{?}\boxed{?} \cdots \boxed{?}.$$

7. Turn over the permutation commitment to $\mathsf{sw}_{y_\ell} \circ \mathsf{sw}_{y_{\ell-1}} \circ \cdots \circ \mathsf{sw}_{y_1} \circ x$ obtained in the previous step and return "accept" if it is id; otherwise return "reject."

4   Security and Performance

In this section, we discuss the security and performance of Protocol 1 described in Sect. 3.

4.1   Security

First, let us check that, for a given sequence $x \in S_n$ and a length ℓ, our protocol performs a zero-knowledge proof for a solution y (of length ℓ); in other words, we need to show that the protocol satisfies the completeness, soundness, and zero-knowledge properties.

Completeness. Suppose that the prover P correctly places integer commitments according to the solution y. In this case, as can be seen from the construction of our protocol, it is not rejected at any step and is also accepted at the final step.

Soundness. Assume that the prover P places illegal commitments as input. There are two cases to be considered; we will show that our protocol eventually rejects the invalid solution in both cases.

(i) If there is an illegal integer commitment (placed by P) which does not consist of one red card and $n - 1$ black cards, then it is detected and rejected when the integer commitment is turned over in Step (3) of our protocol.

(ii) (ii) If the input integer commitments correspond to an incorrect solution $y' = (y'_1, y'_2, \ldots, y'_\ell)$, then the permutation commitment to x is rearranged according to y', as can be seen from the construction of our protocol. However, the rearranged permutation is not id in Step (7) and our protocol rejects it.

Zero-Knowledge. Suppose that the integer commitments corresponding to the solution $y = (y_1, y_2, \ldots, y_\ell)$ are correctly placed. No information about y_i is leaked during the execution of our protocol, because a pile-scramble shuffle is applied immediately before the cards are turned over to be face-up (except in the final step). The identity id that is opened in the final step is public information. Therefore, our protocol is information-theoretically secure.

4.2 Performance

This subsection discusses the number of cards and the number of shuffles required in our protocol.

First, for the number of cards, as described at the beginning of Sect. 3.2, we use ℓ ♡ cards and $(n-1)\ell$ ♣ cards for integer commitments. In addition, we use $n+2$ sets of cards from $\boxed{1}$ to $\boxed{n}$ as additional cards. Thus, $n\ell$ black and red cards and $n(n+2)$ integer cards are used. Therefore, our protocol requires $n^2 + (2+\ell)n$ cards in total.

The only shuffling operation used in the proposed protocol is the pile-scramble shuffle. The pile-scramble shuffle is performed once in Step (3) and once in Step (4), and each of these steps is executed ℓ times. Therefore, in total, the number of shuffles required in our protocol is 2ℓ.

5 Variants

This section presents variants of our protocol.

5.1 Non-interactive Protocol with Fewer Additional Cards

In our protocol, the first integer commitment is

$$E_n(y_1): \boxed{?}\boxed{?}\cdots\boxed{?},$$

where the y_1-th card is ♡ and the other $n-1$ cards are ♣. Let us consider a variant that uses $\boxed{1}$ instead of ♡ and $\boxed{2},\boxed{3},\cdots,\boxed{n}$ instead of ♣. In this case, after $\underbrace{\boxed{?}}_{\text{sw}_{y_1}}$ is identified in Step (3) of our protocol, the opened $\boxed{1},\boxed{2},\boxed{3},\cdots,\boxed{n}$ can be used as additional cards in Step (4), and hence, we can reduce the number of additional cards by n.

5.2 Interactive Protocol with Fewer Additional Cards

Our protocol uses ℓ ♡ cards and $(n-1)\ell$ ♣ cards for integer commitments $E_n(y_1), E_n(y_2), \cdots, E_n(y_\ell)$. Instead of preparing all $E_n(y_1), E_n(y_2), \cdots, E_n(y_\ell)$ in advance, if the prover P places $E_n(y_i)$ every time Steps (3) and (6) are executed, the protocol could be executed with one ♡ card and $n-1$ ♣ cards. Note that the order of permutation commitments $\underbrace{\boxed{?}}_{\text{sw}_{y_1}} \underbrace{\boxed{?}}_{\text{sw}_{y_2}} \cdots \underbrace{\boxed{?}}_{\text{sw}_{y_n}}$ is randomized by the pile-scramble shuffle in Step (3). Hence, the prover can not determine the correct position of the permutation commitment corresponding to the next prefix reversal, and hence, it is impossible for the prover to place a new integer commitment correctly. To address this issue, just after returning the permutation commitment to its original position in Step (5), the prover applies a pile-scramble shuffle, turns over the permutation commitments to be face-up, places a new integer commitment corresponding to the next prefix reversal, and turns over the permutation commitments again to be face-down. After that, the piles of cards are shuffled with a pile-scramble shuffle in Step (3), as invoked by Step (6). Hence, although this variant can reduce the number of required cards, the number of shuffles increases by $\ell - 1$.

Similar to Sect. 5.1, the number of additional cards can be reduced more by using $\boxed{1}\boxed{2}\boxed{3} \cdots \boxed{n}$ instead of one $\boxed{\heartsuit}$ card and $n - 1$ $\boxed{\clubsuit}$ cards.

5.3 Protocol with Fewer Shuffles

Because sw_i satisfies $\mathsf{sw}_i = \mathsf{sw}_i^{-1}$ (namely, $\mathsf{sw}_i \circ \mathsf{sw}_i = \mathsf{sw}_i^{-1} \circ \mathsf{sw}_i = \mathsf{id}$), two consecutive applications of sw_i to a sequence $x \in S_n$ will not change it. If a player tries to find a solution with a shorter length for the pancake sorting problem, the same prefix reversal is never performed twice in a row. Instead of executing Step (3) of our protocol (and the step that is equivalent to Step (3) in Step (6)) for $E_n(y_i)$ one at a time, executing two steps for $E_n(y_i)$ and $E_n(y_{i+1})$ together can reduce the number of shuffles by $\lfloor \ell/2 \rfloor$. This variant applies to both the interactive and non-interactive protocols above.

5.4 Protocol with Fewer Cards

The permutation commitment $\mathsf{sw}_1 = \mathsf{id}$ does not change a sequence $x \in S_n$. Similar to the discussion in Sect. 5.3, if a player tries to find a solution with a shorter length for the pancake sorting problem, $\mathsf{sw}_1 = \mathsf{id}$ is never performed in our protocol as well as the above-mentioned variants. Hence, we can omit the leftmost column in Step (2) of our protocol so that Steps (2), (3), and (5) are performed with $n - 1$ piles (columns) of cards. In this variant, we can reduce the number of cards by $n + \ell$.

6 Conclusion

In this paper, we proposed a physical zero-knowledge proof protocol for the pancake sorting problem. The main idea is to combine permutation and integer commitments so that a prover can efficiently place a solution and efficiently perform prefix reversals secretly.

Because the pancake sorting problem has many variations (e.g., the introduction of settings where pancakes have two distinct sides [12,69,70]), building new or generic protocols for them is one of our future works.

Beyond the pancake sorting problem and its variants, our zero-knowledge proof protocol can be modified for the following general problem[5]: Assuming that a sequence x of length n (which is not necessarily a permutation) and an integer ℓ along with m distinct permutations $\sigma_1, \sigma_2, \ldots, \sigma_m \in S_n$ and a sequence

---

[5] This generalization was pointed out by Koji Nuida.

z of length n are public, the prover wants to convince the verifier that the prover knows $(y_1, y_2, \ldots, y_\ell)$ such that

$$\sigma_{y_\ell} \circ \sigma_{y_{\ell-1}} \circ \cdots \circ \sigma_{y_1}(x) = z,$$

where $\pi(x)$ for a permutation π represents the permuted sequence according to π. This general problem includes solving the Rubik's Cube, for instance.

The graph obtained by connecting two vertices that can be transitioned by a prefix reversal with edges, where each sequence is regarded as a vertex, is called a *pancake network* [19], and is considered to be the origin of the *reconfiguration problem* (e.g., [23,24]), which is currently popular in the study of algorithm theory. Our protocol can be regarded as a technique to show that a vertex can be transitioned from one vertex to another in a pancake network without leaking any information, and we believe that it is an attractive topic to investigate whether card-based cryptography and zero-knowledge proofs can be applied to various other reconfiguration problems.

Acknowledgements. We thank the anonymous referees, whose comments have helped us improve the presentation of the paper. This work was supported by Grant-in-Aid for Scientific Research (JP18H05289, JP21K11881). We thank Koji Nuida for advising us to generalize the problem, as described in the third paragraph of Sect. 6.

References

1. Abe, Y., et al.: Efficient card-based majority voting protocols. New Gener. Comput. **40**, 173–198 (2022). https://doi.org/10.1007/s00354-022-00161-7
2. Asai, S., Kounoike, Y., Shinano, Y., Kaneko, K.: Computing the diameter of 17-pancake graph using a PC cluster. In: Nagel, W.E., Walter, W.V., Lehner, W. (eds.) Euro-Par 2006. LNCS, vol. 4128, pp. 1114–1124. Springer, Heidelberg (2006). https://doi.org/10.1007/11823285_117
3. Bulteau, L., Fertin, G., Rusu, I.: Pancake flipping is hard. In: Rovan, B., Sassone, V., Widmayer, P. (eds.) MFCS 2012. LNCS, vol. 7464, pp. 247–258. Springer, Heidelberg (2012). https://doi.org/10.1007/978-3-642-32589-2_24
4. Bulteau, L., Fertin, G., Rusu, I.: Pancake flipping is hard. J. Comput. Syst. Sci. **81**(8), 1556–1574 (2015). https://www.sciencedirect.com/science/article/pii/S0022000015000124. https://doi.org/10.1016/j.jcss.2015.02.003
5. Bultel, X., Dreier, J., Dumas, J.G., Lafourcade, P.: Physical zero-knowledge proofs for Akari, Takuzu, Kakuro and KenKen. In: Demaine, E.D., Grandoni, F. (eds.) Fun with Algorithms. LIPIcs, vol. 49, pp. 8:1–8:20, Dagstuhl, Germany. Schloss Dagstuhl (2016). https://doi.org/10.4230/LIPIcs.FUN.2016.8
6. Bultel, X., et al.: Physical zero-knowledge proof for Makaro. In: Izumi, T., Kuznetsov, P. (eds.) SSS 2018. LNCS, vol. 11201, pp. 111–125. Springer, Cham (2018). https://doi.org/10.1007/978-3-030-03232-6_8
7. Chien, Y.-F., Hon, W.-K.: Cryptographic and physical zero-knowledge proof: from Sudoku to Nonogram. In: Boldi, P., Gargano, L. (eds.) FUN 2010. LNCS, vol. 6099, pp. 102–112. Springer, Heidelberg (2010). https://doi.org/10.1007/978-3-642-13122-6_12

8. Chitturi, B., et al.: An (18/11)n upper bound for sorting by prefix reversals. Theor. Comput. Sci. **410**(36), 3372–3390 (2009). Graphs, Games and Computation: Dedicated to Professor Burkhard Monien on the Occasion of his 65th Birthday. https://www.sciencedirect.com/science/article/pii/S0304397508003575. https://doi.org/10.1016/j.tcs.2008.04.045

9. Cibulka, J.: On average and highest number of flips in pancake sorting. Theor. Comput. Scie. **412**(8), 822–834 (2011). https://www.sciencedirect.com/science/article/pii/S0304397510006663. https://doi.org/10.1016/j.tcs.2010.11.028

10. Cohen, D.S., Blum, M.: On the problem of sorting burnt pancakes. Discrete Appl. Math. **61**(2), 105–120 (1995). https://www.sciencedirect.com/science/article/pii/0166218X94000093. https://doi.org/10.1016/0166-218X(94)00009-3

11. Dumas, J.-G., Lafourcade, P., Miyahara, D., Mizuki, T., Sasaki, T., Sone, H.: Interactive physical zero-knowledge proof for Norinori. In: Du, D.-Z., Duan, Z., Tian, C. (eds.) COCOON 2019. LNCS, vol. 11653, pp. 166–177. Springer, Cham (2019). https://doi.org/10.1007/978-3-030-26176-4_14

12. Gates, W.H., Papadimitriou, C.H.: Bounds for sorting by prefix reversal. Discret. Math. **27**(1), 47–57 (1979). https://doi.org/10.1016/0012-365X(79)90068-2

13. Goldwasser, S., Micali, S., Rackoff, C.: The knowledge complexity of interactive proof-systems. In: Annual ACM Symposium on Theory of Computing, STOC 1985, pp. 291–304. ACM, New York (1985). https://doi.org/10.1145/22145.22178

14. Gradwohl, R., Naor, M., Pinkas, B., Rothblum, G.N.: Cryptographic and physical zero-knowledge proof systems for solutions of Sudoku puzzles. Theory Comput. Syst. **44**(2), 245–268 (2009). https://doi.org/10.1007/s00224-008-9119-9

15. Haga, R., Hayashi, Y., Miyahara, D., Mizuki, T.: Card-minimal protocols for three-input functions with standard playing cards. In: Batina, L., Daemen, J. (eds.) AFRICACRYPT 2022. LNCS, vol. 13503, pp. 448–468. Springer, Cham (2022). https://doi.org/10.1007/978-3-031-17433-9_19

16. Haga, R., et al.: Card-based secure sorting protocol. In: Cheng, C.-M., Akiyama, M. (eds.) AFRICACRYPT 2022. LNCS, vol. 13504, pp. 224–240. Springer, Cham (2022). https://doi.org/10.1007/978-3-031-17433-9_19

17. Hashimoto, Y., Shinagawa, K., Nuida, K., Inamura, M., Hanaoka, G.: Secure grouping protocol using a deck of cards. In: Shikata, J. (ed.) ICITS 2017. LNCS, vol. 10681, pp. 135–152. Springer, Cham (2017). https://doi.org/10.1007/978-3-319-72089-0_8

18. Hashimoto, Y., Shinagawa, K., Nuida, K., Inamura, M., Hanaoka, G.: Secure grouping protocol using a deck of cards. IEICE Trans. Fundam. Electron. Commun. Comput. Sci. **101**(9), 1512–1524 (2018). https://doi.org/10.1587/transfun.E101.A.1512

19. Heydari, M.H., Sudborough, I.H.: On the diameter of the pancake network. J. Algorithms **25**(1), 67–94 (1997). https://www.sciencedirect.com/science/article/pii/S0196677497908749. https://doi.org/10.1006/jagm.1997.0874

20. Ibaraki, T., Manabe, Y.: A more efficient card-based protocol for generating a random permutation without fixed points. In: Mathematics and Computers in Sciences and in Industry (MCSI), pp. 252–257 (2016). https://doi.org/10.1109/MCSI.2016.054

21. Ishikawa, R., Chida, E., Mizuki, T.: Efficient card-based protocols for generating a hidden random permutation without fixed points. In: Calude, C.S., Dinneen, M.J. (eds.) UCNC 2015. LNCS, vol. 9252, pp. 215–226. Springer, Cham (2015). https://doi.org/10.1007/978-3-319-21819-9_16

22. Isuzugawa, R., Miyahara, D., Mizuki, T.: Zero-knowledge proof protocol for cryptarithmetic using dihedral cards. In: Kostitsyna, I., Orponen, P. (eds.) UCNC 2021. LNCS, vol. 12984, pp. 51–67. Springer, Cham (2021). https://doi.org/10.1007/978-3-030-87993-8_4

23. Ito, T., et al.: On the complexity of reconfiguration problems. Theor. Comput. Sci. **412**(12), 1054–1065 (2011). https://www.sciencedirect.com/science/article/pii/S0304397510006961. https://doi.org/10.1016/j.tcs.2010.12.005

24. Ito, T., Kakimura, N., Kamiyama, N., Kobayashi, Y., Okamoto, Y.: Shortest reconfiguration of perfect matchings via alternating cycles. SIAM J. Discret. Math. **36**(2), 1102–1123 (2022). https://doi.org/10.1137/20M1364370

25. Kimura, K., Takahashi, A., Araki, T., Amano, K.: Maximum number of steps of topswops on 18 and 19 cards. arXiv:2103.08346 (2021). https://arxiv.org/abs/2103.08346

26. Klamkin, M.S.: Problems in Applied Mathematics: Selections from SIAM Review (1990). https://epubs.siam.org/doi/abs/10.1137/1.9781611971729.ch4. https://epubs.siam.org/doi/pdf/10.1137/1.9781611971729.ch4. https://doi.org/10.1137/1.9781611971729.ch4

27. Kleitman, D.J., Kramer, E., Conway, J.H., Bell, S., Dweighter, H.: Elementary problems: E2564-E2569. Am. Math. Mon. **82**(10), 1009–1010 (1975). http://www.jstor.org/stable/2318260

28. Koch, A.: The landscape of optimal card-based protocols. Math. Cryptol. **1**(2), 115–131 (2022). https://journals.flvc.org/mathcryptology/article/view/130529

29. Komano, Y., Mizuki, T.: Physical zero-knowledge proof protocol for Topswops. In: Chunhua, S., Gritzalis, D., Piuri, V. (eds.) ISPEC 2022. LNCS, vol. 13620, pp. 537–553. Springer, Cham (2022). https://doi.org/10.1007/978-3-031-21280-2_30

30. Kounoike, Y., Kaneko, K., Shinano, Y.: Computing the diameters of 14- and 15-pancake graphs. In: 8th International Symposium on Parallel Architectures, Algorithms and Networks (ISPAN 2005), p. 6 (2005). https://doi.org/10.1109/ISPAN.2005.31

31. Kuzuma, T., Isuzugawa, R., Toyoda, K., Miyahara, D., Mizuki, T.: Card-based single-shuffle protocols for secure multiple-input AND and XOR computations. In: ASIA Public-Key Cryptography, pp. 51–58. ACM, New York (2022). https://doi.org/10.1145/3494105.3526236

32. Lafourcade, P., Miyahara, D., Mizuki, T., Robert, L., Sasaki, T., Sone, H.: How to construct physical zero-knowledge proofs for puzzles with a "single loop" condition. Theor. Comput. Sci. **888**, 41–55 (2021). https://doi.org/10.1016/j.tcs.2021.07.019

33. Lafourcade, P., Miyahara, D., Mizuki, T., Sasaki, T., Sone, H.: A physical ZKP for Slitherlink: how to perform physical topology-preserving computation. In: Heng, S.-H., Lopez, J. (eds.) ISPEC 2019. LNCS, vol. 11879, pp. 135–151. Springer, Cham (2019). https://doi.org/10.1007/978-3-030-34339-2_8

34. Manabe, Y., Ono, H.: Secure card-based cryptographic protocols using private operations against malicious players. In: Maimut, D., Oprina, A.-G., Sauveron, D. (eds.) SecITC 2020. LNCS, vol. 12596, pp. 55–70. Springer, Cham (2021). https://doi.org/10.1007/978-3-030-69255-1_5

35. Manabe, Y., Ono, H.: Card-based cryptographic protocols with malicious players using private operations. New Gener. Comput. **40**, 67–93 (2022). https://doi.org/10.1007/s00354-021-00148-w

36. Miyahara, D., Haneda, H., Mizuki, T.: Card-based zero-knowledge proof protocols for graph problems and their computational model. In: Huang, Q., Yu, Yu. (eds.) ProvSec 2021. LNCS, vol. 13059, pp. 136–152. Springer, Cham (2021). https://doi.org/10.1007/978-3-030-90402-9_8

37. Miyahara, D., Hayashi, Y., Mizuki, T., Sone, H.: Practical card-based implementations of Yao's millionaire protocol. Theor. Comput. Sci. **803**, 207–221 (2020). https://doi.org/10.1016/j.tcs.2019.11.005

38. Miyahara, D., Mizuki, T.: Secure computations through checking suits of playing cards. In: Li, M., Sun, X. (eds.) IJTCS-FAW 2022. LNCS, pp. 110–128. Springer, Cham (2022). https://doi.org/10.1007/978-3-031-20796-9_9

39. Miyahara, D., et al.: Card-based ZKP protocols for Takuzu and Juosan. In: Farach-Colton, M., Prencipe, G., Uehara, R. (eds.) Fun with Algorithms. LIPIcs, vol. 157, pp. 20:1–20:21, Dagstuhl, Germany. Schloss Dagstuhl (2020). https://doi.org/10.4230/LIPIcs.FUN.2021.20

40. Miyahara, D., Sasaki, T., Mizuki, T., Sone, H.: Card-based physical zero-knowledge proof for Kakuro. IEICE Trans. Fundam. Electron. Commun. Comput. Sci. **102**(9), 1072–1078 (2019). https://doi.org/10.1587/transfun.E102.A.1072

41. Miyamoto, K., Shinagawa, K.: Graph automorphism shuffles from pile-scramble shuffles. New Gener. Comput. **40**, 199–223 (2022). https://doi.org/10.1007/s00354-022-00164-4

42. Mizuki, T.: Preface: special issue on card-based cryptography. New Gener. Comput. **39**, 1–2 (2021). https://doi.org/10.1007/s00354-021-00127-1

43. Mizuki, T.: Preface: special issue on card-based cryptography 2. New Gener. Comput. **40**, 47–48 (2022). https://doi.org/10.1007/s00354-022-00170-6

44. Mizuki, T., Komano, Y.: Information leakage due to operative errors in card-based protocols. Inf. Comput. **285**, 104910 (2022). https://doi.org/10.1016/j.ic.2022.104910

45. Morales, L., Sudborough, H.: A quadratic lower bound for Topswops. Theor. Comput. Sci. **411**(44), 3965–3970 (2010). https://www.sciencedirect.com/science/article/pii/S0304397510004287. https://doi.org/10.1016/j.tcs.2010.08.011

46. Nakai, T., Misawa, Y., Tokushige, Y., Iwamoto, M., Ohta, K.: Secure computation for threshold functions with physical cards: power of private permutations. New Gener. Comput. **40**, 95–113 (2022). https://doi.org/10.1007/s00354-022-00153-7

47. Nishimura, A., Hayashi, Y.I., Mizuki, T., Sone, H.: Pile-shifting scramble for card-based protocols. IEICE Trans. Fundam. Electron. Commun. Comput. Sci. **101**(9), 1494–1502 (2018). https://doi.org/10.1587/transfun.E101.A.1494

48. Robert, L., Lafourcade, P., Miyahara, D., Mizuki, T.: Card-based ZKP protocol for Nurimisaki. In: Devismes, S., Petit, F., Altisen, K., Di Luna, G.A., Anta, A.F. (eds.) SSS 2022. LNCS, vol. 13751, pp. 285–298. Springer, Cham (2022). https://doi.org/10.1007/978-3-031-21017-4_19

49. Robert, L., Miyahara, D., Lafourcade, P., Mizuki, T.: Physical zero-knowledge proof for Suguru puzzle. In: Devismes, S., Mittal, N. (eds.) SSS 2020. LNCS, vol. 12514, pp. 235–247. Springer, Cham (2020). https://doi.org/10.1007/978-3-030-64348-5_19

50. Robert, L., Miyahara, D., Lafourcade, P., Mizuki, T.: Interactive physical ZKP for connectivity: applications to Nurikabe and Hitori. In: De Mol, L., Weiermann, A., Manea, F., Fernández-Duque, D. (eds.) CiE 2021. LNCS, vol. 12813, pp. 373–384. Springer, Cham (2021). https://doi.org/10.1007/978-3-030-80049-9_37

51. Robert, L., Miyahara, D., Lafourcade, P., Mizuki, T.: Hide a liar: card-based ZKP protocol for Usowan. In: Du, D.Z., Du, D., Wu, C., Xu, D. (eds.) TAMC 2022. LNCS, vol. 13571, pp. 201–217. Springer, Cham (2022). https://doi.org/10.1007/978-3-031-20350-3_17

52. Robert, L., Miyahara, D., Lafourcade, P., Libralesso, L., Mizuki, T.: Physical zero-knowledge proof and NP-completeness proof of Suguru puzzle.

Inf. Comput. 104858 (2021). https://www.sciencedirect.com/science/article/pii/S0890540121001905. https://doi.org/10.1016/j.ic.2021.104858

53. Robert, L., Miyahara, D., Lafourcade, P., Mizuki, T.: Card-based ZKP for connectivity: applications to Nurikabe, Hitori, and Heyawake. New Gener. Comput. 1–23 (2022). https://doi.org/10.1007/s00354-022-00155-5

54. Ruangwises, S.: An improved physical ZKP for Nonogram. In: Du, D.-Z., Du, D., Wu, C., Xu, D. (eds.) COCOA 2021. LNCS, vol. 13135, pp. 262–272. Springer, Cham (2021). https://doi.org/10.1007/978-3-030-92681-6_22

55. Ruangwises, S.: Two standard decks of playing cards are sufficient for a ZKP for Sudoku. In: Chen, C.-Y., Hon, W.-K., Hung, L.-J., Lee, C.-W. (eds.) COCOON 2021. LNCS, vol. 13025, pp. 631–642. Springer, Cham (2021). https://doi.org/10.1007/978-3-030-89543-3_52

56. Ruangwises, S.: Using five cards to encode each integer in Z/6Z. In: Ryan, P.Y.A., Toma, C. (eds.) SecITC 2021. LNCS, vol. 13195, pp. 165–177. Springer, Cham (2021). https://doi.org/10.1007/978-3-031-17510-7_12

57. Ruangwises, S.: Two standard decks of playing cards are sufficient for a ZKP for Sudoku. New Gener. Comput. 1–17 (2022). https://doi.org/10.1007/s00354-021-00146-y

58. Ruangwises, S., Itoh, T.: Physical zero-knowledge proof for Numberlink. In: Farach-Colton, M., Prencipe, G., Uehara, R. (eds.) Fun with Algorithms. LIPIcs, vol. 157, pp. 22:1–22:11, Dagstuhl, Germany. Schloss Dagstuhl (2020). https://doi.org/10.4230/LIPIcs.FUN.2021.22

59. Ruangwises, S., Itoh, T.: Securely computing the n-variable equality function with $2n$ cards. In: Chen, J., Feng, Q., Xu, J. (eds.) TAMC 2020. LNCS, vol. 12337, pp. 25–36. Springer, Cham (2020). https://doi.org/10.1007/978-3-030-59267-7_3

60. Ruangwises, S., Itoh, T.: Physical zero-knowledge proof for Numberlink puzzle and k vertex-disjoint paths problem. New Gener. Comput. 39(1), 3–17 (2021). https://doi.org/10.1007/s00354-020-00114-y

61. Ruangwises, S., Itoh, T.: Physical zero-knowledge proof for Ripple Effect. In: Uehara, R., Hong, S.-H., Nandy, S.C. (eds.) WALCOM 2021. LNCS, vol. 12635, pp. 296–307. Springer, Cham (2021). https://doi.org/10.1007/978-3-030-68211-8_24

62. Ruangwises, S., Itoh, T.: Physical zero-knowledge proof for Ripple Effect. Theor. Comput. Sci. 895, 115–123 (2021). https://doi.org/10.1016/j.tcs.2021.09.034

63. Ruangwises, S., Itoh, T.: Physical ZKP for connected spanning subgraph: applications to Bridges puzzle and other problems. In: Kostitsyna, I., Orponen, P. (eds.) UCNC 2021. LNCS, vol. 12984, pp. 149–163. Springer, Cham (2021). https://doi.org/10.1007/978-3-030-87993-8_10

64. Ruangwises, S., Itoh, T.: Securely computing the n-variable equality function with 2n cards. Theor. Comput. Sci. 887, 99–110 (2021). https://doi.org/10.1016/j.tcs.2021.07.007

65. Ruangwises, S., Itoh, T.: How to physically verify a rectangle in a grid: a physical ZKP for Shikaku. In: Fraigniaud, P., Uno, Y. (eds.) Fun with Algorithms. LIPIcs, vol. 226, pp. 24:1–24:12, Dagstuhl. Schloss Dagstuhl (2022). https://doi.org/10.4230/LIPIcs.FUN.2022.24

66. Ruangwises, S., Itoh, T.: Physical ZKP for Makaro using a standard deck of cards. In: Du, D.Z., Du, D., Wu, C., Xu, D. (eds.) TAMC 2022. LNCS, vol. 13571. Springer, Cham (2022). https://doi.org/10.1007/978-3-031-20350-3_5

67. Sasaki, T., Miyahara, D., Mizuki, T., Sone, H.: Efficient card-based zero-knowledge proof for Sudoku. Theor. Comput. Sci. 839, 135–142 (2020). https://doi.org/10.1016/j.tcs.2020.05.036

68. Sasaki, T., Mizuki, T., Sone, H.: Card-based zero-knowledge proof for Sudoku. In: Ito, H., Leonardi, S., Pagli, L., Prencipe, G. (eds.) Fun with Algorithms. LIPIcs, vol. 100, pp. 29:1–29:10, Dagstuhl, Germany. Schloss Dagstuhl (2018). https://doi.org/10.4230/LIPIcs.FUN.2018.29

69. Sawada, J., Williams, A.: Greedy flipping of pancakes and burnt pancakes. Discret. Appl. Math. **210**, 61–74 (2016). https://doi.org/10.1016/j.dam.2016.02.005

70. Sawada, J., Williams, A.: Successor rules for flipping pancakes and burnt pancakes. Theor. Comput. Sci. **609**, 60–75 (2016). https://doi.org/10.1016/j.tcs.2015.09.007

71. Shikata, H., Toyoda, K., Miyahara, D., Mizuki, T.: Card-minimal protocols for symmetric Boolean functions of more than seven inputs. In: Seidl, H., Liu, Z., Pasareanu, C.S. (eds.) ICTAC 2022. LNCS, vol. 13572, pp. 388–406. Springer, Cham (2022). https://doi.org/10.1007/978-3-031-17715-6_25

72. Shinagawa, K., et al.: Card-based protocols using regular polygon cards. IEICE Trans. Fundam. Electron. Commun. Comput. Sci. **100**(9), 1900–1909 (2017). https://doi.org/10.1587/transfun.E100.A.1900

73. Shinagawa, K., Nuida, K.: A single shuffle is enough for secure card-based computation of any Boolean circuit. Discret. Appl. Math. **289**, 248–261 (2021). https://doi.org/10.1016/j.dam.2020.10.013

74. Shinagawa, K., Nuida, K.: Single-shuffle full-open card-based protocols imply private simultaneous messages protocols. Cryptology ePrint Archive, Paper 2022/1306 (2022). https://eprint.iacr.org/2022/1306

75. Shinoda, Y., Miyahara, D., Shinagawa, K., Mizuki, T., Sone, H.: Card-based covert lottery. In: Maimut, D., Oprina, A.-G., Sauveron, D. (eds.) SecITC 2020. LNCS, vol. 12596, pp. 257–270. Springer, Cham (2021). https://doi.org/10.1007/978-3-030-69255-1_17

76. Suga, Y.: A classification proof for commutative three-element semigroups with local AND structure and its application to card-based protocols. In: 2022 IEEE International Conference on Consumer Electronics - Taiwan, pp. 171–172. IEEE (2022). https://doi.org/10.1109/ICCE-Taiwan55306.2022.9869063

77. Takashima, K., et al.: Card-based protocols for secure ranking computations. Theor. Comput. Sci. **845**, 122–135 (2020). https://doi.org/10.1016/j.tcs.2020.09.008

Activity Detection from Encrypted Remote Desktop Protocol Traffic

Lukasz Lapczyk[✉] and David Skillicorn

Queen's University, Kingston, ON K7L 3N6, Canada
{171116,skill}@queensu.ca
https://cac.queensu.ca, https://www.cs.queensu.ca/

Abstract. An increasing amount of Internet traffic has its content encrypted. We address the question of whether it is possible to predict the activities taking place over an encrypted channel, in particular Microsoft's Remote Desktop Protocol. We show that the presence of five typical activities can be detected with precision greater than 97% and recall greater than 94% in 30-s traces. We also show that the design of the protocol exposes fine-grained actions such as keystrokes and mouse movements which may be leveraged to reveal properties such as lengths of passwords.

Keywords: Encryption · Traffic Classification · Detection · Network Security · Cybersecurity · Analytics · Privacy · User Activity · Side Channel Analysis

1 Introduction

One response to the obvious security weaknesses of networks is to encrypt the payloads of packet traffic. It was estimated in 2018 that encryption was used in more than 70% of network communications [21] but the rate of penetration is quite variable because of the cost and complexity of public key infrastructure, particularly for small enterprises. We explore the question of how much can be detected about interactions, even when payloads are encrypted. In particular, we are concerned with activity detection: what is a user doing?

There are some legitimate reasons to be able to answer this question: determining usage to insure adequate provisioning, for example. It is also important to know how much an adversary could infer [34]. We focus on the Microsoft Remote Desktop Protocol (RDP), a popular protocol that provides an encrypted channel between a client and a host, allowing remote work on the host [10]. Five major interactions occur between client and host: file download, browsing on the host (i.e. a mixture of viewing, typing, and using the mouse), using an editor on the host, watching a video, and copying content from host to client or *vice versa* using the clipboard.

We show that, even though all traffic is encrypted, it is possible to detect which of these activities is underway from the traffic properties, even if two or more simultaneous activities are occurring. A heterogeneous ensemble classifier

G. Bella et al. (Eds.): SecITC 2022, LNCS 13809, pp. 240–260, 2023.
https://doi.org/10.1007/978-3-031-32636-3_14

achieves precision greater than 97% and recall greater than 94%. We also discover that there are markers in the protocol that are directly related to fine-grained user actions.

2 Related Work

Traffic inspection and classification has two main purposes: security (detecting malicious activity [25]), and quality of service management (insuring resources are appropriate for traffic [23]). Traffic analysis can be done using: port structure (services being used) [9], deep packet inspection (signatures in payloads) [9], data analytics (per-packet or per-flow) [5], or behavioral classification (communication pattern graphs) [5].

To overcome the weaknesses associated with the port-based and payload-based approaches, data analytics has been proposed as a solution for network traffic classification [2,13]. In particular, data-analytic approaches can detect novel traffic using anomaly detection [33].

Draper-Gil et al. [11] generated a dataset used by several researchers to predict traffic classes. It contains browsing, email, chat, streaming, file transfer, VoIP, and P2P traffic; each inside and outside of a VPN tunnel. However, each window contains only a single kind of traffic. Draper-Gil used k-Nearest Neighbor and decision tree predictors; Saber et al. [26] used under- and over-sampling, PCA, SVMs; Lotfollahi et al. [19] used stacked autoencoders and convolutional neural networks; and Vu et al. [30] used LSTMs. The best models on this dataset achieve F1 scores up to 0.98 on the single-class prediction problem.

Zhang et al. [32], in the closest work to ours, classify categories of seven types of activities: Browsing, Chat, Online Gaming, Downloading, Uploading, Online Video, and BitTorrent, using windows of different sizes. However, each window contains at most two simultaneous kinds of traffic. They achieve around 80% prediction accuracy for 5-s windows and over 90% accuracy for 1-m traffic windows for the single class problem. Their accuracy decreases for some classes when there are two concurrent activities.

A finer-grained, and harder, version of the problem is to detect not only the kind of traffic but which application is being used. Taylor et al. [28] create an "Appscanner" tool to recognize smartphone apps in encrypted traffic. Their work was later improved by Taylor et al. [29] using bursts, packets grouped within a time window. They analyze one second bursts to deliver near real-time prediction for 110 out of 200 most popular free Google Play applications. Alan and Kaur [1] reduce computational complexity by analyzing only the first 64 packets to identify the application. Saltaformaggio et al. [27] achieve an average of 78% precision and 76% recall using KMeans and multi-class SVM and properties that could be captured by eavesdropping. In addition, they also paid attention to how easy it was to discover user properties from the traffic, and revealed some major privacy issues. Application identification is also possible in encrypted tunnels. Lotfollahi et al. [19] and Yamansavascilar et al. [31] run their experiments on the same VPN dataset by Draper-Gil et al. [11] to detect application instead of the broad traffic category.

A related problem is to detect what actions users are doing on their devices, that is behavioral detection. Conti et al. [7] analyze encrypted traffic from Android devices to discover user behaviors such as sending a new message with Gmail or opening the Dropbox app. Their study included seven Android applications: Facebook, Gmail, Twitter, Tumblr, Dropbox, Google+ and Evernote and they simulated user actions to obtain signatures of flows generated by use of these apps. Coull and Dyer analyze user behaviors in Apple iMessage [8] and showed that users' actions, as well as language and length of messages exchanged, can be predicted. Park and Kim [24] predict KakaoTalk's eleven behaviors in encrypted traffic. Liu et al. [18] predict whether a user is using Wechat, WhatsApp and Facebook and behaviors such as voice calling, video calling or picture sharing. Dubin et al. [12] trained a classifier to predict the most popular YouTube videos titles, basing on encrypted traffic statistics, notably the bits per peak.

3   Approach

A real-world system was used to collect RDP traffic data about five classes of traffic. Derived data were computed from the base traffic data using Discrete Cosine Transform, singular value decomposition, and independent component analysis. A series of predictive models were then built and their performance assessed using standard measures as well as a custom measure designed for the problem. Our models serve as proof of concept demonstrating that activities inside of encrypted RDP communications can be learnt without the need for decryption.

3.1   System Setup

The Remote Desktop Protocol is designed to let a user at a client interact with a host as if sitting at that host. It provides the full interactivity of using the mouse, viewing the screen, and using the keyboard.

The client workstation, called Workstation01, is a 6-core Intel Xeon processor, 36 GB memory, 2 TB storage and Network Interface Card connected to a Local Area Network with an Internet gateway, running Microsoft Windows 10 Professional. For data analysis, Java Runtime Environment 1.8 was installed to run CIC FlowMeter v4.0 for attribute extraction, and Wireshark to capture RDP network traffic into .pcap files. As a Remote Desktop client, Workstation01 is configured to mount local drives, allow clipboard and runs in resolution 1366×768 with full user desktop experience.

Hyper-V service is enabled on Workstation01 for virtualization and there are two virtual machines running on it: Win01 and Centos-Miner. Win01 VM is a plain installation of a Windows 10 Professional 1809 virtual machine that acts as a Remote Desktop host. The VM is configured with 4 virtual cores and 8 GB of RAM. It has a static IP, Network Level Authentication, and a Windows firewall with an exception allowing incoming RDP traffic. This setup ensures that Workstation01 can connect freely to Win01 VM over both TCP and UDP protocols on port 3389.

CentOS-Miner is a CentOS 7.5 VM running on top of Workstation-01 Hyper-V. This Linux virtual machine has a Bash environment and Tshark installed and it is used for data exploration and additional attribute extraction.

A physically remote VM, CAC01, is hosted at Queen's University's Centre for Advanced Computing. The configuration is exactly the same as for Win01 VM except that it runs Windows 10 Education, and resides behind a firewall with NAT. CAC-01 has 4 virtual cores and 4 GB of RAM.

Traffic to Win01 is on the same IP subnet as the client, and only encounters the built-in Windows firewall on Win01 itself. Traffic to CAC01 passes through an Internet connection, the Queen's University campus network, and a physical firewall that accepts connections on port 13389 and forwards them to CAC01 on port 3389. RDP uses TCP only for traffic outside a subnet, and a mixture of TCP and UDP for traffic within a subnet, so two different predictive models had to be developed.

Figure 1 shows the network setup with all the Virtual Machines used for data generation. The red path shows the traffic path for the local subnet scenario and the green path represents the distant scenario, traversing the Internet.

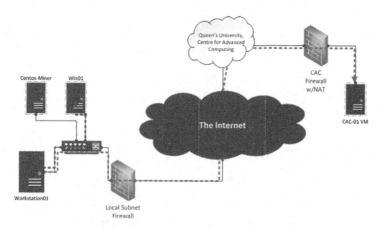

Fig. 1. Network architecture diagram.

3.2   Data Collection

The Remote Desktop traffic attributes were captured for 30 s windows of one or more of the following activity classes:

- Download – file download from host to client;
- Browsing – using a browser (Firefox and Chrome) on the host, driven from the client;
- Notepad – editing on the host from the client (typing for more than 80% of the time window);
- YouTube – playing a video on the host (Youtube or mp4s), viewed on the client; and
- Clipboard – copying content from remote system to local using the clipboard mechanism.

Samples may be pure – a single activity for 30 s – or mixed, with up to four activities simultaneously in a 30-s window.

Attribute collection is performed by CIC Flow Meter and Tshark. The former is a tool developed by University of New Brunswick's Canadian Institute for Cybersecurity [16]. CIC Flow Meter extracts a predefined number of attributes for each network traffic conversation from a .pcap file. There will be one conversation for TCP only traffic samples, and two conversations for TCP and UDP traffic samples. Predictive attributes include properties such as packet lengths, inter-arrival times and TCP SYN flag counts.

A Bash script extracts additional meaningful predictive attributes from the packet-level attributes of Tshark. The additional attributes include Packet Length Statistics from Wireshark, as shown in Fig. 2, and include attributes discovered during exploratory data analysis. All of the data is preprocessed to insure that forward always refers to traffic from local to remote, and backward the converse, based on IP addresses.

Topic / Item	Count	Average	Min val	Max val	Rate (ms)	Percent	Burst rate	Burst start
∨ Packet Lengths	833	88.22	52	295	0.0283	100%	0.1100	23.574
0-19	0	-	-	-	0.0000	0.00%	-	-
20-39	0	-	-	-	0.0000	0.00%	-	-
40-79	316	53.72	52	56	0.0107	37.94%	0.0300	1.109
80-159	491	102.58	92	153	0.0167	58.94%	0.0800	23.574
160-319	26	236.35	171	295	0.0009	3.12%	0.0200	8.472
320-639	0	-	-	-	0.0000	0.00%	-	-
640-1279	0	-	-	-	0.0000	0.00%	-	-
1280-2559	0	-	-	-	0.0000	0.00%	-	-
2560-5119	0	-	-	-	0.0000	0.00%	-	-
5120 and greater	0	-	-	-	0.0000	0.00%	-	-

Fig. 2. Wireshark – packet length statistics.

Several derived attributes of the measured traffic attributes were also computed. The Discrete Cosine Transform expresses a sequence as a sum of cosine functions. It has often been observed that a single component of the DCT integrates the variability within a sequence [22]. We compute this value for each row of the dataset, that is for the collected traffic attributes of each traffic flow.

Singular Value Decomposition is an affine transformation of a vector space into a form where the greatest variability is captured by the first few axes of the transformed space. Truncation of the SVD amounts to a projection of a high-dimensional space into a low-dimensional one in a way that preserves maximal variation. We apply SVD to the matrix of windows × traffic attributes and keep the first 20 columns of the left singular vector matrix.

Independent Component Analysis (ICA) [15] is another matrix transformation that decomposes a matrix into statistically independent components. We apply ICA to the windows × traffic attributes and select the 20 columns of the left decomposition matrix[1].

Table 1. Attributes.

Attributes			
ACK Flag Cnt	Fwd Blk Rate Avg	Subflow Bwd Byts	svd8
Active Max	Fwd Byts/b Avg	Subflow Bwd Pkts	svd9
Active Mean	Fwd Header Len	Subflow Fwd Byts	svd10
Active Min	Fwd IAT Max	Subflow Fwd Pkts	svd11
Active Std	Fwd IAT Mean	Tot Bwd Pkts	svd12
Bwd Blk Rate Avg	Fwd IAT Min	Tot Fwd Pkts	svd13
Bwd Byts/b Avg	Fwd IAT Std	TotLen Bwd Pkts	svd14
Bwd Header Len	Fwd IAT Tot	TotLen Fwd Pkts	svd15
Bwd IAT Max	Fwd PSH Flags	URG Flag Cnt	svd16
Bwd IAT Mean	Fwd Pkt Len Max	FwdFrame91-93	svd17
Bwd IAT Min	Fwd Pkt Len Mean	FwdFrame80-91	svd18
Bwd IAT Std	Fwd Pkt Len Min	FwdFrame90-94	svd19
Bwd IAT Tot	Fwd Pkt Len Std	FwdFrame96-98	ica0
Bwd PSH Flags	Fwd Pkts/b Avg	FwdFrame103-105	ica1
Bwd Pkt Len Max	Fwd Pkts/s	FwdFrame1280-2559	ica2
Bwd Pkt Len Mean	Fwd Seg Size Avg	BwdFrame40-79	ica3
Bwd Pkt Len Min	Fwd URG Flags	BwdFrame80-159	ica4
Bwd Pkt Len Std	Idle Max	BwdFrame160-319	ica5
Bwd Pkts/b Avg	Idle Mean	BwdFrame320-639	ica6
Bwd Pkts/s	Idle Min	BwdFrame640-1279	ica7
Bwd Seg Size Avg	Idle Std	BwdFrame1280-2559	ica8
Bwd URG Flags	Init Bwd Win Byts	BwdPUSH	ica9
CWE Flag Count	Init Fwd Win Byts	FwdPUSH	ica10
ECE Flag Cnt	PSH Flag Cnt	dct_col	ica11
FIN Flag Cnt	Pkt Len Max	svd0	ica12
Flow Byts/s	Pkt Len Mean	svd1	ica13
Flow Duration	Pkt Len Min	svd2	ica14
Flow IAT Max	Pkt Len Std	svd3	ica15
Flow IAT Mean	Pkt Len Var	svd4	ica16
Flow IAT Min	Pkt Size Avg	svd5	ica17
Flow IAT Std	RST Flag Cnt	svd6	ica18
Flow Pkts/s	SYN Flag Cnt	svd7	ica19

---

[1] There are a number of sophisticated ways to select the most important columns, for example those with maximal kurtosis, but we retain the first 20 and leave it to attribute selection to find the best.

The final predictive attribute set is shown in Table 1.

Shapley Values calculate the contributions to a final result made by individual players in a game theory context [17]. They have been successfully applied to attribute selection in predictors because of the development of fast approximation algorithms that avoid the implicit exponential number of attribute combinations to be evaluated. The two most popular Shapley value explainers are TreeExplainer [20], for tree-based predictors, and DeepExplainer, for neural networks predictors.

We use Shapley values for attribute selection. The selection process is run independently five times, each time for a different class. Shapley Values were computed with two different classification techniques as the backend: Neural Network (Deep Explainer) and Extreme Gradient Boosting (XGBoost).

3.3   Individual Techniques and the Ensemble Predictor

For predictors, we use k-Nearest Neighbors, Support Vector Machines [3], decision trees, random forests [4], Adaboost [14], XGBoost [6], and multilayer perceptrons.

Each of the prediction techniques was run with 10-fold cross validation, with binary class labels (traffic class present or not). The final ensemble model consists of the top three most effective classifiers for each traffic class, chosen to maximize the precision, so that the ensemble classifier can determine with a high degree of certainty whenever a specific kind of traffic is present. A specific sample is predicted to contain a specific class of traffic when at least two of the three classifiers predict that class.

The output of the ensemble classifier is 5 binary values, predicting the presence of each of the 5 kinds of traffic in the sample. Three different performance measures are calculated:

- The precision, recall and F1 score for each class;
- A confusion matrix for each class;
- An ensemble score function designed for the problem domain.

The ensemble score function assigns points to each record as follows:

- For a true negative, no points;
- For a true positive, add one point;
- For a false positive, subtract two points;
- For a false negative, no points.

For instance, if the model predicts download and clipboard, where the traffic actually contained download and browsing, it will assign +1 point for download, 0 points for browsing as it was a false negative, 0 points for Notepad and YouTube as they were true negatives, and −2 for false positive on clipboard. The aggregate of scores calculated on all test set rows is divided by the sum of all positive labels in the test set and multiplied by 100. The scoring function severely penalizes the ensemble whenever it predicts a traffic class that is not actually present. This insures that the model is reliable for predicting behavior.

Table 2. Total TCP Samples Count.

Num samples	Download?	Browsing?	Notepad?	YouTube?	Clipboard?
240	1	0	0	0	0
240	0	1	0	0	0
239	0	0	1	0	0
243	0	0	0	1	0
120	0	0	0	0	1
74	0	1	0	0	1
43	1	1	0	0	0
25	1	0	1	0	1
22	1	0	1	0	0
62	0	0	1	1	0
27	1	0	0	1	0
63	0	1	0	1	0
22	0	0	1	0	1
15	1	1	0	0	1
21	1	0	1	1	1
1456	TOTAL				

3.4 Dataset

The dataset consists of 2160 30-s data samples. The information relating to number of samples is summarized in Table 2 for the CAC-01 (Remote VM, TCP transport) and Table 3 for Win01 (Local subnet VM, TCP and UDP transport) traffic respectively. For simplicity, we will refer to the first kind of traffic as TCP and to the latter as UDP.

When TCP is the only protocol used, it is easier to make accurate predictions. When UDP is added, the problem complexity grows because there are at least two conversations – one for the TCP stream and one for the UDP stream, in the same Remote Desktop session. UDP seems to be used for bulk transfers while TCP is used to send user inputs, such as keystrokes and mouse movements, and perhaps RDP session management details.

Every keystroke that is sent from local system to the remote system over Remote Desktop is carried by two 92-byte TCP frames in the forward direction. As a result, the total number of 92-byte frames in a window reveals how many keystrokes have been sent (except that actions such as pressing and holding a Shift key generates 92-byte frames, until the key is released).

The remote system also responds with packets that are revealing. 92-byte upward packets produce PSH-flagged packets whose payload size correlates with the visual change to the screen of the character echo – the more pixels changed,

Table 3. Total UDP Samples Count.

Num samples	Download?	Browsing?	Notepad?	YouTube?	Clipboard?
103	1	0	0	0	0
92	0	1	0	0	0
100	0	0	1	0	0
105	0	0	0	1	0
100	0	0	0	0	1
42	0	1	0	0	1
44	0	1	0	1	0
42	1	0	1	0	0
37	1	0	1	0	1
39	1	0	0	1	0
704	TOTAL				

the larger the payload[2]. This suggests a potential attack against passwords, since the echoed character is typically not the character sent but a filler character. As a result, entering a password may produce an easily detectable signature.

Mouse movements generate packets of either 97 or 104 bytes, with 97-byte packets associated with mouse clicks. Observing the number of such packets allows mouse activity to be estimated; and the mixing with 92-byte packets allows even finer grained estimates – for example, the size of form data might be estimated by observing how many characters are typed in between mouse clicks and small mouse movements.

4   Results

Attribute ranking is computed for ten cases: 5 TCP activities and 5 UDP activities, and for each both the tree-based and neural-net based Shapley value computation. This results in twenty ranked lists of attribute significance. Tree based Shapley values also provide information about whether an attribute is associated with one class label or the other, and how strongly.

The most predictive attributes are fairly consistent using both the tree-based and network-based Shapley values. The 92- and 104-byte attributes rank highly, as do many of the SVD components, suggesting that the original attributes tend to capture traffic properties that are strongly correlated.

---

[2] There are hints that what is being returned is the delta of the character being displayed.

Table 4. Selected Attribute Sets for TCP Classes.

TCP Download	TCP Browsing	TCP Notepad	TCP YouTube	TCP Clipboard
svd0	FwdFrame103-105	svd2	BwdFrame320-639	FwdPUSH
BwdFrame80-159	BwdFrame320-639	FwdFrame91-93	svd1	svd1
BwdFrame320-639	Fwd Pkt Len Mean	svd0	svd6	svd0
Init Fwd Win Byts	Fwd Seg Size Avg	FwdPUSH	svd0	Subflow Bwd Byts
Tot Fwd Pkts	svd8	BwdFrame80-159	svd9	ica7
BwdFrame640-1279	BwdPUSH		FwdPUSH	FwdFrame91-93
Fwd IAT Mean	FwdFrame96-98		TotLen Fwd Pkts	FwdFrame103-105
Pkt Len Std	FwdPUSH		Flow IAT Std	svd6
Bwd IAT Max	BwdFrame1280-2559		BwdFrame640-1279	ica11
ica19	ica7			svd11
Bwd Pkt Len Mean	FwdFrame91-93			ica5
Flow Byts/s	Init Fwd Win Byts			Fwd Pkt Len Mean
	Bwd Pkt Len Mean			BwdFrame320-639
				svd8
				Pkt Len Std

Table 4 shows the best attributes for the TCP traffic classes and Table 5 shows the best attributes for the UDP traffic classes.

Table 6 shows the performance summary for the predictors run on the TCP traffic and Table 7 summarizes performance for the UDP traffic. Accuracies are over 10-fold cross validation.

For each TCP and UDP traffic class we select the top three best performing cross-validated predictors to build two ensemble predictors – the TCP Ensemble and the UDP Ensemble, shown in Figs. 3 and 4.

Table 8 provides the True Positives, False Positives, True Negatives, and False Negatives with five-fold cross-validation for the ensemble predictors. We then calculate Accuracy, Precision, Recall and F1 score.

Table 9 summarizes the single ensemble scores obtained for each fold of the TCP and UDP models, along with the average. Voting makes a significant contribution towards reducing false positives.

For both UDP and TCP traffic, there are similarities when it comes to the most commonly misclassified traffic classes. For both TCP and UDP traffic, the most common misclassification misses the Clipboard class. This is reflected in the recall scores for the UDP Clipboard at only 94.97% and the TCP Clipboard at 95.67%, while other classes all have recall higher than 98%.

The most common error in TCP traffic is a mixture of Browsing and Clipboard being classified as Browsing only. Both Browsing and Clipboard involve mouse movements and mouse clicks, both right- and left-clicks, but it seems slightly surprising that these are difficult to distinguish.

The second most common error occurs when Browsing traffic is classified as Browsing and Clipboard, generating a false positive prediction for Clipboard. The third most common is for the combination of Download, Browsing and Clipboard where the Clipboard traffic is missed. The fourth most common is when a Download and YouTube mixture is classified as Download only.

Table 5. Selected Attribute Sets for UDP Classes.

UDP Download	UDP Browsing	UDP Notepad	UDP YouTube	UDP Clipboard
svd0	svd1	FwdFrame91-93	svd1	svd2
svd1	Fwd Pkt Len Std	BwdFrame40-79	svd0	Bwd IAT Std
svd2	FwdFrame96-98	svd2	svd3	Fwd IAT Mean
Fwd Pkt Len Std	svd0	Fwd IAT Min	svd5	FwdFrame103-105
Bwd Header Len	svd5	svd1	BwdFrame80-159	Flow IAT Mean
	FwdFrame90-94	Bwd IAT Mean	FwdFrame91-93	Flow IAT Std
	BwdFrame320-639		Flow IAT Max	BwdFrame40-79
			Bwd IAT Max	BwdFrame320-639
			Fwd Pkt Len Mean	Bwd IAT Mean
			Fwd Seg Size Avg	FwdFrame91-93
			BwdFrame320-639	Pkt Len Mean
			Bwd IAT Std	FwdFrame90-94
			Fwd IAT Max	Fwd IAT Min
			svd4	
			Bwd Header Len	
			ica8	
			Bwd Pkt Len Max	
			Fwd IAT Tot	
			Bwd IAT Tot	

Table 6. TCP Traffic Individual Techniques – Accuracy and Standard Deviation.

Technique	Download	Browsing	Notepad	YouTube	Clipboard
NN	99.66% (± 0.46%)	98.62% (± 1.27%)	99.66% (± 0.46%)	99.59% (± 0.46%)	95.88% (± 1.23%)
RF	99.18% (± 0.79%)	99.38% (± 0.57%)	99.86% (± 0.27%)	99.59% (± 0.46%)	98.69% (± 0.84%)
XGB	99.52% (± 0.69%)	99.59% (± 0.62%)	99.72% (± 0.46%)	99.59% (± 0.45%)	98.56% (± 1.12%)
SVM	99.73% (± 0.34%)	99.24% (± 0.72%)	99.86% (± 0.28%)	99.59% (± 0.45%)	95.47% (± 2.60%)
Ada	99.66% (± 0.46%)	99.25% (± 0.57%)	99.86% (± 0.28%)	99.52% (± 0.81%)	98.49% (± 0.67%)
KNN	99.45% (± 0.51%)	99.04% (± 0.70%)	99.79% (± 0.31%)	99.31% (± 0.68%)	94.71% (± 1.81%)
DTC	98.63% (± 0.86%)	98.83% (± 0.75%)	99.93% (± 0.21%)	99.52% (± 0.69%)	96.91% (± 1.20%)

Table 7. UDP Traffic Individual Techniques – Accuracy and Standard Deviation.

Technique	Download	Browsing	Notepad	YouTube	Clipboard
NN	99.86% (± 0.42%)	97.72% (± 1.93%)	99.71% (± 0.57%)	99.86% (± 0.42%)	96.02% (± 2.09%)
RF	99.86% (± 0.42%)	99.29% (± 0.71%)	99.43% (± 0.69%)	100.00% (± 0.00%)	98.15% (± 1.28%)
XGB	99.57% (± 0.91%)	99.01% (± 0.90%)	98.72% (± 1.34%)	99.15% (± 0.95%)	97.87% (± 1.30%)
SVM	99.71% (± 0.57%)	98.29% (± 1.39%)	99.72% (± 0.57%)	99.43% (± 0.69%)	95.03% (± 2.73%)
Ada	99.57% (± 0.65%)	99.01% (± 0.91%)	99.57% (± 0.65%)	99.71% (± 0.86%)	98.44% (± 1.00%)
KNN	99.86% (± 0.42%)	98.01% (± 1.45%)	99.72% (± 0.56%)	99.01% (± 1.11%)	94.45% (± 2.17%)
DTC	99.86% (± 0.42%)	98.87% (± 1.76%)	99.58% (± 0.65%)	98.86% (± 1.06%)	96.60% (± 1.69%)

Misclassifications are rare the other way – mixtures of the two rarely get classified as YouTube only. Download has a potential to dominate YouTube, apparently because it generates significantly more and faster traffic; and it is possible that

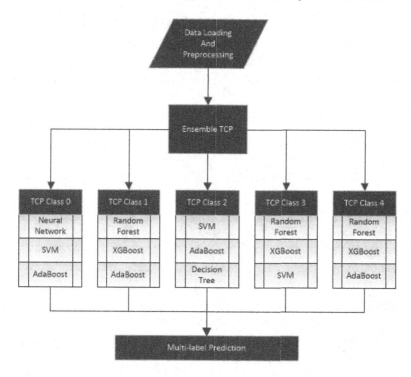

Fig. 3. TCP Ensemble Model.

backward (remote to local) packet lengths could vary, especially when traversing the Internet. This could be caused by TCP adjusting the window size for transfers. Interestingly, there were no misclassifications relating to the 4-class TCP traffic.

For UDP traffic, the most common misclassification is again a False negative for the Clipboard class. Most often, this happens in the mixture of Download, Notepad and Clipboard, where Clipboard is missed and traffic is classified as Download and Notepad. Both Download and Notepad have many more visible traffic attributes than Clipboard does – the total number of backward bytes for Download and 92-byte frames for Notepad. There were some other misclassifications such as Browsing and Clipboard being identified as Browsing alone and Clipboard or Browsing being classified as none of the five classes.

We wondered if Browsing samples from web sites with lots of video and dynamic content would tend to get misclassified as the YouTube class. Such misclassifications are rare and the predictive model is apparently resilient to audio and video contents embedded in websites.

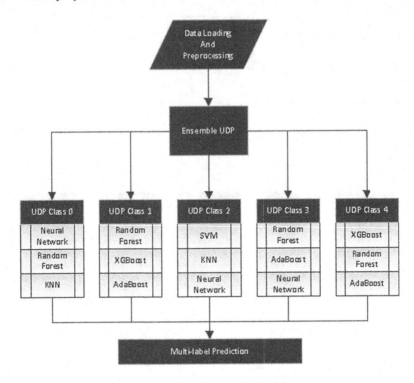

Fig. 4. UDP Ensemble Model.

Table 8. Summary of Each TCP and UDP Traffic Class Results over 5-fold cross-validation.

Class	FP	TP	FN	TN	Accu.	Prec.	Rec.	F1
TCP Download	1	391	2	1062	99.79	99.74	99.49	99.62
TCP Browsing	3	434	1	1018	99.73	99.31	99.77	99.54
TCP Notepad	0	390	1	1065	99.93	100.00	99.74	99.87
TCP YouTube	2	413	3	1038	99.66	99.52	99.28	99.40
TCP Clipboard	5	265	12	1174	98.83	98.15	95.67	96.89
UDP Download	0	221	0	483	100.00	100.00	100.00	100.00
UDP Browsing	2	175	3	524	99.29	98.87	98.31	98.59
UDP Notepad	1	178	1	524	99.72	99.44	99.44	99.44
UDP YouTube	0	188	0	516	100.00	100.00	100.00	100.00
UDP Clipboard	4	170	9	521	98.15	97.70	94.97	96.32

Table 9. Single Ensemble Score Results.

Fold	TCP Ensemble Score	UDP Ensemble Score
1	98.18	95.36
2	97.86	97.47
3	97.19	97.85
4	97.95	96.22
5	98.13	98.90
Average	97.86	97.16

5   Conclusions

We have shown that, for an encrypted protocol such as RDP, it is still possible
to infer five common categories of activities with high reliability from traffic
properties that cannot be concealed by encryption. It is conceivable that some
of these predictions could be defeated by obfuscation in the protocol but protocol
designers are caught between the need to conceal activity and the need to provide
responsiveness. As we have shown, this has led to a design in which keystrokes,
mouse activity, and visual rendering all leave traces in the encrypted traffic which
could potentially be used for attacks.

A limitation of this model is that it only used traffic between Windows 10
systems. Different systems, and RDP updates, could conceivably change traffic
structure in a macroscopic way, although the proof of concept here suggests that
only model retraining would be needed. Other kinds of traffic were not examined:
for example, two-way video such as Zoom or Skype might induce quite different
traffic structure .

Appendix Additional Figures - Shapley Values

(See (Figs. 5, 6, 7 and 8))

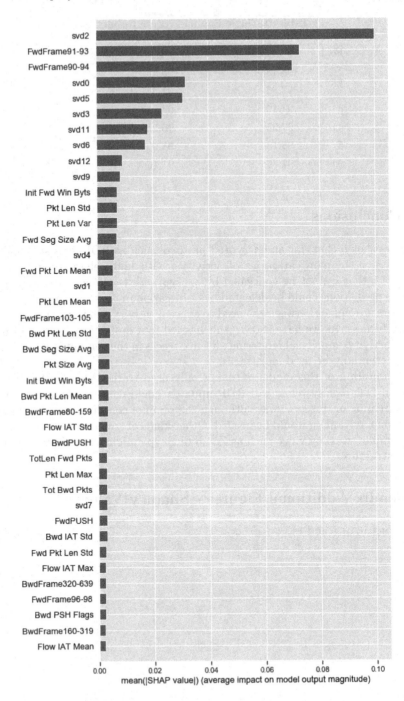

Fig. 5. TCP Attribute Ranking – Notepad, Deep Explainer

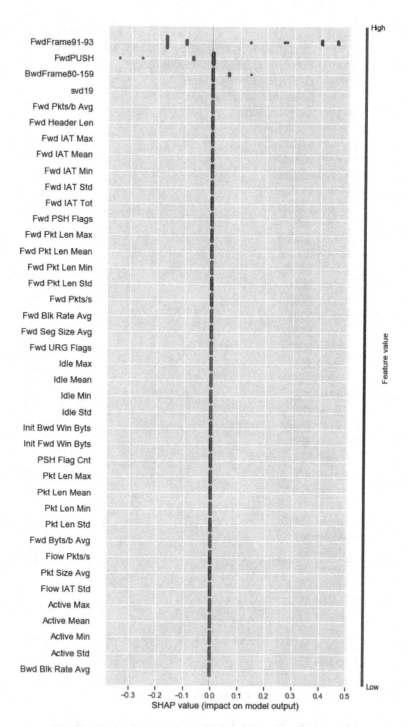

Fig. 6. TCP Attribute Ranking – Notepad, XGBoost Explainer

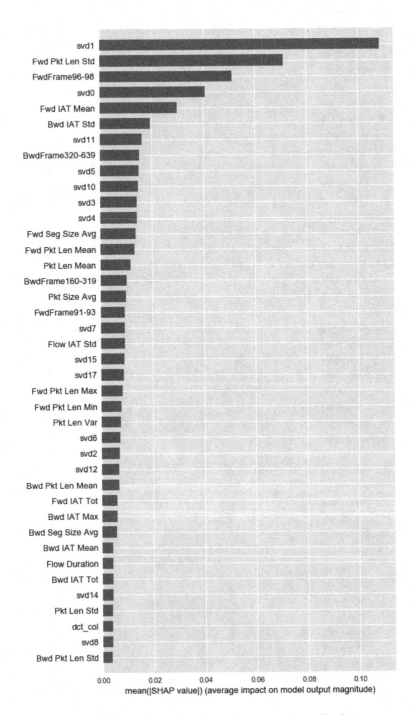

Fig. 7. UDP Attribute Ranking – Browsing, Deep Explainer

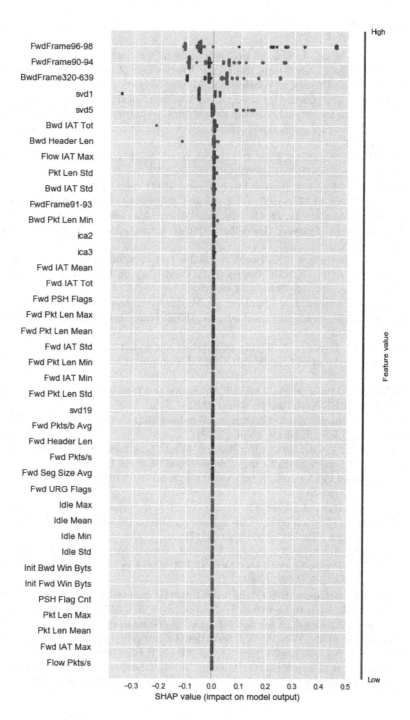

Fig. 8. UDP Attribute Ranking – Browsing, XGBoost Explainer

References

1. Alan, H.F., Kaur, J.: Can android applications be identified using only TCP/IP headers of their launch time traffic? In: Proceedings of the 9th ACM Conference on Security & Privacy in Wireless and Mobile Networks, pp. 61–66. ACM (2016)
2. Alshammari, R., Zincir-Heywood, A.N.: Machine learning based encrypted traffic classification: identifying SSH and Skype. In: Computational Intelligence for Security and Defense Applications, 2009. CISDA 2009. IEEE Symposium on, pp. 1–8. IEEE (2009)
3. Berwick, R.: An idiot's guide to support vector machines (SVMs) (2003). http://svms.org/tutorials/Berwick2003.pdf. Accessed 02 Nov 2019
4. Breiman, L.: Random forests. Mach. Learn. **45**(1), 5–32 (2001)
5. Cao, Z., Xiong, G., Zhao, Y., Li, Z., Guo, L.: A survey on encrypted traffic classification. In: Batten, L., Li, G., Niu, W., Warren, M. (eds.) ATIS 2014. CCIS, vol. 490, pp. 73–81. Springer, Heidelberg (2014). https://doi.org/10.1007/978-3-662-45670-5_8
6. Chen, T., Guestrin, C.: XGBoost: a scalable tree boosting system. In: Proceedings of the 22nd ACM SIGKDD International Conference on Knowledge Discovery and Data Mining, pp. 785–794. ACM (2016)
7. Conti, M., Mancini, L.V., Spolaor, R., Verde, N.V.: Analyzing android encrypted network traffic to identify user actions. IEEE Trans. Inf. Forensics Secur. **11**(1), 114–125 (2016)
8. Coull, S.E., Dyer, K.P.: Traffic analysis of encrypted messaging services: apple iMessage and beyond. ACM SIGCOMM Comput. Commun. Rev. **44**(5), 5–11 (2014)
9. Dainotti, A., Pescape, A., Claffy, K.C.: Issues and future directions in traffic classification. IEEE Netw. **26**(1), 35–40 (2012)
10. Dautis, B.: Installing and Configuring Windows 10:b 70–698 Exam Guide. PACKT Publishing Limited, Birmingham (2018)
11. Draper-Gil, G., Lashkari, A.H., Mamun, M.S.I., Ghorbani, A.A.: Characterization of encrypted and vpn traffic using time-related features. In: Proceedings of the 2nd International Conference on Information Systems Security and Privacy (ICISSP), pp. 407–414 (2016)
12. Dubin, R., Dvir, A., Pele, O., Hadar, O.: I know what you saw last minute - encrypted HTTP adaptive video streaming title classification. IEEE Trans. Inf. Forensics Secur. **12**(12), 3039–3049 (2017)
13. Erman, J., Arlitt, M., Mahanti, A.: Traffic classification using clustering algorithms. In: Proceedings of the 2006 SIGCOMM Workshop on Mining Network Data, pp. 281–286. ACM (2006)
14. Freund, Y., Schapire, R.E.: A decision-theoretic generalization of on-line learning and an application to boosting. J. Comput. Syst. Sci. **55**(1), 119–139 (1997)
15. Hyvarinen, A.: Fast ICA for noisy data using Gaussian moments. In: ISCAS 1999. Proceedings of the 1999 IEEE International Symposium on Circuits and Systems VLSI (Cat. No. 99CH36349), vol. 5, pp. 57–61. IEEE (1999)
16. Lashkari, A.H., Draper-Gil, G., Mamun, M.S.I., Ghorbani, A.A.: Characterization of Tor traffic using time based features. In: ICISSP, pp. 253–262 (2017)

17. Liben-Nowell, D., Sharp, A., Wexler, T., Woods, K.: Computing shapley value in supermodular coalitional games. In: Gudmundsson, J., Mestre, J., Viglas, T. (eds.) COCOON 2012. LNCS, vol. 7434, pp. 568–579. Springer, Heidelberg (2012). https://doi.org/10.1007/978-3-642-32241-9_48

18. Liu, J., Fu, Y., Ming, J., Ren, Y., Sun, L., Xiong, H.: Effective and real-time in-app activity analysis in encrypted internet traffic streams. In: Proceedings of the 23rd ACM SIGKDD International Conference on Knowledge Discovery and Data Mining, pp. 335–344. ACM (2017)

19. Lotfollahi, M., Jafari Siavoshani, M., Shirali Hossein Zade, R., Saberian, M.: Deep packet: a novel approach for encrypted traffic classification using deep learning. Soft Comput. **24**, 1–14 (2017)

20. Lundberg, S.M., et al.: Explainable AI for trees: from local explanations to global understanding. arXiv preprint arXiv:1905.04610 (2019)

21. Maddison, J.: Encrypted traffic reaches a new threshold (2018). https://www.networkcomputing.com/network-security/encrypted-traffic-reaches-new-threshold. Accessed 17 Nov 2019

22. Makhoul, J.: A fast cosine transform in one and two dimensions. IEEE Trans. Acoust. Speech Signal Process. **28**(1), 27–34 (1980)

23. Orsolic, I., Pevec, D., Suznjevic, M., Skorin-Kapov, L.: A machine learning approach to classifying YouTube QoE based on encrypted network traffic. Multimedia Tools Appl. **76**(21), 22267–22301 (2017)

24. Park, K., Kim, H.: Encryption is not enough: inferring user activities on KakaoTalk with traffic analysis. In: Kim, H., Choi, D. (eds.) WISA 2015. LNCS, vol. 9503, pp. 254–265. Springer, Cham (2016). https://doi.org/10.1007/978-3-319-31875-2_21

25. Radivilova, T., Kirichenko, L., Ageyev, D., Tawalbeh, M., Bulakh, V.: Decrypting SSL/TLS traffic for hidden threats detection. In: 2018 IEEE 9th International Conference on Dependable Systems, Services and Technologies (DESSERT), pp. 143–146. IEEE (2018)

26. Saber, A., Fergani, B., Abbas, M.: Encrypted traffic classification: combining over- and under-sampling through a PCA-SVM. In: 2018 3rd International Conference on Pattern Analysis and Intelligent Systems (PAIS), pp. 1–5. IEEE (2018)

27. Saltaformaggio, B., Choi, H., Johnson, K., Kwon, Y., Zhang, Q., Zhang, X.: Eavesdropping on fine-grained user activities within smartphone apps over encrypted network traffic. In: 10th USENIX Workshop on Offensive Technologies (WOOT 16) (2016)

28. Taylor, V.F., Spolaor, R., Conti, M., Martinovic, I.: Appscanner: automatic fingerprinting of smartphone apps from encrypted network traffic. In: 2016 IEEE European Symposium on Security and Privacy (EuroS&P), pp. 439–454. IEEE (2016)

29. Taylor, V.F., Spolaor, R., Conti, M., Martinovic, I.: Robust smartphone app identification via encrypted network traffic analysis. IEEE Trans. Inf. Forensics Secur. **13**(1), 63–78 (2018)

30. Vu, L.: Time series analysis for encrypted traffic classification: a deep learning approach. In: 2018 18th International Symposium on Communications and Information Technologies (ISCIT), pp. 121–126 IEEE (2018)

31. Yamansavascilar, B., Guvensan, M.A., Yavuz, A.G., Karsligil, M.E.: Application identification via network traffic classification. In: 2017 International Conference on Computing, Networking and Communications (ICNC), pp. 843–848. IEEE (2017)

32. Zhang, F., He, W., Liu, X., Bridges, P.G.: Inferring users' online activities through traffic analysis. In: Proceedings of the Fourth ACM Conference on Wireless Network Security, pp. 59–70. ACM (2011)

33. Zhang, J., Chen, X., Xiang, Y., Zhou, W., Jie, W.: Robust network traffic classification. IEEE/ACM Trans. Netw. (TON) **23**(4), 1257–1270 (2015)
34. Zhang, W., Meng, Y., Liu, Y., Zhang, X., Zhang, Y., Zhu, H.: Homonit: monitoring smart home apps from encrypted traffic. In: Proceedings of the 2018 ACM SIGSAC Conference on Computer and Communications Security, pp. 1074–1088. ACM (2018)

Application-Oriented Anonymization Framework for Social Network Datasets and IoT Environments

Jana Medková[(✉)] and Josef Hynek

University of Hradec Králové, Rokitanského 62,
500 03 Hradec Králové, Czech Republic
jana.medkova@uhk.cz

Abstract. Everyday usage of online Internet services and the recent rise of the Internet of Things (IoT) cause the collection of a massive amount of data, including personal and sensitive information. Anonymization enables providers to share their datasets and preserve the privacy of individuals at the same time. It is a valuable tool for preserving individuals' privacy in social network datasets and IoT environments. Researchers recently focused on developing a universal and robust anonymization method to keep privacy and preserve almost all data utility. Many various anonymization methods have been developed; however, none meet the requirements perfectly. The application-oriented anonymization has been recently discussed only for relational datasets. This paper introduces the framework for application-oriented anonymization for social network datasets and IoT environments. In our framework, it is not necessary to preserve all data utility but only the data utility specified by the data recipient. While requesting the anonymized social network data, the data receiver can specify the metrics that should be kept as close to the original graph as possible. While requesting anonymized data from the cloud in an IoT environment, the data receiver can prioritize attributes. It enables the data recipient to customize the anonymized data and the data provider to control the computing over their dataset. Moreover, we discuss the vulnerability of application-oriented anonymization to composition attacks.

Keywords: Anonymization · Task Oriented Privacy · Social network · Internet of things

1 Introduction

An enormous amount of data is stored on servers and computers worldwide daily. The total volume of data created, collected, copied and consumed worldwide is estimated to reach 120 zettabytes[1] by 2023 [25]. People share information with institutions, marketing companies, and various online services. Datasets collected

---

[1] 1 zettabyte = 10^{21} bytes.

G. Bella et al. (Eds.): SecITC 2022, LNCS 13809, pp. 261–274, 2023.
https://doi.org/10.1007/978-3-031-32636-3_15

by service providers usually contain individual personal data and sensitive information. Furthermore, the datasets are a valuable source of information for academic, marketing and business research. Hence, the providers are encouraged to publish their datasets or share them with third parties. However, sharing and publishing datasets with users' information raises privacy-preserving issues.

Privacy is a complex concept of protecting sensitive data and information from unauthorized access [19]. It arises from the users' desire to keep their information confidential and prevent adversaries from misusing them. This paper focuses on the privacy-preserving issue called *identity disclosure*. The considered anonymization methods prevent the adversary from identifying the target user in the published or shared dataset. In the IoT environment, anonymization prevents linking the particular household with records in the dataset stored in the cloud. Providers applied an anonymization method to the original dataset to gain the anonymized dataset that is published or shared.

An anonymization method $\mathcal{M}$ is an algorithm that modifies the original dataset $\mathcal{D}$ to the anonymized dataset $\mathcal{D}^*$ such that $\mathcal{D}^*$ satisfies the required privacy property (ex. k-anonymization for given k). The aim of anonymization methods is also to minimize the information loss caused by the modification from $\mathcal{D}$ to $\mathcal{D}^*$ and keep as much data utility as possible in $\mathcal{D}^*$.

Anonymization was initially proposed for relational datasets [22]. Afterwards, anonymization approaches were extended to social network (SN) datasets [16]. In addition to anonymizing users' records, SN anonymization modifies the graph structure representing the social relationships [9]. Responding to the growth of the Internet of Things (IoT), researchers in anonymization give more attention to stream data. In the IoT environment, data are transferred as the stream from smart homes to the cloud [20,24]. Hence, the associated privacy-preserving issue is how to modify the stream data such that the privacy is preserved in the cloud or other storage where big data are collected.

The objective of most of the anonymization studies has been the development of a universal and robust anonymization method. Such a universal anonymization method should handle perfectly modifying all datasets of the particular type regardless of further usage. The comprehensive survey and analysis of the state-of-the-art SN anonymization methods in [9] suggested that it seemed to be an impossible task, at least for SN anonymization. The application-oriented anonymization is suggested to be potential promising direction for current research in both SN anonymization [9,18] and relational data anonymization [7,17,29].

The application-oriented anonymization is even more befitting in IoT environments. The data collected in smart homes contain personal information; hence applying anonymization is appropriate [24]. Furthermore, the collected data from the group of smart homes are stored in a cloud. Various applications and services further exploit the collected dataset [11,28]. The services will use the anonymized data regularly. They will load new anonymized data every day (or every hour) but exploit the same utilities in the data. Hence, it makes sense to customize the anonymization according to the service's requirements and preserve the specific data utilities.

This paper proposes a framework for application-oriented anonymization using existing anonymization methods. It enables application-oriented anonymization in SN datasets and IoT environments. As far as we know, an application-oriented framework has been offered only for relational datasets yet. The goal is to maximize data utility for the recipients. The crucial idea is to identify metrics that ought to be preserved during the anonymization and select the proper anonymization method that preserves the metrics well. With application-oriented anonymization, the provider can produce the anonymized dataset with a higher level of privacy. The anonymized data are still valuable for further research since the specific data utility is preserved.

Furthermore, the novel concept of information loss measurement is proposed. Instead of measuring the total information loss, the information loss is calculated with respect to the selected metrics. Finally, we discuss the vulnerability of application-oriented anonymization to composition attacks and methods for restraining such an attack. In summary, the main contribution of this paper is

1. to show that application-oriented anonymization is the considerable direction in anonymization research
2. to formalize application-oriented anonymization approach in SN datasets and IoT environments
3. to propose frameworks for the anonymization of SN datasets and IoT environments
4. to introduce a novel method for information loss measurement and a new information loss metric for SN datasets

2 Related Work

The idea of implementing the anonymization method such that the anonymized data suits the further application has been studied in [29] by Xiong and Rangachari. They focused on the anonymization of relational datasets and identified the crucial point of application-oriented anonymization. Each application had a unique need for the data, and the best way of measuring data utility should be based on the analysis task. They presented three types of target applications and two typical scenarios in medical data mining.

A similar approach was proposed in [26], where Sun et al. presented a method that automatically derived the attribute priorities using the concept of entropy to measure the independency among attributes. A data recipient must determine the most useful and least useful attributes. However, specifying the attribute priorities before the data mining can be difficult for data analysts.

The shortcoming was addressed by Jafer et al. in [7] where task-oriented privacy preserving data publishing model was proposed. They considered only the classification task as the potential application of the anonymized relational dataset. The feature selection procedure identified the subset of features most relevant to the classification task in the proposed model, and no prior attribute prioritization was needed.

A similar approach that was not limited to classification tasks was introduced in [17] by Maeda and Yamaoka. They proposed a framework for performing custom-made anonymization by a data analysis program provided by the data recipient. This framework enabled the data receiver to create a program and send it to the data holder. The data holder ran the program on their side. However, the data holder has no guarantee that the program is correct and not malicious.

The task-oriented privacy, custom-made and application-oriented anonymization are different terms for the anonymization approach in which the data are modified with respect to their further usage. In this paper, we considered the similar communication between the data holder and data receiver as in [7,17]. We extended their methods to SN datasets and IoT environments. Moreover, we do not limit the data mining application as in [7] and omit the usage of untrusted programs, unlike [17].

The important part of the framework for SN datasets is evaluation tools that classify the anonymization methods with respect to structural and application metrics. Ji et al. proposed an evaluation tool called SecGraph in [8]. It can be used for anonymizing social network datasets, examining the vulnerability of anonymized data to state-of-the-art deanonymization attacks, and evaluating anonymized data.

A different privacy evaluation framework for graph anonymization is proposed in [1]. The DUEF-GA framework includes generic and task-specific information loss measures and metrics for the examination of re-identification and risk assessment.

3   Privacy Models

To provide insight into the principles of anonymization, we briefly described the concept of SN anonymization and two different approaches to anonymization in an IoT environment. We refer to [9,18] for more detailed descriptions and comprehensive surveys of the state-of-the-art anonymization methods.

3.1   Social Network Anonymization

The SN datasets contain information about users from online social networks. It includes users' characteristics that can be represented as *identifying attributes* (ex. name, username) and *quasi-identifying attributes* (ex. age, gender). The identifying attributes uniquely identify the user; thus, they are removed during the anonymization. The quasi-identifying attributes can be used to re-identify the individual if combined or joined with any external information. Hence, they are modified in the anonymization process. Additionally, the SN dataset includes information about social relations between the SN users. The social relationships can be represented by a graph structure and are considered to be the quasi-identifying attribute as well [9]. More precisely, the social network dataset is represented with the graph $\mathcal{G}_A = (V(\mathcal{G}_A), E(\mathcal{G}_A), U(\mathcal{G}_A))$ where $V(\mathcal{G}_A)$ is the set of nodes representing the users, $E(\mathcal{G}_A)$ is the set of edges representing the relationships between users and $U(\mathcal{G}_A)$ is the set of attributes characterizing the users.

There are two types of SN anonymization methods. Semantic methods focus on anonymizing the whole SN datasets with $U(\mathcal{G}_A)$. On the other hand, the structural methods anonymize only the graph structure. It means that their goal is to anonymize the graph $\mathcal{G} = (V(\mathcal{G}), E(\mathcal{G}))$, where $V(\mathcal{G}) = V(\mathcal{G}_A)$ and $E(\mathcal{G}) = E(\mathcal{G}_A)$. In this scenario, the set $U(\mathcal{G}_A)$ can be anonymized in the same way as the relational datasets.

The structural anonymization methods can be categorized according to the way how they modify the SN datasets as *edge-editing methods* [2, 16, 30], *clustering methods* [27], *noise node addition methods* [3] and *differential privacy* [4].

3.2   Anonymization in IoT Environment

The model of the IoT environment assumed in this paper is shown in Fig. 1. The data from various devices in a single smart home is collected inside the smart home and then sent to the cloud. The cloud collects data from the group of smart homes, and the collected dataset in the cloud can be shared with various applications and services.

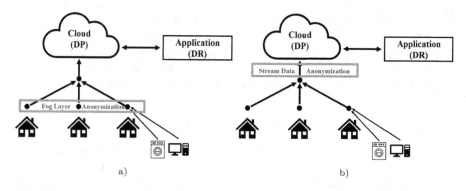

Fig. 1. The scheme of the IoT environment with different anonymization approaches.

Two anonymization approaches have been proposed for IoT environments [20, 21]. Both approaches are illustrated in Fig. 1. It depends on the IoT platform provider how the anonymization is applied in the environment. One possibility is to anonymize the data on the level of households. The data collected from a single household are anonymized before being sent to the cloud, as shown in Fig. 1a. For instance, the fog layer can be employed to handle preserving the privacy of users from the house [21]. The anonymization is applied to the data collected in a single house. Afterwards, the anonymized data collections from particular smart homes are joined. A disadvantage of the approach is that data from more households are not combined during the anonymization process. The other scenario is to anonymize the data before they reach the cloud, as shown in Fig. 1b. The data from the group of households continuously arrive in the cloud as the stream data, and the anonymization is applied to the stream data before they reach the cloud [20]. In both approaches, the cloud gathers already anonymized data since the anonymization is applied before the data get to the cloud.

Note that we address anonymizing datasets collected in IoT environments and shared with third parties. We deal with the protection against privacy leakage caused by exploiting information stored in shared datasets. Privacy and security in the whole IoT environment is a much larger topic, including encrypting, ensuring secure data transfer, or IP address anonymization. Anonymizing IP addresses of the subjects in the IoT environment and their communication is addressed in [5,13].

4   The Proposed Schemes for Application-Oriented Anonymization

In this section, we separately discuss the application-oriented anonymization for SN datasets and IoT environments. In both proposed frameworks, the priority is to keep the required level of privacy according to the privacy model and preserve the data utility specified by the data recipient (DR). Hence, the data provider (DP) can produce anonymized data that satisfy a higher level of privacy and are still valuable for DR. To avoid the inference attack or the execution of malicious programs on the datasets, the data recipient must determine their priorities based only on the dataset information or test data. They are not allowed to submit their program that is run on the original dataset by DP as in [17].

4.1   The Framework for Social Network Datasets

In this section, we focus on anonymizing the graph structure of the SN dataset and the selection and application of the structural anonymization methods. DP can use the already published structural methods and approaches in the proposed framework. As mentioned in Section 3.1, there has been proposed many various SN anonymization methods. None of them can preserve all data utility; however, they differ in preserving particular network and application metrics. The aim is to select the proper method such that the anonymized data is customized for DR. In other words, DR selects which metrics should be preserved in the anonymized data. Certainly, the selected metrics will not have the same values as in the original dataset. Each anonymization method modifies all metrics. However, the aim of the anonymization method should be to keep the selected metrics as close to the metrics of the original graph as possible. Moreover, it is not important how much the other metrics are modified in the anonymization process and how large the total information loss is.

Not considering the total information loss is the crucial point of the proposed framework. Furthermore, it is the most significant difference between the "usual" anonymization and the proposed application-oriented anonymization. The quality measure of the application-oriented anonymization method is not the total information loss but the information loss in the selected metrics. We define the application-oriented information loss of the anonymization method as follows:

Definition 1. *Let $\mathcal{G}$ be a graph representing a social network dataset. Let $\mathcal{M}$ be an anonymization method that modifies $\mathcal{G}$ to the anonymized graph $\mathcal{G}^*$ (which is denoted by $\mathcal{M}(\mathcal{G}) = \mathcal{G}^*$). Let $m_1, \ldots, m_n$ be the set of metrics that should be preserved in the anonymization process with priorities $w_1, \ldots, w_n$, $\sum_{i=1}^{n} w_i = 1$. Let $m_i(\mathcal{G})$ be the metric value in $\mathcal{G}$. Then the* application-oriented information loss *of $\mathcal{M}$ with respect to $m_1, \ldots, m_n$ is defined as*

$$AppIL(\mathcal{M}; m_1, \ldots, m_n) = 1 - \sum_{i=1}^{n} w_i \cdot Eval_i(m_i(\mathcal{G}), m_i(\mathcal{G}^*))$$

where $Eval_i(m_i(\mathcal{G}), m_i(\mathcal{G}^*))$ is the chosen evaluation method for the metric m_i such that $0 \le Eval_i(m_i(\mathcal{G}), m_i(\mathcal{G}^*)) \le 1$ and $Eval_i(m_i(\mathcal{G}), m_i(\mathcal{G})) = 1$.

As mentioned in [8], the possible evaluation method $Eval_i$ in the previous definition can be

- the cosine similarity between the distribution of $m_i(\mathcal{G})$ and $m_i(\mathcal{G}^*)$
- the ratios between the distributions of $m_i(\mathcal{G})$ and $m_i(\mathcal{G}^*)$
- the Jaccard similarity between $m_i(\mathcal{G})$ and $m_i(\mathcal{G}^*)$

Different evaluation methodologies can be applied to different metrics. The evaluation tools like SecGraph [9] or DUEF-GA [1] can be employed. The metrics in the definition can be any network or application metrics. The frequently used network metrics are degree distribution, average path length, local clustering coefficient, closeness centrality, betweenness centrality or the largest eigenvalue of the adjacency metric. The application utility metrics include role extraction, community detection, secure routing, or Sybil account detection [9]. The following example demonstrates the computation of $AppIL$.

Example. For instance, let us compute $AppIL$ for the k-degree anonymization algorithm (kDA) and the union-split clustering algorithm (USC) implemented in SecGraph [8]. Denote $\mathcal{G}$ to be the graph representing Enron dataset [12,14], $\mathcal{G}_k^* = kDA(\mathcal{G})$ with the anonymization parameter $k = 50$ and $\mathcal{G}_U^* = USC(\mathcal{G})$ with the anonymization parameter $k = 50$. Assume that betweenness centrality (BC) and the average path length (PL) metrics should be preserved with weights $w_{BC} = 0.3$ and $w_{PL} = 0.7$. Using SecGraph evaluation and the results published in [8], we get

$$SecGraph(BC(\mathcal{G}_k^*), BC(\mathcal{G})) = 0.9019, \ SecGraph(PL(\mathcal{G}_k^*), PL(\mathcal{G})) = 0.8934$$
$$SecGraph(BC(\mathcal{G}_U^*), BC(\mathcal{G})) = 0.9733, \ SecGraph(PL(\mathcal{G}_U^*), PL(\mathcal{G})) = 0.9905$$

After computing $AppIL$, we find that union-split clustering caused smaller information loss with respect to BC, PL and given weights:

$$AppIL(kDA; BC, PL) = 1 - 0.3 \cdot 0.9019 + 0.7 \cdot 0.8934 = 0.1041$$
$$AppIL(USC; BC, PL) = 1 - 0.3 \cdot 0.9733 + 0.7 \cdot 0.9905 = 0.0147$$

Communication Between DP and DR. Before the actual data sharing, DP has to set up a portfolio of available anonymization methods. From the collection of the published methods, DP selects and implements several methods that differ in preserving network and application metrics. Afterwards, DP evaluates the potential vulnerabilities of the data and sets the anonymization parameters of the selected methods. The anonymized dataset should always satisfy the required level of privacy. It is essential to set the values of anonymization parameters before evaluating the methods since the values of the anonymization parameters influence the effect of the methods on the metrics. Then DP selects an independent evaluation tool like SecGraph [8] of DUEF-GA [1] for the computation of *AppIL*.

After the preparation phase, DP can establish communication with DRs. At first, DP publishes the dataset information. Then DR selects metrics $m_1, \ldots, m_n$ that should be preserved well in anonymized data. Note that DP and DR do not discuss the anonymization method used. They discuss only the properties that should be preserved as a priority in the anonymized data. Thus, DR sends $\{m_1, \ldots, m_n\}$ and $\{w_1, \ldots, w_n\}$ to DP who select the anonymization method with the minimal $AppIL(\mathcal{M}; m_1, \ldots, m_n)$. If the weights are not specified by DR, then $w_i = \frac{1}{n}, \forall i$. The datasets are anonymized with the chosen method, and the anonymized data is transferred to DR. The whole process is summarized in Algorithm 1.

Algorithm 1. Application-oriented framework for SN datasets

Require: DP: SN dataset $\mathcal{G}$, anonymization methods $M_1, \ldots, M_s$, evaluation methods
$Eval_1, \ldots, Eval_s$; DR: network metrics $m_1, \ldots, m_n$
Ensure: anonymized dataset $\mathcal{G}$ with respect to requirements of DR
1: DP: Set the required level of privacy for $\mathcal{G}^*$
2: DP: Set anonymization parameters for $M_1, \ldots, M_s$ with respect to Step 1
3: DP: publishes information about $\mathcal{G}$
4: DR: select $m_1, \ldots, m_n$ and set $w_1, \ldots, w_n$
5: DR $\longrightarrow$ DP: $m_1, \ldots, m_n, w_1, \ldots, w_n$
6: DP: Find M_j: $AppIL(M_j; m_1, \ldots, m_n) = \min_{i=1,\ldots,s} \{AppIL(M_i; m_1, \ldots, m_n)\}$
7: DP: generate $\mathcal{G}^* = M_j(\mathcal{G})$
8: DP $\longrightarrow$ DR: $\mathcal{G}^*$

The above scenario describes the situation of sharing data. While DP publishes the dataset (making it available online), DP anonymizes the dataset with one selected anonymization method and publishes the anonymized data with the additional information, which metric is preserved as a priority in the anonymization process. However, only one version of the same dataset should be published. Otherwise, the published anonymized datasets are vulnerable to the composition attack as discussed in Sect. 5.

4.2   The Framework for IoT Environments

We assume the IoT environment as shown in Fig. 1 where the data collected in smart homes are transferred into the cloud. The data collected from smart homes with their embedded devices and sensors can also be infused with the data from other smart city components. The data collection is used by commercial applications and implied in intelligent products and services. Since the smart case from the personal context is extended to the larger community in the smart city [11], the data from the smart home are exploited not only by its residents but the whole community. For instance, each smart home location can have outdoor sensors monitoring temperature and humidity, and a smart system cloud-based weather station [10]. The data measured by the outdoor sensors and gathered by the smart weather station are sent to the cloud. A weather monitoring system can use the gathered data to analyze weather conditions and weather forecasts in the location [28].

DP is the cloud service provider in this model, and DR is the application. Unlike relational or SN datasets, where DRs are expected to be data analysts or companies that buy the dataset once or a few times a year, DRs in the IoT environments are expected to use the data repeatedly in short periods. For instance, the weather monitoring system can request fresh data daily or every hour. Let us assume that a single DR requests data from the cloud. The DR asks for the data repeatedly; however, the requested data should always have the same utility since the use of the data is always the same. In other words, requirements on data utilities are always the same from the same DR. Thus, the data submitted to the DR are always anonymized with the same priorities.

Let us assume that there are more DRs requesting data from the same cloud. Each DR can have different priorities on the data utility, or some DRs can have similar ones. For instance, a weather monitoring system prioritizes keeping the temperature and humidity values close to the original data, and other agriculture applications can also prioritize the temperature and humidity attributes. On the other hand, an energy management application can prioritize attributes describing how much energy consumes particular devices. Thus, the data submitted to the specific DRs can sometimes be anonymized with the same priorities. Other times, different versions of anonymized data will be submitted to different DRs.

According to the published studies, anonymization is applied when the data are leaving the smart home environment in the fog layer [21] or before they reach the cloud [20] (see Fig. 1). In both cases, the cloud contains anonymized data. If application-oriented anonymization is considered, the same data should be anonymized several times according to different priorities. The cloud contains several anonymized versions of the same data in this scenario. DP has not had the original data available but only several versions of the anonymized data.

Let there be n versions of the anonymized data and let AD_i, $1 \leq i \leq n$, be the identification of the i-th anonymization method. Let there be m participating data recipients. Assume DP to assign the DRs the identification $DR_1, \ldots DR_m$. Let $L_{DP} = \{[DR_i, AD_j]; 1 \leq i \leq m, 1 \leq j \leq n\}$ be a map where DR_i is the key and AD_j is the value. The tuple $[DR_i, AD_j]$ describes that the DR with the identification DR_i requests data anonymized with the method AD_j. Let $\overline{DR}$ be a new data recipient requesting the data from DP. In the preprocessing stage, DP publishes information about the particular versions of the anonymization methods. It is not necessary to publish the actual anonymization algorithm. The important information is which attributes are prioritized during the anonymization. Afterwards, $\overline{DR}$ selects the version of the anonymized data. More precisely, $\overline{DR}$ chooses i such that AD_i is their preferable anonymization method. DP adds to L_{DP} the tuple $[DR_{m+1}; AD_i]$ and send $\overline{DR}$ their identification DR_{m+1}.

The processing stage repeats when $\overline{DR}$ requests the data. $\overline{DR}$ sends the request including the identification DR_{m+1} and time interval $[t_1; t_2]$, where t_1 and t_2 are timestamps. All DRs are assumed to require always data from a specific period (an hour, a day, a week). DP looks into L_{DP} to find the proper anonymization method AD_i. DP selects the data that are anonymized with AD_i and have the timestamp t such that $t_1 \leq t \leq t_2$. DP send the compiled dataset to $\overline{DR}$. The framework is summarized in Algorithm 2.

Algorithm 2. Application-oriented framework for IoT environments

---

Require: DP: dataset with anonymized data $\mathcal{D}^*$, anonymization methods $AD_1, \ldots, AD_n, L_{DP}$
Ensure: anonymized datasets $\mathcal{D}_i^*$'s with respect to requirements of $\overline{DR}$
1: DP: publish information about $\mathcal{D}^*$ and $AD_1, \ldots, AD_n$
2: $\overline{DR}$: select AD_i
3: $\overline{DR} \longrightarrow$ DP: i
4: DP: $L_{DP} = L_{DP} \cup [DR_{m+1}; AD_i]$
5: DP $\longrightarrow \overline{DR}$: $m + 1$
6: **while** $\overline{DR}$ requests data **do**
7:     $\overline{DR}$: select t_1, t_2
8:     $\overline{DR} \longrightarrow$ DP: $t_1, t_2, m + 1$
9:     DP: find AD_i such that $[DR_{m+1}; AD_i] \in L_{DP}$
10:    DP: compile records from $\mathcal{D}^*$ having timestamps in $[t_1; t_2]$ and being anonymized with $AD_i \longrightarrow \mathcal{D}_i^*$
11:    DP $\longrightarrow \overline{DR}$: $\mathcal{D}_i^*$
12:    DP: wait for the next request
13: **end while**

---

5   Vulnerability of Application-Oriented Anonymization to Composition Attacks

The composition attack is the privacy threat for relational datasets [6,15,23] and social network datasets [19]. The composition attack aims to attack the pairs of anonymized datasets with overlapping records or user communities. Let us consider the composition attack on relational datasets. Let us assume that two datasets D_1, D_2 contain the same records. Several records from the dataset D_1 are also included in D_2. The dataset D_1 could have many other records not included in D_2 and vice versa.

Moreover, let both datasets have the same sensitive attribute, and its value is constant for all overlapping records in both datasets. The assumption is realistic, as presented in [15]. If both datasets are anonymized and published independently, the adversary can use the anonymized versions of D_1 and D_2 to perform the composition attack.

Definition 2 (Composition attack *[15]*). *Assume D_1, D_2 to be two datasets with overlapping user communities having the same sensitive attribute. Denote $r_i(I) \in D_i$ to be a record in D_i describing the individual I, $i = 1, 2$. Let D_1^* and D_2^* be the anonymized versions of D_1 and D_2 that are published independently of each other. The attacker with access to D_1^*, D_2^* perform the* composition attack *if he/she finds the nonempty set $\{[r_1(I), r_2(I)]; r_1(I) \in D_1^*, r_2(I) \in D_2^*\}$.*

The result of the composition attack is not the complete re-identification of the individuals linked with the overlapping records; however, it is a significant decrement in the privacy level. The version of the composition attack on SN datasets is similar, and it aims to attack the pair of anonymized SNs with overlapping user communities.

If two or more DRs having different priorities require the anonymized dataset from the same DP, DP can create two or more anonymized versions of the same dataset. Since all those versions are modifications of the same dataset, they certainly have overlapping records (or overlapping user communities in the case of the SN datasets). Thus, they can become targets of composition attacks.

5.1   Methods for Restraining Composition Attacks

Consider publishing SN datasets. The prevention against the composition attack is to publish only one anonymized version of one dataset. Suppose the provider wishes to publish two or more anonymized versions of their data. In that case, he/she should split the dataset into several smaller datasets without overlapping the user community. Then, DP can anonymize each smaller dataset with a different method or with different priorities and publishes all of them.

In this scenario, DRs are expected to be data analysts or companies that buy the data from the same DP once or a few times. The recommendation is not to provide the same DR with different anonymized versions of the same dataset. If the DR receives two different versions of the same dataset, they can perform the composition attack. Moreover, DRs should not be allowed to publish the received dataset themselves or to share it with other parties.

However, preventing the adversary from pretending to be two data recipients DR_1 and DR_2 requesting data with different priorities is difficult. Thus, the prevention against this behaviour is to split the dataset into several smaller datasets without overlapping user communities and anonymize each smaller dataset with a different method or priorities. The DR does not obtain the whole dataset but only the smaller part of it. This recommendation is applicable to large or big data datasets.

Consider the situation in the IoT environment. As discussed in Sect. 4.2, DRs are assumed to be applications that require the data with the same prioritize repeatedly. To prevent the composition attack, DP can submit only one anonymized version of the dataset to each DR. Since there can be many applications benefiting from the data from the same cloud in the smart city, splitting the data collection in the cloud into smaller parts may cause significant information loss. The smaller part may be too small, and the submitted information may not be precise enough.

6   Conclusion

Application-oriented anonymization is a promising research direction in privacy-preserving approaches. This paper introduces the frameworks for employing application-oriented anonymization in social network datasets and IoT environments. The crucial point of the proposed framework is the preference for preserving selected metrics before minimizing the total information loss. The new measure has been introduced to evaluate the information loss caused by SN anonymization with respect to the selected metrics. It can motivate the development of new application-oriented anonymization methods that focus on preserving particular metrics regardless of the total information loss.

However, many open problems should be solved before application-oriented anonymization is employed in practice. In social network anonymization, it will be helpful to find good combinations of state-of-the-art methods such that they differ in preserving particular network and application metrics. The data providers can implement such combinations to have suitable methods for meeting various requirements of data recipients.

Moreover, it is crucial to find effective ways to prevent composition attacks using application-oriented anonymization and prevent the adversary from managing two applications that request the data independently and with different priorities. The authors will continue in the research of application-oriented anonymization and address the issue in future research.

Acknowledgements. This study is supported by the SPEV project 2022 run at the Faculty of Informatics and Management, University of Hradec Kralove, Czech Republic.

References

1. Casas-Roma, J.: DUEF-GA: data utility and privacy evaluation framework for graph anonymization. Int. J. Inf. Secur. **19**, 465–478 (2020). https://doi.org/10.1007/s10207-019-00469-4
2. Cheng, J., Fu, A.W.C., Liu, J.: K-isomorphism: privacy preserving network publication against structural attacks. In: Proceedings of the ACM SIGMOD International Conference on Management of Data, pp. 459–470. ACM Press, New York (2010). https://doi.org/10.1145/1807167.1807218

3. Chester, S., Kapron, B.M., Ramesh, G., Srivastava, G., Thomo, A., Venkatesh, S.: Why waldo befriended the dummy? k-anonymization of social networks with pseudo-nodes. Soc. Netw. Anal. Min. **3**(3), 381–399 (2013). https://doi.org/10.1007/s13278-012-0084-6

4. Dwork, C.: Differential privacy: a survey of results. In: Agrawal, M., Du, D., Duan, Z., Li, A. (eds.) TAMC 2008. LNCS, vol. 4978, pp. 1–19. Springer, Heidelberg (2008). https://doi.org/10.1007/978-3-540-79228-4_1

5. Fan, J., Xu, J., Ammar, M.H., Moon, S.B.: Prefix-preserving IP address anonymization: measurement-based security evaluation and a new cryptography-based scheme. Comput. Netw. **46**(2), 253–272 (2004). https://doi.org/10.1016/j.comnet.2004.03.033

6. Ganta, S.R., Kasiviswanathan, S.P., Smith, A.: Composition attacks and auxiliary information in data privacy. In: Proceedings of the 14th ACM SIGKDD International Conference on Knowledge Discovery and Data Mining, pp. 265–273. ACM (2008). https://doi.org/10.1145/1401890.1401926

7. Jafer, Y., Matwin, S., Sokolova, M.: Task oriented privacy preserving data publishing using feature selection. In: Sokolova, M., van Beek, P. (eds.) AI 2014. LNCS (LNAI), vol. 8436, pp. 143–154. Springer, Cham (2014). https://doi.org/10.1007/978-3-319-06483-3_13

8. Ji, S., Li, W., Mittal, P., Hu, X., Beyah, R.: SecGraph: a uniform and open-source evaluation system for graph data anonymization and de-anonymization. In: 24th USENIX Security Symposium, pp. 303–318 (2015)

9. Ji, S., Mittal, P., Beyah, R.: Graph data anonymization, de-anonymization attacks, and de-anonymizability quantification: a survey. IEEE Commu. Surv. Tutorials **19**(2), 1305–1326 (2016). https://doi.org/10.1109/COMST.2016.2633620

10. Kapoor, P., Barbhuiya, F.A.: Cloud based weather station using IoT devices. In: TENCON 2019–2019 IEEE Region 10 Conference (TENCON), pp. 2357–2362 (2019). https://doi.org/10.1109/TENCON.2019.8929528

11. Kaur, M.J., Maheshwari, P.: Building smart cities applications using IoT and cloud-based architectures. In: 2016 International Conference on Industrial Informatics and Computer Systems (CIICS), pp. 1–5 (2016). https://doi.org/10.1109/ICCSII.2016.7462433

12. Klimt, B., Yang, Y.: Introducing the Enron corpus. In: Proceedings of the 1st Conference on Email and Anti-spam. CEAS (2004)

13. Kouachi, A.I., Bachir, A., Lasla, N.: Anonymizing communication flow identifiers in the internet of things. Comput. Electr. Eng. **91**, 107063 (2021). https://doi.org/10.1016/j.compeleceng.2021.107063

14. Leskovec, J., Lang, K.J., Dasgupta, A., Mahoney, M.W.: Community structure in large networks: natural cluster sizes and the absence of large well-defined clusters. Internet Math. **6**(1), 29–123 (2009)

15. Li, J., Baig, M.M., Sattar, A.S., Ding, X., Liu, J., Vincent, M.: A hybrid approach to prevent composition attacks for independent data releases. Inform Sci. (2016). https://doi.org/10.1016/j.ins.2016.05.009

16. Liu, K., Terzi, E.: Towards identity anonymization on graphs. In: Proceedings of the ACM SIGMOD International Conference on Management of Data, pp. 93–106. ACM Press, Vancouver, Canada (2008). https://doi.org/10.1145/1376616.1376629

17. Maeda, W., Yamaoka, Y.: Custom-made anonymization by data analysis program provided by recipient. In: Proceedings of the 9th ACM Conference on Data and Application Security and Privacy, pp. 149–151. ACM, Richardson Texas USA (2019). https://doi.org/10.1145/3292006.3302380

18. Majeed, A., Lee, S.: Anonymization techniques for privacy preserving data publishing: a comprehensive survey. IEEE Access **9**, 8512–8545 (2021). https://doi.org/10.1109/ACCESS.2020.3045700

19. Medková, J.: Composition attack against social network data. Comput. Secur. **74**, 115–129 (2018). https://doi.org/10.1016/j.cose.2018.01.002

20. Otgonbayar, A., Pervez, Z., Dahal, K., Eager, S.: K-VARP: K-anonymity for varied data streams via partitioning. Inf. Sci. **467**, 238–255 (2018). https://doi.org/10.1016/j.ins.2018.07.057

21. Puri, V., Kaur, P., Sachdeva, S.: Data anonymization for privacy protection in fog-enhanced smart homes. In: 2020 6th International Conference on Signal Processing and Communication (ICSC), pp. 201–205 (2020). https://doi.org/10.1109/ICSC48311.2020.9182761

22. Samarati, P., Sweeney, L.: Protecting privacy when disclosing information: k-anonymity and its enforcement through generalization and suppression. In: Technical Report SRI-CSL-98-04. Computer Science Laboratory, SRI International, Palo Alto, CA (1998)

23. Sattar, A.S., Li, J., Liu, J., Heatherly, R., Malin, B.: A probabilistic approach to mitigate composition attacks on privacy in non-coordinated environments. Knowl. Based Syst. **67**, 361–372 (2014). https://doi.org/10.1016/j.knosys.2014.04.019

24. Seliem, M., Elgazzar, K., Khalil, K.: Towards privacy preserving IoT environments: a survey. Wirel. Commun. Mob. Comput. (2018). https://doi.org/10.1155/2018/1032761

25. Statista: Volume of data/information created, captured, copied, and consumed worldwide from 2010 to 2025 (2022). https://www.statista.com/statistics/871513/worldwide-data-created/. Accessed 07 May 2022

26. Sun, X., Wang, H., Li, J., Zhang, Y.: Injecting purpose and trust into data anonymisation. Comput. Secur. **30**(5), 332–345 (2011). https://doi.org/10.1016/j.cose.2011.05.005

27. Thompson, B., Yao, D.: The union-split algorithm and cluster-based anonymization of social networks. In: Proceedings of the 4th International Symposium on Information, Computer, and Communications Security, pp. 218–227. ACM Press, New York (2009). https://doi.org/10.1145/1533057.1533088

28. Tiwari, M., Narang, D., Goel, P., Gadhwal, A., Gupta, A., Chawla, A.: Weather monitoring system using IoT and cloud computing. Int. J. Adv. Sci. Tech. **29**(12s), 2473–2479 (2020)

29. Xiong, L., Rangachari, K.: Towards application-oriented data anonymization. In: 1st SIAM International Workshop on Practical Privacy-Preserving Data Mining, Atlanta, US, pp. 1–10. Citeseer (2008)

30. Zhou, B., Pei, J.: Preserving privacy in social networks against neighborhood attacks. In: 2008 IEEE 24th International Conference on Data Engineering, pp. 506–515. IEEE, Cancun, Mexico (2008). https://doi.org/10.1109/icde.2008.4497459

AI-Powered Vulnerability Detection for Secure Source Code Development

Sampath Rajapaksha[1]([✉])[ID], Janaka Senanayake[1][ID], Harsha Kalutarage[1][ID], and Mhd Omar Al-Kadri[2][ID]

[1] School of Computing, Robert Gordon University, Aberdeen AB10 7QB, UK
{s.rajapaksha,j.senanayake,h.kalutarage}@rgu.ac.uk
[2] School of Computing and Digital Technology, Birmingham City University, Birmingham B5 5JU, UK
omar.alkadri@bcu.ac.uk
https://www.rgu.ac.uk/

Abstract. Vulnerable source code in software applications is causing paramount reliability and security issues. Software security principles should be integrated to reduce these issues at the early stages of the development lifecycle. Artificial Intelligence (AI) could be applied to detect vulnerabilities in source code. In this research, a Machine Learning (ML) based method is proposed to detect source code vulnerabilities in C/C++ applications. Furthermore, Explainable AI (XAI) was applied to support developers in identifying vulnerable source code tokens and understanding their causes. The proposed model can detect whether the code is vulnerable or not in binary classification with 0.96 F1-Score. In case of vulnerability type detection, a multi-class classification based on CWE-ID, the model achieved 0.85 F1-Score. Several ML classifiers were tested, and the Random Forest (RF) and Extreme Gradient Boosting (XGB) performed well in binary and multi-class approaches respectively. Since the model is trained on a dataset containing actual source codes, the model is highly generalizable.

Keywords: Source code vulnerability · Machine learning · Software security · Vulnerability scanners

1 Introduction

Security threats evolve rapidly, forcing developers to be up to date with the latest security vulnerabilities to minimize the risk of software attacks. Education of security for developers is an ongoing process. To date, many software developers have overlooked security issues throughout the software development lifecycle [22, 24]. One of the main reasons for this could be a possible lack of understanding about how common errors in software development result in exploitable vulnerabilities in software systems [15] and possible pressure towards fast deployment. Also, the communication disconnection between developers and cyber security experts has led to widespread software vulnerabilities [26].

G. Bella et al. (Eds.): SecITC 2022, LNCS 13809, pp. 275–288, 2023.
https://doi.org/10.1007/978-3-031-32636-3_16

Traditional security tools and penetration-testing techniques are considered very complicated, time-consuming and expensive processes in dynamically changing cyber attacks [14]. For example, one of the challenges businesses face today is that the mandate to be agile and release software faster while ensuring that their product is secure against cyber threats. Possible other solutions include static code analysis tools, which can have low detection capability (high false negative rate) due to the lack of up-to-date cyber attack data [9,14]. Therefore, the software development industry is in definite need of automating vulnerability detection with the growing impact of cyber attacks on businesses due to downtime, reputation damage, loss of customers and asset sabotage.

Due to the advancement in computational power, new algorithms and availability of data, AI and ML can be successfully used to address problems in various domains. Many applications in the computer security and privacy domain, have been addressed using AI/ML techniques [28]. Software vulnerabilities are such area in which AI/ML algorithms can be used to detect vulnerabilities in source codes [1,2,19]. In the context of vulnerability detection, use of AI/ML algorithms help to reduce the need of human expertise [29] and automate the process. Programming languages can be considered as languages with words, numbers and different symbols. Hence previous works have used Natural Language Processing (NLP) techniques to detect vulnerabilities in source code, treating code as a form of texts [5]. Extracted features through NLP techniques are used to train AI/ML algorithms to model this problem as a classification model.

A requirement of having a high accuracy source code vulnerability detection method is fulfilled in this work which used AI/ML techniques. In summary, the following contributions are made:

- *Improved data pre-processing approach to identify important features:* Presenting a method using a Concrete Syntax Trees (CST) to identify the most important features of source codes to train a ML model.
- *Generalized vulnerability detection models:* Source code vulnerability detection using binary and multi-class classification models. The generalization capability of the proposed method is high since the models are trained on a carefully generated dataset that includes real-world source codes and a subset of a synthetic dataset.
- *Model explainability:* Visually representing the identified vulnerable source code segments to help make the necessary changes to convert the code from vulnerable to benign. Furthermore, this supports for optimising the data pre-processing approach to improving the model accuracy.

The rest of the paper is organised as follows: Sect. 2 contains background and related work. Section 3 explains the methodology of this work. Section 4 discusses the performance evaluation. Finally, the conclusions and future work directions are discussed in Sect. 5.

2   Background and Related Work

This section sets the base for the study by providing a sound knowledge of source code vulnerabilities and weaknesses, various parsers and scanners, and various vulnerability detection methods while discussing the related studies.

2.1   Source Code Vulnerabilities and Weaknesses

There is a wide scope of human error within the software development process, especially if an extensive testing and validation process is not followed from the initial stage of the software development lifecycle [7]. Due to these potential human errors, several vulnerabilities in the code can occur. Reducing vulnerabilities in source code is identified as a good practice in secure software development [23].

Source code weaknesses are flaws, bugs, faults, or other errors that, if left unaddressed, could result in the software being vulnerable to attack. Software source code weaknesses are identified in Common Weakness Enumeration (CWE) [3] and the known vulnerabilities are identified in Common Vulnerabilities and Exposures (CVE) [4]. Identifying weaknesses in source code at early stages, make the software less vulnerable. Some weaknesses have relationships with other weaknesses (parent-child relationship in CWE category). Therefore, there can be overlaps of codes related to more than one CWE ID (i.e. CWE-120 and CWE-126 are related to buffer sizes).

2.2   Parsers and Scanners

Software developers require supportive tools which can be integrated with their coding to minimize developer errors by detecting vulnerabilities at an initial step to mitigate them after performing the source code analysis [22]. The source code needs to be initially formatted into a generalized form with CST or Abstract Syntax Trees (AST) [25]. Static analysis can be used [9] to create these syntax trees. The rate of false alarms on vulnerabilities depends on the accuracy of formulating the CST/AST and its generalisation mechanism. Tree-sitter[1] is an open-source parser generator tool which can create a CST for a source file. It also can efficiently update the tree when there is a change in the source code.

Using the parsed code, scanners can be used to perform analysis. Few scanners are available which can perform analysis in C/C++ source code with relatively good accuracy [17]. Cppcheck[2] is one of the open source static analysis tools to detect bugs, undefined behaviour and dangerous coding constructs in C/C++ code. It can provide the following data for each alert: filename, line, severity, alert identifier, and CWE. This also can be integrated with other development tools. Flawfinder[3] is another open source tool that can examine C/C++

---

[1] https://tree-sitter.github.io/tree-sitter.

[2] https://cppcheck.sourceforge.io.

[3] https://github.com/david-a-wheeler/flawfinder.

source code and report possible security weaknesses. It works by using a built-in database of C/C++ functions with well-known vulnerable problems, such as format string problems (printf, snprintf, and syslog), buffer overflow risks (strcpy, strcat, gets, sprintf, and scanf), potential shell metacharacter dangers (exec, system, popen), poor random number acquisition (random), and race conditions (access, chown, chgrp, chmod, tmpfile, tmpnam, tempnam, and mktemp).

2.3   Vulnerability Detection Methods

Metric-based and pattern-based techniques have been used in previous works [6] for vulnerability detection. Metric-based techniques use supervised or unsupervised machine learning algorithms using features such as complexity metrics, code churn metrics, token frequency metrics, dependency metrics, developer activity metrics or execution complexity metrics [6]. Pattern-based techniques use static analysis to identify vulnerable codes using known vulnerable codes. However, the technique used in this, limited to function level codes and considered as a pre-step for vulnerability assessment as the proposed solution did not identify the vulnerability type or the possible location of the vulnerability. Additionally, usage of metric based features in compared ML algorithms showed a low detection capability.

Authors in [10] have used text features in source code to predict software defects. They have considered everything as texts separated by space or tab except comments. Naive Bayes (NB) and Logistic Regression (LR) were used as the classification algorithms in this study. This concept was adapted by [20] and used for software vulnerability prediction tasks using the same algorithms with Bag of Words (BoW) as features. Everything except for comment words separated by space or tab have been treated as features for this model. Experimental results showed a lower F1-Score for all selected test cases. This might be due to the poor feature selection without focusing on the proper data pre-processing approach. In [8] n-gram (1-gram, 2-gram and 3-gram) and word2vec were used as the features to predict if a test case contains vulnerability or not. As a solution to the class imbalance problem, the authors used the random oversampling technique. However, both of the above-mentioned models [8,16] are limited to binary classification models to detect the vulnerability states.

Minimum intermediate representation learning was used to source code vulnerability detection in [19]. Unsupervised learning was used in the pre-training stage to solve the lack of vulnerability samples. Convolutions Neural Networks (CNN) were used to generate high-level features. Finally, these features are used in classifiers such as LR, NB, Support Vector Machine (SVM), Multi-Layer Perceptron (MLP), Gradient Boosting (GB), Decision Tree (DT) and RF for vulnerability detection. Only two CWE-IDs of a synthetic dataset were selected as the training dataset and therefore, this model has a low generalization capability for other CWE-IDs and real datasets.

Authors in [27] proposed a method to guide manual source code analysis using vulnerability extrapolation. To this end, the authors generated AST using a parser. This work is limited to vulnerabilities present in a few source code functions. The vulnerability detection method proposed by [1] is also based on the AST representation of source code. Pycparser[4] library was used to generate AST for the C language. It was modelled as a binary classification task using MLP and CNN algorithms. The proposed model used four CWE classes and achieved between 0.09 to 0.59 F1-Score.

Though the trend toward applying ML for vulnerability detection is high, as discussed above, many studies do not provide a high accuracy/F1-Score when detecting source code vulnerabilities. Many of them were not trained on a dataset that includes a real-world dataset, following enhanced preprocessing techniques. Furthermore, they were only limited to binary classification or a limited number of CWE classes. Therefore, our study addresses these problems by using a real-world dataset to achieve an F1-Score of 0.96 in the binary class model and 0.85 in the multi-class classification model for twenty CWE classes.

3 Methodology

3.1 Dataset

Lack of vulnerability dataset is one of the major challenges for developing vulnerability prediction model [11,21]. Authors in [12] showed the importance of using sufficient and accurately labelled data to achieve good accuracy of the vulnerability prediction task. Previous works used different datasets to train proposed algorithms. The proposed method in [20] has used data of 182 releases of 20 apps. It used a source code analyser to identify vulnerabilities without using a vulnerability database. Datasets published by Software Assurance Reference (SARD) and the National Vulnerability Database (NVD)[5] used in [19]. To identify the ground truth of mined open-source code, the authors used static analysis, dynamic analysis with commit-message and bug-report tagging. SARD is a dataset produced by the National Institute of Standards and Technology (NIST) as a result of the Software Assurance Metrics And Tool Evaluation (SAMATE) project[6]. SATE IV juilet test suit[7] of SAMATE project, debian linux distribution and data on public git repositories on GitHub were used in [1].

Since this research focuses on predicting both vulnerable and non-vulnerable codes and detecting the CWE-IDs, both positive and negative classes data is needed. As the vulnerable dataset, synthetic test cases (C and C++ languages) of SATE IV juilet test suit was selected. This dataset was developed to encourage the improvement of static code analysers. The selected dataset includes 52,185 source code samples. Since this dataset is limited to vulnerable codes and CWE-IDs distribution is highly imbalanced, a web crawler was developed to retrieve more C and C++ source codes from public GitHub repositories. The entire

---

[4] https://github.com/eliben/pycparser.

[5] https://cve.mitre.org/.

[6] https://samate.nist.gov/SARD/.

[7] https://www.nist.gov/itl/ssd/software-quality-group/static-analysis-tool-expositio n-sate-iv.

source code was considered as a sample. Existing static analysis tools were used to identify the ground truth of the retrieved source codes. In general, signature-based detection methods have lower false positives. Since they might suffer from higher false negatives, they were used in an ensemble way to obtain the ground truth. The main objective here is to learn the capabilities of these analysers and obtain a lower false negative and positive rate from the ML-based models. To this end, the sample was considered as malicious if one of the analysers identifies the sample as malicious. If all analysers identify the sample as benign, then it was considered as benign. Based on the combined dataset of SATE IV Juilet test suit and GitHub data, twenty highest frequent CWE-IDs were selected as vulnerable code samples, including over 0.3 million source codes. Vulnerability class distribution is depicted in Fig. 1. Similar size of C and C++ source codes were selected as the benign dataset, making it approximately 1:1 positive and negative class distribution.

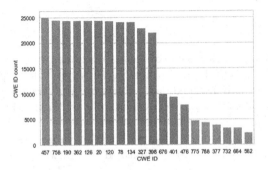

Fig. 1. CWE-ID distribution.

3.2   Model Architecture

The proposed model includes two machine learning models for binary and multi-class classifications. The binary classification model is trained to detect the source code as benign or vulnerable code. Multi-class classification model uses the identified vulnerable code to detect the CWE-IDs associated with it. The XAI is used on the multi-class classification results to explain the model prediction and hence to identify vulnerable code segments. This process is depicted in Fig. 2.

Data Pre-processing. The selected dataset contains C and C++ language source codes. Previous works [1,13,27] used AST and CST representations of codes to identify features. In this research, CST is used to identify the tokens of source code to retain more details in the code using a parser generator tool. Following pre-processing steps were applied to source codes.

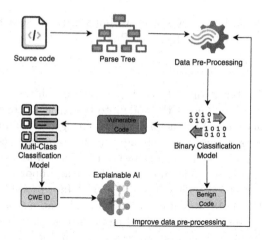

Fig. 2. Model Architecture.

1. Use a parser generator to generate CSTs (parse tree) of source codes.
2. Clean CST outputs to generate tokens.
3. Create numerical vectors for ML models.

All source codes were passed through the parser generator to generate CSTs. CSTs contain much information, such as comments, symbols, hexadecimal numbers and user-defined function names, which cannot use as generalized features for machine learning models. Hence, comments and selected symbols were removed and user-defined function names were replaced with common names such as 'UserDef'. Symbols to remove from the codes were identified with the support of a set of domain experts to avoid important symbol removal. Preprocessed CST outputs were used to generate features for ML models. To this end, Python library CountVectorizer and TfidfVectorizer were used to generate features of Bag-of-words (BoW), n-gram (n = 2, 3) and term frequency-inverse document frequency (TF-IDF). Grid search was used to identify optimal hyper-parameters including maximum (max df) and minimum (min df) document frequencies.

Algorithms: Data pre-processing produced three feature vectors from CST tokens: BoW, n-gram and TF-IDF. The complete dataset of 0.6 million source code samples was used to train the binary classification model, whereas 0.3 million source code samples which included 20 CWE-IDs were used to train the multi-class classification model. Due to class imbalance, stratified random sampling was used to split the dataset into 80:20 ratios for the multi-class classification model. 80% of the data was used to train binary and multi-class algorithms and the rest of the 20% was used to evaluate their performance. NB, RF, LR and XGB algorithms were used with BOW, n-gram (n = 1, 2) and TF-IDF features. Since a vulnerable code might have more than one vulnerability, the top K (K = 3) predictions were used as possible vulnerable classes to address the multi-label cases. Python sklearn library was used to implement these algorithms. Experiments were conducted on a MacBook Pro 2.2 GHz Intel Core i7 with 16 GB RAM.

Vulnerability Explanation: Identifying the vulnerabilities and relevant CWE IDs are not sufficient to convert the code into benign code. Identifying the specific code segments (tokens) is helpful in evaluating the validity of model predictions and making the necessary changes to the vulnerable code to make it a benign code. This helps the developer to use the domain knowledge to make an informed decision. Hence, model interpretability is an important factor in source code vulnerability detection. To this end, Local Interpretable Model-agnostic Explanations (LIME) [18] was used. LIME provides an explanation which is a local linear approximation of the trained model's behaviour [18]. LIME learns a sparse linear model by sampling instances around specific instances, approximating the trained model locally. LIME supports text classifiers and provides visual and textual artefacts that developers can understand. These explanations were used to further fine-tune data pre-processing by removing non-related tokens and keeping the important tokens. In addition, LIME provides the explanation for top K predictions, which helps to identify multiple vulnerabilities of a code.

4 Performance Evaluation

This section presents the results for different classifiers and features described in the previous section. All the results discussed in this section were based on the test set. As mentioned earlier, F1-Score was selected as the evaluation metric as it is the harmonic mean of precision and recall. Labels 0 and 1 represent benign and vulnerable classes of the binary classification model, whereas twenty CWE-IDs represent vulnerability classes of the multi-class classification model.

4.1 Machine Learning Models

As mentioned in the previous section, four machine learning algorithms were used to predict vulnerabilities using three features. N-gram includes 2-gram and 3-gram. Table 1 summarize the F1-Score for binary classification models for BoW, 2-gram, 3-gram and TF-IDF features. The best model performance was obtained with the default parameters. The BoW feature achieved a higher or similar F1-Score than n-gram for all algorithms except the XGB algorithm. XGB algorithm showed a very low detection capability for benign class for all features, even with different hyper-parameters. This might be due to the large number of available hyperparameters of XGB, and the selected grid search values were out of the optimum values for the binary classification. The RF algorithm achieved a significantly higher F1-Score than other algorithms for TF-IDF. RF algorithm with the feature BoW outperformed all other algorithms and features and achieved 0.96 F1-Score.

Table 1. Performance of binary classification ML algorithms with BoW, n-gram, and TF-IDF features (F1-Score).

Class	NB				LR				RF				XGB			
	BoW	2-gram	3-gram	TF-IDF	BoW	2-gram	3-gram	TF-IDF	BoW	2-gram	3-gram	TF-IDF	BoW	2-gram	3-gram	TF-IDF
0	0.72	0.57	0.63	0.84	0.90	0.88	0.89	0.91	0.95	0.95	0.95	0.95	0	0.02	0.03	0
1	0.81	0.76	0.78	0.85	0.89	0.88	0.89	0.91	0.96	0.95	0.95	0.95	0.68	0.63	0.66	0.68
Overall	0.76	0.66	0.71	0.84	0.89	0.88	0.89	0.91	0.96	0.95	0.95	0.95	0.34	0.33	0.37	0.34

Table 2 presents the performance achieved by multi-class algorithms with respective features. NB algorithm achieved the lowest F1-Score for all features. For both NB and LR algorithms, increasing the n-gram caused to achieve the same F1-Score as BoW or slight detection improvement. In contrast, the opposite was observed for RF and XGB algorithms. F1-Score was reduced when increasing the n-gram. RF and XGB algorithms for BoW and TF-IDF showed nearly similar detection capabilities.

According to the results, the best overall F1-Score was obtained as 0.85 for XGB algorithm with BoW features. Overall, BoW features performed better than the n-gram features. Generally, higher n-gram models contain more information about the word (token) contexts. However, this increases the data sparsity with the n. This might be one possible reason for the lower F1-Score for n-gram based models compared to BoW based models. Another possible reason would be the association of key terms with the vulnerabilities than the term combinations. Combining these key terms with the nearby terms might reduce the vulnerability detection capability. CWE-IDs which had over 20,000 source code samples, achieved over 0.80 F1-Scores, whereas other classes showed comparatively low detection capability. However, CWE-ID 676 detection rate is higher for all algorithms regardless of the dataset size. Usage of potentially dangerous functions such as strcat(), strcpy() and sprintf() introduce the CWE-ID 676 vulnerability. The frequent appearance of these vulnerable terms could be a reason for the higher detection rate.

Multi-class classification results indicate the detection rate likely to be associated with the dataset size for each class. To verify this, all classes over 20000 samples were considered and the remaining classes were categorized as 'other' category. This produced 12 unique classes compared to 20 classes used in the previous model. The best performing XGB with BoW feature was used to evaluate the performance. Table 3 presents the performance achieved for increased sample size. As expected, this improved the overall F1-Score by 4%.

Detection latency is a critical criterion in a production environment for real-time predictions. This highly depends on the number of features used and model complexity. Since BoW provided the best detection rate, BoW was used to evaluate the detection latency of four ML algorithms. Table 4 presents the average detection latency (ms) for one source code. NB provides the prediction in a very short time with lower detection rates. In contrast, RF takes much time despite

Table 2. Performance of multi-class classification ML algorithms with BoW, n-gram, and TF-IDF features (F1-Score).

CWE ID	NB				LR				RF				XGB			
	BoW	2-gram	3-gram	TF-IDF	BoW	2-gram	3-gram	TF-IDF	BoW	2-gram	3-gram	TF-IDF	BoW	2-gram	3-gram	TF-IDF
20	0.39	0.39	0.34	0.56	0.63	0.63	0.63	0.70	0.82	0.79	0.74	0.82	0.87	0.83	0.76	0.87
78	0.57	0.57	0.56	0.66	0.78	0.75	0.73	0.83	0.91	0.88	0.84	0.9	0.95	0.91	0.85	0.95
120	0.06	0.34	0.35	0.55	0.59	0.60	0.59	0.62	0.80	0.78	0.75	0.79	0.83	0.82	0.78	0.82
126	0.30	0.32	0.32	0.53	0.58	0.60	0.61	0.66	0.83	0.80	0.75	0.83	0.87	0.84	0.80	0.87
134	0.40	0.43	0.45	0.54	0.65	0.68	0.69	0.69	0.85	0.82	0.80	0.85	0.86	0.84	0.79	0.86
190	0.35	0.29	0.28	0.57	0.70	0.71	0.68	0.73	0.88	0.87	0.83	0.88	0.91	0.89	0.83	0.90
327	0.57	0.53	0.51	0.69	0.87	0.80	0.75	0.84	0.94	0.90	0.85	0.94	0.96	0.91	0.83	0.96
362	0.49	0.50	0.49	0.58	0.71	0.69	0.67	0.71	0.84	0.82	0.79	0.83	0.87	0.84	0.81	0.87
377	0.26	0.23	0.24	0.32	0.36	0.41	0.48	0.62	0.74	0.67	0.62	0.73	0.86	0.72	0.65	0.85
398	0.70	0.73	0.74	0.74	0.86	0.87	0.87	0.86	0.93	0.92	0.91	0.93	0.94	0.94	0.92	0.93
401	0.39	0.42	0.43	0.43	0.42	0.54	0.59	0.62	0.78	0.76	0.73	0.77	0.79	0.80	0.77	0.79
457	0.39	0.40	0.44	0.57	0.65	0.67	0.68	0.69	0.84	0.83	0.81	0.84	0.84	0.82	0.78	0.83
476	0.30	0.32	0.33	0.23	0.40	0.47	0.54	0.47	0.77	0.76	0.75	0.78	0.72	0.72	0.69	0.71
562	0.30	0.31	0.29	0.17	0.47	0.50	0.56	0.38	0.77	0.77	0.76	0.76	0.70	0.71	0.70	0.69
664	0.26	0.26	0.27	0.21	0.34	0.38	0.51	0.48	0.77	0.76	0.74	0.77	0.81	0.82	0.79	0.82
676	0.50	0.48	0.45	0.49	0.79	0.73	0.68	0.80	0.92	0.88	0.80	0.92	0.97	0.91	0.83	0.96
732	0.36	0.40	0.40	0.48	0.66	0.61	0.64	0.70	0.85	0.81	0.75	0.85	0.91	0.89	0.80	0.91
758	0.52	0.53	0.52	0.63	0.70	0.73	0.78	0.76	0.92	0.92	0.91	0.92	0.89	0.87	0.83	0.89
775	0.27	0.27	0.30	0.44	0.38	0.44	0.52	0.52	0.68	0.66	0.64	0.66	0.72	0.73	0.71	0.70
788	0.10	0.29	0.33	0.23	0.16	0.21	0.30	0.43	0.66	0.67	0.65	0.65	0.64	0.67	0.64	0.63
Overall	0.37	0.40	0.40	0.48	0.59	0.60	0.62	0.66	0.82	0.80	0.77	0.82	0.85	0.82	0.78	0.84

Table 3. Performance of XGB algorithm with BoW for 12 classes (F1-Score).

CWE ID	120	126	134	190	208	327	362	398	457	758	780	Other	Overall
F1-Score	0.8	0.88	0.86	0.9	0.87	0.96	0.87	0.94	0.83	0.88	0.96	0.89	0.89

a higher detection rate. Overall, among the selected algorithms, XGB provides the best detection latency and detection rate tradeoff.

Table 4. Average detection latency.

ML Algorithm	Detection latency (ms)
NB	0.005
LR	8.378
RF	175.968
XGB	**14.378**

4.2 Explainable AI

Even though ML algorithms with BoW showed a higher detection rate, this is not much useful unless the reasons behind these predictions are known. Hence, LIME was used to identify the vulnerable code segments of each source code and potential other CWE-IDs which were not available as a ground truth. This is

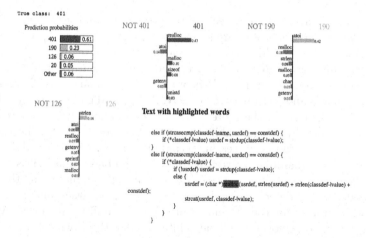

Fig. 3. Explainability of the predictions.

highly important as multiple CWE-IDs might be there due to parent-child relationships. The selected example presented in Fig. 3 includes CWE-ID 401 as the vulnerability. This is relevant to the missing release of memory after an effective Lifetime. Developers should sufficiently track and release allocated memory after it has been used [3]. XGB accurately predicts the CWE-ID 401 as the vulnerability of this source code. LIME provides the prediction probabilities for the top 4 predictions and respective features (tokens) that caused the vulnerability. Further, LIME provides the visualization of highlighted code. Since the original codes were pre-processed, this shows the pre-processed code. In this example, it identified that 'realloc', 'malloc', 'sizeof' and 'unistd' positively affect towards CWE-ID 401. These tokens are highlighted with brown colour in the code. Even though the ground truth was 401, as expected, this identified other possible vulnerabilities as well. CWE-ID 190 is another vulnerability that lies in this code due to inappropriate usage of function 'atoi'. Additionally, inappropriate usage of 'strlen' leads to CWE-ID 126, also identified by the algorithm as the 3rd possible vulnerability.

Based on these features, the developer can examine the code regardless of its number of code lines and convert the vulnerable code into benign code by changing the respective feature usage. These explanations also can be used to optimise the feature pre-processing. There might be some features that are not useful to predict the vulnerability and still, the algorithm identifies them as valid features due to dataset bias. These features can be identified by analysing the LIME output, which helps to perform the required pre-processing to remove such features continuously.

5   Conclusion and Future Works

Vulnerable source code sometime can cause critical security flaws. Therefore, the weaknesses of the source code must be reduced to a great extent. Though a few methods are available to detect source code vulnerabilities, their accuracies and generalization capabilities are low. Existing methods do not provide reasons for the vulnerabilities, which is very important to the developers. The proposed method in this work can detect source code vulnerabilities in C/C++ using an ML-based approach with an F1-Score of 0.96 in binary classification (with RF classifier) and an F1-Score of 0.85 in CWE-ID-based multi-class classification (with XGB classifier). Furthermore, XAI was also applied in this work to explain the causes of particular vulnerabilities. The F1-Score can be further increased by improving the data pre-processing techniques and extending the dataset with more source code examples. Currently, the CWE-ID based multi-class classification model can detect twenty types of weaknesses, and by increasing the sample source code, it can detect more classes with higher accuracy and improve the detection capability for the extremely broad vulnerability categories. An automated solution to perform that is also integrated with a live web portal. Once the dataset contains a high volume of data, it can also be explored as a future improvement since there can be vulnerable source code associated with more than one CWE-ID. Once the vulnerabilities are detected, mitigation methods can also be proposed by integrating more features in XAI for future improvement. Finally, the model will be deployed with a live web portal to validate under real-world settings.

Acknowledgment. This work has been funded by The Scottish Funding Council, we are thankful to the funder for their support.

Appendix: Common Weaknesses in C/C++ Source Code

CWE-ID	CWE-Name	Sample Vulnerable C/C++ Code
CWE-20	Improper Input Validation	board = (board_square_t*) malloc(m * n * sizeof(board_square_t));
CWE-78	Improper Neutralization of Special Elements used in an OS Command ('OS Command Injection')	system(NULL)
CWE-120	Buffer Copy without Checking Size of Input ('Classic Buffer Overflow')	strcpy(buf, string);
CWE-126	Buffer Over-read	strncpy(Filename, argv[1], sizeof(Filename));
CWE-134	Use of Externally-Controlled Format String	snprintf(buf, 128, argv[1]);
CWE-190	Integer Overflow or Wraparound response	xmalloc(nresp*sizeof(char*));
CWE-327	Use of a Broken or Risky Cryptographic Algorithm	EVP_des_ecb();
CWE-362	Concurrent Execution using Shared Resource with Improper Synchronization ('Race Condition')	pthread_mutex_lock(mutex);
CWE-401	Missing Release of Memory after Effective Lifetime	char buf = (char) malloc(BLOCK_SIZE); read(fd, buf, BLOCK_SIZE) != BLOCK_SIZE;
CWE-457	Use of Uninitialized Variable	char *test_string; if (i != err_val) test_string = "Hello World!"; printf("%s", test_string);
CWE-676	Use of Potentially Dangerous Function	char buf[24]; strcpy(buf, string);

References

1. Bilgin, Z., Ersoy, M.A., Soykan, E.U., Tomur, E., Çomak, P., Karaçay, L.: Vulnerability prediction from source code using machine learning. IEEE Access **8**, 150672–150684 (2020)
2. Chakraborty, S., Krishna, R., Ding, Y., Ray, B.: Deep learning based vulnerability detection: are we there yet? IEEE Trans. Softw. Eng. **48**(9), 3280–3296 (2022). https://doi.org/10.1109/TSE.2021.3087402
3. Corporation, M: Common Weakness Enumeration (CWE) (2022). https://cwe.mitre.org/. Accessed 01 Feb 2022
4. Corporation, M: CVE Details (2022). https://www.cvedetails.com/. Accessed 01 Feb 2022
5. Dam, H.K., Tran, T., Pham, T., Ng, S.W., Grundy, J., Ghose, A.: Automatic feature learning for vulnerability prediction. arXiv preprint arXiv:1708.02368 (2017)
6. Du, X., et al.: Leopard: identifying vulnerable code for vulnerability assessment through program metrics. In: 2019 IEEE/ACM 41st International Conference on Software Engineering (ICSE), pp. 60–71. IEEE (2019)
7. Fujdiak, R., et al.: Managing the secure software development. In: 2019 10th IFIP International Conference on New Technologies, Mobility and Security (NTMS), pp. 1–4 (2019). https://doi.org/10.1109/NTMS.2019.8763845
8. Grieco, G., Grinblat, G.L., Uzal, L., Rawat, S., Feist, J., Mounier, L.: Toward large-scale vulnerability discovery using machine learning. In: Proceedings of the Sixth ACM Conference on Data and Application Security and Privacy, pp. 85–96 (2016)
9. Harer, J.A., et al.: Automated software vulnerability detection with machine learning. arXiv preprint arXiv:1803.04497 (2018)
10. Hata, H., Mizuno, O., Kikuno, T.: Fault-prone module detection using large-scale text features based on spam filtering. Empir. Softw. Eng. **15**(2), 147–165 (2010)
11. Jimenez, M.: Evaluating vulnerability prediction models. Ph.D. thesis, University of Luxembourg, Luxembourg (2018)
12. Jimenez, M., Rwemalika, R., Papadakis, M., Sarro, F., Le Traon, Y., Harman, M.: The importance of accounting for real-world labelling when predicting software vulnerabilities. In: Proceedings of the 2019 27th ACM Joint Meeting on European Software Engineering Conference and Symposium on the Foundations of Software Engineering, pp. 695–705 (2019)
13. Jin, Z., Yu, Y.: Current and future research of machine learning based vulnerability detection. In: 2018 Eighth International Conference on Instrumentation & Measurement, Computer, Communication and Control (IMCCC), pp. 1562–1566 (2018). https://doi.org/10.1109/IMCCC.2018.00322
14. Li, Z., et al.: VulDeePecker: a deep learning-based system for vulnerability detection. arXiv preprint arXiv:1801.01681 (2018)
15. Morgan, S.: Is poor software development the biggest cyber threat (2015). https://www.csoonline.com/article/2978858
16. Pang, Y., Xue, X., Namin, A.S.: Predicting vulnerable software components through N-gram analysis and statistical feature selection. In: 2015 IEEE 14th International Conference on Machine Learning and Applications (ICMLA), pp. 543–548 (2015). https://doi.org/10.1109/ICMLA.2015.99
17. Pereira, J.D., Vieira, M.: On the use of open-source C/C++ static analysis tools in large projects. In: 2020 16th European Dependable Computing Conference (EDCC), pp. 97–102. IEEE (2020). https://doi.org/10.1109/EDCC51268.2020.00025

18. Ribeiro, M.T., Singh, S., Guestrin, C.: "Why should I trust you?" explaining the predictions of any classifier. In: Proceedings of the 22nd ACM SIGKDD International Conference on Knowledge Discovery and Data Mining, pp. 1135–1144 (2016)
19. Russell, R., et al.: Automated vulnerability detection in source code using deep representation learning. In: 2018 17th IEEE International Conference on Machine Learning and Applications (ICMLA), pp. 757–762. IEEE (2018)
20. Scandariato, R., Walden, J., Hovsepyan, A., Joosen, W.: Predicting vulnerable software components via text mining. IEEE Trans. Softw. Eng. **40**(10), 993–1006 (2014)
21. Senanayake, J., Kalutarage, H., Al-Kadri, M.O.: Android mobile malware detection using machine learning: a systematic review. Electronics **10**(13) (2021). https://doi.org/10.3390/electronics10131606. https://www.mdpi.com/2079-9292/10/13/1606
22. Senanayake, J., Kalutarage, H., Al-Kadri, M.O., Petrovski, A., Piras, L.: Android source code vulnerability detection: a systematic literature review. ACM Comput. Surv. (2022). https://doi.org/10.1145/3556974, just Accepted
23. Senanayake, J., Kalutarage, H., Al-Kadri, M.O., Petrovski, A., Piras, L.: Developing secured android applications by mitigating code vulnerabilities with machine learning. In: Proceedings of the 2022 ACM on Asia Conference on Computer and Communications Security, ASIA CCS 2022, pp. 1255–1257. Association for Computing Machinery, New York (2022). https://doi.org/10.1145/3488932.3527290
24. Tahaei, M., Vaniea, K.: A survey on developer-centred security. In: 2019 IEEE European Symposium on Security and Privacy Workshops (EuroS&PW), pp. 129–138 (2019). https://doi.org/10.1109/EuroSPW.2019.00021
25. Wile, D.S.: Abstract syntax from concrete syntax. In: Proceedings of the 19th International Conference on Software Engineering, pp. 472–480 (1997)
26. Xie, J., Lipford, H.R., Chu, B.: Why do programmers make security errors? In: 2011 IEEE Symposium on Visual Languages and Human-Centric Computing (VL/HCC), pp. 161–164 (2011). https://doi.org/10.1109/VLHCC.2011.6070393
27. Yamaguchi, F., Lottmann, M., Rieck, K.: Generalized vulnerability extrapolation using abstract syntax trees. In: Proceedings of the 28th Annual Computer Security Applications Conference, pp. 359–368 (2012)
28. Zeng, P., Lin, G., Pan, L., Tai, Y., Zhang, J.: Software vulnerability analysis and discovery using deep learning techniques: a survey. IEEE Access (2020)
29. Zhou, Y., Liu, S., Siow, J., Du, X., Liu, Y.: Devign: Effective vulnerability identification by learning comprehensive program semantics via graph neural networks. In: NeurIPS (2019)

Towards Verifying Physical Assumption in Card-Based Cryptography

Masahisa Shimano[1]([✉])[iD], Kazuo Sakiyama[1][iD], and Daiki Miyahara[1,2][iD]

[1] The University of Electro-Communications, Tokyo, Japan
{m.shimano,sakiyama,miyahara}@uec.ac.jp
[2] National Institute of Advanced Industrial Science and Technology, Tokyo, Japan

Abstract. Card-based cryptography realizes cryptographic tasks, such as secure computation, with a deck of physical cards. The primary research subjects for card-based cryptography are theoretical studies that, for example, propose efficient protocols regarding the number of required cards and procedures. However, almost all prior studies are based on the ideal physical assumption that the backs of all cards are indistinguishable without verification. This study addresses this assumption from a physical perspective to improve the security of card-based cryptography. In the first attempt, we assume a strong attacker who uses ink and a high-performance camera to distinguish the backs of the cards. We experimented with them and confirmed that such an attacker could identify the inked area of the back by analyzing an image captured by the camera. Based on our study, one can address another approach, such as using invisible oil and smartphone cameras to verify the physical assumption. This study is a seminal work that addresses this physical assumption. In addition to the verification, we study secret information that such a strong attacker can obtain during the execution of card-based protocols.

Keywords: Card-based cryptography · Hyperspectral camera · Physical assumption

1 Introduction

Card-based cryptography is a method of realizing cryptographic tasks, such as a secure computation using a deck of physical cards shown in Fig. 1. In card-based cryptography, a value is typically represented by a sequence of cards called a *commitment*. Each player holding an input value places a commitment that represents the value. Then, they shuffle and reveal the cards to obtain only the output value, indicating that no information about the input values is revealed during the computation process. Because card-based cryptography uses a deck of "real" cards to perform secure computations, it is of educational value [12,19].

© The Author(s), under exclusive license to Springer Nature Switzerland AG 2023
G. Bella et al. (Eds.): SecITC 2022, LNCS 13809, pp. 289–305, 2023.
https://doi.org/10.1007/978-3-031-32636-3_17

1.1   Background

Research on card-based cryptography began with a card-based protocol called the five-card trick, invented by Den Boer in 1989 [3]. Since then, various protocols have been proposed [2,8,9,11,13,16,18,20,24]. Further, theoretical studies on the necessary and sufficient number of required cards have been conducted [4,8,9,23]. Most of these theoretical studies are based on the *physical assumption* [7] that the backs of all cards are indistinguishable, as is for poker and other card games. However, this physical assumption is ideal and does not always hold in practice; a malicious player can tamper with cards to secretly distinguish the backs. Hence, we must discuss this from an engineering perspective and understand the actual capabilities of attackers.

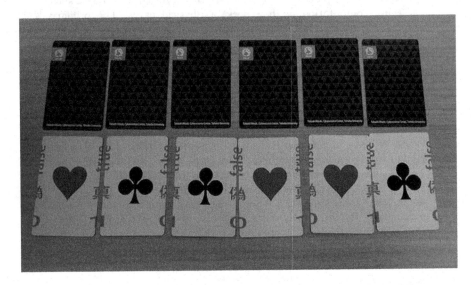

Fig. 1. Sequence of cards typically used in card-based cryptography

1.2   Contributions

We investigate the validity of the physical assumption in card-based cryptography. This study aims to improve the security of card-based cryptography and apply it to daily card games, such as poker games. More precisely, we investigate whether an attacker can identify a card from the back using practical instruments.

This study focuses on cameras because they are suitable for developing the physical security of card-based cryptography. In the first attempt, we assume a strong attacker who uses ink and a high-performance camera, e.g., *hyperspectral camera* introduced in Sect. 2. An attacker secretly inks the back of a card with

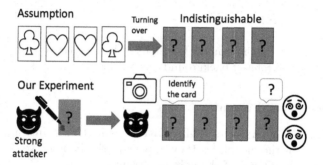

Fig. 2. Our aim and experiment

the same color as the design before starting a protocol, making it inconspicuous to the human eye. When performing the protocol, the attacker takes a picture using a high-performance camera to read the inked area and identify the card. Through experiments, we confirmed that such an attacker could identify the inked card, and the physical assumption used in card-based cryptography does not always hold. Moreover, based on the experimental results, we discuss the physical properties of ink depending on its color and propose countermeasures. Based on this experiment, we can address another approach, such as using invisible oil and smartphone cameras to verify the physical assumption. This study is a seminal work addressing this physical assumption. Our aims and the experiment are summarized in Fig. 2.

We also theoretically examine the information about the input values that can be obtained by such a strong attacker. Because every player should privately make an input commitment at hand, an attacker (i.e., a malicious player) can secretly ink its commitment to identify it later. For instance, an attacker can ink a card under the table or use an ink-stained finger when making its own commitment so that nobody notices. This study selects the five-card trick [3], which computes the logical AND of two inputs, and the six-card AND (a.k.a. MS-AND [15]) to determine whether such an attacker can obtain information about the other player's input value. This attack was found to be effective for both players in the five-card trick, but only for one player in the MS-AND. This implies that the attack depends on protocol procedures.

1.3   Organization

The rest of this paper is organized as follows. In Sect. 2, we introduce a hyperspectral camera and related work. Section 3 describes the experimental tools and the environment. We describe our experimental results and discuss them in Sects. 4 and 5. Section 6 concludes the study. In Appendix A, we discuss secret information that a strong attacker can obtain.

2   Preliminaries

This section describes the general functions of hyperspectral cameras. Furthermore, we introduce related background and work.

2.1   Hyperspectral Camera

Typical cameras are known as RGB cameras. Using these cameras, we obtain a precise picture of the objects as they appear in the human eye. RGB cameras measure only three bands of the light spectrum.

Hyperspectral cameras measure multiple bands of the light spectrum and a regular image. Specifically, hyperspectral cameras can obtain a spectrum with over one hundred wavelengths per pixel of the captured image. Because the way light is reflected and absorbed by objects differs depending on their materials and colors, hyperspectral cameras help identify color differences and materials that are difficult to distinguish with the naked eye. Because of these characteristics, hyperspectral cameras were primarily used in military applications and remote sensing. However, recently, they have been used in various fields because they are less expensive, and their sizes are minimized.

2.2   Related Matters

In 2011, an incident using infrared contact lenses and invisible ink occurred during a casino card game [26]. Cheaters paid casino workers to mark decks of cards with invisible ink and then wore infrared contact lenses to read the ink and distinguish the marked cards.

Hyperspectral imaging techniques can identify the type of ink used in documents. Khan et al. [5] studied ink mismatch detection in the visible spectrum. The basis of this study is that similar colors of different ink products differ in spectrum depending on their materials.

2.3   Related Work

Mizuki and Shizuya [14] proposed a countermeasure to perform secure computations even if the backs of cards were scratched. Table 1 summarizes the differences between our study and their work. The most significant difference is verifying the physical assumption, that is, considering any situation wherein the assumption might not hold and inventing helpful countermeasures. Thus, this study includes their work [14]. Their countermeasures work under the assumption that everyone knows in advance where the cards are scratched. However, in our study, an attacker secretly applies the ink; hence, we should adopt a different approach to invent countermeasures.

Identifying cards by applying markers to their backs is called *card marking* and has been addressed for many years in casinos. Initially, one identifies cards creating small bumps by bending or crimping them, but recently markings have been applied to the designs of cards as the design of the backs has changed. Marking methods using ink are known as block-out. Kneitel [6] presented a case study on judging illegal card marking that occurred in casinos. However, detecting card marking using electronic devices such as hyperspectral cameras has not been studied. We also emphasize that our study is the first attempt to introduce card marking to the field of card-based cryptography.

Using invisible ink in card-based cryptography was first considered by Shinagawa [21]. These protocols legally use invisible ink to encode an integer on a card and "partially" reveal the integer by illuminating the covered card with a black light.

Table 1. Differences between existing work [14] and this study

Difference	[14]	This study
Objective	Secure computations	Verifying the physical assumption
Clue	Scuff (accidental)	Ink (intentional)
How to identify	Human eyes	Additional tools

3   Our Experiment

We experimented with ink and a hyperspectral camera to verify the physical assumption in card-based cryptography. We verified the possibility of distinguishing between inked and left untouched cards by comparing their spectra.

3.1   Hyperspectral Camera, Card, and Ink

This experiment used Specim IQ® (over \$10,000), commercialized by SPECIM, SPECTRAL IMAGING LTD. shown in Fig. 3. The camera has a resolution of 512×512 pixels[1] and can obtain a spectrum in the range of wavelengths from 397 to 1000 nm in steps of 3 nm for each pixel. Figure 4 illustrates the card to be photographed. The card on the left side was not inked, and only the center of the right card was inked. We only photograph the right card. Table 2 summarizes the 10 commercial colored inks (five blue and five black inks) used in this experiment.[2]

---

[1] This resolution is significantly lower than the latest smartphone cameras (about 10 megapixels).

[2] As seen from Fig. 4, one could notice the color difference if one carefully observes the backs. This is because the blue reflection area is the one the human eye can detect. In this study, however, we focus on using a high-performance camera to identify the inked backs. This study does not discuss the card's wear, material, and texture.

Table 2. Commercial ink products used in the experiment

Blue	Black
SARASA CLIP®	JETSTREAM®
Mackeenock®	SARASA CLIP®
Playcolor K®	PENTEL Sign PEN®
uni-ball Signo®	Magic Ink®
Super Petit®	Mackeework®

Fig. 3. Specim IQ®

3.2 Filming Environment

We captured the photos in a darkened room with a halogen lamp illuminating the card to be photographed, as shown in Fig. 5. The reason for using a halogen lamp instead of a fluorescent lamp in a room is that it emits light over a broad wavelength band (refer to the figures in [25] for their spectra).

As shown in Fig. 5, when photographing, a white panel is lined up on the card. This is because a calibration process is required to generate the spectral data. White reflects light of all wavelengths; assuming that light shone on the white plate is all reflected, spectral data in the other areas are generated on this assumption.

As discussed previously, we prepared equipment, such as a halogen lamp, to obtain spectral data; hence, an attacker cannot execute this attack secretly. That is, our filming environment is ideal for an attacker. This is because we assume a strong attacker in this study. We believe that an attacker can create this ideal

Fig. 4. The backs of two cards. Blue ink has adhered to the right one near the center (Color figure online)

environment and photograph the backs of cards without anyone notice it after we execute a card-based protocol. This issue is also discussed in Sect. 6.

3.3 Experimental Procedure

Here, we describe our experimental procedure.

1. Mark specific areas of the back of a card near the center with one of the 10 ink products listed in Table 2 and lightly wipe the inked area with a finger.
2. Place the white plate and the inked card side by side and illuminate them using the halogen lamp.
3. Photograph the inked card and the white plate using Specim IQ® and obtain the spectra of the inked and left untouched areas of the card.
4. Use a standard function called SAM Mask described in Sect. 3.4 to confirm that the entire inked area can be revealed.
5. Observe differences in the spectra of inked and left untouched areas.

3.4 Spectral Angle Mapper

The spectral angle mapper (SAM) compares and classifies spectra [10]. The SAM compares the two spectra by treating them as vectors and calculating their angles. Here, the vector represents a multidimensional vector of the reflectance in each band. The following formula[3] is used in the analysis software attached

---

[3] The SAM initially calculates the angle (in the radian), but this analysis software calculates the cosine of the angle.

Fig. 5. Filming environment

to Specim IQ®:

$$\theta(x, y) = \frac{\sum_{i=1}^{n} x_i y_i}{\sqrt{(\sum_{i=1}^{n} x_i^2)}\sqrt{(\sum_{i=1}^{n} y_i^2)}},$$

where x and y denote the spectra and n denotes the number of bands. This formula implies that the closer the value to one, the more similar the two spectra. This software shows pixels with similar spectra (as shown in Fig. 7) after calculating the angle between each pixel and setting a threshold value. Our experiment used this function to verify whether inked and left untouched areas could be clearly identified.

4   Experimental Result

This section describes the results of the experiments. We examined spectra to determine the differences observed in each wavelength band.

4.1   Blue Ink

We describe the results of photographing the back of a card inked with each blue-ink product. Figure 6 shows the obtained spectra of the back inked with uni-ball Signo® and that of the uninked area. (Due to the space and size limits, let us omit the remaining four spectra.)

The spectra are different in the blue-to-green transition from 397 to 548 nm and in the near-infrared region from 800 nm onward. They can be readily distinguished at approximately 430 nm and 800 nm for certain ink products.

Using the SAM, we could display inked areas for all ink products, where we set a threshold value of 0.9996. Figure 7 depicts the inked area with uni-ball Signo® using the SAM, where the threshold value was 0.9998.

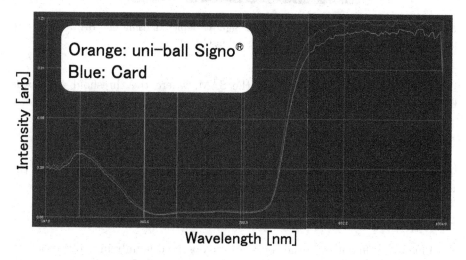

Fig. 6. Obtained spectra of the back inked with uni-ball Signo® (orange-lined) and that of the uninked area (blue-lined) (Color figure online)

4.2   Black Ink

We describe the results of photography for each black-ink product. Figure 8 shows the obtained spectra of the back inked with Magic Ink® and the uninked area.

Because the light in the visible-light range from 397 to 800 nm was absorbed, no discernible difference could be observed. Some differences were observed in the near-infrared region after 800 nm, but they could not be discerned from the graph.

However, for Magic Ink® and Mackeework®, we can display the inked area using the SAM. We identified the inked and left untouched areas for the two inked products, where we set a threshold value of 0.9960. Figure 9 depicts the

Fig. 7. Inked area for blue ink uni-ball Signo® depicted using the SAM where the threshold value was 0.9998 (Color figure online)

inked area with Magic Ink® using the SAM, where the threshold value was 0.9960.

5   Discussion

This section discusses the observed differences in the spectra depending on the type of ink in the experimental results described in Sect. 4.

5.1   Spectrum in Blue Ink

For blue ink, differences in the spectra were observed mainly in two wavelength regions, from 397 to 548 nm and from 800 nm onward. Herein, we discuss the differences in the two wavelength ranges.

Visible-light from 397 to 548 nm is detected by the human eye. The difference in this wavelength region may be due to the pigment composition of ink. More precisely, solvents and colorants composing ink caused the difference in spectra although their colors were similar blue. Among the five blue inks used in this study, only the uni-ball Signo® has a higher reflection rate in the visible-light range, whereas the remaining four inks have almost the same or a lower reflection rate.

Wavelengths above 800 nm are in the infrared wavelength region and cannot be detected by the human eye. Therefore, the difference in this region originates not from their colors, but their ink-specific components. The main components of the ink are solvents and colorants. Solvents are classified as oil- and water-based, whereas colorants are classified as dyes and pigments. Oil-based ink uses volatile organic solvents and is highly viscous, whereas water-based ink uses water and has a low viscosity. The difference between dyes and pigments is that dyes are soluble in solvents, whereas pigments are not.

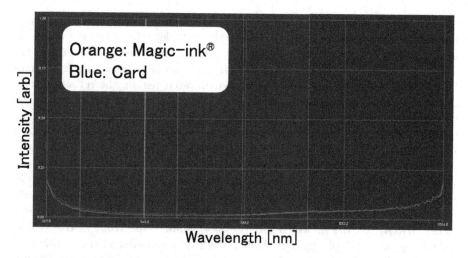

Fig. 8. Obtained spectra of the back inked with Magic Ink® and that of the uninked area (Color figure online)

Fig. 9. Inked area for black-ink Magic Ink® depicted by using the SAM where the threshold value was 0.9960 (Color figure online)

Comparing the shapes of the spectra in the infrared wavelengths, SARASA CLIP®, Playcolor K®, and Super Petit® are similar to the spectrum of the card. Among these three ink products, SARASA CLIP® and Super Petit® use water-based pigments, whereas Playcolor K® uses water-based dyes. Uni-ball Signo® had a slightly lower spectrum than the three ink products. This is possibly because the uni-ball Signo® is called gel ink, which is water-based, but has a higher viscosity than the three ink products. Mackeenock® is oil-based ink; thus, its reflection rate is below that of the others.

The feasibility of attacks using the five ink products depends on the characteristics of the ink used in secretly conducting attacks. The ideal ink for attacks is one such that its spectrum is indistinguishable from that of the card in the visible-light range, but differs in the near-infrared range because such ink cannot be detected by the human eye. In the near-infrared region, the reflection ratio decreases in the order of water-, gel-, and oil-based ink. Although we can identify oil-based ink simply by observing the spectrum in the near-infrared, we can quickly notice that oil-based ink used has adhered to the card visually. Water-based ink has the most similar spectra in the near-infrared region to the card, making it more difficult to distinguish it from the card. However, it is more difficult to visually confirm where the ink adhered compared to oil-based ink. Gel ink is between oil- and water-based, but it is as tricky as water-based to visually confirm the ink adhesion points. Therefore, among the five ink products used, either SARASA CLIP®, which has the most similar spectrum in the visible-light range, or uni-ball Signo®, which is slightly less similar in the visible-light range, but the difference is easily observed in the near-infrared range, is feasible for attacks. We believe that oil-based ink is the most feasible among the three types of ink because its spectra are the most similar to those of the card in the visible-light range; hence, it is interesting to experiment with multiple oil-based ink products.

Although the spectra of blue ink and the blue design on the back of the card are similar, they do not match perfectly because of the components and pigments of the ink. The above discussion holds for any color other than black and white with a unique reflection ratio.

5.2   Spectrum in Black Ink

When photographed with black ink, wavelengths from 397 to 800 nm, which are in the visible-light range, are almost entirely absorbed, and wavelengths after 800 nm are only slightly reflected. This is because black is a light-absorbing color.

For Magic Ink® and Mackeework®, the SAM calculation was able to indicate the inked area. Both of them use oil-based dyes. Regarding the other three ink products, only JETSTREAM® is oil-based, and the other two are water-based. Although JETSTREAM ink® is oil-based, it is characterized by low viscosity.[4]

Magic Ink® and Mackeework® are the only two products that use dyes as coloring agents. Dyes are less sensitive to light than pigments, and their colors fade after prolonged exposure to light. Because black absorbs light, the spectrum may have been affected by light absorption from the lighting during the photoshoot.

In summary, the following two conditions are considered necessary for attacks using black ink: high ink viscosity and weak lightfastness.

---

[4] Refer to the following URL for ink details. https://www.mpuni.co.jp/en/company/rd/index.html.

6 Conclusion

In this study, we used ink and a hyperspectral camera in the experiments to evaluate the validity of the physical assumption in card-based cryptography. Our experimental results showed that it is possible to identify the backs of cards. This indicates that the physical assumption is not always valid. We also conducted theoretical research on the potential leakage of information in certain card-based protocols if the physical assumption is not upheld in practice. Our findings showed that it varies depending on the specific protocol procedures. Overall, this study contributes to both the engineering and theoretical aspects of card-based cryptography.

In future work, we plan to investigate the feasibility of this attack using other invisible materials, such as water or oil. Sebum is also a promising candidate; if a high-performance camera is able to identify a large amount of human-specific sebum on a card, we are able to quickly obtain information about the input values. Additionally, we will examine the persistence and durability of ink attached to a card. While the durability of the ink is not a concern, the persistence of the ink must be verified to ensure that the same results can be obtained from ink that has been attached for several days prior to the capture.

Acknowledgements. We thank the anonymous referees, whose comments have helped us improve the presentation of the paper. This work was supported in part by JSPS KAKENHI Grant Number JP18H05289.

A Theoretical Considerations for Attacks

In Sect. 4, we confirmed that attacks using ink and the hyperspectral camera are possible. This appendix selects the five-card trick [3] and MS-AND [15] as examples and clarifies that such an attack leaks information about input values.

A.1 How to Execute the Protocol

The basic setup is described in Sect. 1. We use two colored cards: ♣ and ♡. A player uses these two cards to encode Boolean values as follows:

$$♣♡ = 0, \qquad ♡♣ = 1.$$

When two face-down cards represent a bit $x \in \{0, 1\}$ based on this encoding, we call these cards a commitment to x and denote it as follows:

In the five-card trick and MS-AND, Alice and Bob place commitments to $a, b \in \{0, 1\}$ on the table, respectively, and use additional cards to obtain only the value of $a \wedge b$.

The five-card trick uses an additional card ♡. First, the commitment to $\overline{a}$ and b are lined up[5]. The additional face-down card is then placed between the two commitments. Note that the three consecutive cards in the middle are reds if and only if $a = b = 1$. Subsequently, a cyclic shuffling operation called *random cut* is performed to randomize the order, and all five cards are finally turned over. Here, we have $a \wedge b = 1$ if the three reds are consecutive apart from the cyclic shift; otherwise, $a \wedge b = 0$ as follows:

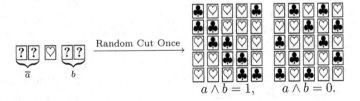

In the MS-AND, we place an additional commitment to 0 between the two commitments as follows:

$$\boxed{?}\boxed{?}\boxed{♣}\boxed{♡}\boxed{?}\boxed{?} \quad \rightarrow \quad \boxed{?}\boxed{?}\boxed{?}\boxed{?}\boxed{?}\boxed{?}.$$

$$\underbrace{}_{a} \quad \underbrace{}_{b} \qquad \underbrace{}_{a} \quad \underbrace{}_{0} \quad \underbrace{}_{b}$$

First, the second card from the left and the two cards in the middle are swapped. Second, a shuffling operation called a random bisection cut is applied to the sequence; that is, the left and right halves are swapped randomly. The second and third cards are then replaced with the fourth card. Finally, the first two cards are revealed, and a commitment to $a \wedge b$ can be obtained as follows:

$$\boxed{♣}\boxed{♡}\boxed{?}\boxed{?}\boxed{?}\boxed{?} \quad \text{or} \quad \boxed{♡}\boxed{♣}\boxed{?}\boxed{?}\boxed{?}\boxed{?}.$$

$$\qquad\underbrace{}_{a \wedge b} \qquad\qquad\qquad \underbrace{}_{a \wedge b}$$

A.2   Information Obtained from This Attack

Recall that the assumed attacker can identify the inked card. Because every player privately manipulates its commitment before starting a protocol, we consider an attacker who secretly inks their own commitment. Let us consider information that the attacker can gain in the two protocols presented previously.

In the five-card trick [3], if both players input commitments to 1, they can quickly determine that the other's input is 1 from the output value. Consider whether information about the other's input can be obtained if the attacker inputs a commitment to 0. We focus on the sequence of cards after shuffling, namely, the following five sequences:

$$\boxed{♡}\boxed{♣}\boxed{♡}\boxed{♣}\boxed{♡}, \quad \boxed{♡}\boxed{♡}\boxed{♣}\boxed{♡}\boxed{♣}, \quad \boxed{♣}\boxed{♡}\boxed{♡}\boxed{♣}\boxed{♡}, \quad \boxed{♡}\boxed{♣}\boxed{♡}\boxed{♡}\boxed{♣}, \quad \boxed{♣}\boxed{♡}\boxed{♡}\boxed{♣}\boxed{♡}.$$

---

[5] The negation of a commitment can be obtained simply by swapping the two cards comprising the commitment.

If one knows the position of one's commitment, the value of the other's commitment can be derived because all the cards are revealed. In summary, if we know which card we have placed, we can always obtain the value of the other's input in the five-card trick.

In the MS-AND [15], however, we found that information gained by an attacker depends on their position. First, we consider the case where Alice is an attacker. Assume that Alice inputs a commitment to 0 and always knows the location of her ♡. Here, if we denote by ? all the cards other than her ♡ when obtaining the output commitment, the sequence is as follows:

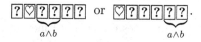

However, to obtain the output commitment, we reveal the two cards on the left. Thus, even if Alice knows the location of her commitment, she obtains no information about Bob's input.

However, Bob can obtain Alice's input value under the same conditions because the sequence when obtaining the output commitment is as follows:

$$\boxed{?}\boxed{?}\boxed{?}\boxed{♡}\boxed{?}\boxed{?} \quad \text{or} \quad \boxed{?}\boxed{?}\boxed{?}\boxed{?}\boxed{?}\boxed{♡}.$$

To obtain the output commitment, the two cards on the left are revealed, which represent a or $\bar{a}$. Knowing the position of Bob's ♡, he can determine whether the two cards represent a or $\bar{a}$. If his ♡ is in the fourth and the first two revealed cards are ♣♡, the two cards represent $\bar{a}$ and Bob has $a = 1$. Thus, Bob can obtain Alice's input, which holds even if the card to be marked is ♣.

It is interesting to discuss why such asymmetry arises, that is, the attack effectiveness changes depending on the protocols, and to elucidate the condition for such asymmetry. In the case of the MS-AND [15], the reason is clear because the two revealed cards before obtaining the output commitment is either a commitment to a or $\bar{a}$ because of the shuffle applied previously. Thus, Alice gains no information even if her commitment is marked by her. However, this property is specific to the MS-AND, and a card-based protocol often reveals one of the attacker's commitment, the other's commitment, and additional cards (e.g., [1,17]); hence, the condition for such asymmetry is not trivial. To discover this, we need to study many card-based protocols, classifying cards possibly revealed in a protocol and clarifying whether an attacker can gain information about the other's input value; we will leave this in our future work.

A.3 Discussion

We discuss whether this attack is realistic. Although our study revealed that the inked areas could be identified as indicated in Sect. 3, this attack is limited because it uses a high-cost camera of over \$10,000. We plan to investigate the use of cameras in smartphones because they are widely available. In addition, conducting this attack during the execution of protocols is impossible without another player noticing because a halogen lamp must be prepared in this attack. This attack will be feasible at the end of the protocol. That is, an attacker remembers the order of the sequence of cards at the end and then conducts this attack without the other players watching it. One might think that this attack is infeasible because all cards are completely shuffled at the end of any card-based protocol to prevent leakage of information. However, no card-based protocol shuffles face-up cards at the end because they simply indicate either the output value, such as the five-card trick [3] or the following action, such as the MS-AND [15] (cf, [22]). Thus, this attack implies a new insight that all cards, including face-up cards, should be shuffled after the end of any card-based protocol.

Based on the experimental results, countermeasures against this attack include making the backs black and white, which have a unique reflection ratio and making the mesh of the backs finer. To physically prevent ink from adhering to the cards, the cards can be covered with sleeves.

References

1. Abe, Y., Hayashi, Y., Mizuki, T., Sone, H.: Five-card AND computations in committed format using only uniform cyclic shuffles. New Gener. Comput. **39**(1), 97–114 (2021). https://doi.org/10.1007/s00354-020-00110-2
2. Costiuc, M., Maimuţ, D., Teşeleanu, G.: Physical cryptography. In: Simion, E., Géraud-Stewart, R. (eds.) SecITC 2019. LNCS, vol. 12001, pp. 156–171. Springer, Cham (2020). https://doi.org/10.1007/978-3-030-41025-4_11
3. Boer, B.: More efficient match-making and satisfiability *the five card trick*. In: Quisquater, J.-J., Vandewalle, J. (eds.) EUROCRYPT 1989. LNCS, vol. 434, pp. 208–217. Springer, Heidelberg (1990). https://doi.org/10.1007/3-540-46885-4_23
4. Kastner, J., et al.: The minimum number of cards in practical card-based protocols. In: Takagi, T., Peyrin, T. (eds.) ASIACRYPT 2017. LNCS, vol. 10626, pp. 126–155. Springer, Cham (2017). https://doi.org/10.1007/978-3-319-70700-6_5
5. Khan, Z., Shafait, F., Mian, A.: Automatic ink mismatch detection for forensic document analysis. Pattern Recogn. **48**(11), 3615–3626 (2015). https://doi.org/10.1016/j.patcog.2015.04.008
6. Kneitel, A.: Casino countermeasures: are casinos cheating. Harv. J. Sports Ent. L. **10**, 55 (2019)
7. Koch, A.: The landscape of security from physical assumptions. In: 2021 IEEE Information Theory Workshop (ITW), Los Alamitos, CA, USA, pp. 1–6. IEEE (2021). https://doi.org/10.1109/ITW48936.2021.9611501
8. Koch, A., Schrempp, M., Kirsten, M.: Card-based cryptography meets formal verification. In: Galbraith, S.D., Moriai, S. (eds.) ASIACRYPT 2019. LNCS, vol. 11921, pp. 488–517. Springer, Cham (2019). https://doi.org/10.1007/978-3-030-34578-5_18
9. Koch, A., Walzer, S., Härtel, K.: Card-based cryptographic protocols using a minimal number of cards. In: Iwata, T., Cheon, J.H. (eds.) ASIACRYPT 2015. LNCS, vol. 9452, pp. 783–807. Springer, Heidelberg (2015). https://doi.org/10.1007/978-3-662-48797-6_32
10. Kruse, F., et al.: The spectral image processing system (SIPS)–interactive visualization and analysis of imaging spectrometer data. Remote Sens. Environ. **44**(2), 145–163 (1993). https://doi.org/10.1016/0034-4257(93)90013-N

11. Manabe, Y., Ono, H.: Secure card-based cryptographic protocols using private operations against malicious players. In: Maimut, D., Oprina, A.-G., Sauveron, D. (eds.) SecITC 2020. LNCS, vol. 12596, pp. 55–70. Springer, Cham (2021). https:// doi.org/10.1007/978-3-030-69255-1_5

12. Marcedone, A., Wen, Z., Shi, E.: Secure dating with four or fewer cards. Cryptology ePrint Archive, Report 2015/1031 (2015). https://eprint.iacr.org/2015/1031

13. Mizuki, T., Kumamoto, M., Sone, H.: The five-card trick can be done with four cards. In: Wang, X., Sako, K. (eds.) ASIACRYPT 2012. LNCS, vol. 7658, pp. 598–606. Springer, Heidelberg (2012). https://doi.org/10.1007/978-3-642-34961-4_36

14. Mizuki, T., Shizuya, H.: Practical card-based cryptography. In: Ferro, A., Luccio, F., Widmayer, P. (eds.) FUN 2014. LNCS, vol. 8496, pp. 313–324. Springer, Cham (2014). https://doi.org/10.1007/978-3-319-07890-8_27

15. Mizuki, T., Sone, H.: Six-card secure AND and four-card secure XOR. In: Deng, X., Hopcroft, J.E., Xue, J. (eds.) FAW 2009. LNCS, vol. 5598, pp. 358–369. Springer, Heidelberg (2009). https://doi.org/10.1007/978-3-642-02270-8_36

16. Nakai, T., Misawa, Y., Tokushige, Y., Iwamoto, M., Ohta, K.: How to solve millionaires' problem with two kinds of cards. New Gener. Comput. **39**(1), 73–96 (2021). https://doi.org/10.1007/s00354-020-00118-8

17. Niemi, V., Renvall, A.: Solitaire zero-knowledge. Fundam. Inf. **38**(1,2), 181–188 (1999). https://doi.org/10.3233/FI-1999-381214

18. Ono, H., Manabe, Y.: Card-based cryptographic logical computations using private operations. New Gener. Comput. **39**(1), 19–40 (2021). https://doi.org/10.1007/ s00354-020-00113-z

19. Pass, R., Shelat, A.: A course in cryptography (2010). https://www.cs.cornell.edu/ rafael/

20. Ruangwises, S., Itoh, T.: Securely computing the n-variable equality function with 2n cards. Theor. Comput. Sci. **887**, 99–110 (2021). https://doi.org/10.1016/j.tcs. 2021.07.007

21. Shinagawa, K.: Card-based cryptography with dihedral symmetry. New Gener. Comput. **39**(1), 41–71 (2021). https://doi.org/10.1007/s00354-020-00117-9

22. Shinagawa, K., Mizuki, T.: The six-card trick: secure computation of three-input equality. In: Lee, K. (ed.) ICISC 2018. LNCS, vol. 11396, pp. 123–131. Springer, Cham (2019). https://doi.org/10.1007/978-3-030-12146-4_8

23. Shinagawa, K., Nuida, K.: A single shuffle is enough for secure card-based computation of any Boolean circuit. Discret. Appl. Math. **289**, 248–261 (2021). https:// doi.org/10.1016/j.dam.2020.10.013

24. Shinoda, Y., Miyahara, D., Shinagawa, K., Mizuki, T., Sone, H.: Card-based covert lottery. In: Maimut, D., Oprina, A.-G., Sauveron, D. (eds.) SecITC 2020. LNCS, vol. 12596, pp. 257–270. Springer, Cham (2021). https://doi.org/10.1007/978-3-030-69255-1_17

25. Specim: Specim IQ user manual. https://www.specim.fi/downloads/iq/manual/ software/iq/topics/illumination.html. Accessed 1 July 2022

26. USA Today: Poker cheat who wore infrared contact lenses gets jail (2013). https:// www.usatoday.com/story/news/world/2013/09/26/france-card-sharp-infrared-contact-lenses-jailed/2878239/. Accessed 1 July 2022

The Security of Quasigroups Based Substitution Permutation Networks

George Teşeleanu[1,2]([✉])([iD])

[1] Advanced Technologies Institute, 10 Dinu Vintilă, Bucharest, Romania
`tgeorge@dcti.ro`
[2] Simion Stoilow Institute of Mathematics of the Romanian Academy,
21 Calea Grivitei, Bucharest, Romania

Abstract. The study of symmetric structures based on quasigroups is relatively new and certain gaps can be found in the literature. In this paper, we want to fill one of these gaps. More precisely, in this work we study substitution permutation networks based on quasigroups that make use of permutation layers that are non-linear relative to the quasigroup operation. We prove that for quasigroups isotopic with a group $\mathbb{G}$, the complexity of mounting a differential attack against this type of substitution permutation network is the same as attacking another symmetric structure based on $\mathbb{G}$. The resulting structure is interesting and new, and we hope that it will form the basis for future secure block ciphers.

1 Introduction

When designing a block cipher, one of the main challenges is to construct a set of permutations that are easy to implement and at the same time behave as random permutations. Keeping this in mind, three main approaches can be found in the literature [22]. Substitution-permutation networks (SPNs) construct a large block random looking permutation using a series of substitution[1] and permutation layers iterated over several rounds. A different approach is used to construct Feistel and Lai-Massey symmetric structures. Instead of using invertible building blocks, these two structures construct permutations using non-invertible components.

One of the most powerful tools used to attack block ciphers is differential cryptanalysis [14]. Introduced by Biham and Shamir [2], this type of attack exploits the way certain plaintext changes propagate to the ciphertext. If we used truly random permutations, we could predict these changes with a probability of $1/2^n$, where n is the number of input bits. Therefore, if n was for example 128 bits the probability would be negligible. Nevertheless, as stated before we should be able to easily describe the permutation and this is not the case for ideal permutations. Hence, in order to build practical block ciphers, designers need to use theoretical estimates based on certain assumptions that are not always valid in practice. In consequence, block ciphers are not ideal and this

---

[1] Comprised of several substitution boxes (s-boxes) with small block length.

G. Bella et al. (Eds.): SecITC 2022, LNCS 13809, pp. 306–319, 2023.
https://doi.org/10.1007/978-3-031-32636-3_18

makes them susceptible to differential cryptanalysis. Because of that, security against differential cryptanalysis is one of the basic design criteria for symmetric primitives [18].

Latin squares are $\ell \times \ell$ matrices which contain only ℓ symbols and have the property that each symbol appears only once in each row and only once in each column [10]. A set endowed with a multiplication table that is a Latin square forms a quasigroup. These structures can be thought of as a group that is not associative and does not have an identity element. Although quasigroups are not a popular choice when constructing cryptographic primitives, various designs based can still be found in the literature [1,6,7,11–13,15,16].

A very recent approach [3–5,8] uses commutative regular subgroups of the symmetric group to design SPN structures that appear secure against classical differential cryptanalysis, but are weaker with respect to a differential attack that uses a different group operation. Specifically, such a symmetrical structure has a level of security, in relation to differential attacks, which is dependent on the intended operation. This methodology is similar to the one used in this paper, because we also consider different operations to construct differential attacks against the proposed SPNs. Nevertheless, the scope of [3–5,8] is to show how a designer can embed a trapdoor into a symmetric structure[2], while ours is to investigate whether changing the group operation to a quasigroup one could strengthen an SPN structure against differential cryptanalysis.

In [20,21] the author introduces a straightforward generalization of the three main symmetric structures: SPNs, Feistel and Lai-Massey. Namely, instead of using a group operation between keys and (intermediary) plaintexts, the generalisations use a quasigroup one. When studying their security the author restricts the study to quasigroup operations that are isotopic with a group operation, since this is the most popular method for constructing quasigroups. We further discuss only the results concerning SPNs, since this is the topic of our paper. The result of the two studies is that in the case of isotopies the resulting symmetric structures are equivalent[3] with another structure that uses a group operation. Although the result is the same, the views considered in the two papers are different. In [21], the author implicitly considers that the permutation layer is linear with respect to the quasigroup operation. Therefore, differential probabilities are induced only by the s-boxes, since the permutation layer and the key mixing operation make differentials predictable with no uncertainty. Hence, we can reduce the analysis of the differential probabilities induced by the round function to those induced by the s-boxes. In the second paper [20], the view is changed from an element wise one to a global one. More precisely, in the first paper the key mixing operation between the key $k = k_1 \| \ldots \| k_n$ and the plaintext $p = p_1 \| \ldots \| p_n$ is $k_1 \otimes p_1 \| \ldots \| k_n \otimes p_n$, while in the subsequent work is simply $k \otimes p$, where $\otimes$ is the quasigroup operation. Keep in mind that the results from [21] still apply since the whole round transformation can be seen as a permutation.

---

[2] The trapdoor consists in knowing the group operation that weakens the structure.
[3] From the point of view of differential attacks.

In this paper we study the remaining case, namely SPN structures with a permutation layer that is non-linear with respect to the quasigroup operation. When this assumption holds, the results from [20, 21] do not apply. Therefore, a new analysis is required. The results obtained using the techniques introduced in this paper are twofold. First of all we confirm the results[4] presented in [20, 21] by using a different approach than the original one. Secondly, we show that when the permutation layer is non-linear relative to the quasigroup operation, then we cannot reduce its security to a group based SPN structure. More precisely, we obtain that the quasigroup based SPN is equivalent to a structure that has an extra substitution layer before the key mixing operation takes place and which uses a group based key mixing step. To the authors' knowledge, this design was never described in the literature. Therefore, we believe that this novel structure is worth attention for future research from both a theoretical and a design point of view.

Structure of the Paper. We introduce notations and definitions in Sect. 2. SPNs with generic permutation layers are studied in Sect. 3. We conclude in Sect. 4.

2 Preliminaries

Notations. Throughout the paper $|\mathbb{G}|$ will denote the cardinality of set $\mathbb{G}$ and $\oplus$ the bitwise xor operation. Also, by $x\|y$ we understand the concatenation of the strings x and y. When defining a permutation π we further use the shorthand $\pi = \{a_0, a_1, \ldots, a_\ell\}$ which translates into $\pi(i) = a_i$ for all i values. We also define the identity permutation $Id = \{0, \ldots, \ell\}$.

2.1 Quasigroups

In this section we introduce a few basic notions about quasigroups. We base our exposition on [19].

Definition 1. *A quasigroup $(\mathbb{G}, \otimes)$ is a set $\mathbb{G}$ equipped with a binary operation of multiplication $\otimes : \mathbb{G} \times \mathbb{G} \to \mathbb{G}$, in which specification of any two of the values x, y, z in the equation $x \otimes y = z$ determines the third uniquely.*

Definition 2. *For a quasigroup $(\mathbb{G}, \otimes)$ we define the left division $x \oslash z = y$ as the unique solution y to $x \otimes y = z$. Similarly, we define the right division $z \oslash y = x$ as the unique solution x to $x \otimes y = z$.*

Lemma 1. *The following identities hold*

$$y \oslash (y \otimes x) = x, \qquad\qquad (x \otimes y) \oslash y = x,$$
$$y \otimes (y \oslash x) = x, \qquad\qquad (x \oslash y) \otimes y = x.$$

---

[4] Restricted to quasigroups isotopic to commutative groups.

Lemma 2. *If* $(\mathbb{G}, \otimes)$ *is a group then* $x \oslash z = x^{-1} \otimes z$ *and* $z \oslash y = z \otimes y^{-1}$.

Definition 3. *Let* $(\mathbb{G}, \otimes)$, $(\mathbb{H}, \star)$ *be two quasigroups. An ordered triple of bijections* π, ρ, ω *of a set* $\mathbb{G}$ *onto the set* $\mathbb{H}$ *is called an isotopy of* $(\mathbb{G}, \otimes)$ *to* $(\mathbb{H}, \star)$ *if for any* $x, y \in \mathbb{G}$ $\pi(x) \star \rho(y) = \omega(x \otimes y)$. *If such an isotopy exists, then* $(\mathbb{G}, \otimes)$, $(\mathbb{H}, \star)$ *are called isotopic.*

A popular method for constructing quasigroups [12,13,15,23] is the following. Choose a group $(\mathbb{G}, \star)$ (*e.g.* $(\mathbb{Z}_{2^n}, \oplus)$ or $(\mathbb{Z}_{2^n}, +)$) and three arbitrary permutations $\pi, \rho, \omega : \mathbb{G} \to \mathbb{G}$. Then, define the quasigroup operation as $x \otimes y = \omega^{-1}(\pi(x) \star \rho(y))$. To see why this leads to a quasigroup, we note that x, y and z are mapped uniquely to $\pi(x)$, $\rho(y)$ and $\omega(z)$, and thus any equation of the form $\pi(x) \star \rho(y) = \omega(z)$ is in fact uniquely resolved in the base group $\mathbb{G}$ given any of $\pi(x)$, $\rho(y)$ and $\omega(z)$.

Example 1. Let $(\mathbb{G}, \star) = (\mathbb{Z}_4, \oplus)$, $\omega^{-1} = \{2,1,0,3\}$, $\pi = \{2,1,3,0\}$ and $\rho = \{2,0,3,1\}$. The corresponding quasigroup operations for $(\mathbb{Z}_4, \otimes)$ can be found in Table 1 [21].

Table 1. Quasigroup operations.

$\otimes$	0	1	2	3
0	2	0	1	3
1	3	1	0	2
2	1	3	2	0
3	0	2	3	1

$\oslash$	0	1	2	3
0	1	2	0	3
1	2	1	3	0
2	3	0	2	1
3	0	3	1	2

$\oslash$	0	1	2	3
0	3	0	1	2
1	2	1	0	3
2	0	3	2	1
3	1	2	3	0

Example 2. Let $(\mathbb{G}, \star) = (\mathbb{Z}_n, -)$. Then $\mathbb{G}$ is isotopic with $(\mathbb{Z}_n, +)$, where $\omega, \pi = Id$ and $\rho(i) = n - i \bmod n$. [23]

2.2 Quasigroup Differential Cryptanalysis

The notion of differential cryptanalysis was first introduced in [2] for analyzing the Data Encryption Standard block cipher. Since the key mixing layer was simply bitwise addition modulo 2 between the key and the (intermediary) plaintext, differential attacks where defined only for $(\mathbb{Z}_{2^n}, \oplus)$. Later on, the concept was extended to commutative groups [17], non-commutative groups [21] and quasigroups [20,21]. We further present the notions of quasigroup differential probabilities for a permutation. Note that when the quasigroup is replaced with a (non-)commutative group the notions are in accordance with [17,21]. Also, in the case of groups the *KDP* notions coincide with the corresponding *DP* probability (*i.e.* are key independent).

Definition 4. *Let* $\mathbb{G}$ *be a set equipped with a binary operation* $\bullet : \mathbb{G} \times \mathbb{G} \to \mathbb{G}$. *The difference between two elements* $X, X' \in (\mathbb{G}, \bullet)$ *is defined as* $\Delta_\bullet(X, X') = X \bullet X'$.

Definition 5. *Let K be a key, $(\mathbb{G}, \otimes)$ a quasigroup and $\bullet \in \{\oslash, \oslash\}$. We define the quasigroup differential probabilities*

$$DP_\bullet(\sigma, \alpha, \beta) = \frac{1}{|\mathbb{G}|} \sum_{\substack{X, X' \in \mathbb{G} \\ \Delta_\bullet(X, X') = \alpha}} [\Delta_\bullet(\sigma(X), \sigma(X')) = \beta],$$

$$KDP_\oslash(\sigma, \alpha, \beta, K) = \frac{1}{|\mathbb{G}|} \sum_{\substack{X, X' \in \mathbb{G} \\ \Delta_\oslash(X, X') = \alpha}} [\Delta_\oslash(\sigma(K \otimes X), \sigma(K \otimes X')) = \beta],$$

$$KDP_\oslash(\sigma, \alpha, \beta, K) = \frac{1}{|\mathbb{G}|} \sum_{\substack{X, X' \in \mathbb{G} \\ \Delta_\oslash(X, X') = \alpha}} [\Delta_\oslash(\sigma(X \otimes K), \sigma(X' \otimes K)) = \beta],$$

where $\sigma : \mathbb{G} \to \mathbb{G}$ is a permutation and $\alpha, \beta \in \mathbb{G}$.

2.3 Quasigroup Substitution Permutation Network

Let n be a positive integer and $(\mathbb{G}, \otimes)$ a quasigroup. An SPN is an iterated structure that processes a plaintext for r rounds. Each round consist of a key mixing operation, a substitution layer and a permutation layer. Also, the SPN has a final round that consists only of a key mixing operation. Note that for each round i the key schedule algorithm derives the subkey k_i from the initial key. We refer the reader to Fig. 1 for some SPN examples that have three rounds.[5]

To exemplify the different types of possible generalisations of the SPN structure we will use Fig. 1 as a reference. Let $p_i = \tilde{p}_i^1 \| \dots \| \tilde{p}_i^8 = \hat{p}_i^1 \| \dots \| \hat{p}_i^4$ and $k_i = \tilde{k}_i^1 \| \dots \| \tilde{k}_i^8 = \hat{k}_i^1 \| \dots \| \hat{k}_i^8$ be the intermediary plaintext and the subkey for round $i \in \{1, 2, 3\}$.

In Fig. 1a we have an example of an element wise key mixing layer $\tilde{p}_i^1 \otimes \tilde{k}_i^1 \| \dots \| \tilde{p}_i^8 \otimes \tilde{k}_i^8$ (right quasigroup operation[6]) and a permutation layer that is linear with respect to $\otimes$. Therefore, is sufficient to study the differential properties of the s-box with respect to $x \bar{\otimes} y = x_1 \otimes y_1 \| x_2 \otimes y_2$, where $x = x_1 \| x_2$ and $y = y_1 \| y_2$. This variant was studied in [21].

In Fig. 1b we have an example of an element wise key mixing layer $\hat{p}_i^1 \otimes \hat{k}_i^1 \| \dots \| \hat{p}_i^4 \otimes \hat{k}_i^4$ (right quasigroup operation) and a permutation layer that is non-linear with respect to $\otimes$. This is the version that we further study in our paper.

The last version is presented in Fig. 1c and represents an example of a global key mixing layer $p_i \otimes k_i$ (right quasigroup operation). Here the permutation layer is inherently non-linear with respect to $\otimes$. This type of SPN was studied in [20].

---

[5] Figure 1 is based on the TikZ found in [9].

[6] Left quasigroup operation: $\tilde{k}_i^1 \otimes \tilde{p}_i^1 \| \dots \| \tilde{k}_i^8 \otimes \tilde{p}_i^8$.

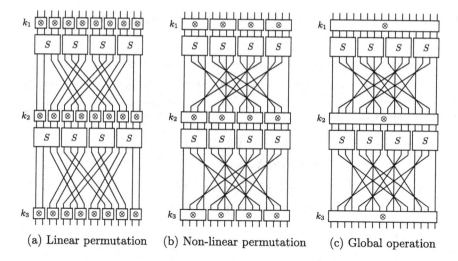

(a) Linear permutation   (b) Non-linear permutation   (c) Global operation

Fig. 1. Variations of the SPN structure

3   Security Analysis

We further assume that the permutation layer P is non-linear with respect to $\otimes$. Since P shuffles b-bit blocks of data we further assume, without loss of generality, that it is linear with respect to addition modulo 2^b, further denoted by $\odot$. In the worse case, the permutation shuffles bits, and thus is linear with respect to $\oplus$. Note that since P shuffles blocks composed of bits that means that the quasigroup operation $\otimes$ must be isotopic to addition modulo some $2^{b'}$, for some $b' > b$.[7] We also assume, without loss of generality, that b' is a multiple of b.[8] In the worse case, we take $b = 1$ and this condition is fulfilled. To simplify our exposition we use the multiplicative notation for the inverse of an element modulo 2^b.

Since the permutation layer is $\odot$-linear, we have to study the following differential properties

$$LKDP_{\odot,\otimes}(\sigma,\alpha,\beta,K) = \frac{1}{|\mathbb{G}|} \sum_{\substack{X,X'\in\mathbb{G} \\ X\odot X'^{-1}=\alpha}} [\sigma(K\otimes X)\odot\sigma(K\otimes X')^{-1} = \beta],$$

$$RKDP_{\odot,\otimes}(\sigma,\alpha,\beta,K) = \frac{1}{|\mathbb{G}|} \sum_{\substack{X,X'\in\mathbb{G} \\ X\odot X'^{-1}=\alpha}} [\sigma(X\otimes K)\odot\sigma(X'\otimes K)^{-1} = \beta],$$

where $\sigma : \mathbb{G} \to \mathbb{G}$ is a permutation and $\alpha,\beta \in \mathbb{G}$.

---

[7] This condition is implied by the fact that the permutation is not linear.

[8] This condition implies that the sets $G = \mathbb{Z}_{2^{b'}}$ and $(\mathbb{Z}_{2^b})^{b'/b}$ are isomorphic.

Lemma 3. *Let $\sigma' = \sigma \circ \omega^{-1}$. We define $x * y = \pi(x) \star \rho(y)$. Then the following identities hold*

$$LKDP_{\odot,\otimes}(\sigma, \alpha, \beta, K) = LKDP_{\odot,*}(\sigma', \alpha, \beta, K),$$
$$RKDP_{\odot,\otimes}(\sigma, \alpha, \beta, K) = RKDP_{\odot,*}(\sigma', \alpha, \beta, K).$$

Proof. First we rewrite

$$\begin{aligned}
\beta &= \sigma(K \otimes X) \odot \sigma(K \otimes X')^{-1} \\
&= \sigma(\omega^{-1}(\pi(K) \star \rho(X))) \odot \sigma(\omega^{-1}(\pi(K) \star \rho(X')))^{-1} \\
&= \sigma'(\pi(K) \star \rho(X)) \odot \sigma'(\pi(K) \star \rho(X'))^{-1} \\
&= \sigma'(K * X) \odot \sigma'(K * X')^{-1}.
\end{aligned}$$

Then we obtain

$$\begin{aligned}
LKDP_{\odot,\otimes}(\sigma, \alpha, \beta, K) &= \frac{1}{|\mathbb{G}|} \sum_{\substack{X,X' \in \mathbb{G} \\ X \odot X'^{-1} = \alpha}} [\sigma(K \otimes X) \odot \sigma(K \otimes X')^{-1} = \beta] \\
&= \frac{1}{|\mathbb{G}|} \sum_{\substack{X,X' \in \mathbb{G} \\ X \odot X'^{-1} = \alpha}} [\sigma'(K * X) \odot \sigma'(K * X')^{-1} = \beta] \\
&= LKDP_{\odot,*}(\sigma', \alpha, \beta, K).
\end{aligned}$$

Similarly, we obtain $RKDP_{\odot,\otimes}(\sigma, \alpha, \beta, K) = RKDP_{\odot,*}(\sigma', \alpha, \beta, K)$. □

Lemma 3 tells us that it is irrelevant from a differential point of view if we define the quasigroup operation with $\omega \neq Id$ or $\omega = Id$. Thus, we further restrict our study to the quasigroup operation $x \otimes y = \pi(x) \star \rho(y)$.

A closer analysis of $LKDP$ and $RKDP$ shows some interesting properties. These are presented in the following lemma.

Lemma 4. *The following equalities hold*

$$LKDP_{\odot,\otimes}(\sigma, \alpha, \beta, K) = LKDP_{\odot,\otimes}(Id, \alpha, \gamma, K) \cdot DP_{\odot}(\sigma, \gamma, \beta),$$
$$RKDP_{\odot,\otimes}(\sigma, \alpha, \beta, K) = RKDP_{\odot,\otimes}(Id, \alpha, \gamma, K) \cdot DP_{\odot}(\sigma, \gamma, \beta).$$

Proof. We only prove the lemma for $LKDP$, since the proof for $RKPD$ is similar. Therefore, we have

$$\begin{aligned}
LKDP_{\odot,\otimes}(\sigma, \alpha, \beta, K) &= \frac{1}{|\mathbb{G}|} \sum_{\substack{X,X' \in \mathbb{G} \\ X \odot X'^{-1} = \alpha}} [\sigma(K \otimes X) \odot \sigma(K \otimes X')^{-1} = \beta] \\
&= \frac{1}{|\mathbb{G}|^2} \sum_{\substack{X,X' \in \mathbb{G} \\ X \odot X'^{-1} = \alpha}} \sum_{\substack{Y,Y'^{-1} \in \mathbb{G} \\ Y \odot Y'^{-1} = \gamma}} [(K \otimes X) \odot (K \otimes X')^{-1} = \gamma]
\end{aligned}$$

$$\cdot \, [\sigma(Y) \odot \sigma(Y')^{-1} = \beta]$$

$$= \left\{ \frac{1}{|G|} \sum_{\substack{X,X' \in G \\ X \odot X'^{-1} = \alpha}} [(K \otimes X) \odot (K \otimes X')^{-1} = \gamma] \right\}$$

$$\cdot \left\{ \frac{1}{|G|} \sum_{\substack{Y,Y' \in G \\ Y \odot Y'^{-1} = \gamma}} [\sigma(Y) \odot \sigma(Y')^{-1} = \beta] \right\}$$

$$= LKDP_{\odot,\otimes}(Id, \alpha, \gamma, K) \cdot DP_{\odot}(\sigma, \gamma, \beta),$$

as desired. $\qquad\qquad\square$

Looking more closely at Lemma 4 we can observe that $DP_{\odot}(\sigma, \gamma, \beta)$ is independent of $\otimes$. Hence, the only components that need to be studied further are $LKDP_{\odot,\otimes}(Id, \alpha, \gamma, K)$ and $RKDP_{\odot,\otimes}(Id, \alpha, \gamma, K)$. Using a similar argument as in Lemma 4 we can further breakdown the two differential probabilities.

Lemma 5. *We define $x *_1 y = \pi(x) \star y$ and $x *_2 y = x \star \rho(y)$. Then the following identities hold*

$$LKDP_{\odot,\otimes}(Id, \alpha, \gamma, K) = DP_{\odot}(\rho, \alpha, \delta) \cdot LKDP_{\odot,*_1}(Id, \delta, \gamma, K),$$
$$RKDP_{\odot,\otimes}(Id, \alpha, \gamma, K) = DP_{\odot}(\rho, \alpha, \delta) \cdot RKDP_{\odot,*_2}(Id, \delta, \gamma, K).$$

Proof. For $LKDP$ the following relations hold

$$LKDP_{\odot,\otimes}(Id, \alpha, \gamma, K) = \frac{1}{|G|} \sum_{\substack{X,X' \in G \\ X \odot X'^{-1} = \alpha}} [(K \otimes X) \odot (K \otimes X')^{-1} = \gamma]$$

$$= \frac{1}{|G|^2} \sum_{\substack{X,X' \in G \\ X \odot X'^{-1} = \alpha}} \sum_{\substack{Y,Y'^{-1} \in G \\ Y \odot Y'^{-1} = \delta}} [\rho(X) \odot \rho(X')^{-1} = \delta]$$

$$\cdot \, [(\pi(K) \star Y) \odot (\pi(K) \star Y')^{-1} = \gamma]$$

$$= \left\{ \frac{1}{|G|} \sum_{\substack{X,X' \in G \\ X \odot X'^{-1} = \alpha}} [\rho(X) \odot \rho(X')^{-1} = \delta] \right\}$$

$$\cdot \left\{ \frac{1}{|G|} \sum_{\substack{Y,Y' \in G \\ Y \odot Y'^{-1} = \delta}} [(K *_1 Y) \odot (K *_1 Y')^{-1} = \gamma] \right\}$$

$$= DP_{\odot}(\rho, \alpha, \delta) \cdot LKDP_{\odot,*_1}(Id, \delta, \gamma, K).$$

Similarly, we obtain the result for $RKDP$. $\qquad\qquad\square$

Corollary 1. *The following properties are true*

$$LKDP_{\odot,\otimes}(\sigma, \alpha, \beta, K) = DP_{\odot}(\rho, \alpha, \delta) \cdot LKDP_{\odot,*_1}(Id, \delta, \gamma, K) \cdot DP_{\odot}(\sigma, \gamma, \beta),$$
$$RKDP_{\odot,\otimes}(\sigma, \alpha, \beta, K) = DP_{\odot}(\rho, \alpha, \delta) \cdot RKDP_{\odot,*_2}(Id, \delta, \gamma, K) \cdot DP_{\odot}(\sigma, \gamma, \beta).$$

The following corollary tell us that if P is linear with respect to $\star$ then $LKDP$ and $RKDP$ are key independent.

Corollary 2. If $\star = \odot$, then following properties are true

$$LKDP_{\odot,\otimes}(\sigma, \alpha, \beta, K) = RKDP_{\odot,\otimes}(\sigma, \alpha, \beta, K) = DP_\odot(\rho, \alpha, \delta) \cdot DP_\odot(\sigma, \delta, \beta).$$

Proof. Let $X \odot X' = \delta$. Then

$$
\begin{aligned}
\gamma &= (K *_1 X) \odot (K *_1 X')^{-1} \\
&= \pi(K) \odot X \odot \pi(K)^{-1} \odot X'^{-1} \\
&= X \odot X'^{-1} \\
&= \delta,
\end{aligned}
$$

and thus $LKDP_{\odot,*_1}(Id, \delta, \gamma, K) = 1$ if and only if $\gamma = \delta$. Similarly, we have $RKDP_{\odot,*_2}(Id, \delta, \gamma, K) = 1$ if and only if $\gamma = \delta$. Therefore, we obtain the desired results. □

According to Corollary 2 the notions of $LKDP$ and $RKDP$ coincide if $\star = \odot$. A consequence of this is the following result from [20]. Note that our proof is different from the one given in the original paper.

Corollary 3. *The left and right quasigroup SPNs derived from a commutative group SPN using an isotopy are equivalent from a differential point of view.*

Corollary 4. Let $\sigma' = \sigma \circ \rho$. If $\star = \odot$, then following equalities hold

$$LKDP_{\odot,\otimes}(\sigma, \alpha, \beta, K) = RKDP_{\odot,\otimes}(\sigma, \alpha, \beta, K) = DP_\odot(\sigma, \alpha, \beta).$$

Proof. From Corollary 2 we know that

$$LKDP_{\odot,\otimes}(\sigma, \alpha, \beta, K) = DP_\odot(\rho, \alpha, \delta) \cdot DP_\odot(\sigma, \delta, \beta).$$

Rewriting the right hand side RHS term of the equality we obtain

$$
RHS = \left\{ \frac{1}{|\mathbb{G}|} \sum_{\substack{X,X' \in \mathbb{G} \\ X \odot X'^{-1} = \alpha}} [\rho(X) \odot \rho(X')^{-1} = \delta] \right\}
$$

$$
\cdot \left\{ \frac{1}{|\mathbb{G}|} \sum_{\substack{Y,Y' \in \mathbb{G} \\ Y \odot Y'^{-1} = \delta}} [\sigma(Y) \odot \sigma(Y')^{-1} = \beta] \right\}
$$

$$
= \frac{1}{|\mathbb{G}|^2} \sum_{\substack{X,X' \in \mathbb{G} \\ X \odot X'^{-1} = \alpha}} \sum_{\substack{\rho(X),\rho(X') \in \mathbb{G} \\ \rho(X) \odot \rho(X')^{-1} = \delta}} [\sigma(\rho(X)) \odot \sigma(\rho(X'))^{-1} = \beta]
$$

$$
\cdot [\rho(X) \odot \rho(X')^{-1} = \delta]
$$

$$
= \frac{1}{|\mathbb{G}|} \sum_{\substack{X,X' \in \mathbb{G} \\ X \odot X'^{-1} = \alpha}} [\sigma'(X) \odot \sigma(X')^{-1} = \beta],
$$

which leads to

$$LKDP_{\odot,\otimes}(\sigma,\alpha,\beta,K) = DP_{\odot}(\sigma',\alpha,\beta),$$

as desired. □

When $\otimes = \odot$, Corollary 4 tells us that is irrelevant from a differential point of view if we replace the group operation with a quasigroup one isotopic to a commutative group operation. Therefore, using different techniques we arrive at the main result from [21].

Corollary 5. *A quasigroup SPN derived from a commutative group SPN using an isotopy has the same differential security as the same group SPN instantiated with a different s-box.*

Remark that in $LKDP_{\odot,*_1}$ and $RKDP_{\odot,*_2}$ we apply a permutation to the key K. Since K and, for example, π are generated as a pair, it suffices from a differential point of view to simply consider $K' = \pi(K)$ as being the key that we want to recover. This is possible, since our final scope is to recover the plaintexts and not the initial key used by the block cipher. As a consequence, it suffices to study $LKDP_{\odot,*}$ and $RKDP_{\odot,*}$. Therefore, we can rewrite the results presented in Corollary 1 as follows

$$LKDP_{\odot,\otimes}(\sigma,\alpha,\beta,K) = DP_{\odot}(\rho,\alpha,\delta) \cdot LKDP_{\odot,*}(Id,\delta,\gamma,K') \cdot DP_{\odot}(\sigma,\gamma,\beta),$$
$$RKDP_{\odot,\otimes}(\sigma,\alpha,\beta,K) = DP_{\odot}(\rho,\alpha,\delta) \cdot RKDP_{\odot,*}(Id,\delta,\gamma,K') \cdot DP_{\odot}(\sigma,\gamma,\beta).$$

Using the results obtained so far the SPN construction shown in Fig. 1b is equivalent with the symmetric structure presented in Fig. 2. To summarise all the lemmas and observations we provide the reader with Proposition 1.

Proposition 1. *Let $(\mathbb{G},\otimes)$ be a quasigroup isotopic with a group $(\mathbb{G},\star)$. Then, in the case of SPNs that use element wise key mixing based on $\otimes$ and a permutation that is non-linear relative to $\otimes$, the equivalent structure[9] is composed of*

a. *$r-1$ rounds consisting of a substitution layer, a key mixing operation based on $\star$, a substitution layer and a permutation layer,*
b. *a final round consisting only of a substitution layer and a key mixing operation based on $\star$.*

The last thing we will prove is that it does not matter if we use the left or right differential probability. As a consequence, the left and right versions of structure presented in Fig. 2 are equivalent from a differential point of view.

Lemma 6. *Let $i(x) = x^{-1}$, where the inverse is with respect to $\star$. Then*

$$LKDP_{\odot,\star}(Id,\delta,\gamma,K) = RKDP_{\odot,\star}(i,\delta,\gamma,i(K)),$$
$$RKDP_{\odot,\star}(Id,\delta,\gamma,K) = LKDP_{\odot,\star}(i,\delta,\gamma,i(K)).$$

---

[9] From a differential point of view.

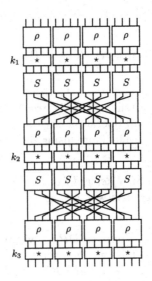

Fig. 2. Equivalent symmetric structure

Proof. Let $Z = i(Y)$, $Z' = i(Y')$ and $K' = i(K)$. Then we have

$$LKDP_{\odot,\star}(Id, \delta, \gamma, K) = \frac{1}{|\mathbb{G}|} \sum_{\substack{Y,Y' \in \mathbb{G} \\ Y \odot Y'^{-1} = \delta}} [(K \star Y) \odot (K \star Y')^{-1} = \gamma]$$

$$= \frac{1}{|\mathbb{G}|} \sum_{\substack{Y,Y' \in \mathbb{G} \\ Y \odot Y'^{-1} = \delta}} [i(i(Y) \star i(K)) \odot (i(i(Y') \star i(K)))^{-1} = \gamma]$$

$$= \frac{1}{|\mathbb{G}|} \sum_{\substack{Z,Z' \in \mathbb{G} \\ Z \odot Z'^{-1} = \delta}} [i(Z \star K') \odot (i(Z' \star K'))^{-1} = \gamma]$$

$$= RKDP_{\odot,\star}(i, \delta, \gamma, K'),$$

as desired. □

Corollary 6. *Let $i(x) = x^{-1}$, where the inverse is with respect to $\star$. Then*

$$LKDP_{\odot,\otimes}(\sigma, \alpha, \beta, K) = DP_{\odot}(\rho, \alpha, \delta) \cdot RKDP_{\odot,\star}(i, \delta, \gamma, i(K)) \cdot DP_{\odot}(\sigma, \gamma, \beta),$$
$$RKDP_{\odot,\otimes}(\sigma, \alpha, \beta, K) = DP_{\odot}(\rho, \alpha, \delta) \cdot LKDP_{\odot,\star}(i, \delta, \gamma, i(K)) \cdot DP_{\odot}(\sigma, \gamma, \beta).$$

Lemma 7. *Let $i(x) = x^{-1}$, where the inverse is with respect to $\star$. Then*

$$LKDP_{\odot,\star}(i, \delta, \gamma, K) = LKDP_{\odot,\star}(Id, \delta, \eta, K) \cdot DP_{\odot}(i, \eta, \gamma),$$
$$RKDP_{\odot,\star}(i, \delta, \gamma, K) = RKDP_{\odot,\star}(Id, \delta, \eta, K) \cdot DP_{\odot}(i, \eta, \gamma).$$

Proof. For the left version, we have

$$LKDP_{\odot,\star}(i,\delta,\gamma,K) = \frac{1}{|G|} \sum_{\substack{X,X'\in G \\ X\odot X'^{-1}=\delta}} [i(K\star X)\odot i(K\star X')^{-1}=\gamma]$$

$$= \frac{1}{|G|^2} \sum_{\substack{X,X'\in G \\ X\odot X'^{-1}=\delta}} \sum_{\substack{Y,Y'^{-1}\in G \\ Y\odot Y'^{-1}=\eta}} [(K\star X)\odot(K\star X')^{-1}=\eta]$$

$$\cdot [i(Y)\odot i(Y')^{-1}=\gamma]$$

$$= \left\{ \frac{1}{|G|} \sum_{\substack{X,X'\in G \\ X\odot X'^{-1}=\delta}} [(K\star X)\odot(K\star X')^{-1}=\eta] \right\}$$

$$\cdot \left\{ \frac{1}{|G|} \sum_{\substack{Y,Y'\in G \\ Y\odot Y'^{-1}=\eta}} [i(Y)\odot i(Y')^{-1}=\gamma] \right\}$$

$$= LKDP_{\odot,\star}(Id,\delta,\eta,K)\cdot DP_{\odot}(i,\eta,\gamma),$$

as desired. Similarly, we obtain the relation for the right version.   □

Lemma 8. *Let $i(x) = x^{-1}$, where the inverse is with respect to $\star$. Also, let $\sigma' = i\circ\sigma$. Then*

$$DP_{\odot}(i,\eta,\gamma)\cdot DP_{\odot}(\sigma,\gamma,\beta) = DP_{\odot}(\sigma',\eta,\beta),$$
$$DP_{\odot}(i,\eta,\gamma)\cdot DP_{\odot}(\sigma,\gamma,\beta) = DP_{\odot}(\sigma',\eta,\beta).$$

Proof. For the first relation we have

$$LHS = \left\{ \frac{1}{|G|} \sum_{\substack{X,X'\in G \\ X\odot X'^{-1}=\eta}} [i(X)\odot(i(X'))^{-1}=\gamma] \right\}$$

$$\cdot \left\{ \frac{1}{|G|} \sum_{\substack{Y,Y'\in G \\ Y\odot Y'^{-1}=\gamma}} [\sigma(Y)\odot\sigma(Y')^{-1}=\beta] \right\}$$

$$= \frac{1}{|G|^2} \sum_{\substack{X,X'\in G \\ X\odot X'^{-1}=\eta}} \sum_{\substack{i(X),i(X')\in G \\ i(X)\odot i(X')^{-1}=\gamma}} [\sigma(i(X))\odot\sigma(i(X'))^{-1}=\beta]$$

$$\cdot [i(X)\odot i(X')^{-1}=\gamma]$$

$$= \frac{1}{|G|} \sum_{\substack{X,X'\in G \\ X\odot X'^{-1}=\eta}} [\sigma'(X)\odot\sigma'(X')^{-1}=\beta],$$

as desired. The second relation is proven similarly.   □

Corollary 7. *Let $i(x) = x^{-1}$, where the inverse is with respect to $\star$. Also, let $\sigma' = i \circ \sigma$. Then*

$$LKDP_{\odot,\otimes}(\sigma, \alpha, \beta, K) = DP_{\odot}(\rho, \alpha, \delta) \cdot RKDP_{\odot,\star}(Id, \delta, \gamma, i(K)) \cdot DP_{\odot}(\sigma', \gamma, \beta),$$
$$RKDP_{\odot,\otimes}(\sigma, \alpha, \beta, K) = DP_{\odot}(\rho, \alpha, \delta) \cdot LKDP_{\odot,\star}(Id, \delta, \gamma, i(K)) \cdot DP_{\odot}(\sigma', \eta, \beta).$$

Proof. We only prove the corollary for the first equality. Using Corollary 6 and Lemmas 7 and 6 we obtain

$$\begin{aligned} LHS &= DP_{\odot}(\rho, \alpha, \delta) \cdot RKDP_{\odot,\star}(i, \delta, \gamma, i(K)) \cdot DP_{\odot}(\sigma, \gamma, \beta) \\ &= DP_{\odot}(\rho, \alpha, \delta) \cdot RKDP_{\odot,\star}(Id, \delta, \eta, i(K)) \cdot DP_{\odot}(i, \eta, \gamma) \cdot DP_{\odot}(\sigma, \gamma, \beta) \\ &= DP_{\odot}(\rho, \alpha, \delta) \cdot RKDP_{\odot,\star}(Id, \delta, \eta, i(K)) \cdot DP_{\odot}(\sigma', \eta, \beta). \end{aligned}$$

Hence, we obtain the equality.   □

4   Conclusions

In this paper we filled a gap found in the literature. Namely, the study of SPN structures that use a quasigroup operation to mix keys and plaintexts, and a permutation layer that is non-linear relative to the quasigroup operation. Therefore, we studied the effect of quasigroups isotopic to groups in the design of these SPN structures. We managed to link their security to another symmetric structure that has an extra substitution layer before key mixing takes place. Also, in the case of the equivalent structure, the key and the plaintext are combined using the initial group operation. Note that, to our knowledge, the resulting structure is novel, and thus can lead to a new designs of secure block ciphers.

References

1. Bakhtiari, S., Safavi-Naini, R., Pieprzyk, J.: A message authentication code based on Latin squares. In: Varadharajan, V., Pieprzyk, J., Mu, Y. (eds.) ACISP 1997. LNCS, vol. 1270, pp. 194–203. Springer, Heidelberg (1997). https://doi.org/10.1007/BFb0027926
2. Biham, E., Shamir, A.: Differential cryptanalysis of DES-like cryptosystems. In: Menezes, A.J., Vanstone, S.A. (eds.) CRYPTO 1990. LNCS, vol. 537, pp. 2–21. Springer, Heidelberg (1991). https://doi.org/10.1007/3-540-38424-3_1
3. Brunetta, C., Calderini, M., Sala, M.: On hidden sums compatible with a given block cipher diffusion layer. Discret. Math. **342**(2), 373–386 (2019)
4. Calderini, M., Civino, R., Sala, M.: On properties of translation groups in the affine general linear group with applications to cryptography. J. Algebra **569**, 658–680 (2021)
5. Calderini, M., Sala, M.: On differential uniformity of maps that may hide an algebraic trapdoor. In: Maletti, A. (ed.) CAI 2015. LNCS, vol. 9270, pp. 70–78. Springer, Cham (2015). https://doi.org/10.1007/978-3-319-23021-4_7
6. Chauhan, D., Gupta, I., Verma, R.: Construction of cryptographically strong S-boxes from ternary quasigroups of order 4. Cryptologia **569**, 658–680 (2021)

7. Chauhan, D., Gupta, I., Verma, R.: Quasigroups and their applications in cryptography. Cryptologia **45**(3), 227–265 (2021)
8. Civino, R., Blondeau, C., Sala, M.: Differential attacks: using alternative operations. Des. Codes Cryptogr. **87**(2–3), 225–247 (2019)
9. Delporte, F.: TikZ for Cryptographers (2016). https://www.iacr.org/authors/tikz/
10. Dénes, J., Keedwell, A.D.: Latin Squares: New Developments in the Theory and Applications, Annals of Discrete Mathematics, vol. 46. Elsevier (1991)
11. Dénes, J., Keedwell, A.D.: A new authentication scheme based on Latin squares. Discret. Math. **106**, 157–161 (1992)
12. Gligoroski, D., Markovski, S., Knapskog, S.J.: The stream cipher Edon80. In: Robshaw, M., Billet, O. (eds.) New Stream Cipher Designs. LNCS, vol. 4986, pp. 152–169. Springer, Heidelberg (2008). https://doi.org/10.1007/978-3-540-68351-3_12
13. Gligoroski, D., Markovski, S., Kocarev, L.: Edon-R, an infinite family of cryptographic hash functions. I.J. Netw. Secur. **8**(3), 293–300 (2009)
14. Knudsen, L.R., Robshaw, M.: The Block Cipher Companion. Springer, Heidelberg (2011)
15. Kościelny, C.: A method of constructing quasigroup-based stream-ciphers. Appl. Math. Comput. Sci. **6**, 109–122 (1996)
16. Lai, X., Massey, J.L.: A proposal for a new block encryption standard. In: Damgård, I.B. (ed.) EUROCRYPT 1990. LNCS, vol. 473, pp. 389–404. Springer, Heidelberg (1991). https://doi.org/10.1007/3-540-46877-3_35
17. Lai, X., Massey, J.L., Murphy, S.: Markov ciphers and differential cryptanalysis. In: Davies, D.W. (ed.) EUROCRYPT 1991. LNCS, vol. 547, pp. 17–38. Springer, Heidelberg (1991). https://doi.org/10.1007/3-540-46416-6_2
18. Mouha, N.: On proving security against differential cryptanalysis. In: CFAIL 2019 (2019)
19. Smith, J.D.: Four lectures on quasigroup representations. Quasigroups Rel. Syst. **15**, 109–140 (2007)
20. Teşeleanu, G.: Cryptographic Symmetric Structures Based on Quasigroups. Cryptologia (2021, to appear). https://eprint.iacr.org/2021/1676
21. Teşeleanu, G.: Quasigroups and substitution permutation networks: a failed experiment. Cryptologia **45**(3), 266–281 (2021)
22. Vaudenay, S.: A Classical Introduction to Cryptography: Applications for Communications Security. Springer, Heidelberg (2005)
23. Vojvoda, M., Sỳs, M., Jókay, M.: A note on algebraic properties of quasigroups in Edon80. Technical report, eSTREAM report 2007/005 (2007)

Unbounded Revocable Decentralized Multi-Authority Attribute-Based Encryption Supporting Non-monotone Access Structures

Takuya Ishibashi[1], Toshihiro Ohigashi[1], and Hikaru Tsuchida[2(✉)]

[1] Tokai University, Minato City, Japan
t_ishibashi@star.tokai-u.jp, ohigashi@tsc.u-tokai.ac.jp
[2] NEC Corporation, Kawasaki City, Japan
h_tsuchida@nec.com

Abstract. Ciphertext-policy attribute-based encryption (CP-ABE) is a cryptographic technology that enforces an access control mechanism over encrypted data by specifying an access policy with encrypted data and introducing an attribute authority (AA) that manages user's attributes. A CP-ABE with multiple attribute authorities and no central authority, a decentralized multi-authority CP-ABE (DMA-CP-ABE), can achieve more realistic attribute management than CP-ABE with a single authority.

However, DMA-CP-ABE has an attribute revocation problem. As a different problem, the size of the public parameters of each AA is proportional to the size of the attribute universe managed by each AA. Moreover, since most existing DMA-CP-ABE schemes support only monotonic access structures, the size of the access policy specified in the ciphertext becomes large when an encryptor specifies a non-monotonic access policy in the ciphertext. Therefore, the DMA-CP-ABE that supports the attribute revocation, constant-size public and secret parameters (a.k.a unboundedness), and non-monotonic access structure is required. However, to the best of our knowledge, no one has proposed it yet.

In this paper, we propose a new unbounded revocable DMA-CP-ABE (UR-DMA-CP-ABE) that supports a non-monotone access structure. We prove that our scheme achieves adaptively payload-hiding against chosen-plaintext attacks under the decisional linear (DLIN) assumption.

Keywords: Attribute-based encryption · Revocation · Unboundedness · Non-monotone access structure

1 Introduction

1.1 Background

Attribute-based encryption (ABE) is a cryptographic technology that enforces an access control mechanism over encrypted data by using access policies and

---

The order of authors is alphabetical.

© The Author(s), under exclusive license to Springer Nature Switzerland AG 2023
G. Bella et al. (Eds.): SecITC 2022, LNCS 13809, pp. 320–339, 2023.
https://doi.org/10.1007/978-3-031-32636-3_19

associated attributes among ciphertexts and the user's private keys and introducing an attribute authority (AA) that manages attributes. Loosely speaking,
there are two types of ABE schemes: *ciphertext-policy ABE* (CP-ABE) and *key-
policy ABE* (KP-ABE). In CP-ABE systems, the AA specifies the attributes
associated with the user in the user's private keys and issues it to the user
using the AA's master secret key. The encryptor specifies an access policy to the
ciphertext when encrypting the message by using public keys for access policies
issued by the AA. Loosely speaking, KP-ABE is almost the same as CP-ABE
except that the AA specifies the access policy in the user's private keys and the
encryptor specifies several attributes to the ciphertext. In this paper, we focus
on CP-ABE. Suppose that users with private keys for attributes that do not
satisfy the access policy specified in the ciphertext collude. Even if the colluding
users combine their private keys, they cannot decrypt the CP-ABE ciphertext.

In most existing CP-ABE schemes, the AA is a single authority. However, CP-
ABE with a single AA suffers from some drawbacks. For example, the malicious
AA can decrypt all ciphertexts using the AA's master secret key. A different
issue is that the AA must be online when the user's private keys are issued.
Thus, if the AA is a single authority, the AA can be a single point of failure. In
addition, managing all attributes in a single AA is not practical when trying to
perform access control using attributes managed by different systems.

The CP-ABE schemes with multiple AAs and the central authority (MA-
CP-ABE) has been proposed to mitigate these drawbacks. After that, the CP-
ABE schemes with multiple AAs and no central authority, *decentralized multi-
authority CP-ABE* (DMA-CP-ABE), have been proposed as a generalization of
CP-ABE schemes. However, to the best of our knowledge, no DMA-CP-ABE
that supports all of the following useful three features has been proposed:

1. **Key revocation:** CP-ABE supporting key revocation is required when managing dynamic attributes. For example, suppose that access control in a company's human resource system is to be realized by CP-ABE schemes. The
   system must revoke the private keys held by departing employees. If the
   system cannot revoke these keys, it cannot prevent unauthorized access by
   departing employees. It is more difficult for DMA-CP-ABE to support key
   revocation than for single-authority CP-ABE or MA-CP-ABE because it is
   necessary to revoke the user's private key for attributes that are managed
   independently by each AA.
2. **Constant-size parameters independent of the size of the attribute
   universe (a.k.a unboundedness):** CP-ABE supporting constant-size
   parameters independent of the size of the attribute universe is required when
   managing attributes with a vast universe. In most existing CP-ABE schemes,
   the size of public parameters of the AA is proportional to the size of the
   attribute universe managed by the AA. Since an encryptor needs to obtain
   the public keys for the attributes managed by each AA from each AA in
   DMA-CP-ABE schemes, the public key size should not depend on the size of
   the attribute universe so that the burden on the encryptor is small.

Table 1. Comparison of the existing schemes and ours.

Schemes	DMA-CP-ABE	Key revocation	Unboundedness	Non-monotone access structure
[8]	(KP-ABE)	✓	✓	✓
[20,31]	(MA-CP-ABE)	✓	(Bounded)	(Not supporting)
[12]	(MA-CP-ABE)	✓	✓	(Not supporting)
[9,14,15]	✓	(Not supporting)	(Bounded)	(Not supporting)
[23]	✓	(Not supporting)	(Bounded)	✓
[26]	✓	(Not supporting)	✓	(Not supporting)
[17]	✓	✓	✓	(Not supporting)
[29]	✓	✓	(Bounded)	✓
Ours	✓	✓	✓	✓

3. **Non-monotone access structure:** Loosely speaking, if any superset of the attribute set (satisfying the access structure) satisfies the access structure, then the access structure is called the *monotone* access structure. On the other hand, if the attribute set's superset (satisfying the access structure) exists that does not satisfy the access structure, then the access structure is called the *non-monotone* access structure. CP-ABE supporting non-monotone access structures is required when the access policy specified in the ciphertext includes the NOT operator. Let $U = \{a_0, a_1, a_2, a_3\}$ be the attribute universe containing four attributes, a_0, a_1, a_2 and a_3. If an encryptor would like to generate the ciphertext with the access policy expressed as "NOT a_0", the encryptor using the CP-ABE scheme that supports only monotone access structure needs to specify the monotonic access policy expressed as "a_1 OR a_2 OR a_3" that is equivalent to the original access policy because "NOT a_0" is non-monotonic. When an encryptor uses the CP-ABE scheme supporting only a monotone access structure to generate the ciphertext specified with the access policy, including the NOT operator, the size of the access policy and ciphertexts may increase in proportion to the size of the attribute universe.

1.2 Our Contributions

We propose a DMA-CP-ABE scheme supporting key revocation, unboundedness, and non-monotone access structure. Table 1 shows that no DMA-CP-ABE scheme supports these features except ours. We prove that our scheme achieves adaptively payload-hiding against chosen-plaintext attacks under the decisional linear (DLIN) assumption.

1.3 Related Works

To the best of our knowledge, no DMA-CP-ABE that supports key revocation, unboundedness, and non-monotone access structure has been proposed, as discussed below.

Single-Authority ABE: As the origin of the research on ABE, Sahai and Waters proposed the fuzzy identity-based encryption (FIBE) [28] that is a special case of ABE where an access policy specified in a ciphertext (or key) a threshold function. After FIBE introduced, there proposed some ABE schemes, for example, KP-ABE [11], CP-ABE [5] and ABE that supports more complex access structures [1,4,10,21]. There has also been research on ABE schemes supporting some of the three features as follows.

- **Existing schemes achieving one of the three features:** Sahai et al. proposed the revocable ABE by using update keys and updating ciphertexts [27]. Lee et al. introduced the new time-evolution revocation scheme for ABE with modularity [13]. Meanwhile, Attrapadung and Imai proposed the revocable ABE without update keys by specifying revoked users in ciphertexts [3]. After that, they proposed the ABE scheme supporting the hybrid revocation by using the update keys and specifying revoked users in ciphertexts [2]. In recent years, Yamada et al. proposed the generic constructions of the revocable ABE [32].
  Ostrovsky et al. proposed the ABE scheme supporting non-monotone access structure [24]. Okamoto and Takashima proposed the ABE schemes supporting general predicates, i.e., non-monotone access structure using inner-product relations [21].
  Lewko and Waters proposed the unbounded ABE scheme in composite order bilinear groups [16]. Rouselakis and Waters proposed the unbounded ABE scheme in prime order bilinear groups [25].
- **Existing scheme achieving two of the three features:** Okamoto and Takashima proposed the unbounded ABE scheme supporting non-monotone access structure [22].
- **Existing scheme achieving all of the three features:** Datta et al. proposed the KP-ABE supporting key revocation, unboundedness, and non-monotone access structure [8]. However, their scheme [8] is a single-authority KP-ABE, not DMA-CP-ABE.

(D)MA-CP-ABE: Chase proposed the first MA-CP-ABE scheme [6]. Then, some improved MA-CP-ABE schemes [7,18] and revocable MA-CP-ABE schemes [12,20,31] have been proposed, but those schemes require the central authority.

Lewko and Waters proposed the first DMA-CP-ABE, i.e., multi-authority CP-ABE scheme without the central authority in the composite order bilinear groups [15]. After that, Lewko proposed the DMA-CP-ABE in the prime order bilinear groups [14]. Okamoto and Takashima proposed the DMA-CP-ABE that supports the non-monotone access structure using inner-product relations [23]. In recent years, Datta et al. proposed the first DMA-CP-ABE from the learning with error assumption [9].

Rouselakis and Waters proposed the unbounded DMA-CP-ABE [26]. However, their scheme [26] does not support key revocation and non-monotone access structure. Li et al. proposed the revocable and unbounded DMA-CP-ABE [17], but it does not support the non-monotone access structure. Tsuchida et al. proposed the revocable DMA-CP-ABE that supports the non-monotone access structure using inner-product relations [29] based on [23]. However, their scheme [29] is not unbounded.

In recent years, Venema and Alpár broke the eleven ABE schemes in [30]. Their attack does not affect the security of [23] (the DMA-CP-ABE scheme used to construct our scheme) and our scheme.

2 Preliminaries

2.1 Notations

We follow the notations in [13,23,29].

When A is a random variable or distribution, we denote that a is randomly selected from A according to its distribution as $a \xleftarrow{\mathsf{R}} A$. When A is a set, we denote that a is uniformly selected from A as $a \xleftarrow{\mathsf{U}} A$. Let $\mathbb{F}_q$ and $\mathbb{F}_q^\times$ be the finite field of order q and $\mathbb{F}_q \setminus \{0\}$, respectively.

We denote the n-dimensional vector with elements on $\mathbb{F}_q$ as $\vec{x} = (x_1, \ldots, x_n) \in \mathbb{F}_q^n$. We also denote the inner-product of two vectors $\vec{x} = (x_1, \ldots, x_n)$ and $\vec{v} = (v_1, \ldots, v_n)$ as $\vec{x} \cdot \vec{v} (= \sum_{i=1}^n x_i v_i \bmod q)$. Let X^T be the transpose of matrix X.

2.2 Security Assumption

We follow the definition of DLIN assumption described in [23].

Definition 1 (DLIN: Decisional Linear Assumption). *The DLIN problem is to guess* $\beta \in \{0,1\}$, *given* $(\mathsf{param}_{\mathbb{G}}, G, \xi G, \kappa G, \delta\xi G, \sigma\kappa G, Y_\beta) \xleftarrow{\mathsf{R}} \mathcal{G}_\beta^{\mathsf{DLIN}}(1^\lambda)$, *where*

$$\mathcal{G}_\beta^{\mathsf{DLIN}}(1^\lambda):$$

$$\mathsf{param}_{\mathbb{G}} := (q, \mathbb{G}, \mathbb{G}_T, G, e) \xleftarrow{\mathsf{R}} \mathcal{G}_{\mathsf{sbpg}}(1^\lambda),$$

$$\kappa, \delta, \xi, \sigma \xleftarrow{\mathsf{U}} \mathbb{F}_q, Y_0 := (\delta + \sigma)G, Y_1 \xleftarrow{\mathsf{U}} \mathbb{G},$$

$$return\ (\mathsf{param}_{\mathbb{G}}, G, \xi G, \kappa G, \delta\xi G, \sigma\kappa G, Y_\beta),$$

for $\beta \xleftarrow{\mathsf{U}} \{0,1\}$. *For a probabilistic machine* $\mathcal{E}$, *we define the advantage of* $\mathcal{E}$ *for the DLIN problem as:* $\mathsf{Adv}_{\mathcal{E}}^{\mathsf{DLIN}}(\lambda) := |\Pr[\mathcal{E}(1^\lambda, \varrho) \to 1 \| \varrho \xleftarrow{\mathsf{R}} \mathcal{G}_0^{\mathsf{DLIN}}(1^\lambda)] - \Pr[\mathcal{E}(1^\lambda, \varrho) \to 1 \| \varrho \xleftarrow{\mathsf{R}} \mathcal{G}_1^{\mathsf{DLIN}}(1^\lambda)]|$.

The DLIN assumption is: For any probabilistic polynomial-time adversary $\mathcal{E}$, *the advantage* $\mathsf{Adv}_{\mathcal{E}}^{\mathsf{DLIN}}(\lambda)$ *is negligible in* λ.

2.3 Dual Pairing Vector Spaces by Direct Product of Symmetric Pairing Groups

In this paper, we follow the definitions in [23].

Definition 2 (Symmetric Bilinear Pairing Groups (SBPG) [23]). *SBPG is a tuple, $(q, \mathbb{G}, \mathbb{G}_T, G, e)$. q is a prime. $\mathbb{G}$ and $\mathbb{G}_T$ are cyclic additive group of order q and multiplicative group of order q, respectively. Note that $G \neq 0 \in \mathbb{G}$. e is a polynomial time computable non-degenerate bilinear pairing. We also note that $e : \mathbb{G} \times \mathbb{G} \to \mathbb{G}_T$, i.e., $e(sG, tG) = e(G, G)^{st}$ and $e(G, G) \neq 1$. Let $\mathcal{G}_{\mathsf{sbpg}}$ be an algorithm that takes an input 1^λ and outputs a description of SBPG $(q, \mathbb{G}, \mathbb{G}_T, G, e)$ with security parameter λ.*

Definition 3 (Dual Pairing Vector Spaces (DPVS) [23]). *DPVS is a tuple, $(q, \mathbb{V}, \mathbb{G}_T, \mathbb{A}, e)$. q is a prime. $\mathbb{V}(= \overbrace{\mathbb{G} \times \cdots \times \mathbb{G}}^{N})$ is a N-dimensional vector space over $\mathbb{F}_q$. $\mathbb{G}_T$ is a multiplicative group of order q. $\mathbb{A} = \{\boldsymbol{a}_1, \ldots, \boldsymbol{a}_N\}$ is a canonical basis of $\mathbb{V}$ where $\boldsymbol{a}_i = (\overbrace{0, \ldots, 0}^{i-1}, G, \overbrace{0, \ldots, 0}^{N-i})$. The pairing e is defined by $e(\boldsymbol{x}, \boldsymbol{y}) = \prod_{i=1}^{N} e(G_i, H_i) \in \mathbb{G}_T$ where $\boldsymbol{x} = (G_1, \ldots, G_N) \in \mathbb{V}$ and $\boldsymbol{y} = (H_1, \ldots, H_N) \in \mathbb{V}$. We note that e is non-degenerate bilinear, i.e., $e(s\boldsymbol{x}, t\boldsymbol{y}) = e(\boldsymbol{x}, \boldsymbol{y})^{st}$ for $s, t \in \mathbb{F}_q$. If $e(\boldsymbol{x}, \boldsymbol{y}) = 1$ for all $\boldsymbol{y} \in \mathbb{V}$, then $\boldsymbol{x} = (0, \ldots, 0)$. For all i and j, $e(\boldsymbol{a}_i, \boldsymbol{a}_j) = e(G, G)^{\delta_{i,j}}$ where $e(G, G) \neq 1 \in \mathbb{G}_T$ and $\delta_{i,j} = \begin{cases} 0 & (i \neq j) \\ 1 & (i = j) \end{cases}$.*

DPVS generation algorithm, $\mathcal{G}_{\mathsf{dpvs}}$, takes an input 1^λ and outputs a description of $\mathsf{param}_{\mathbb{V}} = (q, \mathbb{V}, \mathbb{G}_T, \mathbb{A}, e)$ with the security parameter $\lambda \in \mathbb{N}$ and the $N(\in \mathbb{N})$-dimensional $\mathbb{V}$. Note that $\mathcal{G}_{\mathsf{dpvs}}$ can be constructed by using $\mathcal{G}_{\mathsf{sbpg}}$.

For bases $\mathbb{B} := (\boldsymbol{b}_1, \ldots, \boldsymbol{b}_N)$ and $\mathbb{B}^* := (\boldsymbol{b}_1^*, \ldots, \boldsymbol{b}_N^*)$, let $(x_1, \ldots, x_N)_{\mathbb{B}}$ and $(y_1, \ldots, y_N)_{\mathbb{B}^*}$ be $\sum_{i=1}^{N} x_i \boldsymbol{b}_i$ and $\sum_{i=1}^{N} y_i \boldsymbol{b}_i^*$, respectively.

2.4 General Predicates: Non-monotone Access Structures with Inner-Product Relations

In this paper, we follow the definitions in [23]. See Appendix A and B for details on span programs and linear secret sharing schemes, respectively.

Definition 4 (Inner-Products of Attribute Vectors and Access Structures). $\mathcal{U}_t = \bigcup_{i'=1}^{c_t} \mathcal{U}_{t,i'}$ *($t = 1, \ldots, d$ and $\mathcal{U}_t \subset \{0,1\}^*$) is a t-th sub-universe. $\mathcal{U}_{t,i'}$ is a set of attributes, each of which is expressed by a pair of sub-universe id, category id and value of attribute, i.e., (t, i', x), where $t \in \{1, \ldots, d\}$, $i' \in \{1, \ldots, c_t\}$ and $x_{t,i'} \in \mathbb{F}_q \setminus \{0\}$.*

We now define such an attribute to be a variable p of a span program $\mathbb{S} := (M, \rho)$, *i.e.,* $p := (t, i', v_{t,i'})$. *An access structure* $\mathbb{A}$ *is a span program* $\mathbb{S} := (M, \rho)$ *along with variables* $p := (t, i', v_{t,i'}), \ldots,$ *i.e.,* $\mathbb{A} := (M, \rho)$ *such that* $\rho : \{1, \ldots, \ell\} \to \{(t, i', v_{t,i'}), \ldots, \neg(t, i', v_{t,i'}), \ldots\}$. *Let* Γ *be a set of attributes, i.e.,* $\Gamma := \{(t, i', x_{t,i'}) \mid x_{t,i'} \in \mathbb{F}q \setminus \{0\}, 1 \le t \le d, 1 \le i' \le c_t\}$, *where* t *and* i' *run through some subset of* $\{1, \ldots, d\}$ *and* $\{1, \ldots, c_t\}$, *respectively, not necessarily the whole indices.*

When Γ *is given to access structure* $\mathbb{S}$, *map* $\gamma : \{1, \ldots, \ell\} \to \{0, 1\}$ *for span program* $\hat{M} := (M, \rho)$ *is defined as follows: For* $i = 1, \ldots, \ell$, *set* $\gamma(i) = 1$ *if* $[\rho(i) = (t, i', v_{t,i'})] \wedge [(t, i', x_{t,i'}) \in \Gamma] \wedge [(v_{t,i'}, -1) \cdot (1, x_{t,i'}) = 0]$ *or* $[\rho(i) = \neg(t, i', v_{t,i'})] \wedge [(t, i', x_{t,i'}) \in \Gamma] \wedge [(v_{t,i'}, -1) \cdot (1, x_{t,i'}) \ne 0]$. *Set* $\gamma(i) = 0$ *otherwise. Access structure* $\mathbb{A} := (M, \rho)$ *accepts* Γ *if and only if* $\vec{1} \in \mathsf{span}\langle (M_i)_{\gamma(i)=1}\rangle$.

We note that we define $\mathcal{U}_t$ as the attribute sub-universe managed by t-th AA in the same way as [23]. However, unlike [23], we also define $\mathcal{U}_t = \bigcup_{i'=1}^{c_t} \mathcal{U}_{t,i'}$. We assume that t-th AA manages the attributes by dividing them into c_t categories. The reason for this split management of attributes is that it is useful when using the NOT operator in the access policy. See Appendix C.

2.5   Revocation Framework Based on Full Binary Tree

To support key revocation, we use the full binary tree, $\mathcal{BT}$ and the complete subtree (CS) method, CS [19]. For more details, see Appendix D and E.

3   Unbounded Revocable DMA-CP-ABE Supporting Non-monotone Access Structures

3.1   Syntax of Unbounded Revocable DMA-CP-ABE (UR-DMA-CP-ABE)

A UR-DMA-CP-ABE scheme consists of the following five algorithms. These are randomized algorithms except for Dec. We assume that the number of AAs is d. The t-th AA ($1 \le t \le d$) manages attributes split into $c_t(\in \mathbb{N})$ categories.

1. GSetup(1^λ): This algorithm takes a security parameter λ as input and outputs a global parameter gparam.
2. ASetup(gparam, t, c_t, $\{N_{max,t,i'}\}_{i'=1}^{c_t}$): This algorithm takes a global parameter gparam, index of AA t, total number of attribute category managed by AA_t c_t and set of maximum number of users per attribute category $\{N_{max,t,i'}\}_{i'=1}^{c_t}$ as inputs. It outputs master secret keys of AA_t, msk_t, master public keys of AA_t, mpk_t, and user management information $\{(\mathcal{BT}_{t,i'}, R_{t,i'})\}_{i'=1}^{c_t}$ where

$\mathcal{BT}_{t,i'}$ is a full binary tree assigned users in i'-th attribute category and $R_{t,i'}$ is the set of revoked users[1] in i'-th attribute category[2].

3. KeyGen(gparam, gid, $x_{t,i'}$, msk_t, $\mathcal{BT}_{t,i'}$): This algorithm takes a global parameter gparam, global identifier of user gid, attribute in i'-th category managed by AA_t $x_{t,i'}$, master secret keys of AA_t msk_t and full binary tree of i'-th category managed by AA_t $\mathcal{BT}_{t,i'}$ as inputs. It outputs private keys of user who has gid associated with the attribute $x_{t,i'}$, $\mathsf{usk}_{\mathsf{gid},(t,i',x_{t,i'})}$.

4. Enc(gparam, $\{\mathsf{mpk}_t, \{(\mathcal{BT}_{t,i'}, R_{t,i'})\}_{i'}\}_t$, m, $\mathbb{A} = (M, \rho)$): This algorithm takes a global parameter gparam, master public keys of AA_t mpk_t, full binary tree and set of revoked users of i'-th category managed by AA_t $(\mathcal{BT}_{t,i'}, R_{t,i'})$, message m and access structure $\mathcal{A}$ as inputs. It outputs the ciphertext $\mathsf{ct}_{\mathbb{A},\{R_{t,i'}\}}$. Note that an encryptor specifies the revocation list to the ciphertext in this algorithm.

5. Dec(gparam, $\mathsf{ct}_{\mathbb{A},\{R_{t,i'}\}}$, $\{\mathsf{usk}_{\mathsf{gid},(t,i',x_{t,i'})}\}$): This algorithm takes a global parameter gparam, ciphertext $\mathsf{ct}_{\mathbb{A},\{R_{t,i'}\}}$ and set of private keys of user who has gid $\{\mathsf{usk}_{\mathsf{gid},(t,i',x_{t,i'})}\}$ as inputs. It outputs a message m or a special symbol $\perp$.

A UR-DMA-CP-ABE scheme should have the following correctness property: for all security parameter λ, all index of AA_t, all n_t, all $N_{max,t,i'}$, all attribute sets $\Gamma := \{(t, i', x_{t,i'})\}$, all gid, all messages m, and all access structures $\mathbb{A}$, it holds that $m = $ Dec(gparam, $\mathsf{ct}_{\mathbb{A},\{R_{t,i'}\}}$, $\{\mathsf{usk}_{\mathsf{gid},(t,i',x_{t,i'})}\}$) with overwhelming probability, if $\mathbb{A}$ accepts Γ and there exists δ related with Γ, i.e., $\vec{1} \in \mathsf{span}\langle M_\delta \rangle$ s.t. $M_\delta := (M_j)_{\gamma(j)=1}$ where gid $\notin R_{t,i'}$ for all j s.t. $\gamma(j) = 1$ and $\rho(j) = (t, i', x_{t,i'})$ or $\neg(t, i', x_{t,i'})$, where

$$\text{gparam} \xleftarrow{\mathsf{R}} \mathsf{GSetup}(1^\lambda),$$

$$(\mathsf{msk}_t, \mathsf{mpk}_t, \{(\mathcal{BT}_{t,i'}, R_{t,i'})\}_{i'=1}^{c_t}) \xleftarrow{\mathsf{R}} \mathsf{ASetup}(\text{gparam}, t, c_t, \{N_{max,t,i'}\}_{i'=1}^{c_t}),$$

$$\mathsf{usk}_{\mathsf{gid},(t,i',x_{t,i'})} \xleftarrow{\mathsf{R}} \mathsf{KeyGen}(\text{gparam}, \text{gid}, x_{t,i'}, \mathsf{msk}_t, \mathcal{BT}_{t,i'}),$$

$$\mathsf{ct}_{\mathbb{A},\{R_{t,i'}\}} \xleftarrow{\mathsf{R}} \mathsf{Enc}(\text{gparam}, \{\mathsf{mpk}_t, \{(\mathcal{BT}_{t,i'}, R_{t,i'})\}_{i'}\}_t, m, \mathbb{A} = (M, \rho)).$$

---

[1] In ASetup, AA_t initializes as $R_{t,i'} = \phi$. After running ASetup, AA_t publishes $R_{t,i'}$ and adds the revoked user's identifier to $R_{t,i'}$ whenever the revocation event happens.

[2] We note that the size of master secret and public keys of AA_t does not depend on n_t and $N_{max,t,i'}$, but the size of user management information $\{(\mathcal{BT}_{t,i'}, R_{t,i'})\}_{i'=1}^{c_t}$ depends on it. We emphasize that we are attempting to achieve the unboundedness to the parameters of DMA-CP-ABE managed by AA_t, i.e., msk_t and mpk_t, not user management information. The user management information is just like text. Hence, the data size of it is sufficiently smaller than that of msk_t and mpk_t, even if the size of user management information depends on n_t and $N_{max,t,i'}$

We also note that key revocation with a revocation list and user tree for each attribute category is inefficient in terms of ciphertext and key size. However, attribute-level revocation is efficient in the sense that it reduces the cost of key redistribution for each revocation event.

3.2 Security of UR-DMA-CP-ABE

For an adversary $\mathcal{A}$, the advantage of $\mathcal{A}$ in the following game is defined as $\mathsf{Adv}_{\mathcal{A}}^{\mathsf{PH}}(\lambda) := |\Pr[b' = b] - 1/2|$ for any security parameter λ. A UR-DMA-CP-ABE scheme is adaptively payload-hiding secure against chosen-plaintext attacks if all polynomial time adversaries have at most a negligible advantage in the following game:

Setup

Given 1^λ, the challenger gives gparam $\xleftarrow{\mathsf{R}}$ GSetup(1^λ) to $\mathcal{A}$. The challenger runs $(\mathsf{msk}_t, \mathsf{mpk}_t, \{(\mathcal{BT}_{t,i'}, R_{t,i'})\}_{i'=1}^{c_t}) \xleftarrow{\mathsf{R}}$ ASetup(gparam, t, c_t, $\{N_{max,t,i'}\}_{i'=1}^{c_t}$) for $t = 1, \ldots, d$ and gives $\{\mathsf{mpk}_t, \{(\mathcal{BT}_{t,i'}, R_{t,i'})\}_{i'=1}^{c_t}\}_{t=1}^{d}$ to $\mathcal{A}$.

Phase 1

$\mathcal{A}$ is allowed to issue a polynomial number of queries, $(\mathsf{gid}, (t, i', x_{t,i'}))$, to the challenger or oracle KeyGen(gparam, gid, $x_{t,i'}$, msk_t, $\mathcal{BT}_{t,i'}$) for user's private keys.

Challenge

Let $\Gamma_{\mathsf{gid}_j} := \{(t, i', x_{t,i'})\}(j = 1, \ldots, \nu)$ be the queries set to the KeyGen oracle with gid_j. $\mathcal{A}$ submits two challenge messages m_0^*, m_1^*, challenge access structure $\mathbb{A}^* := (M, \rho)$ and the challenge set of revoked users $\{R_{t,i'}^*\}$ to the challenger. $\mathbb{A}^*$ and $\{R_{t,i'}^*\}$ must satisfy at least one of the following restrictions for each j:

Restriction I

$\mathbb{A}^*$ does not accept any Γ_{gid_j} for $j = 1, \ldots, \nu$.

Restriction II

For $j = 1, \ldots, \nu$, if $\mathbb{A}^*$ accepts Γ_{gid_j}, there exists $R_{t,i'}^*$ containing gid_j s.t. $\rho(i) = (t, i', x_{t,i'})$ or $\neg(t, i', x_{t,i'})$ for $i \in I$ where $\vec{1} \in \mathsf{span}\langle(M_i)_{\gamma(i)=1}\rangle$ and $I \subseteq \{i \in \{1, \ldots, \ell\} \mid \gamma(i) = 1\}$.

The challenger flips a random coin $b \xleftarrow{\mathsf{U}} \{0,1\}$ and run $\mathsf{ct}_{\mathbb{A}^*, \{R_{t,i'}^*\}}^* \xleftarrow{\mathsf{R}}$ Enc(gparam, $\{\mathsf{mpk}_t, \{(\mathcal{BT}_{t,i'}, R_{t,i'}^*)\}_{i'}\}_t$, m_b^*, $\mathbb{A}^*$). Then, the challenger sends $\mathsf{ct}_{\mathbb{A}^*, \{R_{t,i'}^*\}}^*$ to $\mathcal{A}$.

Phase 2

$\mathcal{A}$ is allowed to issue a polynomial number of queries, $(\mathsf{gid}, (t, i', x_{t,i'}))$, to the challenger or oracle KeyGen(gparam, gid, $x_{t,i'}$, msk_t, $\mathcal{BT}_{t,i'}$) for user's private keys subject to the same restriction as before.

Guess

$\mathcal{A}$ outputs a guess b' of b.

3.3 Our Construction

Key Idea. A straightforward way to construct the UR-DMA-CP-ABE scheme supporting the non-monotone access structure seems is to extend the existing revocable DMA-CP-ABE scheme [29] to the variant of it with unboundedness by applying the existing technologies for unboundedness (indexing and consistent randomness amplification) [22]. However, we cannot employ this approach. The scheme of [29] needs to represent the user for each attribute category as an $O(\log N_{max,t,i'})$-dimensional vector on DPVS for key revocation. The consistent randomness amplification [22] can realize the unboundedness only for the number of attribute categories or dimension of vector. Hence, if we were to try to realize the unboundedness for the number of attribute categories while using multiple attribute categories in the system, the consistent randomness amplification [22] could not be applied to the scheme of [29].

To overcome this technical difficulty, we introduce the novel encoding that represents the user for each attribute category as a two-dimensional vector on DPVS for key revocation and modify the existing revocable DMA-CP-ABE scheme [29] by using the introduced encoding. In addition, unlike [29], we restrict the attribute vector to be two-dimensional. In this way, we can apply the technologies for unboundedness [22] to the modified revocable DMA-CP-ABE scheme based on [29] and construct the UR-DMA-CP-ABE scheme supporting the non-monotone access structure. We show the algorithms of our scheme as follows:

1. $\mathsf{GSetup}(1^\lambda)$:

   Trusted third party (TTP) runs $\mathsf{param}_{\mathbb{G}} := (q, \mathbb{G}, \mathbb{G}_T, G, e) \xleftarrow{\text{R}} \mathcal{G}_{\mathsf{sbpg}}(1^\lambda)$. Let $H : \{0,1\}^* \to \mathbb{G}$ be the hash function. TTP publishes $\mathsf{gparam} = (\mathsf{param}_{\mathbb{G}}, H)$. Note that anyone can compute the following value by using gparam: $G_0 := H(0^\lambda)$, $G_1 := H(0^{\lambda-1} \| 1)$, $g_T := e(G_0, G_1)$.

2. $\mathsf{ASetup}(\mathsf{gparam}, t, c_t, \{N_{max,t,i'}\}_{i'=1}^{c_t})$:

   AA_t $(1 \leq t \leq d)$ computes $\mathsf{param}_{\mathbb{V}_{A,t}} = (q, \mathbb{V}_{A,t}, \mathbb{G}_T, \mathbb{A}_{A,t}, e)$ and $\mathsf{param}_{\mathbb{V}_{R,t}} = (q, \mathbb{V}_{R,t}, \mathbb{G}_T, \mathbb{A}_{R,t}, e)$ by running $\mathcal{G}_{\mathsf{dpvs}}(1^\lambda, 24, \mathbb{F}_q)$ and $\mathcal{G}_{\mathsf{dpvs}}(1^\lambda, 24, \mathbb{F}_q)$, respectively.

   Then, AA_t computes $X_{A,t}, X_{R,t} \xleftarrow{\text{U}} GL(24, \mathbb{F}_q)$, $\boldsymbol{b}_{A,t,j} = X_{A,t}((0^{j-1}, G_0, 0^{24-j}))$ and $\boldsymbol{b}_{R,t,j} = X_{R,t}((0^{j-1}, G_0, 0^{24-j}))$ for $j = 1, \ldots, 24$. AA_t sets $\hat{\mathbb{B}}_{A,t} = (\boldsymbol{b}_{A,t,1}, \ldots, \boldsymbol{b}_{A,t,6}, \boldsymbol{b}_{A,t,21}, \ldots, \boldsymbol{b}_{A,t,24})$ and $\hat{\mathbb{B}}_{R,t} = (\boldsymbol{b}_{R,t,1}, \ldots, \boldsymbol{b}_{R,t,6}, \boldsymbol{b}_{R,t,21}, \ldots, \boldsymbol{b}_{R,t,24})$.

   Next, AA_t runs $\mathsf{CS.Setup}(N_{max,t,i'})$ and obtain $\mathcal{BT}_{t,i'}$ for $i' = 1, \ldots, c_t$. AA_t initializes the set of revoked users $R_{t,i'} = \phi$ for $i' = 1, \ldots, c_t$. If an user gid is revoked, AA_t updates as $R_{t,i'} \cup \{\mathsf{gid}\}$ and publishes it.

   Finally, AA_t sets $\mathsf{msk}_t = (X_{A,t}, X_{R,t})$, $\mathsf{mpk}_t = (\mathsf{param}_{\mathbb{V}_{A,t}}, \hat{\mathbb{B}}_{A,t}, \mathsf{param}_{\mathbb{V}_{R,t}}, \hat{\mathbb{B}}_{R,t})$. AA_t publishes mpk_t and $\{(\mathcal{BT}_{t,i'}, R_{t,i'})\}_{i'=1}^{c_t}$.

3. $\mathsf{KeyGen}(\mathsf{gparam}, \mathsf{gid}, x_{t,i'}, \mathsf{msk}_t, \mathcal{BT}_{t,i'})$:

   AA_t computes $G_{\mathsf{gid}} = (\delta G_1) = H(\mathsf{gid}) \in \mathbb{G}$ and $\sigma_{A,i'}, \varphi_{A,i',1}, \varphi_{A,i',2}, \xi_{\mathsf{gid}} \xleftarrow{\text{U}} \mathbb{F}_q$. Then, AA_t computes

$$k^*_{t,i',A} = (X_{A,t}^{-1})^T((\overbrace{\sigma_{A,i'}(1,i')G_1}^{2}, \overbrace{(1, x_{t,i'})G_1}^{2}, \overbrace{(1, x_{t,i'})G_{\mathsf{gid}}}^{2},$$
$$\overbrace{0, \ldots, 0}^{12}, \overbrace{(\varphi_{A,i',1}, \varphi_{A,i',2})G_1}^{2}, \overbrace{\xi_{\mathsf{gid}}(1, x_{t,i'})G_1}^{2}, \overbrace{0, 0}^{2})).$$

AA_t runs CS.Assign($\mathcal{BT}_{t,i'}$, gid) and obtains $PV_{t,i',\text{gid}} = \{S_{t,i',\text{gid},j_0}, \ldots, S_{t,i',\text{gid},j_{h_{t,i'}}}\}$ where $h_{t,i'}$ is the depth of $\mathcal{BT}_{t,i'}$.

Next, AA_t computes $\sigma_{R,i',j'}, \varphi_{R,i',j',1}, \varphi_{R,i',j',2} \xleftarrow{\mathsf{U}} \mathbb{F}_q$ for $j' = j_0, \ldots, j_{h_{t,i'}}$. Then, AA_t computes

$$k^*_{t,i',R,j'} = (X_{R,t}^{-1})^T((\overbrace{\sigma_{R,i',j'}(1,i')G_1}^{2}, \overbrace{(1,j')G_1}^{2}, \overbrace{(1,j')G_{\text{gid}}}^{2},$$
$$\overbrace{0,\ldots,0}^{12}, \overbrace{(\varphi_{R,i',j'1}, \varphi_{R,i',j',2})G_1}^{2}, \overbrace{\xi_{\text{gid}}(1,j')G_1}^{2}, \overbrace{0,0}^{2}))$$

for $j' = j_0, \ldots, j_{h_{t,i'}}$.

Finally, AA_t issues the user's private key $\mathsf{usk}_{\text{gid},t,i',x_{t,i'}} = (k^*_{t,i',A}, \{k^*_{t,i',R,j'}\}_{j'=j_0}^{j_{h_{t,i'}}}, PV_{t,i',\text{gid}})$ to the user gid.

4. Enc(gparam, $\{\mathsf{mpk}_t, \{(\mathcal{BT}_{t,i'}, R_{t,i'})\}_{i'}\}_t$, m, $\mathbb{A} = (M, \rho)$):

An encryptor computes $\vec{f}_m \xleftarrow{\mathsf{U}} \mathbb{F}_q^r$, $\vec{s}_m^T = (s_{m,1}, \ldots, s_{m,\ell})^T = M \cdot \vec{f}_m^T$ and $s_{m,0} = \vec{1} \cdot \vec{f}_m^T$ for $m = A, R$. He/she also computes $\vec{f'}_m \xleftarrow{\mathsf{U}} \mathbb{F}_q^r$ s.t. $\vec{1} \cdot \vec{f'}_m^T = 0$ and $\vec{s'}_m^T = (s'_{m,1}, \ldots, s'_{m,\ell})^T = M \cdot \vec{f'}_m^T$ for $m = A, R$.

Next, the encryptor obtains $\mu_{A,i}, \theta_{A,i}, \theta'_{A,i}, \theta''_{A,i}, \eta_{A,i,1}, \eta_{A,i,2} \xleftarrow{\mathsf{U}} \mathbb{F}_q$ and $w_i \xleftarrow{\mathsf{U}} \mathbb{F}_q^\times$ for $i = 1, \ldots, \ell$.

If $\rho(i) = (t, i', v_{t,i'})$, the encryptor computes

$$c_{A,i} = (\overbrace{\mu_{A,i}(i',-1)}^{2}, \overbrace{s_{A,i}(1,0) + \theta_{A,i}(v_{t,i'},-1)}^{2}, \overbrace{s'_{A,i}(1,0) + \theta'_{A,i}(v_{t,i'},-1)}^{2},$$
$$\overbrace{0,\ldots,0}^{12}, \overbrace{0,0}^{2}, \overbrace{w_i(1,0) + \theta''_{A,i}(v_{t,i'},-1)}^{2}, \overbrace{\eta_{A,i,1}, \eta_{A,i,2}}^{2})_{\mathbb{B}_{A,t}}.$$

If $\rho(i) = \neg(t, i', v_{t,i'})$, the encryptor computes

$$c_{A,i} = (\overbrace{\mu_{A,i}(i',-1)}^{2}, \overbrace{s_{A,i}(v_{t,i'},-1)}^{2}, \overbrace{s'_{A,i}(v_{t,i'},-1)}^{2},$$
$$\overbrace{0,\ldots,0}^{12}, \overbrace{0,0}^{2}, \overbrace{w_i(v_{t,i'},-1)}^{2}, \overbrace{\eta_{A,i,1}, \eta_{A,i,2}}^{2})_{\mathbb{B}_t}.$$

Then, the encryptor runs CS.Cover($\mathcal{BT}_{t,i'}, R_{t,i'}$) and obtains $CV_{R_{t,i'}} = \{S_{t,i',i_1}, \ldots, S_{t,i',i_m}\}$. He/she computes $\mu_{R,i,i''}, \theta_{R,i,i''}, \theta'_{R,i,i''}, \theta''_{R,i,i''}, \eta_{R,i,i'',1}, \eta_{R,i,i'',2} \xleftarrow{\mathsf{U}} \mathbb{F}_q$ for $i = 1, \ldots, \ell$; $i'' = i_1, \ldots, i_{m'}$. After that, he/she computes

$$c_{R,i,i''} = (\overbrace{\mu_{R,i,i''}(i',-1)}^{2}, \overbrace{s_{R,i}(1,0)+\theta_{R,i,i''}(i'',-1)}^{2}, \overbrace{s'_{R,i}(1,0)+\theta'_{R,i,i''}(i'',-1)}^{2},$$

$$\overbrace{0,\ldots,0}^{12}, \overbrace{0,0}^{2}, \overbrace{(-w_i)(1,0)+\theta''_{R,i,i''}(i'',-1)}^{2}, \overbrace{\eta_{R,i,i'',1},\eta_{R,i,i'',2}}^{2})_{\mathbb{B}_{R,t}},$$

for $i'' = i_1,\ldots,i_{m'}$.

Finally, the encryptor computes $c_0 = m \cdot g_T^{s_{A,0}+s_{R,0}}$ and outputs $\mathsf{ct}_{\mathbb{A},\{R_{t,i'}\}} = (\mathbb{A}, \{c_{A,i}, CV_{R_{\tilde{\rho}(i)}}, \{c_{R,i,i''}\}_{i''=i_1}^{i_{m'}}\}_{i=1}^{\ell}, c_0)$ where $\tilde{\rho}$ is an injective function such that $\tilde{\rho}(i) = (t,i')$ if $\rho(i) = (t,i',v_{t,i'})$ or $\neg(t,i',v_{t,i'})$.

5. $\mathsf{Dec}(\mathsf{gparam}, \mathsf{ct}_{\mathbb{A},\{R_{t,i'}\}}, \{\mathsf{usk}_{\mathsf{gid},(t,i',x_{t,i'})}\})$:

A decryptor who has the set of attributes $\Gamma = \{(t,i',x_{t,i'}) \in \mathsf{usk}_{\mathsf{gid},t,i',x_{t,i'}}\}$ can compute $\{\alpha_i\}_{i\in I}$ if $\mathbb{A} = (M,\rho)$ accepts Γ such that $\vec{1} \in \sum_{i\in I}\alpha_i M_i$ and $I \subseteq \{i \in \{1,\ldots,\ell\} \mid [\rho(i) = (t,i',v_{t,i'}) \wedge (t,i',x_{t,i'}) \in \Gamma \wedge v_{t,i'} = x_{t,i'}] \vee [\rho(i) = \neg(t,i',v_{t,i'}) \wedge (t,i',x_{t,i'}) \in \Gamma \wedge v_{t,i'} \neq x_{t,i'}]\}$.

The decryptor runs $\mathsf{CS.Match}(CV_{R_{t,i'}}, PV_{t,i',\mathsf{gid}})$ for $\tilde{\rho}(i) = (t,i')$ and $i \in I$. If $\mathsf{gid} \notin R_{t,i'}$, he/she can obtain $S_{t,i',k}$ such that $S_{t,i',k} \in CV_{R_{t,i'}}$ and $S_{t,i',k} \in PV_{t,i',\mathsf{gid}}$. Otherwise, he/she outputs $\perp$.

Next, the decryptor computes

$$K = \prod_{i\in I \wedge \rho(i)=(t,i',v_{t,i'})} (e(c_{A,i},k^*_{t,i',A}) \cdot e(c_{R,i,k},k^*_{t,i',R,k}))^{\alpha_i}$$

$$\cdot \prod_{i\in I \wedge \rho(i)=\neg(t,i',v_{t,i'})} (e(c_{A,i},k^*_{t,i',A})^{1/(v_{t,i'}-x_{t,i'})} \cdot e(c_{R,i,k},k^*_{t,i',R,k}))^{\alpha_i}$$

Finally, the decryptor outputs $m = c_0/K$.

[**Correctness**] If $\mathbb{A}$ accepts Γ and $\mathsf{gid} \notin R_{t,i'}$ for $\tilde{\rho}(i) = (t,i')$ and $i \in I$,

$$K = \prod_{i\in I \wedge \rho(i)=(t,i',v_{t,i'})} (g^{\mu_{A,i}\cdot\sigma_{A,i'}\cdot 0+s_{A,i}+\delta s'_{A,i}+\xi_{\mathsf{gid}}\cdot w_i}$$

$$\cdot g_T^{\mu_{R,i,i''}\cdot\sigma_{R,i',j'}\cdot 0+s_{R,i}+\delta s'_{R,i}-\xi_{\mathsf{gid}}\cdot w_i})^{\alpha_i}$$

$$\cdot \prod_{i\in I \wedge \rho(i)=\neg(t,i',v_{t,i'})} (g^{(\mu_{A,i}\cdot\sigma_{A,i'}\cdot 0+(s_{A,i}+\delta s'_{A,i}+\xi_{\mathsf{gid}}\cdot w_i)(v_{t,i'}-x_{t,i'}))/(v_{t,i'}-x_{t,i'})}$$

$$\cdot g_T^{\mu_{R,i,i''}\cdot\sigma_{R,i',j'}\cdot 0+s_{R,i}+\delta s'_{R,i}-\xi_{\mathsf{gid}}\cdot w_i})^{\alpha_i}$$

$$= g_T^{\sum_{i\in I}(\alpha_i s_{A,i}+\delta\alpha_i s'_{A,i}+\alpha_i s_{R,i}+\delta\alpha_i s'_{R,i})} = g_T^{s_{A,0}+s_{R,0}},$$

since $\sum_{i\in I}\alpha_i s_{A,i} = s_{A,0}$, $\sum_{i\in I}\alpha_i s_{R,i} = s_{R,0}$ and $\sum_{i\in I}\alpha_i s'_{A,i} = \sum_{i\in I}\alpha_i s'_{R,i} = 0$.

To show that our scheme is more practical than [29], we compare the structure of ciphertexts and secret keys and the performance in Appendix F.

3.4 Security Proof Sketch

Theorem 1 *The proposed UR-DMA-CP-ABE scheme is adaptively payload-hiding against chosen plaintext attacks under the DLIN assumption in the random oracle model. For any adversary, $\mathcal{A}$, there exist probabilistic machines $\mathcal{E}_1$, $\mathcal{E}_2$ and $\mathcal{E}_3$, whose running times are essentially the same as that of $\mathcal{A}$, s.t. for any λ,*

$$\mathsf{Adv}_{\mathcal{A}}^{\mathsf{PH}}(\lambda) \leq \mathsf{Adv}_{\mathcal{E}_1}^{\mathsf{DLIN}}(\lambda) + \sum_{h=1}^{\nu}(\mathsf{Adv}_{\mathcal{E}_2}^{\mathsf{DLIN}}(\lambda) + \mathsf{Adv}_{\mathcal{E}_3}^{\mathsf{DLIN}}(\lambda)) + \epsilon,$$

where ν is the maximum number of queries to the random oracle, and ϵ is the constant value dependent on d (the number of AAs), ν, and q.

We use the DLIN assumption and follow the dual system encryption strategy employed in [23] to achieve adaptively payload-hiding security against chosen-plaintext attacks. However, since our scheme supports key revocation and unboundedness, we cannot straightforwardly use the dual system encryption strategy employed in [23].

To achieve the security while supporting key revocation, we use **Restrictions I** and **II** in the security game in Sect. 3.2 as well as the existing revocable ABE [8, 29]. If we try to prove the security by using the dual system encryption strategy employed in [23] straightforwardly, the adversary can distinguish the games in Lemma 21 in [23] because the adversary can obtain the whole of the variables about user's keys and distinguish between the pre-semi-functional ciphertext and the semi-functional ciphertext. By splitting the user's key into the keys for attributes and revocations and employing **Restrictions I** and **II** in the security game, we can prevent the adversary from being able to distinguish security games.

To achieve security while supporting unboundedness, we use the consistent randomness amplification as well as [8,22] in the game sequences. Like [8,22], we replace the intra-subspace information theoretical transformation in the game sequences by the unbounded intra-subspace transformation assumption that is reduced to a swapping assumption.

4 Conclusion

We proposed a novel UR-DMA-CP-ABE that supports a non-monotone access structure achieving the adaptively payload-hiding against chosen-plaintext attacks under the DLIN assumption. The parameter sizes of the user's secret keys and ciphertexts in ours are smaller than that of the existing revocable DMA-CP-ABE supporting non-monotone access structures [29] even if $n_t = 2$. Hence, our scheme is more practical than [29].

Appendix

A   Span Programs

Definition 5 (Span Programs [23]). *We define* $\{p_1, \ldots, p_m\}$ *as a set of variables. A span program over* $\mathbb{F}_q$ *is a labeled matrix* $\mathbb{S} := (M, \rho)$. *Note that* M *is a* $\ell \times r$ *matrix over* $\mathbb{F}_q$. *We also note that* ρ *is a labeling of the rows of* M *by literals from* $\{p_1, \ldots, p_m, \neg p_1, \ldots, \neg p_m\}$. *Every row is labeled by one literal, i.e.,* $\rho : \{1, \ldots, \ell\} \to \{p_1, \ldots, p_m, \neg p_1, \ldots, \neg p_m\}$.

$\mathbb{S}$ *accepts or rejects an input by the following criterion. For every input sequence* $\delta \in \{0,1\}^m$ *define the submatrix* M_δ *of* M *consisting of those rows whose labels are set to 1 by the input* δ, *i.e., either rows labeled by some* p_i *such that* $\delta_i = 1$ *or rows labeled by some* $\neg p_i$ *such that* $\delta_i = 0$. *(i.e.,* $\gamma : \{1, \ldots, \ell\} \to \{0,1\}$ *is defined by* $\gamma(j) = 1$ *if* $[\rho(j) = p_i] \wedge [\delta_i = 1]$ *or* $[\rho(j) = \neg p_i] \wedge [\delta_i = 0]$, *and* $\gamma(j) = 0$ *otherwise.* $M_\delta := (M_j)_{\gamma(j)=1}$, *where* M_j *is the* j-*th row of* M.*)*

$\mathbb{S}$ *accepts* δ *if and only if* $\vec{1} = (\overbrace{1, \ldots, 1}^{r}) \in \mathsf{span}\langle M_\delta \rangle$. *That is, the some linear combination of the rows of* M_δ, $\mathsf{span}\langle M_\delta \rangle$, *gives* $\vec{1}$ *such that the row vector has the value 1 in each coordinate.* $\mathbb{S}$ *computes a Boolean function* f *if it accepts exactly those inputs* δ *where* $f(\delta) = 1$.

$\mathbb{S}$ *is called monotone if the labels of the rows are only the positive literals* $\{p_1, \ldots, p_m\}$. *Monotone span programs compute monotone functions. In other words, a span program in general is "non"-monotone.*

Assume that no row $M_i (i = 1, \ldots, \ell)$ of the matrix M is $\vec{0} = (\overbrace{0, \ldots, 0}^{r})$, i.e., the row vector has the value 0 in each coordinate. We introduce a non-monotone access structure with evaluating map γ by using the inner-product of attribute vectors, which is employed in our scheme in the same way as [23].

B   Linear Secret Sharing Schemes

Definition 6 (Linear Secret Sharing Schemes [23]). *Let* M *be an* $\ell \times r$ *matrix. Let column vector* $\vec{f}^T := (f_1, \ldots, f_r)^T \xleftarrow{\mathsf{U}} \mathbb{F}_q^r$. *Then,* $s_0 = \vec{1} \cdot \vec{f}^T = \sum_{k=1}^{r} f_k$ *is the secret to be shared, and* $\vec{s}^T = (s_1, \ldots, s_\ell)^T = M \cdot \vec{f}^T$ *is the vector of* ℓ *shares of the secret* s_0. *Each share* s_i *belongs to* $\rho(i)$.

If span program $\mathbb{S} := (M, \rho)$ *accepts* δ, *or access structure* $\mathbb{A} := (M, \rho)$ *accepts* Γ, *i.e.,* $\vec{1} \in \mathsf{span}\langle (M_i)_{\gamma(i)=1} \rangle$ *with* $\gamma : \{1, \ldots, \ell\} \to \{0,1\}$, *then there exist constants* $\{\alpha_i \in \mathbb{F}_q \mid i \in I\}$ *such that* $I \subseteq \{i \in \{1, \ldots \ell\} \mid \gamma(i) = 1\}$ *and* $\sum_{i \in I} \alpha_i s_i = s_0$. *Note that* $\{\alpha_i\}$ *can be computed in time polynomial in the size of matrix* M.

C Usefulness of Splitting the Attribute Universe When Using the NOT Operator

For example, we assume that t-th AA is a company and manages attributes about employees split into two categories, "department"(={Human Resource Department, Accounting Department, General Affairs Department, Manufacturing Department}) and "length of service"(={1,2,3,4,5}). If an encryptor encrypts the message so that only employees with five years of service outside of the Human Resources Department can decrypt it, the encryptor would like to specify the access policy such as (NOT(department = "Human Resources Department")) AND (length of service = "5") in the ciphertext. If t-th AA manages all attributes in one category, the expression of access policy would be complicated, and the ciphertext size may increase. In the previous example, an encryptor needs to specify the access policy such as ("Accounting Department" AND "5") OR ("General Affairs Department" AND "5") OR ("Manufacturing Department" AND "5") because the encryptor cannot use NOT operator. If t-th AA manages all attributes in one category, an access policy (NOT "Human Resources Department") equals "Accounting Department" OR "General Affairs Department" OR "1" OR "2" OR "3" OR "4" OR "5".

Hence, the AA in the DMA-CP-ABE system supporting non-monotone access structures (e.g., [23]) is required to manage attributes in multiple categories. However, we emphasize that the size of the public parameters managed by each AA would be proportional to the number of categories. Therefore, the non-monotone ABE scheme supporting unboundedness for the number of attribute categories (that means the size of the public parameter must be independent of the number of attribute categories) is desirable.

D Full Binary Tree

A full binary tree $\mathcal{BT}$ is a tree data structure such that every node except leaf nodes has two child nodes. If we let h be the depth[3] of $\mathcal{BT}$, the number of leaf nodes of $\mathcal{BT}$ is denoted as $N_{max} = 2^h$. Note that the depth of the root node is 0. The total number of nodes is $2N_{max} - 1 (= 2^{h+1} - 1)$.

For any index $0 \leq i \leq 2N_{max} - 1$, we let ν_i be a i-th node in $\mathcal{BT}$. Note that we assign the index 0 to the root node and other indices to other nodes using a breadth-first search. That is, for any ν_i, the index of its left child node is $2i + 1$ and the index of its right child node is $2i + 2$, while the index of its parent node is $\lfloor \frac{i-1}{2} \rfloor$. Siblings are nodes sharing the same parent node.

We define ID as a mapping from the node ν_i to its index i. That is, it holds that $ID(\nu_i) = i$.

---

[3] The depth of a node is the length of the path from the root node to the node.

E   The Subset-Cover Revocation Framework (SC)

Naor et al. introduced SC as a general methodology for the construction of efficient revocation systems [19]. We let $\mathcal{N} = \{1, \ldots, N_{max}\}$ be the set of all users. SC for $\mathcal{N}$ consists of the following four probabilistic polynomial-time algorithms.

1. Setup(N_{max}): The setup algorithm takes the maximum number of users N_{max} as input and outputs a collection $\mathcal{SUB}$ of subsets $S_1, \ldots, S_w$ where $S_i \subseteq \mathcal{N}$.
2. Assign($\mathcal{SUB}, u$): The assigning algorithm takes the collection $\mathcal{SUB}$ and a user $u \in \mathcal{N}$. It outputs a private set $PV_u = \{S_{j_1}, \ldots, S_{j_n}\}$ that is associated with the user u.
3. Cover($\mathcal{SUB}, R$): The covering algorithm takes as the collection $\mathcal{SUB}$ and a revoked set $R \subset \mathcal{N}$ of users, and it outputs a covering set $CV_R = \{S_{i_1}, \ldots, S_{i_m}\}$ that is a partition of the unrevoked users $\mathcal{N} \setminus R$ into disjoint subsets $S_{i_1}, \ldots, S_{i_m}$, that is, they are disjoint, and it holds that $\mathcal{N} \setminus R = \bigcup_{k=1}^{m} S_{i_k}$.
4. Match(CV_R, PV_u) : The matching algorithm takes as input a covering set $CV_R = \{S_{i_1}, \ldots, S_{i_m}\}$ and a private set $PV_u = \{S_{j_1}, \ldots, S_{j_n}\}$. It outputs $(S_{i_k}, S_{j_{k'}})$ such that $S_{i_k} \in CV_R$, $u \in S_{i_k}$ and $S_{j_{k'}} \in PV_u$, or it outputs $\perp$.

The correctness of SC is defined as follows: For all $\mathcal{SUB}$ generated by Setup(N_{max}), all PV_u generated by Assign($\mathcal{SUB}, u$) for any u, and all CV_R generated by Cover($\mathcal{SUB}, R$) for any R, it is required that:

- If $u \notin R$, then Match(CV_R, PV_u) outputs $(S_{i_k}, S_{j_{k'}})$ such that $S_{i_k} \in CV_R$, $u \in S_{i_k}$ and $S_{j_{k'}} \in PV_u$.
- If $u \in R$, then Match(CV_R, PV_u) outputs $\perp$.

In particular, we use the complete subtree (CS) method in [19]. For $\mathcal{BT}$ and a subset R of leaf nodes, we let $ST(\mathcal{BT}, R)$ be the Steiner Tree induced by the set R and the root node. That is, $ST(\mathcal{BT}, R)$ is the minimal subtree of $\mathcal{BT}$ connecting all the leaf nodes in R and the root node. Hereafter, we simply denote $ST(\mathcal{BT}, R)$ by $ST(R)$. The CS method consists of the following four probabilistic polynomial-time algorithms.

1. CS.Setup(N_{max}): The setup algorithm takes the maximum number of users $N_{max} = 2^h$ as input. It first sets $\mathcal{BT}$ of depth h. Each user is assigned a different leaf node in $\mathcal{BT}$[4]. The collection $\mathcal{SUB}$ of CS is $\{S_i : \nu_i \in \mathcal{BT}\}$. Recall that S_i is the set of all the leaf nodes in the subtree $\mathcal{T}_i$. Then, it outputs $\mathcal{BT}$.
2. CS.Assign($\mathcal{SUB}, u$): The assign algorithm takes $\mathcal{BT}$ and a user $u \in \mathcal{N}$ as inputs. We let ν_u be the leaf node of $\mathcal{BT}$ that is assigned to u. Let $(\nu_{j_0}, \nu_{j_1}, \ldots, \nu_{j_h})$ be the path from the root node $\nu_{j_0} = \nu_0$ to the leaf node $\nu_{j_h} = \nu_u$. It sets $PV_u = \{S_{j_0}, \ldots, S_{j_h}\}$, and outputs the private set PV_u.

---

[4] In our scheme, if a user with an assigned leaf node ν becomes revoked and unrevoked again. Then, the user cannot reuse the same leaf node ν, and in this case, a new different leaf node needs to be assigned to the user. We emphasize that the leaf node ν cannot be reused for other users.

3. CS.Cover(SUB, R): The covering algorithm takes BT and a revoked set R of users as inputs. It first computes $ST(R)$. Let $T_{i_1}, \ldots, T_{i_m}$ be all the subtrees of BT that hang off $ST(R)$, that is, all subtrees whose roots $\nu_{i_1}, \ldots, \nu_{i_m}$ are not in $ST(R)$ but adjacent to nodes of outdegree 1 in $ST(R)$. It outputs a covering set $CV_R = \{S_{i_1}, \ldots, S_{i_m}\}$.
4. CS.Match(CV_R, PV_u): The matching algorithm takes a covering set $CV_R = \{S_{i_1}, \ldots, S_{i_m}\}$ and a private set $PV_u = \{S_{j_0}, \ldots, S_{j_h}\}$ as inputs. It finds a subset S_k such that $S_k \in CV_R$ and $S_k \in PV_u$. If there is such a subset, it outputs (S_k, S_k). Otherwise, it outputs $\perp$.

F   Comparison Between Existing DMA-CP-ABE and Ours

F.1   Structure of Ciphertexts and Secret Keys

We compare our scheme and the existing schemes [23, 29]. These schemes and ours achieve adaptively payload-hiding against chosen-plaintext attacks under DLIN assumption.

Okamoto and Takashima gave a DMA-CP-ABE scheme achieving adaptively payload-hiding against chosen-plaintext attacks on the DPVS framework [23]. In [23], ciphertexts (CT) and secret keys (SK) vectors have dimension $5n_t + 1 = 2n_t + 2n_t + n_t + 1$, where the first $2n_t$ dimension is the real-encoding part (real part, for short) for CT and SK vectors, the second $2n_t$ is the hidden part for temporary, pre-semi-functional and semi-functional CT and SK vectors, the third n_t is the SK randomness part and the fourth is the CT randomness part. However, DMA-CP-ABE [23] is not supporting the revocation of the user's attributes.

To realize the revocation, the authors of [29] introduced two types of CT and SK, CT (and SK) for access control and revocation, respectively. In addition, they increased double possession resistance part (resist. part, for short), i.e., $n_{f,t}$−dimensional with $6n_{f,t} + 1 = 2n_{f,t} + 2n_{f,t} + n_{f,t} + n_{f,t} + 1$ inner−structure. "Double possession" means having SK, each of which has a different value (different vector $\vec{x}_{f,t}$) for the same category t. However, revocable DMA-CP-ABE [29] is not supporting unboundedness.

To realize the unboundedness, we employ the indexing and consistent randomness amplification [22] in the same way as [8]. Hence, we increased the indexing part in CT and SK. We note that the consistent randomness amplification can realize the unboundedness for the number of attribute categories or dimensions of a vector. Therefore, in our scheme, the dimension of the attribute vector in CT and SK is fixed, i.e., 2.

$$\text{CT \& SK vector in [23] : } (\underbrace{\text{real}}_{2n_t} \; \underbrace{\text{hidden}}_{2n_t} \; \underbrace{\text{SK ran.}}_{n_t} \; \underbrace{\text{CT ran.}}_{1}),$$

$$\text{CT \& SK vector in [29] : } (\underbrace{\text{real}}_{2n_{f,t}} \; \underbrace{\text{hidden}}_{2n_{f,t}} \; \underbrace{\text{SK ran.}}_{n_{f,t}} \; \underbrace{\text{resist.}}_{n_{f,t}} \; \underbrace{\text{CT ran.}}_{1}),$$

$$\text{CT \& SK vector in ours: } (\underbrace{\text{indexing}}_{2} \; \underbrace{\text{real}}_{4} \; \underbrace{\text{hidden}}_{12} \; \underbrace{\text{SK ran.}}_{2} \; \underbrace{\text{resist.}}_{2} \; \underbrace{\text{CT ran.}}_{2}),$$

F.2   Performance

Table 2. Comparison of the parameter size of public parameters (PP) and master secret keys (MSK) between existing DMA-ABE and ours ($|\mathbb{G}|$: the size of $\mathbb{G}$, $|\mathbb{G}_T|$: the size of $\mathbb{G}_T$, $|\mathbb{F}_q|$: the size of $\mathbb{F}_q$, n_t: the dimension of the attribute vector, φ_t: the upper bound for the number of subsets in the cover, h_t: the height of the tree of users).

Schemes	PP	MSK
[26]	$|\mathbb{G}_T| + |\mathbb{G}|$	$|\mathbb{F}_q|$
[23]	$(10n_t^2 + 7n_t + 1)|\mathbb{G}|$	$(25n_t^2 + 10n_t + 1)|\mathbb{F}_q|$
[29]	$(18n_t^2 + 9n_t + 18\varphi_t^2 + 99\varphi_t$ $+ 36h_t\varphi_t + 48h_t + 101)|\mathbb{G}|$	$(18n_t^2 + 9n_t + 14h_t^2 + \varphi_t^2 + 6h_t\varphi_t$ $+16h_t + 8\varphi_t + 2^{h_t} + 17)|\mathbb{F}_q|$
This work	$480|\mathbb{G}|$	$576|\mathbb{F}_q|$

Table 3. Comparison of the parameter size of user's secret key (SK) and ciphertexts (CT) between existing DMA-ABE and ours ($|\Gamma|$: the size of the attribute set, R_t: the number of revoked users in AA_t).

Schemes	SK	CT
[26]	$2|\Gamma||\mathbb{G}|$	$(\ell + 1)|\mathbb{G}_T| + 3\ell|\mathbb{G}|$
[23]	$\sum_{i=1}^{|\Gamma|}(n_t|\mathbb{F}_q| + (5n_t + 1)|\mathbb{G}|)$	$|\mathbb{G}_T| + \sum_{i=1}^{\ell}(5n_t + 1)|\mathbb{G}|$
[29]	$\sum_{i=1}^{|\Gamma|}(n_t|\mathbb{F}_q|$ $+ (6n_t + 12h_t + 6\varphi_t + 26)|\mathbb{G}|)$	$|\mathbb{G}_T| + \sum_{i=1}^{\ell}(6n_t + 1 +$ $\mathsf{R}_t\log_2(2^{h_t}/\mathsf{R}_t)(24h_t + 12\varphi_t + 50)|\mathbb{G}|)$
This work	$\sum_{i=1}^{|\Gamma|}(|\mathbb{F}_q| + (24 + 24h_t)|\mathbb{G}|)$	$|\mathbb{G}_T| + \sum_{i=1}^{\ell}(24 + 24\mathsf{R}_t\log_2(2^{h_t}/\mathsf{R}_t)|\mathbb{G}|)$

We compare the parameter size between existing DMA-CP-ABE and ours in Tables 2 and 3. For simplicity, we assume that each AA manages one attribute category.

Table 2 shows the comparison of the parameter size of public parameters and master secret keys (managed by each AA) between existing schemes and ours. It shows that our parameter sizes are independent of the number of attributes and attribute categories.

Table 3 compares the parameter size of the user's secret keys and ciphertexts between existing schemes and ours. Our parameter sizes are smaller than that of the existing revocable DMA-CP-ABE supporting non-monotone access structures [29] even if $n_t = 2$.

References

1. Attrapadung, N.: Unbounded dynamic predicate compositions in attribute-based encryption. In: Ishai, Y., Rijmen, V. (eds.) EUROCRYPT 2019. LNCS, vol. 11476, pp. 34–67. Springer, Cham (2019). https://doi.org/10.1007/978-3-030-17653-2_2

2. Attrapadung, N., Imai, H.: Attribute-based encryption supporting direct/indirect revocation modes. In: Parker, M.G. (ed.) IMACC 2009. LNCS, vol. 5921, pp. 278–300. Springer, Heidelberg (2009). https://doi.org/10.1007/978-3-642-10868-6_17

3. Attrapadung, N., Imai, H.: Conjunctive broadcast and attribute-based encryption. In: Shacham, H., Waters, B. (eds.) Pairing 2009. LNCS, vol. 5671, pp. 248–265. Springer, Heidelberg (2009). https://doi.org/10.1007/978-3-642-03298-1_16

4. Attrapadung, N., Tomida, J.: Unbounded dynamic predicate compositions in ABE from standard assumptions. In: Moriai, S., Wang, H. (eds.) ASIACRYPT 2020. LNCS, vol. 12493, pp. 405–436. Springer, Cham (2020). https://doi.org/10.1007/978-3-030-64840-4_14

5. Bethencourt, J., Sahai, A., Waters, B.: Ciphertext-policy attribute-based encryption. In: IEEE Symposium on Security and Privacy, pp. 321–334. IEEE Computer Society (2007)

6. Chase, M.: Multi-authority attribute based encryption. In: Vadhan, S.P. (ed.) TCC 2007. LNCS, vol. 4392, pp. 515–534. Springer, Heidelberg (2007). https://doi.org/10.1007/978-3-540-70936-7_28

7. Chase, M., Chow, S.S.M.: Improving privacy and security in multi-authority attribute-based encryption. In: CCS, pp. 121–130. ACM (2009)

8. Datta, P., Dutta, R., Mukhopadhyay, S.: Adaptively secure unrestricted attribute-based encryption with subset difference revocation in bilinear groups of prime order. In: Pointcheval, D., Nitaj, A., Rachidi, T. (eds.) AFRICACRYPT 2016. LNCS, vol. 9646, pp. 325–345. Springer, Cham (2016). https://doi.org/10.1007/978-3-319-31517-1_17

9. Datta, P., Komargodski, I., Waters, B.: Decentralized multi-authority ABE for DNFs from LWE. In: Canteaut, A., Standaert, F.-X. (eds.) EUROCRYPT 2021. LNCS, vol. 12696, pp. 177–209. Springer, Cham (2021). https://doi.org/10.1007/978-3-030-77870-5_7

10. Garg, S., Gentry, C., Halevi, S., Sahai, A., Waters, B.: Attribute-based encryption for circuits from multilinear maps. In: Canetti, R., Garay, J.A. (eds.) CRYPTO 2013. LNCS, vol. 8043, pp. 479–499. Springer, Heidelberg (2013). https://doi.org/10.1007/978-3-642-40084-1_27

11. Goyal, V., Pandey, O., Sahai, A., Waters, B.: Attribute-based encryption for fine-grained access control of encrypted data. In: CCS, pp. 89–98. ACM (2006)

12. Huang, K.: Secure efficient revocable large universe multi-authority attribute-based encryption for cloud-aided IoT. IEEE Access 9, 53576–53588 (2021)

13. Lee, K., Choi, S.G., Lee, D.H., Park, J.H., Yung, M.: Self-updatable encryption: time constrained access control with hidden attributes and better efficiency. In: Sako, K., Sarkar, P. (eds.) ASIACRYPT 2013. LNCS, vol. 8269, pp. 235–254. Springer, Heidelberg (2013). https://doi.org/10.1007/978-3-642-42033-7_13

14. Lewko, A.B.: Functional encryption: new proof technique and advancing capabilities. Ph.D. thesis, University of Texas at Austin (2012)

15. Lewko, A., Waters, B.: Decentralizing attribute-based encryption. In: Paterson, K.G. (ed.) EUROCRYPT 2011. LNCS, vol. 6632, pp. 568–588. Springer, Heidelberg (2011). https://doi.org/10.1007/978-3-642-20465-4_31

16. Lewko, A., Waters, B.: Unbounded HIBE and attribute-based encryption. In: Paterson, K.G. (ed.) EUROCRYPT 2011. LNCS, vol. 6632, pp. 547–567. Springer, Heidelberg (2011). https://doi.org/10.1007/978-3-642-20465-4_30

17. Li, D., Chen, J., Liu, J., Wu, Q., Liu, W.: Efficient CCA2 secure revocable multi-authority large-universe attribute-based encryption. In: Wen, S., Wu, W., Castiglione, A. (eds.) CSS 2017. LNCS, vol. 10581, pp. 103–118. Springer, Cham (2017). https://doi.org/10.1007/978-3-319-69471-9_8

18. Müller, S., Katzenbeisser, S., Eckert, C.: Distributed attribute-based encryption. In: Lee, P.J., Cheon, J.H. (eds.) ICISC 2008. LNCS, vol. 5461, pp. 20–36. Springer, Heidelberg (2009). https://doi.org/10.1007/978-3-642-00730-9_2

19. Naor, D., Naor, M., Lotspiech, J.: Revocation and tracing schemes for stateless receivers. In: Kilian, J. (ed.) CRYPTO 2001. LNCS, vol. 2139, pp. 41–62. Springer, Heidelberg (2001). https://doi.org/10.1007/3-540-44647-8_3

20. Nomura, K., Mohri, M., Shiraishi, Y., Morii, M.: Attribute revocable multi-authority attribute-based encryption with forward secrecy for cloud storage. IEICE Trans. Inf. Syst. $\mathbf{E100.D}(10)$, 2420–2431 (2017)

21. Okamoto, T., Takashima, K.: Fully secure functional encryption with general relations from the decisional linear assumption. In: Rabin, T. (ed.) CRYPTO 2010. LNCS, vol. 6223, pp. 191–208. Springer, Heidelberg (2010). https://doi.org/10.1007/978-3-642-14623-7_11

22. Okamoto, T., Takashima, K.: Fully secure unbounded inner-product and attribute-based encryption. In: Wang, X., Sako, K. (eds.) ASIACRYPT 2012. LNCS, vol. 7658, pp. 349–366. Springer, Heidelberg (2012). https://doi.org/10.1007/978-3-642-34961-4_22

23. Okamoto, T., Takashima, K.: Decentralized attribute-based signatures. In: Kurosawa, K., Hanaoka, G. (eds.) PKC 2013. LNCS, vol. 7778, pp. 125–142. Springer, Heidelberg (2013). https://doi.org/10.1007/978-3-642-36362-7_9

24. Ostrovsky, R., Sahai, A., Waters, B.: Attribute-based encryption with non-monotonic access structures. In: CCS, pp. 195–203. ACM (2007)

25. Rouselakis, Y., Waters, B.: Practical constructions and new proof methods for large universe attribute-based encryption. In: CCS, pp. 463–474. ACM (2013)

26. Rouselakis, Y., Waters, B.: Efficient statically-secure large-universe multi-authority attribute-based encryption. In: Böhme, R., Okamoto, T. (eds.) FC 2015. LNCS, vol. 8975, pp. 315–332. Springer, Heidelberg (2015). https://doi.org/10.1007/978-3-662-47854-7_19

27. Sahai, A., Seyalioglu, H., Waters, B.: Dynamic credentials and ciphertext delegation for attribute-based encryption. In: Safavi-Naini, R., Canetti, R. (eds.) CRYPTO 2012. LNCS, vol. 7417, pp. 199–217. Springer, Heidelberg (2012). https://doi.org/10.1007/978-3-642-32009-5_13

28. Sahai, A., Waters, B.: Fuzzy identity-based encryption. In: Cramer, R. (ed.) EUROCRYPT 2005. LNCS, vol. 3494, pp. 457–473. Springer, Heidelberg (2005). https://doi.org/10.1007/11426639_27

29. Tsuchida, H., Nishide, T., Okamoto, E., Kim, K.: Revocable decentralized multi-authority functional encryption. In: Dunkelman, O., Sanadhya, S.K. (eds.) INDOCRYPT 2016. LNCS, vol. 10095, pp. 248–265. Springer, Cham (2016). https://doi.org/10.1007/978-3-319-49890-4_14

30. Venema, M., Alpár, G.: A bunch of broken schemes: a simple yet powerful linear approach to analyzing security of attribute-based encryption. In: Paterson, K.G. (ed.) CT-RSA 2021. LNCS, vol. 12704, pp. 100–125. Springer, Cham (2021). https://doi.org/10.1007/978-3-030-75539-3_5

31. Wu, Z., Zhang, Y., Xu, E.: Multi-authority revocable access control method based on CP-ABE in NDN. Future Internet $\mathbf{12}(1)$, 15 (2020)

32. Yamada, K., Attrapadung, N., Emura, K., Hanaoka, G., Tanaka, K.: Generic constructions for fully secure revocable attribute-based encryption. In: Foley, S.N., Gollmann, D., Snekkenes, E. (eds.) ESORICS 2017. LNCS, vol. 10493, pp. 532–551. Springer, Cham (2017). https://doi.org/10.1007/978-3-319-66399-9_29

Author Index

G. Bella et al. (Eds.): SecITC 2022, LNCS 13809, pp. 341–342, 2023.
https://doi.org/10.1007/978-3-031-32636-3

Printed in the United States
by Baker & Taylor Publisher Services